THE GOLDEN BOUGH

ROLF BOLDREWOOD: Robbery Under Arms

A. C. BRADLEY: Shakespearean Tragedy

LEWIS CARROLL: Alice's Adventures in Wonderland *and* Through the Looking-Glass (with all the original illustrations by Sir John Tenniel). *Together in one volume*

SIR J. G. FRAZER: The Golden Bough (Abridged Edition). *In two volumes*

SIR W. S. GILBERT: The Savoy Operas. *In two volumes*

THOMAS HARDY: Far from the Madding Crowd; Jude the Obscure; Tess of the D'Urbervilles; The Mayor of Casterbridge; The Return of the Native; The Woodlanders; Under the Greenwood Tree

THOMAS HUGHES: Tom Brown's School-Days (with illustrations by Edmund J. Sullivan)

A. G. MACDONELL: England, Their England

MARGARET MITCHELL: Gone with the Wind. *In two volumes*

CHARLES MORGAN: Portrait in a Mirror; The Fountain

SEAN O'CASEY: Three Plays (Juno and the Paycock; The Shadow of a Gunman; The Plough and the Stars); Five One-act Plays (The End of the Beginning; A Pound on Demand; Hall of Healing; Bedtime Story; Time to Go)

SIR OSBERT SITWELL: Left Hand, Right Hand!; The Scarlet Tree; Great Morning; Laughter in the Next Room.

SIR HUGH WALPOLE: Jeremy; Rogue Herries; Judith Paris

THE GOLDEN BOUGH

A Study in Magic and Religion

BY

SIR JAMES GEORGE FRAZER

F.R.S., F.B.A.

Fellow of Trinity College, Cambridge

Hon. D.C.L., Oxford; Hon. Litt.D., Cambridge and Durham;
Hon. LL.D., Glasgow; Doctor Honoris Causa of the
Universities of Paris and Strasbourg

ABRIDGED EDITION

VOLUME I

LONDON

MACMILLAN & CO LTD

1960

MACMILLAN AND COMPANY LIMITED
London Bombay Calcutta Madras Melbourne

THE MACMILLAN COMPANY OF CANADA LIMITED
Toronto

ST MARTIN'S PRESS INC
New York

*First issued in St Martin's Library 1957
Reprinted 1960*

PRINTED IN GREAT BRITAIN

PREFACE

THE primary aim of this book is to explain the remarkable rule which regulated the succession to the priesthood of Diana at Aricia. When I first set myself to solve the problem more than thirty years ago, I thought that the solution could be propounded very briefly, but I soon found that to render it probable or even intelligible it was necessary to discuss certain more general questions, some of which had hardly been broached before. In successive editions the discussion of these and kindred topics has occupied more and more space, the enquiry has branched out in more and more directions, until the two volumes of the original work have expanded into twelve. Meantime a wish has often been expressed that the book should be issued in a more compendious form. This abridgment is an attempt to meet the wish and thereby to bring the work within the range of a wider circle of readers. While the bulk of the book has been greatly reduced, I have endeavoured to retain its leading principles, together with an amount of evidence sufficient to illustrate them clearly. The language of the original has also for the most part been preserved, though here and there the exposition has been somewhat condensed. In order to keep as much of the text as possible I have sacrificed all the notes, and with them all exact references to my authorities. Readers who desire to ascertain the source of any particular statement must therefore consult the larger work, which is fully documented and provided with a complete bibliography.

In the abridgment I have neither added new matter nor altered the views expressed in the last edition; for the evidence which has come to my knowledge in the meantime has on the whole served either to confirm my former conclusions or to furnish fresh illustrations of old principles. Thus, for example, on the crucial question of the practice of putting kings to death either at the end of a fixed period or whenever their health and strength began to fail, the body of evidence which points to the wide prevalence of such a custom has been considerably augmented in the interval. A striking instance of a limited monarchy of this sort is furnished by the powerful mediaeval kingdom of the Khazars in Southern Russia, where the kings were liable to be put to death either on the expiry of a set term or whenever some public calamity, such as drought, dearth, or defeat in war, seemed to indicate a failure of their natural powers. The evidence for the systematic killing of the Khazar kings, drawn from the accounts of old Arab travellers, has been collected by me elsewhere.[1] Africa, again, has supplied several fresh examples of a similar practice of regicide. Among them the most notable perhaps is the custom formerly observed in Bunyoro of choosing every year from a particular clan a mock king, who was supposed to incarnate the late king, cohabited with his widows at his temple-tomb, and after reigning for a week was strangled.[2] The custom presents a close parallel to the ancient Babylonian festival of the Sacaea, at which a mock king was dressed in the royal robes, allowed to enjoy the real king's concubines, and after reigning for five days was stripped, scourged, and put to death. That festival in its turn has lately received fresh light from certain Assyrian inscriptions,[3] which seem to confirm the interpretation which I formerly gave of the festival as a New Year celebration and the parent of the Jewish festival of Purim.[4] Other recently discovered parallels to the priestly kings of Aricia are African priests and kings who used to be put to death at the end of seven or of two years, after being liable in the interval to be attacked and killed by a strong man, who thereupon succeeded to the priesthood or the kingdom.[5]

[1] J. G. Frazer, "The Killing of the Khazar Kings," *Folk-lore*, xxviii, (1917) pp. 382-407.

[2] Rev. J. Roscoe, *The Soul of Central Africa* (London, 1922), p. 200. Compare J. G. Frazer, "The Mackie Ethnological Expedition to Central Africa," *Man*, xx, (1920), p. 181.

[3] H. Zimmern, *Zum babylonischen Neujahrsfest* (Leipzig, 1918). Compare A. H. Sayce, in *Journal of the Royal Asiatic Society*, July 1921, pp. 440-442.

[4] *The Golden Bough*, Part VI. *The Scapegoat*, pp. 354 *sqq.*, 412 *sqq.*

[5] P. Amaury Talbot, in *Journal of the African Society*, July 1916, pp. 309 *sq.*; *id.*, in *Folklore*, xxvi., (1916), pp. 79 *sq.*; H. R. Palmer, in *Journal of the African Society*, July 1912, pp. 403, 407 *sq.*

With these and other instances of like customs before us it is no longer possible to regard the rule of succession to the priesthood of Diana at Aricia as exceptional ; it clearly exemplifies a widespread institution, of which the most numerous and the most similar cases have thus far been found in Africa. How far the facts point to an early influence of Africa on Italy, or even to the existence of an African population in Southern Europe, I do not presume to say. The prehistoric relations between the two continents are still obscure and still under investigation.

Whether the explanation which I have offered of the institution is correct or not must be left to the future to determine. I shall always be ready to abandon it if a better can be suggested. Meantime in committing the book in its new form to the judgment of the public I desire to guard against a misapprehension of its scope which appears to be still rife, though I have sought to correct it before now. If in the present work I have dwelt at some length on the worship of trees, it is not, I trust, because I exaggerate its importance in the history of religion, still less because I would deduce from it a whole system of mythology; it is simply because I could not ignore the subject in attempting to explain the significance of a priest who bore the title of King of the Wood, and one of whose titles to office was the plucking of a bough—the Golden Bough — from a tree in the sacred grove. But I am so far from regarding the reverence for trees as of supreme importance for the evolution of religion that I consider it to have been altogether subordinate to other factors, and in particular to the fear of the human dead, which, on the whole, I believe to have been probably the most powerful force in the making of primitive religion. I hope that after this explicit disclaimer I shall no longer be taxed with embracing a system of mythology which I look upon not merely as false but as preposterous and absurd. But I am too familiar with the hydra of error to expect that by lopping off one of the monster's heads I can prevent another, or even the same, from sprouting again. I can only trust to the candour and intelligence of my readers to rectify this serious misconception of my views by a comparison with my own express declaration.

J. G. FRAZER

1 BRICK COURT, TEMPLE,
LONDON, JUNE 1922.

Contents

Contents

CHAPTER I

THE KING OF THE WOOD

§ 1. *Diana and Virbius.* — Who does not know Turner's picture of the Golden Bough? The scene, suffused with the golden glow of imagination in which the divine mind of Turner steeped and transfigured even the fairest natural landscape, is a dream-like vision of the little woodland lake of Nemi — 'Diana's Mirror,' as it was called by the ancients. No one who has seen that calm water, lapped in a green hollow of the Alban hills, can ever forget it. The two characteristic Italian villages which slumber on its banks, and the equally Italian palace whose terraced gardens descend steeply to the lake, hardly break the stillness and even the solitariness of the scene. Dian herself might still linger by this lonely shore, still haunt those woodlands wild.

In antiquity this sylvan landscape was the scene of a strange and recurring tragedy. On the northern shore of the lake, right under the precipitous cliffs on which the modern village of Nemi is perched, stood the sacred grove and sanctuary of Diana Nemorensis, or Diana of the Wood. The lake and the grove were sometimes known as the lake and grove of Aricia. But the town of Aricia (the modern La Riccia) was situated about three miles off, at the foot of the Alban Mount, and separated by a steep descent from the lake, which lies in a small crater-like hollow on the mountain side. In this sacred grove there grew a certain tree round which at any time of the day, and probably far into the night, a grim figure might be seen to prowl. In his hand he carried a drawn sword, and he kept peering warily about him as if at every instant he expected to be set upon by an enemy. He was a priest and a murderer; and the man for whom he looked was sooner or later to murder him and hold the priesthood in his stead. Such was the rule of the sanctuary. A candidate for the priesthood could only succeed to office by slaying the priest, and

1

having slain him, he retained office till he was himself slain by a stronger or craftier.

The post which he held by this precarious tenure carried with it the title of king; but surely no crowned head ever lay uneasier, or was visited by more evil dreams, than his. For year in year out, in summer and winter, in fair weather and in foul, he had to keep his lonely watch, and whenever he snatched a troubled slumber it was at the peril of his life. The least relaxation of his vigilance, the smallest abatement of his strength of limb or skill of fence, put him in jeopardy; grey hairs might seal his death-warrant. To gentle and pious pilgrims at the shrine the sight of him might well seem to darken the fair landscape, as when a cloud suddenly blots the sun on a bright day. The dreamy blue of Italian skies, the dappled shade of summer woods, and the sparkle of waves in the sun, can have accorded but ill with that stern and sinister figure. Rather we picture to ourselves the scene as it may have been witnessed by a belated wayfarer on one of those wild autumn nights when the dead leaves are falling thick, and the winds seem to sing the dirge of the dying year. It is a sombre picture, set to melancholy music — the background of forest showing black and jagged against a lowering and stormy sky, the sighing of the wind in the branches, the rustle of the withered leaves under foot, the lapping of the cold water on the shore, and in the foreground, pacing to and fro, now in twilight and now in gloom, a dark figure with a glitter of steel at the shoulder whenever the pale moon, riding clear of the cloud-rack, peers down at him through the matted boughs.

The strange rule of this priesthood has no parallel in classical antiquity, and cannot be explained from it. To find an explanation we must go farther afield. No one will probably deny that such a custom savours of a barbarous age, and, surviving into imperial times, stands out in striking isolation from the polished Italian society of the day, like a primaeval rock rising from a smooth-shaven lawn. It is the very rudeness and barbarity of the custom which allow us a hope of explaining it. For recent researches into the early history of man have revealed the essential similarity with which, under many superficial differences, the human mind has elaborated its first crude philosophy of life. Accordingly, if we can show that a barbarous custom, like that of the priesthood of Nemi, has existed elsewhere; if we can detect the motives which led to its institution; if we can prove that these motives have operated widely, perhaps universally, in human society, producing in varied circumstances a variety of institutions specifically different but generically alike; if we can show, lastly, that these very motives, with some of their derivative institutions, were actually at work in classical antiquity; then we may fairly infer that at a remoter age the same motives gave birth to the priesthood of Nemi. Such an inference, in default of direct evidence as to how the priesthood did actually arise, can never amount to demonstration. But it will be more or less probable according to the degree of completeness with which it fulfils the conditions I have indicated. The object of this book is, by meeting these conditions, to offer a fairly probable explanation of the priesthood of Nemi.

I begin by setting forth the few facts and legends which have come down to us on the subject. According to one story the worship of Diana at Nemi was instituted by Orestes, who, after killing Thoas, king of the Tauric Chersonese (the Crimea), fled with his sister to Italy, bringing with him the image of the Tauric Diana hidden in a faggot of sticks. After his death his bones were transported from Aricia to Rome and buried in front of the temple of Saturn, on the Capitoline slope, beside the temple of Concord. The bloody ritual which legend ascribed to the Tauric Diana is familiar to classical readers; it is said that every stranger who landed on the shore was sacrificed on her altar. But transported to Italy, the rite assumed a milder form. Within the sanctuary at Nemi grew a certain tree of which no branch might be broken. Only a runaway slave was allowed to break off, if he could, one of its boughs. Success in the attempt entitled him to fight the priest in single combat, and if he slew him he reigned in his stead with the title of King of the Wood (*Rex Nemorensis*). According to the public opinion of the ancients the fateful branch was that Golden Bough which, at the Sibyl's bidding, Aeneas plucked before he essayed the perilous journey to the world of the dead. The flight of the slave represented, it was said, the flight of Orestes; his combat with the priest was a reminiscence of the human sacrifices once offered to the Tauric Diana. This rule of succession **by the sword was observed down to imperial times; for amongst** his other freaks Caligula, thinking that the priest of Nemi had held office too long, hired a more stalwart ruffian to slay him; and a Greek traveller, who visited Italy in the age of the Antonines, remarks that down to his time the priesthood was still the prize of victory in a single combat.

Of the worship of Diana at Nemi some leading features can still be made out. From the votive offerings which have been found on the site, it appears that she was conceived of especially as a huntress, and further as blessing men and women with offspring, and granting expectant mothers an easy delivery. Again, fire seems to have played a foremost part in her ritual. For during her annual festival, held on the thirteenth of August, at the hottest time of the year, her grove shone with a multitude of torches, whose ruddy glare was reflected by the lake; and throughout the length and breadth of Italy the day was kept with holy rites at every domestic hearth. Bronze statuettes found in her precinct represent the goddess herself holding a torch in her raised right hand; and women whose prayers had been heard by her came crowned with wreaths and bearing lighted torches to the sanctuary in fulfilment of their vows. Some one unknown dedicated a perpetually burning lamp in a little shrine at Nemi for the safety of the Emperor Claudius and his family. The terra-cotta lamps which have been discovered in the grove may perhaps have served a like purpose for humbler persons. If so, the analogy of the custom to the Catholic practice of dedicating holy candles in churches would be obvious. Further, the title of Vesta borne by Diana at Nemi points clearly to the maintenance of a perpetual holy fire in her sanctuary. A large circular basement at the north-east corner of the temple, raised on three steps and bearing traces of a mosaic pavement, probably supported a round temple of Diana in her character of Vesta, like the round temple of Vesta in the Roman Forum. Here the sacred fire would seem to have been tended by Vestal Virgins, for the head of a Vestal in terra-cotta was found on the spot, and the worship of a perpetual fire, cared for by holy maidens, appears to have been common in Latium from the earliest to the latest times. Further, at the annual festival of the goddess, hunting dogs were crowned and wild beasts were not molested; young people went through a purificatory ceremony in her honour; wine was brought forth,

and the feast consisted of a kid, cakes served piping hot on plates of leaves, and apples still hanging in clusters on the boughs.

But Diana did not reign alone in her grove at Nemi. Two lesser divinities shared her forest sanctuary. One was Egeria, the nymph of the clear water which, bubbling from the basaltic rocks, used to fall in graceful cascades into the lake at the place called Le Mole, because here were established the mills of the modern village of Nemi. The purling of the stream as it ran over the pebbles is mentioned by Ovid, who tells us that he had often drunk of its water. Women with child used to sacrifice to Egeria, because she was believed, like Diana, to be able to grant them an easy delivery. Tradition ran that the nymph had been the wife or mistress of the wise king Numa, that he had consorted with her in the secrecy of the sacred grove, and that the laws which he gave the Romans had been inspired by communion with her divinity. Plutarch compares the legend with other tales of the loves of goddesses for mortal men, such as the love of Cybele and the Moon for the fair youths Attis and Endymion. According to some, the trysting-place of the lovers was not in the woods of Nemi but in a grove outside the dripping Porta Capena at Rome, where another sacred spring of Egeria gushed from a dark cavern. Every day the Roman Vestals fetched water from this spring to wash the temple of Vesta, carrying it in earthenware pitchers on their heads. In Juvenal's time the natural rock had been encased in marble, and the hallowed spot was profaned by gangs of poor Jews, who were suffered to squat, like gypsies, in the grove. We may suppose that the spring which fell into the lake of Nemi was the true original Egeria, and that when the first settlers moved down from the Alban hills to the banks of the Tiber they brought the nymph with them and found a new home for her in a grove outside the gates. The remains of baths which have been discovered within the sacred precinct, together with many terra-cotta models of various parts of the human body, suggest that the waters of Egeria were used to heal the sick, who may have signified their hopes or testified their gratitude by dedicating likenesses of the diseased members to the goddess, in accordance with a custom which is still observed in many parts of Europe. To this day it would seem that the spring retains medicinal virtues.

The other of the minor deities at Nemi was Virbius. Legend had it that Virbius was the young Greek hero Hippolytus, chaste and fair, who learned the art of venery from the centaur Chiron, and spent all his days in the greenwood chasing wild beasts with the virgin huntress Artemis (the Greek counterpart of Diana) for his only comrade. Proud of her divine society, he spurned the love of women, and this proved his bane. For Aphrodite, stung by his scorn, inspired his stepmother Phaedra with love of him; and when he disdained her wicked advances she falsely accused him to his father Theseus. The slander was believed, and Theseus prayed to his sire Poseidon to avenge the imagined wrong. So while Hippolytus drove in a chariot by the shore of the Saronic Gulf, the sea-god sent a fierce bull forth from the waves. The terrified horses bolted, threw Hippolytus from the chariot, and dragged him at their hoofs to death. But Diana, for the love she bore Hippolytus, persuaded the leech Aesculapius to bring her fair young hunter back to life by his simples. Jupiter, indignant that a mortal man should return from the gates of death, thrust down the meddling leech himself to Hades. But Diana hid her favourite from the angry god in a thick cloud, disguised his features by adding years to his life, and then bore him far away to the dells of Nemi, where she entrusted him to the nymph Egeria, to live there, unknown and solitary, under the name of Virbius, in the depth of the Italian forest. There he reigned a king, and there he dedicated a precinct to Diana. He had a comely son, Virbius, who, undaunted by his father's fate, drove a team of fiery steeds to join the Latins in the war against Aeneas and the Trojans. Virbius was worshipped as a god not only at Nemi but elsewhere; for in Campania we hear of a special priest devoted to his service. Horses were excluded from the Arician grove and sanctuary because horses had killed Hippolytus. It was unlawful to touch his image. Some thought that he was the sun. 'But the truth is,' says Servius, 'that he is a deity associated with Diana, as Attis is associated with the Mother of the Gods, and Erichthonius with Minerva, and Adonis with Venus.' What the nature of that association was we shall enquire presently. Here it is worth observing that in his long and chequered career this mythical personage has displayed a remarkable tenacity of life. For we can hardly doubt that the Saint Hippolytus of the

Roman calendar, who was dragged by horses to death on the thirteenth of August, Diana's own day, is no other than the Greek hero of the same name, who, after dying twice over as a heathen sinner, has been happily resuscitated as a Christian saint.

It needs no elaborate demonstration to convince us that the stories told to account for Diana's worship at Nemi are unhistorical. Clearly they belong to that large class of myths which are made up to explain the origin of a religious ritual and have no other foundation than the resemblance, real or imaginary, which may be traced between it and some foreign ritual. The incongruity of these Nemi myths is indeed transparent, since the foundation of the worship is traced now to Orestes and now to Hippolytus, according as this or that feature of the ritual has to be accounted for. The real value of such tales is that they serve to illustrate the nature of the worship by providing a standard with which to compare it; and further, that they bear witness indirectly to its venerable age by showing that the true origin was lost in the mists of a fabulous antiquity. In the latter respect these Nemi legends are probably more to be trusted than the apparently historical tradition, vouched for by Cato the Elder, that the sacred grove was dedicated to Diana by a certain Egerius Baebius or Laevius of Tusculum, a Latin dictator, on behalf of the peoples of Tusculum, Aricia, Lanuvium, Laurentum, Cora, Tibur, Pometia, and Ardea. This tradition indeed speaks for the great age of the sanctuary, since it seems to date its foundation sometime before 495 B.C., the year in which Pometia was sacked by the Romans and disappears from history. But we cannot suppose that so barbarous a rule as that of the Arician priesthood was deliberately instituted by a league of civilised communities, such as the Latin cities undoubtedly were. It must have been handed down from a time beyond the memory of man, when Italy was still in a far ruder state than any known to us in the historical period. The credit of the tradition is rather shaken than confirmed by another story which ascribes the foundation of the sanctuary to a certain Manius Egerius, who gave rise to the saying, 'There are many Manii at Aricia.' This proverb some explained by alleging that Manius Egerius was the ancestor of a long and distinguished line, whereas others thought it meant that there were many ugly and deformed people at Aricia, and they derived the

name Manius from *Mania,* a bogy or bugbear to frighten children.
A Roman satirist uses the name Manius as typical of the beggars
who lay in wait for pilgrims on the Arician slopes. These
differences of opinion, together with the discrepancy between
Manius Egerius of Aricia and Egerius Laevius of Tusculum, as
well as the resemblance of both names to the mythical Egeria,
excite our suspicion. Yet the tradition recorded by Cato seems
too circumstantial, and its sponsor too respectable, to allow us to
dismiss it as an idle fiction. Rather we may suppose that it refers
to some ancient restoration or reconstruction of the sanctuary,
which was actually carried out by the confederate states. At any
rate it testifies to a belief that the grove had been from early times
a common place of worship for many of the oldest cities of the
country, if not for the whole Latin confederacy.

§ 2. *Artemis and Hippolytus.* — I have said that the Arician
legends of Orestes and Hippolytus, though worthless as history,
have a certain value in so far as they may help us to understand
the worship at Nemi better by comparing it with the ritual and
myths of other sanctuaries. We must ask ourselves, Why did the
authors of these legends pitch upon Orestes and Hippolytus in
order to explain Virbius and the King of the Wood? In regard
to Orestes, the answer is obvious. He and the image of the Tauric
Diana, which could only be appeased with human blood, were
dragged in to render intelligible the murderous rule of succession
to the Arician priesthood. In regard to Hippolytus the case is
not so plain. The manner of his death suggests readily enough
a reason for the exclusion of horses from the grove; but this by
itself seems hardly enough to account for the identification. We
must try to probe deeper by examining the worship as well as
the legend or myth of Hippolytus.

He had a famous sanctuary at his ancestral home of Troezen,
situated on that beautiful, almost landlocked bay, where groves
of oranges and lemons, with tall cypresses soaring like dark
spires above the garden of the Hesperides, now clothe the strip
of fertile shore at the foot of the rugged mountains. Across the
blue water of the tranquil bay, which it shelters from the open
sea, rises Poseidon's sacred island, its peaks veiled in the sombre
green of the pines. On this fair coast Hippolytus was worshipped.
Within his sanctuary stood a temple with an ancient image. His

service was performed by a priest who held office for life: every year a sacrificial festival was held in his honour; and his untimely fate was yearly mourned, with weeping and doleful chants, by unwedded maids. Youths and maidens dedicated locks of their hair in his temple before marriage. His grave existed at Troezen, though the people would not show it. It has been suggested, with great plausibility, that in the handsome Hippolytus, beloved of Artemis, cut off in his youthful prime, and yearly mourned by damsels, we have one of those mortal lovers of a goddess who appear so often in ancient religion, and of whom Adonis is the most familiar type. The rivalry of Artemis and Phaedra for the affection of Hippolytus reproduces, it is said, under different names, the rivalry of Aphrodite and Proserpine for the love of Adonis, for Phaedra is merely a double of Aphrodite. The theory probably does no injustice either to Hippolytus or to Artemis. For Artemis was originally a great goddess of fertility, and, on the principles of early religion, she who fertilises nature must herself be fertile, and to be that she must necessarily have a male consort. On this view, Hippolytus was the consort of Artemis of Troezen, and the shorn tresses offered to him by the Troezenian youths and maidens before marriage were designed to strengthen his union with the goddess, and so promote the fruitfulness of the earth, of cattle, and of mankind. It is some confirmation of this view that within the precinct of Hippolytus at Troezen there were worshipped two female powers named Damia and Auxesia, whose connexion with the fertility of the ground is unquestionable. When Epidaurus suffered from a dearth, the people, in obedience to an oracle, carved images of Damia and Auxesia out of sacred olive-wood, and no sooner had they done so and set them up than the earth bore fruit again. Moreover, at Troezen itself, and apparently within the precinct of Hippolytus, a curious festival of stone-throwing was held in honour of these maidens, as the Troezenians called them; and it is easy to show that similar customs have been practised in many lands for the express purpose of ensuring good crops. In the story of the tragic death of the youthful Hippolytus we may discern an analogy with similar tales of other fair but mortal youths who paid with their lives for the brief rapture of the love of an immortal goddess. These hapless lovers were probably not always mere myths, and the legends which traced their spilt blood in the purple bloom of the violet, the scarlet stain of the anemone, or the crimson flush of the rose were no idle poetic emblems of youth and beauty fleeting as the summer flowers. Such fables contain a deeper philosophy of the relation of the life of man to the life of nature — a sad philosophy which gave birth to a tragic practice. What that philosophy and that practice were, we shall learn later on.

§ 3. *Recapitulation.* — We can now perhaps understand why the ancients identified Hippolytus, the consort of Artemis, with Virbius, who, according to Servius, stood to Diana as Adonis to Venus, or Attis to the Mother of the Gods. For Diana, like Artemis, was a goddess of fertility in general, and of childbirth in particular. As such she, like her Greek counterpart, needed a male partner. That partner, if Servius is right, was Virbius. In his character of the founder of the sacred grove and first king of Nemi, Virbius is clearly the mythical predecessor or archetype of the line of priests who served Diana under the title of Kings of the Wood, and who came, like him, one after the other, to a violent end. It is natural, therefore, to conjecture that they stood to the goddess of the grove in the same relation in which Virbius stood to her; in short, that the mortal King of the Wood had for his queen the woodland Diana herself. If the sacred tree which he guarded with his life was supposed, as seems probable, to be her special embodiment, her priest may not only have worshipped it as his goddess but embraced it as his wife. There is at least nothing absurd in the supposition, since even in the time of Pliny a noble Roman used thus to treat a beautiful beech-tree in another sacred grove of Diana on the Alban hills. He embraced it, he kissed it, he lay under its shadow, he poured wine on its trunk. Apparently he took the tree for the goddess. The custom of physically marrying men and women to trees is still practised in India and other parts of the East. Why should it not have obtained in ancient Latium?

Reviewing the evidence as a whole, we may conclude that the worship of Diana in her sacred grove at Nemi was of great importance and immemorial antiquity; that she was revered as the goddess of woodlands and of wild creatures, probably also of domestic cattle and of the fruits of the earth; that she was believed to bless men and women with offspring and to aid mothers in childbed; that her holy fire, tended by chaste virgins, burned perpetually in a round temple within the precinct; that associated with her was a water-nymph Egeria who discharged one of Diana's own functions by succouring women in travail, and who was popularly supposed to have mated with an old Roman king in the sacred grove; further, that Diana of the Wood herself had a male companion Virbius by name, who was to her what Adonis was to Venus, or Attis to Cybele; and, lastly, that this mythical Virbius was represented in historical times by a line of priests known as Kings of the Wood, who regularly perished by the swords of their successors, and whose lives were in a manner bound up with a certain tree in the grove, because so long as that tree was uninjured they were safe from attack.

Clearly these conclusions do not of themselves suffice to explain the peculiar rule of succession to the priesthood. But perhaps the survey of a wider field may lead us to think that they contain in germ the solution of the problem. To that wider survey we must now address ourselves. It will be long and laborious, but may possess something of the interest and charm of a voyage of discovery, in which we shall visit many strange foreign lands, with strange foreign peoples, and still stranger customs. The wind is in the shrouds: we shake out our sails to it, and leave the coast of Italy behind us for a time.

CHAPTER II

PRIESTLY KINGS

THE questions which we have set ourselves to answer are mainly two: first, why had Diana's priest at Nemi, the King of the Wood, to slay his predecessor? second, why before doing so had he to pluck the branch of a certain tree which the public opinion of the ancients identified with Virgil's Golden Bough?

The first point on which we fasten is the priest's title. Why was he called the King of the Wood? Why was his office spoken of as a kingdom?

The union of a royal title with priestly duties was common in ancient Italy and Greece. At Rome and in other cities of Latium there was a priest called the Sacrificial King or King of the Sacred Rites, and his wife bore the title of Queen of the Sacred Rites. In republican Athens the second annual magistrate of the state was called the King, and his wife the Queen; the functions of both were religious. Many other Greek democracies had titular kings, whose duties, so far as they are known, seem to have been priestly, and to have centred round the Common Hearth of the state. Some Greek states had several of these titular kings, who held office simultaneously. At Rome the tradition was that the Sacrificial King had been appointed after the abolition of the monarchy in order to offer the sacrifices which before had been offered by the kings. A similar view as to the origin of the priestly kings appears to have prevailed in Greece. In itself the opinion is not improbable, and it is borne out by the example of Sparta, almost the only purely Greek state which retained the kingly form of government in historical times. For in Sparta all state sacrifices were offered by the kings as descendants of the god. One of the two Spartan kings held the priesthood of Zeus Lacedaemon, the other the priesthood of Heavenly Zeus.

This combination of priestly functions with royal authority is familiar to every one. Asia Minor, for example, was the seat of various great religious capitals peopled by thousands of sacred slaves, and ruled by pontiffs who wielded at once temporal and spiritual authority, like the popes of mediaeval Rome. Such priest-ridden cities were Zela and Pessinus. Teutonic kings, again, in the old heathen days seem to have stood in the position, and to have exercised the powers, of high priests. The Emperors of China offered public sacrifices, the details of which were regulated by the ritual books. The King of Madagascar was high-priest of the realm. At the great festival of the new year, when a bullock was sacrificed for the good of the kingdom, the king stood over the sacrifice to offer prayer and thanksgiving, while his attendants slaughtered the animal. In the monarchical states which still maintain their independence among the Gallas of Eastern Africa, the king sacrifices on the mountain tops and regulates the immolation of human victims; and the dim light of tradition reveals a similar union of temporal and spiritual power, of royal and priestly duties, in the kings of that delightful region of Central America whose ancient capital, now buried under the rank growth of the tropical forest, is marked by the stately and mysterious ruins of Palenque.

When we have said that the ancient kings were commonly priests also, we are far from having exhausted the religious aspect of their office. In those days the divinity that hedges a king was no empty form of speech, but the expression of a sober belief. Kings were revered, in many cases not merely as priests, that is, as intercessors between man and god, but as themselves gods, able to bestow upon their subjects and worshippers those blessings which are commonly supposed to be beyond the reach of mortals, and are sought, if at all, only by prayer and sacrifice offered to superhuman and invisible beings. Thus kings are often expected to give rain and sunshine in due season, to make the crops grow, and so on. Strange as this expectation appears to us, it is quite of a piece with early modes of thought. A savage hardly conceives the distinction commonly drawn by more advanced peoples between the natural and the supernatural. To him the world is to a great extent worked by supernatural agents, that is, by personal beings acting on impulses and motives like his own, liable like him to be moved by appeals to their pity, their hopes, and their fears. In a world so conceived he sees no limit to his power of influencing the course of nature to his own advantage. Prayers, promises, or threats may secure him fine weather and an abundant crop from the gods; and if a god should happen, as he sometimes believes, to become incarnate in his own person, then he need appeal to no higher being; he, the savage, possesses in himself all the powers necessary to further his own well-being and that of his fellow-men.

This is one way in which the idea of a man-god is reached. But there is another. Along with the view of the world as pervaded by spiritual forces, savage man has a different, and probably still older, conception in which we may detect a germ of the modern notion of natural law or the view of nature as a series of events occurring in an invariable order without the intervention of personal agency. The germ of which I speak is involved in that sympathetic magic, as it may be called, which plays a large part in most systems of superstition. In early society the king is frequently a magician as well as a priest; indeed he appears to have often attained to power by virtue of his supposed proficiency in the black or white art. Hence in order to understand the evolution of the kingship and the sacred character with which the office has commonly been invested in the eyes of savage or barbarous peoples, it is essential to have some acquaintance with the principles of magic and to form some conception of the extraordinary hold which that ancient system of superstition has had on the human mind in all ages and all countries. Accordingly I propose to consider the subject in some detail.

CHAPTER III

SYMPATHETIC MAGIC

§ 1. *The Principles of Magic.* — If we analyse the principles of thought on which magic is based, they will probably be found to resolve themselves into two: first, that like produces like, or that an effect resembles its cause; and, second, that things which have once been in contact with each other continue to act on each other at a distance after the physical contact has been severed. The former principle may be called the Law of Similarity, the latter the Law of Contact or Contagion. From the first of these principles, namely the Law of Similarity, the magician infers that he can produce any effect he desires merely by imitating it: from the second he infers that whatever he does to a material object will affect equally the person with whom the object was once in contact, whether it formed part of his body or not. Charms based on the Law of Similarity may be called Homoeopathic or Imitative Magic. Charms based on the Law of Contact or Contagion may be called Contagious Magic. To denote the first of these branches of magic the term Homoeopathic is perhaps preferable, for the alternative term Imitative or Mimetic suggests, if it does not imply, a conscious agent who imitates, thereby limiting the scope of magic too narrowly. For the same principles which the magician applies in the practice of his art are implicitly believed by him to regulate the operations of inanimate nature;

in other words, he tacitly assumes that the Laws of Similarity and Contact are of universal application and are not limited to human actions. In short, magic is a spurious system of natural law as well as a fallacious guide of conduct; it is a false science as well as an abortive art. Regarded as a system of natural law, that is, as a statement of the rules which determine the sequence of events throughout the world, it may be called Theoretical Magic: regarded as a set of precepts which human beings observe in order to compass their ends, it may be called Practical Magic. At the same time it is to be borne in mind that the primitive magician knows magic only on its practical side; he never analyses the mental processes on which his practice is based, never reflects on the abstract principles involved in his actions. With him, as with the vast majority of men, logic is implicit, not explicit: he reasons just as he digests his food in complete ignorance of the intellectual and physiological processes which are essential to the one operation and to the other. In short, to him magic is always an art, never a science; the very idea of science is lacking in his undeveloped mind. It is for the philosophic student to trace the train of thought which underlies the magician's practice; to draw out the few simple threads of which the tangled skein is composed; to disengage the abstract principles from their concrete applications; in short, to discern the spurious science behind the bastard art.

If my analysis of the magician's logic is correct, its two great principles turn out to be merely two different misapplications of the association of ideas. Homoeopathic magic is founded on the association of ideas by similarity; contagious magic is founded on the association of ideas by contiguity. Homoeopathic magic commits the mistake of assuming that things which resemble each other are the same: contagious magic commits the mistake of assuming that things which have once been in contact with each other are always in contact. But in practice the two branches are often combined; or, to be more exact, while homoeopathic or imitative magic may be practised by itself, contagious magic will generally be found to involve an application of the homoeopathic or imitative principle. Thus generally stated the two things may be a little difficult to grasp, but they will readily become intelligible when they are illustrated by particular examples. Both trains of thought are in fact extremely simple and elementary. It could hardly be otherwise, since they are familiar in the concrete, though certainly not in the abstract, to the crude intelligence not only of the savage, but of ignorant and dull-witted people everywhere. Both branches of magic, the homoeopathic and the contagious, may conveniently be comprehended under the general name of Sympathetic Magic, since both assume that things act on each other at a distance through a secret sympathy, the impulse being transmitted from one to the other by means of what we may conceive as a kind of invisible ether, not unlike that which is postulated by modern science for a precisely similar purpose, namely, to explain how things can physically affect each other through a space which appears to be empty.

It may be convenient to tabulate as follows the branches of magic according to the laws of thought which underlie them:

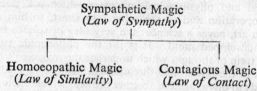

Sympathetic Magic
(*Law of Sympathy*)

Homoeopathic Magic   Contagious Magic
(*Law of Similarity*)   (*Law of Contact*)

I will now illustrate these two great branches of sympathetic magic by examples, beginning with homoeopathic magic.

§ 2. *Homoeopathic or Imitative Magic.* — Perhaps the most familiar application of the principle that like produces like is the attempt which has been made by many peoples in many ages to injure or destroy an enemy by injuring or destroying an image of him, in the belief that, just as the image suffers, so does the man, and that when it perishes he must die. A few instances out of many may be given to prove at once the wide diffusion of the practice over the world and its remarkable persistence through the ages. For thousands of years ago it was known to the sorcerers of ancient India, Babylon, and Egypt, as well as of Greece and Rome, and at this day it is still resorted to by cunning and malignant savages in Australia, Africa, and Scotland. Thus the North American Indians, we are told, believe that by drawing the figure of a person in sand, ashes, or clay, or by considering any object as his body, and then pricking it with a sharp stick or doing it any other injury, they inflict a corresponding injury on the person represented. For example, when an Ojebway Indian desires to work evil on any one, he makes a little wooden image of his enemy and runs a needle into its head or heart, or he shoots an arrow into it, believing that wherever the needle pierces or the arrow strikes the image, his foe will the same instant be seized with a sharp pain in the corresponding part of his body; but if he intends to kill the person outright, he burns or buries the puppet, uttering certain magic words as he does so. The Peruvian Indians moulded images of fat mixed with grain to imitate the persons whom they disliked or feared, and then burned the effigy on the road where the intended victim was to pass. This they called burning his soul.

A Malay charm of the same sort is as follows. Take parings of nails, hair, eyebrows, spittle, and so forth of your intended victim, enough to represent every part of his person, and then make them up into his likeness with wax from a deserted bees' comb. Scorch the figure slowly by holding it over a lamp every night for seven nights, and say:

> '*It is not wax that I am scorching,*
> *It is the liver, heart, and spleen of So-and-so that I scorch.*'

After the seventh time burn the figure, and your victim will die. This charm obviously combines the principles of homoeopathic and contagious magic; since the image which is made in the likeness of an enemy contains things which once were in contact with him, namely, his nails, hair, and spittle. Another form of the Malay charm, which resembles the Ojebway practice still more closely, is to make a corpse of wax from an empty bees' comb and of the length of a footstep; then pierce the eye of the image, and your enemy is blind; pierce the stomach, and he is sick; pierce the head, and his head aches; pierce the breast, and his breast will suffer. If you would kill him outright, transfix the image from the head downwards; enshroud it as you would a corpse; pray over it as if you were praying over the dead; then bury it in the middle of a path where your victim will be sure to step over it. In order that his blood may not be on your head, you should say:

> '*It is not I who am burying him,*
> *It is Gabriel who is burying him.*'

Thus the guilt of the murder will be laid on the shoulders of the archangel Gabriel, who is a great deal better able to bear it than you are.

If homoeopathic or imitative magic, working by means of images, has commonly been practised for the spiteful purpose of putting obnoxious people out of the world, it has also, though far more rarely, been employed with the benevolent intention of helping others into it. In other words, it has been used to facilitate childbirth and to procure offspring for barren women. Thus among the Bataks of Sumatra a barren woman, who would become a mother, will make a wooden image of a child and hold it in her lap, believing that this will lead to the fulfilment of her wish. In the Babar Archipelago, when a woman desires to have a child, she invites a man who is himself the father of a large family to pray on her behalf to Upulero, the spirit of the sun. A doll is made of red cotton, which the woman clasps in her arms, as if she would suckle it. Then the father of many children takes a fowl and holds it by the legs to the woman's head, saying, 'O Upulero, make use of the fowl; let it fall, let descend a child, I beseech you, I entreat you, let a child fall and descend into my hands and on my lap.' Then he asks the woman, 'Has the child come?' and she answers, 'Yes, it is sucking already.' After that the man holds the fowl on the husband's head, and mumbles some form of words. Lastly, the bird is killed and laid, together with some betel, on the domestic place of sacrifice. When the ceremony is over, word goes about in the village that the woman has been brought to bed, and her friends come and congratulate her. Here the pretence that a child has been born is a purely magical rite designed to secure, by means of imitation or mimicry, that a child really shall be born; but an attempt is made to add to the efficacy of the rite by means of prayer and sacrifice. To put it otherwise, magic is here blent with and reinforced by religion.

Among some of the Dyaks of Borneo, when a woman is in hard labour, a wizard is called in, who essays to facilitate the delivery in a rational manner by manipulating the body of the sufferer. Meantime another wizard outside the room exerts himself to attain the same end by means which we should regard as wholly irrational. He, in fact, pretends to be the expectant mother; a large stone attached to his stomach by a cloth wrapt round his body represents the child in the womb, and, following the directions shouted to him by his colleague on the real scene of operations, he moves this make-believe baby about on his body in exact imitation of the movements of the real baby till the infant is born.

The same principle of make-believe, so dear to children, has led other peoples to employ a simulation of birth as a form of adoption, and even as a mode of restoring a supposed dead person to life. If you pretend to give birth to a boy, or even to a great bearded man who has not a drop of your blood in his veins, then, in the eyes of primitive law and philosophy, that boy or man is really your son to all intents and purposes. Thus Diodorus tells us that when Zeus persuaded his jealous wife Hera to adopt Hercules, the goddess got into bed, and clasping the burly hero to her bosom, pushed him through her robes and let him fall to the ground in imitation of a real birth; and the historian adds that in his own day the same mode of adopting children was practised by the barbarians. At the present time it is said to be still in use in Bulgaria and among the Bosnian Turks. A woman will take a boy whom she intends to adopt and push or pull him through her clothes ; ever afterwards he is regarded as her very son, and inherits the whole property of his adoptive parents. Among the Berawans of Sarawak, when a woman desires to adopt a grown-up man or woman, a great many people assemble and have a feast. The adopting mother, seated in public on a raised and covered seat, allows the adopted person to crawl from behind between her legs. As soon as he appears in front he is stroked with the sweet-scented blossoms of the areca palm, and tied to the woman. Then the adopting mother and the adopted son or daughter, thus bound together, waddle to the end of the house and back again in front of all the spectators. The tie established between the two by this graphic imitation of childbirth is very strict; an offence committed against an adopted child is reckoned more heinous than one committed against a real child. In ancient Greece any man who had been supposed erroneously to be dead, and for whom in his absence funeral rites had been performed, was treated as dead to society till he had gone through the form of being born again. He was passed through a woman's lap, then washed, dressed in swaddling-clothes, and put out to nurse.

Not until this ceremony had been punctually performed might he mix freely with living folk. In ancient India, under similar circumstances, the supposed dead man had to pass the first night after his return in a tub filled with a mixture of fat and water; there he sat with doubled-up fists and without uttering a syllable, like a child in the womb; while over him were performed all the sacraments that were wont to be celebrated over a pregnant woman. Next morning he got out of the tub and went through once more all the other sacraments he had formerly partaken of from his youth up; in particular, he married a wife or espoused his old one over again with due solemnity.

Another beneficent use of homoeopathic magic is to heal or prevent sickness. The ancient Hindoos performed an elaborate ceremony, based on homoeopathic magic, for the cure of jaundice. Its main drift was to banish the yellow colour to yellow creatures and yellow things, such as the sun, to which it properly belongs, and to procure for the patient a healthy red colour from a living, vigorous source, namely a red bull. With this intention, a priest recited the following spell: 'Up to the sun shall go thy heart-ache and thy jaundice: in the colour of the red bull do we envelop thee! We envelop thee in red tints, unto long life. May this person go unscathed and be free of yellow colour! The cows whose divinity is Rohini, they who, moreover, are themselves red (*rohinih*) — in their every form and every strength we do envelop thee. Into the parrots, into the thrush, do we put thy jaundice, and, furthermore, into the yellow wagtail do we put thy jaundice.' While he uttered these words, the priest, in order to infuse the rosy hue of health into the sallow patient, gave him water to sip which was mixed with the hair of a red bull; he poured water over the animal's back and made the sick man drink it; he seated him on the skin of a red bull and tied a piece of the skin to him. Then in order to improve his colour by thoroughly eradicating the yellow taint, he proceeded thus. He first daubed him from head to foot with a yellow porridge made of turmeric or curcuma (a yellow plant), set him on a bed, tied three yellow birds, to wit a parrot, a thrush, and a yellow wagtail, by means of a yellow string to the foot of the bed; then pouring water over the patient, he washed off the yellow porridge, and with it no doubt the jaundice, from him to the birds. After that, by way of giving a final bloom to his complexion, he took some hairs of a red bull, wrapt them in gold leaf, and glued them to the patient's skin. The ancients held that if a person suffering from jaundice looked sharply at a stone-curlew, and the bird looked steadily at him, he was cured of the disease. 'Such is the nature,' says Plutarch, 'and such the temperament of the creature that it draws out and receives the malady which issues, like a stream, through the eyesight.' So well recognised among bird-fanciers was this valuable property of the stone-curlew that when they had one of these birds for sale they kept it carefully covered, lest a jaundiced person should look at it and be cured for nothing. The virtue of the bird lay not in its colour but in its large golden eye, which naturally drew out the yellow jaundice. Pliny tells of another, or perhaps the same, bird, to which the Greeks gave their name for jaundice, because if a jaundiced man saw it, the disease left him and slew the bird. He mentions also a stone which was supposed to cure jaundice because its hue resembled that of a jaundiced skin.

One of the great merits of homoeopathic magic is that it enables the cure to be performed on the person of the doctor instead of on that of his victim, who is thus relieved of all trouble and inconvenience, while he sees his medical man writhe in anguish before him. For example, the peasants of Perche, in France, labour under the impression that a prolonged fit of vomiting is brought about by the patient's stomach becoming unhooked, as they call it, and so falling down. Accordingly, a practitioner is called in to restore the organ to its proper place. After hearing the symptoms he at once throws himself into the most horrible contortions, for the purpose of unhooking his own stomach. Having succeeded in the effort, he next hooks it up again in another series of contortions and grimaces, while the patient experiences a corresponding relief. Fee five francs. In like manner a Dyak medicine-man, who has been fetched in a case of illness, will lie down and pretend to be dead. He is accordingly treated like a corpse, is bound up in mats, taken out of the house, and deposited on the ground. After about an hour the other medicine-men loose the pretended dead man and bring him to life; and as he recovers, the sick person is supposed to recover too. A cure for a tumour, based on the principle of homoeopathic

B

magic, is prescribed by Marcellus of Bordeaux, court physician to Theodosius the First, in his curious work on medicine. It is as follows. Take a root of vervain, cut it across, and hang one end of it round the patient's neck, and the other in the smoke of the fire. As the vervain dries up in the smoke, so the tumour will also dry up and disappear. If the patient should afterwards prove ungrateful to the good physician, the man of skill can avenge himself very easily by throwing the vervain into water; for as the root absorbs the moisture once more, the tumour will return. The same sapient writer recommends you, if you are troubled with pimples, to watch for a falling star, and then instantly, while the star is still shooting from the sky, to wipe the pimples with a cloth or anything that comes to hand. Just as the star falls from the sky, so the pimples will fall from your body; only you must be very careful not to wipe them with your bare hand, or the pimples will be transferred to it.

Further, homoeopathic and in general sympathetic magic plays a great part in the measures taken by the rude hunter or fisherman to secure an abundant supply of food. On the principle that like produces like, many things are done by him and his friends in deliberate imitation of the result which he seeks to attain; and, on the other hand, many things are scrupulously avoided because they bear some more or less fanciful resemblance to others which would really be disastrous.

Nowhere is the theory of sympathetic magic more systematically carried into practice for the maintenance of the food supply than in the barren regions of Central Australia. Here the tribes are divided into a number of totem clans, each of which is charged with the duty of multiplying their totem for the good of the community by means of magical ceremonies. Most of the totems are edible animals and plants, and the general result supposed to be accomplished by these ceremonies is that of supplying the tribe with food and other necessaries. Often the rites consist of an imitation of the effect which the people desire to produce; in other words, their magic is homoeopathic or imitative. Thus among the Warramunga the headman of the white cockatoo totem seeks to multiply white cockatoos by holding an effigy of the bird and mimicking its harsh cry. Among the Arunta the men of the witchetty grub totem perform ceremonies for multiplying the grub which the other members of the tribe use as food. One of the ceremonies is a pantomime representing the fully developed insect in the act of emerging from the chrysalis. A long narrow structure of branches is set up to imitate the chrysalis case of the grub. In this structure a number of men, who have the grub for their totem, sit and sing of the creature in its various stages. Then they shuffle out of it in a squatting posture, and as they do so they sing of the insect emerging from the chrysalis. This is supposed to multiply the numbers of the grubs. Again, in order to multiply emus, which are an important article of food, the men of the emu totem paint on the ground the sacred design of their totem, especially the parts of the emu which they like best to eat, namely, the fat and the eggs. Round this painting the men sit and sing. Afterwards performers, wearing head-dresses to represent the long neck and small head of the emu, mimic the appearance of the bird as it stands aimlessly peering about in all directions.

The Indians of British Columbia live largely upon the fish which abound in their seas and rivers. If the fish do not come in due season, and the Indians are hungry, a Nootka wizard will make an image of a swimming fish and put it into the water in the direction from which the fish generally appear. This ceremony, accompanied by a prayer to the fish to come, will cause them to arrive at once. The islanders of Torres Straits use models of dugong and turtles to charm dugong and turtle to their destruction. The Toradjas of Central Celebes believe that things of the same sort attract each other by means of their indwelling spirits or vital ether. Hence they hang up the jawbones of deer and wild pigs in their houses, in order that the spirits which animate these bones may draw the living creatures of the same kind into the path of the hunter. In the island of Nias, when a wild pig has fallen into the pit prepared for it, the animal is taken out and its back is rubbed with nine fallen leaves, in the belief that this will make nine more wild pigs fall into the pit, just as the nine leaves fell from the tree. In the East Indian islands of Saparoea, Haroekoe, and Noessa Laut, when a fisherman is about to set a trap for fish in the sea, he looks out for a tree, of which the fruit has been much pecked at by birds. From such a tree he cuts a stout branch and makes of it the principal post in his fish-trap; for he believes that, just as the tree lured many birds to its fruit, so the branch cut from that tree will lure many fish to the trap.

The western tribes of British New Guinea employ a charm to aid the hunter in spearing dugong or turtle. A small beetle, which haunts coco-nut trees, is placed in the hole of the spear-haft into which the spear-head fits. This is supposed to make the spear-head stick fast in the dugong or turtle, just as the beetle sticks fast to a man's skin when it bites him. When a Cambodian hunter has set his nets and taken nothing, he strips himself naked, goes some way off, then strolls up to the net as if he did not see it, lets himself be caught in it, and cries, 'Hillo! what's this? I'm afraid I'm caught.' After that the net is sure to catch game. A pantomime of the same sort has been acted within living memory in our Scottish Highlands. The Rev. James Macdonald, now of Reay in Caithness, tells us that in his boyhood when he was fishing with companions about Loch Aline and they had had no bites for a long time, they used to make a pretence of throwing one of their fellows overboard and hauling him out of the water, as if he were a fish; after that the trout or silloch would begin to nibble, according as the boat was on fresh or salt water. Before a Carrier Indian goes out to snare martens, he sleeps by himself for about ten nights beside the fire with a little stick pressed down on his neck. This naturally causes the fall-stick of his trap to drop down on the neck of the marten. Among the Galelareese, who inhabit a district in the northern part of Halmahera, a large island to the west of New Guinea, it is a maxim that when you are loading your gun to go out shooting, you should always put the bullet in your mouth before you insert it in the gun; for by so doing you practically eat the game that is to be hit by the bullet, which therefore cannot possibly miss the mark. A Malay who has baited a trap for crocodiles, and is awaiting results, is careful in eating his curry always to begin by swallowing three lumps of rice successively; for this helps the bait to slide more easily down the crocodile's throat. He is equally scrupulous not to take any bones out of his curry; for, if he did, it seems clear that the sharp-pointed stick on which the bait is skewered would similarly work itself loose, and the crocodile would get off with the bait. Hence in these circumstances it is prudent for the hunter, before he begins his meal, to get somebody else to take the bones out of his curry, otherwise he may at any moment have to choose between swallowing a bone and losing the crocodile.

This last rule is an instance of the things which the hunter abstains from doing lest, on the principle that like produces like, they should spoil his luck. For it is to be observed that the system of sympathetic magic is not merely composed of positive precepts; it comprises a very large number of negative precepts, that is, prohibitions. It tells you not merely what to do, but also what to leave undone. The positive precepts are charms; the negative precepts are taboos. In fact the whole doctrine of taboo, or at all events a large part of it, would seem to be only a special application of sympathetic magic, with its two great laws of similarity and contact. Though these laws are certainly not formulated in so many words nor even conceived in the abstract by the savage, they are nevertheless implicitly believed by him to regulate the course of nature quite independently of human will. He thinks that if he acts in a certain way, certain consequences will inevitably follow in virtue of one or other of these laws; and if the consequences of a particular act appear to him likely to prove disagreeable or dangerous, he is naturally careful not to act in that way lest he should incur them. In other words, he abstains from doing that which, in accordance with his mistaken notions of cause and effect, he falsely believes would injure him; in short, he subjects himself to a taboo. Thus taboo is so far a negative application of practical magic. Positive magic or sorcery says, 'Do this in order that so and so may happen.' Negative magic or taboo says, 'Do not do this, lest so and so should happen.' The aim of positive magic or sorcery is to produce a desired event; the aim of negative magic or taboo is to avoid an undesirable one. But both consequences, the desirable and the undesirable, are supposed to be brought about in accordance with the laws of similarity and contact. And just as the desired consequence is not really effected by the observance of a magical ceremony, so the dreaded consequence does not really result from the violation of a taboo. If the supposed evil necessarily followed a breach of taboo, the taboo would not be a taboo but a precept of morality or common sense. It is not a taboo to say, 'Do not put your hands in the fire'; it is a rule of common sense, because the forbidden action entails a real, not an imaginary evil. In short, those negative precepts which we call taboo are just as vain and futile as those positive precepts which we call sorcery. The two things are merely opposite sides or poles of one great disastrous fallacy, a mistaken conception of the association of ideas. Of that fallacy, sorcery is the positive, and taboo the negative pole. If we give the general name of magic to the whole erroneous system, both theoretical and practical, then taboo may be defined as the negative side of practical magic. To put this in tabular form:

Magic

Theoretical
(Magic as a pseudo-science)

Practical
(Magic as a pseudo-art)

Positive Magic
or
Sorcery

Negative Magic
or
Taboo

I have made these remarks on taboo and its relations to magic because I am about to give some instances of taboos observed by hunters, fishermen, and others, and I wished to show that they fall under the head of Sympathetic Magic, being only particular applications of that general theory. Thus, among the Esquimaux, boys are forbidden to play cat's cradle, because if they did so their fingers might in later life become entangled in the harpoon-line. Here the taboo is obviously an application of the law of similarity, which is the basis of homoeopathic magic: as the child's fingers are entangled by the string in playing cat's cradle, so they will be entangled by the harpoon-line when he is a man and hunts whales. Again, among the Huzuls of the Carpathian Mountains the wife of a hunter may not spin while her husband is hunting, or the game will turn and wind like the spindle, and the hunter will be unable to hit it. Here again the taboo is clearly derived from the law of similarity. So, too, in most parts of ancient Italy women were forbidden by law to spin on the highroads as they walked, or even to carry their spindles openly, because any such action was believed to injure the crops. Probably the notion was that the twirling of the spindle would twirl the corn-stalks and prevent them from growing straight. So, too, among the Ainos of Saghalien a pregnant woman may not spin nor twist ropes for two months before her delivery, because they think that if she did so the child's guts might be entangled like the thread. For a like reason in Bilaspore, a district of India, when the chief men of a village meet in council, no one present should twirl a spindle; for they think that if such a thing were to happen, the discussion, like the spindle, would move in a circle and never be wound up. In some of the East Indian islands any one who comes to the house of a hunter must walk straight in; he may not loiter at the door, for were he to do so, the game would in like manner stop in front of the hunter's snares and then turn back, instead of being caught in the trap. For a similar reason it is a rule with the Toradjas of Central Celebes that no one may stand or loiter on the ladder of a house where there is a pregnant woman, for such delay would retard the birth of the child; and in various parts of Sumatra the woman herself in these circumstances is forbidden to stand at the door or on the top rung of the house-ladder under pain of suffering hard labour for her imprudence in neglecting so elementary a precaution. Malays engaged in the search for camphor eat their food dry and take care not to pound their salt fine. The reason is that the camphor occurs in the form of small grains deposited in the cracks of the trunk of the camphor-tree. Accordingly it seems plain to the Malay that if, while seeking for camphor, he were to eat his salt finely ground, the camphor would be found also in fine grains; whereas by eating his salt coarse he ensures that the grains of the camphor will also be large. Camphor hunters in Borneo use the leathery sheath of the leaf-stalk of the Penang palm as a plate for food, and during the whole of the expedition they will never wash the plate, for fear that the camphor might dissolve and disappear from the crevices of the tree. Apparently they think that to wash their plates would be to wash out the camphor crystals from the trees in which they are imbedded. The chief product of some parts of Laos, a province of Siam, is lac. This is a resinous gum exuded by a red insect on the young branches of trees, to which the little creatures have to be attached by hand. All who engage in the business of gathering the gum abstain from washing themselves and especially from cleansing their heads, lest by removing the parasites from their hair they should detach the other insects from the boughs. Again, a Blackfoot Indian who has set a trap for eagles, and is watching it, would not eat rosebuds on any account; for he argues that if he did so, and an eagle alighted near the trap, the rosebuds in his own stomach would make the bird itch, with the result that instead of swallowing the bait the eagle would merely sit and scratch himself. Following this train of thought the eagle hunter also refrains from using an awl when he is looking after his snares; for surely if he were to scratch with an awl, the eagles would scratch him. The same disastrous consequence would follow if his wives and children at home used an awl while he is out after eagles, and accordingly they are forbidden to handle the tool in his absence for fear of putting him in bodily danger.

Among the taboos observed by savages none perhaps are more numerous or important than the prohibitions to eat certain foods, and of such prohibitions many are demonstrably derived from the law of similarity and are accordingly examples of negative magic. Just as the savage eats many animals or plants in order to acquire certain desirable qualities with which he believes them to be endowed, so he avoids eating many other animals and plants lest he should acquire certain undesirable qualities with which he believes them to be infected. In eating the former he practises positive magic; in abstaining from the latter he practises negative magic. Many examples of such positive magic will meet us later on; here I will give a few instances of such negative magic or taboo. For example, in Madagascar soldiers are forbidden to eat a number of foods lest on the principle of homoeopathic magic they should be tainted by certain dangerous or undesirable properties which are supposed to inhere in these particular viands. Thus they may not taste hedgehog, 'as it is feared that this animal, from its propensity of coiling up into a ball when alarmed, will impart a timid shrinking disposition to those who partake of it.' Again, no soldier should eat an ox's knee, lest like an ox he should become weak in the knees and unable to march. Further, the warrior should be careful to avoid partaking of a cock that has died fighting or anything that has been speared to death; and no male animal may on any account be killed in his house while he is away at the wars. For it seems obvious that if he were to eat a cock that had died fighting, he would himself be slain on the field of battle; if he were to partake of an animal that had been speared, he would be speared himself; if a male animal were killed in his house during his absence, he would himself be killed in like manner and perhaps at the same instant. Further, the Malagasy soldier must eschew kidneys, because in the Malagasy language the word for kidney is the same as that for 'shot'; so shot he would certainly be if he ate a kidney.

The reader may have observed that in some of the foregoing examples of taboos the magical influence is supposed to operate at considerable distances; thus among the Blackfoot Indians the wives and children of an eagle hunter are forbidden to use an awl during his absence, lest the eagles should scratch the distant husband and father; and again no male animal may be killed in the house of a Malagasy soldier while he is away at the wars, lest the killing of the animal should entail the killing of the man. This belief in the sympathetic influence exerted on each other by persons or things at a distance is of the essence of magic. Whatever doubts science may entertain as to the possibility of action at a distance, magic has none; faith in telepathy is one of its first principles. A modern advocate of the influence of mind upon mind at a distance would have no difficulty in convincing a savage; the savage believed in it long ago, and what is more, he acted on his belief with a logical consistency such as his civilised brother in the faith has not yet, so far as I am aware, exhibited in his conduct. For the savage is convinced not only that magical ceremonies affect persons and things afar off, but that the simplest acts of daily life may do so too. Hence on important occasions the behaviour of friends and relations at a distance is often regulated by a more or less elaborate code of rules, the neglect of which by the one set of persons would, it is supposed, entail misfortune or even death on the absent ones. In particular when a party of men are out hunting or fighting, their kinsfolk at home are often expected to do certain things or to abstain from doing certain others, for the sake of ensuring the safety and success of the distant hunters or warriors. I will now give some instances of this magical telepathy both in its positive and in its negative aspect.

In Laos when an elephant hunter is starting for the chase, he warns his wife not to cut her hair or oil her body in his absence; for if she cut her hair the elephant would burst the toils, if she oiled herself it would slip through them. When a Dyak village has turned out to hunt wild pigs in the jungle, the people who stay at home may not touch oil or water with their hands during the absence of their friends; for if they did so, the hunters would all be 'butter-fingered' and the prey would slip through their hands.

Elephant-hunters in East Africa believe that, if their wives prove unfaithful in their absence, this gives the elephant power over his pursuer, who will accordingly be killed or severely wounded. Hence if a hunter hears of his wife's misconduct, he abandons the chase and returns home. If a Wagogo hunter is unsuccessful, or is attacked by a lion, he attributes it to his wife's misbehaviour at home, and returns to her in great wrath. While he is away hunting, she may not let any one pass behind her or stand in front of her as she sits; and she must lie on her face in bed. The Moxos Indians of Bolivia thought that if a hunter's wife was unfaithful to him in his absence he would be bitten by a serpent or a jaguar. Accordingly, if such an accident happened to him, it was sure to entail the punishment, and often the death, of the woman, whether she was innocent or guilty. An Aleutian hunter of sea-otters thinks that he cannot kill a single animal if during his absence from home his wife should be unfaithful or his sister unchaste.

The Huichol Indians of Mexico treat as a demi-god a species of cactus which throws the eater into a state of ecstasy. The plant does not grow in their country, and has to be fetched every year by men who make a journey of forty-three days for the purpose. Meanwhile the wives at home contribute to the safety of their absent husbands by never walking fast, much less running, while the men are on the road. They also do their best to ensure the benefits which, in the shape of rain, good crops, and so forth, are expected to flow from the sacred mission. With this intention they subject themselves to severe restrictions like those imposed upon their husbands. During the whole of the time which elapses till the festival of the cactus is held, neither party washes except on certain occasions, and then only with water brought from the distant country where the holy plant grows. They also fast much, eat no salt, and are bound to strict continence. Any one who breaks this law is punished with illness, and, moreover, jeopardises the result which all are striving for. Health, luck, and life are to be gained by gathering the cactus, the gourd of the God of Fire; but inasmuch as the pure fire cannot benefit the impure, men and women must not only remain chaste for the time being, but must also purge themselves from the taint of past sin. Hence four days after the men have started the women gather and confess to Grandfather Fire with what men they have been in love from childhood till now. They may not omit a single one, for if they did so the men would not find a single cactus. So to refresh their memories each one prepares a string with as many knots as she has had lovers. This she brings to the temple, and, standing before the fire, she mentions aloud all the men she has scored on her string, name after name. Having ended her confession, she throws the string into the fire, and when the god has consumed it in his pure flame, her sins are forgiven her and she departs in peace. From now on the women are averse even to letting men pass near them. The cactus-seekers themselves make in like manner a clean breast of all their frailties. For every peccadillo they tie a knot on a string, and after they have 'talked to all the five winds' they deliver the rosary of their sins to the leader, who burns it in the fire.

Many of the indigenous tribes of Sarawak are firmly persuaded that were the wives to commit adultery while their husbands are searching for camphor in the jungle, the camphor obtained by the men would evaporate. Husbands can discover, by certain knots in the tree, when their wives are unfaithful; and it is said that in former days many women were killed by jealous husbands on no better evidence than that of these knots. Further, the wives dare not touch a comb while their husbands are away collecting the camphor; for if they did so, the interstices between the fibres of the tree, instead of being filled with the precious crystals, would be empty like the spaces between the teeth of a comb. In the Kei Islands, to the south-west of New Guinea, as soon as a vessel that is about to sail for a distant port has been launched, the part of the beach on which it lay is covered as speedily as possible with palm branches, and becomes sacred. No one may thenceforth cross that spot till the ship comes home. To cross it sooner would cause the vessel to perish. Moreover, all the time that the voyage lasts three or four young girls, specially chosen for the duty, are supposed to remain in sympathetic connexion with the mariners and to contribute by their behaviour to the safety and success of the voyage. On no account, except for the most necessary purpose, may they quit the room that has been assigned to them. More than that, so long as the vessel is believed to be at sea they must remain absolutely motionless, crouched on their mats with their hands clasped between their knees. They may not turn their heads to the left or to the right or make any other movement whatsoever. If they did, it would cause the boat to pitch and toss; and they may not eat any sticky stuff, such as rice boiled in coco-nut milk, for the stickiness of the food would clog the passage of the boat through the water. When the sailors are supposed to have reached their destination, the strictness of these rules is somewhat relaxed; but during the whole time that the voyage lasts the girls are forbidden to eat fish which have sharp bones or stings, such as the sting-ray, lest their friends at sea should be involved in sharp, stinging trouble.

Where beliefs like these prevail as to the sympathetic connexion between friends at a distance, we need not wonder that above everything else war, with its stern yet stirring appeal to some of the deepest and tenderest of human emotions, should quicken in the anxious relations left behind a desire to turn the sympathetic bond to the utmost account for the benefit of the dear ones who may at any moment be fighting and dying far away. Hence, to secure an end so natural and laudable, friends at home are apt to resort to devices which will strike us as pathetic or ludicrous, according as we consider their object or the means adopted to effect it. Thus in some districts of Borneo, when a Dyak is out head-hunting, his wife or, if he is unmarried, his sister must wear a sword day and night in order that he may always be thinking of his weapons; and she may not sleep during the day nor go to bed before two in the morning, lest her husband or brother should thereby be surprised in his sleep by an enemy. Among the Sea Dyaks of Banting in Sarawak the women strictly observe an elaborate code of rules while the men are away fighting. Some of the rules are negative and some are positive, but all alike are based on the principles of magical homoeopathy and telepathy. Amongst them are the following. The women must wake very early in the morning and open the windows as soon as it is light; otherwise their absent husbands will oversleep themselves. The women may not oil their hair, or the men will slip. The women may neither sleep nor doze by day, or the men will be drowsy on the march. The women must cook and scatter popcorn on the verandah every morning; so will the men be agile in their movements. The rooms must be kept very tidy, all boxes being placed near the walls; for if any one were to stumble over them, the absent husbands would fall and be at the mercy of the foe. At every meal a little rice must be left in the pot and put aside; so will the men far away always have something to eat and need never go hungry. On no account may the women sit at the loom till their legs grow cramped, otherwise their husbands will likewise be stiff in their joints and unable to rise up quickly or to run away from the foe. So in order to keep their husbands' joints supple the women often vary their labours at the loom by walking up and down the verandah. Further, they may not cover up their faces, or the men would not be able to find their way through the tall grass or jungle. Again, the women may not sew with a needle, or the men will tread on the sharp spikes set by the enemy in the path. Should a wife prove unfaithful while her husband is away, he will lose his life in the enemy's country. Some years ago all these rules and more were observed by the women of Banting, while their husbands were fighting for the English against rebels. But alas! these tender precautions availed them little; for many a man, whose faithful wife was keeping watch and ward for him at home, found a soldier's grave.

In the island of Timor, while war is being waged, the high-priest never quits the temple; his food is brought to him or cooked inside; day and night he must keep the fire burning, for if he were to let it die out, disaster would befall the warriors and would continue so long as the hearth was cold. Moreover, he must drink only hot water during the time the army is absent; for every draught of cold water would damp the spirits of the people, so that they could not vanquish the enemy. In the Kei Islands, when the warriors have departed, the women return indoors and bring out certain baskets containing fruits and stones. These fruits and stones they anoint and place on a board, murmuring as they do so, 'O lord sun, moon, let the bullets rebound from our husbands, brothers, betrothed, and other relations, just as raindrops rebound from these objects which are smeared with oil.' As soon as the first shot is heard, the baskets are put aside, and the women, seizing their fans, rush out of the houses. Then, waving their fans in the direction of the enemy, they run through the village, while they sing, 'O golden fans! let our bullets hit, and those of the enemy miss.' In this custom the ceremony of anointing stones, in order that the bullets may recoil from the men like raindrops from the stones, is a piece of pure homoeopathic or imitative magic; but the prayer to the sun, that he will be pleased to give effect to the charm, is a religious and perhaps later addition. The waving of the fans seems to be a charm to direct the bullets towards or away from their mark, according as they are discharged from the guns of friends or foes.

An old historian of Madagascar informs us that 'while the men are at the wars, and until their return, the women and girls cease not day and night to dance, and neither lie down nor take food in their own houses. And although they are very voluptuously inclined, they would not for anything in the world have an intrigue with another man while their husband is at the war, believing firmly that if that happened, their husband would be either killed or wounded. They believe that by dancing they impart strength, courage, and good fortune to their husbands; accordingly during such times they give themselves no rest, and this custom they observe very religiously.'

Among the Tshi-speaking peoples of the Gold Coast the wives of men who are away with the army paint themselves white, and adorn their persons with beads and charms. On the day when a battle is expected to take place, they run about armed with guns, or sticks carved to look like guns, and taking green paw-paws (fruits shaped somewhat like a melon), they hack them with knives, as if they were chopping off the heads of the foe. The pantomime is no doubt merely an imitative charm, to enable the men to do to the enemy as the women do to the paw-paws. In the West African town of Framin, while the Ashantee war was raging some years ago, Mr. Fitzgerald Marriott saw a dance performed by women whose husbands had gone as carriers to the war. They were painted white and wore nothing but a short petticoat. At their head was a shrivelled old sorceress in a very short white petticoat, her black hair arranged in a sort of long projecting horn, and her black face, breasts, arms, and legs profusely adorned with white circles and crescents. All carried long white brushes made of buffalo or horse tails, and as they danced they sang, 'Our husbands have gone to Ashanteeland; may they sweep their enemies off the face of the earth!'

Among the Thompson Indians of British Columbia, when the men were on the war-path, the women performed dances at frequent intervals. These dances were believed to ensure the success of the expedition. The dancers flourished their knives, threw long sharp-pointed sticks forward, or drew sticks with hooked ends repeatedly backward and forward. Throwing the sticks forward was symbolic of piercing or warding off the enemy, and drawing them back was symbolic of drawing their own men from danger. The hook at the end of the stick was particularly well adapted to serve the purpose of a life-saving apparatus. The women always pointed their weapons towards the enemy's country. They painted their faces red and sang as they danced, and they prayed to the weapons to preserve their husbands and help them to kill many foes. Some had eagle-down stuck on the points of their sticks. When the dance was over, these weapons were hidden. If a woman whose husband was at the war thought she saw hair or a piece of a scalp on the weapon when she took it out, she knew that her husband had killed an enemy. But if she saw a stain of blood on it, she knew he was wounded or dead. When the men of the Yuki tribe in California were away fighting, the women at home did not sleep; they danced continually in a circle, chanting and waving leafy wands. For they said that if they danced all the time, their husbands would not grow tired. Among the Haida Indians of the Queen Charlotte Islands, when the men had gone to war, the women at home would get up very early in the morning and pretend to make war by falling upon their children and feigning to take them for slaves. This was supposed to help their husbands to go and do likewise. If a wife were unfaithful to her husband while he was away on the war-path, he would probably be killed. For ten nights all the women at home lay with their heads towards the point of the compass to which the war-canoes had paddled away. Then they changed about, for the warriors were supposed to be coming home across the sea. At Masset the Haida women danced and sang war-songs all the time their husbands were away at the wars, and they had to keep everything about them in a certain order. It was thought that a wife might kill her husband by not observing these customs. When a band of Carib Indians of the Orinoco had gone on the war-path, their friends left in the village used to calculate as nearly as they could the exact moment when the absent warriors would be advancing to attack the enemy. Then they took two lads, laid them down on a bench, and inflicted a most severe scourging on their bare backs. This the youths submitted to without a murmur, supported in their sufferings by the firm conviction, in which they had been bred from childhood, that on the constancy and fortitude with which they bore the cruel ordeal depended the valour and success of their comrades in the battle.

Among the many beneficent uses to which a mistaken ingenuity has applied the principle of homoeopathic or imitative magic, is that of causing trees and plants to bear fruit in due season. In Thüringen the man who sows flax carries the seed in a long bag which reaches from his shoulders to his knees, and he walks with long strides, so that the bag sways to and fro on his back. It is believed that this will cause the flax to wave in the wind. In the interior of Sumatra rice is sown by women who, in sowing, let their hair hang loose down their back, in order that the rice may grow luxuriantly and have long stalks. Similarly, in ancient Mexico a festival was held in honour of the goddess of maize, or 'the long-haired mother,' as she was called. It began at the time 'when the plant had attained its full growth, and fibres shooting forth from the top of the green ear indicated that the grain was fully formed. During this festival the women wore their long hair unbound, shaking and tossing it in the dances which were the chief feature in the ceremonial, in order that the tassel of the maize might grow in like profusion, that the grain might be correspondingly large and flat, and that the people might have abundance.' In many parts of Europe dancing or leaping high in the air are approved homoeopathic modes of making the crops grow high. Thus in Franche-Comté they say that you should dance at the Carnival in order to make the hemp grow tall.

The notion that a person can influence a plant homoeopathically by his act or condition comes out clearly in a remark made by a Malay woman. Being asked why she stripped the upper part of her body naked in reaping the rice, she explained that she did it to make the rice-husks thinner, as she was tired of pounding thick-husked rice. Clearly, she thought that the less clothing she wore the less husk there would be on the rice. The magic virtue of a pregnant woman to communicate fertility is known to Bavarian and Austrian peasants, who think that if you give the first fruit of a tree to a woman with child to eat, the tree will bring forth abundantly next year. On the other hand, the Baganda believe that a barren wife infects her husband's garden with her own sterility and prevents the trees from bearing fruit; hence a childless woman is generally divorced. The Greeks and Romans sacrificed pregnant victims to the goddesses of the corn and of the earth, doubtless in order that the earth might teem and the corn swell in the ear. When a Catholic priest remonstrated with the Indians of the Orinoco on allowing their women to sow the fields in the blazing sun, with infants at their breasts, the men answered, 'Father, you don't understand these things, and that is why they vex you. You know that women are accustomed to bear children, and that we men are not. When the women sow, the stalk of the maize bears two or three ears, the root of the yucca yields two or three basketfuls, and everything multiplies in proportion. Now why is that? Simply because the women know how to bring forth, and know how to make the seed which they sow bring forth also. Let them sow, then; we men don't know as much about it as they do.'

Thus on the theory of homoeopathic magic a person can influence vegetation either for good or for evil according to the good or the bad character of his acts or states: for example, a fruitful woman makes plants fruitful, a barren woman makes them barren. Hence this belief in the noxious and infectious nature of certain personal qualities or accidents has given rise to a number of prohibitions or rules of avoidance: people abstain from doing certain things lest they should homoeopathically infect the fruits of the earth with their own undesirable state or condition. All such customs of abstention or rules of avoidance are examples of negative magic or taboo. Thus, for example, arguing from what may be called the infectiousness of personal acts or states, the Galelareese say that you ought not to shoot with a bow and arrows under a fruit-tree, or the tree will cast its fruit even as the arrows fall to the ground; and that when you are eating water-melon you ought not to mix the pips which you spit out of your mouth with the pips which you have put aside to serve as seed; for if you do, though the pips you spat out may certainly spring up and blossom, yet the blossoms will keep falling off just as the pips fell from your mouth, and thus these pips will never bear fruit. Precisely the same train of thought leads the Bavarian peasant to believe that if he allows the graft of a fruit-tree to fall on the ground, the tree that springs from that graft will let its fruit fall untimely. When the Chams of Cochinchina are sowing their dry ricefields and desire that no shower should fall, they eat their rice dry in order to prevent rain from spoiling the crop.

In the foregoing cases a person is supposed to influence vegetation homoeopathically. He infects trees or plants with qualities or accidents, good or bad, resembling and derived from his own. But on the principle of homoeopathic magic the influence is mutual: the plant can infect the man just as much as the man can infect the plant. In magic, as I believe in physics, action and reaction are equal and opposite. The Cherokee Indians are adepts in practical botany of the homoeopathic sort. Thus wiry roots of the catgut plant are so tough that they can almost stop a plough-share in the furrow. Hence Cherokee women wash their heads with a decoction of the roots to make the hair strong, and Cherokee ball-players wash themselves with it to toughen their muscles. It is a Galelareese belief that if you eat a fruit which has fallen to the ground, you will yourself contract a disposition to stumble and fall; and that if you partake of something which has been forgotten (such as a sweet potato left in the pot or a banana in the fire), you will become forgetful. The Galelareese are also of opinion that if a woman were to consume two bananas growing from a single head she would give birth to twins. The Guarani Indians of South America thought that a woman would become a mother of twins if she ate a double grain of millet. In Vedic times a curious application of this principle supplied a charm by which a banished prince might be restored to his kingdom. He had to eat food cooked on a fire which was fed with wood which had grown out of the stump of a tree which had been cut down. The recuperative power manifested by such a tree would in due course be communicated through the fire to the food, and so to the prince, who ate the food which was cooked on the fire which was fed with the wood which grew out of the tree. The Sundanese think that if a house is built of the wood of thorny trees, the life of the people who dwell in that house will likewise be thorny and full of trouble.

There is a fruitful branch of homoeopathic magic which works by means of the dead; for just as the dead can neither see nor hear nor speak, so you may on homoeopathic principles render people blind, deaf, and dumb by the use of dead men's bones or anything else that is tainted by the infection of death. Thus among the Galelareese, when a young man goes a-wooing at night, he takes a little earth from a grave and strews it on the roof of his sweetheart's house just above the place where her parents sleep. This, he fancies, will prevent them from waking while he converses with his beloved, since the earth from the grave will make them sleep as sound as the dead. Burglars in all ages and many lands have been patrons of this species of magic, which is very useful to them in the exercise of their profession. Thus a South Slavonian housebreaker sometimes begins operations by throwing a dead man's bone over the house, saying, with pungent sarcasm, 'As this bone may waken, so may these people waken'; after that not a soul in the house can keep his or her eyes open. Similarly, in Java the burglar takes earth from a grave and sprinkles it round the house which he intends to rob; this throws the inmates into a deep sleep. With the same intention a Hindoo will strew ashes from a pyre at the door of the house; Indians of Peru scatter the dust of dead men's bones; and Ruthenian burglars remove the marrow from a human shin-bone, pour tallow into it, and having kindled the tallow, march thrice round the house with this candle burning, which causes the inmates to sleep a death-like sleep. Or the Ruthenian will make a flute out of a human leg-bone and play upon it; whereupon all persons within hearing are overcome with drowsiness. The Indians of Mexico employed for this maleficent purpose the left forearm of a woman who had died in giving birth to her first child; but the arm had to be stolen. With it they beat the ground before they entered the house which they designed to plunder; this caused every one in the house to lose all power of speech and motion; they were as dead, hearing and seeing everything, but perfectly powerless; some of them, however, really slept and even snored. In Europe similar properties were ascribed to the Hand of Glory, which was the dried and pickled hand of a man who had been hanged. If a candle made of the fat of a malefactor who had also died on the gallows was lighted and placed in the Hand of Glory as in a candlestick, it rendered motionless all persons to whom it was presented; they could not stir a finger any more than if they were dead. Sometimes the dead man's hand is itself the candle, or rather bunch of candles, all its withered fingers being set on fire; but should any member of the household be awake, one of the fingers will not kindle. Such nefarious lights can only be extinguished with milk. Often it is prescribed that the thief's candle should be made of the finger of a new-born or, still better, unborn child; sometimes it is thought needful that the thief should have one such candle for every person in the house, for if he has one candle too little somebody in the house will wake and catch him. Once these tapers begin to burn, there is nothing but milk that will put them out. In the seventeenth century robbers used to murder pregnant women in order thus to extract candles from their wombs. An ancient Greek robber or burglar thought he could silence and put to flight the fiercest watchdogs by carrying with him a brand plucked from a funeral pyre. Again, Servian and Bulgarian women who chafe at the restraints of domestic life will take the copper coins from the eyes of a corpse, wash them in wine or water, and give the liquid to their husbands to drink. After swallowing it, the husband will be as blind to his wife's peccadilloes as the dead man was on whose eyes the coins were laid.

Further, animals are often conceived to possess qualities or properties which might be useful to man, and homoeopathic or imitative magic seeks to communicate these properties to human beings in various ways. Thus some Bechuanas wear a ferret as a charm, because, being very tenacious of life, it will make them difficult to kill. Others wear a certain insect, mutilated, but living, for a similar purpose. Yet other Bechuana warriors wear the hair of a hornless ox among their own hair, and the skin of a frog on their mantle, because a frog is slippery, and the ox, having no horns, is hard to catch; so the man who is provided with these charms believes that he will be as hard to hold as the ox and the frog. Again, it seems plain that a South African warrior who twists tufts of rats' hair among his own curly black locks will have just as many chances of avoiding the enemy's spear as the nimble rat has of avoiding things thrown at it; hence in these regions rats' hair is in great demand when war is expected. One of the ancient books of India prescribes that when a sacrifice is offered for victory, the earth out of which the altar is to be made should be taken from a place where a boar has been wallowing, since the strength of the boar will be in that earth. When you are playing the one-stringed lute, and your fingers are stiff, the thing to do is to catch some long-legged field spiders and roast them, and then rub your fingers with the ashes; that will make your fingers as lithe and nimble as the spiders' legs—at least so think the Galelareese. To bring back a runaway slave an Arab will trace a magic circle on the ground, stick a nail in the middle of it, and attach a beetle by a thread to the nail, taking care that the sex of the beetle is that of the fugitive. As the beetle crawls round and round, it will coil the thread about the nail, thus shortening the tether and drawing nearer to the centre at every circuit. So by virtue of homoeopathic magic the runaway slave will be drawn back to his master.

Among the western tribes of British New Guinea, a man who has killed a snake will burn it and smear his legs with the ashes when he goes into the forest; for no snake will bite him for some days afterwards. If a South Slavonian has a mind to pilfer and steal at market, he has nothing to do but to burn a blind cat, and then throw a pinch of its ashes over the person with whom he is higgling; after that he can take what he likes from the booth, and the owner will not be a bit the wiser, having become as blind as the deceased cat with whose ashes he has been sprinkled. The thief may even ask boldly, 'Did I pay for it?' and the deluded huckster will reply, 'Why, certainly.' Equally simple and effectual is the expedient adopted by natives of Central Australia who desire to cultivate their beards. They prick the chin all over with a pointed bone, and then stroke it carefully with a magic stick or stone, which represents a kind of rat that has very long whiskers.

The virtue of these whiskers naturally passes into the representative stick or stone, and thence by an easy transition to the chin, which, consequently, is soon adorned with a rich growth of beard. The ancient Greeks thought that to eat the flesh of the wakeful nightingale would prevent a man from sleeping; that to smear the eyes of a blear-sighted person with the gall of an eagle would give him the eagle's vision; and that a raven's eggs would restore the blackness of the raven to silvery hair. Only the person who adopted this last mode of concealing the ravages of time had to be most careful to keep his mouth full of oil at the time he applied the eggs to his venerable locks, else his teeth as well as his hair would be dyed raven black, and no amount of scrubbing and scouring would avail to whiten them again. The hair-restorer was in fact a shade too powerful, and in applying it you might get more than you bargained for.

The Huichol Indians admire the beautiful markings on the backs of serpents. Hence when a Huichol woman is about to weave or embroider, her husband catches a large serpent and holds it in a cleft stick, while the woman strokes the reptile with one hand down the whole length of its back; then she passes the same hand over her forehead and eyes, that she may be able to work as beautiful patterns in the web as the markings on the back of the serpent.

On the principle of homoeopathic magic, inanimate things, as well as plants and animals, may diffuse blessing or bane around them, according to their own intrinsic nature and the skill of the wizard to tap or dam, as the case may be, the stream of weal or woe. In Samarcand women give a baby sugar-candy to suck and put glue in the palm of its hand, in order that, when the child grows up, his words may be sweet and precious things may stick to his hands as if they were glued. The Greeks thought that a garment made from the fleece of a sheep that had been torn by a wolf would hurt the wearer, setting up an itch or irritation in his skin. They were also of opinion that if a stone which had been bitten by a dog were dropped in wine, it would make all who drank of that wine fall out among themselves. Among the Arabs of Moab a childless woman often borrows the robe of a woman who has had many children, hoping with the robe to acquire the fruitfulness of its owner. The Caffres of

Sofala, in East Africa, had a great dread of being struck with anything hollow, such as a reed or a straw, and greatly preferred being thrashed with a good thick cudgel or an iron bar, even though it hurt very much. For they thought that if a man were beaten with anything hollow, his inside would waste away till he died. In Eastern seas there is a large shell which the Buginese of Celebes call the 'old man' (*kadjâwo*). On Fridays they turn these 'old men' upside down and place them on the thresholds of their houses, believing that whoever then steps over the threshold of the house will live to be old. At initiation a Brahman boy is made to tread with his right foot on a stone, while the words are repeated, 'Tread on this stone; like a stone be firm'; and the same ceremony is performed, with the same words, by a Brahman bride at her marriage. In Madagascar a mode of counteracting the levity of fortune is to bury a stone at the foot of the heavy house-post. The common custom of swearing upon a stone may be based partly on a belief that the strength and stability of the stone lend confirmation to an oath. Thus the old Danish historian Saxo Grammaticus tells us that 'the ancients, when they were to choose a king, were wont to stand on stones planted in the ground, and to proclaim their votes, in order to foreshadow from the steadfastness of the stones that the deed would be lasting'.

But while a general magical efficacy may be supposed to reside in all stones by reason of their common properties of weight and solidity, special magical virtues are attributed to particular stones, or kinds of stone, in accordance with their individual or specific qualities of shape and colour. For example, the Indians of Peru employed certain stones for the increase of maize, others for the increase of potatoes, and others again for the increase of cattle. The stones used to make maize grow were fashioned in the likeness of cobs of maize, and the stones destined to multiply cattle had the shape of sheep.

In some parts of Melanesia a like belief prevails that certain sacred stones are endowed with miraculous powers which correspond in their nature to the shape of the stone. Thus a piece of water-worn coral on the beach often bears a surprising likeness to a bread-fruit. Hence in the Banks Islands a man who finds such a coral will lay it at the root of one of his bread-fruit trees in the expectation that it will make the tree bear well. If the result answers his expectation, he will then, for a proper remuneration, take stones of less marked character from other men and let them lie near his, in order to imbue them with the magic virtue which resides in it. Similarly a stone with little discs upon it is good to bring in money; and if a man found a large stone with a number of small ones under it, like a sow among her litter, he was sure that to offer money upon it would bring him pigs. In these and similar cases, the Melanesians ascribe the marvellous power, not to the stone itself, but to its indwelling spirit; and sometimes, as we have just seen, a man endeavours to propitiate the spirit by laying down offerings on the stone. But the conception of spirits that must be propitiated lies outside the sphere of magic, and within that of religion. Where such a conception is found, as here, in conjunction with purely magical ideas and practices, the latter may generally be assumed to be the original stock on which the religious conception has been at some later time engrafted. For there are strong grounds for thinking that, in the evolution of thought, magic has preceded religion. But to this point we shall return presently.

The ancients set great store on the magical qualities of precious stones; indeed it has been maintained, with great show of reason, that such stones were used as amulets long before they were worn as mere ornaments. Thus the Greeks gave the name of tree-agate to a stone which exhibits tree-like markings, and they thought that if two of these gems were tied to the horns or necks of oxen at the plough, the crop would be sure to be plentiful. Again, they recognised a milk-stone which produced an abundant supply of milk in women if only they drank it dissolved in honey-mead. Milk-stones are used for the same purpose by Greek women in Crete and Melos at the present day; in Albania nursing mothers wear the stones in order to ensure an abundant flow of milk. Again, the Greeks believed in a stone which cured snake-bites, and hence was named the snake-stone; to test its efficacy you had only to grind the stone to powder and sprinkle the powder on the wound. The wine-coloured amethyst received its name, which means 'not drunken,' because it was supposed to keep the wearer of it sober; and two brothers who desired to live at unity were advised to carry magnets about with them, which, by drawing the twain together, would clearly prevent them from falling out.

The ancient books of the Hindoos lay down a rule that after sunset on his marriage night a man should sit silent with his wife till the stars begin to twinkle in the sky. When the pole-star appears, he should point it out to her, and, addressing the star, say, 'Firm art thou; I see thee, the firm one. Firm be thou with me, O thriving one!' Then, turning to his wife, he should say, 'To me Brihaspati has given thee; obtaining offspring through me, thy husband, live with me a hundred autumns.' The intention of the ceremony is plainly to guard against the fickleness of fortune and the instability of earthly bliss by the steadfast influence of the constant star. It is a wish expressed in Keats's last sonnet:

> '*Bright star! would I were steadfast as thou art—*
> *Not in lone splendour hung aloft the night.*'

Dwellers by the sea cannot fail to be impressed by the sight of its ceaseless ebb and flow, and are apt, on the principles of that rude philosophy of sympathy and resemblance which here engages our attention, to trace a subtle relation, a secret harmony, between its tides and the life of man, of animals, and of plants. In the flowing tide they see not merely a symbol, but a cause of exuberance, of prosperity, and of life, while in the ebbing tide they discern a real agent as well as a melancholy emblem of failure, of weakness, and of death. The Breton peasant fancies that clover sown when the tide is coming in will grow well, but that if the plant be sown at low water or when the tide is going out, it will never reach maturity, and that the cows which feed on it will burst. His wife believes that the best butter is made when the tide has just turned and is beginning to flow, that milk which foams in the churn will go on foaming till the hour of high water is past, and that water drawn from the well or milk extracted from the cow while the tide is rising will boil up in the pot or saucepan and overflow into the fire. According to some of the ancients, the skins of seals, even after they had been parted from their bodies, remained in secret sympathy with the sea, and were observed to ruffle when the tide was on the ebb. Another ancient belief, attributed to Aristotle, was that no creature can die except at ebb tide. The belief, if we can trust Pliny, was confirmed by experience, so far as regards human beings, on the coast of France. Philostratus also assures us that at Cadiz dying people never yielded up the ghost while the water was high. A like fancy still lingers in some parts of Europe. On the Cantabrian coast they think that persons who die of chronic or acute disease expire at the moment when the tide begins to recede. In Portugal, all along the coast of Wales, and on some parts of the coast of Brittany, a belief is said to prevail that people are born when the tide comes in, and die when it goes out. Dickens attests the existence of the same superstition in England. 'People can't die, along the coast,' said Mr. Peggotty, 'except when the tide's pretty nigh out. They can't be born, unless it's pretty nigh in — not properly born till flood.' The belief that most deaths happen at ebb tide is said to be held along the east coast of England from Northumberland to Kent. Shakespeare must have been familiar with it, for he makes Falstaff die, 'even just between twelve and one, e'en at the turning o' the tide.' We meet the belief again on the Pacific coast of North America among the Haidas. Whenever a good Haida is about to die he sees a canoe manned by some of his dead friends, who come with the tide to bid him welcome to the spirit land. 'Come with us now,' they say, 'for the tide is about to ebb and we must depart.' At Port Stephens, in New South Wales, the natives always buried their dead at flood tide, never at ebb, lest the retiring water should bear the soul of the departed to some distant country.

To ensure a long life the Chinese have recourse to certain complicated charms, which concentrate in themselves the magical essence emanating, on homoeopathic principles, from times and seasons, from persons and from things. The vehicles employed to transmit these happy influences are no other than grave-clothes. These are provided by many Chinese in their lifetime, and most people have them cut out and sewn by an unmarried girl or a very young woman, wisely calculating that, since such a person is likely to live a great many years to come, a part of her capacity to live long must surely pass into the clothes, and thus stave off for many years the time when they shall be put to their proper use. Further, the garments are made by preference in a year which has an intercalary month; for to the Chinese mind it seems plain that grave-clothes made in a year which is unusually long will possess the capacity of prolonging life in an unusually high degree. Amongst the clothes there is one robe in particular on which special pains have been lavished to imbue it with this priceless quality. It is a long silken gown of the deepest blue colour, with the word 'longevity' embroidered all over it in thread of gold. To present an aged parent with one of these costly and splendid mantles, known as 'longevity garments,' is esteemed by the Chinese an act of filial piety and a delicate mark of attention. As the garment purports to prolong the life of its owner, he often wears it, especially on festive occasions, in order to allow the influence of longevity, created by the many golden letters with which it is bespangled, to work their full effect upon his person. On his birthday, above all, he hardly ever fails to don it, for in China common sense bids a man lay in a large stock of vital energy on his birthday, to be expended in the form of health and vigour during the rest of the year. Attired in the gorgeous pall, and absorbing its blessed influence at every pore, the happy owner receives complacently the congratulations of friends and relations, who warmly express their admiration of these magnificent cerements, and of the filial piety which prompted the children to bestow so beautiful and useful a present on the author of their being.

Another application of the maxim that like produces like is seen in the Chinese belief that the fortunes of a town are deeply affected by its shape, and that they must vary according to the character of the thing which that shape most nearly resembles. Thus it is related that long ago the town of Tsuen-cheu-fu, the outlines of which are like those of a carp, frequently fell a prey to the depredations of the neighbouring city of Yung-chun, which is shaped like a fishing-net, until the inhabitants of the former town conceived the plan of erecting two tall pagodas in their midst. These pagodas, which still tower above the city of Tsuen-cheu-fu, have ever since exercised the happiest influence over its destiny by intercepting the imaginary net before it could descend and entangle in its meshes the imaginary carp. Some forty years ago the wise men of Shanghai were much exercised to discover the cause of a local rebellion. On careful enquiry they ascertained that the rebellion was due to the shape of a large new temple which had most unfortunately been built in the shape of a tortoise, an animal of the very worst character. The difficulty was serious, the danger was pressing; for to pull down the temple would have been impious, and to let it stand as it was would be to court a succession of similar or worse disasters. However, the genius of the local professors of geomancy, rising to the occasion, triumphantly surmounted the difficulty and obviated the danger. By filling up two wells, which represented the eyes of the tortoise, they at once blinded that disreputable animal and rendered him incapable of doing further mischief.

Sometimes homoeopathic or imitative magic is called in to annul an evil omen by accomplishing it in mimicry. The effect is to circumvent destiny by substituting a mock calamity for a real one. In Madagascar this mode of cheating the fates is reduced to a regular system. Here every man's fortune is determined by the day or hour of his birth, and if that happens to be an unlucky one his fate is sealed, unless the mischief can be extracted, as the phrase goes, by means of a substitute. The ways of extracting the mischief are various. For example, if a man is born on the first day of the second month (February), his house will be burnt down when he comes of age. To take time by the forelock and avoid this catastrophe, the friends of the infant will set up a shed in a field or in the cattle-fold and burn it. If the ceremony is to be really effective, the child and his mother should be placed in the shed and only plucked, like brands, from the burning hut before it is too late. Again, dripping November is the month of tears, and he who is born in it is born to sorrow. But in order to disperse the clouds that thus gather over his future, he has nothing to do but to take the lid off a boiling pot and wave it about. The drops that fall from it will accomplish his destiny and so prevent the tears from trickling from his eyes. Again, if fate has decreed that a young girl, still unwed, should see her children, still unborn, descend before her with sorrow to the grave, she can avert the calamity as follows. She kills a grasshopper, wraps it in a rag to represent a shroud, and mourns over it like Rachel weeping for her children and refusing to be comforted. Moreover, she takes a dozen or more other grasshoppers, and having removed some of their superfluous legs and wings she lays them about their dead and shrouded fellow. The buzz of the tortured insects and the agitated motions of their mutilated limbs represent the shrieks and contortions of the mourners at a funeral. After burying the deceased grasshopper she leaves the rest to continue their mourning till death releases them from their pain; and having bound up her dishevelled hair she retires from the grave with the step and carriage of a person plunged in grief. Thenceforth she looks cheerfully forward to seeing her children survive her; for it cannot be that she should mourn and bury them twice over. Once more, if fortune has frowned on a man at his birth and penury has marked him for her own, he can easily erase the mark in question by purchasing a couple of cheap pearls, price three halfpence, and burying them. For who but the rich of this world can thus afford to fling pearls away?

§ 3. *Contagious Magic.* — Thus far we have been considering chiefly that branch of sympathetic magic which may be called homoeopathic or imitative. Its leading principle, as we have seen, is that like produces like, or, in other words, that an effect resembles its cause. The other great branch of sympathetic magic, which I have called Contagious Magic, proceeds upon the notion that things which have once been conjoined must remain ever afterwards, even when quite dissevered from each other, in such a sympathetic relation that whatever is done to the one must similarly affect the other. Thus the logical basis of Contagious Magic, like that of Homoeopathic Magic, is a mistaken association of ideas; its physical basis, if we may speak of such a thing, like the physical basis of Homoeopathic Magic, is a material medium of some sort which, like the ether of modern physics, is assumed to unite distant objects and to convey impressions from one to the other. The most familiar example of Contagious Magic is the magical sympathy which is supposed to exist between a man and any severed portion of his person, as his hair or nails; so that whoever gets possession of human hair or nails may work his will, at any distance, upon the person from whom they were cut. This superstition is world-wide; instances of it in regard to hair and nails will be noticed later on in this work.

Among the Australian tribes it was a common practice to knock out one or more of a boy's front teeth at those ceremonies of initiation to which every male member had to submit before he could enjoy the rights and privileges of a full-grown man. The reason of the practice is obscure; all that concerns us here is the belief that a sympathetic relation continued to exist between the lad and his teeth after the latter had been extracted from his gums. Thus among some of the tribes about the River Darling, in New South Wales, the extracted tooth was placed under the bark of a tree near a river or water-hole; if the bark grew over the tooth, or if the tooth fell into the water, all was well; but if it were exposed and the ants ran over it, the natives believed that the boy would suffer from a disease of the mouth. Among the Murring and other tribes of New South Wales the extracted tooth was first taken care of by an old man, and then passed from one headman to another, until it had gone all round the community, when it came back to the lad's father, and finally to the lad himself. But however it was thus conveyed from hand to hand, it might on no account be placed in a bag containing magical substances, for to do so would, they believed, put the owner of the tooth in great danger. The late Dr. Howitt once acted as custodian of the teeth which had been extracted from some novices at a ceremony of initiation, and the old men earnestly besought him not to carry them in a bag in which they knew that he had some quartz crystals. They declared that if he did so the magic of the crystals would pass into the teeth, and so injure the boys. Nearly a year after Dr. Howitt's return from the ceremony he was visited by one of the principal men of the Murring tribe, who had travelled some two hundred and fifty miles from his home to fetch back the teeth. This man explained that he had been sent for them because one of the boys had fallen into ill health, and it was believed that the teeth had received some injury which had affected him. He was assured that the teeth had been kept in a box apart from any substances, like quartz crystals, which could influence them; and he returned home bearing the teeth with him carefully wrapt up and concealed.

The Basutos are careful to conceal their extracted teeth, lest these should fall into the hands of certain mythical beings who haunt graves, and who could harm the owner of the tooth by working magic on it. In Sussex some fifty years ago a maid-servant remonstrated strongly against the throwing away of children's cast teeth, affirming that should they be found and gnawed by any animal, the child's new tooth would be, for all the world, like the teeth of the animal that had bitten the old one. In proof of this she named Old Master Simmons, who had a very large pig's tooth in his upper jaw, a personal defect that he always averred was caused by his mother, who threw away one of his cast teeth by accident into the hog's trough. A similar belief has led to practices intended, on the principles of homoeopathic magic, to replace old teeth by new and better ones. Thus in many parts of the world it is customary to put extracted teeth in some place where they will be found by a mouse or a rat, in the hope that, through the sympathy which continues to subsist between them and their former owner, his other teeth may acquire the same firmness and excellence as the teeth of these rodents. For example in Germany it is said to be an almost universal maxim among the people that when you have had a tooth taken out you should insert it in a mouse's hole. To do so with a child's milk-tooth which has fallen out will prevent the child from having toothache. Or you should go behind the stove and throw your tooth backwards over your head, saying, 'Mouse, give me your iron tooth; I will give you my bone tooth.' After that your other teeth will remain good. Far away from Europe, at Raratonga, in the Pacific, when a child's tooth was extracted, the following prayer used to be recited:

> *'Big rat! little rat!*
> *Here is my old tooth.*
> *Pray give me a new one.'*

Then the tooth was thrown on the thatch of the house, because rats make their nests in the decayed thatch. The reason assigned for invoking the rats on these occasions was that rats' teeth were the strongest known to the natives.

Other parts which are commonly believed to remain in a sympathetic union with the body, after the physical connexion has been severed, are the navel-string and the afterbirth, including the placenta. So intimate, indeed, is the union conceived to be, that the fortunes of the individual for good or evil throughout life are often supposed to be bound up with one or other of these portions of his person, so that if his navel-string or afterbirth is preserved and properly treated, he will be prosperous; whereas if it be injured or lost, he will suffer accordingly. Thus certain tribes of Western Australia believe that a man swims well or ill, according as his mother at his birth threw the navel-string into water or not. Among the natives of the Pennefather River in

Queensland it is believed that a part of the child's spirit (*cho-i*)
stays in the afterbirth. Hence the grandmother takes the afterbirth
away and buries it in the sand. She marks the spot by a number
of twigs which she sticks in the ground in a circle, tying their
tops together so that the structure resembles a cone. When
Anjea, the being who causes conception in women by putting
mud babies into their wombs, comes along and sees the place, he
takes out the spirit and carries it away to one of his haunts,
such as a tree, a hole in a rock, or a lagoon, where it may remain
for years. But some time or other he will put the spirit again
into a baby, and it will be born once more into the world. In
Ponape, one of the Caroline Islands, the navel-string is placed
in a shell and then disposed of in such a way as shall best adapt
the child for the career which the parents have chosen for him;
for example, if they wish to make him a good climber, they will
hang the navel-string on a tree. The Kei islanders regard the
navel-string as the brother or sister of the child, according to
the sex of the infant. They put it in a pot with ashes, and set it
in the branches of a tree, that it may keep a watchful eye on the
fortunes of its comrade. Among the Bataks of Sumatra, as
among many other peoples of the Indian Archipelago, the placenta
passes for the child's younger brother or sister, the sex being
determined by the sex of the child, and it is buried under the
house. According to the Bataks it is bound up with the child's
welfare, and seems, in fact, to be the seat of the transferable
soul, of which we shall hear something later on. The Karo Bataks
even affirm that of a man's two souls it is the true soul that lives
with the placenta under the house; that is the soul, they say,
which begets children.

The Baganda believe that every person is born with a double,
and this double they identify with the afterbirth, which they regard
as a second child. The mother buries the afterbirth at the root of
a plantain tree, which then becomes sacred until the fruit has
ripened, when it is plucked to furnish a sacred feast for the family.
Among the Cherokees the navel-string of a girl is buried under a
corn-mortar, in order that the girl may grow up to be a good
baker; but the navel-string of a boy is hung up on a tree in the
woods, in order that he may be a hunter. The Incas of Peru
preserved the navel-string with the greatest care, and gave it to the

child to suck whenever it fell ill. In ancient Mexico they used to give a boy's navel-string to soldiers, to be buried by them on a field of battle, in order that the boy might thus acquire a passion for war. But the navel-string of a girl was buried beside the domestic hearth, because this was believed to inspire her with a love of home and a taste for cooking and baking.

Even in Europe many people still believe that a person's destiny is more or less bound up with that of his navel-string or afterbirth. Thus in Rhenish Bavaria the navel-string is kept for a while wrapt up in a piece of old linen, and then cut or pricked to pieces according as the child is a boy or a girl, in order that he or she may grow up to be a skilful workman or a good sempstress. In Berlin the midwife commonly delivers the dried navel-string to the father with a strict injunction to preserve it carefully, for so long as it is kept the child will live and thrive and be free from sickness. In Beauce and Perche the people are careful to throw the navel-string neither into water nor into fire, believing that if that were done the child would be drowned or burned.

Thus in many parts of the world the navel-string, or more commonly the afterbirth, is regarded as a living being, the brother or sister of the infant, or as the material object in which the guardian spirit of the child or part of its soul resides. Further, the sympathetic connexion supposed to exist between a person and his afterbirth or navel-string comes out very clearly in the widespread custom of treating the afterbirth or navel-string in ways which are supposed to influence for life the character and career of the person, making him, if it is a man, a nimble climber, a strong swimmer, a skilful hunter, or a brave soldier, and making her, if it is a woman, a cunning sempstress, a good baker, and so forth. Thus the beliefs and usages concerned with the afterbirth or placenta, and to a less extent with the navel-string, present a remarkable parallel to the widespread doctrine of the transferable or external soul and the custom founded on it. Hence it is hardly rash to conjecture that the resemblance is no mere chance coincidence, but that in the afterbirth or placenta we have a physical basis (not necessarily the only one) for the theory and practice of the external soul. The consideration of that subject is reserved for a later part of this work.

A curious application of the doctrine of contagious magic is the

c

relation commonly believed to exist between a wounded man
and the agent of the wound, so that whatever is subsequently done
by or to the agent must correspondingly affect the patient either
for good or evil.   Thus Pliny tells us that if you have wounded a
man and are sorry for it, you have only to spit on the hand that
gave the wound, and the pain of the sufferer will be instantly
alleviated.   In Melanesia, if a man's friends get possession of the
arrow which wounded him, they keep it in a damp place or in cool
leaves, for then the inflammation will be trifling and will soon
subside.   Meantime the enemy who shot the arrow is hard at
work to aggravate the wound by all the means in his power.   For
this purpose he and his friends drink hot burning juices and
chew irritating leaves, for this will clearly inflame and irritate
the wound.   Further, they keep the bow near the fire to make the
wound which it has inflicted hot; and for the same reason they put
the arrow-head, if it has been recovered, into the fire.   Moreover,
they are careful to keep the bow-string taut and to twang it
occasionally, for this will cause the wounded man to suffer from
tension of the nerves and spasms of tetanus.   'It is constantly
received and avouched,' says Bacon, 'that the anointing of the
weapon that maketh the wound will heal the wound itself.   In this
experiment, upon the relation of men of credit (though myself, as
yet, am not fully inclined to believe it), you shall note the points
following; first, the ointment wherewith this is done is made of
divers ingredients, whereof the strangest and hardest to come by
are the moss upon the skull of a dead man unburied, and the fats
of a boar and a bear killed in the act of generation.'   The precious
ointment compounded out of these and other ingredients was
applied, as the philosopher explains, not to the wound but to the
weapon, and that even though the injured man was at a great
distance and knew nothing about it.   The experiment, he tells us,
had been tried of wiping the ointment off the weapon without the
knowledge of the person hurt, with the result that he was presently
in a great rage of pain until the weapon was anointed again.
Moreover, 'it is affirmed that if you cannot get the weapon, yet
if you put an instrument of iron or wood resembling the weapon
into the wound, whereby it bleedeth, the anointing of that instrument will serve and work the effect.'   Remedies of the sort which
Bacon deemed worthy of his attention are still in vogue in the

eastern counties of England. Thus in Suffolk if a man cuts himself with a bill-hook or a scythe he always takes care to keep the weapon bright, and oils it to prevent the wound from festering. If he runs a thorn or, as he calls it, a bush into his hand, he oils or greases the extracted thorn. A man came to a doctor with an inflamed hand, having run a thorn into it while he was hedging. On being told that the hand was festering, he remarked, 'That didn't ought to, for I greased the bush well arter I pulled it out.' If a horse wounds its foot by treading on a nail, a Suffolk groom will invariably preserve the nail, clean it, and grease it every day, to prevent the foot from festering. Similarly Cambridgeshire labourers think that if a horse has run a nail into its foot, it is necessary to grease the nail with lard or oil and put it away in some safe place, or the horse will not recover. A few years ago a veterinary surgeon was sent for to attend a horse which had ripped its side open on the hinge of a farm gatepost. On arriving at the farm he found that nothing had been done to the wounded horse, but that a man was busy trying to prise the hinge out of the gatepost in order that it might be greased and put away, which, in the opinion of the Cambridge wiseacres, would conduce to the recovery of the animal. Similarly Essex rustics opine that, if a man has been stabbed with a knife, it is essential to his recovery that the knife should be greased and laid across the bed on which the sufferer is lying. So in Bavaria you are directed to anoint a linen rag with grease and tie it on the edge of the axe that cut you, taking care to keep the sharp edge upwards. As the grease on the axe dries, your wound heals. Similarly in the Harz Mountains they say that if you cut yourself, you ought to smear the knife or the scissors with fat and put the instrument away in a dry place in the name of the Father, of the Son, and of the Holy Ghost. As the knife dries, the wound heals. Other people, however, in Germany say that you should stick the knife in some damp place in the ground, and that your hurt will heal as the knife rusts. Others again, in Bavaria, recommend you to smear the axe or whatever it is with blood and put it under the eaves.

The train of reasoning which thus commends itself to English and German rustics, in common with the savages of Melanesia and America, is carried a step farther by the aborigines of Central Australia, who conceive that under certain circumstances the near relations of a wounded man must grease themselves, restrict their diet, and regulate their behaviour in other ways in order to ensure his recovery. Thus when a lad has been circumcised and the wound is not yet healed, his mother may not eat opossum, or a certain kind of lizard, or carpet snake, or any kind of fat, for otherwise she would retard the healing of the boy's wound. Every day she greases her digging-sticks and never lets them out of her sight; at night she sleeps with them close to her head. No one is allowed to touch them. Every day also she rubs her body all over with grease, as in some way this is believed to help her son's recovery. Another refinement of the same principle is due to the ingenuity of the German peasant. It is said that when one of his pigs or sheep breaks its leg, a farmer of Rhenish Bavaria or Hesse will bind up the leg of a chair with bandages and splints in due form. For some days thereafter no one may sit on that chair, move it, or knock up against it; for to do so would pain the injured pig or sheep and hinder the cure. In this last case it is clear that we have passed wholly out of the region of contagious magic and into the region of homoeopathic or imitative magic; the chair-leg, which is treated instead of the beast's leg, in no sense belongs to the animal, and the application of bandages to it is a mere simulation of the treatment which a more rational surgery would bestow on the real patient.

The sympathetic connexion supposed to exist between a man and the weapon which has wounded him is probably founded on the notion that the blood on the weapon continues to feel with the blood in his body. For a like reason the Papuans of Tumleo, an island off New Guinea, are careful to throw into the sea the bloody bandages with which their wounds have been dressed, for they fear that if these rags fell into the hands of an enemy he might injure them magically thereby. Once when a man with a wound in his mouth, which bled constantly, came to the missionaries to be treated, his faithful wife took great pains to collect all the blood and cast it into the sea. Strained and unnatural as this idea may seem to us, it is perhaps less so than the belief that magic sympathy is maintained between a person and his clothes, so that whatever is done to the clothes will be felt by the man himself, even though he may be far away at the time. In the Wotjobaluk tribe of Victoria a wizard would sometimes get hold of a man's opossum rug and roast it slowly in the fire, and as he did so the owner of the rug would fall sick. If the wizard consented to undo the charm, he would give the rug back to the sick man's friends, bidding them put it in water, 'so as to wash the fire out.' When that happened, the sufferer would feel a refreshing coolness and probably recover. In Tanna, one of the New Hebrides, a man who had a grudge at another and desired his death would try to get possession of a cloth which had touched the sweat of his enemy's body. If he succeeded, he rubbed the cloth carefully over with the leaves and twigs of a certain tree, rolled and bound cloth, twigs, and leaves into a long sausage-shaped bundle, and burned it slowly in the fire. As the bundle was consumed, the victim fell ill, and when it was reduced to ashes, he died. In this last form of enchantment, however, the magical sympathy may be supposed to exist not so much between the man and the cloth as between the man and the sweat which issued from his body. But in other cases of the same sort it seems that the garment by itself is enough to give the sorcerer a hold upon his victim. The witch in Theocritus, while she melted an image or lump of wax in order that her faithless lover might melt with love of her, did not forget to throw into the fire a shred of his cloak which he had dropped in her house. In Prussia they say that if you cannot catch a thief, the next best thing you can do is to get hold of a garment which he may have shed in his flight; for if you beat it soundly, the thief will fall sick. This belief is firmly rooted in the popular mind. Some eighty or ninety years ago, in the neighbourhood of Berend, a man was detected trying to steal honey, and fled, leaving his coat behind him. When he heard that the enraged owner of the honey was mauling his lost coat, he was so alarmed that he took to his bed and died.

Again, magic may be wrought on a man sympathetically, not only through his clothes and severed parts of himself, but also through the impressions left by his body in sand or earth. In particular, it is a world-wide superstition that by injuring foot-prints you injure the feet that made them. Thus the natives of South-eastern Australia think that they can lame a man by placing sharp pieces of quartz, glass, bone, or charcoal in his footprints. Rheumatic pains are often attributed by them to this cause. Seeing a Tatungolung man very lame, Mr. Howitt asked him what

was the matter. He said, 'Some fellow has put *bottle* in my foot.'
He was suffering from rheumatism, but believed that an enemy
had found his foot-track and had buried in it a piece of broken
bottle, the magical influence of which had entered his foot.

Similar practices prevail in various parts of Europe. Thus in
Mecklenburg it is thought that if you drive a nail into a man's
footprint he will fall lame; sometimes it is required that the nail
should be taken from a coffin. A like mode of injuring an enemy
is resorted to in some parts of France. It is said that there was an
old woman who used to frequent Stow in Suffolk, and she was a
witch. If, while she walked, any one went after her and stuck a
nail or a knife into her footprint in the dust, the dame could not
stir a step till it was withdrawn. Among the South Slavs a girl
will dig up the earth from the footprints of the man she loves and
put it in a flower-pot. Then she plants in the pot a marigold, a
flower that is thought to be fadeless. And as its golden blossom
grows and blooms and never fades, so shall her sweetheart's love
grow and bloom, and never, never fade. Thus the love-spell acts
on the man through the earth he trod on. An old Danish mode of
concluding a treaty was based on the same idea of the sympathetic
connexion between a man and his footprints: the covenanting
parties sprinkled each other's footprints with their own blood, thus
giving a pledge of fidelity. In ancient Greece superstitions of the
same sort seem to have been current, for it was thought that if a
horse stepped on the track of a wolf he was seized with numbness;
and a maxim ascribed to Pythagoras forbade people to pierce a
man's footprints with a nail or a knife.

The same superstition is turned to account by hunters in many
parts of the world for the purpose of running down the game.
Thus a German huntsman will stick a nail taken from a coffin
into the fresh spoor of the quarry, believing that this will hinder
the animal from escaping. The aborigines of Victoria put hot
embers in the tracks of the animals they were pursuing. Hottentot
hunters throw into the air a handful of sand taken from the
footprints of the game, believing that this will bring the animal
down. Thompson Indians used to lay charms on the tracks of
wounded deer; after that they deemed it superfluous to pursue
the animal any farther that day, for being thus charmed it could
not travel far and would soon die. Similarly, Ojebway Indians

placed 'medicine' on the track of the first deer or bear they met with, supposing that this would soon bring the animal into sight, even if it were two or three days' journey off; for this charm had power to compress a journey of several days into a few hours. Ewe hunters of West Africa stab the footprints of game with a sharp-pointed stick in order to maim the quarry and allow them to come up with it.

But though the footprint is the most obvious it is not the only impression made by the body through which magic may be wrought on a man. The aborigines of South-eastern Australia believe that a man may be injured by burying sharp fragments of quartz, glass, and so forth in the mark made by his reclining body; the magical virtue of these sharp things enters his body and causes those acute pains which the ignorant European puts down to rheumatism. We can now understand why it was a maxim with the Pythagoreans that in rising from bed you should smooth away the impression left by your body on the bed-clothes. The rule was simply an old precaution against magic, forming part of a whole code of superstitious maxims which antiquity fathered on Pythagoras, though doubtless they were familiar to the barbarous forefathers of the Greeks long before the time of that philosopher.

§ 4. *The Magician's Progress.* — We have now concluded our examination of the general principles of sympathetic magic. The examples by which I have illustrated them have been drawn for the most part from what may be called private magic, that is from magical rites and incantations practised for the benefit or the injury of individuals. But in savage society there is commonly to be found in addition what we may call public magic, that is, sorcery practised for the benefit of the whole community. Wherever ceremonies of this sort are observed for the common good, it is obvious that the magician ceases to be merely a private practitioner and becomes to some extent a public functionary. The development of such a class of functionaries is of great importance for the political as well as the religious evolution of society. For when the welfare of the tribe is supposed to depend on the performance of these magical rites, the magician rises into a position of much influence and repute, and may readily acquire the rank and authority of a chief or king. The profession accordingly draws into its ranks some of the ablest and most ambitious men of the tribe, because it holds out to them a prospect of honour, wealth, and power such as hardly any other career could offer. The acuter minds perceive how easy it is to dupe their weaker brother and to play on his superstition for their own advantage. Not that the sorcerer is always a knave and impostor; he is often sincerely convinced that he really possesses those wonderful powers which the credulity of his fellows ascribes to him. But the more sagacious he is, the more likely he is to see through the fallacies which impose on duller wits. Thus the ablest members of the profession must tend to be more or less conscious deceivers; and it is just these men who in virtue of their superior ability will generally come to the top and win for themselves positions of the highest dignity and the most commanding authority. The pitfalls which beset the path of the professional sorcerer are many, and as a rule only the man of coolest head and sharpest wit will be able to steer his way through them safely. For it must always be remembered that every single profession and claim put forward by the magician as such is false; not one of them can be maintained without deception, conscious or unconscious. Accordingly the sorcerer who sincerely believes in his own extravagant pretensions is in far greater peril and is much more likely to be cut short in his career than the deliberate impostor. The honest wizard always expects that his charms and incantations will produce their supposed effect; and when they fail, not only really, as they always do, but conspicuously and disastrously, as they often do, he is taken aback: he is not, like his knavish colleague, ready with a plausible excuse to account for the failure, and before he can find one he may be knocked on the head by his disappointed and angry employers.

The general result is that at this stage of social evolution the supreme power tends to fall into the hands of men of the keenest intelligence and the most unscrupulous character. If we could balance the harm they do by their knavery against the benefits they confer by their superior sagacity, it might well be found that the good greatly outweighed the evil. For more mischief has probably been wrought in the world by honest fools in high places than by intelligent rascals. Once your shrewd rogue has attained the height of his ambition, and has no longer any selfish end to further, he may, and often does, turn his talents, his experience, his resources, to the service of the public. Many men who have been least scrupulous in the acquisition of power have been most beneficent in the use of it, whether the power they aimed at and won was that of wealth, political authority, or what not. In the field of politics the wily intriguer, the ruthless victor, may end by being a wise and magnanimous ruler, blessed in his lifetime, lamented at his death, admired and applauded by posterity. Such men, to take two of the most conspicuous instances, were Julius Caesar and Augustus. But once a fool always a fool, and the greater the power in his hands the more disastrous is likely to be the use he makes of it. The heaviest calamity in English history, the breach with America, might never have occurred if George the Third had not been an honest dullard.

Thus, so far as the public profession of magic affected the constitution of savage society, it tended to place the control of affairs in the hands of the ablest man: it shifted the balance of power from the many to the one: it substituted a monarchy for a democracy, or rather for an oligarchy of old men; for in general the savage community is ruled, not by the whole body of adult males, but by a council of elders. The change, by whatever causes produced, and whatever the character of the early rulers, was on the whole very beneficial. For the rise of monarchy appears to be an essential condition of the emergence of mankind from savagery. No human being is so hidebound by custom and tradition as your democratic savage; in no state of society consequently is progress so slow and difficult. The old notion that the savage is the freest of mankind is the reverse of the truth. He is a slave, not indeed to a visible master, but to the past, to the spirits of his dead forefathers, who haunt his steps from birth to death, and rule him with a rod of iron. What they did is the pattern of right, the unwritten law to which he yields a blind unquestioning obedience. The least possible scope is thus afforded to superior talent to change old customs for the better. The ablest man is dragged down by the weakest and dullest, who necessarily sets the standard, since he cannot rise, while the other can fall. The surface of such a society presents a uniform dead level, so far as it is humanly possible to reduce the natural inequalities, the immeasurable real differences of inborn capacity and temper, to a false superficial appearance of equality. From this low and stagnant condition of affairs, which demagogues and dreamers in later times have lauded as the ideal state, the Golden Age, of humanity, everything that helps to raise society by opening a career to talent and proportioning the degrees of authority to men's natural abilities, deserves to be welcomed by all who have the real good of their fellows at heart. Once these elevating influences have begun to operate — and they cannot be for ever suppressed — the progress of civilisation becomes comparatively rapid. The rise of one man to supreme power enables him to carry through changes in a single lifetime which previously many generations might not have sufficed to effect; and if, as will often happen, he is a man of intellect and energy above the common, he will readily avail himself of the opportunity. Even the whims and caprices of a tyrant may be of service in breaking the chain of custom which lies so heavy on the savage. And as soon as the tribe ceases to be swayed by the timid and divided counsels of the elders, and yields to the direction of a single strong and resolute mind, it becomes formidable to its neighbours and enters on a career of aggrandisement, which at an early stage of history is often highly favourable to social, industrial, and intellectual progress. For extending its sway, partly by force of arms, partly by the voluntary submission of weaker tribes, the community soon acquires wealth and slaves, both of which, by relieving some classes from the perpetual struggle for a bare subsistence, afford them an opportunity of devoting themselves to that disinterested pursuit of knowledge which is the noblest and most powerful instrument to ameliorate the lot of man.

Intellectual progress, which reveals itself in the growth of art and science and the spread of more liberal views, cannot be dissociated from industrial or economic progress, and that in its turn receives an immense impulse from conquest and empire. It is no mere accident that the most vehement outbursts of activity of the human mind have followed close on the heels of victory, and that the great conquering races of the world have commonly done most to advance and spread civilisation, thus healing in peace the wounds they inflicted in war. The Babylonians, the Greeks, the Romans, the Arabs are our witnesses in the past : we may yet live to see a similar outburst in Japan. Nor, to remount the stream of history to its sources, is it an accident that all the first great strides towards civilisation have been made under despotic and theocratic governments, like those of Egypt, Babylon, and Peru, where the supreme ruler claimed and received the servile allegiance of his subjects in the double character of a king and a god. It is hardly too much to say that at this early epoch despotism is the best friend of humanity and, paradoxical as it may sound, of liberty. For after all there is more liberty in the best sense — liberty to think our own thoughts and to fashion our own destinies — under the most absolute despotism, the most grinding tyranny, than under the apparent freedom of savage life, where the individual's lot is cast from the cradle to the grave in the iron mould of hereditary custom.

So far, therefore, as the public profession of magic has been one of the roads by which the ablest men have passed to supreme power, it has contributed to emancipate mankind from the thraldom of tradition and to elevate them into a larger, freer life, with a broader outlook on the world. This is no small service rendered to humanity. And when we remember further that in another direction magic has paved the way for science, we are forced to admit that if the black art has done much evil, it has also been the source of much good; that if it is the child of error, it has yet been the mother of freedom and truth.

CHAPTER IV

MAGIC AND RELIGION

THE examples collected in the last chapter may suffice to illustrate the general principles of sympathetic magic in its two branches, to which we have given the names of Homoeopathic and Contagious respectively. In some cases of magic which have come before us we have seen that the operation of spirits is assumed, and that an attempt is made to win their favour by prayer and sacrifice. But these cases are on the whole exceptional; they exhibit magic tinged and alloyed with religion. Wherever sympathetic magic occurs in its unadulterated form, it assumes that in nature one event follows another necessarily and invariably without the intervention of any spiritual or personal agency. Thus its fundamental conception is identical with that of modern science; underlying the whole system is a faith, implicit but real and firm, in the order and uniformity of nature. The magician does not doubt that the same causes will always produce the same effects, that the performance of the proper ceremony, accompanied by the appropriate spell, will inevitably be attended by the desired result, unless, indeed, his incantations should chance to be thwarted and foiled by the more potent charms of another sorcerer. He supplicates no higher power: he sues the favour of no fickle and wayward being: he abases himself before no awful deity. Yet his power, great as he believes it to be, is by no means arbitrary and unlimited. He can wield it only so long as he strictly conforms to the rules of his art, or to what may be called the laws of nature as conceived by him. To neglect these rules, to break these laws in the smallest particular, is to incur failure, and may even expose the unskilful practitioner himself to the utmost peril. If he claims a sovereignty over nature, it is a constitutional sovereignty rigorously limited in its scope and exercised in exact conformity with ancient usage. Thus the analogy between the magical and the scientific conceptions of the world is close. In both of them the succession of events is assumed to be perfectly regular and certain, being determined by immutable laws, the operation of which can be foreseen and calculated precisely; the elements of caprice, of chance, and of accident are banished from the course of nature. Both of them open up a seemingly boundless vista of possibilities to him who knows the causes of things and can touch the secret springs that set in motion the vast and intricate mechanism of the world. Hence the strong attraction which magic and science alike have exercised on the human mind; hence the powerful stimulus that both have given to the pursuit of knowledge. They lure the weary enquirer, the footsore seeker, on through the wilderness of disappointment in the present by their endless promises of the future; they take him up to the top of an exceedingly high mountain and show him, beyond the dark clouds and rolling mists at his feet, a vision of the celestial city, far off, it may be, but radiant with unearthly splendour, bathed in the light of dreams.

The fatal flaw of magic lies not in its general assumption of a sequence of events determined by law, but in its total misconception of the nature of the particular laws which govern that sequence. If we analyse the various cases of sympathetic magic which have been passed in review in the preceding pages, and which may be taken as fair samples of the bulk, we shall find, as I have already indicated, that they are all mistaken applications of one or other of two great fundamental laws of thought, namely, the association of ideas by similarity and the association of ideas by contiguity in space or time. A mistaken association of similar ideas produces homoeopathic or imitative magic: a mistaken association of contiguous ideas produces contagious magic. The principles of association are excellent in themselves, and indeed absolutely essential to the working of the human mind. Legitimately applied they yield science; illegitimately applied they yield magic, the bastard sister of science. It is therefore a truism, almost a tautology, to say that all magic is necessarily false and barren; for were it ever to become true and fruitful, it would no longer be magic but science. From the earliest times man has been engaged in a search for general rules whereby to turn the order of natural phenomena to his own advantage, and in the long search he has scraped together a great hoard of such maxims, some of them golden and some of them mere dross. The true or golden rules constitute the body of applied science which we call the arts; the false are magic.

If magic is thus next of kin to science, we have still to enquire how it stands related to religion. But the view we take of that relation will necessarily be coloured by the idea which we have formed of the nature of religion itself; hence a writer may reasonably be expected to define his conception of religion before he proceeds to investigate its relation to magic. There is probably no subject in the world about which opinions differ so much as the nature of religion, and to frame a definition of it which would satisfy every one must obviously be impossible. All that a writer can do is, first, to say clearly what he means by religion, and afterwards to employ the word consistently in that sense throughout his work. By religion, then, I understand a propitiation or conciliation of powers superior to man which are believed to direct and control the course of nature and of human life. Thus defined, religion consists of two elements, a theoretical and a practical, namely, a belief in powers higher than man and an attempt to propitiate or please them. Of the two, belief clearly comes first, since we must believe in the existence of a divine being before we can attempt to please him. But unless the belief leads to a corresponding practice, it is not a religion but merely a theology; in the language of St. James, 'faith, if it hath not works, is dead, being alone.' In other words, no man is religious who does not govern his conduct in some measure by the fear or love of God. On the other hand, mere practice, divested of all religious belief, is also not religion. Two men may behave in exactly the same way, and yet one of them may be religious and the other not. If the one acts from the love or fear of God, he is religious; if the other acts from the love or fear of man, he is moral or immoral according as his behaviour comports or conflicts with the general good. Hence belief and practice or, in theological language, faith and works are equally essential to religion, which cannot exist without both of them. But it is not necessary that religious practice should always take the form of a ritual; that is, it need not consist in the offering of sacrifice, the recitation of prayers, and other outward ceremonies. Its aim is to please the deity, and if the deity is one who delights in charity and mercy and purity more than in oblations of blood, the chanting of hymns, and the fumes of incense, his worshippers will best please him, not by prostrating themselves before him, by intoning his praises, and by filling his temples with costly gifts, but by being pure and merciful and charitable towards men, for in so doing they will imitate, so far as human infirmity allows, the perfections of the divine nature. It was this ethical side of religion which the Hebrew prophets, inspired with the noble ideal of God's goodness and holiness, were never weary of inculcating. Thus Micah says: 'He hath shewed thee, O man, what is good; and what doth the Lord require of thee, but to do justly, and to love mercy, and to walk humbly with thy God?' And at a later time much of the force by which Christianity conquered the world was drawn from the same high conception of God's moral nature and the duty laid on men of conforming themselves to it. 'Pure religion and undefiled,' says St. James, 'before God and the Father is this, To visit the fatherless and widows in their affliction, and to keep himself unspotted from the world.'

But if religion involves, first, a belief in superhuman beings who rule the world, and, second, an attempt to win their favour, it clearly assumes that the course of nature is to some extent elastic or variable, and that we can persuade or induce the mighty beings who control it to deflect, for our benefit, the current of events from the channel in which they would otherwise flow. Now this implied elasticity or variability of nature is directly opposed to the principles of magic as well as of science, both of which assume that the processes of nature are rigid and invariable in their operation, and that they can as little be turned from their course by persuasion and entreaty as by threats and intimidation. The distinction between the two conflicting views of the universe turns on their answer to the crucial question, Are the forces which govern the world conscious and personal, or unconscious and impersonal? Religion, as a conciliation of the superhuman powers, assumes the former member of the alternative. For all conciliation implies that the being conciliated is a conscious or personal agent, that his conduct is in some measure uncertain, and that he can be prevailed upon to vary it in the desired direction by a judicious appeal to his interests, his appetites, or his emotions. Conciliation is never employed towards things which are regarded as inanimate, nor towards persons whose behaviour in the particular circumstances is known to be determined with absolute certainty. Thus in so far as religion assumes the world to be directed by conscious agents who may be turned from their purpose by persuasion, it stands in fundamental antagonism to magic as well as to science, both of which take for granted that the course of nature is determined, not by the passions or caprice of personal beings, but by the operation of immutable laws acting mechanically. In magic, indeed, the assumption is only implicit, but in science it is explicit. It is true that magic often deals with spirits, which are personal agents of the kind assumed by religion; but whenever it does so in its proper form, it treats them exactly in the same fashion as it treats inanimate agents, that is, it constrains or coerces instead of conciliating or propitiating them as religion would do. Thus it assumes that all personal beings, whether human or divine, are in the last resort subject to those impersonal forces which control all things, but which nevertheless can be turned to account by any one who knows how to manipulate them by the appropriate ceremonies and spells. In ancient Egypt, for example, the magicians claimed the power of compelling even the highest gods to do their bidding, and actually threatened them with destruction in case of disobedience. Sometimes, without going quite so far as that, the wizard declared that he would scatter the bones of Osiris or reveal his sacred legend, if the god proved contumacious. Similarly in India at the present day the great Hindoo trinity itself of Brahma, Vishnu, and Siva is subject to the sorcerers, who, by means of their spells, exercise such an ascendancy over the mightiest deities, that these are bound submissively to execute on earth below, or in heaven above, whatever commands their masters the magicians may please to issue. There is a saying everywhere current in India: 'The whole universe is subject to the gods; the gods are subject to the spells (*mantras*); the spells to the Brahmans; therefore the Brahmans are our gods.'

This radical conflict of principle between magic and religion sufficiently explains the relentless hostility with which in history the priest has often pursued the magician. The haughty self-sufficiency of the magician, his arrogant demeanour towards the higher powers, and his unabashed claim to exercise a sway like theirs could not but revolt the priest, to whom, with his awful sense of divine majesty, and his humble prostration in presence of it, such claims and such a demeanour must have appeared an impious and blasphemous usurpation of prerogatives that belong to God alone. And sometimes, we may suspect, lower motives concurred to whet the edge of the priest's hostility. He professed to be the proper medium, the true intercessor between God and man, and no doubt his interests as well as his feelings were often injured by a rival practitioner, who preached a surer and smoother road to fortune than the rugged and slippery path of divine favour.

Yet this antagonism, familiar as it is to us, seems to have made its appearance comparatively late in the history of religion. At an earlier stage the functions of priest and sorcerer were often combined or, to speak perhaps more correctly, were not yet differentiated from each other. To serve his purpose man wooed the good-will of gods or spirits by prayer and sacrifice, while at the same time he had recourse to ceremonies and forms of words which he hoped would of themselves bring about the desired result without the help of god or devil. In short, he performed religious and magical rites simultaneously; he uttered prayers and incantations almost in the same breath, knowing or recking little of the theoretical inconsistency of his behaviour, so long as by hook or crook he contrived to get what he wanted. Instances of this fusion or confusion of magic with religion have already met us in the practices of Melanesians and of other peoples.

The same confusion of magic and religion has survived among peoples that have risen to higher levels of culture. It was rife in ancient India and ancient Egypt; it is by no means extinct among European peasantry at the present day. With regard to ancient India we are told by an eminent Sanscrit scholar that 'the sacrificial ritual at the earliest period of which we have detailed information is pervaded with practices that breathe the spirit of the most primitive magic.' Speaking of the importance of magic in the East, and especially in Egypt, Professor Maspero remarks that 'we ought not to attach to the word magic the degrading idea which it almost inevitably calls up in the mind of a modern. Ancient magic was the very foundation of religion. The faithful who desired to obtain some favour from a god had no chance of succeeding except by laying hands on the deity, and this arrest could only be effected by means of a certain number of rites, sacrifices, prayers, and chants, which the god himself had revealed, and which obliged him to do what was demanded of him.'

Among the ignorant classes of modern Europe the same confusion of ideas, the same mixture of religion and magic, crops up in various forms. Thus we are told that in France 'the majority of the peasants still believe that the priest possesses a secret and irresistible power over the elements. By reciting certain prayers which he alone knows and has the right to utter, yet for the utterance of which he must afterwards demand absolution, he can, on an occasion of pressing danger, arrest or reverse for a moment the action of the eternal laws of the physical world. The winds, the storms, the hail, and the rain are at his command and obey his will. The fire also is subject to him, and the flames of a conflagration are extinguished at his word.' For example, French peasants used to be, perhaps are still, persuaded that the priests could celebrate, with certain special rites, a Mass of the Holy Spirit, of which the efficacy was so miraculous that it never met with any opposition from the divine will; God was forced to grant whatever was asked of Him in this form, however rash and importunate might be the petition. No idea of impiety or irreverence attached to the rite in the minds of those who, in some of the great extremities of life, sought by this singular means to take the kingdom of heaven by storm. The secular priests generally refused to say the Mass of the Holy Spirit; but the monks, especially the Capuchin friars, had the reputation of yielding with less scruple to the entreaties of the anxious and distressed. In the constraint thus supposed by Catholic peasantry to be laid by the priest upon the deity we seem to have an exact counterpart of the power which the ancient Egyptians ascribed to their magicians. Again, to take another example, in many villages of Provence the priest is still reputed to possess the faculty of averting storms. It is not every priest who enjoys this reputation; and in some villages, when a change of pastors takes place, the parishioners are eager to learn whether the new incumbent has the power (*pouder*), as they call it. At the first sign of a heavy storm they put him to the proof by inviting him to exorcise the threatening clouds; and if the result answers to their hopes, the new shepherd is assured of the sympathy and respect of his flock. In some parishes, where the reputation of the curate in this respect stood higher than that of his rector, the relations between the two have been so strained in consequence that the bishop has had to translate the rector to another benefice. Again, Gascon peasants believe that to revenge themselves on their enemies bad men will sometimes induce a priest to say a mass called the Mass of Saint Sécaire. Very few priests know this mass, and threefourths of those who do know it would not say it for love or money. None but wicked priests dare to perform the gruesome ceremony, and you may be quite sure that they will have a very heavy account to render for it at the last day. No curate or bishop, not even the archbishop of Auch, can pardon them; that right belongs to the Pope of Rome alone. The Mass of Saint Sécaire may be said only in a ruined or deserted church, where owls mope and hoot, where bats flit in the gloaming, where gypsies lodge of nights, and where toads squat under the desecrated altar. Thither the bad priest comes by night with his light o' love, and at the first stroke of eleven he begins to mumble the mass backwards, and ends just as the clocks are knelling the midnight hour. His leman acts as clerk. The host he blesses is black and has three points; he consecrates no wine, but instead he drinks the water of a well into which the body of an unbaptized infant has been flung. He makes the sign of the cross, but it is on the ground and with his left foot. And many other things he does which no good Christian could look upon without being struck blind and deaf and dumb for the rest of his life. But the man for whom the mass is said withers away little by little, and nobody can say what is the matter with him; even the doctors can make nothing of it. They do not know that he is slowly dying of the Mass of Saint Sécaire.

Yet though magic is thus found to fuse and amalgamate with religion in many ages and in many lands, there are some grounds for thinking that this fusion is not primitive, and that there was a time when man trusted to magic alone for the satisfaction of such wants as transcended his immediate animal cravings. In the first place a consideration of the fundamental notions of magic and religion may incline us to surmise that magic is older than religion in the history of humanity. We have seen that on the one hand magic is nothing but a mistaken application of the very simplest and most elementary processes of the mind, namely the association of ideas by virtue of resemblance or contiguity; and that on the other hand religion assumes the operation of conscious or personal agents, superior to man, behind the visible screen of nature. Obviously the conception of personal agents is more complex than a simple recognition of the similarity or contiguity of ideas; and a theory which assumes that the course of nature is determined by conscious agents is more abstruse and recondite, and requires for its apprehension a far higher degree of intelligence and reflection, than the view that things succeed each other simply by reason of their contiguity or resemblance. The very beasts associate the ideas of things that are like each other or that have been found together in their experience; and they could hardly survive for a day if they ceased to do so. But who attributes to the animals a belief that the phenomena of nature are worked by a multitude of invisible animals or by one enormous and prodigiously strong animal behind the scenes? It is probably no injustice to the brutes to assume that the honour of devising a theory of this latter sort must be reserved for human reason.

Thus, if magic be deduced immediately from elementary processes of reasoning, and be, in fact, an error into which the mind falls almost spontaneously, while religion rests on conceptions which the merely animal intelligence can hardly be supposed to have yet attained to, it becomes probable that magic arose before religion in the evolution of our race, and that man essayed to bend nature to his wishes by the sheer force of spells and enchantments before he strove to coax and mollify a coy, capricious, or irascible deity by the soft insinuation of prayer and sacrifice.

The conclusion which we have thus reached deductively from a consideration of the fundamental ideas of magic and religion is confirmed inductively by the observation that among the aborigines of Australia, the rudest savages as to whom we possess accurate information, magic is universally practised, whereas religion in the sense of a propitiation or reconciliation of the higher powers seems to be nearly unknown. Roughly speaking, all men in Australia are magicians, but not one is a priest; everybody fancies he can influence his fellows or the course of nature by sympathetic magic, but nobody dreams of propitiating gods by prayer and sacrifice.

But if in the most backward state of human society now known to us we find magic thus conspicuously present and religion conspicuously absent, may we not reasonably conjecture that the civilised races of the world have also at some period of their history passed through a similar intellectual phase, that they attempted to force the great powers of nature to do their pleasure before they thought of courting their favour by offerings and prayer — in short that, just as on the material side of human culture there has everywhere been an Age of Stone, so on the intellectual side there has everywhere been an Age of Magic? There are reasons for answering this question in the affirmative. When we survey the existing races of mankind from Greenland to Tierra del Fuego, or from Scotland to Singapore, we observe that they are distinguished one from the other by a great variety of religions, and that these distinctions are not, so to speak, merely coterminous with the broad distinctions of race, but descend into the minuter sub-divisions of states and common-wealths, nay, that they honeycomb the town, the village, and even the family, so that the surface of society all over the world is cracked and seamed, sapped and mined with rents and fissures and yawning crevasses opened up by the disintegrating influence of religious dissension. Yet when we have penetrated through these differences, which affect mainly the intelligent and thoughtful part of the community, we shall find underlying them all a solid stratum of intellectual agreement among the dull, the weak, the ignorant, and the superstitious, who constitute, unfortunately, the vast majority of mankind. One of the great achievements of the nineteenth century was to run shafts down into this low mental stratum in many parts of the world, and thus to discover its substantial identity everywhere. It is beneath our feet — and not very far beneath them — here in Europe at the present day, and it crops up on the surface in the heart of the Australian wilderness and wherever the advent of a higher civilisation has not crushed it underground. This universal faith, this truly Catholic creed, is a belief in the efficacy of magic. While religious systems differ not only in different countries, but in the same country in different ages, the system of sympathetic magic remains everywhere and at all times substantially alike in its principles and practice. Among the ignorant and superstitious classes of modern Europe it is very much what it was thousands of years ago in Egypt and India, and what it now is among the lowest savages surviving in the remotest corners of the world. If the test of truth lay in a show of hands or a counting of heads, the system of magic might appeal, with far more reason than the Catholic Church, to the proud motto, '*Quod semper, quod ubique, quod ab omnibus*,' as the sure and certain credential of its own infallibility.

It is not our business here to consider what bearing the permanent existence of such a solid layer of savagery beneath the surface of society, and unaffected by the superficial changes of religion and culture, has upon the future of humanity. The dispassionate observer, whose studies have led him to plumb its depths, can hardly regard it otherwise than as a standing menace to civilisation. We seem to move on a thin crust which may at any moment be rent by the subterranean forces slumbering below. From time to time a hollow murmur underground or a sudden spirt of flame into the air tells of what is going on beneath our feet. Now and then the polite world is startled by a paragraph in a newspaper which tells how in Scotland an image has been found stuck full of pins for the purpose of killing an obnoxious laird or minister, how a woman has been slowly roasted to death as a witch in Ireland, or how a girl has been murdered and chopped up in Russia to make those candles of human tallow by whose light thieves hope to pursue their midnight trade unseen. But whether the influences that make for further progress, or those that threaten to undo what has already been accomplished, will ultimately prevail; whether the impulsive energy of the minority or the dead weight of the majority of mankind will prove the stronger force to carry us up to higher heights or to sink us into lower depths, are questions rather for the sage, the moralist, and the statesman, whose eagle vision scans the future, than for the humble student of the present and the past. Here we are only concerned to ask how far the uniformity, the universality, and the permanence of a belief in magic, compared with the endless variety and the shifting character of religious creeds, raises a presumption that the former represents a ruder and earlier phase of the human mind, through which all the races of mankind have passed or are passing on their way to religion and science.

If an Age of Religion has thus everywhere, as I venture to surmise, been preceded by an Age of Magic, it is natural that we should enquire what causes have led mankind, or rather a portion of them, to abandon magic as a principle of faith and practice and to betake themselves to religion instead. When we reflect upon the multitude, the variety, and the complexity of the facts to be explained, and the scantiness of our information regarding them, we shall be ready to acknowledge that a full and satisfactory solution of so profound a problem is hardly to be hoped for, and that the most we can do in the present state of our knowledge is to hazard a more or less plausible conjecture. With all due diffidence, then, I would suggest that a tardy recognition of the inherent falsehood and barrenness of magic set the more thoughtful part of mankind to cast about for a truer theory of nature and a more fruitful method of turning her resources to account. The shrewder intelligences must in time have come to perceive that magical ceremonies and incantations did not really effect the results which they were designed to produce, and which the majority of their simpler fellows still believed that they did actually produce. This great discovery of the inefficacy of magic must have wrought a radical though probably slow revolution in the minds of those who had the sagacity to make it. The discovery amounted to this, that men for the first time recognised their inability to manipulate at pleasure certain natural forces which hitherto they had believed to be completely within their control. It was a confession of human ignorance and weakness. Man saw that he had taken for causes what were no causes, and that all his efforts to work by means of these imaginary causes had been vain. His painful toil had been wasted, his curious ingenuity had been squandered to no purpose. He had been pulling at strings to which nothing was attached; he had been marching, as he thought, straight to the goal, while in reality he had only been treading in a narrow circle. Not that the effects which he had striven so hard to produce did not continue to manifest themselves. They were still produced, but not by him. The rain still fell on the thirsty ground: the sun still pursued his daily, and the moon her nightly journey across the sky: the silent procession of the seasons still moved in light and shadow, in cloud and sunshine across the earth: men were still born to labour and sorrow, and still, after a brief sojourn here, were gathered to their fathers in the long home hereafter. All things indeed went on as before, yet all seemed different to him from whose eyes the old scales had fallen. For he could no longer cherish the pleasing illusion that it was he who guided the earth and the heaven in their courses, and that they would cease to perform their great revolutions were he to take his feeble hand from the wheel. In the death of his enemies and his friends he no longer saw a proof of the resistless potency of his own or of hostile enchantments; he now knew that friends and foes alike had succumbed to a force stronger than any that he could wield, and in obedience to a destiny which he was powerless to control.

Thus cut adrift from his ancient moorings and left to toss on a troubled sea of doubt and uncertainty, his old happy confidence in himself and his powers rudely shaken, our primitive philosopher must have been sadly perplexed and agitated till he came to rest, as in a quiet haven after a tempestuous voyage, in a new system of faith and practice, which seemed to offer a solution of his harassing doubts and a substitute, however precarious, for that sovereignty over nature which he had reluctantly abdicated. If the great world went on its way without the help of him or his fellows, it must surely be because there were other beings, like himself, but far stronger, who, unseen themselves, directed its course and brought about all the varied series of events which he had hitherto believed to be dependent on his own magic. It was they, as he now believed, and not he himself, who made the stormy wind to blow, the lightning to flash, and the thunder to roll; who had laid the foundations of the solid earth and set bounds to the restless sea that it might not pass; who caused all the glorious lights of heaven to shine; who gave the fowls of the air their meat and the wild beasts of the desert their prey; who bade the fruitful land to bring forth in abundance, the high hills to be clothed with forests, the bubbling springs to rise under the rocks in the valleys, and green pastures to grow by still waters; who breathed into man's nostrils and made him live, or turned him to destruction by famine and pestilence and war. To these mighty beings, whose handiwork he traced in all the gorgeous and varied pageantry of nature, man now addressed himself, humbly confessing his dependence on their invisible power, and beseeching them of their mercy to furnish him with all good things, to defend him from the perils and dangers by which our mortal life is compassed about on every hand, and finally to bring his immortal spirit, freed from the burden of the body, to some happier world, beyond the reach of pain and sorrow, where he might rest with them and with the spirits of good men in joy and felicity for ever.

In this, or some such way as this, the deeper minds may be conceived to have made the great transition from magic to religion. But even in them the change can hardly ever have been sudden; probably it proceeded very slowly, and required long ages for its more or less perfect accomplishment. For the recognition of man's powerlessness to influence the course of nature on a grand scale must have been gradual; he cannot have been shorn of the whole of his fancied dominion at a blow. Step by step he must have been driven back from his proud position; foot by foot he must have yielded, with a sigh, the ground which he had once viewed as his own. Now it would be the wind, now the rain, now the sunshine, now the thunder, that he confessed himself unable to wield at will; and as province after province of nature thus fell from his grasp, till what had once seemed a kingdom threatened to shrink into a prison, man must have been more and more profoundly impressed with a sense of his own helplessness and the might of the invisible beings by whom he believed himself to be surrounded. Thus religion, beginning as a slight and partial acknowledgment of powers superior to man, tends with the growth of knowledge to deepen into a confession of man's entire and absolute dependence on the divine; his old free bearing is exchanged for an attitude of lowliest prostration before the mysterious powers of the unseen, and his highest virtue is to submit his will to theirs: *In la sua volontade è nostra pace.* But this deepening sense of religion, this more perfect submission to the divine will in all things, affects only those higher intelligences who have breadth of view enough to comprehend the vastness of the universe and the littleness of man. Small minds cannot grasp great ideas; to their narrow comprehension, their purblind vision, nothing seems really great and important but themselves. Such minds hardly rise into religion at all. They are, indeed, drilled by their betters into an outward conformity with its precepts and a verbal profession of its tenets; but at heart they cling to their old magical superstitions, which may be discountenanced and forbidden, but cannot be eradicated by religion, so long as they have their roots deep down in the mental framework and constitution of the great majority of mankind.

The reader may well be tempted to ask, How was it that intelligent men did not sooner detect the fallacy of magic? How could they continue to cherish expectations that were invariably doomed to disappointment? With what heart persist in playing venerable antics that led to nothing, and mumbling solemn balderdash that remained without effect? Why cling to beliefs which were so flatly contradicted by experience? How dare to repeat experiments that had failed so often? The answer seems to be that the fallacy was far from easy to detect, the failure by no means obvious, since in many, perhaps in most, cases the desired event did actually follow, at a longer or shorter interval, the performance of the rite which was designed to bring it about;

and a mind of more than common acuteness was needed to perceive that, even in these cases, the rite was not necessarily the cause of the event. A ceremony intended to make the wind blow or the rain fall, or to work the death of an enemy, will always be followed, sooner or later, by the occurrence it is meant to bring to pass; and primitive man may be excused for regarding the occurrence as a direct result of the ceremony, and the best possible proof of its efficacy. Similarly, rites observed in the morning to help the sun to rise, and in spring to wake the dreaming earth from her winter sleep, will invariably appear to be crowned with success, at least within the temperate zones; for in these regions the sun lights his golden lamp in the east every morning, and year by year the vernal earth decks herself afresh with a rich mantle of green. Hence the practical savage, with his conservative instincts, might well turn a deaf ear to the subtleties of the theoretical doubter, the philosophic radical, who presumed to hint that sunrise and spring might not, after all, be direct consequences of the punctual performance of certain daily or yearly ceremonies, and that the sun might perhaps continue to rise and trees to blossom though the ceremonies were occasionally intermitted, or even discontinued altogether. These sceptical doubts would naturally be repelled by the other with scorn and indignation as airy reveries subversive of the faith and manifestly contradicted by experience. 'Can anything be plainer,' he might say, 'than that I light my twopenny candle on earth and that the sun then kindles his great fire in heaven? I should be glad to know whether, when I have put on my green robe in spring, the trees do not afterwards do the same? These are facts patent to everybody, and on them I take my stand. I am a plain practical man, not one of your theorists and splitters of hairs and choppers of logic. Theories and speculation and all that may be very well in their way, and I have not the least objection to your indulging in them, provided, of course, you do not put them in practice. But give me leave to stick to facts; then I know where I am.' The fallacy of this reasoning is obvious to us, because it happens to deal with facts about which we have long made up our minds. But let an argument of precisely the same calibre be applied to matters which are still under debate, and it may be questioned whether a British audience would not applaud it as sound, and esteem the speaker who used it a safe man — not brilliant or showy, perhaps, but thoroughly sensible and hard-headed. If such reasonings could pass muster among ourselves, need we wonder that they long escaped detection by the savage?

CHAPTER V

THE MAGICAL CONTROL OF THE WEATHER

§ 1. *The Public Magician.* — The reader may remember that we were led to plunge into the labyrinth of magic by a consideration of two different types of man-god. This is the clue which has guided our devious steps through the maze, and brought us out at last on higher ground, whence, resting a little by the way, we can look back over the path we have already traversed and forward to the longer and steeper road we have still to climb.

As a result of the foregoing discussion, the two types of human gods may conveniently be distinguished as the religious and the magical man-god respectively. In the former, a being of an order different from and superior to man is supposed to become incarnate, for a longer or a shorter time, in a human body, manifesting his super-human power and knowledge by miracles wrought and prophecies uttered through the medium of the fleshly tabernacle in which he has deigned to take up his abode. This may also appropriately be called the inspired or incarnate type of man-god. In it the human body is merely a frail earthly vessel filled with a divine and immortal spirit. On the other hand, a man-god of the magical sort is nothing but a man who possesses in an unusually high degree powers which most of his fellows arrogate to themselves on a smaller scale; for in rude society there is hardly a person who does not dabble in magic. Thus, whereas a man-god of the former or inspired type derives his divinity from a deity who has stooped to hide his heavenly radiance behind a dull mask of earthly mould, a man-god of the latter type draws his extraordinary power from a certain physical sympathy with nature. He is not merely the receptacle of a divine spirit. His whole being, body and soul, is so delicately attuned to the harmony of the world that a touch of his hand or a turn of his head may send a thrill vibrating through the universal framework of things; and conversely his divine organism is acutely sensitive to such slight changes of environment as would leave ordinary mortals wholly unaffected. But the line between these two types of man-god, however sharply we may draw it in theory, is seldom to be traced with precision in practice, and in what follows I shall not insist on it.

We have seen that in practice the magic art may be employed for the benefit either of individuals or of the whole community, and that according as it is directed to one or other of these two objects it may be called private or public magic. Further, I pointed out that the public magician occupies a position of great influence, from which, if he is a prudent and able man, he may advance step by step to the rank of a chief or king. Thus an examination of public magic conduces to an understanding of the early kingship, since in savage and barbarous society many chiefs and kings appear to owe their authority in great measure to their reputation as magicians.

Among the objects of public utility which magic may be employed to secure, the most essential is an adequate supply of food. The examples cited in preceding pages prove that the purveyors of food — the hunter, the fisher, the farmer — all resort to magical practices in the pursuit of their various callings; but they do so as private individuals for the benefit of themselves and their families, rather than as public functionaries acting in the interest of the whole people. It is otherwise when the rites are performed, not by the hunters, the fishers, the farmers themselves, but by professional magicians on their behalf. In primitive society, where uniformity of occupation is the rule, and the distribution of the community into various classes of workers has hardly begun, every man is more or less his own magician; he practises charms and incantations for his own good and the injury of his enemies. But a great step in advance has been taken when a special class of magicians has been instituted; when, in other words, a number of men have been set apart for the express purpose of benefiting the whole community by their skill, whether that skill be directed to the healing of diseases, the forecasting of the future, the regulation of the weather, or any other object of general utility. The impotence of the means adopted by most of these practitioners to accomplish their ends ought not to bind us to the immense importance of the institution itself. Here is a body of men relieved, at least in the higher stages of savagery, from the need of earning their livelihood by hard manual toil, and allowed, nay, expected and encouraged, to prosecute researches into the secret ways of nature. It was at once their duty and their interest to know more than their fellows, to acquaint themselves with everything that could aid man in his arduous struggle with nature, everything that could mitigate his sufferings and prolong his life. The properties of drugs and minerals, the causes of rain and drought, of thunder and lightning, the changes of the seasons, the phases of the moon, the daily and yearly journeys of the sun, the motions of the stars, the mystery of life, and the mystery of death, all these things must have excited the wonder of these early philosophers, and stimulated them to find solutions of problems that were doubtless often thrust on their attention in the most practical form by the importunate demands of their clients, who expected them not merely to understand but to regulate the great processes of nature for the good of man. That their first shots fell very far wide of the mark could hardly be helped. The slow, the never-ending approach to truth consists in perpetually forming and testing hypotheses, accepting those which at the time seem to fit the facts and rejecting the others. The views of natural causation embraced by the savage magician no doubt appear to us manifestly false and absurd; yet in their day they were legitimate hypotheses, though they have not stood the test of experience. Ridicule and blame are the just meed, not of those who devised these crude theories, but of those who obstinately adhered to them after better had been propounded. Certainly no men ever had stronger incentives in the pursuit of truth than these savage sorcerers. To maintain at least a show of knowledge was absolutely necessary; a single mistake detected might cost them their life. This no doubt led them to practise imposture for the purpose of concealing their ignorance; but it also supplied them with the most powerful motive for substituting a real for a sham knowledge, since, if you would appear to know anything, by far the best way is actually to know it. Thus, however justly we may reject the extravagant pretensions of magicians and condemn the deceptions which they have practised on mankind, the original institution of this class of men has, take it all in all, been productive of incalculable good to humanity. They were the direct predecessors, not merely of our physicians and surgeons, but of our investigators and discoverers in every branch of natural science. They began the work which has since been carried to such glorious and beneficent issues by their successors in after ages; and if the beginning was poor and feeble, this is to be imputed to the inevitable difficulties which beset the path of knowledge rather than to the natural incapacity or wilful fraud of the men themselves.

§ 2. *The Magical Control of Rain.* — Of the things which the public magician sets himself to do for the good of the tribe, one of the chief is to control the weather and especially to ensure an adequate fall of rain. Water is an essential of life, and in most countries the supply of it depends upon showers. Without rain vegetation withers, animals and men languish and die. Hence in savage communities the rain-maker is a very important personage; and often a special class of magicians exists for the purpose of regulating the heavenly water supply. The methods by which they attempt to discharge the duties of their office are commonly, though not always, based on the principle of homoeopathic or imitative magic. If they wish to make rain they simulate it by sprinkling water or mimicking clouds: if their object is to stop rain and cause drought, they avoid water and resort to warmth and fire for the sake of drying up the too abundant moisture. Such attempts are by no means confined, as the cultivated reader might imagine, to the naked inhabitants of those sultry lands like Central Australia and some parts of Eastern and Southern Africa, where often for months together the pitiless sun beats down out of a blue and cloudless sky on the parched and gaping earth. They are, or used to be, common enough among outwardly civilised folk in the moister climate of Europe. I will now illustrate them by instances drawn from the practice both of public and private magic.

Thus, for example, in a village near Dorpat, in Russia, when rain was much wanted, three men used to climb up the fir-trees of an old sacred grove. One of them drummed with a hammer on a kettle or small cask to imitate thunder; the second knocked two fire-brands together and made the sparks fly, to imitate lightning; and the third, who was called 'the rain-maker,' had a bunch of twigs with which he sprinkled water from a vessel on all sides. To put an end to drought and bring down rain, women and girls of the village of Ploska are wont to go naked by night to the boundaries of the village and there pour water on the ground. In Halmahera, or Gilolo, a large island to the west of New Guinea, a wizard makes rain by dipping a branch of a particular kind of tree in water and then scattering the moisture from the dripping bough over the ground. In New Britain the rain-maker wraps some leaves of a red and green striped creeper in a banana-leaf, moistens the bundle with water, and buries it in the ground; then he imitates with his mouth the plashing of rain. Amongst the Omaha Indians of North America, when the corn is withering for want of rain, the members of the sacred Buffalo Society fill a large vessel with water and dance four times round it. One of them drinks some of the water and spirts it into the air, making a fine spray in imitation of a mist or drizzling rain. Then he upsets the vessel, spilling the water on the ground; whereupon the dancers fall down and drink up the water, getting mud all over their faces. Lastly, they squirt the water into the air, making a fine mist. This saves the corn. In spring-time the Natchez of North America used to club together to purchase favourable weather for their crops from the wizards. If rain was needed, the wizards fasted and danced with pipes full of water in their mouths. The pipes were perforated like the nozzle of a watering-can, and through the holes the rain-maker blew the water towards that part of the sky where the clouds hung heaviest. But if fine weather was wanted, he mounted the roof of his hut, and with extended arms, blowing with all his might, he beckoned to the clouds to pass by. When the rains do not come in due season the people of Central Angoniland repair to what is called the rain-temple. Here they clear away the grass, and the leader pours beer into a pot which is buried in the ground, while he says, 'Master *Chauta*, you have hardened your heart towards us, what would you have us do? We must perish indeed. Give your children the rains, there is the beer we have given you.' Then they all partake of the beer that is left over, even the children being made to sip it. Next they take branches of trees and dance and sing for rain.

When they return to the village they find a vessel of water set at
the doorway by an old woman; so they dip their branches in it
and wave them aloft, so as to scatter the drops. After that the
rain is sure to come driving up in heavy clouds. In these practices
we see a combination of religion with magic; for while the
scattering of the water-drops by means of branches is a purely
magical ceremony, the prayer for rain and the offering of beer
are purely religious rites. In the Mara tribe of Northern Australia
the rain-maker goes to a pool and sings over it his magic song.
Then he takes some of the water in his hands, drinks it, and
spits it out in various directions. After that he throws water all
over himself, scatters it about, and returns quietly to the camp.
Rain is supposed to follow. The Arab historian Makrizi describes
a method of stopping rain which is said to have been resorted to
by a tribe of nomads called Alqamar in Hadramaut. They cut
a branch from a certain tree in the desert, set it on fire, and then
sprinkled the burning brand with water. After that the vehemence
of the rain abated, just as the water vanished when it fell on the
glowing brand. Some of the Eastern Angamis of Manipur are
said to perform a somewhat similar ceremony for the opposite
purpose, in order, namely, to produce rain. The head of the
village puts a burning brand on the grave of a man who has
died of burns, and quenches the brand with water, while he prays
that rain may fall. Here the putting out the fire with water, which
is an imitation of rain, is reinforced by the influence of the dead
man, who, having been burnt to death, will naturally be anxious
for the descent of rain to cool his scorched body and assuage his
pangs.

Other people besides the Arabs have used fire as a means of
stopping rain. Thus the Sulka of New Britain heat stones red
hot in the fire and then put them out in the rain, or they throw
hot ashes in the air. They think that the rain will soon cease to
fall, for it does not like to be burned by the hot stones or ashes.
The Telugus send a little girl out naked into the rain with a burning
piece of wood in her hand, which she has to show to the rain.
That is supposed to stop the downpour. At Port Stephens in
New South Wales the medicine-men used to drive away rain by
throwing fire-sticks into the air, while at the same time they
puffed and shouted. Any man of the Anula tribe in Northern

Australia can stop rain by simply warming a green stick in the fire, and then striking it against the wind.

In time of severe drought the Dieri of Central Australia, loudly lamenting the impoverished state of the country and their own half-starved condition, call upon the spirits of their remote predecessors whom they call Mura-muras, to grant them power to make a heavy rainfall. For they believe that the clouds are bodies in which rain is generated by their own ceremonies or those of neighbouring tribes, through the influence of the Mura-muras. The way in which they set about drawing rain from the clouds is this. A hole is dug about twelve feet long and eight or ten broad, and over this hole a conical hut of logs and branches is made. Two wizards, supposed to have received a special inspiration from the Mura-muras, are bled by an old and influential man with a sharp flint; and the blood, drawn from their arms below the elbow, is made to flow on the other men of the tribe, who sit huddled together in the hut. At the same time the two bleeding men throw handfuls of down about, some of which adheres to the blood-stained bodies of their comrades, while the rest floats in the air. The blood is thought to represent the rain, and the down the clouds. During the ceremony two large stones are placed in the middle of the hut; they stand for gathering clouds and presage rain. Then the wizards who were bled carry away the two stones for about ten or fifteen miles, and place them as high as they can in the tallest tree. Meanwhile the other men gather gypsum, pound it fine, and throw it into a water-hole. This the Mura-muras see, and at once they cause clouds to appear in the sky. Lastly, the men, young and old, surround the hut, and, stooping down, butt at it with their heads, like so many rams. Thus they force their way through it and reappear on the other side, repeating the process till the hut is wrecked. In doing this they are forbidden to use their hands or arms; but when the heavy logs alone remain, they are allowed to pull them out with their hands. 'The piercing of the hut with their heads symbolises the piercing of the clouds; the fall of the hut, the fall of the rain.' Obviously, too, the act of placing high up in trees the two stones, which stand for clouds, is a way of making the real clouds to mount up in the sky. The Dieri also imagine that the foreskins taken from lads at circumcision have a great power of producing

D

rain. Hence the Great Council of the tribe always keeps a small stock of foreskins ready for use. They are carefully concealed, being wrapt up in feathers with the fat of the wild dog and of the carpet snake. A woman may not see such a parcel opened on any account. When the ceremony is over, the foreskin is buried, its virtue being exhausted. After the rains have fallen, some of the tribe always undergo a surgical operation, which consists in cutting the skin of their chest and arms with a sharp flint. The wound is then tapped with a flat stick to increase the flow of blood, and red ochre is rubbed into it. Raised scars are thus produced. The reason alleged by the natives for this practice is that they are pleased with the rain, and that there is a connexion between the rain and the scars. Apparently the operation is not very painful, for the patient laughs and jokes while it is going on. Indeed, little children have been seen to crowd round the operator and patiently take their turn; then after being operated on, they ran away, expanding their little chests and singing for the rain to beat upon them. However, they were not so well pleased next day, when they felt their wounds stiff and sore. In Java, when rain is wanted, two men will sometimes thrash each other with supple rods till the blood flows down their backs; the streaming blood represents the rain, and no doubt is supposed to make it fall on the ground. The people of Egghiou, a district of Abyssinia, used to engage in sanguinary conflicts with each other, village against village, for a week together every January for the purpose of procuring rain. Some years ago the emperor Menelik forbade the custom. However, the following year the rain was deficient, and the popular outcry so great that the emperor yielded to it, and allowed the murderous fights to be resumed, but for two days a year only. The writer who mentions the custom regards the blood shed on these occasions as a propitiatory sacrifice offered to spirits who control the showers; but perhaps, as in the Australian and Javanese ceremonies, it is an imitation of rain. The prophets of Baal, who sought to procure rain by cutting themselves with knives till the blood gushed out, may have acted on the same principle.

There is a widespread belief that twin children possess magical powers over nature, especially over rain and the weather. This curious superstition prevails among some of the Indian tribes of British Columbia, and has led them often to impose certain singular restrictions or taboos on the parents of twins, though the exact meaning of these restrictions is generally obscure. Thus the Tsimshian Indians of British Columbia believe that twins control the weather; therefore they pray to wind and rain, 'Calm down, breath of the twins.' Further, they think that the wishes of twins are always fulfilled; hence twins are feared, because they can harm the man they hate. They can also call the salmon and the olachen or candle-fish, and so they are known by a name which means 'making plentiful.' In the opinion of the Kwakiutl Indians of British Columbia, twins are transformed salmon; hence they may not go near water, lest they should be changed back again into the fish. In their childhood they can summon any wind by motions of their hands, and they can make fair or foul weather, and also cure diseases by swinging a large wooden rattle. The Nootka Indians of British Columbia also believe that twins are somehow related to salmon. Hence among them twins may not catch salmon, and they may not eat or even handle the fresh fish. They can make fair or foul weather, and can cause rain to fall by painting their faces black and then washing them, which may represent the rain dripping from the dark clouds. The Shuswap Indians, like the Thompson Indians, associate twins with the grizzly bear, for they call them 'young grizzly bears.' According to them, twins remain throughout life endowed with supernatural powers. In particular they can make good or bad weather. They produce rain by spilling water from a basket in the air; they make fine weather by shaking a small flat piece of wood attached to a stick by a string; they raise storms by strewing down on the ends of spruce branches.

The same power of influencing the weather is attributed to twins by the Baronga, a tribe of Bantu negroes who inhabit the shores of Delagoa Bay in South-eastern Africa. They bestow the name of *Tilo* — that is, the sky — on a woman who has given birth to twins, and the infants themselves are called the children of the sky. Now when the storms which generally burst in the months of September and October have been looked for in vain, when a drought with its prospect of famine is threatening, and all nature, scorched and burnt up by a sun that has shone for six months from a cloudless sky, is panting for the beneficent showers of the South African spring, the women perform ceremonies to bring down the longed-for rain on the parched earth. Stripping themselves of all their garments, they assume in their stead girdles and head-dresses of grass, or short petticoats made of the leaves of a particular sort of creeper. Thus attired, uttering peculiar cries and singing ribald songs, they go about from well to well, cleansing them of the mud and impurities which have accumulated in them. The wells, it may be said, are merely holes in the sand where a little turbid unwholesome water stagnates. Further, the women must repair to the house of one of their gossips who has given birth to twins, and must drench her with water, which they carry in little pitchers. Having done so they go on their way, shrieking out their loose songs and dancing immodest dances. No man may see these leaf-clad women going their rounds. If they meet a man, they maul him and thrust him aside. When they have cleansed the wells, they must go and pour water on the graves of their ancestors in the sacred grove. It often happens, too, that at the bidding of the wizard they go and pour water on the graves of twins. For they think that the grave of a twin ought always to be moist, for which reason twins are regularly buried near a lake. If all their efforts to procure rain prove abortive, they will remember that such and such a twin was buried in a dry place on the side of a hill. 'No wonder,' says the wizard in such a case, 'that the sky is fiery. Take up his body and dig him a grave on the shore of the lake.' His orders are at once obeyed, for this is supposed to be the only means of bringing down the rain.

Some of the foregoing facts strongly support an interpretation which Professor Oldenberg has given of the rules to be observed by a Brahman who would learn a particular hymn of the ancient Indian collection known as the Samaveda. The hymn, which bears the name of the Ṣakvarī song, was believed to embody the might of Indra's weapon, the thunderbolt; and hence, on account of the dreadful and dangerous potency with which it was thus charged, the bold student who essayed to master it had to be isolated from his fellow-men, and to retire from the village into the forest. Here for a space of time, which might vary, according to different doctors of the law, from one to twelve years, he had to observe certain rules of life, among which were the following.

Thrice a day he had to touch water; he must wear black garments and eat black food; when it rained, he might not seek the shelter of a roof, but had to sit in the rain and say, 'Water is the Śakvarī song'; when the lightning flashed, he said, 'That is like the Śakvarī song'; when the thunder pealed, he said, 'The Great One is making a great noise.' He might never cross a running stream without touching water; he might never set foot on a ship unless his life were in danger, and even then he must be sure to touch water when he went on board; 'for in water,' so ran the saying, 'lies the virtue of the Śakvarī song.' When at last he was allowed to learn the song itself, he had to dip his hands in a vessel of water in which plants of all sorts had been placed. If a man walked in the way of all these precepts, the rain-god Parjanya, it was said, would send rain at the wish of that man. It is clear, as Professor Oldenberg well points out, that 'all these rules are intended to bring the Brahman into union with water, to make him, as it were, an ally of the water powers, and to guard him against their hostility. The black garments and the black food have the same significance; no one will doubt that they refer to the rain-clouds when he remembers that a black victim is sacrificed to procure rain; "it is black, for such is the nature of rain." In respect of another rain-charm it is said plainly, "He puts on a black garment edged with black, for such is the nature of rain." We may therefore assume that here in the circle of ideas and ordinances of the Vedic schools there have been preserved magical practices of the most remote antiquity, which were intended to prepare the rain-maker for his office and dedicate him to it.'

It is interesting to observe that where an opposite result is desired, primitive logic enjoins the weather-doctor to observe precisely opposite rules of conduct. In the tropical island of Java, where the rich vegetation attests the abundance of the rainfall, ceremonies for the making of rain are rare, but ceremonies for the prevention of it are not uncommon. When a man is about to give a great feast in the rainy season and has invited many people, he goes to a weather-doctor and asks him to 'prop up the clouds that may be lowering.' If the doctor consents to exert his professional powers, he begins to regulate his behaviour by certain rules as soon as his customer has departed. He must observe a fast, and may neither drink nor bathe; what little he eats must be eaten dry, and in no case may he touch water. The host, on his side, and his servants, both male and female, must neither wash clothes nor bathe so long as the feast lasts, and they have all during its continuance to observe strict chastity. The doctor seats himself on a new mat in his bedroom, and before a small oil-lamp he murmurs, shortly before the feast takes place, the following prayer or incantation: 'Grandfather and Grandmother Sroekoel' (the name seems to be taken at random; others are sometimes used), 'return to your country. Akkemat is your country. Put down your water-cask, close it properly, that not a drop may fall out.' While he utters this prayer the sorcerer looks upwards, burning incense the while. So among the Toradjas the rain-doctor, whose special business it is to drive away rain, takes care not to touch water before, during, or after the discharge of his professional duties. He does not bathe, he eats with unwashed hands, he drinks nothing but palm wine, and if he has to cross a stream he is careful not to step in the water. Having thus prepared himself for his task he has a small hut built for himself outside of the village in a rice-field, and in this hut he keeps up a little fire, which on no account may be suffered to go out. In the fire he burns various kinds of wood, which are supposed to possess the property of driving off rain; and he puffs in the direction from which the rain threatens to come, holding in his hand a packet of leaves and bark which derive a similar cloud-compelling virtue, not from their chemical composition, but from their names, which happen to signify something dry or volatile. If clouds should appear in the sky while he is at work, he takes lime in the hollow of his hand and blows it towards them. The lime, being so very dry, is obviously well adapted to disperse the damp clouds. Should rain afterwards be wanted, he has only to pour water on his fire, and immediately the rain will descend in sheets.

The reader will observe how exactly the Javanese and Toradja observances, which are intended to prevent rain, form the antithesis of the Indian observances, which aim at producing it. The Indian sage is commanded to touch water thrice a day regularly as well as on various special occasions; the Javanese and Toradja wizards may not touch it at all. The Indian lives out in the forest, and even when it rains he may not take shelter;

the Javanese and the Toradja sit in a house or a hut. The one signifies his sympathy with water by receiving the rain on his person and speaking of it respectfully; the others light a lamp or a fire and do their best to drive the rain away. Yet the principle on which all three act is the same; each of them, by a sort of childish make-believe, identifies himself with the phenomenon which he desires to produce. It is the old fallacy that the effect resembles its cause: if you would make wet weather, you must be wet; if you would make dry weather, you must be dry.

In South-eastern Europe at the present day ceremonies are observed for the purpose of making rain which not only rest on the same general train of thought as the preceding, but even in their details resemble the ceremonies practised with the same intention by the Baronga of Delagoa Bay. Among the Greeks of Thessaly and Macedonia, when a drought has lasted a long time, it is customary to send a procession of children round to all the wells and springs of the neighbourhood. At the head of the procession walks a girl adorned with flowers, whom her companions drench with water at every halting-place, while they sing an invocation, of which the following is part:

> *'Perperia, all fresh bedewed,*   *Send thou us a still, small rain;*
> *Freshen all the neighbourhood;*   *That the fields may fruitful be,*
> *By the woods, on the highway,*   *And vines in blossom we may see;*
> *As thou goest, to God now*   *That the grain be full and sound,*
>   *pray!*   *And wealthy grow the folks*
> *O my God, upon the plain,*   *around.'*

In time of drought the Serbians strip a girl to her skin and clothe her from head to foot in grass, herbs, and flowers, even her face being hidden behind a veil of living green. Thus disguised she is called the Dodola and goes through the village with a troop of girls. They stop before every house; the Dodola keeps turning herself round and dancing, while the other girls form a ring about her singing one of the Dodola songs, and the housewife pours a pail of water over her. One of the songs they sing runs thus:

> *'We go through the village;*   *Faster go the clouds;*
> *The clouds go in the sky;*   *They have overtaken us,*
> *We go faster,*   *And wetted the corn and the vine.'*

At Poona in India, when rain is needed, the boys dress up one of their number in nothing but leaves and call him King of Rain. Then they go round to every house in the village, where the householder or his wife sprinkles the Rain King with water, and gives the party food of various kinds. When they have thus visited all the houses, they strip the Rain King of his leafy robes and feast upon what they have gathered.

Bathing is practised as a rain-charm in some parts of Southern and Western Russia. Sometimes after service in church the priest in his robes has been thrown down on the ground and drenched with water by his parishioners. Sometimes it is the women who, without stripping off their clothes, bathe in crowds on the day of St. John the Baptist, while they dip in the water a figure made of branches, grass, and herbs, which is supposed to represent the saint. In Kursk, a province of Southern Russia, when rain is much wanted, the women seize a passing stranger and throw him into the river, or souse him from head to foot. Later on we shall see that a passing stranger is often taken for a deity or the personification of some natural power. It is recorded in official documents that during a drought in 1790 the peasants of Scheroutz and Werboutz collected all the women and compelled them to bathe, in order that rain may fall. An Armenian rain-charm is to throw the wife of a priest into the water and drench her. The Arabs of North Africa fling a holy man, willy-nilly, into a spring as a remedy for drought. In Minahassa, a province of North Celebes, the priest bathes as a rain-charm. In Central Celebes when there has been no rain for a long time and the rice-stalks begin to shrivel up, many of the villagers, especially the young folk, go to a neighbouring brook and splash each other with water, shouting noisily, or squirt water on one another through bamboo tubes. Sometimes they imitate the plump of rain by smacking the surface of the water with their hands, or by placing an inverted gourd on it and drumming on the gourd with their fingers.

Women are sometimes supposed to be able to make rain by ploughing, or pretending to plough. Thus the Pshaws and Chewsurs of the Caucasus have a ceremony called 'ploughing the rain,' which they observe in time of drought. Girls yoke themselves to a plough and drag it into a river, wading in the water up to their girdles. In the same circumstances Armenian girls and women do the same. The oldest woman, or the priest's wife, wears the priest's dress, while the others, dressed as men, drag the plough through the water against the stream. In the Caucasian province of Georgia, when a drought has lasted long, marriageable girls are yoked in couples with an ox-yoke on their shoulders, a priest holds the reins, and thus harnessed they wade through rivers, puddles, and marshes, praying, screaming, weeping, and laughing. In a district of Transylvania, when the ground is parched with drought, some girls strip themselves naked, and, led by an older woman, who is also naked, they steal a harrow and carry it across the fields to a brook, where they set it afloat. Next they sit on the harrow and keep a tiny flame burning on each corner of it for an hour. Then they leave the harrow in the water and go home. A similar rain-charm is resorted to in some parts of India; naked women drag a plough across a field by night, while the men keep carefully out of the way, for their presence would break the spell.

Sometimes the rain-charm operates through the dead. Thus in New Caledonia the rain-makers blackened themselves all over, dug up a dead body, took the bones to a cave, jointed them, and hung the skeleton over some taro leaves. Water was poured over the skeleton to run down on the leaves. They believed that the soul of the deceased took up the water, converted it into rain, and showered it down again. In Russia, if common report may be believed, it is not long since the peasants of any district that chanced to be afflicted with drought used to dig up the corpse of some one who had drunk himself to death and sink it in the nearest swamp or lake, fully persuaded that this would ensure the fall of the needed rain. In 1868 the prospect of a bad harvest, caused by a prolonged drought, induced the inhabitants of a village in the Tarashchansk district to dig up the body of a Raskolnik, or Dissenter, who had died in the preceding December. Some of the party beat the corpse, or what was left of it, about the head, exclaiming, 'Give us rain!' while others poured water on it through a sieve. Here the pouring of water through a sieve seems plainly an imitation of a shower, and reminds us of the manner in which Strepsiades in Aristophanes imagined that rain was made by Zeus. Sometimes, in order to procure rain, the

Toradjas make an appeal to the pity of the dead. Thus, in the village of Kalingooa there is the grave of a famous chief, the grandfather of the present ruler. When the land suffers from unseasonable drought, the people go to this grave, pour water on it, and say, 'O grandfather, have pity on us; if it is your will that this year we should eat, then give rain.' After that they hang a bamboo full of water over the grave; there is a small hole in the lower end of the bamboo, so that the water drips from it continually. The bamboo is always refilled with water until rain drenches the ground. Here, as in New Caledonia, we find religion blent with magic, for the prayer to the dead chief, which is purely religious, is eked out with a magical imitation of rain at his grave. We have seen that the Baronga of Delagoa Bay drench the tombs of their ancestors, especially the tombs of twins, as a rain-charm. Among some of the Indian tribes in the region of the Orinoco it was customary for the relations of a deceased person to disinter his bones a year after burial, burn them, and scatter the ashes to the winds, because they believed that the ashes were changed into rain, which the dead man sent in return for his obsequies. The Chinese are convinced that when human bodies remain unburied, the souls of their late owners feel the discomfort of rain, just as living men would do if they were exposed without shelter to the inclemency of the weather. These wretched souls, therefore, do all in their power to prevent the rain from falling, and often their efforts are only too successful. Then drought ensues, the most dreaded of all calamities in China, because bad harvests, dearth, and famine follow in its train. Hence it has been a common practice of the Chinese authorities in time of drought to inter the dry bones of the unburied dead for the purpose of putting an end to the scourge and conjuring down the rain.

Animals, again, often play an important part in these weather-charms. The Anula tribe of Northern Australia associate the dollar-bird with rain, and call it the rain-bird. A man who has the bird for his totem can make rain at a certain pool. He catches a snake, puts it alive into the pool, and after holding it under the water for a time takes it out, kills it, and lays it down by the side of the creek. Then he makes an arched bundle of grass stalks in imitation of a rainbow, and sets it up over the snake. After that all he does is to sing over the snake and the mimic rainbow; sooner or later the rain will fall. They explain this procedure by saying that long ago the dollar-bird had as a mate at this spot a snake, who lived in the pool and used to make rain by spitting up into the sky till a rainbow and clouds appeared and rain fell. A common way of making rain in many parts of Java is to bathe a cat or two cats, a male and a female; sometimes the animals are carried in procession with music. Even in Batavia you may from time to time see children going about with a cat for this purpose; when they have ducked it in a pool, they let it go.

Among the Wambugwe of East Africa, when the sorcerer desires to make rain, he takes a black sheep and a black calf in bright sunshine, and has them placed on the roof of the common hut in which the people live together. Then he slits the stomachs of the animals and scatters their contents in all directions. After that he pours water and medicine into a vessel; if the charm has succeeded, the water boils up and rain follows. On the other hand, if the sorcerer wishes to prevent rain from falling, he withdraws into the interior of the hut, and there heats a rock-crystal in a calabash. In order to procure rain the Wagogo sacrifice black fowls, black sheep, and black cattle at the graves of dead ancestors, and the rain-maker wears black clothes during the rainy season. Among the Matabele the rain-charm employed by sorcerers was made from the blood and gall of a black ox. In a district of Sumatra, in order to procure rain, all the women of the village, scantily clad, go to the river, wade into it, and splash each other with the water. A black cat is thrown into the stream and made to swim about for a while, then allowed to escape to the bank, pursued by the splashing of the women. The Garos of Assam offer a black goat on the top of a very high mountain in time of drought. In all these cases the colour of the animal is part of the charm; being black, it will darken the sky with rain-clouds. So the Bechuanas burn the stomach of an ox at evening, because they say, 'The black smoke will gather the clouds and cause the rain to come.' The Timorese sacrifice a black pig to the Earth-goddess for rain, a white or red one to the Sun-god for sunshine. The Angoni sacrifice a black ox for rain and a white one for fine weather. Among the high mountains of Japan there is a district in which, if rain has not fallen for a long time, a party of villagers goes in procession to the bed of a mountain torrent, headed by a priest, who leads a black dog. At the chosen spot they tether the beast to a stone, and make it a target for their bullets and arrows. When its life-blood bespatters the rocks, the peasants throw down their weapons and lift up their voices in supplication to the dragon divinity of the stream, exhorting him to send down forthwith a shower to cleanse the spot from its defilement. Custom has prescribed that on these occasions the colour of the victim shall be black, as an emblem of the wished-for rain-clouds. But if fine weather is wanted, the victim must be white, without a spot.

The intimate association of frogs and toads with water has earned for these creatures a widespread reputation as custodians of rain; and hence they often play a part in charms designed to draw needed showers from the sky. Some of the Indians of the Orinoco held the toad to be the god or lord of the waters, and for that reason feared to kill the creature. They have been known to keep frogs under a pot and to beat them with rods when there was a drought. It is said that the Aymara Indians often make little images of frogs and other aquatic animals and place them on the tops of the hills as a means of bringing down rain. The Thompson Indians of British Columbia and some people in Europe think that to kill a frog will cause rain to fall. In order to procure rain people of low caste in the Central Provinces of India will tie a frog to a rod covered with green leaves and branches of the *nîm* tree (*Azadirachta Indica*) and carry it from door to door singing:

> '*Send soon, O frog, the jewel of water!
> And ripen the wheat and millet in the field.*'

The Kapus or Reddis are a large caste of cultivators and land-owners in the Madras Presidency. When rain falls, women of the caste will catch a frog and tie it alive to a new winnowing fan made of bamboo. On this fan they spread a few margosa leaves and go from door to door singing, 'Lady frog must have her bath. O rain-god, give a little water for her at least.' While the Kapu women sing this song, the woman of the house pours water over the frog and gives an alms, convinced that by so doing she will soon bring rain down in torrents.

Sometimes, when a drought has lasted a long time, people drop the usual hocus-pocus of imitative magic altogether, and being far too angry to waste their breath in prayer they seek by threats and curses or even downright physical force to extort the waters of heaven from the supernatural being who has, so to say, cut them off at the main. In a Japanese village, when the guardian divinity had long been deaf to the peasants' prayers for rain, they at last threw down his image and, with curses loud and long, hurled it head foremost into a stinking rice-field. 'There,' they said, 'you may stay yourself for a while, to see how *you* feel after a few days' scorching in this broiling sun that is burning the life from our cracking fields.' In the like circumstances the Feloupes of Senegambia cast down their fetishes and drag them about the fields, cursing them till rain falls.

The Chinese are adepts in the art of taking the kingdom of heaven by storm. Thus, when rain is wanted they make a huge dragon of paper or wood to represent the rain-god, and carry it about in procession; but if no rain follows, the mock-dragon is execrated and torn to pieces. At other times they threaten and beat the god if he does not give rain; sometimes they publicly depose him from the rank of deity. On the other hand, if the wished-for rain falls, the god is promoted to a higher rank by an imperial decree. In April 1888 the mandarins of Canton prayed to the god Lung-wong to stop the incessant downpour of rain; and when he turned a deaf ear to their petitions they put him in a lock-up for five days. This had a salutary effect. The rain ceased and the god was restored to liberty. Some years before, in time of drought, the same deity had been chained and exposed to the sun for days in the courtyard of his temple in order that he might feel for himself the urgent need of rain. So when the Siamese need rain, they set out their idols in the blazing sun; but if they want dry weather, they unroof the temples and let the rain pour down on the idols. They think that the inconvenience to which the gods are thus subjected will induce them to grant the wishes of their worshippers.

The reader may smile at the meteorology of the Far East; but precisely similar modes of procuring rain have been resorted to in Christian Europe within our own lifetime. By the end of April 1893 there was great distress in Sicily for lack of water. The drought had lasted six months. Every day the sun rose and set in a sky of cloudless blue. The gardens of the Conca d'Oro, which surround Palermo with a magnificent belt of verdure, were withering. Food was becoming scarce. The people were in great alarm. All the most approved methods of procuring rain had been tried without effect. Processions had traversed the streets and the fields. Men, women, and children, telling their beads, had lain whole nights before the holy images. Consecrated candles had burned day and night in the churches. Palm branches, blessed on Palm Sunday, had been hung on the trees. At Solaparuta, in accordance with a very old custom, the dust swept from the churches on Palm Sunday had been spread on the fields. In ordinary years these holy sweepings preserve the crops; but that year, if you will believe me, they had no effect whatever. At Nicosia the inhabitants, bare-headed and bare-foot, carried the crucifixes through all the wards of the town and scourged each other with iron whips. It was all in vain. Even the great St. Francis of Paolo himself, who annually performs the miracle of rain and is carried every spring through the market-gardens, either could not or would not help. Masses, vespers, concerts, illuminations, fireworks — nothing could move him. At last the peasants began to lose patience. Most of the saints were banished. At Palermo they dumped St. Joseph in a garden to see the state of things for himself, and they swore to leave him there in the sun till rain fell. Other saints were turned, like naughty children, with their faces to the wall. Others again, stripped of their beautiful robes, were exiled far from their parishes, threatened, grossly insulted, ducked in horse-ponds. At Caltanisetta the golden wings of St. Michael the Archangel were torn from his shoulders and replaced with wings of pasteboard; his purple mantle was taken away and a clout wrapt about him instead. At Licata the patron saint, St. Angelo, fared even worse, for he was left without any garments at all; he was reviled, he was put in irons, he was threatened with drowning or hanging. 'Rain or the rope!' roared the angry people at him, as they shook their fists in his face.

Sometimes an appeal is made to the pity of the gods. When their corn is being burnt up by the sun, the Zulus look out for a 'heaven bird,' kill it, and throw it into a pool. Then the heaven melts with tenderness for the death of the bird; 'it wails for it by raining, wailing a funeral wail.' In Zululand women sometimes bury their children up to the neck in the ground, and then retiring to a distance keep up a dismal howl for a long time. The sky is supposed to melt with pity at the sight. Then the women dig the children out and feel sure that rain will soon follow. They say that they call to 'the lord above' and ask him to send rain. If it comes they declare that 'Usondo rains.' In times of drought the Guanches of Teneriffe led their sheep to sacred ground, and there they separated the lambs from their dams, that their plaintive bleating might touch the heart of the god. In Kumaon a way of stopping rain is to pour hot oil in the left ear of a dog. The animal howls with pain, his howls are heard by Indra, and out of pity for the beast's sufferings the god stops the rain. Sometimes the Toradjas attempt to procure rain as follows. They place the stalks of certain plants in water, saying, 'Go and ask for rain, and so long as no rain falls I will not plant you again, but there shall you die.' Also they string some fresh-water snails on a cord, and hang the cord on a tree, and say to the snails, 'Go and ask for rain, and so long as no rain comes, I will not take you back to the water.' Then the snails go and weep, and the gods take pity and send rain. However, the foregoing ceremonies are religious rather than magical, since they involve an appeal to the compassion of higher powers.

Stones are often supposed to possess the property of bringing on rain, provided they be dipped in water or sprinkled with it, or treated in some other appropriate manner. In a Samoan village a certain stone was carefully housed as the representative of the rain-making god, and in time of drought his priests carried the stone in procession and dipped it in a stream. Among the Ta-ta-thi tribe of New South Wales the rain-maker breaks off a piece of quartz-crystal and spits it towards the sky; the rest of the crystal he wraps in emu feathers, soaks both crystal and feathers in water, and carefully hides them. In the Keramin tribe of New South Wales the wizard retires to the bed of a creek, drops water on a round flat stone, then covers up and conceals it. Among some tribes of North-western Australia the rain-maker repairs to a piece of ground which is set apart for the purpose of rain-making. There he builds a heap of stones or sand, places on the top of it his magic stone, and walks or dances round the pile chanting his incantations for hours, till sheer exhaustion obliges him to desist, when his place is taken by his assistant. Water is sprinkled on the stone and huge fires are kindled. No layman may approach the sacred spot while the mystic ceremony is being performed. When the Sulka of New Britain wish to procure rain they blacken stones with the ashes of certain fruits and set them out, along with certain other plants and buds, in the sun. Then a handful of twigs is dipped in water and weighted with stones, while a spell is chanted. After that rain should follow. In Manipur, on a lofty hill to the east of the capital, there is a stone which the popular imagination likens to an umbrella. When rain is wanted, the rajah fetches water from a spring below and sprinkles it on the stone. At Sagami in Japan there is a stone which draws down rain whenever water is poured on it. When the Wakondyo, a tribe of Central Africa, desire rain, they send to the Wawamba, who dwell at the foot of snowy mountains, and are the happy possessors of a 'rain-stone.' In consideration of a proper payment, the Wawamba wash the precious stone, anoint it with oil, and put it in a pot full of water. After that the rain cannot fail to come. In the arid wastes of Arizona and New Mexico the Apaches sought to make rain by carrying water from a certain spring and throwing it on a particular point high up on a rock; after that they imagined that the clouds would soon gather, and that rain would begin to fall.

But customs of this sort are not confined to the wilds of Africa and Asia or the torrid deserts of Australia and the New World. They have been practised in the cool air and under the grey skies of Europe. There is a fountain called Barenton, of romantic fame, in those 'wild woods of Broceliande,' where, if legend be true, the wizard Merlin still sleeps his magic slumber in the hawthorn shade. Thither the Breton peasants used to resort when they needed rain. They caught some of the water in a tankard and threw it on a slab near the spring. On Snowdon there is a lonely tarn called Dulyn, or the Black Lake, lying 'in a dismal dingle surrounded by high and dangerous rocks.' A row of stepping-stones runs out into the lake, and if any one steps on the stones and throws water so as to wet the farthest stone, which is called the Red Altar, 'it is but a chance that you do not get rain before night, even when it is hot weather.' In these cases it appears probable that, as in Samoa, the stone is regarded as more or less divine. This appears from the custom sometimes observed of dipping a cross in the Fountain of Barenton to procure rain, for this is plainly a Christian substitute for the old pagan way of throwing water on the stone. At various places in France it is, or used till lately to be, the practice to dip the image of a saint in water as a means of procuring rain. Thus, beside the old priory of Commagny there is a spring of St. Gervais, whither the inhabitants go in procession to obtain rain or fine weather according to the needs of the crops. In times of great drought they throw into the basin of the fountain an ancient stone image of the saint that stands in a sort of niche from which the fountain flows. At Collobrières and Carpentras a similar practice was observed with the images of St. Pons and St. Gens respectively. In several villages of Navarre prayers for rain used to be offered to St. Peter, and by way of enforcing them the villagers carried the image of the saint in procession to the river, where they thrice invited him to reconsider his resolution and to grant their prayers; then, if he was still obstinate, they plunged him in the water, despite the remonstrances of the clergy, who pleaded with as much truth as piety that a simple caution or admonition administered to the image would produce an equally good effect. After this the rain was sure to fall within twenty-four hours. Catholic countries do not enjoy a monopoly of making rain by ducking holy images in water. In Mingrelia, when the crops are suffering from want of rain, they take a particularly holy image and dip it in water every day till a shower falls; and in the Far East the Shans drench the images of Buddha with water when the rice is perishing of drought. In all such cases the practice is probably at bottom a sympathetic charm, however it may be disguised under the appearance of a punishment or a threat.

Like other peoples, the Greeks and Romans sought to obtain rain by magic, when prayers and processions had proved ineffectual. For example, in Arcadia, when the corn and trees were parched with drought, the priest Zeus dipped an oak branch into a certain spring on Mount Lycaeus. Thus troubled, the water sent up a misty cloud, from which rain soon fell upon the land. A similar mode of making rain is still practised, as we have seen, in Halmahera near New Guinea. The people of Crannon in Thessaly had a bronze chariot which they kept in a temple. When they desired a shower they shook the chariot and the shower fell. Probably the rattling of the chariot was meant to imitate thunder; we have already seen that mock thunder and lightning form part of a rain-charm in Russia and Japan. The legendary Salmoneus, King of Elis, made mock thunder by dragging bronze kettles behind his chariot, or by driving over a bronze bridge, while he hurled blazing torches in imitation of lightning. It was his impious wish to mimic the thundering car of Zeus as it rolled across the vault of heaven. Indeed he declared that he was actually Zeus, and caused sacrifices to be offered to himself as such. Near a temple of Mars, outside the walls of Rome, there was kept a certain stone known as the *lapis manalis*. In time of drought the stone was dragged into Rome, and this was supposed to bring down rain immediately.

§ 3. *The Magical Control of the Sun.* — As the magician thinks he can make rain, so he fancies he can cause the sun to shine, and can hasten or stay its going down. At an eclipse the Ojebways used to imagine that the sun was being extinguished. So they shot fire-tipped arrows in the air, hoping thus to rekindle his expiring light. The Sencis of Peru also shot burning arrows at the sun during an eclipse, but apparently they did this not so much to relight his lamp as to drive away a savage beast with which they supposed him to be struggling. Conversely during an eclipse of the moon some tribes of the Orinoco used to bury lighted brands in the ground; because, they said, if the moon were to be extinguished, all fire on earth would be extinguished with her, except such as was hidden from her sight. During an eclipse of the sun the Kamtchatkans were wont to bring out fire from their huts and pray the great luminary to shine as before. But the prayer addressed to the sun shows that this ceremony was religious rather than magical. Purely magical, on the other hand, was the ceremony observed on similar occasions by the Chilcotin Indians. Men and women tucked up their robes, as they do in travelling, and then leaning on staves, as if they were heavy laden, they continued to walk in a circle till the eclipse was over. Apparently they thought thus to support the failing steps of the sun as he trod his weary round in the sky. Similarly in

ancient Egypt the king, as
solemnly round the walls of
sun should perform his daily
interruption of an eclipse or ot...
autumnal equinox the ancient Egyptians ... sun, walked
'the nativity of the sun's walking-stick,' because ... that the
declined daily in the sky, and his light and heat dimi...
was supposed to need a staff on which to lean. In New Caled...
when a wizard desires to make sunshine he takes some plants and
corals to the burial-ground and fashions them into a bundle,
adding two locks of hair cut from a living child of his family,
also two teeth or an entire jawbone from the skeleton of an
ancestor. He then climbs a mountain whose top catches the
first rays of the morning sun. Here he deposits three sorts of
plants on a flat stone, places a branch of dry coral beside them,
and hangs the bundle of charms over the stone. Next morning
he returns to the spot and sets fire to the bundle at the moment
when the sun rises from the sea. As the smoke curls up, he rubs
the stone with the dry coral, invokes his ancestors, and says:
'Sun! I do this that you may be burning hot, and eat up all the
clouds in the sky.' The same ceremony is repeated at sunset.
The New Caledonians also make a drought by means of a disc-
shaped stone with a hole in it. At the moment when the sun
rises, the wizard holds the stone in his hand and passes a burning
brand repeatedly into the hole, while he says: 'I kindle the sun,
in order that he may eat up the clouds and dry up our land, so
that it may produce nothing.' The Banks Islanders make sunshine by means of a mock sun. They take a very round stone,
called a *vat loa* or sunstone, wind red braid about it, and stick it
with owls' feathers to represent rays, singing the proper spell in
a low voice. Then they hang it on some high tree, such as a
banyan or a casuarina, in a sacred place.

The offering made by the Brahman in the morning is supposed
to produce the sun, and we are told that 'assuredly it would not
rise, were he not to make that offering.' The ancient Mexicans
conceived the sun as the source of all vital force; hence they
named him Ipalnemohuani, 'He by whom men live.' But if he
bestowed life on the world, he needed also to receive life from it.
And as the heart is the seat and symbol of life, bleeding hearts of

presented to the sun to maintain him in
...m to run his course across the sky. Thus
...crifices to the sun were magical rather than
men...g designed, not so much to please and propitiate
...ysically to renew his energies of heat, light, and motion.
...nstant demand for human victims to feed the solar fire was
... by waging war every year on the neighbouring tribes and
bringing back troops of captives to be sacrificed on the altar.
Thus the ceaseless wars of the Mexicans and their cruel system
of human sacrifices, the most monstrous on record, sprang in
great measure from a mistaken theory of the solar system. No
more striking illustration could be given of the disastrous consequences that may flow in practice from a purely speculative
error. The ancient Greeks believed that the sun drove in a
chariot across the sky; hence the Rhodians, who worshipped the
sun as their chief deity, annually dedicated a chariot and four
horses to him, and flung them into the sea for his use. Doubtless
they thought that after a year's work his old horses and chariot
would be worn out. From a like motive, probably, the idolatrous
kings of Judah dedicated chariots and horses to the sun, and the
Spartans, Persians, and Massagetae sacrificed horses to him. The
Spartans performed the sacrifice on the top of Mount Taygetus,
the beautiful range behind which they saw the great luminary set
every night. It was as natural for the inhabitants of the valley of
Sparta to do this as it was for the islanders of Rhodes to throw
the chariot and horses into the sea, into which the sun seemed to
them to sink at evening. For thus, whether on the mountain or
in the sea, the fresh horses stood ready for the weary god where
they would be most welcome, at the end of his day's journey.

As some people think they can light up the sun or speed him
on his way, so others fancy they can retard or stop him. In a
pass of the Peruvian Andes stand two ruined towers on opposite
hills. Iron hooks are clamped into their walls for the purpose of
stretching a net from one tower to the other. The net is intended
to catch the sun. Stories of men who have caught the sun in a
noose are widely spread. When the sun is going southward in
the autumn, and sinking lower and lower in the Arctic sky, the
Esquimaux of Iglulik play the game of cat's cradle in order to
catch him in the meshes of the string and so prevent his dis-

appearance. On the contrary, when the sun is moving northward in the spring, they play the game of cup-and-ball to hasten his return. When an Australian blackfellow wishes to stay the sun from going down till he gets home, he puts a sod in the fork of a tree, exactly facing the setting sun. On the other hand, to make it go down faster, the Australians throw sand into the air and blow with their mouths towards the sun, perhaps to waft the lingering orb westward and bury it under the sands into which it appears to sink at night.

As some people imagine they can hasten the sun, so others fancy they can jog the tardy moon. The natives of New Guinea reckon months by the moon, and some of them have been known to throw stones and spears at the moon, in order to accelerate its progress and so to hasten the return of their friends, who were away from home for twelve months working on a tobacco plantation. The Malays think that a bright glow at sunset may throw a weak person into a fever. Hence they attempt to extinguish the glow by spitting out water and throwing ashes at it. The Shuswap Indians believe that they can bring on cold weather by burning the wood of a tree that has been struck by lightning. The belief may be based on the observation that in their country cold follows a thunder-storm. Hence in spring, when these Indians are travelling over the snow on high ground, they burn splinters of such wood in the fire in order that the crust of the snow may not melt.

§ 4. *The Magical Control of the Wind.* — Once more, the savage thinks he can make the wind to blow or to be still. When the day is hot and a Yakut has a long way to go, he takes a stone which he has chanced to find in an animal or fish, winds a horse-hair several times round it, and ties it to a stick. He then waves the stick about, uttering a spell. Soon a cool breeze begins to blow. In order to procure a cool wind for nine days the stone should first be dipped in the blood of a bird or beast and then presented to the sun, while the sorcerer makes three turns contrary to the course of the luminary. If a Hottentot desires the wind to drop, he takes one of his fattest skins and hangs it on the end of a pole, in the belief that by blowing the skin down the wind will lose all its force and must itself fall. Fuegian wizards throw shells against the wind to make it drop. The

natives of the island of Bibili, off New Guinea, are reputed to
make wind by blowing with their mouths. In stormy weather
the Bogadjim people say, 'The Bibili folk are at it again, blowing
away.' Another way of making wind which is practised in New
Guinea is to strike a 'wind-stone' lightly with a stick; to strike
it hard would bring on a hurricane. So in Scotland witches used
to raise the wind by dipping a rag in water and beating it thrice
on a stone, saying:

> '*I knok this rag upone this stane*
> *To raise the wind in the divellis name,*
> *It sall not lye till I please againe.*'

In Greenland a woman in child-bed and for some time after
delivery is supposed to possess the power of laying a storm. She
has only to go out of doors, fill her mouth with air, and coming
back into the house blow it out again. In antiquity there was a
family at Corinth which enjoyed the reputation of being able to
still the raging wind; but we do not know in what manner its
members exercised a useful function, which probably earned for
them a more solid recompense than mere repute among the sea-
faring population of the isthmus. Even in Christian times, under
the reign of Constantine, a certain Sopater suffered death at
Constantinople on a charge of binding the winds by magic,
because it happened that the corn-ships of Egypt and Syria were
detained afar off by calms or head-winds, to the rage and disappointment of the hungry Byzantine rabble. Finnish wizards
used to sell wind to storm-stayed mariners. The wind was enclosed
in three knots; if they undid the first knot, a moderate wind
sprang up; if the second, it blew a gale; if the third, a hurricane.
Indeed the Esthonians, whose country is divided from Finland
only by an arm of the sea, still believe in the magical powers of
their northern neighbours. The bitter winds that blow in spring
from the north and north-east, bringing ague and rheumatic
inflammations in their train, are set down by the simple Esthonian
peasantry to the machinations of the Finnish wizards and witches.
In particular they regard with special dread three days in spring
to which they give the name of Days of the Cross; one of them
falls on the Eve of Ascension Day. The people in the neighbourhood of Fellin fear to go out on these days lest the cruel winds

from Lappland should smite them dead. A popular Esthonian song runs:

> *'Wind of the Cross! rushing and mighty!*
> *Heavy the blow of thy wings sweeping past!*
> *Wild wailing wind of misfortune and sorrow,*
> *Wizards of Finland ride by on the blast.'*

It is said, too, that sailors, beating up against the wind in the Gulf of Finland, sometimes see a strange sail heave in sight astern and overhaul them hand over hand. On she comes with a cloud of canvas — all her studding-sails out — right in the teeth of the wind, forging her way through the foaming billows, dashing back the spray in sheets from her cutwater, every sail swollen to bursting, every rope strained to cracking. Then the sailors know that she hails from Finland.

The art of tying up the wind in three knots, so that the more knots are loosed the stronger will blow the wind, has been attributed to wizards in Lappland and to witches in Shetland, Lewis, and the Isle of Man. Shetland seamen still buy winds in the shape of knotted handkerchiefs or threads from old women who claim to rule the storms. There are said to be ancient crones in Lerwick now who live by selling wind. Ulysses received the winds in a leathern bag from Aeolus, King of the Winds. The Motumotu in New Guinea think that storms are sent by an Oiabu sorcerer; for each wind he has a bamboo which he opens at pleasure. On the top of Mount Agu in Togo, a district of West Africa, resides a fetish called Bagba, who is supposed to control the wind and the rain. His priest is said to keep the winds shut up in great pots.

Often the stormy wind is regarded as an evil being who may be intimidated, driven away, or killed. When storms and bad weather have lasted long and food is scarce with the Central Esquimaux, they endeavour to conjure the tempest by making a long whip of seaweed, armed with which they go down to the beach and strike out in the direction of the wind, crying, '*Taba* (it is enough)!' Once when north-westerly winds had kept the ice long on the coast and food was becoming scarce, the Esquimaux performed a ceremony to make a calm. A fire was kindled on the shore, and the men gathered round it and chanted. An old man then stepped up to the fire and in a coaxing voice invited the demon of the wind to come under the fire and warm himself. When he was supposed to have arrived, a vessel of water, to which each man present had contributed, was thrown on the flames by an old man, and immediately a flight of arrows sped towards the spot where the fire had been. They thought that the demon would not stay where he had been so badly treated. To complete the effect guns were discharged in various directions, and the captain of a European vessel was invited to fire on the wind with cannon. On the twenty-first of February 1883 a similar ceremony was performed by the Esquimaux of Point Barrow, Alaska, with the intention of killing the spirit of the wind. Women drove the demon from their houses with clubs and knives, with which they made passes in the air; and the men, gathering round a fire, shot him with their rifles and crushed him under a heavy stone the moment that steam rose in a cloud from the smouldering embers, on which a tub of water had just been thrown.

The Lengua Indians of the Gran Chaco ascribe the rush of a whirlwind to the passage of a spirit and they fling sticks at it to frighten it away. When the wind blows down their huts, the Payaguas of South America snatch up firebrands and run against the wind, menacing it with the blazing brands, while others beat the air with their fists to frighten the storm. When the Guaycurus are threatened by a severe storm, the men go out armed, and the women and children scream their loudest to intimidate the demon. During a tempest the inhabitants of a Batak village in Sumatra have been seen to rush from their houses armed with sword and lance. The rajah placed himself at their head, and with shouts and yells they hewed and hacked at the invisible foe. An old woman was observed to be specially active in the defence of her house, slashing the air right and left with a long sabre. In a violent thunderstorm, the peals sounding very near, the Kayans of Borneo have been seen to draw their swords threateningly half out of their scabbards, as if to frighten away the demons of the storm. In Australia the huge columns of red sand that move rapidly across a desert tract are thought by the natives to be spirits passing along. Once an athletic young black ran after one of these moving columns to kill it with boomerangs. He was away two or three hours, and came back very weary, saying he had killed Koochee (the demon), but that Koochee had growled at him and he must die. Of the Bedouins of Eastern Africa it is said that 'no whirlwind ever sweeps across the path without being pursued by a dozen savages with drawn creeses, who stab into the centre of the dusty column in order to drive away the evil spirit that is believed to be riding on the blast.'

In the light of these examples a story told by Herodotus, which his modern critics have treated as a fable, is perfectly credible. He says, without however vouching for the truth of the tale, that once in the land of the Psylli, the modern Tripoli, the wind blowing from the Sahara had dried up all the water-tanks. So the people took counsel and marched in a body to make war on the south wind. But when they entered the desert the simoom swept down on them and buried them to a man. The story may well have been told by one who watched them disappearing, in battle array, with drums and cymbals beating, into the red cloud of whirling sand.

CHAPTER VI

MAGICIANS AS KINGS

THE foregoing evidence may satisfy us that in many lands and many races magic has claimed to control the great forces of nature for the good of man. If that has been so, the practitioners of the art must necessarily be personages of importance and influence in any society which puts faith in their extravagant pretensions, and it would be no matter for surprise if, by virtue of the reputation which they enjoy and of the awe which they inspire, some of them should attain to the highest position of authority over their credulous fellows. In point of fact magicians appear to have often developed into chiefs and kings.

Let us begin by looking at the lowest race of men as to whom we possess comparatively full and accurate information, the aborigines of Australia. These savages are ruled neither by chiefs nor kings. So far as their tribes can be said to have a political constitution, it is a democracy or rather an oligarchy of old and influential men, who meet in council and decide on all measures of importance to the practical exclusion of the younger men. Their deliberative assembly answers to the senate of later times: if we had to coin a word for such a government of elders we might call it a *gerontocracy*. The elders who in aboriginal Australia thus meet and direct the affairs of their tribe appear to be for the most part the headmen of their respective totem clans. Now in Central Australia, where the desert nature of the country and the almost complete isolation from foreign influences have retarded progress and preserved the natives on the whole in their most primitive state, the headmen of the various totem clans are charged with the important task of performing magical ceremonies for the multiplication of the totems, and as the great majority of the totems are edible animals or plants, it follows that these men are commonly expected to provide the people with food by means of magic. Others have to make the rain to fall or to render other services to the community. In short, among the tribes of Central Australia the headmen are public magicians. Further, their most important function is to take charge of the sacred storehouse, usually a cleft in the rocks or a hole in the ground, where are kept the holy stones and sticks (*churinga*) with which the souls of all the people, both living and dead, are apparently supposed to be in a manner bound up. Thus while the headmen have certainly to perform what we should call civil duties, such as to inflict punishment for breaches of tribal custom, their principal functions are sacred or magical.

When we pass from Australia to New Guinea we find that, though the natives stand at a far higher level of culture than the Australian aborigines, the constitution of society among them is still essentially democratic or oligarchic, and chieftainship exists only in embryo. Thus Sir William MacGregor tells us that in British New Guinea no one has ever arisen wise enough, bold enough, and strong enough to become the despot even of a single district. 'The nearest approach to this has been the very distant one of some person becoming a renowned wizard; but that has only resulted in levying a certain amount of blackmail.'

According to a native account, the origin of the power of Melanesian chiefs lies entirely in the belief that they have communication with mighty ghosts, and wield that supernatural power whereby they can bring the influence of the ghosts to bear. If a chief imposed a fine, it was paid because the people universally dreaded his ghostly power, and firmly believed that he could inflict calamity and sickness upon such as resisted him. As soon as any considerable number of his people began to disbelieve in his influence with the ghosts, his power to levy fines was shaken. Again, Dr. George Brown tells us that in New Britain 'a ruling chief was always supposed to exercise priestly functions, that is, he professed to be in constant communication with the *tebarans* (spirits), and through their influence he was enabled to bring rain or sunshine, fair winds or foul ones, sickness or health, success or disaster in war, and generally to procure any blessing or curse for which the applicant was willing to pay a sufficient price.'

Still rising in the scale of culture we come to Africa, where both the chieftainship and the kingship are fully developed; and here the evidence for the evolution of the chief out of the magician, and especially out of the rainmaker, is comparatively plentiful. Thus among the Wambugwe, a Bantu people of East Africa, the original form of government was a family republic, but the enormous power of the sorcerers, transmitted by inheritance, soon raised them to the rank of petty lords or chiefs. Of the three chiefs living in the country in 1894 two were much dreaded as magicians, and the wealth of cattle they possessed came to them almost wholly in the shape of presents bestowed for their services in that capacity. Their principal art was that of rainmaking. The chiefs of the Watataru, another people of East Africa, are said to be nothing but sorcerers destitute of any direct political influence. Again, among the Wagogo of East Africa the main power of the chiefs, we are told, is derived from their art of rain-making. If a chief cannot make rain himself, he must procure it from some one who can.

Again, among the tribes of the Upper Nile the medicine-men are generally the chiefs. Their authority rests above all upon their supposed power of making rain, for 'rain is the one thing which matters to the people in those districts, as if it does not come down at the right time it means untold hardships for the community. It is therefore small wonder that men more cunning than their fellows should arrogate to themselves the power of producing it, or that having gained such a reputation, they should trade on the credulity of their simpler neighbours.' Hence, 'most of the chiefs of these tribes are rain-makers, and enjoy a popularity in proportion to their powers to give rain to their people at the proper season. . . . Rain-making chiefs always build their villages on the slopes of a fairly high hill, as they no doubt know that the hills attract the clouds, and that they are, therefore, fairly safe in their weather forecasts.' Each of these rain-makers has a number of rain-stones, such as rock-crystal, aventurine, and amethyst, which he keeps in a pot. When he wishes to produce rain he plunges the stones in water, and taking in his hand a peeled cane, which is split at the top, he beckons with it to the clouds to come or waves them away in the way they should go, muttering an incantation the while. Or he pours water and the entrails of a sheep or goat into a hollow in a stone and then sprinkles the water towards the sky. Though the chief acquires wealth by the exercise of his supposed magical powers, he often, perhaps generally, comes to a violent end; for in time of drought the angry people assemble and kill him, believing that it is he who prevents the rain from falling. Yet the office is usually hereditary and passes from father to son. Among the tribes which cherish these beliefs and observe these customs are the Latuka, Bari, Laluba, and Lokoiya.

In Central Africa, again, the Lendu tribe, to the west of Lake Albert, firmly believe that certain people possess the power of making rain. Among them the rain-maker either is a chief or almost invariably becomes one. The Banyoro also have a great respect for the dispensers of rain, whom they load with a profusion of gifts. The great dispenser, he who has absolute and uncontrollable power over the rain, is the king; but he can depute his power to other persons, so that the benefit may be distributed and the heavenly water laid on over the various parts of the kingdom.

In Western as well as in Eastern and Central Africa we meet with the same union of chiefly with magical functions. Thus in the Fan tribe the strict distinction between chief and medicine-man does not exist. The chief is also a medicine-man and a smith to boot; for the Fans esteem the smith's craft sacred, and none but chiefs may meddle with it.

As to the relation between the offices of chief and rain-maker in South Africa a well-informed writer observes: 'In very old days the chief was the great Rain-maker of the tribe. Some chiefs allowed no one else to compete with them, lest a successful Rain-maker should be chosen as chief. There was also another reason: the Rain-maker was sure to become a rich man if he gained a great reputation, and it would manifestly never do for the chief to allow any one to be too rich. The Rain-maker exerts tremendous control over the people, and so it would be most important to keep this function connected with royalty. Tradition always places the power of making rain as the fundamental glory of ancient chiefs and heroes, and it seems probable that it may have been the origin of chieftainship. The man who made the rain would naturally become the chief. In the same way Chaka [the famous Zulu despot] used to declare that he was the only diviner in the country, for if he allowed rivals his life would be insecure.' Similarly speaking of the South African tribes in general, Dr. Moffat says that 'the rain-maker is in the estimation of the people no mean personage, possessing an influence over the minds of the people superior even to that of the king, who is likewise compelled to yield to the dictates of this arch-official.'

The foregoing evidence renders it probable that in Africa the king has often been developed out of the public magician, and especially out of the rain-maker. The unbounded fear which the magician inspires and the wealth which he amasses in the exercise of his profession may both be supposed to have contributed to his promotion. But if the career of a magician and especially of a rain-maker offers great rewards to the successful practitioner of the art, it is beset with many pitfalls into which the unskilful or unlucky artist may fall. The position of the public sorcerer is indeed a very precarious one; for where the people firmly believe that he has it in his power to make the rain to fall, the sun to shine, and the fruits of the earth to grow, they naturally impute drought and dearth to his culpable negligence or wilful obstinacy, and they punish him accordingly. Hence in Africa the chief who fails to procure rain is often exiled or killed. Thus, in some parts of West Africa, when prayers and offerings presented to the king have failed to procure rain, his subjects bind him with ropes and take him by force to the grave of his forefathers that he may obtain from them the needed rain. The Banjars in West Africa ascribe to their king the power of causing rain or fine weather. So long as the weather is fine they load him with presents of grain and cattle. But if long drought or rain threatens to spoil the crops, they insult and beat him till the weather changes. When the harvest fails or the surf on the coast is too heavy to allow of fishing, the people of Loango accuse their king of a 'bad heart' and depose him. On the Grain Coast the high priest or fetish king, who bears the title of Bodio, is responsible for the health of the community, the fertility of the earth, and the abundance of fish in the sea and rivers; and if the country suffers in any of these respects the Bodio is deposed from his office. In Ussukuma, a great district on the southern bank of the Victoria Nyanza, 'the rain and locust question is part and parcel of the Sultan's government. He, too, must know how to make rain and drive away the locusts. If he and his medicine-men are unable to accomplish this, his whole existence is at stake in times of distress. On a certain occasion, when the rain so greatly desired by the people did not come, the Sultan was simply driven out (in Ututwa, near Nassa). The people, in fact, hold that rulers must have power over Nature and her phenomena.' Again, we are told of the natives of the Nyanza region generally that 'they are persuaded that rain only falls as a result of magic, and the important duty of causing it to descend devolves on the chief of the tribe. If rain does not come at the proper time, everybody complains. More than one petty king has been banished his country because of drought.' Among the Latuka of the Upper Nile, when the crops are withering, and all the efforts of the chief to draw down rain have proved fruitless, the people commonly attack him by night, rob him of all he possesses, and drive him away. But often they kill him.

In many other parts of the world kings have been expected to regulate the course of nature for the good of their people and have been punished if they failed to do so. It appears that the Scythians, when food was scarce, used to put their king in bonds. In ancient Egypt the sacred kings were blamed for the failure of the crops, but the sacred beasts were also held responsible for the course of nature. When pestilence and other calamities had fallen on the land, in consequence of a long and severe drought, the priests took the animals by night and threatened them, but if the evil did not abate they slew the beasts. On the coral island of Niuē or Savage Island, in the South Pacific, there formerly reigned a line of kings. But as the kings were also high priests, and were supposed to make the food grow, the people became angry with them in times of scarcity and killed them; till at last, as one after another was killed, no one would be king, and the monarchy came to an end. Ancient Chinese writers inform us that in Corea the blame was laid on the king whenever too much or too little rain fell and the crops did not ripen. Some said that he must be deposed, others that he must be slain.

Among the American Indians the furthest advance towards civilisation was made under the monarchical and theocratic governments of Mexico and Peru; but we know too little of the early history of these countries to say whether the predecessors of their deified kings were medicine-men or not. Perhaps a trace of such a succession may be detected in the oath which the Mexican kings, when they mounted the throne, swore that they would make the sun shine, the clouds to give rain, the rivers to flow, and the earth to bring forth fruits in abundance. Certainly, in aboriginal America the sorcerer or medicine-man, surrounded by a halo of mystery and an atmosphere of awe, was a personage of great influence and importance, and he may well have developed into a chief or king in many tribes, though positive evidence of such a development appears to be lacking. Thus Catlin tells us that in North America the medicine-men 'are valued as dignitaries in the tribe, and the greatest respect is paid to them by the whole community; not only for their skill in their *materia medica*, but more especially for their tact in magic and mysteries, in which they all deal to a very great extent. . . . In all tribes their doctors are conjurers—are magicians—are sooth-sayers, and I had like to have said high-priests, inasmuch as they superintend and conduct all their religious ceremonies; they are looked upon by all as oracles of the nation. In all councils of war and peace, they have a seat with the chiefs, are regularly consulted before any public step is taken, and the greatest deference and respect is paid to their opinions.' Similarly in California 'the shaman was, and still is, perhaps the most important individual among the Maidu. In the absence of any definite system of government, the word of a shaman has great weight: as a class they are regarded with much awe, and as a rule are obeyed much more than the chief.'

In South America also the magicians or medicine-men seem

to have been on the highroad to chieftainship or kingship. One
of the earliest settlers on the coast of Brazil, the Frenchman
Thevet, reports that the Indians 'hold these *pages* (or medicine-
men) in such honour and reverence that they adore, or rather
idolise them. You may see the common folk go to meet them,
prostrate themselves, and pray to them, saying, "Grant that I
be not ill, that I do not die, neither I nor my children," or some
such request. And he answers, "You shall not die, you shall not
be ill," and such like replies. But sometimes if it happens that
these *pages* do not tell the truth, and things turn out otherwise
than they predicted, the people make no scruple of killing them
as unworthy of the title and dignity of *pages*.' Among the
Lengua Indians of the Gran Chaco every clan has its cazique or
chief, but he possesses little authority. In virtue of his office he
has to make many presents, so he seldom grows rich and is generally
more shabbily clad than any of his subjects. 'As a matter of fact
the magician is the man who has most power in his hands, and
he is accustomed to receive presents instead of to give them.' It
is the magician's duty to bring down misfortune and plagues on
the enemies of his tribe, and to guard his own people against
hostile magic. For these services he is well paid, and by them
he acquires a position of great influence and authority.

Throughout the Malay region the rajah or king is commonly
regarded with superstitious veneration as the possessor of
supernatural powers, and there are grounds for thinking that he
too, like apparently so many African chiefs, has been developed
out of a simple magician. At the present day the Malays firmly
believe that the king possesses a personal influence over the works
of nature, such as the growth of the crops and the bearing of
fruit-trees. The same prolific virtue is supposed to reside, though
in a lesser degree, in his delegates, and even in the persons of
Europeans who chance to have charge of districts. Thus in
Selangor, one of the native states of the Malay Peninsula, the
success or failure of the rice crops is often attributed to a change
of district officers. The Toorateyas of Southern Celebes hold
that the prosperity of the rice depends on the behaviour of their
princes, and that bad government, by which they mean a government which does not conform to ancient custom, will result in
a failure of the crops.

The Dyaks of Sarawak believed that their famous English ruler, Rajah Brooke, was endowed with a certain magical virtue which, if properly applied, could render the rice-crops abundant. Hence when he visited a tribe, they used to bring him the seed which they intended to sow next year, and he fertilised it by shaking over it the women's necklaces, which had been previously dipped in a special mixture. And when he entered a village, the women would wash and bathe his feet, first with water, and then with the milk of a young coco-nut, and lastly with water again, and all this water which had touched his person they preserved for the purpose of distributing it on their farms, believing that it ensured an abundant harvest. Tribes which were too far off for him to visit used to send him a small piece of white cloth and a little gold or silver, and when these things had been impregnated by his generative virtue they buried them in their fields, and confidently expected a heavy crop. Once when a European remarked that the rice-crops of the Samban tribe were thin, the chief immediately replied that they could not be otherwise, since Rajah Brooke had never visited them, and he begged that Mr. Brooke might be induced to visit his tribe and remove the sterility of their land.

The belief that kings possess magical or supernatural powers by virtue of which they can fertilise the earth and confer other benefits on their subjects would seem to have been shared by the ancestors of all the Aryan races from India to Ireland, and it has left clear traces of itself in our own country down to modern times. Thus the ancient Hindoo law-book called *The Laws of Manu* describes as follows the effects of a good king's reign: 'In that country where the king avoids taking the property of mortal sinners, men are born in due time and are long-lived. And the crops of the husbandmen spring up, each as it was sown, and the children die not, and no misshaped offspring is born.' In Homeric Greece kings and chiefs were spoken of as sacred or divine; their houses, too, were divine and their chariots sacred; and it was thought that the reign of a good king caused the black earth to bring forth wheat and barley, the trees to be loaded with fruit, the flocks to multiply, and the sea to yield fish. In the Middle Ages, when Waldemar I., King of Denmark, travelled in Germany, mothers brought their infants and husbandmen their seed for him to lay his hands on, thinking that children would both thrive the better for the royal touch, and for a like reason farmers asked him to throw the seed for them. It was the belief of the ancient Irish that when their kings observed the customs of their ancestors, the seasons were mild, the crops plentiful, the cattle fruitful, the waters abounded with fish, and the fruit trees had to be propped up on account of the weight of their produce. A canon attributed to St. Patrick enumerates among the blessings that attend the reign of a just king 'fine weather, calm seas, crops abundant, and trees laden with fruit.' On the other hand, dearth, dryness of cows, blight on fruit, and scarcity of corn were regarded as infallible proofs that the reigning king was bad.

Perhaps the last relic of such superstitions which lingered about our English kings was the notion that they could heal scrofula by their touch. The disease was accordingly known as the King's Evil. Queen Elizabeth often exercised this miraculous gift of healing. On Midsummer Day 1633, Charles the First cured a hundred patients at one swoop in the chapel royal at Holyrood. But it was under his son Charles the Second that the practice seems to have attained its highest vogue. It is said that in the course of his reign Charles the Second touched near a hundred thousand persons for scrofula. The press to get near him was something terrific. On one occasion six or seven of those who came to be healed were trampled to death. The cool-headed William the Third contemptuously refused to lend himself to the hocus-pocus; and when his palace was besieged by the usual unsavoury crowd, he ordered them to be turned away with a dole. On the only occasion when he was importuned into laying his hand on a patient, he said to him, 'God give you better health and more sense.' However, the practice was continued, as might have been expected, by the dull bigot James the Second and his dull daughter Queen Anne.

The kings of France also claimed to possess the same gift of healing by touch, which they are said to have derived from Clovis or from St. Louis, while our English kings inherited it from Edward the Confessor. Similarly the savage chiefs of Tonga were believed to heal scrofula and cases of indurated liver by the touch of their feet; and the cure was strictly homoeopathic, for the disease as well as the cure was thought to be caused by contact with the royal person or with anything that belonged to it.

On the whole, then, we seem to be justified in inferring that in many parts of the world the king is the lineal successor of the old magician or medicine-man. When once a special class of sorcerers has been segregated from the community and entrusted by it with the discharge of duties on which the public safety and welfare are believed to depend, these men gradually rise to wealth and power, till their leaders blossom out into sacred kings. But the great social revolution which thus begins with democracy and ends in despotism is attended by an intellectual revolution which affects both the conception and the functions of royalty. For as time goes on, the fallacy of magic becomes more and more apparent to the acuter minds and is slowly displaced by religion; in other words, the magician gives way to the priest, who renouncing the attempt to control directly the processes of nature for the good of man, seeks to attain the same end indirectly by appealing to the gods to do for him what he no longer fancies he can do for himself. Hence the king, starting as a magician, tends gradually to exchange the practice of magic for the priestly functions of prayer and sacrifice. And while the distinction between the human and the divine is still imperfectly drawn, it is often imagined that men may themselves attain to godhead, not merely after their death, but in their lifetime, through the temporary or permanent possession of their whole nature by a great and powerful spirit. No class of the community has benefited so much as kings by this belief in the possible incarnation of a god in human form. The doctrine of that incarnation, and with it the theory of the divinity of kings in the strict sense of the word, will form the subject of the following chapter.

CHAPTER VII

INCARNATE HUMAN GODS

THE instances which in the preceding chapters I have drawn from the beliefs and practices of rude peoples all over the world, may suffice to prove that the savage fails to recognise those limitations to his power over nature which seem so obvious to us. In a society where every man is supposed to be endowed more or less with powers which we should call supernatural, it is plain that the distinction between gods and men is somewhat blurred, or rather has scarcely emerged. The conception of gods as super-human beings endowed with powers to which man possesses nothing comparable in degree and hardly even in kind, has been slowly evolved in the course of history. By primitive peoples the supernatural agents are not regarded as greatly, if at all, superior to man; for they may be frightened and coerced by him into doing his will. At this stage of thought the world is viewed as a great democracy; all beings in it, whether natural or supernatural, are supposed to stand on a footing of tolerable equality. But with the growth of his knowledge man learns to realise more clearly the vastness of nature and his own littleness and feebleness in presence of it. The recognition of his helplessness does not, however, carry with it a corresponding belief in the impotence of those supernatural beings with which his imagination peoples the universe. On the contrary, it enhances his conception of their power. For the idea of the world as a system of impersonal forces acting in accordance with fixed and invariable laws has not yet fully dawned or darkened upon him. The germ of the idea he certainly has, and he acts upon it, not only in magic art, but in much of the business of daily life. But the idea remains undeveloped, and so far as he attempts to explain the world he lives in, he pictures it as the manifestation of conscious will and personal agency. If then he feels himself to be so frail and slight, how vast and powerful must he deem the beings who control the gigantic machinery of nature! Thus as his old sense of equality with the gods slowly vanishes, he resigns at the same time the hope of directing the course of nature by his own unaided resources, that is, by magic, and looks more and more to the gods as the sole repositories of those supernatural powers which he once claimed to share with them. With the advance of know-ledge, therefore, prayer and sacrifice assume the leading place in religious ritual; and magic, which once ranked with them as a legitimate equal, is gradually relegated to the background and sinks to the level of a black art. It is now regarded as an encroachment, at once vain and impious, on the domain of the gods, and as such encounters the steady opposition of the priests, whose reputation and influence rise or fall with those of their gods. Hence, when at a late period the distinction between religion and superstition has emerged, we find that sacrifice and prayer are the resource of the pious and enlightened portion of the community, while magic is the refuge of the superstitious and ignorant. But when, still later, the conception of the elemental forces as personal agents is giving way to the recognition of natural law; then magic, based as it implicitly is on the idea of a necessary and invariable sequence of cause and effect, independent of personal will, reappears from the obscurity and discredit into which it had fallen, and by investigating the causal sequences in nature, directly prepares the way for science. Alchemy leads up to chemistry.

The notion of a man-god, or of a human being endowed with divine or supernatural powers, belongs essentially to that earlier period of religious history in which gods and men are still viewed as beings of much the same order, and before they are divided by the impassable gulf which, to later thought, opens out between them. Strange, therefore, as may seem to us the idea of a god incarnate in human form, it has nothing very startling for early man, who sees in a man-god or a god-man only a higher degree of the same supernatural powers which he arrogates in perfect good faith to himself. Nor does he draw any very sharp distinction between a god and a powerful sorcerer. His gods are often merely invisible magicians who behind the veil of nature work the same sort of charms and incantations which the human magician works in a visible and bodily form among his fellows. And as the gods are commonly believed to exhibit themselves in the likeness of men to their worshippers, it is easy for the magician, with his supposed miraculous powers, to acquire the reputation of being an incarnate deity. Thus beginning as little more than a simple conjurer, the medicine-man or magician tends to blossom out into a full-blown god and king in one. Only in speaking of him as a god we must beware of importing into the savage conception of deity those very abstract and complex ideas which we attach to the term. Our ideas on this profound subject are the fruit of a long intellectual and moral evolution, and they are so far from being shared by the savage that he cannot even understand them when they are explained to him. Much of the controversy which has raged as to the religion of the lower races has sprung merely from a mutual misunderstanding. The savage does not understand the thoughts of the civilised man, and few civilised men understand the thoughts of the savage. When the savage uses his word for god, he has in his mind a being of a certain sort: when the civilised man uses his word for god, he has in his mind a being of a very different sort; and if, as commonly happens, the two men are equally unable to place themselves at the other's point of view, nothing but confusion and mistakes can result from their discussions. If we civilised men insist on limiting the name of God to that particular conception of the divine nature which we ourselves have formed, then we must confess that the savage has no god at all. But we shall adhere more closely to the facts of history if we allow most of the higher savages at least to possess a rudimentary notion of certain supernatural beings who may fittingly be called gods, though not in the full sense in which we use the word. That rudimentary notion represents in all probability the germ out of which the civilised peoples have gradually evolved their own high conceptions of deity; and if we could trace the whole course of religious development, we might find that the chain which links our idea of the Godhead with that of the savage is one and unbroken.

With these explanations and cautions I will now adduce some examples of gods who have been believed by their worshippers to be incarnate in living human beings, whether men or women. The persons in whom a deity is thought to reveal himself are by no means always kings or descendants of kings; the supposed incarnation may take place even in men of the humblest rank. In India, for example, one human god started in life as a cotton-bleacher and another as the son of a carpenter. I shall therefore not draw my examples exclusively from royal personages, as I wish to illustrate the general principle of the deification of living men, in other words, the incarnation of a deity in human form. Such incarnate gods are common in rude society. The incarnation may be temporary or permanent. In the former case, the incarnation — commonly known as inspiration or possession —

reveals itself in supernatural knowledge rather than in super-natural power. In other words, its usual manifestations are divination and prophecy rather than miracles. On the other hand, when the incarnation is not merely temporary, when the divine spirit has permanently taken up its abode in a human body, the god-man is usually expected to vindicate his character by working miracles. Only we have to remember that by men at this stage of thought miracles are not considered as breaches of natural law. Not conceiving the existence of natural law, primitive man cannot conceive a breach of it. A miracle is to him merely an unusually striking manifestation of a common power.

The belief in temporary incarnation or inspiration is world-wide. Certain persons are supposed to be possessed from time to time by a spirit or deity; while the possession lasts, their own personality lies in abeyance, the presence of the spirit is revealed by convulsive shiverings and shakings of the man's whole body, by wild gestures and excited looks, all of which are referred, not to the man himself, but to the spirit which has entered into him; and in this abnormal state all his utterances are accepted as the voice of the god or spirit dwelling in him and speaking through him. Thus, for example, in the Sandwich Islands, the king, personating the god, uttered the responses of the oracle from his concealment in a frame of wicker-work. But in the southern islands of the Pacific the god 'frequently entered the priest, who, inflated as it were with the divinity, ceased to act or speak as a voluntary agent, but moved and spoke as entirely under supernatural influence. In this respect there was a striking resemblance between the rude oracles of the Polynesians, and those of the celebrated nations of ancient Greece. As soon as the god was supposed to have entered the priest, the latter became violently agitated, and worked himself up to the highest pitch of apparent frenzy, the muscles of the limbs seemed convulsed, the body swelled, the countenance became terrific, the features distorted, and the eyes wild and strained. In this state he often rolled on the earth, foaming at the mouth, as if labouring under the influence of the divinity by whom he was possessed, and in shrill cries, and violent and often indistinct sounds, revealed the will of the god. The priests, who were attending, and versed in the mysteries, received, and reported to the people, the declarations which had been thus received. When the priest had uttered the response of the oracle, the violent paroxysm gradually subsided, and comparative composure ensued. The god did not, however, always leave him as soon as the communication had been made. Sometimes the same *taura*, or priest, continued for two or three days possessed by the spirit or deity; a piece of native cloth, of a peculiar kind, worn round one arm, was an indication of inspiration, or of the indwelling of the god with the individual who wore it. The acts of the man during this period were considered as those of the god, and hence the greatest attention was paid to his expressions, and the whole of his deportment. . . . When *uruhia* (under the inspiration of the spirit), the priest was always considered as sacred as the god, and was called, during this period, *atua*, god, though at other times only denominated *taura* or priest.'

But examples of such temporary inspiration are so common in every part of the world and are now so familiar through books on ethnology that it is needless to multiply illustrations of the general principle. It may be well, however, to refer to two particular modes of producing temporary inspiration, because they are perhaps less known than some others, and because we shall have occasion to refer to them later on. One of these modes of producing inspiration is by sucking the fresh blood of a sacrificed victim. In the temple of Apollo Diradiotes at Argos, a lamb was sacrificed by night once a month; a woman, who had to observe the rule of chastity, tasted the blood of the lamb, and thus being inspired by the god she prophesied or divined. At Aegira in Achaia the priestess of Earth drank the fresh blood of a bull before she descended into the cave to prophesy. Similarly among the Kuruvikkarans, a class of bird-catchers and beggars in Southern India, the goddess Kali is believed to descend upon the priest, and he gives oracular replies after sucking the blood which streams from the cut throat of a goat. At a festival of the Alfoors of Minahassa, in Northern Celebes, after a pig has been killed, the priest rushes furiously at it, thrusts his head into the carcase, and drinks of the blood. Then he is dragged away from it by force and set on a chair, whereupon he begins to prophesy how the rice-crop will turn out that year. A second

time he runs at the carcase and drinks of the blood; a second
time he is forced into the chair and continues his predictions.
It is thought that there is a spirit in him which possesses the
power of prophecy.

The other mode of producing temporary inspiration, to which
I shall here refer, consists in the use of a sacred tree or plant.
Thus in the Hindoo Koosh a fire is kindled with twigs of the
sacred cedar; and the Dainyal or sibyl, with a cloth over her
head, inhales the thick pungent smoke till she is seized with
convulsions and falls senseless to the ground. Soon she rises and
raises a shrill chant, which is caught up and loudly repeated by
her audience. So Apollo's prophetess ate the sacred laurel and
was fumigated with it before she prophesied. The Bacchanals
ate ivy, and their inspired fury was by some believed to be due
to the exciting and intoxicating properties of the plant. In Uganda
the priest, in order to be inspired by his god, smokes a pipe of
tobacco fiercely till he works himself into a frenzy; the loud
excited tones in which he then talks are recognised as the voice
of the god speaking through him. In Madura, an island off the
north coast of Java, each spirit has its regular medium, who is
oftener a woman than a man. To prepare herself for the reception
of the spirit she inhales the fumes of incense, sitting with her
head over a smoking censer. Gradually she falls into a sort of
trance accompanied by shrieks, grimaces, and violent spasms.
The spirit is now supposed to have entered into her, and when
she grows calmer her words are regarded as oracular, being the
utterances of the indwelling spirit, while her own soul is
temporarily absent.

The person temporarily inspired is believed to acquire, not
merely divine knowledge, but also, at least occasionally, divine
power. In Cambodia, when an epidemic breaks out, the
inhabitants of several villages unite and go with a band of music
at their head to look for the man whom the local god is supposed
to have chosen for his temporary incarnation. When found, the
man is conducted to the altar of the god, where the mystery of
incarnation takes place. Then the man becomes an object of
veneration to his fellows, who implore him to protect the village
against the plague. A certain image of Apollo, which stood in
a sacred cave at Hylae near Magnesia, was thought to impart

superhuman strength. Sacred men, inspired by it, leaped down precipices, tore up huge trees by the roots, and carried them on their backs along the narrowest defiles. The feats performed by inspired dervishes belong to the same class.

Thus far we have seen that the savage, failing to discern the limits of his ability to control nature, ascribes to himself and to all men certain powers which we should now call supernatural. Further, we have seen that, over and above this general supernaturalism, some persons are supposed to be inspired for short periods by a divine spirit, and thus temporarily to enjoy the knowledge and power of the indwelling deity. From beliefs like these it is an easy step to the conviction that certain men are permanently possessed by a deity, or in some other undefined way are endued with so high a degree of supernatural power as to be ranked as gods and to receive the homage of prayer and sacrifice. Sometimes these human gods are restricted to purely supernatural or spiritual functions. Sometimes they exercise supreme political power in addition. In the latter case they are kings as well as gods, and the government is a theocracy. Thus in the Marquesas or Washington Islands there was a class of men who were deified in their lifetime. They were supposed to wield a supernatural power over the elements: they could give abundant harvests or smite the ground with barrenness; and they could inflict disease or death. Human sacrifices were offered to them to avert their wrath. There were not many of them, at the most one or two in each island. They lived in mystic seclusion. Their powers were sometimes, but not always, hereditary. A missionary has described one of these human gods from personal observation. The god was a very old man who lived in a large house within an enclosure. In the house was a kind of altar, and on the beams of the house and on the trees round it were hung human skeletons, head down. No one entered the enclosure except the persons dedicated to the service of the god; only on days when human victims were sacrificed might ordinary people penetrate into the precinct. This human god received more sacrifices than all the other gods; often he would sit on a sort of scaffold in front of his house and call for two or three human victims at a time. They were always brought, for the terror he inspired was extreme. He was invoked all over the island, and offerings were sent to him from every side. Again, of the South Sea Islands in general we are told that each island had a man who represented or personified the divinity. Such men were called gods, and their substance was confounded with that of the deity. The man-god was sometimes the king himself; oftener he was a priest or subordinate chief.

The ancient Egyptians, far from restricting their adoration to cats and dogs and such small deer, very liberally extended it to men. One of these human deities resided at the village of Anabis, and burnt sacrifices were offered to him on the altars; after which, says Porphyry, he would eat his dinner just as if he were an ordinary mortal. In classical antiquity the Sicilian philosopher Empedocles gave himself out to be not merely a wizard but a god. Addressing his fellow-citizens in verse he said:

> '*O friends, in this great city that climbs the yellow slope*
> *Of Agrigentum's citadel, who make good works your scope,*
> *Who offer to the stranger a haven quiet and fair,*
> *All hail! Among you honoured I walk with lofty air.*
> *With garlands, blooming garlands you crown my noble brow.*
> *A mortal man no longer, a deathless godhead now.*
> *Where e'er I go, the people crowd round and worship pay,*
> *And thousands follow seeking to learn the better way.*
> *Some crave prophetic visions, some smit with anguish sore*
> *Would fain hear words of comfort and suffer pain no more.*'

He asserted that he could teach his disciples how to make the wind to blow or be still, the rain to fall and the sun to shine, how to banish sickness and old age and to raise the dead. When Demetrius Poliorcetes restored the Athenian democracy in 307 B.C., the Athenians decreed divine honours to him and his father Antigonus, both of them being then alive, under the title of the Saviour Gods. Altars were set up to the Saviours, and a priest appointed to attend to their worship. The people went forth to meet their deliverer with hymns and dances, with garlands and incense and libations; they lined the streets and sang that he was the only true god, for the other gods slept, or dwelt far away, or were not. In the words of a contemporary poet, which were chanted in public and sung in private:

'*Of all the gods the greatest and
        the dearest
To the city are come.
For Demeter and Demetrius
Together time has brought.
She comes to hold the Maiden's
        awful rites,
And he joyous and fair and
        laughing,
As befits a god.
A glorious sight, with all his
        friends about him,*

*He in their midst,
They like to stars, and he the sun.
Son of Poseidon the mighty,
        Aphrodite's son,
All hail!
The other gods dwell far away,
Or have no ears,
Or are not, or pay us no heed.
But thee we present see,
No god of wood or stone, but
        godhead true.
Therefore to thee we pray.*'

The ancient Germans believed that there was something holy in women, and accordingly consulted them as oracles. Their sacred women, we are told, looked on the eddying rivers and listened to the murmur or the roar of the water, and from the sight and sound foretold what would come to pass. But often the veneration of the men went further, and they worshipped women as true and living goddesses. For example, in the reign of Vespasian a certain Veleda, of the tribe of the Bructeri, was commonly held to be a deity, and in that character reigned over her people, her sway being acknowledged far and wide. She lived in a tower on the river Lippe, a tributary of the Rhine. When the people of Cologne sent to make a treaty with her, the ambassadors were not admitted to her presence; the negotiations were conducted through a minister, who acted as the mouthpiece of her divinity and reported her oracular utterances. The example shows how easily among our rude forefathers the ideas of divinity and royalty coalesced. It is said that among the Getae down to the beginning of our era there was always a man who personified a god and was called God by the people. He dwelt on a sacred mountain and acted as adviser to the king.

According to the early Portuguese historian, Dos Santos, the Zimbas, or Muzimbas, a people of South-eastern Africa, 'do not adore idols or recognise any god, but instead they venerate and honour their king, whom they regard as a divinity, and they say he is the greatest and best in the world. And the said king says of himself that he alone is god of the earth, for which reason if it rains when he does not wish it to do so, or is too hot, he shoots arrows at the sky for not obeying him.' The Mashona of Southern Africa informed their bishop that they had once had a god, but that the Matabeles had driven him away. 'This last was in reference to a curious custom in some villages of keeping a man they called their god. He seemed to be consulted by the people and had presents given to him. There was one at a village belonging to a chief Magondi, in the old days. We were asked not to fire off any guns near the village, or we should frighten him away.' This Mashona god was formerly bound to render an annual tribute to the king of the Matabele in the shape of four black oxen and one dance. A missionary has seen and described the deity discharging the latter part of his duty in front of the royal hut. For three mortal hours, without a break, to the banging of a tambourine, the click of castanettes, and the drone of a monotonous song, the swarthy god engaged in a frenzied dance, crouching on his hams like a tailor, sweating like a pig, and bounding about with an agility which testified to the strength and elasticity of his divine legs.

The Baganda of Central Africa believed in a god of Lake Nyanza, who sometimes took up his abode in a man or woman. The incarnate god was much feared by all the people, including the king and the chiefs. When the mystery of incarnation had taken place, the man, or rather the god, removed about a mile and a half from the margin of the lake, and there awaited the appearance of the new moon before he engaged in his sacred duties. From the moment that the crescent moon appeared faintly in the sky, the king and all his subjects were at the command of the divine man, or *Lubare* (god), as he was called, who reigned supreme not only in matters of faith and ritual, but also in questions of war and state policy. He was consulted as an oracle; by his word he could inflict or heal sickness, withhold rain, and cause famine. Large presents were made him when his advice was sought. The chief of Urua, a large region to the west of Lake Tanganyika, 'arrogates to himself divine honours and power and pretends to abstain from food for days without feeling its necessity; and, indeed, declares that as a god he is altogether above requiring food and only eats, drinks, and smokes for the pleasure it affords him.' Among the Gallas, when a woman grows tired of the cares of housekeeping, she begins to talk incoherently and to demean herself extravagantly. This is a sign of the descent of the holy spirit Callo upon her. Immediately her husband prostrates himself and adores her; she ceases to bear the humble title of wife and is called 'Lord'; domestic duties have no further claim on her, and her will is a divine law.

The king of Loango is honoured by his people 'as though he were a god; and he is called Sambee and Pango, which mean god. They believe that he can let them have rain when he likes; and once a year, in December, which is the time they want rain, the people come to beg of him to grant it to them.' On this occasion the king, standing on his throne, shoots an arrow into the air, which is supposed to bring on rain. Much the same is said of the king of Mombasa. Down to a few years ago, when his spiritual reign on earth was brought to an abrupt end by the carnal weapons of English marines and bluejackets, the king of Benin was the chief object of worship in his dominions. 'He occupies a higher post here than the Pope does in Catholic Europe; for he is not only God's vicegerent upon earth, but a god himself, whose subjects both obey and adore him as such, although I believe their adoration to arise rather from fear than love.' The king of Iddah told the English officers of the Niger Expedition, 'God made me after his own image; I am all the same as God; and he appointed me a king.'

A peculiarly bloodthirsty monarch of Burma, by name Badonsachen, whose very countenance reflected the inbred ferocity of his nature, and under whose reign more victims perished by the executioner than by the common enemy, conceived the notion that he was something more than mortal, and that this high distinction had been granted him as a reward for his numerous good works. Accordingly he laid aside the title of king and aimed at making himself a god. With this view, and in imitation of Buddha, who, before being advanced to the rank of a divinity, had quitted his royal palace and seraglio and retired from the world, Badonsachen withdrew from his palace to an immense pagoda, the largest in the empire, which he had been engaged in constructing for many years. Here he held conferences with the most learned monks, in which he sought to persuade them that the five thousand years assigned for the observance of the law of Buddha were now elapsed, and that he himself was the god who was destined to appear after that period, and to abolish the old law by substituting his own. But to his great mortification many of the monks undertook to demonstrate the contrary; and this disappointment, combined with his love of power and his impatience under the restraints of an ascetic life, quickly disabused him of his imaginary godhead, and drove him back to his palace and his harem. The king of Siam 'is venerated equally with a divinity. His subjects ought not to look him in the face; they prostrate themselves before him when he passes, and appear before him on their knees, their elbows resting on the ground.' There is a special language devoted to his sacred person and attributes, and it must be used by all who speak to or of him. Even the natives have difficulty in mastering this peculiar vocabulary. The hairs of the monarch's head, the soles of his feet, the breath of his body, indeed every single detail of his person, both outward and inward, have particular names. When he eats or drinks, sleeps or walks, a special word indicates that these acts are being performed by the sovereign, and such words cannot possibly be applied to the acts of any other person whatever. There is no word in the Siamese language by which any creature of higher rank or greater dignity than a monarch can be described; and the missionaries, when they speak of God, are forced to use the native word for king.

But perhaps no country in the world has been so prolific of human gods as India; nowhere has the divine grace been poured out in a more liberal measure on all classes of society from kings down to milkmen. Thus amongst the Todas, a pastoral people of the Neilgherry Hills of Southern India, the dairy is a sanctuary, and the milkman who attends to it has been described as a god. On being asked whether the Todas salute the sun, one of these divine milkmen replied, 'Those poor fellows do so, but I,' tapping his chest, 'I, a god! why should I salute the sun?' Every one, even his own father, prostrates himself before the milkman, and no one would dare to refuse him anything. No human being, except another milkman, may touch him; and he gives oracles to all who consult him, speaking with the voice of a god.

Further, in India 'every king is regarded as little short of a present god.' The Hindoo law-book of Manu goes farther and says that 'even an infant king must not be despised from an idea that he is a mere mortal; for he is a great deity in human form.'

There is said to have been a sect in Orissa some years ago who worshipped the late Queen Victoria in her lifetime as their chief divinity. And to this day in India all living persons remarkable for great strength or valour or for supposed miraculous powers run the risk of being worshipped as gods. Thus, a sect in the Punjaub worshipped a deity whom they called Nikkal Sen. This Nikkal Sen was no other than the redoubted General Nicholson, and nothing that the general could do or say damped the ardour of his adorers. The more he punished them, the greater grew the religious awe with which they worshipped him. At Benares not many years ago a celebrated deity was incarnate in the person of a Hindoo gentleman who rejoiced in the euphonious name of Swami Bhaskaranandaji Saraswati, and looked uncommonly like the late Cardinal Manning, only more ingenuous. His eyes beamed with kindly human interest, and he took what is described as an innocent pleasure in the divine honours paid him by his confiding worshippers.

At Chinchvad, a small town about ten miles from Poona in Western India, there lives a family of whom one in each generation is believed by a large proportion of the Mahrattas to be an incarnation of the elephant-headed god Gunputty. That celebrated deity was first made flesh about the year 1640 in the person of a Brahman of Poona, by name Mooraba Gosseyn, who sought to work out his salvation by abstinence, mortification, and prayer. His piety had its reward. The god himself appeared to him in a vision of the night and promised that a portion of his, that is, of Gunputty's holy spirit should abide with him and with his seed after him even to the seventh generation. The divine promise was fulfilled. Seven successive incarnations, transmitted from father to son, manifested the light of Gunputty to a dark world. The last of the direct line, a heavy-looking god with very weak eyes, died in the year 1810. But the cause of truth was too sacred, and the value of the church property too considerable, to allow the Brahmans to contemplate with equanimity the unspeakable loss that would be sustained by a world which knew not Gunputty. Accordingly they sought and found a holy vessel in whom the divine spirit of the master had revealed itself anew, and the revelation has been happily continued in an unbroken succession of vessels from that time to this. But a mysterious law of spiritual economy, whose operation in the history of religion we may deplore though we cannot alter, has decreed that the miracles wrought by the god-man in these degenerate days cannot compare with those which were wrought by his predecessors in days gone by; and it is even reported that the only sign vouchsafed by him to the present generation of vipers is the miracle of feeding the multitude whom he annually entertains to dinner at Chinchvad.

A Hindoo sect, which has many representatives in Bombay and Central India, holds that its spiritual chiefs or Maharajas, as they are called, are representatives or even actual incarnations on earth of the god Krishna. And as Krishna looks down from heaven with most favour on such as minister to the wants of his successors and vicars on earth, a peculiar rite called Self-devotion has been instituted, whereby his faithful worshippers make over their bodies, their souls, and, what is perhaps still more important, their worldly substance to his adorable incarnations; and women are taught to believe that the highest bliss for themselves and their families is to be attained by yielding themselves to the embraces of those beings in whom the divine nature mysteriously coexists with the form and even the appetites of true humanity.

Christianity itself has not uniformly escaped the taint of these unhappy delusions; indeed it has often been sullied by the extravagances of vain pretenders to a divinity equal to or even surpassing that of its great Founder. In the second century Montanus the Phrygian claimed to be the incarnate Trinity, uniting in his single person God the Father, God the Son, and God the Holy Ghost. Nor is this an isolated case, the exorbitant pretension of a single ill-balanced mind. From the earliest times down to the present day many sects have believed that Christ, nay God himself, is incarnate in every fully initiated Christian, and they have carried this belief to its logical conclusion by adoring each other. Tertullian records that this was done by his fellow-Christians at Carthage in the second century; the disciples of St. Columba worshipped him as an embodiment of Christ; and in the eighth century Elipandus of Toledo spoke of Christ as 'a god among gods,' meaning that all believers were gods just as truly as Jesus himself. The adoration of each other was customary among the Albigenses, and is noticed hundreds of times in the records of the Inquisition at Toulouse in the early part of the fourteenth century.

In the thirteenth century there arose a sect called the Brethren and Sisters of the Free Spirit, who held that by long and assiduous contemplation any man might be united to the deity in an ineffable manner and become one with the source and parent of all things, and that he who had thus ascended to God and been absorbed in his beatific essence, actually formed part of the Godhead, was the Son of God in the same sense and manner with Christ himself, and enjoyed thereby a glorious immunity from the trammels of all laws human and divine. Inwardly transported by this blissful persuasion, though outwardly presenting in their aspect and manners a shocking air of lunacy and distraction, the sectaries roamed from place to place, attired in the most fantastic apparel and begging their bread with wild shouts and clamour, spurning indignantly every kind of honest labour and industry as an obstacle to divine contemplation and to the ascent of the soul towards the Father of spirits. In all their excursions they were followed by women with whom they lived on terms of the closest familiarity. Those of them who conceived they had made the greatest proficiency in the higher spiritual life dispensed with the use of clothes altogether in their assemblies, looking upon decency and modesty as marks of inward corruption, characteristics of a soul that still grovelled under the dominion of the flesh and had not yet been elevated into communion with the divine spirit, its centre and source. Sometimes their progress towards this mystic communion was accelerated by the Inquisition, and they expired in the flames, not merely with unclouded serenity, but with the most triumphant feelings of cheerfulness and joy.

About the year 1830 there appeared, in one of the States of the American Union bordering on Kentucky, an impostor who declared that he was the Son of God, the Saviour of mankind, and that he had reappeared on earth to recall the impious, the unbelieving, and sinners to their duty. He protested that if they did not mend their ways within a certain time, he would give the signal, and in a moment the world would crumble to ruins. These extravagant pretensions were received with favour even by persons of wealth and position in society. At last a German humbly besought the new Messiah to announce the dreadful catastrophe to his fellow-countrymen in the German language, as they did not understand English, and it seemed a pity that they should be damned merely on that account. The would-be Saviour in reply confessed with great candour that he did not know German. 'What!' retorted the German, 'you the Son of God, and don't speak all languages, and don't even know German? Come, come; you are a knave, a hypocrite, and a madman. Bedlam is the place for you.' The spectators laughed, and went away ashamed of their credulity.

Sometimes, at the death of the human incarnation, the divine spirit transmigrates into another man. The Buddhist Tartars believe in a great number of living Buddhas, who officiate as Grand Lamas at the head of the most important monasteries. When one of these Grand Lamas dies his disciples do not sorrow, for they know that he will soon reappear, being born in the form of an infant. Their only anxiety is to discover the place of his birth. If at this time they see a rainbow they take it as a sign sent them by the departed Lama to guide them to his cradle. Sometimes the divine infant himself reveals his identity. 'I am the Grand Lama,' he says, 'the living Buddha of such and such a temple. Take me to my old monastery. I am its immortal head.' In whatever way the birthplace of the Buddha is revealed, whether by the Buddha's own avowal or by the sign in the sky, tents are struck, and the joyful pilgrims, often headed by the king or one of the most illustrious of the royal family, set forth to find and bring home the infant god. Generally he is born in Tibet, the holy land, and to reach him the caravan has often to traverse the most frightful deserts. When at last they find the child they fall down and worship him. Before, however, he is acknowledged as the Grand Lama whom they seek he must satisfy them of his identity. He is asked the name of the monastery of which he claims to be the head, how far off it is, and how many monks live in it; he must also describe the habits of the deceased Grand Lama and the manner of his death. Then various articles, as prayer-books, tea-pots, and cups, are placed before him, and he has to point out those used by himself in his previous life. If he does so without a mistake his claims are admitted, and he is conducted in triumph to the monastery. At the head of all the Lamas is the Dalai Lama of Lhasa, the Rome of Tibet. He is regarded as a living god, and at death his divine and immortal spirit is born again in a child. According to some accounts the mode of discovering the Dalai Lama is similar to the method, already described, of discovering an ordinary Grand Lama. Other accounts speak of an election by drawing lots from a golden jar. Wherever he is born, the trees and plants put forth green leaves: at his bidding flowers bloom and springs of water rise; and his presence diffuses heavenly blessings.

But he is by no means the only man who poses as a god in these regions. A register of all the incarnate gods in the Chinese empire is kept in the *Li fan yüan* or Colonial Office at Peking. The number of gods who have thus taken out a licence is one hundred and sixty. Tibet is blessed with thirty of them, Northern Mongolia rejoices in nineteen, and Southern Mongolia basks in the sunshine of no less than fifty-seven. The Chinese government, with a paternal solicitude for the welfare of its subjects, forbids the gods on the register to be reborn anywhere but in Tibet. They fear lest the birth of a god in Mongolia should have serious political consequences by stirring the dormant patriotism and warlike spirit of the Mongols, who might rally round an ambitious native deity of royal lineage and seek to win for him, at the point of the sword, a temporal as well as a spiritual kingdom. But besides these public or licensed gods there are a great many little private gods, or unlicensed practitioners of divinity, who work miracles and bless their people in holes and corners; and of late years the Chinese government has winked at the rebirth of these pettifogging deities outside of Tibet. However, once they are born, the government keeps its eye on them as well as on the regular practitioners, and if any of them misbehaves he is promptly degraded, banished to a distant monastery, and strictly forbidden ever to be born again in the flesh.

From our survey of the religious position occupied by the king in rude societies we may infer that the claim to divine and supernatural powers put forward by the monarchs of great historical empires like those of Egypt, Mexico, and Peru, was not the simple outcome of inflated vanity or the empty expression of a grovelling adulation; it was merely a survival and extension of the old savage apotheosis of living kings. Thus, for example, as children of the Sun the Incas of Peru were revered like gods;

they could do no wrong, and no one dreamed of offending against the person, honour, or property of the monarch or of any of the royal race. Hence, too, the Incas did not, like most people, look on sickness as an evil. They considered it a messenger sent from their father the Sun to call them to come and rest with him in heaven. Therefore the usual words in which an Inca announced his approaching end were these: 'My father calls me to come and rest with him.' They would not oppose their father's will by offering sacrifice for recovery, but openly declared that he had called them to his rest. Issuing from the sultry valleys upon the lofty table-land of the Colombian Andes, the Spanish conquerors were astonished to find, in contrast to the savage hordes they had left in the sweltering jungles below, a people enjoying a fair degree of civilisation, practising agriculture, and living under a government which Humboldt has compared to the theocracies of Tibet and Japan. These were the Chibchas, Muyscas, or Mozcas, divided into two kingdoms, with capitals at Bogota and Tunja, but united apparently in spiritual allegiance to the high pontiff of Sogamozo or Iraca. By a long and ascetic novitiate, this ghostly ruler was reputed to have acquired such sanctity that the waters and the rain obeyed him, and the weather depended on his will. The Mexican kings at their accession, as we have seen, took an oath that they would make the sun to shine, the clouds to give rain, the rivers to flow, and the earth to bring forth fruits in abundance. We are told that Montezuma, the last king of Mexico, was worshipped by his people as a god.

The early Babylonian kings, from the time of Sargon I. till the fourth dynasty of Ur or later, claimed to be gods in their lifetime. The monarchs of the fourth dynasty of Ur in particular had temples built in their honour; they set up their statues in various sanctuaries and commanded the people to sacrifice to them; the eighth month was especially dedicated to the kings, and sacrifices were offered to them at the new moon and on the fifteenth of each month. Again, the Parthian monarchs of the Arsacid house styled themselves brothers of the sun and moon and were worshipped as deities. It was esteemed sacrilege to strike even a private member of the Arsacid family in a brawl.

The kings of Egypt were deified in their lifetime, sacrifices were offered to them, and their worship was celebrated in special temples and by special priests. Indeed the worship of kings sometimes cast that of the gods into the shade. Thus in the reign of Merenra a high official declared that he had built many holy places in order that the spirits of the king, the ever-living Merenra, might be invoked 'more than all the gods.' 'It has never been doubted that the king claimed actual divinity; he was the "great god," the "golden Horus," and son of Ra. He claimed authority not only over Egypt, but over "all lands and nations," "the whole world in its length and its breadth, the east and the west," "the entire compass of the great circuit of the sun," "the sky and what is in it, the earth and all that is upon it," "every creature that walks upon two or upon four legs, all that fly or flutter, the whole world offers her productions to him." Whatever in fact might be asserted of the Sun-god, was dogmatically predicable of the king of Egypt. His titles were directly derived from those of the Sun-god.' ' In the course of his existence,' we are told, 'the kings of Egypt exhausted all the possible conceptions of divinity which the Egyptians had framed for themselves. A superhuman god by his birth and by his royal office, he became the deified man after his death. Thus all that was known of the divine was summed up in him.'

We have now completed our sketch, for it is no more than a sketch, of the evolution of that sacred kingship which attained its highest form, its most absolute expression, in the monarchies of Peru and Egypt. Historically, the institution appears to have originated in the order of public magicians or medicine-men; logically it rests on a mistaken deduction from the association of ideas. Men mistook the order of their ideas for the order of nature, and hence imagined that the control which they have, or seem to have, over their thoughts, permitted them to exercise a corresponding control over things. The men who for one reason or another, because of the strength or the weakness of their natural parts, were supposed to possess these magical powers in the highest degree, were gradually marked off from their fellows and became a separate class, who were destined to exercise a most far-reaching influence on the political, religious, and intellectual evolution of mankind. Social progress, as we know, consists mainly in a successive differentiation of functions, or, in simpler language, a division of labour. The work which in primitive society is done by all alike and by all equally ill, or nearly so, is gradually distributed among different classes of workers and executed more and more perfectly; and so far as the products, material or immaterial, of this specialised labour are shared by all, the whole community benefits by the increasing specialisation. Now magicians or medicine-men appear to constitute the oldest artificial or professional class in the evolution of society. For sorcerers are found in every savage tribe known to us; and among the lowest savages, such as the Australian aborigines, they are the only professional class that exists. As time goes on, and the process of differentiation continues, the order of medicine-men is itself subdivided into such classes as the healers of disease, the makers of rain, and so forth; while the most powerful member of the order wins for himself a position as chief and gradually develops into a sacred king, his old magical functions falling more and more into the background and being exchanged for priestly or even divine duties, in proportion as magic is slowly ousted by religion. Still later, a partition is effected between the civil and the religious aspect of the kingship, the temporal power being committed to one man and the spiritual to another. Meanwhile the magicians, who may be repressed but cannot be extirpated by the predominance of religion, still addict themselves to their old occult arts in preference to the newer ritual of sacrifice and prayer; and in time the more sagacious of their number perceive the fallacy of magic and hit upon a more effectual mode of manipulating the forces of nature for the good of man; in short, they abandon sorcery for science. I am far from affirming that the course of development has everywhere rigidly followed these lines: it has doubtless varied greatly in different societies. I merely mean to indicate in the broadest outline what I conceive to have been its general trend. Regarded from the industrial point of view the evolution has been from uniformity to diversity of function: regarded from the political point of view, it has been from democracy to despotism. With the later history of monarchy, especially with the decay of despotism and its displacement by forms of government better adapted to the higher needs of humanity, we are not concerned in this enquiry: our theme is the growth, not the decay, of a great and, in its time, beneficent institution.

done by all alike and by all equally ill, or nearly so, is gradually distributed among different classes of workers, and executed more and more perfectly .... produces, material or immaterial, of this specialised labour are shared by all, the whole community .... magicians, or medicine-men appear to constitute the oldest

CHAPTER VIII

DEPARTMENTAL KINGS OF NATURE

THE preceding investigation has proved that the same union of sacred functions with a royal title which meets us in the King of the Wood at Nemi, the Sacrificial King at Rome, and the magistrate called the King at Athens, occurs frequently outside the limits of classical antiquity and is a common feature of societies at all stages from barbarism to civilisation. Further, it appears that the royal priest is often a king, not only in name but in fact, swaying the sceptre as well as the crosier. All this confirms the traditional view of the origin of the titular and priestly kings in the republics of ancient Greece and Italy. At least by showing that the combination of spiritual and temporal power, of which Graeco-Italian tradition preserved the memory, has actually existed in many places, we have obviated any suspicion of improbability that might have attached to the tradition. Therefore we may now fairly ask, May not the King of the Wood have had an origin like that which a probable tradition assigns to the Sacrificial King of Rome and the titular King of Athens? In other words, may not his predecessors in office have been a line of kings whom a republican revolution stripped of their political power, leaving them only their religious functions and the shadow of a crown? There are at least two reasons for answering this question in the negative. One reason is drawn from the abode of the priest of Nemi; the other from his title, the King of the Wood. If his predecessors had been kings in the ordinary sense, he would surely have been found residing, like the fallen kings of Rome and Athens, in the city of which the sceptre had passed from him. This city must have been Aricia, for there was none nearer. But Aricia was three miles off from his forest sanctuary by the lake shore. If he reigned, it was not in the city, but in the greenwood. Again his title, King of the Wood, hardly allows us to suppose that he had ever been a king in the common sense of the word. More likely he was a king of nature, and of a special side of nature, namely, the woods from which he took his title. If we could find instances of what we may call departmental kings of nature, that is of persons supposed to rule over particular elements or aspects of nature, they would probably present a closer analogy to the King of the Wood than the divine kings we have been hitherto considering, whose control of nature is general rather than special. Instances of such departmental kings are not wanting.

On a hill at Bomma near the mouth of the Congo dwells Namvulu Vumu, King of the Rain and Storm. Of some of the tribes on the Upper Nile we are told that they have no kings in the common sense; the only persons whom they acknowledge as such are the Kings of the Rain, *Mata Kodou*, who are credited with the power of giving rain at the proper time, that is, in the rainy season. Before the rains begin to fall at the end of March the country is a parched and arid desert; and the cattle, which form the people's chief wealth, perish for lack of grass. So, when the end of March draws on, each householder betakes himself to the King of the Rain and offers him a cow that he may make the blessed waters of heaven to drip on the brown and withered pastures. If no shower falls, the people assemble and demand that the king shall give them rain; and if the sky still continues cloudless, they rip up his belly, in which he is believed to keep the storms. Amongst the Bari tribe one of these Rain Kings made rain by sprinkling water on the ground out of a handbell.

Among tribes on the outskirts of Abyssinia a similar office exists and has been thus described by an observer: 'The priesthood of the Alfai, as he is called by the Barea and Kunama, is a remarkable one; he is believed to be able to make rain. This office formerly existed among the Algeds and appears to be still common to the Nuba negroes. The Alfai of the Barea, who is also consulted by the northern Kunama, lives near Tembadere on a mountain alone with his family. The people bring him a tribute in the form of clothes and fruits, and cultivate for him a large field of his own. He is a kind of king, and his office passes by inheritance to his brother or sister's son. He is supposed to conjure down rain and to drive away the locusts. But if he disappoints the people's expectation and a great drought arises in the land, the Alfai is stoned to death, and his nearest relations are obliged to cast the first stone at him. When we passed through the country, the office of Alfai was still held by an old man; but I heard that rain-making had proved too dangerous for him and that he had renounced his office.'

In the backwoods of Cambodia live two mysterious sovereigns known as the King of the Fire and the King of the Water. Their fame is spread all over the south of the great Indo-Chinese peninsula; but only a faint echo of it has reached the West. Down to a few years ago no European, so far as is known, had ever seen either of them; and their very existence might have passed for a fable, were it not that till lately communications were regularly maintained between them and the King of Cambodia, who year by year exchanged presents with them. Their royal functions are of a purely mystic or spiritual order; they have no political authority; they are simple peasants, living by the sweat of their brow and the offerings of the faithful. According to one account they live in absolute solitude, never meeting each other and never seeing a human face. They inhabit successively seven towers perched upon seven mountains, and every year they pass from one tower to another. People come furtively and cast within their reach what is needful for their subsistence. The kingship lasts seven years, the time necessary to inhabit all the towers successively; but many die before their time is out. The offices are hereditary in one or (according to others) two royal families, who enjoy high consideration, have revenues assigned to them, and are exempt from the necessity of tilling the ground. But naturally the dignity is not coveted, and when a vacancy occurs, all eligible men (they must be strong and have children) flee and hide themselves. Another account, admitting the reluctance of the hereditary candidates to accept the crown, does not countenance the report of their hermit-like seclusion in the seven towers. For it represents the people as prostrating themselves before the mystic kings whenever they appear in public, it being thought that a terrible hurricane would burst over the country if this mark of homage were omitted. Like many other sacred kings, of whom we shall read in the sequel, the Kings of Fire and Water are not allowed to die a natural death, for that would lower their reputation. Accordingly when one of them is seriously ill, the elders hold a consultation and if they think he cannot recover they stab him to death. His body is burned and the ashes are piously collected and publicly honoured for five years. Part of them is given to the widow, and she keeps them in an urn, which she must carry on her back when she goes to weep on her husband's grave.

We are told that the Fire King, the more important of the two, whose supernatural powers have never been questioned, officiates at marriages, festivals, and sacrifices in honour of the *Yan* or spirit. On these occasions a special place is set apart for him; and the path by which he approaches is spread with white cotton cloths. A reason for confining the royal dignity to the same family is that this family is in possession of certain famous talismans which would lose their virtue or disappear if they passed out of the family. These talismans are three: the fruit of a creeper called *Cui*, gathered ages ago at the time of the last deluge, but still fresh and green; a rattan, also very old but bearing flowers that never fade; and lastly, a sword containing a *Yan* or spirit, who guards it constantly and works miracles with it. The spirit is said to be that of a slave, whose blood chanced to fall upon the blade while it was being forged, and who died a voluntary death to expiate his involuntary offence. By means of the two former talismans the Water King can raise a flood that would drown the whole earth. If the Fire King draws the magic sword a few inches from its sheath, the sun is hidden and men and beasts fall into a profound sleep; were he to draw it quite out of the scabbard, the world would come to an end. To this wondrous brand sacrifices of buffaloes, pigs, fowls, and ducks are offered for rain. It is kept swathed in cotton and silk; and amongst the annual presents sent by the King of Cambodia were rich stuffs to wrap the sacred sword.

Contrary to the common usage of the country, which is to bury the dead, the bodies of both these mystic monarchs are burnt, but their nails and some of their teeth and bones are religiously preserved as amulets. It is while the corpse is being consumed on the pyre that the kinsmen of the deceased magician flee to the forest and hide themselves, for fear of being elevated to the invidious dignity which he has just vacated. The people go and search for them, and the first whose lurking place they discover is made King of Fire or Water.

These, then, are examples of what I have called departmental kings of nature. But it is a far cry to Italy from the forests of

Cambodia and the sources of the Nile. And though Kings of Rain, Water, and Fire have been found, we have still to discover a King of the Wood to match the Arician priest who bore that title. Perhaps we shall find him nearer home.

CHAPTER IX

THE WORSHIP OF TREES

§ 1. *Tree-spirits*. — In the religious history of the Aryan race in Europe the worship of trees has played an important part. Nothing could be more natural. For at the dawn of history Europe was covered with immense primaeval forests, in which the scattered clearings must have appeared like islets in an ocean of green. Down to the first century before our era the Hercynian forest stretched eastward from the Rhine for a distance at once vast and unknown; Germans whom Caesar questioned had travelled for two months through it without reaching the end. Four centuries later it was visited by the Emperor Julian, and the solitude, the gloom, the silence of the forest appear to have made a deep impression on his sensitive nature. He declared that he knew nothing like it in the Roman empire. In our own country the wealds of Kent, Surrey, and Sussex are remnants of the great forest of Anderida, which once clothed the whole of the south-eastern portion of the island. Westward it seems to have stretched till it joined another forest that extended from Hampshire to Devon. In the reign of Henry II the citizens of London still hunted the wild bull and the boar in the woods of Hampstead. Even under the later Plantagenets the royal forests were sixty-eight in number. In the forest of Arden it was said that down to modern times a squirrel might leap from tree to tree for nearly the whole length of Warwickshire. The excavation of ancient pile-villages in the valley of the Po has shown that long before the rise and probably the foundation of Rome the north of Italy was covered with dense woods of elms, chestnuts, and especially of oaks. Archaeology is here confirmed by history; for classical writers contain many references to Italian forests which have now disappeared. As late as the fourth century before our era Rome was divided from central Etruria by the dreaded Ciminian forest, which Livy compares to the woods of Germany. No merchant, if we may trust the Roman historian, had ever penetrated its pathless solitudes: and it was deemed a most daring feat when a Roman general, after sending two scouts to explore its intricacies, led his army into the forest and, making his way to a ridge of the wooded mountains, looked down on the rich Etrurian fields spread out below. In Greece beautiful woods of pine, oak, and other trees still linger on the slopes of the high Arcadian mountains, still adorn with their verdure the deep gorge through which the Ladon hurries to join the sacred Alpheus, and were still, down to a few years ago, mirrored in the dark blue waters of the lonely lake of Pheneus; but they are mere fragments of the forests which clothed great tracts in antiquity, and which at a more remote epoch may have spanned the Greek peninsula from sea to sea.

From an examination of the Teutonic words for 'temple' Grimm has made it probable that amongst the Germans the oldest sanctuaries were natural woods. However that may be, tree-worship is well attested for all the great European families of the Aryan stock. Amongst the Celts the oak-worship of the Druids is familiar to every one, and their old word for a sanctuary seems to be identical in origin and meaning with the Latin *nemus*, a grove or woodland glade, which still survives in the name of Nemi. Sacred groves were common among the ancient Germans, and tree-worship is hardly extinct amongst their descendants at the present day. How serious that worship was in former times may be gathered from the ferocious penalty appointed by the old German laws for such as dared to peel the bark of a standing tree. The culprit's navel was to be cut out and nailed to the part of the tree which he had peeled, and he was to be driven round and round the tree till all his guts were wound about its trunk. The intention of the punishment clearly was to replace the dead bark by a living substitute taken from the culprit; it was a life for a life, the life of a man for the life of a tree. At Upsala, the old religious capital of Sweden, there was a sacred grove in which every tree was regarded as divine. The heathen Slavs worshipped trees and groves. The Lithuanians were not converted to Christianity till towards the close of the fourteenth century, and amongst them at the date of their conversion the worship of trees was prominent. Some of them revered remarkable oaks and other great shady trees, from which they received oracular responses. Some maintained holy groves about their villages or houses, where even to break a twig would have been a sin. They thought that he who cut a bough in such a grove either died suddenly or was crippled in one of his limbs. Proofs of the prevalence of tree-worship in ancient Greece and Italy are abundant. In the sanctuary of Aesculapius at Cos, for example, it was forbidden to cut down the cypress-trees under a penalty of a thousand drachms. But nowhere, perhaps, in the ancient world was this antique form of religion better preserved than in the heart of the great metropolis itself. In the Forum, the busy centre of Roman life, the sacred fig-tree of Romulus was worshipped down to the days of the empire, and the withering of its trunk was enough to spread consternation through the city. Again, on the slope of the Palatine Hill grew a cornel-tree which was esteemed one of the most sacred objects in Rome. Whenever the tree appeared to a passer-by to be drooping, he set up a hue and cry which was echoed by the people in the street, and soon a crowd might be seen running helter-skelter from all sides with buckets of water, as if (says Plutarch) they were hastening to put out a fire.

Among the tribes of the Finnish-Ugrian stock in Europe the heathen worship was performed for the most part in sacred groves, which were always enclosed with a fence. Such a grove often consisted merely of a glade or clearing with a few trees dotted about, upon which in former times the skins of the sacrificial victims were hung. The central point of the grove, at least among the tribes of the Volga, was the sacred tree, beside which everything else sank into insignificance. Before it the worshippers assembled and the priest offered his prayers, at its roots the victim was sacrificed, and its boughs sometimes served as a pulpit. No wood might be hewn and no branch broken in the grove, and women were generally forbidden to enter it.

But it is necessary to examine in some detail the notions on which the worship of trees and plants is based. To the savage the world in general is animate, and trees and plants are no exception to the rule. He thinks that they have souls like his own, and he treats them accordingly. 'They say,' writes the ancient vegetarian

Porphyry, 'that primitive men led an unhappy life, for their superstition did not stop at animals but extended even to plants. For why should the slaughter of an ox or a sheep be a greater wrong than the felling of a fir or an oak, seeing that a soul is implanted in these trees also?' Similarly, the Hidatsa Indians of North America believe that every natural object has its spirit, or to speak more properly, its shade. To these shades some consideration or respect is due, but not equally to all. For example, the shade of the cottonwood, the greatest tree in the valley of the Upper Missouri, is supposed to possess an intelligence which, if properly approached, may help the Indians in certain undertakings; but the shades of shrubs and grasses are of little account. When the Missouri, swollen by a freshet in spring, carries away part of its banks and sweeps some tall tree into its current, it is said that the spirit of the tree cries, while the roots still cling to the land and until the trunk falls with a splash into the stream. Formerly the Indians considered it wrong to fell one of these giants, and when large logs were needed they made use only of trees which had fallen of themselves. Till lately some of the more credulous old men declared that many of the misfortunes of their people were caused by this modern disregard for the rights of the living cottonwood. The Iroquois believed that each species of tree, shrub, plant, and herb had its own spirit, and to these spirits it was their custom to return thanks. The Wanika of Eastern Africa fancy that every tree, and especially every coco-nut tree, has its spirit; 'the destruction of a coco-nut tree is regarded as equivalent to matricide, because that tree gives them life and nourishment, as a mother does her child.' Siamese monks, believing that there are souls everywhere, and that to destroy anything whatever is forcibly to dispossess a soul, will not break a branch of a tree, 'as they will not break the arm of an innocent person.' These monks, of course, are Buddhists. But Buddhist animism is not a philosophical theory. It is simply a common savage dogma incorporated in the system of an historical religion. To suppose, with Benfey and others, that the theories of animism and transmigration current among rude peoples of Asia are derived from Buddhism, is to reverse the facts.

Sometimes it is only particular sorts of trees that are supposed to be tenanted by spirits. At Grbalj in Dalmatia it is said that among great beeches, oaks, and other trees there are some that are endowed with shades or souls, and whoever fells one of them must die on the spot, or at least live an invalid for the rest of his days. If a woodman fears that a tree which he has felled is one of this sort, he must cut off the head of a live hen on the stump of the tree with the very same axe with which he cut down the tree. This will protect him from all harm, even if the tree be one of the animated kind. The silk-cotton trees, which rear their enormous trunks to a stupendous height, far out-topping all the other trees of the forest, are regarded with reverence throughout West Africa, from the Senegal to the Niger, and are believed to be the abode of a god or spirit. Among the Ewe-speaking peoples of the Slave Coast the indwelling god of this giant of the forest goes by the name of Huntin. Trees in which he specially dwells — for it is not every silk-cotton tree that he thus honours — are surrounded by a girdle of palm-leaves; and sacrifices of fowls, and occasionally of human beings, are fastened to the trunk or laid against the foot of the tree. A tree distinguished by a girdle of palm-leaves may not be cut down or injured in any way; and even silk-cotton trees which are not supposed to be animated by Huntin may not be felled unless the woodman first offers a sacrifice of fowls and palm-oil to purge himself of the proposed sacrilege. To omit the sacrifice is an offence which may be punished with death. Among the Kangra mountains of the Punjaub a girl used to be annually sacrificed to an old cedar-tree, the families of the village taking it in turn to supply the victim. The tree was cut down not very many years ago.

If trees are animate, they are necessarily sensitive and the cutting of them down becomes a delicate surgical operation, which must be performed with as tender a regard as possible for the feelings of the sufferers, who otherwise may turn and rend the careless or bungling operator. When an oak is being felled 'it gives a kind of shriekes or groanes, that may be heard a mile off, as if it were the genius of the oake lamenting. E. Wyld, Esq., hath heard it severall times.' The Ojebways 'very seldom cut down green or living trees, from the idea that it puts them to pain, and some of their medicine-men profess to have heard the wailing of the trees under the axe.' Trees that bleed and utter cries of pain or indignation when they are hacked or burned occur very often in Chinese books, even in Standard Histories. Old peasants in some parts of Austria still believe that forest-trees are animate, and will not allow an incision to be made in the bark without special cause; they have heard from their fathers that the tree feels the cut not less than a wounded man his hurt. In felling a tree they beg its pardon. It is said that in the Upper Palatinate also old woodmen still secretly ask a fine, sound tree to forgive them before they cut it down. So in Jarkino the woodman craves pardon of the tree he fells. Before the Ilocanes of Luzon cut down trees in the virgin forest or on the mountains, they recite some verses to the following effect: 'Be not uneasy, my friend, though we fell what we have been ordered to fell.' This they do in order not to draw down on themselves the hatred of the spirits who live in the trees, and who are apt to avenge themselves by visiting with grievous sickness such as injure them wantonly. The Basoga of Central Africa think that, when a tree is cut down, the angry spirit which inhabits it may cause the death of the chief and his family. To prevent this disaster they consult a medicine-man before they fell a tree. If the man of skill gives leave to proceed, the woodman first offers a fowl and a goat to the tree; then as soon as he has given the first blow with the axe, he applies his mouth to the cut and sucks some of the sap. In this way he forms a brotherhood with the tree, just as two men become blood-brothers by sucking each other's blood. After that he can cut down his tree-brother with impunity.

But the spirits of vegetation are not always treated with deference and respect. If fair words and kind treatment do not move them, stronger measures are sometimes resorted to. The durian-tree of the East Indies, whose smooth stem often shoots up to a height of eighty or ninety feet without sending out a branch, bears a fruit of the most delicious flavour and the most disgusting stench. The Malays cultivate the tree for the sake of its fruit, and have been known to resort to a peculiar ceremony for the purpose of stimulating its fertility. Near Jugra in Selangor there is a small grove of durian-trees, and on a specially chosen day the villagers used to assemble in it. Thereupon one of the local sorcerers would take a hatchet and deliver several shrewd blows on the trunk of the most barren of the trees, saying, 'Will you now bear fruit or not? If you do not, I shall fell you.' To

F

this the tree replied through the mouth of another man who had climbed a mangostin-tree hard by (the durian-tree being unclimbable), 'Yes, I will now bear fruit; I beg you not to fell me.' So in Japan to make trees bear fruit two men go into an orchard. One of them climbs up a tree and the other stands at the foot with an axe. The man with the axe asks the tree whether it will yield a good crop next year and threatens to cut it down if it does not. To this the man among the branches replies on behalf of the tree that it will bear abundantly. Odd as this mode of horticulture may seem to us, it has its exact parallels in Europe. On Christmas Eve many a South Slavonian and Bulgarian peasant swings an axe threateningly against a barren fruit-tree, while another man standing by intercedes for the menaced tree, saying, 'Do not cut it down; it will soon bear fruit.' Thrice the axe is swung, and thrice the impending blow is arrested at the entreaty of the intercessor. After that the frightened tree will certainly bear fruit next year.

The conception of trees and plants as animated beings naturally results in treating them as male and female, who can be married to each other in a real, and not merely a figurative or poetical, sense of the word. The notion is not purely fanciful, for plants like animals have their sexes and reproduce their kind by the union of the male and female elements. But whereas in all the higher animals the organs of the two sexes are regularly separated between different individuals, in most plants they exist together in every individual of the species. This rule, however, is by no means universal, and in many species the male plant is distinct from the female. The distinction appears to have been observed by some savages, for we are told that the Maoris 'are acquainted with the sex of trees, etc., and have distinct names for the male and female of some trees.' The ancients knew the difference between the male and the female date-palm, and fertilised them artificially by shaking the pollen of the male tree over the flowers of the female. The fertilisation took place in spring. Among the heathen of Harran the month during which the palms were fertilised bore the name of the Date Month, and at this time they celebrated the marriage festival of all the gods and goddesses. Different from this true and fruitful marriage of the palm are the false and barren marriages of plants which play a part in Hindoo superstition. For example, if a Hindoo has planted a grove of mangos, neither he nor his wife may taste of the fruit until he has formally married one of the trees, as a bridegroom, to a tree of a different sort, commonly a tamarind-tree, which grows near it in the grove. If there is no tamarind to act as bride, a jasmine will serve the turn. The expenses of such a marriage are often considerable, for the more Brahmans are feasted at it, the greater the glory of the owner of the grove. A family has been known to sell its golden and silver trinkets and to borrow all the money they could in order to marry a mango-tree to a jasmine with due pomp and ceremony. On Christmas Eve German peasants used to tie fruit-trees together with straw ropes to make them bear fruit, saying that the trees were thus married.

In the Moluccas, when the clove-trees are in blossom, they are treated like pregnant women. No noise may be made near them; no light or fire may be carried past them at night; no one may approach them with his hat on, all must uncover in their presence. These precautions are observed lest the tree should be alarmed and bear no fruit, or should drop its fruit too soon, like the untimely delivery of a woman who has been frightened in her pregnancy. So in the East the growing rice-crop is often treated with the same considerate regard as a breeding woman. Thus in Amboyna, when the rice is in bloom, the people say that it is pregnant and fire no guns and make no other noises near the field, for fear lest, if the rice were thus disturbed, it would miscarry, and the crop would be all straw and no grain.

Sometimes it is the souls of the dead which are believed to animate trees. The Dieri tribe of Central Australia regard as very sacred certain trees which are supposed to be their fathers transformed; hence they speak with reverence of these trees, and are careful that they shall not be cut down or burned. If the settlers require them to hew down the trees, they earnestly protest against it, asserting that were they to do so they would have no luck, and might be punished for not protecting their ancestors. Some of the Philippine Islanders believe that the souls of their ancestors are in certain trees, which they therefore spare. If they are obliged to fell one of these trees, they excuse themselves to it by saying that it was the priest who made them do it. The spirits take up their abode, by preference, in tall and stately trees with great spreading branches. When the wind rustles the leaves, the natives fancy it is the voice of the spirit; and they never pass near one of these trees without bowing respectfully and asking pardon of the spirit for disturbing his repose. Among the Ignorrotes, every village has its sacred tree, in which the souls of the dead forefathers of the hamlet reside. Offerings are made to the tree, and any injury done to it is believed to entail some misfortune on the village. Were the tree cut down, the village and all its inhabitants would inevitably perish.

In Corea the souls of people who die of the plague or by the roadside, and of women who expire in childbed, invariably take up their abode in trees. To such spirits offerings of cake, wine, and pork are made on heaps of stones piled under the trees. In China it has been customary from time immemorial to plant trees on graves in order thereby to strengthen the soul of the deceased and thus to save his body from corruption; and as the evergreen cypress and pine are deemed to be fuller of vitality than other trees, they have been chosen by preference for this purpose. Hence the trees that grow on graves are sometimes identified with the souls of the departed. Among the Miao-Kia, an aboriginal race of Southern and Western China, a sacred tree stands at the entrance of every village, and the inhabitants believe that it is tenanted by the soul of their first ancestor and that it rules their destiny. Sometimes there is a sacred grove near a village, where the trees are suffered to rot and die on the spot. Their fallen branches cumber the ground, and no one may remove them unless he has first asked leave of the spirit of the tree and offered him a sacrifice. Among the Maraves of Southern Africa the burial-ground is always regarded as a holy place where neither a tree may be felled nor a beast killed, because everything there is supposed to be tenanted by the souls of the dead.

In most, if not all, of these cases the spirit is viewed as incorporate in the tree; it animates the tree and must suffer and die with it. But, according to another and probably later opinion, the tree is not the body, but merely the abode of the tree-spirit, which can quit it and return to it at pleasure. The inhabitants of Siaoo, an East Indian island, believe in certain sylvan spirits who dwell in forests or in great solitary trees. At full moon the spirit comes forth from his lurking-place and roams about. He has a big head, very long arms and legs, and a ponderous body. In order to propitiate the wood-spirits people bring offerings of food, fowls, goats, and so forth to the places which they are supposed to haunt. The people of Nias think that, when a tree dies, its liberated spirit becomes a demon, which can kill a coco-nut palm by merely lighting on its branches, and can cause the death of all the children in a house by perching on one of the posts that support it. Further, they are of opinion that certain trees are at all times inhabited by roving demons who, if the trees were damaged, would be set free to go about on errands of mischief. Hence the people respect these trees, and are careful not to cut them down.

Not a few ceremonies observed at cutting down haunted trees are based on the belief that the spirits have it in their power to quit the trees at pleasure or in case of need. Thus when the Pelew Islanders are felling a tree, they conjure the spirit of the tree to leave it and settle on another. The wily negro of the Slave Coast, who wishes to fell an *ashorin* tree, but knows that he cannot do it so long as the spirit remains in the tree, places a little palm-oil on the ground as a bait, and then, when the unsuspecting spirit has quitted the tree to partake of this dainty, hastens to cut down its late abode. When the Toboongkoos of Celebes are about to clear a piece of forest in order to plant rice, they build a tiny house and furnish it with tiny clothes and some food and gold. Then they call together all the spirits of the wood, offer them the little house with its contents, and beseech them to quit the spot. After that they may safely cut down the wood without fearing to wound themselves in so doing. Before the Tomori, another tribe of Celebes, fell a tall tree they lay a quid of betel at its foot, and invite the spirit who dwells in the tree to change his lodging; moreover, they set a little ladder against the trunk to enable him to descend with safety and comfort. The Mandelings of Sumatra endeavour to lay the blame of all such misdeeds at the door of the Dutch authorities. Thus when a man is cutting a road through a forest and has to fell a tall tree which blocks the way, he will not begin to ply his axe until he has said: 'Spirit who lodgest in this tree, take it not ill that I cut down thy dwelling, for it is done at no wish of mine but by order of the Controller.' And when he wishes to clear a piece of forest-land for cultivation, it is necessary that he should come to a satisfactory understanding with the

woodland spirits who live there before he lays low their leafy
dwellings. For this purpose he goes to the middle of the plot of
ground, stoops down, and pretends to pick up a letter. Then
unfolding a bit of paper he reads aloud an imaginary letter from
the Dutch Government, in which he is strictly enjoined to set
about clearing the land without delay. Having done so, he says:
'You hear that, spirits. I must begin clearing at once, or I shall
be hanged.'

Even when a tree has been felled, sawn into planks, and used
to build a house, it is possible that the woodland spirit may still
be lurking in the timber, and accordingly some people seek to
propitiate him before or after they occupy the new house. Hence,
when a new dwelling is ready the Toradjas of Celebes kill a goat,
a pig, or a buffalo, and smear all the woodwork with its blood.
If the building is a *lobo* or spirit-house, a fowl or a dog is killed
on the ridge of the roof, and its blood allowed to flow down on
both sides. The ruder Tonapoo in such a case sacrifice a human
being on the roof. This sacrifice on the roof of a *lobo* or temple
serves the same purpose as the smearing of blood on the woodwork of an ordinary house. The intention is to propitiate the
forest-spirits who may still be in the timber; they are thus put in
good humour and will do the inmates of the house no harm. For
a like reason people in Celebes and the Moluccas are much afraid
of planting a post upside down at the building of a house; for the
forest-spirit, who might still be in the timber, would very naturally
resent the indignity and visit the inmates with sickness. The
Kayans of Borneo are of opinion that tree-spirits stand very stiffly
on the point of honour and visit men with their displeasure for
any injury done to them. Hence after building a house, whereby
they have been forced to ill-treat many trees, these people observe
a period of penance for a year, during which they must abstain
from many things, such as the killing of bears, tiger-cats, and
serpents.

§ 2. *Beneficent Powers of Tree-Spirits.* — When a tree comes to
be viewed, no longer as the body of the tree-spirit, but simply as
its abode which it can quit at pleasure, an important advance has
been made in religious thought. Animism is passing into poly-
theism. In other words, instead of regarding each tree as a living
and conscious being, man now sees in it merely a lifeless, inert

mass, tenanted for a longer or shorter time by a supernatural being who, as he can pass freely from tree to tree, thereby enjoys a certain right of possession or lordship over the trees, and, ceasing to be a tree-soul, becomes a forest god. As soon as the tree-spirit is thus in a measure disengaged from each particular tree, he begins to change his shape and assume the body of a man, in virtue of a general tendency of early thought to clothe all abstract spiritual beings in concrete human form. Hence in classical art the sylvan deities are depicted in human shape, their woodland character being denoted by a branch or some equally obvious symbol. But this change of shape does not affect the essential character of the tree-spirit. The powers which he exercised as a tree-soul incorporate in a tree, he still continues to wield as a god of trees. This I shall now attempt to prove in detail. I shall show, first, that trees considered as animate beings are credited with the power of making the rain to fall, the sun to shine, flocks and herds to multiply, and women to bring forth easily; and, second, that the very same powers are attributed to tree-gods conceived as anthropomorphic beings or as actually incarnate in living men.

First, then, trees or tree-spirits are believed to give rain and sunshine. When the missionary Jerome of Prague was persuading the heathen Lithuanians to fell their sacred groves, a multitude of women besought the Prince of Lithuania to stop him, saying that with the woods he was destroying the house of god from which they had been wont to get rain and sunshine. The Mundaris in Assam think that if a tree in the sacred grove is felled the sylvan gods evince their displeasure by withholding rain. In order to procure rain the inhabitants of Monyo, a village in the Sagaing district of Upper Burma, chose the largest tamarind-tree near the village and named it the haunt of the spirit (*nat*) who controls the rain. Then they offered bread, coco-nuts, plantains, and fowls to the guardian spirit of the village and to the spirit who gives rain, and they prayed, 'O Lord *nat* have pity on us poor mortals, and stay not the rain. Inasmuch as our offering is given ungrudgingly, let the rain fall day and night.' Afterwards libations were made in honour of the spirit of the tamarind-tree; and still later three elderly women, dressed in fine clothes and wearing necklaces and earrings, sang the Rain Song.

Again, tree-spirits make the crops to grow. Amongst the Mundaris every village has its sacred grove, and 'the grove deities are held responsible for the crops, and are especially honoured at all the great agricultural festivals.' The negroes of the Gold Coast are in the habit of sacrificing at the foot of certain tall trees, and they think that if one of these were felled all the fruits of the earth would perish. The Gallas dance in couples round sacred trees, praying for a good harvest. Every couple consists of a man and woman, who are linked together by a stick, of which each holds one end. Under their arms they carry green corn or grass. Swedish peasants stick a leafy branch in each furrow of their corn-fields, believing that this will ensure an abundant crop. The same idea comes out in the German and French custom of the Harvest-May. This is a large branch or a whole tree, which is decked with ears of corn, brought home on the last waggon from the harvest-field, and fastened on the roof of the farmhouse or of the barn, where it remains for a year. Mannhardt has proved that this branch or tree embodies the tree-spirit conceived as the spirit of vegetation in general, whose vivifying and fructifying influence is thus brought to bear upon the corn in particular. Hence in Swabia the Harvest-May is fastened amongst the last stalks of corn left standing on the field; in other places it is planted on the corn-field and the last sheaf cut is attached to its trunk.

Again, the tree-spirit makes the herds to multiply and blesses women with offspring. In Northern India the *Emblica officinalis* is a sacred tree. On the eleventh of the month Phalgun (February) libations are poured at the foot of the tree, a red or yellow string is bound about the trunk, and prayers are offered to it for the fruitfulness of women, animals, and crops. Again, in Northern India the coco-nut is esteemed one of the most sacred fruits, and is called Sriphala, or the fruit of Sri, the goddess of prosperity. It is the symbol of fertility, and all through Upper India is kept in shrines and presented by the priests to women who desire to become mothers. In the town of Qua, near Old Calabar, there used to grow a palm-tree which ensured conception to any barren woman who ate a nut from its branches. In Europe the May-tree or May-pole is apparently supposed to possess similar powers over both women and cattle. Thus in some parts of Germany on the first of May the peasants set up May-trees or May-bushes at the doors of stables and byres, one for each horse and cow; this is thought to make the cows yield much milk. Of the Irish we are told that 'they fancy a green bough of a tree, fastened on May-day against the house, will produce plenty of milk that summer.'

On the second of July some of the Wends used to set up an oak-tree in the middle of the village with an iron cock fastened to its top; then they danced round it, and drove the cattle round it to make them thrive. The Circassians regard the pear-tree as the protector of cattle. So they cut down a young pear-tree in the forest, branch it, and carry it home, where it is adored as a divinity. Almost every house has one such pear-tree. In autumn, on the day of the festival, the tree is carried into the house with great ceremony to the sound of music and amid the joyous cries of all the inmates, who compliment it on its fortunate arrival. It is covered with candles, and a cheese is fastened to its top. Round about it they eat, drink, and sing. Then they bid the tree good-bye and take it back to the courtyard, where it remains for the rest of the year, set up against the wall, without receiving any mark of respect.

In the Tuhoe tribe of Maoris 'the power of making women fruitful is ascribed to trees. These trees are associated with the navel-strings of definite mythical ancestors, as indeed the navel-strings of all children used to be hung upon them down to quite recent times. A barren woman had to embrace such a tree with her arms, and she received a male or a female child according as she embraced the east or the west side.' The common European custom of placing a green bush on May Day before or on the house of a beloved maiden probably originated in the belief of the fertilising power of the tree-spirit. In some parts of Bavaria such bushes are set up also at the houses of newly-married pairs, and the practice is only omitted if the wife is near her confinement; for in that case they say that the husband has 'set up a May-bush for himself.' Among the South Slavonians a barren woman, who desires to have a child, places a new chemise upon a fruitful tree on the eve of St. George's Day. Next morning before sunrise she examines the garment, and if she finds that some living creature has crept on it, she hopes that her wish will be fulfilled within the year. Then she puts on the chemise, confident that she will be as fruitful as the tree on which the garment has passed the night. Among the Kara-Kirghiz barren women roll themselves on the ground under a solitary apple-tree in order to obtain offspring. Lastly, the power of granting to women an easy delivery at child-birth is ascribed to trees both in Sweden and Africa. In some districts of Sweden there was formerly a *bårdträd* or guardian-tree (lime, ash, or elm) in the neighbourhood of every farm. No one would pluck a single leaf of the sacred tree, any injury to which was punished by ill-luck or sickness. Pregnant women used to clasp the tree in their arms in order to ensure an easy delivery. In some negro tribes of the Congo region pregnant women make themselves garments out of the bark of a certain sacred tree, because they believe that this tree delivers them from the dangers that attend child-bearing. The story that Leto clasped a palm-tree and an olive-tree or two laurel-trees, when she was about to give birth to the divine twins Apollo and Artemis, perhaps points to a similar Greek belief in the efficacy of certain trees to facilitate delivery.

CHAPTER X

RELICS OF TREE-WORSHIP IN MODERN EUROPE

FROM the foregoing review of the beneficent qualities commonly ascribed to tree-spirits, it is easy to understand why customs like the May-tree or May-pole have prevailed so widely and figured so prominently in the popular festivals of European peasants. In spring or early summer or even on Midsummer Day, it was and still is in many parts of Europe the custom to go out to the woods, cut down a tree and bring it into the village, where it is set up amid general rejoicings; or the people cut branches in the woods, and fasten them on every house. The intention of these customs is to bring home to the village, and to each house, the blessings which the tree-spirit has in its power to bestow. Hence the custom in some places of planting a May-tree before every house, or of carrying the village May-tree from door to door, that every household may receive its share of the blessing. Out of the mass of evidence on this subject a few examples may be selected.

Sir Henry Piers, in his *Description of Westmeath*, writing in

1682 says: 'On May-eve, every family sets up before their door a green bush, strewed over with yellow flowers, which the meadows yield plentifully. In countries where timber is plentiful, they erect tall slender trees, which stand high, and they continue almost the whole year; so as a stranger would go nigh to imagine that they were all signs of ale-sellers, and that all houses were ale-houses.' In Northamptonshire a young tree ten or twelve feet high used to be planted before each house on May Day so as to appear growing; flowers were thrown over it and strewn about the door. 'Among ancient customs still retained by the Cornish, may be reckoned that of decking their doors and porches on the first of May with green boughs of sycamore and hawthorn, and of planting trees, or rather stumps of trees, before their houses.' In the north of England it was formerly the custom for young people to rise a little after midnight on the morning of the first of May, and go out with music and the blowing of horns into the woods, where they broke branches and adorned them with nosegays and crowns of flowers. This done, they returned about sunrise and fastened the flower-decked branches over the doors and windows of their houses. At Abingdon in Berkshire young people formerly went about in groups on May morning, singing a carol of which the following are two of the verses:

' *We've been rambling all the night,*   *A garland gay we bring you here;*
   And sometime of this day;   *And at your door we stand;*
And now returning back again,   *It is a sprout well budded out,*
   We bring a garland gay.   *The work of our Lord's hand.*'

At the towns of Saffron Walden and Debden in Essex on the first of May little girls go about in parties from door to door singing a song almost identical with the above and carrying garlands; a doll dressed in white is usually placed in the middle of each garland. Similar customs have been and indeed are still observed in various parts of England. The garlands are generally in the form of hoops intersecting each other at right angles. It appears that a hoop wreathed with rowan and marsh marigold, and bearing suspended within it two balls, is still carried on May Day by villagers in some parts of Ireland. The balls, which are sometimes covered with gold and silver paper, are said to have originally represented the sun and moon.

In some villages of the Vosges Mountains on the first Sunday of May young girls go in bands from house to house, singing a song in praise of May, in which mention is made of the 'bread and meal that come in May.' If money is given them, they fasten a green bough to the door; if it is refused, they wish the family many children and no bread to feed them. In the French department of Mayenne, boys who bore the name of *Maillotins* used to go about from farm to farm on the first of May singing carols, for which they received money or a drink; they planted a small tree or a branch of a tree. Near Saverne in Alsace bands of people go about carrying May-trees. Amongst them is a man dressed in a white shirt with his face blackened; in front of him is carried a large May-tree, but each member of the band also carries a smaller one. One of the company bears a huge basket, in which he collects eggs, bacon, and so forth.

On the Thursday before Whitsunday the Russian villagers 'go out into the woods, sing songs, weave garlands, and cut down a young birch-tree, which they dress up in woman's clothes, or adorn with many-coloured shreds and ribbons. After that comes a feast, at the end of which they take the dressed-up birch-tree, carry it home to their village with joyful dance and song, and set it up in one of the houses, where it remains as an honoured guest till Whitsunday. On the two intervening days they pay visits to the house where their "guest" is; but on the third day, Whitsunday, they take her to a stream and fling her into its waters,' throwing their garlands after her. In this Russian custom the dressing of the birch in woman's clothes shows how clearly the tree is personified; and the throwing it into a stream is most probably a rain-charm.

In some parts of Sweden on the eve of May Day lads go about carrying each a bunch of fresh birch twigs wholly or partly in leaf. With the village fiddler at their head, they make the round of the houses singing May songs; the burden of their songs is a prayer for fine weather, a plentiful harvest, and worldly and spiritual blessings. One of them carries a basket in which he collects gifts of eggs and the like. If they are well received, they stick a leafy twig in the roof over the cottage door. But in Sweden midsummer is the season when these ceremonies are chiefly observed. On the Eve of St. John (the twenty-third of June) the houses are thoroughly cleansed and garnished with green boughs and flowers. Young fir-trees are raised at the doorway and elsewhere about the homestead; and very often small umbrageous arbours are constructed in the garden. In Stockholm on this day a leaf-market is held at which thousands of May-poles (*Maj Stånger*), from six inches to twelve feet high, decorated with leaves, flowers, slips of coloured paper, gilt egg-shells strung on reeds, and so on, are exposed for sale. Bonfires are lit on the hills, and the people dance round them and jump over them. But the chief event of the day is setting up the May-pole. This consists of a straight and tall spruce-pine tree, stripped of its branches. 'At times hoops and at others pieces of wood, placed crosswise, are attached to it at intervals; whilst at others it is provided with bows, representing, so to say, a man with his arms akimbo. From top to bottom not only the "Maj Stäng" (Maypole) itself, but the hoops, bows, etc., are ornamented with leaves, flowers, slips of various cloth, gilt egg-shells, etc.; and on the top of it is a large vane, or it may be a flag.' The raising of the May-pole, the decoration of which is done by the village maidens, is an affair of much ceremony; the people flock to it from all quarters, and dance round it in a great ring. Midsummer customs of the same sort used to be observed in some parts of Germany. Thus in the towns of the Upper Harz Mountains tall fir-trees, with the bark peeled off their lower trunks, were set up in open places and decked with flowers and eggs, which were painted yellow and red. Round these trees the young folk danced by day and the old folk in the evening. In some parts of Bohemia also a May-pole or midsummer-tree is erected on St. John's Eve. The lads fetch a tall fir or pine from the wood and set it up on a height, where the girls deck it with nosegays, garlands, and red ribbons. It is afterwards burned.

It would be needless to illustrate at length the custom, which has prevailed in various parts of Europe, such as England, France, and Germany, of setting up a village May-tree or May-pole on May Day. A few examples will suffice. The puritanical writer Phillip Stubbes in his *Anatomie of Abuses*, first published at London in 1583, has described with manifest disgust how they used to bring in the May-pole in the days of good Queen Bess. His description affords us a vivid glimpse of merry England in the olden time. 'Against May, Whitsonday, or other time, all the yung men and maides, olde men and wives, run gadding over night to the woods, groves, hils, and mountains, where they spend all the night in plesant pastimes; and in the morning they return, bringing with them birch and branches of trees, to deck their assemblies withall. And no mervaile, for there is a great Lord present among them, as superintendent and Lord over their pastimes and sportes, namely, Sathan, prince of hel. But the chiefest jewel they bring from thence is their May-pole, which they bring home with great veneration, as thus. They have twentie or fortie yoke of oxen, every oxe having a sweet nose-gay of flouers placed on the tip of his hornes, and these oxen drawe home this May-pole (this stinkyng ydol, rather), which is covered all over with floures and hearbs, bound round about with strings, from the top to the bottome, and sometime painted with variable colours, with two or three hundred men, women and children following it with great devotion. And thus beeing reared up, with handkercheefs and flags hovering on the top, they straw the ground rounde about, binde green boughes about it, set up sommer haules, bowers, and arbors hard by it. And then fall they to daunce about it, like as the heathen people did at the dedication of the Idols, whereof this is a perfect pattern, or rather the thing itself. I have heard it credibly reported (and that *viva voce*) by men of great gravitie and reputation, that of fortie, threescore, or a hundred maides going to the wood over night, there have scaresly the third part of them returned home againe undefiled.'

In Swabia on the first of May a tall fir-tree used to be fetched into the village, where it was decked with ribbons and set up; then the people danced round it merrily to music. The tree stood on the village green the whole year through, until a fresh tree was brought in next May Day. In Saxony 'people were not content with bringing the summer symbolically (as king or queen) into the village; they brought the fresh green itself from the woods even into the houses: that is the May or Whitsuntide trees, which are mentioned in documents from the thirteenth century onwards. The fetching in of the May-tree was also a festival. The people went out into the woods to seek the May (*majum quaerere*), brought young trees, especially firs and birches, to the village and set them up before the doors of the houses or of the cattle-stalls or in the rooms. Young fellows erected such May-trees, as we have already said, before the chambers of their sweethearts. Besides these household Mays, a great May-tree or May-pole, which had also been brought in solemn procession to the village, was set up in the middle of the village or in the market-place of the town. It had been chosen by the whole community, who watched over it most carefully. Generally the tree was stripped of its branches and leaves, nothing but the crown being left, on which were displayed, in addition to many-coloured ribbons and cloths, a variety of victuals such as sausages, cakes, and eggs. The young folk exerted themselves to obtain these prizes. In the greasy poles which are still to be seen at our fairs we have a relic of these old May-poles. Not uncommonly there was a race on foot or on horseback to the May-tree — a Whitsunday pastime which in course of time has been divested of its goal and survives as a popular custom to this day in many parts of Germany.' At Bordeaux on the first of May the boys of each street used to erect in it a May-pole, which they adorned with garlands and a great crown; and every evening during the whole of the month the young people of both sexes danced singing about the pole. Down to the present day May-trees decked with flowers and ribbons are set up on May Day in every village and hamlet of gay Provence. Under them the young folk make merry and the old folk rest.

In all these cases, apparently, the custom is or was to bring in a new May-tree each year. However, in England the village May-pole seems as a rule, at least in later times, to have been permanent, not renewed annually. Villages of Upper Bavaria renew their May-pole once every three, four, or five years. It is a fir-tree fetched from the forest, and amid all the wreaths, flags, and inscriptions with which it is bedecked, an essential part is the bunch of dark green foliage left at the top 'as a memento that in it we have to do, not with a dead pole, but with a living tree from the greenwood.' We can hardly doubt that originally the practice everywhere was to set up a new May-tree every year. As the object of the custom was to bring in the fructifying spirit of vegetation, newly awakened in spring, the end would have been defeated if, instead of a living tree, green and sappy, an old withered one had been erected year after year or allowed to stand permanently. When, however, the meaning of the custom had been forgotten, and the May-tree was regarded simply as a centre for holiday merry-making, people saw no reason for felling a fresh tree every year, and preferred to let the same tree stand permanently, only decking it with fresh flowers on May Day. But even when the May-pole had thus become a fixture, the need of giving it the appearance of being a green tree, not a dead pole, was sometimes felt. Thus at Weverham in Cheshire, 'are two May-poles, which are decorated on this day (May Day) with all due attention to the ancient solemnity; the sides are hung with garlands, and the top terminated by a birch or other tall slender tree with its leaves on; the bark being peeled, and the stem spliced to the pole, so as to give the appearance of one tree from the summit.' Thus the renewal of the May-tree is like the renewal of the Harvest-May; each is intended to secure a fresh portion of the fertilising spirit of vegetation, and to preserve it throughout the year. But whereas the efficacy of the Harvest-May is restricted to promoting the growth of the crops, that of the May-tree or May-branch extends also, as we have seen, to women and cattle. Lastly, it is worth noting that the old May-tree is sometimes burned at the end of the year. Thus in the district of Prague young people break pieces of the public May-tree and place them behind the holy pictures in their rooms, where they remain till next May Day, and are then burned on the hearth. In Würtemberg the bushes which are set up on the houses on Palm Sunday are sometimes left there for a year and then burnt.

So much for the tree-spirit conceived as incorporate or immanent in the tree. We have now to show that the tree-spirit is often conceived and represented as detached from the tree and clothed in human form, and even as embodied in living men and women. The evidence for this anthropomorphic representation of the tree-spirit is largely to be found in the popular customs of European peasantry.

There is an instructive class of cases in which the tree-spirit is represented simultaneously in vegetable form and in human form, which are set side by side as if for the express purpose of explaining each other. In these cases the human representative of the tree-spirit is sometimes a doll or puppet, sometimes a living person, but whether a puppet or a person, it is placed beside a tree or bough; so that together the person or puppet, and the tree or bough, form a sort of bilingual inscription, the one being, so to speak, a translation of the other. Here, therefore, there is no room left for doubt that the spirit of the tree is actually represented in human form. Thus in Bohemia, on the fourth Sunday in Lent, young people throw a puppet called Death into the water; then the girls go into the wood, cut down a young tree, and fasten to it a puppet dressed in white clothes to look like a woman; with this tree and puppet they go from house to house collecting gratuities and singing songs with the refrain:

> '*We carry Death out of the village,*
> *We bring Summer into the village.*'

Here, as we shall see later on, the 'Summer' is the spirit of vegetation returning or reviving in spring. In some parts of our own country children go about asking for pence with some small imitations of May-poles, and with a finely-dressed doll which they call the Lady of the May. In these cases the tree and the puppet are obviously regarded as equivalent.

At Thann, in Alsace, a girl called the Little May Rose, dressed in white, carries a small May-tree, which is gay with garlands and ribbons. Her companions collect gifts from door to door, singing a song:

> '*Little May Rose turn round three times,*
> *Let us look at you round and round!*
> *Rose of the May, come to the greenwood away,*
> *We will be merry all.*
> *So we go from the May to the roses.*'

In the course of the song a wish is expressed that those who give nothing may lose their fowls by the marten, that their vine may bear no clusters, their tree no nuts, their field no corn; the produce of the year is supposed to depend on the gifts offered to these May singers. Here and in the cases mentioned above, where children go about with green boughs or garlands on May Day singing and collecting money, the meaning is that with the spirit of vegetation they bring plenty and good luck to the house, and they expect to be paid for the service. In Russian Lithuania on the first of May, they used to set up a green tree before the village. Then the rustic swains chose the prettiest girl, crowned her, swathed her in birch branches and set her beside the May-tree, where they danced, sang, and shouted 'O May! O May!' In Brie (Isle de France) a May-tree is erected in the midst of the village; its top is crowned with flowers; lower down it is twined with leaves and twigs, still lower with huge green branches. The girls dance round it, and at the same time a lad wrapt in leaves and called Father May is led about. In the small towns of the Franken Wald mountains in Northern Bavaria, on the second of May, a *Walber* tree is erected before a tavern, and a man dances round it, enveloped in straw from head to foot in such a way that the ears of corn unite above his head to form a crown. He is called the *Walber*, and used to be led in procession through the streets, which were adorned with sprigs of birch.

Amongst the Slavs of Carinthia, on St. George's Day (the twenty-third of April), the young people deck with flowers and garlands a tree which has been felled on the eve of the festival. The tree is then carried in procession, accompanied with music and joyful acclamations, the chief figure in the procession being the Green George, a young fellow clad from head to foot in green birch branches. At the close of the ceremonies the Green George, that is an effigy of him, is thrown into the water. It is the aim of the lad who acts Green George to step out of his leafy envelope and substitute the effigy so adroitly that no one shall perceive the change. In many places, however, the lad himself who plays the part of Green George, is ducked in a river or pond, with the express intention of thus ensuring rain to make the fields and meadows green in summer. In some places the cattle are crowned and driven from their stalls to the accompaniment of a song:

> '*Green George we bring,*
> *Green George we accompany,*
> *May he feed our herds well.*
> *If not, to the water with him.*'

Here we see that the same powers of making rain and fostering the cattle, which are ascribed to the tree-spirit regarded as incorporate in the tree, are also attributed to the tree-spirit represented by a living man.

Among the gypsies of Transylvania and Roumania the festival of Green George is the chief celebration of spring. Some of them keep it on Easter Monday, others on St. George's Day (the twenty-third of April). On the eve of the festival a young willow tree is cut down, adorned with garlands and leaves, and set up in the ground. Women with child place one of their garments under the tree, and leave it there over night; if next morning they find a leaf of the tree lying on the garment, they know that their delivery will be easy. Sick and old people go to the tree in the evening, spit on it thrice, and say, 'You will soon die, but let us live.' Next morning the gypsies gather about the willow. The chief figure of the festival is Green George, a lad who is concealed from top to toe in green leaves and blossoms. He throws a few handfuls of grass to the beasts of the tribe, in order that they may have no lack of fodder throughout the year. Then he takes three iron nails, which have lain for three days and nights in water, and knocks them into the willow; after which he pulls them out and flings them into a running stream to propitiate the water-spirits. Finally, a pretence is made of throwing Green George into the water, but in fact it is only a puppet made of branches and leaves which is ducked in the stream. In this version of the custom the powers of granting an easy delivery to women and of communicating vital energy to the sick and the old are clearly ascribed to the willow; while Green George, the human double of the tree, bestows food on the cattle, and further ensures the favour of the water-spirits by putting them in indirect communication with the tree.

Without citing more examples to the same effect, we may sum up the results of the preceding pages in the words of Mannhardt: 'The customs quoted suffice to establish with certainty the conclusion that in these spring processions the spirit of vegetation is often represented both by the May-tree and in addition by a man dressed in green leaves or flowers or by a girl similarly adorned. It is the same spirit which animates the tree and is active in the inferior plants and which we have recognised in the May-tree and the Harvest-May. Quite consistently the spirit is also supposed to manifest his presence in the first flower of spring and reveals himself both in a girl representing a May-rose, and also, as giver of harvest, in the person of the *Walber*. The procession with this representative of the divinity was supposed to produce the same beneficial effects on the fowls, the fruit-trees, and the crops as the presence of the deity himself. In other words, the mummer was regarded not as an image but as an actual representative of the spirit of vegetation; hence the wish expressed by the attendants of the May-rose and the May-tree that those who refuse them gifts of eggs, bacon, and so forth, may have no share in the blessings which it is in the power of the itinerant spirit to bestow. We may conclude that these begging processions with May-trees or May-boughs from door to door ("bringing the May or the summer") had everywhere originally a serious and, so to speak, sacramental significance; people really believed that the god of growth was present unseen in the bough; by the procession he was brought to each house to bestow his blessing. The names May, Father May, May Lady, Queen of the May, by which the anthropomorphic spirit of vegetation is often denoted, show that the idea of the spirit of vegetation is blent with a personification of the season at which his powers are most strikingly manifested.'

So far we have seen that the tree-spirit or the spirit of vegetation in general is represented either in vegetable form alone, as by a tree, bough, or flower; or in vegetable and human form simultaneously, as by a tree, bough, or flower in combination with a puppet or a living person. It remains to show that the representation of him by a tree, bough, or flower is sometimes entirely dropped, while the representation of him by a living person remains. In this case the representative character of the person is generally marked by dressing him or her in leaves or flowers; sometimes, too, it is indicated by the name he or she bears.

Thus in some parts of Russia on St. George's Day (the twenty-third of April) a youth is dressed out, like our Jack-in-the-Green, with leaves and flowers. The Slovenes call him the Green George. Holding a lighted torch in one hand and a pie in the other, he goes out to the corn-fields, followed by girls singing appropriate songs. A circle of brushwood is next lighted, in the middle of which is set the pie. All who take part in the ceremony then sit down around the fire and divide the pie among them. In this custom the Green George dressed in leaves and flowers is plainly identical with the similarly disguised Green George who is associated with a tree in the Carinthian, Transylvanian, and Roumanian customs observed on the same day. Again, we saw that in Russia at Whitsuntide a birch-tree is dressed in woman's clothes and set up in the house. Clearly equivalent to this is the custom observed on Whit-Monday by Russian girls in the district of Pinsk. They choose the prettiest of their number, envelop her in a mass of foliage taken from the birch-trees and maples, and carry her about through the village.

In Ruhla as soon as the trees begin to grow green in spring, the children assemble on a Sunday and go out into the woods, where they choose one of their playmates to be the Little Leaf Man. They break branches from the trees and twine them about the child till only his shoes peep out from the leafy mantle. Holes are made in it for him to see through, and two of the children lead the Little Leaf Man that he may not stumble or fall. Singing and dancing they take him from house to house, asking for gifts of food such as eggs, cream, sausages, and cakes. Lastly, they sprinkle the Leaf Man with water and feast on the food they have collected. In the Fricktal, Switzerland, at Whitsuntide boys go out into a wood and swathe one of their number in leafy boughs. He is called the Whitsuntide-lout, and being mounted on horseback with a green branch in his hand he is led back into the village. At the village-well a halt is called and the leaf-clad lout is dismounted and ducked in the trough. Thereby he acquires the right of sprinkling water on everybody, and he exercises the right specially on girls and street urchins. The urchins march before him in bands begging him to give them a Whitsuntide wetting.

In England the best-known example of these leaf-clad mummers is the Jack-in-the-Green, a chimney-sweeper who walks encased in a pyramidal framework of wickerwork, which is covered with holly and ivy, and surmounted by a crown of flowers and ribbons. Thus arrayed he dances on May Day at the head of a troop of chimney-sweeps, who collect pence. In Fricktal a similar frame of basketwork is called the Whitsuntide Basket. As soon as the trees begin to bud, a spot is chosen in the wood, and here the village lads make the frame with all secrecy, lest others should forestall them. Leafy branches are twined round two hoops, one of which rests on the shoulders of the wearer, the other encircles his calves; holes are made for his eyes and mouth; and a large nosegay crowns the whole. In this guise he appears suddenly in the village at the hour of vespers, preceded by three boys blowing on horns made of willow bark. The great object of his supporters is to set up the Whitsuntide Basket on the village well, and to keep it and him there, despite the efforts of the lads from neighbouring villages, who seek to carry off the Whitsuntide Basket and set it up on their own well.

In the class of cases of which the foregoing are specimens it is obvious that the leaf-clad person who is led about is equivalent to the May-tree, May-bough, or May-doll, which is carried from house to house by children begging. Both are representatives of the beneficent spirit of vegetation, whose visit to the house is recompensed by a present of money or food.

Often the leaf-clad person who represents the spirit of vegetation is known as the king or the queen; thus, for example, he or she is called the May King, Whitsuntide King, Queen of May, and so on. These titles, as Mannhardt observes, imply that the spirit incorporate in vegetation is a ruler, whose creative power extends far and wide.

In a village near Salzwedel a May-tree is set up at Whitsuntide and the boys race to it; he who reaches it first is king; a garland of flowers is put round his neck and in his hand he carries a May-bush, with which, as the procession moves along, he sweeps away the dew. At each house they sing a song, wishing the inmates good luck, referring to the 'black cow in the stall milking white milk, black hen on the nest laying white eggs,' and begging a gift of eggs, bacon, and so on. At the village of Ellgoth in Silesia a ceremony called the King's Race is observed at Whitsuntide. A pole with a cloth tied to it is set up in a meadow, and the young men ride past it on horseback, each trying to snatch away the cloth as he gallops by. The one who succeeds in carrying it off and dipping it in the neighbouring Oder is proclaimed King. Here the pole is clearly a substitute for a May-tree. In some villages of Brunswick at Whitsuntide a May King is completely enveloped in a May-bush. In some parts of Thüringen also they have a May King at Whitsuntide, but he is dressed up rather differently. A frame of wood is made in which a man can stand; it is completely covered with birch boughs and is surmounted by a crown of birch and flowers, in which a bell is fastened. This frame is placed in the wood and the May King gets into it. The rest go out and look for him, and when they have found him they lead him back into the village to the magistrate, the clergyman, and others, who have to guess who is in the verdurous frame. If they guess wrong, the May King rings his bell by shaking his head, and a forfeit of beer or the like must be paid by the unsuccessful guesser. At Wahrstedt the boys at Whitsuntide choose by lot a king and a high-steward. The latter is completely concealed in a May-bush, wears a wooden crown wreathed with flowers, and carries a wooden sword. The king, on the other hand, is only distinguished by a nosegay in his cap, and a reed, with a red ribbon tied to it, in his hand. They beg for eggs from house to house, threatening that, where none are given, none will be laid by the hens throughout the year. In this custom the high-steward appears, for some reason, to have usurped the insignia of the king. At Hildesheim five or six young fellows go about on the afternoon of Whit-Monday cracking long whips in measured time and collecting eggs from the houses. The chief person of the band is the Leaf King, a lad swathed so completely in birchen twigs that nothing of him can be seen but his feet. A huge head-dress of birchen twigs adds to his apparent stature. In his hand he carries a long crook, with which he tries to catch stray dogs and children. In some parts of Bohemia on Whit-Monday the young fellows disguise themselves in tall caps of birch bark adorned with flowers. One of them is dressed as a king and dragged on a sledge to the village green, and if on the way they pass a pool the sledge is always overturned into it. Arrived at the green they gather round the king; the crier jumps on a stone or climbs up a tree and recites lampoons about each house and its inmates. Afterwards the disguises of bark are stripped off and they go about the village in holiday attire, carrying a May-tree and begging. Cakes, eggs, and corn are sometimes given them. At Grossvargula, near Langensalza, in the eighteenth century a Grass King used to be led about in procession at Whitsuntide. He was encased in a pyramid of poplar branches, the top of which was adorned with a royal crown of branches and flowers. He rode on horseback with the leafy pyramid over him, so that its lower end touched the ground, and an opening was left in it only for his face. Surrounded by a cavalcade of young fellows, he rode in procession to the town hall, the parsonage, and so on, where they all got a drink of beer. Then under the seven lindens of the neighbouring Sommerberg, the Grass King was stripped of his green casing; the crown was handed to the Mayor, and the branches were stuck in the flax fields in order to make the flax grow tall. In this last trait the fertilising influence ascribed to the representative of the tree-spirit comes out clearly. In the neighbourhood of Pilsen (Bohemia) a conical hut of green branches, without any door, is erected at Whitsuntide in the midst of the village. To this hut rides a troop of village lads with a king at their head. He wears a sword at his side and a sugar-loaf hat of rushes on his head. In his train are a judge, a crier, and a personage called the Frog-flayer or Hangman. The last is a sort of ragged merry-andrew, wearing a rusty old sword and bestriding a sorry hack. On reaching the hut the crier dismounts and goes round it looking for a door. Finding none, he says, 'Ah, this is perhaps an enchanted castle; the witches creep through the leaves and need no door.' At last he draws his sword and hews his way into the hut, where there is a chair, on which he seats himself and proceeds to criticise in rhyme the girls, farmers, and farm-servants of the neighbourhood. When this is over, the Frog-flayer steps forward and, after exhibiting a cage with frogs in it, sets up a gallows on which he hangs the frogs in a row. In the neighbourhood of Plas the ceremony differs in some points. The king and his soldiers are completely clad in bark, adorned with flowers and ribbons; they all carry swords and ride horses, which are gay with green branches and flowers. While the village dames and girls are being criticised at the arbour, a frog is secretly pinched and poked by the crier till it quacks. Sentence of death is passed on the frog by the king; the hangman beheads it and flings the bleeding body among the spectators. Lastly, the king is driven from the hut and pursued by the soldiers. The pinching and beheading of the frog are doubtless, as Mannhardt observes, a rain-charm. We have seen that some Indians of the Orinoco beat frogs for the express purpose of producing rain, and that killing a frog is a European rain-charm.

Often the spirit of vegetation in spring is represented by a queen instead of a king. In the neighbourhood of Libchowic (Bohemia), on the fourth Sunday in Lent, girls dressed in white and wearing the first spring flowers, as violets and daisies, in their hair, lead about the village a girl who is called the Queen and is crowned with flowers. During the procession, which is conducted with great solemnity, none of the girls may stand still, but must keep whirling round continually and singing. In every house the Queen announces the arrival of spring and wishes the inmates good luck and blessings, for which she receives presents. In German Hungary the girls choose the prettiest girl to be their Whitsuntide Queen, fasten a towering wreath on her brow, and carry her singing through the streets. At every house they stop, sing old ballads, and receive presents. In the south-east of Ireland on May Day the prettiest girl used to be chosen Queen of the district for twelve months. She was crowned with wild flowers; feasting, dancing, and rustic sports followed, and were closed by a grand procession in the evening. During her year of office she presided over rural gatherings of young people at dances and merry-makings. If she married before next May Day, her authority was at an end, but her successor was not elected till that day came round. The May Queen is common in France and familiar in England.

Again the spirit of vegetation is sometimes represented by a king and queen, a lord and lady, or a bridegroom and bride. Here again the parallelism holds between the anthropomorphic and the vegetable representation of the tree-spirit, for we have seen above that trees are sometimes married to each other. At Halford in south Warwickshire the children go from house to house on May Day, walking two and two in procession and headed by a king and queen. Two boys carry a May-pole some six or seven feet high, which is covered with flowers and greenery. Fastened to it near the top are two cross-bars at right angles to each other. These are also decked with flowers, and from the ends of the bars hang hoops similarly adorned. At the houses the children sing May songs and receive money, which is used to provide tea for them at the schoolhouse in the afternoon. In a Bohemian village near Königgrätz on Whit-Monday the children play the king's game, at which a king and queen march about under a canopy, the queen wearing a garland, and the youngest girl carrying two wreaths on a plate behind them. They are attended by boys and girls called groomsmen and bridesmaids, and they go from house to house collecting gifts. A regular feature in the popular celebration of Whitsuntide in Silesia used to be, and to some extent still is, the contest for the kingship. The contest took various forms, but the mark or goal was generally the May-tree or May-pole. Sometimes the youth who succeeded in climbing the smooth pole and bringing down the prize was proclaimed the Whitsuntide King and his sweetheart the Whitsuntide Bride. Afterwards the king, carrying the May-bush, repaired with the rest of the company to the alehouse, where a dance and a feast ended the merry-making. Often the young farmers and labourers raced on horseback to the May-pole, which was adorned with flowers, ribbons, and a crown. He who first reached the pole was the Whitsuntide King, and the rest had to obey his orders for that day. The worst rider became the clown. At the May-tree all dismounted and hoisted the king on their shoulders. He nimbly swarmed up the pole and brought down the May-bush and the crown, which had been fastened to the top. Meantime the clown hurried to the alehouse and proceeded to bolt thirty rolls of bread and to swig four quart bottles of brandy with the utmost possible despatch. He was followed by the king, who bore the May-bush and crown at the head of the company. If on their arrival the clown had already disposed of the rolls and the brandy, and greeted the king with a speech and a glass of beer, his score was paid by the king; otherwise he had to settle it himself. After church time the stately procession wound through the village. At the head of it rode the king, decked with flowers and carrying the May-bush. Next came the clown with his clothes turned inside out, a great flaxen beard on his chin, and the Whitsuntide crown on his head. Two riders disguised as guards followed. The procession drew up before every farmyard; the two guards dismounted, shut the clown into the house, and claimed a contribution from the housewife to buy soap with which to wash the clown's beard. Custom allowed them to carry off any victuals which were not under lock and key. Last of all they came to the house in which the king's sweetheart lived. She was greeted as Whitsuntide Queen and received suitable presents — to wit, a many-coloured sash, a cloth, and an apron. The king got as a prize, a vest, a neckcloth, and so forth, and had the right of setting up the May-bush or Whitsuntide-tree before his master's yard, where it remained as an honourable token till the same day next year. Finally the procession took its way to the tavern, where the king and queen opened the dance. Sometimes the Whitsuntide King and Queen succeeded to office in a different way. A man of straw, as large as life and crowned with a red cap, was conveyed in a cart, between two men armed and disguised as guards, to a place where a mock court was waiting to try him. A great crowd followed the cart. After a formal trial the straw man was condemned to death and fastened to a stake on the execution ground. The young men with bandaged eyes tried to stab him with a spear. He who succeeded became king and his sweetheart queen. The straw man was known as the Goliath.

In a parish of Denmark it used to be the custom at Whitsuntide to dress up a little girl as the Whitsun-bride and a little boy as her groom. She was decked in all the finery of a grown-up bride, and wore a crown of the freshest flowers of spring on her head. Her groom was as gay as flowers, ribbons and knots could make him. The other children adorned themselves as best they could with the yellow flowers of the trollius and caltha. Then they went in great state from farmhouse to farmhouse, two little girls walking at the head of the procession as bridesmaids, and six or eight outriders galloping ahead on hobby-horses to announce their coming. Contributions of eggs, butter, loaves, cream, coffee, sugar, and tallow-candles were received and conveyed away in baskets. When they had made the round of the farms, some of the farmers' wives helped to arrange the wedding feast, and the children danced merrily in clogs on the stamped clay floor till the sun rose and the birds began to sing. All this is now a thing of the past. Only the old folks still remember the little Whitsun-bride and her mimic pomp.

We have seen that in Sweden the ceremonies associated elsewhere with May Day or Whitsuntide commonly take place at Midsummer. Accordingly we find that in some parts of the Swedish province of Blekinge they still choose a Midsummer's Bride, to whom the 'church coronet' is occasionally lent. The girl selects for herself a Bridegroom, and a collection is made for the pair, who for the time being are looked on as man and wife. The other youths also choose each his bride. A similar ceremony seems to be still kept up in Norway.

In the neighbourhood of Briançon (Dauphiné) on May Day the lads wrap up in green leaves a young fellow whose sweetheart has deserted him or married another. He lies down on the ground and feigns to be asleep. Then a girl who likes him, and would marry him, comes and wakes him, and raising him up offers him her arm and a flag. So they go to the alehouse, where the pair lead off the dancing. But they must marry within the year, or they are treated as old bachelor and old maid, and are debarred the company of the young folk. The lad is called the Bridegroom of the month of May. In the alehouse he puts off his garment of leaves, out of which, mixed with flowers, his partner in the dance makes a nosegay, and wears it at her breast next day, when she leads her again to the alehouse. Like this is a Russian custom observed in the district of Nerechta on the Thursday before Whitsunday. The girls go out into a birch-wood, wind a girdle or band round a stately birch, twist its lower branches into a wreath, and kiss each other in pairs through the wreath. The girls who kiss through the wreath call each other gossips. Then one of the girls steps forward, and mimicking a drunken man, flings herself on the ground, rolls on the grass, and feigns to fall fast asleep. Another girl wakens the pretended sleeper and kisses him; then the whole bevy trips singing through the wood to twine garlands, which they throw into the water. In the fate of the garlands floating on the stream they read their own. Here the part of the sleeper was probably at one time played by a lad. In these French and Russian customs we have a forsaken bridegroom, in the following a forsaken bride. On Shrove Tuesday the Slovenes of Oberkrain drag a straw puppet with joyous cries up and down the village; then they throw it into the water or burn it, and from the height of the flames they judge of the abundance of the next harvest. The noisy crew is followed by a female masker, who drags a great board by a string and gives out that she is a forsaken bride.

Viewed in the light of what has gone before, the awakening of the forsaken sleeper in these ceremonies probably represents the revival of vegetation in spring. But it is not easy to assign their respective parts to the forsaken bridegroom and to the girl who wakes him from his slumber. Is the sleeper the leafless forest or the bare earth of winter? Is the girl who wakens him the fresh verdure or the genial sunshine of spring? It is hardly possible, on the evidence before us, to answer these questions.

In the Highlands of Scotland the revival of vegetation in spring used to be graphically represented on St. Bride's Day, the first of February. Thus in the Hebrides 'the mistress and servants of each family take a sheaf of oats, and dress it up in women's apparel, put it in a large basket, and lay a wooden club by it, and this they call Briid's bed; and then the mistress and servants cry three times "Briid is come, Briid is welcome." This they do just before going to bed, and when they rise in the morning they look among the ashes, expecting to see the impression of Briid's club there; which if they do, they reckon it a true presage of a good crop and prosperous year, and the contrary they take as an ill omen.' The same custom is described by another witness thus: 'Upon the night before Candlemas it is usual to make a bed with corn and hay, over which some blankets are laid, in a part of the house, near the door. When it is ready, a person goes out and repeats three times, . . . "Bridget, Bridget, come in; thy bed is ready." One or more candles are left burning near it all night.' Similarly in the Isle of Man 'on the eve of the first of February, a festival was formerly kept, called, in the Manks language, *Laa'l Breeshey*, in honour of the Irish lady who went over to the Isle of Man to receive the veil from St. Maughold. The custom was to gather a bundle of green rushes, and standing with them in the hand on the threshold of the door, to invite the holy Saint Bridget to come and lodge with them that night. In the Manks language, the invitation ran thus: "*Brede, Brede, tar gys my thie tar dyn thie ayms noght. Foshil jee yn dorrys da Brede, as lhig da Brede e heet staigh.*" In English: "Bridget, Bridget, come to my house, come to my house tonight. Open the door for Bridget, and let Bridget come in." After these words were repeated, the rushes were strewn on the floor by way of a carpet or bed for St. Bridget. A custom very similar to this was also observed in some of the Out-Isles of the ancient kingdom of Man.' In these Manx and Highland ceremonies it is obvious that St. Bride, or St. Bridget, is an old heathen goddess of fertility, disguised in a threadbare

Christian cloak. Probably she is no other than Brigit, the Celtic goddess of fire and apparently of the crops.

Often the marriage of the spirit of vegetation in spring, though not directly represented, is implied by naming the human representative of the spirit, 'the Bride,' and dressing her in wedding attire. Thus in some villages of Altmark at Whitsuntide, while the boys go about carrying a May-tree or leading a boy enveloped in leaves and flowers, the girls lead about the May Bride, a girl dressed as a bride with a great nosegay in her hair. They go from house to house, the May Bride singing a song in which she asks for a present, and tells the inmates of each house that if they give her something they will themselves have something the whole year through; but if they give her nothing they will themselves have nothing. In some parts of Westphalia two girls lead a flower-crowned girl called the Whitsuntide Bride from door to door, singing a song in which they ask for eggs.

CHAPTER XI

THE INFLUENCE OF THE SEXES ON VEGETATION

FROM the preceding examination of the spring and summer festivals of Europe we may infer that our rude forefathers personified the powers of vegetation as male and female, and attempted, on the principle of homoeopathic or imitative magic, to quicken the growth of trees and plants by representing the marriage of the sylvan deities in the persons of a King and Queen of May, a Whitsun Bridegroom and Bride, and so forth. Such representations were accordingly no mere symbolic or allegorical dramas, pastoral plays designed to amuse or instruct a rustic audience. They were charms intended to make the woods to grow green, the fresh grass to sprout, the corn to shoot, and the flowers to blow. And it was natural to suppose that the more closely the mock marriage of the leaf-clad or flower-decked mummers aped the real marriage of the woodland sprites, the more effective would be the charm. Accordingly we may assume with a high degree of probability that the profligacy which notoriously attended these ceremonies was at one time not an accidental excess but an essential part of the rites, and that in the opinion of those who performed them the marriage of trees and plants could not be fertile without the real union of the human sexes. At the present day it might perhaps be vain to look in civilised Europe for customs of this sort observed for the explicit purpose of promoting the growth of vegetation. But ruder races in other parts of the world have consciously employed the intercourse of the sexes as a means to ensure the fruitfulness of the earth; and some rites which are still, or were till lately, kept up in Europe can be reasonably explained only as stunted relics of a similar practice. The following facts will make this plain.

For four days before they committed the seed to the earth the Pipiles of Central America kept apart from their wives 'in order that on the night before planting they might indulge their passions to the fullest extent; certain persons are even said to have been appointed to perform the sexual act at the very moment when the first seeds were deposited in the ground.' The use of their wives at that time was indeed enjoined upon the people by the priests as a religious duty, in default of which it was not lawful to sow the seed. The only possible explanation of this custom seems to be that the Indians confused the process by which human beings reproduce their kind with the process by which plants discharge the same function, and fancied that by resorting to the former they were simultaneously forwarding the latter. In some parts of Java, at the season when the bloom will soon be on the rice, the husbandman and his wife visit their fields by night and there engage in sexual intercourse for the purpose of promoting the growth of the crop. In the Leti, Sarmata, and some other groups of islands which lie between the western end of New Guinea and the northern part of Australia, the heathen population regard the sun as the male principle by whom the earth or female principle is fertilised. They call him Upu-lera or Mr. Sun, and represent him under the form of a lamp made of coco-nut leaves, which may be seen hanging everywhere in their homes and in the sacred fig-tree. Under the tree lies a large flat stone, which serves as a sacrificial table. On it the heads of slain foes were and are still placed in some of the islands. Once a year, at the beginning of the rainy season, Mr. Sun comes down into the holy fig-tree to fertilise the earth, and to facilitate his descent a ladder with seven rungs is considerately placed at his disposal. It is set up under the tree and is adorned with carved figures of the birds whose shrill clarion heralds the approach of the sun in the East. On this occasion pigs and dogs are sacrificed in profusion; men and women alike indulge in a saturnalia; and the mystic union of the sun and the earth is dramatically represented in public, amid song and dance, by the real union of the sexes under the tree. The object of the festival, we are told, is to procure rain, plenty of food and drink, abundance of cattle and children and riches from Grandfather Sun. They pray that he may make every she-goat to cast two or three young, the people to multiply, the dead pigs to be replaced by living pigs, the empty rice-baskets to be filled, and so on. And to induce him to grant these requests they offer him pork and rice and liquor, and invite him to fall to. In the Babar Islands a special flag is hoisted at this festival as a symbol of the creative energy of the sun; it is of white cotton, about nine feet high, and consists of the figure of a man in an appropriate attitude. It would be unjust to treat these orgies as a mere outburst of unbridled passion; no doubt they are deliberately and solemnly organised as essential to the fertility of the earth and the welfare of man.

The same means which are thus adopted to stimulate the growth of the crops are naturally employed to ensure the fruitfulness of trees. In some parts of Amboyna, when the state of the clove plantation indicates that the crop is likely to be scanty, the men go naked to the plantations by night, and there seek to fertilise the trees precisely as they would impregnate women, while at the same time they call out for 'More cloves!' This is supposed to make the trees bear fruit more abundantly.

The Baganda of Central Africa believe so strongly in the intimate relation between the intercourse of the sexes and the fertility of the ground that among them a barren wife is generally sent away, because she is supposed to prevent her husband's garden from bearing fruit. On the contrary, a couple who have given proof of extraordinary fertility by becoming the parents of twins are believed by the Baganda to be endowed with a corresponding power of increasing the fruitfulness of the plantain-trees, which furnish them with their staple food. Some little time after the birth of the twins a ceremony is performed, the object of which clearly is to transmit the reproductive virtue of the parents to the plantains. The mother lies down on her back in the thick grass near the house and places a flower of the plantain between her legs; then the husband comes and knocks the flower away with his genital member. Further, the parents go through the country, performing dances in the gardens of favoured friends, apparently for the purpose of causing the plantain-trees to bear fruit more abundantly.

In various parts of Europe customs have prevailed both at spring and harvest which are clearly based on the same crude notion that the relation of the human sexes to each other can be so used as to quicken the growth of plants. For example, in the Ukraine on St. George's Day (the twenty-third of April) the priest in his robes, attended by his acolytes, goes out to the fields of the village, where the crops are beginning to show green above the ground, and blesses them. After that the young married people lie down in couples on the sown fields and roll several times over on them, in the belief that this will promote the growth of the crops. In some parts of Russia the priest himself is rolled by women over the sprouting crop, and that without regard to the mud and holes which he may encounter in his beneficent progress. If the shepherd resists or remonstrates, his flock murmurs, 'Little Father, you do not really wish us well, you do not wish us to have corn, although you do wish to live on our corn.' In some parts of Germany at harvest the men and women, who have reaped the corn, roll together on the field. This again is probably a mitigation of an older and ruder custom designed to impart fertility to the fields by methods like those resorted to by the Pipiles of Central America long ago and by the cultivators of rice in Java at the present time.

To the student who cares to track the devious course of the human mind in its gropings after truth, it is of some interest to observe that the same theoretical belief in the sympathetic influence of the sexes on vegetation, which has led some peoples to indulge their passions as a means of fertilising the earth, has led others to seek the same end by directly opposite means. From the moment that they sowed the maize till the time that

G

they reaped it, the Indians of Nicaragua lived chastely, keeping apart from their wives and sleeping in a separate place. They ate no salt, and drank neither cocoa nor *chicha*, the fermented liquor made from maize; in short the season was for them, as the Spanish historian observes, a time of abstinence. To this day some of the Indian tribes of Central America practise continence for the purpose of thereby promoting the growth of the crops. Thus we are told that before sowing the maize the Kekchi Indians sleep apart from their wives, and eat no flesh for five days, while among the Lanquineros and Cajaboneros the period of abstinence from these carnal pleasures extends to thirteen days. So amongst some of the Germans of Transylvania it is a rule that no man may sleep with his wife during the whole of the time that he is engaged in sowing his fields. The same rule is observed at Kalotaszeg in Hungary; the people think that if the custom were not observed the corn would be mildewed. Similarly a Central Australian headman of the Kaitish tribe strictly abstains from marital relations with his wife all the time that he is performing magical ceremonies to make the grass grow; for he believes that a breach of this rule would prevent the grass seed from sprouting properly. In some of the Melanesian islands, when the yam vines are being trained, the men sleep near the gardens and never approach their wives; should they enter the garden after breaking this rule of continence the fruits of the garden would be spoilt.

If we ask why it is that similar beliefs should logically lead, among different peoples, to such opposite modes of conduct as strict chastity and more or less open debauchery, the reason, as it presents itself to the primitive mind, is perhaps not very far to seek. If rude man identifies himself, in a manner, with nature; if he fails to distinguish the impulses and processes in himself from the methods which nature adopts to ensure the reproduction of plants and animals, he may leap to one of two conclusions. Either he may infer that by yielding to his appetites he will thereby assist in the multiplication of plants and animals; or he may imagine that the vigour which he refuses to expend in reproducing his own kind will form as it were a store of energy whereby other creatures, whether vegetable or animal, will somehow benefit in propagating their species. Thus from the same crude philosophy, the same primitive notions of nature and life, the savage may derive by different channels a rule either of profligacy or of asceticism.

To readers bred in a religion which is saturated with the ascetic idealism of the East, the explanation which I have given of the rule of continence observed under certain circumstances by rude or savage peoples may seem far-fetched and improbable. They may think that moral purity, which is so intimately associated in their minds with the observance of such a rule, furnishes a sufficient explanation of it; they may hold with Milton that chastity in itself is a noble virtue, and that the restraint which it imposes on one of the strongest impulses of our animal nature marks out those who can submit to it as men raised above the common herd, and therefore worthy to receive the seal of the divine approbation. However natural this mode of thought may seem to us, it is utterly foreign and indeed incomprehensible to the savage. If he resists on occasion the sexual instinct, it is from no high idealism, no ethereal aspiration after moral purity, but for the sake of some ulterior yet perfectly definite and concrete object, to gain which he is prepared to sacrifice the immediate gratification of his senses. That this is or may be so, the examples I have cited are amply sufficient to prove. They show that where the instinct of self-preservation, which manifests itself chiefly in the search of food, conflicts or appears to conflict with the instinct which conduces to the propagation of the species, the former instinct, as the primary and more fundamental, is capable of overmastering the latter. In short, the savage is willing to restrain his sexual propensity for the sake of food. Another object for the sake of which he consents to exercise the same self-restraint is victory in war. Not only the warrior in the field but his friends at home will often bridle their sensual appetites from a belief that by so doing they will the more easily overcome their enemies. The fallacy of such a belief, like the belief that the chastity of the sower conduces to the growth of the seed, is plain enough to us; yet perhaps the self-restraint which these and the like beliefs, vain and false as they are, have imposed on mankind, has not been without its utility in bracing and strengthening the breed. For strength of character in the race as in the individual consists mainly in the power of sacrificing the present to the future, of disregarding the immediate temptations of ephemeral pleasure for more distant and lasting sources of satisfaction. The more the power is exercised the higher and stronger becomes the character; till the height of heroism is reached in men who renounce the pleasures of life and even life itself for the sake of keeping or winning for others, perhaps in distant ages, the blessings of freedom and truth.

CHAPTER XII

THE SACRED MARRIAGE

§ 1. *Diana as a Goddess of Fertility.* — We have seen that according to a widespread belief, which is not without a foundation of fact, plants reproduce their kinds through the sexual union of male and female elements, and that on the principle of homoeopathic or imitative magic this reproduction is supposed to be stimulated by the real or mock marriage of men and women, who masquerade for the time being as spirits of vegetation. Such magical dramas have played a great part in the popular festivals of Europe, and based as they are on a very crude conception of natural law, it is clear that they must have been handed down from a remote antiquity. We shall hardly, therefore, err in assuming that they date from a time when the forefathers of the civilised nations of Europe were still barbarians, herding their cattle and cultivating patches of corn in the clearings of the vast forests, which then covered the greater part of the continent, from the Mediterranean to the Arctic Ocean. But if these old spells and enchantments for the growth of leaves and blossoms, of grass and flowers and fruit, have lingered down to our own time in the shape of pastoral plays and popular merry-makings, is it not reasonable to suppose that they survived in less attenuated forms some two thousand years ago among the civilised peoples of antiquity? Or, to put it otherwise, is it not likely that in certain festivals of the ancients we may be able to detect the equivalents of our May Day, Whitsuntide, and Midsummer celebrations, with this difference, that in those days the ceremonies had not dwindled into mere shows and pageants, but were still religious or magical rites, in which the

actors consciously supported the high parts of gods and goddesses?
Now in the first chapter of this book we found reason to believe
that the priest who bore the title of King of the Wood at Nemi
had for his mate the goddess of the grove, Diana herself. May not
he and she, as King and Queen of the Wood, have been serious
counterparts of the merry mummers who play the King and
Queen in May, the Whitsuntide Bridegroom and Bride in modern
Europe? and may not their union have been yearly celebrated in
a *theogamy* or divine marriage? Such dramatic weddings of
gods and goddesses, as we shall see presently, were carried out
as solemn religious rites in many parts of the ancient world;
hence there is no intrinsic improbability in the supposition that
the sacred grove at Nemi may have been the scene of an annual
ceremony of this sort. Direct evidence that it was so there is
none, but analogy pleads in favour of the view, as I shall now
endeavour to show.

Diana was essentially a goddess of the woodlands, as Ceres
was a goddess of the corn and Bacchus a god of the vine. Her
sanctuaries were commonly in groves, indeed every grove was
sacred to her, and she is often associated with the forest god
Silvanus in dedications. But whatever her origin may have been,
Diana was not always a mere goddess of trees. Like her Greek
sister Artemis, she appears to have developed into a personification
of the teeming life of nature, both animal and vegetable. As
mistress of the greenwood she would naturally be thought to
own the beasts, whether wild or tame, that ranged through it,
lurking for their prey in its gloomy depths, munching the fresh
leaves and shoots among the boughs, or cropping the herbage in
the open glades and dells. Thus she might come to be the patron
goddess both of hunters and herdsmen, just as Silvanus was the
god not only of woods, but of cattle. Similarly in Finland, the
wild beasts of the forest were regarded as the herds of the
woodland god Tapio and of his stately and beautiful wife. No
man might slay one of these animals without the gracious permission of their divine owners. Hence the hunter prayed to the
sylvan deities and vowed rich offerings to them if they would
drive the game across his path. And cattle also seem to have
enjoyed the protection of those spirits of the woods, both when
they were in their stalls and while they strayed in the forest.

Before the Gayos of Sumatra hunt deer, wild goats, or wild pigs with hounds in the woods, they deem it necessary to obtain leave of the unseen Lord of the forest. This is done according to a prescribed form by a man who has special skill in woodcraft. He lays down a quid of betel before a stake which is cut in a particular way to represent the Lord of the Wood, and having done so he prays to the spirit to signify his consent or refusal. In his treatise on hunting, Arrian tells us that the Celts used to offer an annual sacrifice to Artemis on her birthday, purchasing the sacrificial victim with the fines which they had paid into her treasury for every fox, hare, and roe that they had killed in the course of the year. The custom clearly implied that the wild beasts belonged to the goddess, and that she must be compensated for their slaughter.

But Diana was not merely a patroness of wild beasts, a mistress of woods and hills, of lonely glades and sounding rivers; conceived as the moon, and especially, it would seem, as the yellow harvest moon, she filled the farmer's grange with goodly fruits, and heard the prayers of women in travail. In her sacred grove at Nemi, as we have seen, she was especially worshipped as a goddess of childbirth, who bestowed offspring on men and women. Thus Diana, like the Greek Artemis, with whom she was constantly identified, may be described as a goddess of nature in general and of fertility in particular. We need not wonder, therefore, that in her sanctuary on the Aventine she was represented by an image copied from the many-breasted idol of the Ephesian Artemis, with all its crowded emblems of exuberant fecundity. Hence too we can understand why an ancient Roman law, attributed to King Tullus Hostilius, prescribed that when incest had been committed, an expiatory sacrifice should be offered by the pontiffs in the grove of Diana. For we know that the crime of incest is commonly supposed to cause a dearth; hence it would be meet that atonement for the offence should be made to the goddess of fertility.

Now on the principle that the goddess of fertility must herself be fertile, it behoved Diana to have a male partner. Her mate, if the testimony of Servius may be trusted, was that Virbius who had his representative, or perhaps rather his embodiment, in the King of the Wood at Nemi. The aim of their union would be to promote the fruitfulness of the earth, of animals, and of mankind; and it might naturally be thought that this object would be more surely attained if the sacred nuptials were celebrated every year, the parts of the divine bride and bridegroom being played either by their images or by living persons. No ancient writer mentions that this was done in the grove at Nemi; but our knowledge of the Arician ritual is so scanty that the want of information on this head can hardly count as a fatal objection to the theory. That theory, in the absence of direct evidence, must necessarily be based on the analogy of similar customs practised elsewhere. Some modern examples of such customs, more or less degenerate, were described in the last chapter. Here we shall consider their ancient counterparts.

§ 2. *The Marriage of the Gods.* — At Babylon the imposing sanctuary of Bel rose like a pyramid above the city in a series of eight towers or stories, planted one on the top of the other. On the highest tower, reached by an ascent which wound about all the rest, there stood a spacious temple, and in the temple a great bed, magnificently draped and cushioned, with a golden table beside it. In the temple no image was to be seen, and no human being passed the night there, save a single woman, whom, according to the Chaldean priests, the god chose from among all the women of Babylon. They said that the deity himself came into the temple at night and slept in the great bed; and the woman, as a consort of the god, might have no intercourse with mortal man.

At Thebes in Egypt a woman slept in the temple of Ammon as the consort of the god, and, like the human wife of Bel at Babylon, she was said to have no commerce with a man. In Egyptian texts she is often mentioned as 'the divine consort,' and usually she was no less a personage than the Queen of Egypt herself. For, according to the Egyptians, their monarchs were actually begotten by the god Ammon, who assumed for the time being the form of the reigning king, and in that disguise had intercourse with the queen. The divine procreation is carved and painted in great detail on the walls of two of the oldest temples in Egypt, those of Deir el Bahari and Luxor; and the inscriptions attached to the paintings leave no doubt as to the meaning of the scenes.

At Athens the god of the vine, Dionysus, was annually married to the Queen, and it appears that the consummation of the divine union, as well as the espousals, was enacted at the ceremony; but whether the part of the god was played by a man or an image we do not know. We learn from Aristotle that the ceremony took place in the old official residence of the King, known as the Cattle-stall, which stood near the Prytaneum or Town-hall on the north-eastern slope of the Acropolis. The object of the marriage can hardly have been any other than that of ensuring the fertility of the vines and other fruit-trees, of which Dionysus was the god. Thus both in form and in meaning the ceremony would answer to the nuptials of the King and Queen of May.

In the great mysteries solemnised at Eleusis in the month of September the union of the sky-god Zeus with the corn-goddess Demeter appears to have been represented by the union of the hierophant with the priestess of Demeter, who acted the parts of god and goddess. But their intercourse was only dramatic or symbolical, for the hierophant had temporarily deprived himself of his virility by an application of hemlock. The torches having been extinguished, the pair descended into a murky place, while the throng of worshippers awaited in anxious suspense the result of the mystic congress, on which they believed their own salvation to depend. After a time the hierophant reappeared, and in a blaze of light silently exhibited to the assembly a reaped ear of corn, the fruit of the divine marriage. Then in a loud voice he proclaimed, 'Queen Brimo has brought forth a sacred boy Brimos,' by which he meant, 'The Mighty One has brought forth the Mighty.' The corn-mother in fact had given birth to her child, the corn, and her travail-pangs were enacted in the sacred drama. The revelation of the reaped corn appears to have been the crowning act of the mysteries. Thus through the glamour shed round these rites by the poetry and philosophy of later ages there still looms, like a distant landscape through a sunlit haze, a simple rustic festival designed to cover the wide Eleusinian plain with a plenteous harvest by wedding the goddess of the corn to the sky-god, who fertilised the bare earth with genial showers. Every few years the people of Plataea, in Boeotia, held a festival called the Little Daedala, at which they felled an oak-tree in an ancient oak forest. Out of the tree they carved an image, and having dressed it as a bride, they set it on a bullock-cart with a bridesmaid beside it. The image seems then to have been drawn to the bank of the river Asopus and back to the town, attended by a piping and dancing crowd. Every sixty years the festival of the Great Daedala was celebrated by all the people of Boeotia; and at it all the images, fourteen in number, which had accumulated at the lesser festivals, were dragged on wains in procession to the river Asopus and then to the top of Mount Cithaeron, where they were burnt on a great pyre. The story told to explain the festival suggests that they celebrated the marriage of Zeus to Hera, represented by the oaken image in bridal array. In Sweden every year a life-size image of Frey, the god of fertility, both animal and vegetable, was drawn about the country in a waggon attended by a beautiful girl who was called the god's wife. She acted also as his priestess in his great temple at Upsala. Wherever the waggon came with the image of the god and his blooming young bride, the people crowded to meet them and offered sacrifices for a fruitful year.

Thus the custom of marrying gods either to images or to human beings was widespread among the nations of antiquity. The ideas on which such a custom is based are too crude to allow us to doubt that the civilised Babylonians, Egyptians, and Greeks inherited it from their barbarous or savage forefathers. This presumption is strengthened when we find rites of a similar kind in vogue among the lower races. Thus, for example, we are told that once upon a time the Wotyaks of the Malmyz district in Russia were distressed by a series of bad harvests. They did not know what to do, but at last concluded that their powerful but mischievous god Keremet must be angry at being unmarried. So a deputation of elders visited the Wotyaks of Cura and came to an understanding with them on the subject. Then they returned home, laid in a large stock of brandy, and having made ready a gaily decked waggon and horses, they drove in procession with bells ringing, as they do when they are fetching home a bride, to the sacred grove at Cura. There they ate and drank merrily all night, and next morning they cut a square piece of turf in the grove and took it home with them. After that, though it fared well with the people of Malmyz, it fared ill with the people of Cura; for in Malmyz the bread was good, but in Cura it was bad. Hence the men of Cura who had consented to the marriage were blamed and roughly handled by their indignant fellow-villagers. 'What they meant by this marriage ceremony,' says the writer who reports it, 'it is not easy to imagine. Perhaps, as Bechterew thinks, they meant to marry Keremet to the kindly and fruitful Mukylcin, the Earth-wife, in order that she might influence him for good.' When wells are dug in Bengal, a wooden image of a god is made and married to the goddess of water.

Often the bride destined for the god is not a log or a clod, but a living woman of flesh and blood. The Indians of a village in Peru have been known to marry a beautiful girl, about fourteen years of age, to a stone shaped like a human being, which they regarded as a god (*huaca*). All the villagers took part in the marriage ceremony, which lasted three days, and was attended with much revelry. The girl thereafter remained a virgin and sacrificed to the idol for the people. They showed her the utmost reverence and deemed her divine. Every year about the middle of March, when the season for fishing with the dragnet began, the Algonquins and Hurons married their nets to two young girls, aged six or seven. At the wedding feast the net was placed between the two maidens, and was exhorted to take courage and catch many fish. The reason for choosing the brides so young was to make sure that they were virgins. The origin of the custom is said to have been this. One year, when the fishing season came round, the Algonquins cast their nets as usual, but took nothing. Surprised at their want of success, they did not know what to make of it, till the soul or genius (*oki*) of the net appeared to them in the likeness of a tall well-built man, who said to them in a great passion, 'I have lost my wife and I cannot find one who has known no other man but me; that is why you do not succeed, and why you never will succeed till you give me satisfaction on this head.' So the Algonquins held a council and resolved to appease the spirit of the net by marrying him to two such very young girls that he could have no ground of complaint on that score for the future. They did so, and the fishing turned out all that could be wished. The thing got wind among their neighbours the Hurons, and they adopted the custom. A share of the catch was always given to the families of the two girls who acted as brides of the net for the year.

The Oraons of Bengal worship the Earth as a goddess, and annually celebrate her marriage with the Sun-god Dharmē at the time when the *sāl* tree is in blossom. The ceremony is as follows. All bathe, then the men repair to the sacred grove (*sarnā*), while the women assemble at the house of the village priest. After sacrificing some fowls to the Sun-god and the demon of the grove, the men eat and drink. 'The priest is then carried back to the village on the shoulders of a strong man. Near the village the women meet the men and wash their feet. With beating of drums and singing, dancing, and jumping, all proceed to the priest's house, which has been decorated with leaves and flowers. Then the usual form of marriage is performed between the priest and his wife, symbolising the supposed union between Sun and Earth. After the ceremony all eat and drink and make merry; they dance and sing obscene songs, and finally indulge in the vilest orgies. The object is to move the mother earth to become fruitful.' Thus the Sacred Marriage of the Sun and Earth, personated by the priest and his wife, is celebrated as a charm to ensure the fertility of the ground; and for the same purpose, on the principle of homoeopathic magic, the people indulge in a licentious orgy.

It deserves to be remarked that the supernatural being to whom women are married is often a god or spirit of water. Thus Mukasa, the god of the Victoria Nyanza lake, who was propitiated by the Baganda every time they undertook a long voyage, had virgins provided for him to serve as his wives. Like the Vestals they were bound to chastity, but unlike the Vestals they seem to have been often unfaithful. The custom lasted until Mwanga was converted to Christianity. The Akikuyu of British East Africa worship the snake of a certain river, and at intervals of several years they marry the snake-god to women, but especially to young girls. For this purpose huts are built by order of the medicine-men, who there consummate the sacred marriage with the credulous female devotees. If the girls do not repair to the huts of their own accord in sufficient numbers, they are seized and dragged thither to the embraces of the deity. The offspring of these mystic unions appears to be fathered on God (*Ngai*); certainly there are children among the Akikuyu who pass for children of God. It is said that once, when the inhabitants of Cayeli in Buru — an East Indian Island — were threatened with destruction by a swarm of crocodiles, they ascribed the misfortune to a passion which the prince of crocodiles had conceived for a certain girl. Accordingly, they compelled the damsel's father to dress her in bridal array and deliver her over to the clutches of her crocodile lover.

A usage of the same sort is reported to have prevailed in the Maldive Islands before the conversion of the inhabitants to Islam. The famous Arab traveller Ibn Batutah has described the custom and the manner in which it came to an end. He was assured by several trustworthy natives, whose names he gives, that when the people of the islands were idolaters there appeared to them every month an evil spirit among the jinn, who came from across the sea in the likeness of a ship full of burning lamps. The wont of the inhabitants, as soon as they perceived him, was to take a young virgin, and, having adorned her, to lead her to a heathen temple that stood on the shore, with a window looking out to sea. There they left the damsel for the night, and when they came back in the morning they found her a maid no more, and dead. Every month they drew lots, and he upon whom the lot fell gave up his daughter to the jinnee of the sea. The last of the maidens thus offered to the demon was rescued by a pious Berber, who by reciting the Koran succeeded in driving the jinnee back into the sea.

Ibn Batutah's narrative of the demon lover and his mortal brides closely resembles a well-known type of folk-tale, of which versions have been found from Japan and Annam in the East to Senegambia, Scandinavia, and Scotland in the West. The story varies in details from people to people, but as commonly told it runs thus. A certain country is infested by a many-headed serpent, dragon, or other monster, which would destroy the whole people if a human victim, generally a virgin, were not delivered up to him periodically. Many victims have perished, and at last it has fallen to the lot of the king's own daughter to be sacrificed. She is exposed to the monster, but the hero of the tale, generally a young man of humble birth, interposes in her behalf, slays the monster, and receives the hand of the princess as his reward. In many of the tales the monster, who is sometimes described as a serpent, inhabits the water of a sea, a lake, or a fountain. In other versions he is a serpent or dragon who takes possession of the springs of water, and only allows the water to flow or the people to make use of it on condition of receiving a human victim.

It would probably be a mistake to dismiss all these tales as pure inventions of the story-teller. Rather we may suppose that they reflect a real custom of sacrificing girls or women to be the wives of water-spirits, who are very often conceived as great serpents or dragons.

CHAPTER XIII

THE KINGS OF ROME AND ALBA

§ 1. *Numa and Egeria.* — From the foregoing survey of custom and legend we may infer that the sacred marriage of the powers both of vegetation and of water has been celebrated by many peoples for the sake of promoting the fertility of the earth, on which the life of animals and men ultimately depends, and that in such rites the part of the divine bridegroom or bride is often sustained by a man or woman. The evidence may, therefore, lend some countenance to the conjecture that in the sacred grove at Nemi, where the powers of vegetation and of water manifested themselves in the fair forms of shady woods, tumbling cascades and glassy lake, a marriage like that of our King and Queen of May was annually celebrated between the mortal King of the Wood and the immortal Queen of the Wood, Diana. In this connexion an important figure in the grove was the water-nymph Egeria, who was worshipped by pregnant women because she, like Diana, could grant them an easy delivery. From this it seems fairly safe to conclude that, like many other springs, the water of Egeria was credited with a power of facilitating conception as well as delivery. The votive offerings found on the spot, which clearly refer to the begetting of children, may possibly have been dedicated to Egeria rather than to Diana, or perhaps we should rather say that the water-nymph Egeria is only another form of the great nature-goddess Diana herself, the mistress of sounding rivers as well as of umbrageous woods, who had her home by the lake and her mirror in its calm waters, and whose Greek counter-part Artemis loved to haunt meres and springs. The identification of Egeria with Diana is confirmed by a statement of Plutarch that Egeria was one of the oak-nymphs whom the Romans believed to preside over every green oak-grove; for, while Diana was a goddess of the woodlands in general, she appears to have been intimately associated with oaks in particular, especially at her sacred grove of Nemi. Perhaps, then, Egeria was the fairy of a spring that flowed from the roots of a sacred oak. Such a spring is said to have gushed from the foot of the great oak at Dodona, and from its murmurous flow the priestess drew oracles. Among the Greeks a draught of water from certain sacred springs or wells was supposed to confer prophetic powers. This would explain the more than mortal wisdom with which, according to tradition, Egeria inspired her royal husband or lover Numa. When we remember how very often in early society the king is held responsible for the fall of rain and the fruitfulness of the earth, it seems hardly rash to conjecture that in the legend of the nuptials of Numa and Egeria we have a reminiscence of a sacred marriage which the old Roman kings regularly contracted with a goddess of vegetation and water for the purpose of enabling him to discharge his divine or magical functions. In such a rite the part of the goddess might be played either by an image or a woman, and if by a woman, probably by the Queen. If there is any truth in this conjecture, we may suppose that the King and Queen of Rome masqueraded as god and goddess at their marriage, extactly as the King and Queen of Egypt appear to have done. The legend of Numa and Egeria points to a sacred grove rather than to a house as the scene of the nuptial union, which, like the marriage of the King and Queen of May, or of the vine-god and the Queen of Athens, may have been annually celebrated as a charm to ensure the fertility not only of the earth but of man and beast. Now, according to some accounts, the scene of the marriage was no other than the sacred grove of Nemi, and on quite independent grounds we have been led to suppose that in that same grove the King of the Wood was wedded to Diana. The convergence of the two distinct lines of enquiry suggests that the legendary union of the Roman king with Egeria may have been a reflection or duplicate of the union of the King of the Wood with Egeria or her double, Diana. This does not imply that the Roman kings ever served as Kings of the Wood in the Arician grove, but only that they may originally have been invested with a sacred character of the same general kind, and may have held office on similar terms. To be more explicit, it is possible that they reigned, not by right of birth, but in virtue of their supposed divinity as representatives or embodiments of a god, and that as such they mated with a goddess, and had to prove their fitness from time to time to discharge their divine functions by engaging in a severe bodily struggle, which may often have proved fatal to them, leaving the crown to their victorious adversary. Our knowledge of the Roman kingship is far too scanty to allow us to affirm any one of these propositions with confidence; but at least there are some scattered hints or indications of a similarity in all these respects between the priests of Nemi and the kings of Rome, or perhaps rather between their remote predecessors in the dark ages which preceded the dawn of legend.

§ 2. *The King as Jupiter.* — In the first place, then, it would seem that the Roman king personated no less a deity than Jupiter himself. For down to imperial times victorious generals celebrating a triumph, and magistrates presiding at the games in the Circus, wore the costume of Jupiter, which was borrowed for the occasion from his great temple on the Capitol; and it has been held with a high degree of probability both by ancients and moderns that in so doing they copied the traditionary attire and insignia of the Roman kings. They rode a chariot drawn by four laurel-crowned horses through the city, where every one else went on foot; they wore purple robes embroidered or spangled with gold; in the right hand they bore a branch of laurel, and in the left hand an ivory sceptre topped with an eagle: a wreath of laurel crowned their brows: their face was reddened with vermilion; and over their head a slave held a heavy crown of massy gold fashioned in the likeness of oak leaves. In this attire the assimilation of the man to the god comes out above all in the eagle-topped sceptre, the oaken crown, and the reddened face. For the eagle was the bird of Jove, the oak was his sacred tree, and the face of his image standing in his four-horse chariot on the Capitol was in like manner regularly dyed red on festivals; indeed, so important was it deemed to keep the divine features properly rouged that one of the first duties of the censors was to contract for having this done. As the triumphal procession always ended in the temple of Jupiter on the Capitol, it was peculiarly appropriate that the head of the victor should be graced by a crown of oak leaves, for not only was every oak consecrated to Jupiter, but the Capitoline temple of the god was said to have been built by Romulus beside a sacred oak, venerated by shepherds, to which the king attached the spoils won by him from the enemy's general in battle. We are expressly told that the oak crown was sacred to Capitoline Jupiter; a passage of Ovid proves that it was regarded as the god's special emblem.

According to a tradition which we have no reason to reject, Rome was founded by settlers from Alba Longa, a city situated on the slope of the Alban hills, overlooking the lake and Campagna. Hence if the Roman kings claimed to be representatives or embodiments of Jupiter, the god of the sky, of the thunder, and of the oak, it is natural to suppose that the kings of Alba, from whom the founder of Rome traced his descent, may have set up the same claim before them. Now the Alban dynasty bore the name of Silvii or Woods, and it can hardly be without significance that in the vision of the historic glories of Rome revealed to Aeneas in the underworld, Virgil, an antiquary as well as a poet, should represent all the line of Silvii as crowned with oak. A chaplet of oak leaves would thus seem to have been part of the insignia of the old kings of Alba Longa as of their successors the kings of Rome; in both cases it marked the monarch as the human representative of the oak-god. The Roman annals record that one of the kings of Alba, Romulus, Remulus, or Amulius Silvius by name, set up for being a god in his own person, the equal or superior of Jupiter. To support his pretensions and overawe his subjects, he constructed machines whereby he mimicked the clap of thunder and the flash of lightning. Diodorus relates that in the season of fruitage, when thunder is loud and frequent, the king commanded his soldiers to drown the roar of heaven's artillery by clashing their swords against their shields. But he paid the penalty of his impiety, for he perished, he and his house, struck by a thunderbolt in the midst of a dreadful storm. Swollen by the rain, the Alban lake rose in flood and drowned his palace. But still, says an ancient historian, when the water is low and the surface unruffled by a breeze, you may see the ruins of the palace at the bottom of the clear lake. Taken along with the similar story of Salmoneus, king of Elis, this legend points to a real custom observed by the early kings of Greece and Italy, who, like their fellows in Africa down to modern times, may have been expected to produce rain and thunder for the good of the crops. The priestly king Numa passed for an adept in the art of drawing down lightning from the sky. Mock thunder, we know, has been made by various peoples as a rain-charm in modern times; why should it not have been made by kings in antiquity?

Thus, if the kings of Alba and Rome imitated Jupiter as god of the oak by wearing a crown of oak leaves, they seem also to have copied him in his character of a weather-god by pretending to make thunder and lightning. And if they did so, it is probable that, like Jupiter in heaven and many kings on earth, they also acted as public rain-makers, wringing showers from the dark sky by their enchantments whenever the parched earth cried out for the refreshing moisture. At Rome the sluices of heaven were opened by means of a sacred stone, and the ceremony appears to have formed part of the ritual of Jupiter Elicius, the god who elicits from the clouds the flashing lightning and the dripping rain. And who so well fitted to perform the ceremony as the king, the living representative of the sky-god?

If the kings of Rome aped Capitoline Jove, their predecessors the kings of Alba probably laid themselves out to mimic the great Latian Jupiter, who had his seat above the city on the summit of the Alban Mountain. Latinus, the legendary ancestor of the dynasty, was said to have been changed into Latian Jupiter after vanishing from the world in the mysterious fashion characteristic of the old Latin kings. The sanctuary of the god on the top of the mountain was the religious centre of the Latin League, as Alba was its political capital till Rome wrested the supremacy from its ancient rival. Apparently no temple, in our sense of the word, was ever erected to Jupiter on this his holy mountain; as god of the sky and thunder he appropriately received the homage of his worshippers in the open air. The massive wall, of which some remains still enclose the old garden of the Passionist monastery, seems to have been part of the sacred precinct which Tarquin the Proud, the last king of Rome, marked out for the solemn annual assembly of the Latin League. The god's oldest sanctuary on this airy mountain-top was a grove; and bearing in mind not merely the special consecration of the oak to Jupiter, but also the traditional oak crown of the Alban kings and the analogy of the Capitoline Jupiter at Rome, we may suppose that the trees in the grove were oaks. We know that in antiquity Mount Algidus, an outlying group of the Alban hills, was covered with dark forests of oak; and among the tribes who belonged to the Latin League, in the earliest days, and were entitled to share the flesh of the white bull sacrificed on the Alban Mount, there was one whose members styled themselves the Men of the Oak, doubtless on account of the woods among which they dwelt.

But we should err if we pictured to ourselves the country as covered in historical times with an unbroken forest of oaks. Theophrastus has left us a description of the woods of Latium as they were in the fourth century before Christ. He says: 'The land of the Latins is all moist. The plains produce laurels, myrtles, and wonderful beeches; for they fell trees of such a size that a single stem suffices for the keel of a Tyrrhenian ship. Pines and firs grow in the mountains. What they call the land of Circe is a lofty headland thickly wooded with oak, myrtle, and luxuriant laurels. The natives say that Circe dwelt there, and they show the grave of Elpenor, from which grow myrtles such as wreaths are made of, whereas the other myrtle-trees are tall.' Thus the prospect from the top of the Alban Mount in the early days of Rome must have been very different in some respects from what it is today. The purple Apennines, indeed, in their eternal calm on the one hand, and the shining Mediterranean in its eternal unrest on the other, no doubt looked then much as they look now, whether bathed in sunshine or chequered by the fleeting shadows of clouds; but instead of the desolate brown expanse of the fever-stricken Campagna, spanned by its long lines of ruined aqueducts, like the broken arches of the bridge in the vision of Mirza, the eye must have ranged over woodlands that stretched away, mile after mile, on all sides, till their varied hues of green or autumnal scarlet and gold melted insensibly into the blue of the distant mountains and sea.

But Jupiter did not reign alone on the top of his holy mountain. He had his consort with him, the goddess Juno, who was worshipped here under the same title, Moneta, as on the Capitol at Rome. As the oak crown was sacred to Jupiter and Juno on the Capitol, so we may suppose it was on the Alban Mount, from which the Capitoline worship was derived. Thus the oak-god would have his oak-goddess in the sacred oak grove. So at Dodona the oak-god Zeus was coupled with Dione, whose very name is only a dialectically different form of Juno; and so on the top of Mount Cithaeron, as we have seen, he appears to have been periodically wedded to an oaken image of Hera. It is probable, though it cannot be positively proved, that the sacred marriage of Jupiter and Juno was annually celebrated by all the peoples of the Latin stock in the month which they named after the goddess, the midsummer month of June.

If at any time of the year the Romans celebrated the sacred marriage of Jupiter and Juno, as the Greeks commonly celebrated the corresponding marriage of Zeus and Hera, we may suppose that under the Republic the ceremony was either performed over images of the divine pair or acted by the Flamen Dialis and his wife the Flaminica. For the Flamen Dialis was the priest of Jove; indeed, ancient and modern writers have regarded him, with much probability, as a living image of Jupiter, a human embodiment of the sky-god. In earlier times the Roman king, as representative of Jupiter, would naturally play the part of the heavenly bridegroom at the sacred marriage, while his queen would figure as the heavenly bride, just as in Egypt the king and queen masqueraded in the character of deities, and as at Athens the queen annually wedded the vine-god Dionysus. That the Roman king and queen should act the parts of Jupiter and Juno would seem all the more natural because these deities themselves bore the title of King and Queen.

Whether that was so or not, the legend of Numa and Egeria appears to embody a reminiscence of a time when the priestly king himself played the part of the divine bridegroom; and as we have seen reason to suppose that the Roman kings personated the oak-god, while Egeria is expressly said to have been an oak-nymph, the story of their union in the sacred grove raises a presumption that at Rome in the regal period a ceremony was periodically performed exactly analogous to that which was annually celebrated at Athens down to the time of Aristotle.

The marriage of the King of Rome to the oak-goddess, like the wedding of the vine-god to the Queen of Athens, must have been intended to quicken the growth of vegetation by homoeopathic magic. Of the two forms of the rite we can hardly doubt that the Roman was the older, and that long before the northern invaders met with the vine on the shores of the Mediterranean their forefathers had married the tree-god to the tree-goddess in the vast oak forests of Central and Northern Europe. In the England of our day the forests have mostly disappeared, yet still on many a village green and in many a country lane a faded image of the sacred marriage lingers in the rustic pageantry of May Day.

CHAPTER XIV

THE SUCCESSION TO THE KINGDOM IN ANCIENT LATIUM

IN regard to the Roman king, whose priestly functions were inherited by his successor the King of Sacred Rites, the foregoing discussion has led us to the following conclusions. He represented and indeed personated Jupiter, the great god of the sky, the thunder, and the oak, and in that character made rain, thunder, and lightning for the good of his subjects, like many more kings of the weather in other parts of the world. Further, he not only mimicked the oak-god by wearing an oak wreath and other insignia of divinity, but he was married to an oak-nymph Egeria, who appears to have been merely a local form of Diana in her character of a goddess of woods, of waters, and of childbirth. All these conclusions, which we have reached mainly by a considera-tion of the Roman evidence, may with great probability be applied to the other Latin communities. They too probably had of old their divine or priestly kings, who transmitted their religious functions, without their civil powers, to their successors the Kings of the Sacred Rites.

But we have still to ask, What was the rule of succession to the kingdom among the old Latin tribes? According to tradition, there were in all eight kings of Rome, and with regard to the five last of them, at all events, we can hardly doubt that they actually sat on the throne, and that the traditional history of their reigns is, in its main outlines, correct. Now it is very remarkable that though the first king of Rome, Romulus, is said to have descended from the royal house of Alba, in which the kingship is represented as hereditary in the male line, not one of the Roman kings was immediately succeeded by his son on the throne. Yet several left sons or grandsons behind them. On the other hand, one of them was descended from a former king through his mother, not through his father, and three of the kings, namely Tatius, the elder Tarquin, and Servius Tullius, were succeeded by their sons-in-law, who were all either foreigners or of foreign descent. This suggests that the right to kingship was transmitted in the female line, and was actually exercised by foreigners who married the royal princesses. To put it in technical language, the succession to the kingship at Rome and probably in Latium generally would seem to have been determined by certain rules which have moulded early society in many parts of the world, namely, exogamy, *beena* marriage, and female kinship or mother-kin. Exogamy is the rule which obliges a man to marry a woman of a different clan from his own: *beena* marriage is the rule that he must leave the home of his birth and live with his wife's people; and female kinship or mother-kin is the system of tracing relationship and transmitting the family name through women instead of through men. If these principles regulated descent of the kingship among the ancient Latins, the state of things in this respect would be somewhat as follows. The political and religious centre of each community would be the perpetual fire on the king's hearth tended by Vestal Virgins of the royal clan. The king would be a man of another clan, perhaps of another town or even of another race, who had married a daughter of his predecessor and received the kingdom with her. The children whom he had by her would inherit their mother's name, not his; the daughters would remain at home; the sons, when they grew up, would go away into the world, marry, and settle in their wives' country, whether as kings or commoners. Of the daughters who stayed at home, some or all would be dedicated as Vestal Virgins for a longer or shorter time to the service of the fire on the hearth, and one of them would in time become the consort of her father's successor.

This hypothesis has the advantage of explaining in a simple and natural way some obscure features in the traditional history of the Latin kingship. Thus the legends which tell how Latin kings were born of virgin mothers and divine fathers become at least more intelligible. For, stripped of their fabulous element, tales of this sort mean no more than that a woman has been gotten with child by a man unknown; and this uncertainty as to fatherhood is more easily compatible with a system of kinship which ignores paternity than with one which makes it all-important. If at the birth of the Latin kings their fathers were really unknown, the fact points either to a general looseness of life in the royal family or to a special relaxation of moral rules on certain occasions, when men and women reverted for a season to the licence of an earlier age. Such Saturnalias are not uncommon at some stages of social evolution. In our own country traces of them long survived in the practices of May Day and Whitsuntide, if not of Christmas. Children born of the more or less promiscuous intercourse which characterises festivals of this kind would naturally be fathered on the god to whom the particular festival was dedicated.

In this connexion it may be significant that a festival of jollity and drunkenness was celebrated by the plebeians and slaves at Rome on Midsummer Day, and that the festival was specially associated with the fireborn King Servius Tullius, being held in honour of Fortuna, the goddess who loved Servius as Egeria loved Numa. The popular merrymakings at this season included foot-races and boat-races; the Tiber was gay with flower-wreathed boats, in which the young folk sat quaffing wine. The festival appears to have been a sort of Midsummer Saturnalia answering to the real Saturnalia which fell at Midwinter. In modern Europe, as we shall learn later on, the great Midsummer festival has been above all a festival of lovers and of fire; one of its principal features is the pairing of sweethearts, who leap over the bonfires hand in hand or throw flowers across the flames to each other. And many omens of love and marriage are drawn from the flowers which bloom at this mystic season. It is the time of the roses and of love. Yet the innocence and beauty of such festivals in modern times ought not to blind us to the likelihood that in earlier days they were marked by coarser features, which were probably of the essence of the rites. Indeed, among the rude Esthonian peasantry these features seem to have lingered down to our own generation, if not to the present day. One other feature in the Roman celebration of Midsummer deserves to be specially noticed. The custom of rowing in flower-decked boats on the river on this day proves that it was to some extent a water festival; and water has always, down to modern times, played a conspicuous part in the rites of Midsummer Day, which explains why the Church, in throwing its cloak over the old heathen festival, chose to dedicate it to St. John the Baptist.

The hypothesis that the Latin kings may have been begotten at an annual festival of love is necessarily a mere conjecture, though the traditional birth of Numa at the festival of the Parilia, when shepherds leaped across the spring bonfires, as lovers leap across the Midsummer fires, may perhaps be thought to lend it a faint colour of probability. But it is quite possible that the uncertainty as to their fathers may not have arisen till long after the death of the kings, when their figures began to melt away into the cloudland of fable, assuming fantastic shapes and gorgeous colouring as they passed from earth to heaven. If they were alien immigrants, strangers and pilgrims in the land they ruled over, it would be natural enough that the people should forget their lineage, and forgetting it should provide them with another, which made up in lustre what it lacked in truth. The final apotheosis, which represented the kings not merely as sprung from gods but as themselves deities incarnate, would be much facilitated if in their lifetime, as we have seen reason to think, they had actually laid claim to divinity.

If among the Latins the women of royal blood always stayed at home and received as their consorts men of another stock, and often of another country, who reigned as kings in virtue of their marriage with a native princess, we can understand not only why foreigners wore the crown at Rome, but also why foreign names occur in the list of the Alban kings. In a state of society where nobility is reckoned only through women — in other words, where descent through the mother is everything, and descent through the father is nothing — no objection will be felt to uniting girls of the highest rank to men of humble birth, even to aliens or slaves, provided that in themselves the men appear to be suitable mates.

What really matters is that the royal stock, on which the prosperity and even the existence of the people is supposed to depend, should be perpetuated in a vigorous and efficient form, and for this purpose it is necessary that the women of the royal family should bear children to men who are physically and mentally fit, according to the standard of early society, to discharge the important duty of procreation. Thus the personal qualities of the kings at this stage of social evolution are deemed of vital importance. If they, like their consorts, are of royal and divine descent, so much the better; but it is not essential that they should be so.

At Athens, as at Rome, we find traces of succession to the throne by marriage with a royal princess; for two of the most ancient kings of Athens, namely Cecrops and Amphictyon, are said to have married the daughters of their predecessors. This tradition is to a certain extent confirmed by evidence, pointing to the conclusion that at Athens male kinship was preceded by female kinship.

Further, if I am right in supposing that in ancient Latium the royal families kept their daughters at home and sent forth their sons to marry princesses and reign among their wives' people, it will follow that the male descendants would reign in successive generations over different kingdoms. Now this seems to have happened both in ancient Greece and in ancient Sweden; from which we may legitimately infer that it was a custom practised by more than one branch of the Aryan stock in Europe. Many Greek traditions relate how a prince left his native land, and going to a far country married the king's daughter and succeeded to the kingdom. Various reasons are assigned by ancient Greek writers for these migrations of the princes. A common one is that the king's son had been banished for murder. This would explain very well why he fled his own land, but it is no reason at all why he should become king of another. We may suspect that such reasons are afterthoughts devised by writers, who, accustomed to the rule that a son should succeed to his father's property and kingdom, were hard put to it to account for so many traditions of kings' sons who quitted the land of their birth to reign over a foreign kingdom. In Scandinavian tradition we meet with traces of similar customs. For we read of daughters' husbands who received a share of the kingdoms of their royal fathers-in-law, even when these fathers-in-law had sons of their own; in particular, during the five generations which preceded Harold the Fair-haired, male members of the Ynglingar family, which is said to have come from Sweden, are reported in the *Heimskringla* or *Sagas of the Norwegian Kings* to have obtained at least six provinces in Norway by marriage with the daughters of the local kings.

Thus it would seem that among some Aryan peoples, at a certain stage of their social evolution, it has been customary to regard women and not men as the channels in which royal blood flows, and to bestow the kingdom in each successive generation on a man of another family, and often of another country, who marries one of the princesses and reigns over his wife's people. A common type of popular tale, which relates how an adventurer, coming to a strange land, wins the hand of the king's daughter and with her the half or the whole of the kingdom, may well be a reminiscence of a real custom.

Where usages and ideas of this sort prevail, it is obvious that the kingship is merely an appanage of marriage with a woman of the blood royal. The old Danish historian Saxo Grammaticus puts this view of the kingship very clearly in the mouth of Hermutrude, a legendary queen of Scotland. 'Indeed she was a queen,' says Hermutrude, 'and but that her sex gainsaid it, might be deemed a king; nay (and this is yet truer), whomsoever she thought worthy of her bed was at once a king, and she yielded her kingdom with herself. Thus her sceptre and her hand went together.' The statement is all the more significant because it appears to reflect the actual practice of the Pictish kings. We know from the testimony of Bede that, whenever a doubt arose as to the succession, the Picts chose their kings from the female rather than the male line.

The personal qualities which recommended a man for a royal alliance and succession to the throne would naturally vary according to the popular ideas of the time and the character of the king or his substitute, but it is reasonable to suppose that among them in early society physical strength and beauty would hold a prominent place.

Sometimes apparently the right to the hand of the princess and to the throne has been determined by a race. The Alitemnian

Libyans awarded the kingdom to the fleetest runner. Amongst the old Prussians, candidates for nobility raced on horseback to the king, and the one who reached him first was ennobled. According to tradition the earliest games at Olympia were held by Endymion, who set his sons to run a race for the kingdom. His tomb was said to be at the point of the racecourse from which the runners started. The famous story of Pelops and Hippodamia is perhaps only another version of the legend that the first races at Olympia were run for no less a prize than a kingdom.

These traditions may very well reflect a real custom of racing for a bride, for such a custom appears to have prevailed among various peoples, though in practice it has degenerated into a mere form or pretence. Thus 'there is one race, called "Love Chase," which may be considered a part of the form of marriage among the Kirghiz. In this the bride, armed with a formidable whip, mounts a fleet horse, and is pursued by all the young men who make any pretensions to her hand. She will be given as a prize to the one who catches her, but she has the right, besides urging on her horse to the utmost, to use her whip, often with no mean force, to keep off those lovers who are unwelcome to her, and she will probably favour the one whom she has already chosen in her heart.' The race for the bride is found also among the Koryaks of North-eastern Asia. It takes place in a large tent, round which many separate compartments called *pologs* are arranged in a continuous circle. The girl gets a start and is clear of the marriage if she can run through all the compartments without being caught by the bridegroom. The women of the encampment place every obstacle in the man's way, tripping him up, belabouring him with switches, and so forth, so that he has little chance of succeeding unless the girl wishes it and waits for him. Similar customs appear to have been practised by all the Teutonic peoples; for the German, Anglo-Saxon, and Norse languages possess in common a word for marriage which means simply bride-race. Moreover, traces of the custom survived into modern times.

Thus it appears that the right to marry a girl, and especially a princess, has often been conferred as a prize in an athletic contest. There would be no reason, therefore, for surprise if the Roman kings, before bestowing their daughters in marriage, should have resorted to this ancient mode of testing the personal qualities of their future sons-in-law and successors. If my theory is correct, the Roman king and queen personated Jupiter and his divine consort, and in the character of these divinities went through the annual ceremony of a sacred marriage for the purpose of causing the crops to grow and men and cattle to be fruitful and multiply. Thus they did what in more northern lands we may suppose the King and Queen of May were believed to do in days of old. Now we have seen that the right to play the part of the King of May and to wed the Queen of May has sometimes been determined by an athletic contest, particularly a race. This may have been a relic of an old marriage custom of the sort we have examined, a custom designed to test the fitness of a candidate for matrimony. Such a test might reasonably be applied with peculiar rigour to the king in order to ensure that no personal defect should incapacitate him for the performance of those sacred rites and ceremonies on which, even more than on the despatch of his civil and military duties, the safety and prosperity of the community were believed to depend. And it would be natural to require of him that from time to time he should submit himself afresh to the same ordeal for the sake of publicly demonstrating that he was still equal to the discharge of his high calling. A relic of that test perhaps survived in the ceremony known as the Flight of the King (*regifugium*), which continued to be annually observed at Rome down to imperial times. On the twenty-fourth day of February a sacrifice used to be offered in the Comitium, and when it was over the King of the Sacred Rites fled from the Forum. We may conjecture that the Flight of the King was originally a race for an annual kingship, which may have been awarded as a prize to the fleetest runner. At the end of the year the king might run again for a second term of office; and so on, until he was defeated and deposed or perhaps slain. In this way what had once been a race would tend to assume the character of a flight and a pursuit. The king would be given a start: he ran and his competitors ran after him, and if he were overtaken he had to yield the crown and perhaps his life to the lightest of foot among them. In time a man of masterful character might succeed in seating himself permanently on the throne and reducing the annual race or flight to the empty form which it seems always to have been within historical times. The rite was sometimes interpreted as a commemoration of the expulsion of the kings from Rome; but this appears to have been a mere afterthought devised to explain a ceremony of which the old meaning was forgotten. It is far more likely that in acting thus the King of the Sacred Rites was merely keeping up an ancient custom which in the regal period had been annually observed by his predecessors the kings. What the original intention of the rite may have been must probably always remain more or less a matter of conjecture. The present explanation is suggested with a full sense of the difficulty and obscurity in which the subject is involved.

Thus, if my theory is correct, the yearly flight of the Roman king was a relic of a time when the kingship was an annual office awarded, along with the hand of a princess, to the victorious athlete or gladiator, who thereafter figured along with his bride as a god and goddess at a sacred marriage designed to ensure the fertility of the earth by homoeopathic magic. If I am right in supposing that in very early times the old Latin kings personated a god and were regularly put to death in that character, we can better understand the mysterious or violent ends to which so many of them are said to have come. We have seen that, according to tradition, one of the kings of Alba was killed by a thunderbolt for impiously mimicking the thunder of Jupiter. Romulus is said to have vanished mysteriously like Aeneas, or to have been cut to pieces by the patricians whom he had offended, and the seventh of July, the day on which he perished, was a festival which bore some resemblance to the Saturnalia. For on that day the female slaves were allowed to take certain remarkable liberties. They dressed up as free women in the attire of matrons and maids, and in this guise they went forth from the city, scoffed and jeered at all whom they met, and engaged among themselves in a fight, striking and throwing stones at each other. Another Roman king who perished by violence was Tatius, the Sabine colleague of Romulus. It is said that he was at Lavinium offering a public sacrifice to the ancestral gods, when some men, to whom he had given umbrage, despatched him with the sacrificial knives and spits which they had snatched from the altar. The occasion and the manner of his death suggest that the slaughter may have been a sacrifice rather than an assassination. Again, Tullus

Hostilius, the successor of Numa, was commonly said to have been killed by lightning, but many held that he was murdered at the instigation of Ancus Marcius, who reigned after him. Speaking of the more or less mythical Numa, the type of the priestly king, Plutarch observes that 'his fame was enhanced by the fortunes of the later kings. For of the five who reigned after him the last was deposed and ended his life in exile, and of the remaining four not one died a natural death; for three of them were assassinated and Tullus Hostilius was consumed by thunderbolts.'

These legends of the violent ends of the Roman kings suggest that the contest by which they gained the throne may sometimes have been a mortal combat rather than a race. If that were so, the analogy which we have traced between Rome and Nemi would be still closer. At both places the sacred kings, the living representatives of the godhead, would thus be liable to suffer deposition and death at the hand of any resolute man who could prove his divine right to the holy office by the strong arm and the sharp sword. It would not be surprising if among the early Latins the claim to the kingdom should often have been settled by single combat; for down to historical times the Umbrians regularly submitted their private disputes to the ordeal of battle, and he who cut his adversary's throat was thought thereby to have proved the justice of his cause beyond the reach of cavil.

CHAPTER XV

THE WORSHIP OF THE OAK

THE worship of the oak tree or of the oak god appears to have been shared by all the branches of the Aryan stock in Europe. Both Greeks and Italians associated the tree with their highest god, Zeus or Jupiter, the divinity of the sky, the rain, and the thunder. Perhaps the oldest and certainly one of the most famous sanctuaries in Greece was that of Dodona, where Zeus was revered in the oracular oak. The thunderstorms which are said to rage at Dodona more frequently than anywhere else in Europe, would render the spot a fitting home for the god whose voice was heard alike in the rustling of the oak leaves and in the crash of thunder. Perhaps the bronze gongs which kept up a humming in the wind round the sanctuary were meant to mimic the thunder that might so often be heard rolling and rumbling in the coombs of the stern and barren mountains which shut in the gloomy valley. In Boeotia, as we have seen, the sacred marriage of Zeus and Hera, the oak god and the oak goddess, appears to have been celebrated with much pomp by a religious federation of states. And on Mount Lycaeus in Arcadia the character of Zeus as god both of the oak and of the rain comes out clearly in the rain charm practised by the priest of Zeus, who dipped an oak branch in a sacred spring. In his latter capacity Zeus was the god to whom the Greeks regularly prayed for rain. Nothing could be more natural; for often, though not always, he had his seat on the mountains where the clouds gather and the oaks grow. On the acropolis at Athens there was an image of Earth praying to Zeus for rain. And in time of drought the Athenians themselves prayed, 'Rain, rain, O dear Zeus, on the cornland of the Athenians and on the plains.'

Again, Zeus wielded the thunder and lightning as well as the rain. At Olympia and elsewhere he was worshipped under the surname of Thunderbolt; and at Athens there was a sacrificial hearth of Lightning Zeus on the city wall, where some priestly officials watched for lightning over Mount Parnes at certain seasons of the year. Further, spots which had been struck by lightning were regularly fenced in by the Greeks and consecrated to Zeus the Descender, that is, to the god who came down in the flash from heaven. Altars were set up within these enclosures and sacrifices offered on them. Several such places are known from inscriptions to have existed in Athens.

Thus when ancient Greek kings claimed to be descended from Zeus, and even to bear his name, we may reasonably suppose that they also attempted to exercise his divine functions by making thunder and rain for the good of their people or the terror and confusion of their foes. In this respect the legend of Salmoneus probably reflects the pretensions of a whole class of petty sovereigns who reigned of old, each over his little canton, in the oak-clad highlands of Greece. Like their kinsmen the Irish kings, they were expected to be a source of fertility to the land and of fecundity to the cattle; and how could they fulfil these expectations better than by acting the part of their kinsman Zeus, the great god of the oak, the thunder and the rain? They personified him, apparently, just as the Italian kings personified Jupiter.

In ancient Italy every oak was sacred to Jupiter, the Italian counterpart of Zeus; and on the Capitol at Rome the god was worshipped as the deity not merely of the oak, but of the rain and the thunder. Contrasting the piety of the good old times with the scepticism of an age when nobody thought that heaven was heaven, or cared a fig for Jupiter, a Roman writer tells us that in former days noble matrons used to go with bare feet, streaming hair, and pure minds, up the long Capitoline slope, praying to Jupiter for rain. And straightway, he goes on, it rained bucketsful, then or never, and everybody returned dripping like drowned rats. 'But nowadays,' says he, 'we are no longer religious, so the fields lie baking.'

When we pass from southern to central Europe we still meet with the great god of the oak and the thunder among the barbarous Aryans who dwelt in the vast primaeval forests. Thus among the Celts of Gaul the Druids esteemed nothing more sacred than the mistletoe and the oak on which it grew; they chose groves of oaks for the scene of their solemn service, and they performed none of their rites without oak leaves. 'The Celts,' says a Greek writer, 'worship Zeus, and the Celtic image of Zeus is a tall oak.' The Celtic conquerors, who settled in Asia in the third century before our era, appear to have carried the worship of the oak with them to their new home; for in the heart of Asia Minor the Galatian senate met in a place which bore the pure Celtic name of Drynemetum, 'the sacred oak grove,' or 'the temple of the oak.' Indeed the very name of Druids is believed by good authorities to mean no more than 'oak men.'

In the religion of the ancient Germans the veneration for sacred groves seems to have held the foremost place, and according to Grimm the chief of their holy trees was the oak. It appears to have been especially dedicated to the god of thunder, Donar or Thunar, the equivalent of the Norse Thor; for a sacred oak near Geismar, in Hesse, which Boniface cut down in the eighth century, went among the heathen by the name of Jupiter's oak (*robur Jovis*), which in old German would be *Donares eih*, 'the oak of Donar.' That the Teutonic thunder god Donar, Thunar, Thor was identified with the Italian thunder god Jupiter appears from our word Thursday, Thunar's day, which is merely a rendering of the Latin *dies Jovis*. Thus among the ancient Teutons, as among the Greeks and Italians, the god of the oak was also the god of the thunder. Moreover, he was regarded as the great fertilising power, who sent rain and caused the earth to bear fruit; for Adam of Bremen tells us that 'Thor presides in the air; he it is who rules thunder and lightning, wind and rains, fine weather and crops.' In these respects, therefore, the Teutonic thunder god again resembled his southern counterparts Zeus and Jupiter.

Amongst the Slavs also the oak appears to have been the sacred tree of the thunder god Perun, the counterpart of Zeus and Jupiter. It is said that at Novgorod there used to stand an image of Perun in the likeness of a man with a thunder-stone in his hand. A fire of oak wood burned day and night in his honour; and if ever it went out the attendants paid for their negligence with their lives. Perun seems, like Zeus and Jupiter, to have been the chief god of his people; for Procopius tells us that the Slavs 'believe that one god, the maker of lightning, is alone lord of all things, and they sacrifice to him oxen and every victim.'

The chief deity of the Lithuanians was Perkunas or Perkuns, the god of thunder and lightning, whose resemblance to Zeus and Jupiter has often been pointed out. Oaks were sacred to him, and when they were cut down by the Christian missionaries, the people loudly complained that their sylvan deities were destroyed. Perpetual fires, kindled with the wood of certain oak trees, were kept up in honour of Perkunas; if such a fire went out, it was lighted again by friction of the sacred wood. Men sacrificed to oak-trees for good crops, while women did the same to lime-trees; from which we may infer that they regarded oaks as male and lime-trees as female. And in time of drought, when they wanted rain, they used to sacrifice a black heifer, a black he-goat, and a black cock to the thunder god in the depths of the woods. On such occasions the people assembled in great numbers from the country round about, ate and drank, and called upon Perkunas. They carried a bowl of beer thrice round the fire, then poured the liquor on the flames, while they prayed to the god to send showers. Thus the chief Lithuanian deity presents a close resemblance to Zeus and Jupiter, since he was the god of the oak, the thunder, and the rain.

From the foregoing survey it appears that a god of the oak, the thunder, and the rain was worshipped of old by all the main branches of the Aryan stock in Europe, and was indeed the chief deity of their pantheon.

CHAPTER XVI

DIANUS AND DIANA

In this chapter I propose to recapitulate the conclusions to which the enquiry has thus far led us, and drawing together the scattered rays of light, to turn them on the dark figure of the priest of Nemi.

We have found that at an early stage of society men, ignorant of the secret processes of nature and of the narrow limits within which it is in our power to control and direct them, have commonly arrogated to themselves functions which in the present state of knowledge we should deem superhuman or divine. The illusion has been fostered and maintained by the same causes which begot it, namely, the marvellous order and uniformity with which nature conducts her operations, the wheels of her great machine revolving with a smoothness and precision which enable the patient observer to anticipate in general the season, if not the very hour, when they will bring round the fulfilment of his hopes or the accomplishment of his fears. The regularly recurring events of this great cycle, or rather series of cycles, soon stamp themselves even on the dull mind of the savage. He foresees them, and foreseeing them mistakes the desired recurrence for an effect of his own will, and the dreaded recurrence for an effect of the will of his enemies. Thus the springs which set the vast machine in motion, though they lie far beyond our ken, shrouded in a mystery which we can never

H

hope to penetrate, appear to ignorant man to lie within his reach: he fancies he can touch them and so work by magic art all manner of good to himself and evil to his foes. In time the fallacy of this belief becomes apparent to him: he discovers that there are things he cannot do, pleasures which he is unable of himself to procure, pains which even the most potent magician is powerless to avoid. The unattainable good, the inevitable ill, are now ascribed by him to the action of invisible powers, whose favour is joy and life, whose anger is misery and death. Thus magic tends to be displaced by religion, and the sorcerer by the priest. At this stage of thought the ultimate causes of things are conceived to be personal beings, many in number and often discordant in character, who partake of the nature and even of the frailty of man, though their might is greater than his, and their life far exceeds the span of his ephemeral existence. Their sharply-marked individualities, their clear-cut outlines have not yet begun, under the powerful solvent of philosophy, to melt and coalesce into that single unknown substratum of phenomena which, according to the qualities with which our imagination invests it, goes by one or other of the high-sounding names which the wit of man has devised to hide his ignorance. Accordingly, so long as men look on their gods as beings akin to themselves and not raised to an unapproachable height above them, they believe it to be possible for those of their own number who surpass their fellows to attain to the divine rank after death or even life. Incarnate human deities of this latter sort may be said to halt midway between the age of magic and the age of religion. If they bear the names and display the pomp of deities, the powers which they are supposed to wield are commonly those of their predecessor the magician. Like him, they are expected to guard their people against hostile enchantments, to heal them in sickness, to bless them with offspring, and to provide them with an abundant supply of food by regulating the weather and performing the other ceremonies which are deemed necessary to ensure the fertility of the earth and the multiplication of animals. Men who are credited with powers so lofty and far-reaching naturally hold the highest place in the land, and while the rift between the spiritual and the temporal spheres has not yet widened too far, they are supreme in civil as well as religious matters: in a word, they are kings as well as gods. Thus the divinity which hedges a king has its roots deep down in human history, and long ages pass before these are sapped by a profounder view of nature and man.

In the classical period of Greek and Latin antiquity the reign of kings was for the most part a thing of the past; yet the stories of their lineage, titles, and pretensions suffice to prove that they too claimed to rule by divine right and to exercise superhuman powers. Hence we may without undue temerity assume that the King of the Wood at Nemi, though shorn in later times of his glory and fallen on evil days, represented a long line of sacred kings who had once received not only the homage but the adoration of their subjects in return for the manifold blessings which they were supposed to dispense. What little we know of the functions of Diana in the Arician grove seems to prove that she was here conceived as a goddess of fertility, and particularly as a divinity of childbirth. It is reasonable, therefore, to suppose that in the discharge of these important duties she was assisted by her priest, the two figuring as King and Queen of the Wood in a solemn marriage, which was intended to make the earth gay with blossoms of spring and the fruits of autumn, and to gladden the hearts of men and women with healthful offspring.

If the priest of Nemi posed not merely as a king, but as a god of the grove, we have still to ask, What deity in particular did he personate? The answer of antiquity is that he represented Virbius, the consort or lover of Diana. But this does not help much, for of Virbius we know little more than the name. A clue to the mystery is perhaps supplied by the Vestal fire which burned in the grove. For the perpetual holy fires of the Aryans in Europe appear to have been commonly kindled and fed with oak wood, and in Rome itself, not many miles from Nemi, the fuel of the Vestal fire consisted of oaken sticks or logs, as has been proved by a microscopic analysis of the charred embers of the Vestal fire, which were discovered by Commendatore G. Boni in the course of the memorable excavations which he conducted in the Roman forum at the end of the nineteenth century. But the ritual of the various Latin towns seems to have been marked by great uniformity; hence it is reasonable to conclude that wherever in Latium a Vestal fire was maintained, it was fed, as at Rome, with wood of the sacred oak. If this was so at Nemi, it becomes probable that the hallowed grove there consisted of a natural oak-wood, and that therefore the tree which the King of the Wood had to guard at the peril of his life was itself an oak; indeed, it was from an evergreen oak, according to Virgil, that Aeneas plucked the Golden Bough. Now the oak was the sacred tree of Jupiter, the supreme god of the Latins. Hence it follows that the King of the Wood, whose life was bound up in a fashion with an oak, personated no less a deity than Jupiter himself. At least the evidence, slight as it is, seems to point to this conclusion. The old Alban dynasty of the Silvii or Woods, with their crown of oak leaves, apparently aped the style and emulated the powers of Latian Jupiter, who dwelt on the top of the Alban Mount. It is not impossible that the King of the Wood, who guarded the sacred oak a little lower down the mountain, was the lawful successor and representative of this ancient line of the Silvii or Woods. At all events, if I am right in supposing that he passed for a human Jupiter, it would appear that Virbius, with whom legend identified him, was nothing but a local form of Jupiter, considered perhaps in his original aspect as a god of the greenwood.

The hypothesis that in later times at all events the King of the Wood played the part of the oak-god Jupiter, is confirmed by an examination of his divine partner Diana. For two distinct lines of argument converge to show that if Diana was a queen of the woods in general, she was at Nemi a goddess of the oak in particular. In the first place, she bore the title of Vesta, and as such presided over a perpetual fire, which we have seen reason to believe was fed with oak wood. But a goddess of fire is not far removed from a goddess of the fuel which burns in the fire; primitive thought perhaps drew no sharp line of distinction between the blaze and the wood that blazes. In the second place, the nymph Egeria at Nemi appears to have been merely a form of Diana, and Egeria is definitely said to have been a Dryad, a nymph of the oak. Elsewhere in Italy the goddess had her home on oak-clad mountains. Thus Mount Algidus, a spur of the Alban hills, was covered in antiquity with dark forests of oak, both of the evergreen and the deciduous sort. In winter the snow lay long on these cold hills, and their gloomy oak-woods were believed to be a favourite haunt of Diana, as they have been of brigands in modern times. Again,

Mount Tifata, the long abrupt ridge of the Apennines which looks down on the Campanian plain behind Capua, was wooded of old with evergreen oaks, among which Diana had a temple. Here Sulla thanked the goddess for his victory over the Marians in the plain below, attesting his gratitude by inscriptions which were long afterwards to be seen in the temple. On the whole, then, we conclude that at Nemi the King of the Wood personated the oak-god Jupiter and mated with the oak-goddess Diana in the sacred grove. An echo of their mystic union has come down to us in the legend of the loves of Numa and Egeria, who according to some had their trysting-place in these holy woods.

To this theory it may naturally be objected that the divine consort of Jupiter was not Diana but Juno, and that if Diana had a mate at all he might be expected to bear the name not of Jupiter, but of Dianus or Janus, the latter of these forms being merely a corruption of the former. All this is true, but the objection may be parried by observing that the two pairs of deities, Jupiter and Juno on the one side, and Dianus and Diana, or Janus and Jana, on the other side, are merely duplicates of each other, their names and their functions being in substance and origin identical. With regard to their names, all four of them come from the same Aryan root *DI*, meaning ' bright,' which occurs in the names of the corresponding Greek deities, Zeus and his old female consort Dione. In regard to their functions, Juno and Diana were both goddesses of fecundity and childbirth, and both were sooner or later identified with the moon. As to the true nature and functions of Janus the ancients themselves were puzzled; and where they hesitated, it is not for us confidently to decide. But the view mentioned by Varro that Janus was the god of the sky is supported not only by the etymological identity of his name with that of the sky-god Jupiter, but also by the relation in which he appears to have stood to Jupiter's two mates, Juno and Juturna. For the epithet Junonian bestowed on Janus points to a marriage union between the two deities; and according to one account Janus was the husband of the water nymph Juturna, who according to others was beloved by Jupiter. Moreover, Janus, like Jove, was regularly invoked, and commonly spoken of, under the title of Father. Indeed, he was identified with Jupiter not merely by the logic of the learned St. Augustine, but by the piety of a pagan worshipper who dedicated an offering to Jupiter Dianus. A trace of his relation to the oak may be found in the oak-woods of the Janiculum, the hill on the right bank of the Tiber, where Janus is said to have reigned as a king in the remotest ages of Italian history.

Thus, if I am right, the same ancient pair of deities was variously known among the Greek and Italian peoples as Zeus and Dione, Jupiter and Juno, or Dianus (Janus) and Diana (Jana), the names of the divinities being identical in substance, though varying in form with the dialect of the particular tribe which worshipped them. At first, when the peoples dwelt near each other, the difference between the deities would be hardly more than one of name; in other words, it would be almost purely dialectical. But the gradual dispersion of the tribes, and their consequent isolation from each other, would favour the growth of divergent modes of conceiving and worshipping the gods whom they had carried with them from their old home, so that in time discrepancies of myth and ritual would tend to spring up and thereby to convert a nominal into a real distinction between the divinities. Accordingly when, with the slow progress of culture, the long period of barbarism and separation was passing away, and the rising political power of a single strong community had begun to draw or hammer its weaker neighbours into a nation, the confluent peoples would throw their gods, like their dialects, into a common stock; and thus it might come about that the same ancient deities, which their forefathers had worshipped together before the dispersion, would now be so disguised by the accumulated effect of dialectical and religious divergencies that their original identity might fail to be recognised, and they would take their places side by side as independent divinities in the national pantheon.

This duplication of deities, the result of the final fusion of kindred tribes who had long lived apart, would account for the appearance of Janus beside Jupiter, and of Diana or Jana beside Juno in the Roman religion. At least this appears to be a more probable theory than the opinion, which has found favour with some modern scholars, that Janus was originally nothing but the god of doors. That a deity of his dignity and importance, whom the Romans revered as a god of gods and the father of his people, should have started in life as a humble, though doubtless respectable, doorkeeper appears very unlikely. So lofty an end hardly consorts with so lowly a beginning. It is more probable that the door (*janua*) got its name from Janus than that he got his name from it. This view is strengthened by a consideration of the word *janua* itself. The regular word for door is the same in all the languages of the Aryan family from India to Ireland. It is *dur* in Sanscrit, *thura* in Greek, *tür* in German, *door* in English, *dorus* in old Irish, and *foris* in Latin. Yet besides this ordinary name for door, which the Latins shared with all their Aryan brethren, they had also the name *janua*, to which there is no corresponding term in any Indo-European speech. The word has the appearance of being an adjectival form derived from the noun *Janus*. I conjecture that it may have been customary to set up an image or symbol of Janus at the principal door of the house in order to place the entrance under the protection of the great god. A door thus guarded might be known as a *janua foris*, that is, a Januan door, and the phrase might in time be abridged into *janua*, the noun *foris* being understood but not expressed. From this to the use of *janua* to designate a door in general, whether guarded by an image of Janus or not, would be an easy and natural transition.

If there is any truth in this conjecture, it may explain very simply the origin of the double head of Janus, which has so long exercised the ingenuity of mythologists. When it had become customary to guard the entrance of houses and towns by an image of Janus, it might well be deemed necessary to make the sentinel god look both ways, before and behind, at the same time, in order that nothing should escape his vigilant eye. For if the divine watchman always faced in one direction, it is easy to imagine what mischief might have been wrought with impunity behind his back. This explanation of the double-headed Janus at Rome is confirmed by the double-headed idol which the Bush negroes in the interior of Surinam regularly set up as a guardian at the entrance of a village. The idol consists of a block of wood with a human face rudely carved on each side; it stands under a gateway composed of two uprights and a cross-bar. Beside the idol generally lies a white rag intended to keep off the devil; and sometimes there is also a stick which seems to represent a bludgeon or weapon of some sort. Further, from the cross-bar hangs a small log which serves the useful purpose of knocking on the head any evil spirit who might attempt to pass through the gateway.

Clearly this double-headed fetish at the gateway of the negro villages in Surinam bears a close resemblance to the double-headed images of Janus which, grasping a stick in one hand and a key in the other, stood sentinel at Roman gates and doorways; and we can hardly doubt that in both cases the heads facing two ways are to be similarly explained as expressive of the vigilance of the guardian god, who kept his eye on spiritual foes behind and before, and stood ready to bludgeon them on the spot. We may, therefore, dispense with the tedious and unsatisfactory explanations with which, if we may trust Ovid, the wily Janus himself fobbed off an anxious Roman enquirer.

To apply these conclusions to the priest of Nemi, we may suppose that as the mate of Diana he represented originally Dianus or Janus rather than Jupiter, but that the difference between these deities was of old merely superficial, going little deeper than the names, and leaving practically unaffected the essential functions of the god as a power of the sky, the thunder, and the oak. It was fitting, therefore, that his human representative at Nemi should dwell, as we have seen reason to believe he did, in an oak grove. His title of King of the Wood clearly indicates the sylvan character of the deity whom he served; and since he could only be assailed by him who had plucked the bough of a certain tree in the grove, his own life might be said to be bound up with that of the sacred tree. Thus he not only served but embodied the great Aryan god of the oak; and as an oak-god he would mate with the oak-goddess, whether she went by the name of Egeria or Diana. Their union, however consummated, would be deemed essential to the fertility of the earth and the fecundity of man and beast. Further, as the oak-god was also a god of the sky, the thunder, and the rain, so his human representative would be required, like many other divine kings, to cause the clouds to gather, the thunder to peal, and the rain to descend in due season, that the fields and orchards might bear fruit and the pastures be covered with luxuriant herbage. The reputed possessor of powers so exalted must have been a very important personage; and the remains of buildings and of votive offerings which have been found on the site of the sanctuary combine with the testimony of classical writers to prove that in later times it was one of the greatest and most popular shrines in Italy. Even in the old days, when the champaign country around was still parcelled out among the petty tribes who composed the Latin League, the sacred grove is known to have been an object of their common reverence and care. And just as the kings of Cambodia used to send offerings to the mystic kings of Fire and Water far in the dim depths of the tropical forest, so, we may well believe, from all sides of the broad Latian plain the eyes and footsteps of Italian pilgrims turned to the quarter where, standing sharply out against the faint blue line of the Apennines or the deeper blue of the distant sea, the Alban Mountain rose before them, the home of the mysterious priest of Nemi, the King of the Wood. There, among the green woods and beside the still waters of the lonely hills, the ancient Aryan worship of the god of the oak, the thunder, and the dripping sky lingered in its early, almost Druidical form, long after a great political and intellectual revolution had shifted the capital of Latin religion from the forest to the city, from Nemi to Rome.

CHAPTER XVII

THE BURDEN OF ROYALTY

§ 1. *Royal and Priestly Taboos.* — At a certain stage of early society the king or priest is often thought to be endowed with supernatural powers or to be an incarnation of a deity, and consistently with this belief the course of nature is supposed to be more or less under his control, and he is held responsible for bad weather, failure of the crops, and similar calamities. To some extent it appears to be assumed that the king's power over nature, like that over his subjects and slaves, is exerted through definite acts of will; and therefore if drought, famine, pestilence, or storms arise, the people attribute the misfortune to the negligence or guilt of their king, and punish him accordingly with stripes and bonds, or, if he remains obdurate, with deposition and death. Sometimes, however, the course of nature, while regarded as dependent on the king, is supposed to be partly independent of his will. His person is considered, if we may express it so, as the dynamical centre of the universe, from which lines of force radiate to all quarters of the heaven; so that any motion of his — the turning of his head, the lifting of his hand — instantaneously affects and may seriously disturb some part of nature. He is the point of support on which hangs the balance of the world, and the slightest irregularity on his part may overthrow the delicate equipoise. The greatest care must, therefore, be taken both by and of him; and his whole life, down to its minutest details, must be so regulated that no act of his, voluntary or involuntary, may disarrange or upset the established order of nature. Of this class of monarchs the Mikado or Dairi, the spiritual emperor of Japan, is or rather used to be a typical example. He is an incarnation of the sun goddess, the deity who rules the universe, gods and men included; once a year all the gods wait upon him and spend a month at his court. During that month, the name of which means 'without gods,' no one frequents the temples, for they are believed to be deserted. The Mikado receives from his people and assumes in his official proclamations and decrees the title of 'manifest or incarnate deity,' and he claims a general authority over the gods of Japan. For example, in an official decree of the year 646 the emperor is described as 'the incarnate god who governs the universe.'

The following description of the Mikado's mode of life was written about two hundred years ago:

'Even to this day the princes descended of this family, more particularly those who sit on the throne, are looked upon as persons most holy in themselves, and as Popes by birth. And, in order to preserve these advantageous notions in the minds of their subjects, they are obliged to take an uncommon care of their sacred persons, and to do such things, which, examined according to the customs of other nations, would be thought ridiculous and impertinent. It will not be improper to give a few instances of it. He thinks that it would be very prejudicial to his dignity and holiness to touch the ground with his feet; for this reason, when he intends to go anywhere, he must be carried thither on men's shoulders. Much less will they suffer that he should expose his sacred person to the open air, and the sun is not thought worthy to shine on his head. There is such a holiness ascribed to all the parts of his body that he dares to cut off neither his hair, nor his beard, nor his nails. However, lest he should grow too dirty, they may clean him in the night when he is asleep; because, they say, that which is taken from his body at that time, hath been stolen from him, and that such a theft doth not prejudice his holiness or dignity. In ancient times, he was obliged to sit on the throne for some hours every morning, with the imperial crown on his head, but to sit altogether like a statue, without stirring either hands or feet, head or eyes, nor indeed any part of his body, because, by this means, it was thought that he could preserve peace and tranquillity in his empire; for if, unfortunately, he turned himself on one side or the other, or if he looked a good while towards any part of his dominions, it was apprehended that war, famine, fire, or some other great misfortune was near at hand to desolate the country. But it having been afterwards discovered, that the imperial crown was the palladium, which by its immobility could preserve peace in the empire, it was thought expedient to deliver his imperial person, consecrated only to idleness and pleasures, from this burthensome duty, and therefore the crown is at present placed on the throne for some hours every morning. His victuals must be dressed every time in new pots, and served at table in new dishes: both are very clean and neat, but made only of common clay; that without any considerable expense they may be laid aside, or broke, after they have served once. They are generally broke, for fear they should come into the hands of laymen, for they believe religiously, that if any layman should presume to eat his food out of these sacred dishes, it would swell and inflame his mouth and throat. The like ill effect is dreaded from the Dairi's sacred habits; for they believe that if a layman should wear them, without the Emperor's express leave or command, they would occasion swellings and pains in all parts of his body.' To the same effect an earlier account of the Mikado says: 'It was considered as a shameful degradation for him even to touch the ground with his foot. The sun and moon were not even permitted to shine upon his head. None of the superfluities of the body were ever taken from him, neither his hair, his beard, nor his nails were cut. Whatever he ate was dressed in new vessels.'

Similar priestly or rather divine kings are found, at a lower level of barbarism, on the west coast of Africa. At Shark Point near Cape Padron, in Lower Guinea, lives the priestly king Kukulu, alone in a wood. He may not touch a woman nor leave his house;

indeed he may not even quit his chair, in which he is obliged to sleep sitting, for if he lay down no wind would arise and navigation would be stopped. He regulates storms, and in general maintains a wholesome and equable state of the atmosphere. On Mount Agu in Togo there lives a fetish or spirit called Bagba, who is of great importance for the whole of the surrounding country. The power of giving or withholding rain is ascribed to him, and he is lord of the winds, including the Harmattan, the dry, hot wind which blows from the interior. His priest dwells in a house on the highest peak of the mountain, where he keeps the winds bottled up in huge jars. Applications for rain, too, are made to him, and he does a good business in amulets, which consist of the teeth and claws of leopards. Yet though his power is great and he is indeed the real chief of the land, the rule of the fetish forbids him ever to leave the mountain, and he must spend the whole of his life on its summit. Only once a year may he come down to make purchases in the market; but even then he may not set foot in the hut of any mortal man, and must return to his place of exile the same day. The business of government in the villages is conducted by subordinate chiefs, who are appointed by him. In the West African kingdom of Congo there was a supreme pontiff called Chitomé or Chitombé, whom the negroes regarded as a god on earth and all-powerful in heaven. Hence before they would taste the new crops they offered him the first-fruits, fearing that manifold misfortunes would befall them if they broke this rule. When he left his residence to visit other places within his jurisdiction, all married people had to observe strict continence the whole time he was out; for it was supposed that any act of incontinence would prove fatal to him. And if he were to die a natural death, they thought that the world would perish, and the earth, which he alone sustained by his power and merit, would immediately be annihilated. Amongst the semi-barbarous nations of the New World, at the date of the Spanish conquest, there were found hierarchies or theocracies like those of Japan; in particular, the high pontiff of the Zapotecs appears to have presented a close parallel to the Mikado. A powerful rival to the king himself, this spiritual lord governed Yopaa, one of the chief cities of the kingdom, with absolute dominion. It is impossible, we are told, to overrate the reverence in which he was held. He was looked on as a god whom the earth was not worthy to hold nor the sun to shine upon. He profaned his sanctity if he even touched the ground with his foot. The officers who bore his palanquin on their shoulders were members of the highest families: he hardly deigned to look on anything around him; and all who met him fell with their faces to the earth, fearing that death would overtake them if they saw even his shadow. A rule of continence was regularly imposed on the Zapotec priests, especially upon the high pontiff; but 'on certain days in each year, which were generally celebrated with feasts and dances, it was customary for the high priest to become drunk. While in this state, seeming to belong neither to heaven nor to earth, one of the most beautiful of the virgins consecrated to the service of the gods was brought to him.' If the child she bore him was a son, he was brought up as a prince of the blood, and the eldest son succeeded his father on the pontifical throne. The supernatural powers attributed to this pontiff are not specified, but probably they resembled those of the Mikado and Chitomé.

Wherever, as in Japan and West Africa, it is supposed that the order of nature, and even the existence of the world, is bound up with the life of the king or priest, it is clear that he must be regarded by his subjects as a source both of infinite blessing and of infinite danger. On the one hand, the people have to thank him for the rain and sunshine which foster the fruits of the earth, for the wind which brings ships to their coasts, and even for the solid ground beneath their feet. But what he gives he can refuse; and so close is the dependence of nature on his person, so delicate the balance of the system of forces whereof he is the centre, that the least irregularity on his part may set up a tremor which shall shake the earth to its foundations. And if nature may be disturbed by the slightest involuntary act of the king, it is easy to conceive the convulsion which his death might provoke. The natural death of the Chitomé, as we have seen, was thought to entail the destruction of all things. Clearly, therefore, out of a regard for their own safety, which might be imperilled by any rash act of the king, and still more by his death, the people will exact of their king or priest a strict conformity to those rules, the observance of which is deemed necessary for his own preservation, and consequently for the preservation of his people and the world. The idea that early kingdoms are despotisms in which the people exist only for the sovereign, is wholly inapplicable to the monarchies we are considering. On the contrary, the sovereign in them exists only for his subjects; his life is only valuable so long as he discharges the duties of his position by ordering the course of nature for his people's benefit. So soon as he fails to do so, the care, the devotion, the religious homage which they had hitherto lavished on him cease and are changed into hatred and contempt; he is dismissed ignominiously, and may be thankful if he escapes with his life. Worshipped as a god one day, he is killed as a criminal the next. But in this changed behaviour of the people there is nothing capricious or inconsistent. On the contrary, their conduct is entirely of a piece. If their king is their god, he is or should be also their preserver; and if he will not preserve them, he must make room for another who will. So long, however, as he answers their expectations, there is no limit to the care which they take of him, and which they compel him to take of himself. A king of this sort lives hedged in by a ceremonious etiquette, a network of prohibitions and observances, of which the intention is not to contribute to his dignity, much less to his comfort, but to restrain him from conduct which, by disturbing the harmony of nature, might involve himself, his people, and the universe in one common catastrophe. Far from adding to his comfort, these observances, by trammelling his every act, annihilate his freedom and often render the very life, which it is their object to preserve, a burden and sorrow to him.

Of the supernaturally endowed kings of Loango it is said that the more powerful a king is, the more taboos is he bound to observe; they regulate all his actions, his walking and his standing, his eating and drinking, his sleeping and waking. To these restraints the heir to the throne is subject from infancy; but as he advances in life the number of abstinences and ceremonies which he must observe increases, 'until at the moment that he ascends the throne he is lost in the ocean of rites and taboos.' In the crater of an extinct volcano, enclosed on all sides by grassy slopes, lie the scattered huts and yam-fields of Riabba, the capital of the native king of Fernando Po. This mysterious being lives in the lowest depths of the crater, surrounded by a harem of forty women, and covered, it is said, with old silver coins. Naked savage as he is, he yet exercises far more influence in the island than the Spanish governor at Santa Isabel. In him the conservative spirit of the Boobies or aboriginal inhabitants of the island is, as it were, incorporate. He has never seen a white man and, according to the firm conviction of all the Boobies, the sight of a pale face would cause his instant death. He cannot bear to look upon the sea; indeed it is said that he may never see it even in the distance, and that therefore he wears away his life with shackles on his legs in the dim twilight of his hut. Certain it is that he has never set foot on the beach. With the exception of his musket and knife, he uses nothing that comes from the whites; European cloth never touches his person, and he scorns tobacco, rum, and even salt.

Among the Ewe-speaking peoples of the Slave Coast 'the king is at the same time high priest. In this quality he was, particularly in former times, unapproachable by his subjects. Only by night was he allowed to quit his dwelling in order to bathe and so forth. None but his representative, the so-called "visible king," with three chosen elders might converse with him, and even they had to sit on an ox-hide with their backs turned to him. He might not see any European nor any horse, nor might he look upon the sea, for which reason he was not allowed to quit his capital even for a few moments. These rules have been disregarded in recent times.' The king of Dahomey himself is subject to the prohibition of beholding the sea, and so are the kings of Loango and Great Ardra in Guinea. The sea is the fetish of the Eyeos, to the north-west of Dahomey, and they and their king are threatened with death by their priests if ever they dare to look on it. It is believed that the king of Cayor in Senegal would infallibly die within the year if he were to cross a river or an arm of the sea. In Mashona-land down to recent times the chiefs would not cross certain rivers, particularly the Rurikwi and the Nyadiri; and the custom was still strictly observed by at least one chief within recent years. 'On no account will the chief cross the river. If it is absolutely necessary for him to do so, he is blindfolded and carried across with shouting and singing. Should he walk across, he will go blind or die and certainly lose his chieftainship.' So among the Mahafalys and Sakalavas in the south of Madagascar some kings are forbidden to sail on the sea or to cross certain rivers.

Among the Sakalavas the chief is regarded as a sacred being, but 'he is held in leash by a crowd of restrictions, which regulate his behaviour like that of the emperor of China. He can undertake nothing whatever unless the sorcerers have declared the omens favourable: he may not eat warm food: on certain days he may not quit his hut; and so on.' Among some of the hill tribes of Assam both the headman and his wife have to observe many taboos in respect of food; thus they may not eat buffalo, pork, dog, fowl, or tomatoes. The headman must be chaste, the husband of one wife, and he must separate himself from her on the eve of a general or public observance of taboo. In one group of tribes the headman is forbidden to eat in a strange village, and under no provocation whatever may he utter a word of abuse. Apparently the people imagine that the violation of any of these taboos by a headman would bring down misfortune on the whole village.

The ancient kings of Ireland, as well as the kings of the four provinces of Leinster, Munster, Connaught, and Ulster, were subject to certain quaint prohibitions or taboos, on the due observance of which the prosperity of the people and the country, as well as their own, was supposed to depend. Thus, for example, the sun might not rise on the king of Ireland in his bed at Tara, the old capital of Erin; he was forbidden to alight on Wednesday at Magh Breagh, to traverse Magh Cuillinn after sunset, to incite his horse at Fan-Chomair, to go in a ship upon the water the Monday after Bealltaine (May Day), and to leave the track of his army upon Ath Maighne the Tuesday after All-Hallows. The king of Leinster might not go round Tuath Laighean left-hand-wise on Wednesday, nor sleep between the Dothair (Dodder) and the Duibhlinn with his head inclining to one side, nor encamp for nine days on the plains of Cualann, nor travel the road of Duibhlinn on Monday, nor ride a dirty black-heeled horse across Magh Maistean. The king of Munster was prohibited from enjoying the feast of Loch Lein from one Monday to another; from banqueting by night in the beginning of harvest before Geim at Leitreacha; from encamping for nine days upon the Siuir; and from holding a border meeting at Gabhran. The king of Connaught might not conclude a treaty respecting his ancient palace of Cruachan after making peace on All-Hallows Day, nor go in a speckled garment on a grey speckled steed on the heath of Dal Chais, nor repair to an assembly of women at Seaghais, nor sit in autumn on the sepulchral mounds of the wife of Maine, nor contend in running with the rider of a grey one-eyed horse at Ath Gallta between two posts. The king of Ulster was forbidden to attend the horse fair at Rath Line among the youths of Dal Araidhe, to listen to the fluttering of the flocks of birds of Linn Saileach after sunset, to celebrate the feast of the bull of Daire-mic-Daire, to go into Magh Cobha in the month of March, and to drink of the water of Bo Neimhidh between two darknesses. If the kings of Ireland strictly observed these and many other customs, which were enjoined by immemorial usage, it was believed that they would never meet with mischance or misfortune, and would live for ninety years without experiencing the decay of old age; that no epidemic or mortality would occur during their reigns; and that the seasons would be favourable and the earth yield its fruit in abundance; whereas, if they set the ancient usages at naught, the country would be visited with plague, famine, and bad weather.

The kings of Egypt were worshipped as gods, and the routine of their daily life was regulated in every detail by precise and unvarying rules. 'The life of the kings of Egypt,' says Diodorus, 'was not like that of other monarchs who are irresponsible and may do just what they choose; on the contrary, everything was fixed for them by law, not only their official duties, but even the details of their daily life. . . . The hours both of day and night were arranged at which the king had to do, not what he pleased, but what was prescribed for him. . . . For not only were the times appointed at which he should transact public business or sit in judgment; but the very hours for his walking and bathing and sleeping with his wife, and, in short, performing every act of life were all settled. Custom enjoyed a simple diet; the only flesh he might eat was veal and goose, and he might only drink a prescribed quantity of wine.' However, there is reason to think that these rules were observed, not by the ancient Pharaohs, but by the priestly kings who reigned at Thebes and in Ethiopia at the close of the twentieth dynasty.

Of the taboos imposed on priests we may see a striking example in the rules of life prescribed for the Flamen Dialis at Rome, who has been interpreted as a living image of Jupiter, or a human embodiment of the sky-spirit. They were such as the following: The Flamen Dialis might not ride or even touch a horse, nor see an army under arms, nor wear a ring which was not broken, nor have a knot on any part of his garments; no fire except a sacred fire might be taken out of his house; he might not touch wheaten flour or leavened bread; he might not touch or even name a goat, a dog, raw meat, beans, and ivy; he might not walk under a vine; the feet of his bed had to be daubed with mud; his hair could be cut only by a free man and with a bronze knife, and his hair and nails when cut had to be buried under a lucky tree; he might not touch a dead body nor enter a place where one was burned; he might not see work being done on holy days; he might not be uncovered in the open air; if a man in bonds were taken into his house, the captive had to be unbound and the cords had to be drawn up through a hole in the roof and so let down into the street. His wife, the Flaminica, had to observe nearly the same rules, and others of her own besides. She might not ascend more than three steps of the kind of staircase called Greek; at a certain festival she might not comb her hair; the leather of her shoes might not be made from a beast that had died a natural death, but only from one that had been slain or sacrificed; if she heard thunder she was tabooed till she had offered an expiatory sacrifice.

Among the Grebo people of Sierra Leone there is a pontiff who bears the title of Bodia and has been compared, on somewhat slender grounds, to the high priest of the Jews. He is appointed in accordance with the behest of an oracle. At an elaborate ceremony of installation he is anointed, a ring is put on his ankle as a badge of office, and the door-posts of his house are sprinkled with the blood of a sacrificed goat. He has charge of the public talismans and idols, which he feeds with rice and oil every new moon; and he sacrifices on behalf of the town to the dead and to demons. Nominally his power is very great, but in practice it is very limited; for he dare not defy public opinion, and he is held responsible, even with his life, for any adversity that befalls the country. It is expected of him that he should cause the earth to bring forth abundantly, the people to be healthy, war to be driven far away, and witchcraft to be kept in abeyance. His life is trammelled by the observance of certain restrictions or taboos. Thus he may not sleep in any house but his own official residence, which is called the 'anointed house' with reference to the ceremony of anointing him at inauguration. He may not drink water on the highway. He may not eat while a corpse is in the town, and he may not mourn for the dead. If he dies while in office, he must be buried at the dead of night; few may hear of his burial, and none may mourn for him when his death is made public. Should he have fallen a victim to the poison ordeal by drinking a decoction of sassywood, as it is called, he must be buried under a running stream of water.

Among the Todas of Southern India the holy milkman, who acts as priest of the sacred dairy, is subject to a variety of irksome and burdensome restrictions during the whole time of his incumbency, which may last many years. Thus he must live at the sacred dairy and may never visit his home or an ordinary village. He must be celibate; if he is married he must leave his wife. On no account may an ordinary person touch the holy milkman or the holy dairy; such a touch would so defile his holiness that he would forfeit his office. It is only on two days a week, namely Mondays and Thursdays, that a mere layman may even approach the milkman; on other days, if he has any business with him, he must stand at a distance (some say a quarter of a mile) and shout his message across the intervening space. Further, the holy milkman never cuts his hair or pares his nails so long as he holds office; he never crosses a river by a bridge, but wades through a ford and only certain fords; if a death occurs in his clan, he may not attend any of the funeral ceremonies, unless he first resigns his office and descends from the exalted rank of milkman to that of a mere common mortal. Indeed it appears that in old days he had to resign the seals, or rather the pails, of office whenever any member of his clan departed this life. However, these heavy restraints are laid in their entirety only on milkmen of the very highest class.

§ 2. *Divorce of the Spiritual from the Temporal Power.* — The burdensome observances attached to the royal or priestly office produced their natural effect. Either men refused to accept the office, which hence tended to fall into abeyance; or accepting it, they sank under its weight into spiritless creatures, cloistered recluses, from whose nerveless fingers the reins of government slipped into the firmer grasp of men who were often content to wield the reality of sovereignty without its name. In some countries this rift in the supreme power deepened into a total and permanent separation of the spiritual and temporal powers, the old royal house retaining their purely religious functions, while the civil government passed into the hands of a younger and more vigorous race.

To take examples. In a previous part of this work we saw that in Cambodia it is often necessary to force the kingships of Fire and Water upon the reluctant successors, and that in Savage Island the monarchy actually came to an end because at last no one could be induced to accept the dangerous distinction. In some parts of West Africa, when the king dies, a family council is secretly held to determine his successor. He on whom the choice falls is suddenly seized, bound, and thrown into the fetish-house, where he is kept in durance till he consents to accept the crown. Sometimes the heir finds means of evading the honour which it is sought to thrust upon him; a ferocious chief has been known to go about constantly armed, resolute to resist by force any attempt to set him on the throne. The savage Timmes of Sierra Leone, who elect their king, reserve to themselves the right of beating him on the eve of his coronation; and they avail themselves of this constitutional privilege with such hearty goodwill that sometimes the unhappy monarch does not long survive his elevation to the throne. Hence when the leading chiefs have a spite at a man and wish to rid themselves of him, they elect him king. Formerly, before a man was proclaimed king of Sierra Leone, it used to be the custom to load him with chains and thrash him. Then the fetters were knocked off, the kingly robe placed on him, and he received in his hands the symbol of royal dignity, which was nothing but the axe of the executioner. It is not therefore surprising to read that in Sierra Leone, where such customs have prevailed, 'except among the Mandingoes and Suzees, few kings are natives of the countries they govern. So different are their ideas from ours, that very few are solicitous of the honour, and competition is very seldom heard of.'

The Mikados of Japan seem early to have resorted to the expedient of transferring the honours and burdens of supreme power to their infant children; and the rise of the Tycoons, long the temporal sovereigns of the country, is traced to the abdication of a certain Mikado in favour of his three-year-old son. The sovereignty having been wrested by a usurper from the infant prince, the cause of the Mikado was championed by Yoritomo, a man of spirit and conduct, who overthrew the usurper and restored to the Mikado the shadow, while he retained for himself the substance, of power. He bequeathed to his descendants the dignity he had won, and thus became the founder of the line of Tycoons. Down to the latter half of the sixteenth century the Tycoons were active and efficient rulers; but the same fate overtook them which had befallen the Mikados. Immeshed in the same inextricable web of custom and law, they degenerated into mere puppets, hardly stirring from their palaces and occupied in a perpetual round of empty ceremonies, while the real business of government was managed by the council of state. In Tonquin the monarchy ran a similar course. Living like his predecessors in effeminacy and sloth, the king was driven from the throne by an ambitious adventurer named Mack, who from a fisherman had risen to be Grand Mandarin. But the king's brother Tring put down the usurper and restored the king, retaining, however, for himself and his descendants the dignity of general of all the forces. Thenceforward the kings, though invested with the title and pomp of sovereignty, ceased to govern. While they lived secluded in their palaces, all real political power was wielded by the hereditary generals.

In Mangaia, a Polynesian island, religious and civil authority were lodged in separate hands, spiritual functions being discharged by a line of hereditary kings, while the temporal government was entrusted from time to time to a victorious war-chief, whose investiture, however, had to be completed by the king. Similarly in Tonga, besides the civil king whose right to the throne was partly hereditary and partly derived from his warlike reputation and the number of his fighting men, there was a great divine chief who ranked above the king and the other chiefs in virtue of his supposed descent from one of the chief gods. Once a year the first-fruits of the ground were offered to him at a solemn ceremony, and it was believed that if these offerings were not made the vengeance of the gods would fall in a signal manner on the people. Peculiar forms of speech, such as were applied to no one else, were used in speaking of him, and everything that he chanced to touch became sacred or tabooed. When he and the king met, the monarch had to sit down on the ground in token of respect, until his holiness passed by. Yet though he enjoyed the highest venera-tion by reason of his divine origin, this sacred personage possessed no political authority, and if he ventured to meddle with affairs of state it was at the risk of receiving a rebuff from the king, to whom the real power belonged, and who finally succeeded in ridding himself of his spiritual rival.

In some parts of Western Africa two kings reign side by side, a fetish or religious king and a civil king, but the fetish king is really supreme. He controls the weather and so forth, and can put a stop to everything. When he lays his red staff on the ground, no one may pass that way. This division of power between a sacred and a secular ruler is to be met with wherever the true negro culture has been left unmolested, but where the negro form of society has been disturbed, as in Dahomey and Ashantee, there is a tendency to consolidate the two powers in a single king.

In some parts of the East Indian island of Timor we meet with a partition of power like that which is represented by the civil king and the fetish king of Western Africa. Some of the Timorese tribes recognise two rajahs, the ordinary or civil rajah, who governs the people, and the fetish or taboo rajah, who is charged with the control of everything that concerns the earth and its products. This latter ruler has the right of declaring anything taboo; his permission must be obtained before new land may be brought under cultivation, and he must perform certain necessary ceremonies when the work is being carried out. If drought or blight threatens the crops, his help is invoked to save them. Though he ranks below the civil rajah, he exercises a momentous influence on the course of events, for his secular colleague is bound to consult him in all important matters. In some of the neighbouring islands, such as Rotti and eastern Flores, a spiritual ruler of the same sort is recognised under various native names, which all mean 'lord of the ground.' Similarly in the Mekeo district of British New Guinea there is a double chieftainship. The people are divided into two groups according to families, and each of the groups has its chief. One of the two is the war chief, the other is the taboo chief. The office of the latter is hereditary; his duty is to impose a taboo on any of the crops, such as the coco-nuts and areca nuts, whenever he thinks it desirable to prohibit their use. In his office we may perhaps detect the beginning of a priestly dynasty, but as yet his functions appear to be more magical than religious, being concerned with the control of the harvests rather than with the propitiation of higher powers.

CHAPTER XVIII

THE PERILS OF THE SOUL

§ 1. *The Soul as a Mannikin.* — The foregoing examples have taught us that the office of a sacred king or priest is often hedged in by a series of burdensome restrictions or taboos, of which a principal purpose appears to be to preserve the life of the divine man for the good of his people. But if the object of the taboos is to save his life, the question arises, How is their observance supposed to effect this end? To understand this we must know the nature of the danger which threatens the king's life, and which it is the intention of these curious restrictions to guard against. We must, therefore, ask: What does early man understand by death? To what causes does he attribute it? And how does he think it may be guarded against?

As the savage commonly explains the processes of inanimate nature by supposing that they are produced by living beings working in or behind the phenomena, so he explains the phenomena of life itself. If an animal lives and moves, it can only be, he thinks, because there is a little animal inside which moves it: if a man lives and moves, it can only be because he has a little man or animal inside who moves him. The animal inside the animal, the man inside the man, is the soul. And as the activity of an animal or man is explained by the presence of the soul, so the repose of sleep or death is explained by its absence; sleep or trance being the temporary, death being the permanent absence of the soul. Hence if death be the permanent absence of the soul, the way to guard against it is either to prevent the soul from leaving the body, or, if it does depart, to ensure that it shall return.

The precautions adopted by savages to secure one or other of these ends take the form of certain prohibitions or taboos, which are nothing but rules intended to ensure either the continued presence or the return of the soul. In short, they are life-preservers or life-guards. These general statements will now be illustrated by examples.

Addressing some Australian blacks, a European missionary said, 'I am not one, as you think, but two'. Upon this they laughed. 'You may laugh as much as you like,' continued the missionary. 'I tell you that I am two in one; this great body that you see is one; within that there is another little one which is not visible. The great body dies, and is buried, but the little body flies away when the great one dies.' To this some of the blacks replied, 'Yes, yes. We also are two, we also have a little body within the breast.' On being asked where the little body went after death, some said it went behind the bush, others said it went into the sea, and some said they did not know. The Hurons thought that the soul had a head and body, arms and legs; in short, that it was a complete little model of the man himself. The Esquimaux believe that 'the soul exhibits the same shape as the body it belongs to, but is of a more subtle and ethereal nature.' According to the Nootkas the soul has the shape of a tiny man; its seat is the crown of the head. So long as it stands erect, its owner is hale and hearty; but when from any cause it loses its upright position, he loses his senses. Among the Indian tribes of the Lower Fraser River, man is held to have four souls, of which the principal one has the form of a mannikin, while the other three are shadows of it. The Malays conceive the human soul as a little man, mostly invisible and of the bigness of a thumb, who corresponds exactly in shape, proportion, and even in complexion to the man in whose body he resides. This mannikin is of a thin unsubstantial nature, though not so impalpable but that it may cause displacement on entering a physical object, and it can flit quickly from place to place; it is temporarily absent from the body in sleep, trance, and disease, and permanently absent after death.

So exact is the resemblance of the mannikin to the man, in other words, of the soul to the body, that, as there are fat bodies and thin bodies, so there are fat souls and thin souls; as there are heavy bodies and light bodies, long bodies and short bodies, so there are heavy souls and light souls, long souls and short souls. The people of Nias think that every man, before he is born, is asked how long or how heavy a soul he would like, and a soul of the desired weight or length is measured out to him. The heaviest soul ever given out weighs ten grammes. The length of a man's life is proportioned to the length of his soul; children who die young had short souls. The Fijian conception of the soul as a tiny human being comes clearly out in the customs observed at the death of a chief among the Nakelo tribe. When a chief dies, certain men, who are the hereditary undertakers, call him, as he lies, oiled and ornamented, on fine mats, saying, 'Rise, sir, the chief, and let us be going. The day has come over the land.' Then they conduct him to the river side, where the ghostly ferry-man comes to ferry Nakelo ghosts across the stream. As they thus attend the chief on his last journey, they hold their great fans close to the ground to shelter him, because, as one of them explained to a missionary, 'His soul is only a little child.' People in the Punjaub who tattoo themselves believe that at death the soul, 'the little entire man or woman' inside the mortal frame, will go to heaven blazoned with the same tattoo patterns which adorned the body in life. Sometimes, however, as we shall see, the human soul is conceived not in human but in animal form.

§ 2. *Absence and Recall of the Soul.*—The soul is commonly supposed to escape by the natural openings of the body, especially the mouth and nostrils. Hence in Celebes they sometimes fasten fish-hooks to a sick man's nose, navel, and feet, so that if his soul should try to escape it may be hooked and held fast. A Turik on the Baram River, in Borneo, refused to part with some hook-like stones, because they, as it were, hooked his soul to his body, and so prevented the spiritual portion of him from becoming detached from the material. When a Sea Dyak sorcerer or medicine-man is initiated, his fingers are supposed to be furnished with fish-hooks, with which he will thereafter clutch the human soul in the act of flying away, and restore it to the body of the sufferer. But hooks, it is plain, may be used to catch the souls of enemies as well as of friends. Acting on this principle head-hunters in Borneo hang wooden hooks beside the skulls of their slain enemies in the belief that this helps them on their forays to hook in fresh heads. One of the implements of a Haida medicine-man is a hollow bone, in which he bottles up departing souls, and so restores them to their owners. When any one yawns in their presence the Hindoos always snap their thumbs, believing this will hinder the soul from issuing through the open mouth. The Marquesans used to hold the mouth and nose of a dying man, in order to keep him in life by preventing his soul from escaping; the same custom is reported of the New Caledonians; and with the like intention the Bagobos of the Philippine Islands put rings of brass wire on the wrists or ankles of their sick. On the other hand, the Itonamas of South America seal up the eyes, nose, and mouth of a dying person, in case his ghost should get out and carry off others; and for a similar reason the people of Nias, who fear the spirits of the recently deceased and identify them with the breath, seek to confine the vagrant soul in its earthly tabernacle by bunging up the nose or tying up the jaws of the corpse. Before leaving a corpse the Wakelbura of Australia used to place hot coals in its ears in order to keep the ghost in the body, until they had got such a good start that he could not overtake them. In Southern Celebes, to hinder the escape of a woman's soul in childbed, the nurse ties a band as tightly as possible round the body of the expectant mother. The Minang-kabauers of Sumatra observe a similar custom; a skein of thread or a string is sometimes fastened round the wrist or loins of a woman in childbed, so that when her soul seeks to depart in her hour of travail it may find the egress barred. And lest the soul of a babe should escape and be lost as soon as it is born, the Alfoors of Celebes, when a birth is about to take place, are careful to close every opening in the house, even the keyhole; and they stop up every chink and cranny in the walls. Also they tie up the mouths of all animals inside and outside the house, for fear one of them might swallow the child's soul. For a similar reason all persons present in the house, even the mother herself, are obliged to keep their mouths shut the whole time the birth is taking place. When the question was put, Why they did not hold their noses also, lest the child's soul should get into one of them? the answer was that breath being exhaled as well as inhaled through the nostrils, the soul would be expelled before it could have time to settle down. Popular expressions in the language of civilised peoples, such as to have one's heart in one's mouth, or the soul on the lips or in the nose, show how natural is the idea that the life or soul may escape by the mouth or nostrils.

Often the soul is conceived as a bird ready to take flight. This conception has probably left traces in most languages, and it lingers as a metaphor in poetry. The Malays carry out the conception of the bird-soul in a number of odd ways. If the soul is a bird on the wing, it may be attracted by rice, and so either prevented from flying away or lured back again from its perilous flight. Thus in Java when a child is placed on the ground for the first time (a moment which uncultured people seem to regard as especially dangerous), it is put in a hen-coop and the mother makes a clucking sound, as if she were calling hens. And in Sintang, a district of Borneo, when a person, whether man, woman, or child, has fallen out of a house or off a tree, and has been brought home, his wife or other kinswoman goes as speedily as possible to the spot where the accident happened, and there strews rice, which has been coloured yellow, while she utters the words, 'Cluck! cluck! soul! So-and-so is in his house again. Cluck! cluck! soul!' Then she gathers up the rice in a basket, carries it to the sufferer, and drops the grains from her hand on his head, saying again, 'Cluck! cluck! soul!' Here the intention clearly is to decoy back the loitering bird-soul and replace it in the head of its owner.

The soul of a sleeper is supposed to wander away from his body and actually to visit the places, to see the persons, and to perform the acts of which he dreams. For example, when an Indian of Brazil or Guiana wakes up from a sound sleep, he is firmly convinced that his soul has really been away hunting, fishing, felling trees, or whatever else he has dreamed of doing, while all the time his body has been lying motionless in his hammock. A whole Bororo village has been thrown into a panic and nearly deserted because somebody had dreamed that he saw enemies stealthily approaching it. A Macusi Indian in weak health, who dreamed that his employer had made him haul the canoe up a series of difficult cataracts, bitterly reproached his master next morning for his want of consideration in thus making a poor invalid go out and toil during the night. The Indians of the Gran Chaco are often heard to relate the most incredible stories as things which they have themselves seen and heard; hence strangers who do not know them intimately say in their haste that these Indians are liars. In point of fact the Indians are firmly convinced of the truth of what they relate; for these wonderful adventures are simply their dreams, which they do not distinguish from waking realities.

Now the absence of the soul in sleep has its dangers, for if from any cause the soul should be permanently detained away from the body, the person thus deprived of the vital principle must die. There is a German belief that the soul escapes from a sleeper's mouth in the form of a white mouse or a little bird, and that to prevent the return of the bird or animal would be fatal to the sleeper. Hence in Transylvania they say that you should not let a child sleep with its mouth open, or its soul will slip out in the shape of a mouse, and the child will never wake. Many causes may detain the sleeper's soul. Thus, his soul may meet the soul of another sleeper and the two souls may fight; if a Guinea negro wakens with sore bones in the morning, he thinks that his soul has been thrashed by another soul in sleep. Or it may meet the soul of a person just deceased and be carried off by it; hence in the Aru Islands the inmates of a house will not sleep the night after a death has taken place in it, because the soul of the deceased is supposed to be still in the house and they fear to meet it in a dream. Again, the soul of the sleeper may be prevented by accident or by physical force from returning to his body. When a Dyak dreams of falling into the water, he supposes that this accident has really befallen his spirit, and he sends for a wizard, who fishes for the spirit with a hand-net in a basin of water till he catches it and restores it to its owner. The Santals tell how a man fell asleep, and growing very thirsty, his soul, in the form of a lizard, left his body, and entered a pitcher of water to drink. Just then the owner of the pitcher happened to cover it; so the soul could not return to the body and the man died. While his friends were preparing to burn the body some one uncovered the pitcher to get water. The lizard thus escaped and returned to the body, which immediately revived; so the man rose up and asked his friends why they were weeping. They told him they thought he was dead and were about to burn his body. He said he had been down a well to get water, but had found it hard to get out and had just returned. So they saw it all.

It is a common rule with primitive people not to waken a sleeper, because his soul is away and might not have time to get back; so if the man wakened without his soul, he would fall sick. If it is absolutely necessary to rouse a sleeper, it must be done very gradually, to allow the soul time to return. A Fijian in Matuku, suddenly wakened from a nap by somebody treading on his foot, has been heard bawling after his soul and imploring it to return. He had just been dreaming that he was far away in Tonga, and great was his alarm on suddenly wakening to find his body in Matuku. Death stared him in the face unless his soul could be induced to speed at once across the sea and reanimate its deserted tenement. The man would probably have died of fright if a missionary had not been at hand to allay his terror.

Still more dangerous is it in the opinion of primitive man to move a sleeper or alter his appearance, for if this were done the soul on its return might not be able to find or recognise its body, and so the person would die. The Minangkabauers deem it highly improper to blacken or dirty the face of a sleeper, lest the absent soul should shrink from re-entering a body thus disfigured. Patani Malays fancy that if a person's face be painted while he sleeps, the soul which has gone out of him will not recognise him, and he will sleep on till his face is washed. In Bombay it is thought equivalent to murder to change the aspect of a sleeper, as by painting his face in fantastic colours or giving moustaches to a sleeping woman. For when the soul returns it will not know its own body, and the person will die.

But in order that a man's soul should quit his body, it is not necessary that he should be asleep. It may quit him in his waking hours, and then sickness, insanity, or death will be the result. Thus a man of the Wurunjeri tribe in Australia lay at his last gasp because his spirit had departed from him. A medicine-man went in pursuit and caught the spirit by the middle just as it was about to plunge into the sunset glow, which is the light cast by the souls of the dead as they pass in and out of the under-world, where the sun goes to rest. Having captured the vagrant spirit, the doctor brought it back under his opossum rug, laid himself down on the dying man, and put the soul back into him, so that after a time he revived. The Karens of Burma are perpetually anxious about their souls, lest these should go roving from their bodies, leaving the owners to die. When a man has reason to fear that his soul is about to take this fatal step, a ceremony is performed to retain or recall it, in which the whole family must take part. A meal is prepared consisting of a cock and hen, a special kind of rice, and a bunch of bananas. Then the head of the family takes the bowl which is used to skim rice, and knocking with it thrice on the top of the house-ladder says: '*Prrrroo!* Come back, soul, do not tarry outside! If it rains, you will be wet. If the sun shines, you will be hot. The gnats will sting you, the leeches will bite you, the tigers will devour you, the thunder will crush you. *Prrrroo!* Come back, soul! Here it will be well with you. You shall want for nothing. Come and eat under shelter from the wind and the storm.' After that the family partakes of the meal, and the ceremony ends with everybody tying his right wrist with a string which has been charmed by a sorcerer. Similarly the Lolos of South-western China believe that the soul leaves the body in chronic illness. In that case they read a sort of elaborate litany, calling on the soul by name and beseeching it to return from the hills, the vales, the rivers, the forests, the fields, or from wherever it may be straying. At the same time cups of water, wine, and rice are set at the door for the refreshment of the weary wandering spirit. When the ceremony is over, they tie a red cord round the arm of the sick man to tether the soul, and this cord is worn by him until it decays or drops off.

Some of the Congo tribes believe that when a man is ill, his soul has left his body and is wandering at large. The aid of the sorcerer is then called in to capture the vagrant spirit and restore it to the invalid. Generally the physician declares that he has successfully chased the soul into the branch of a tree. The whole town thereupon turns out and accompanies the doctor to the tree, where the strongest men are deputed to break off the branch in which the soul of the sick man is supposed to be lodged. This they do and carry the branch back to the town, insinuating by their gestures that the burden is heavy and hard to bear. When the branch has been brought to the sick man's hut, he is placed in an upright position by its side, and the sorcerer performs the enchantments by which the soul is believed to be restored to its owner.

Pining, sickness, great fright, and death are ascribed by the Bataks of Sumatra to the absence of the soul from the body. At first they try to beckon the wanderer back, and to lure him, like a fowl, by strewing rice. Then the following form of words is commonly repeated: 'Come back, O soul, whether thou art lingering in the wood, or on the hills, or in the dale. See, I call thee with a *toemba bras*, with an egg of the fowl Rajah *moelija*, with the eleven healing leaves. Detain it not, let it come straight here, detain it not, neither in the wood, nor on the hill, nor in the dale. That may not be. O come straight home!' Once when a popular traveller was leaving a Kayan village, the mothers, fearing that their children's souls might follow him on his journey, brought him the boards on which they carry their infants and begged him to pray that the souls of the little ones would return to the familiar boards and not go away with him into the far country. To each board was fastened a looped string for the purpose of tethering the vagrant spirits, and through the loop each baby was made to pass a chubby finger to make sure that its tiny soul would not wander away.

In an Indian story a king conveys his soul into the dead body of a Brahman, and a hunchback conveys his soul into the deserted body of the king. The hunchback is now king and the king is a Brahman. However, the hunchback is induced to show his skill by transferring his soul to the dead body of a parrot, and the king seizes the opportunity to regain possession of his own body. A tale of the same type, with variations of detail, reappears among the Malays. A king has incautiously transferred his soul to an ape, upon which the vizier adroitly inserts his own soul into the king's body and so takes possession of the queen and the kingdom, while the true king languishes at court in the outward semblance of an ape. But one day the false king, who played for high stakes, was watching a combat of rams, and it happened that the animal on which he had laid his money fell down dead. All efforts to restore animation proved unavailing till the false king, with the instinct of a true sportsman, transferred his own soul to the body of the deceased ram, and thus renewed the fray. The real king in the body of the ape saw his chance, and with great presence of mind darted back into his own body, which the vizier had rashly vacated. So he came to his own again, and the usurper in the ram's body met with the fate he richly deserved. Similarly the Greeks told how the soul of Hermotimus of Clazomenae used to quit his body and roam far and wide, bringing back intelligence of what he had seen on his rambles to his friends at home; until one day, when his spirit was abroad, his enemies contrived to seize his deserted body and committed it to the flames.

The departure of the soul is not always voluntary. It may be extracted from the body against its will by ghosts, demons, or sorcerers. Hence, when a funeral is passing the house, the Karens tie their children with a special kind of string to a particular part of the house, lest the souls of the children should leave their bodies and go into the corpse which is passing. The children are kept tied in this way until the corpse is out of sight. And after the corpse has been laid in the grave, but before the earth has been shovelled in, the mourners and friends range themselves round the grave, each with a bamboo split lengthwise in one hand and a little stick in the other; each man thrusts his bamboo into the grave, and drawing the stick along the groove of the bamboo points out to his soul that in this way it may easily climb up out of the tomb. While the earth is being shovelled in, the bamboos are kept out of the way, lest the souls should be in them, and so should be inadvertently buried with the earth as it is being thrown into the grave; and when the people leave the spot they carry away the bamboos, begging their souls to come with them. Further, on returning from the grave each Karen provides himself with three little hooks made of branches of trees, and calling his spirit to follow him, at short intervals, as he returns, he makes a motion as if hooking it, and then thrusts the hook into the ground. This is done to prevent the soul of the living from staying behind with the soul of the dead. When the Karo-Bataks have buried somebody and are filling in the grave, a sorceress runs about beating the air with a stick. This she does in order to drive away the souls of the survivors, for if one of these souls happened to slip into the grave and to be covered up with earth, its owner would die.

In Uea, one of the Loyalty Islands, the souls of the dead seem to have been credited with the power of stealing the souls of the living. For when a man was sick the soul-doctor would go with a large troop of men and women to the graveyard. Here the men played on flutes and the women whistled softly to lure the soul home. After this had gone on for some time they formed in procession and moved homewards, the flutes playing and the women whistling all the way, while they led back the wandering soul and drove it gently along with open palms. On entering the patient's dwelling they commanded the soul in a loud voice to enter his body.

Often the abduction of a man's soul is set down to demons. Thus fits and convulsions are generally ascribed by the Chinese to the agency of certain mischievous spirits who love to draw men's souls out of their bodies. At Amoy the spirits who serve babies and children in this way rejoice in the high-sounding titles of 'celestial agencies bestriding galloping horses' and 'literary graduates residing half-way up in the sky.' When an infant is writhing in convulsions, the frightened mother hastens to the roof of the house, and, waving about a bamboo pole to which one of the child's garments is attached cries out several times, 'My child So-and-so, come back, return home!' Meantime another inmate of the house bangs away at a gong in the hope of attracting the attention of the strayed soul, which is supposed to recognise the familiar garment and to slip into it. The garment containing the soul is then placed on or beside the child and if the child does not die recovery is sure to follow, sooner or later. Similarly some Indians catch a man's lost soul in his boots and restore it to his body by putting his feet into them.

In the Moluccas when a man is unwell it is thought that some devil has carried away his soul to the tree, mountain, or hill where he (the devil) resides. A sorcerer having pointed out the devil's abode, the friends of the patient carry thither cooked rice, fruit, fish, raw eggs, a hen, a chicken, a silken robe, gold armlets, and so forth. Having set out the food in order they pray, saying: 'We come to offer to you, O devil, this offering of food, clothes, gold, and so on; take it and release the soul of the patient for whom we pray. Let it return to his body, and he who now is sick shall be made whole.' Then they eat a little and let the hen loose as a ransom for the soul of the patient; also they put down the raw eggs; but the silken robe, the gold, and the armlets they take home with them. As soon as they are come to the house they place a flat bowl containing the offerings which have been brought back at the sick man's head, and say to him: 'Now is your soul released, and you shall fare well and live to grey hairs on the earth.'

Demons are especially feared by persons who have just entered a new house. Hence at a house-warming among the Alfoors of

I

Minahassa in Celebes the priest performs a ceremony for the purpose of restoring their souls to the inmates. He hangs up a bag at the place of sacrifice and then goes through a list of the gods. There are so many of them that this takes him the whole night through without stopping. In the morning he offers the gods an egg and some rice. By this time the souls of the household are supposed to be gathered in the bag. So the priest takes the bag, and holding it on the head of the master of the house, says, 'Here you have your soul; go (soul) to-morrow away again.' He then does the same, saying the same words, to the housewife and all the other members of the family. Amongst the same Alfoors one way of recovering a sick man's soul is to let down a bowl by a belt out of a window and fish for the soul till it is caught in the bowl and hauled up. And among the same people, when a priest is bringing back a sick man's soul which he has caught in a cloth, he is preceded by a girl holding the large leaf of a certain palm over his head as an umbrella to keep him and the soul from getting wet, in case it should rain; and he is followed by a man brandishing a sword to deter other souls from any attempt at rescuing the captured spirit.

Sometimes the lost soul is brought back in a visible shape. The Salish or Flathead Indians of Oregon believe that a man's soul may be separated for a time from his body without causing death and without the man being aware of his loss. It is necessary, however, that the lost soul should be soon found and restored to its owner or he will die. The name of the man who has lost his soul is revealed in a dream to the medicine-man, who hastens to inform the sufferer of his loss. Generally a number of men have sustained a like loss at the same time; all their names are revealed to the medicine-man, and all employ him to recover their souls. The whole night long these soulless men go about the village from lodge to lodge, dancing and singing. Towards daybreak they go into a separate lodge, which is closed up so as to be totally dark. A small hole is then made in the roof, through which the medicine-man, with a bunch of feathers, brushes in the souls, in the shape of bits of bone and the like, which he receives on a piece of matting. A fire is next kindled, by the light of which the medicine-man sorts out the souls. First he puts aside the souls of dead people, of which there are usually several; for if he were to give the soul of a dead person to a living man, the man would die instantly. Next he picks out the souls of all the persons present, and making them all to sit down before him, he takes the soul of each, in the shape of a splinter of bone, wood, or shell, and placing it on the owner's head, pats it with many prayers and contortions till it descends into the heart and so resumes its proper place.

Again, souls may be extracted from their bodies or detained on their wanderings not only by ghosts and demons but also by men, especially by sorcerers. In Fiji, if a criminal refused to confess, the chief sent for a scarf with which 'to catch away the soul of the rogue.' At the sight or even at the mention of the scarf the culprit generally made a clean breast. For if he did not, the scarf would be waved over his head till his soul was caught in it, when it would be carefully folded up and nailed to the end of a chief's canoe; and for want of his soul the criminal would pine and die. The sorcerers of Danger Island used to set snares for souls. The snares were made of stout cinet, about fifteen to thirty feet long, with loops on either side of different sizes, to suit the different sizes of souls; for fat souls there were large loops, for thin souls there were small ones. When a man was sick against whom the sorcerers had a grudge, they set up these soul-snares near his house and watched for the flight of his soul. If in the shape of a bird or an insect it was caught in the snare, the man would infallibly die. In some parts of West Africa, indeed, wizards are continually setting traps to catch souls that wander from their bodies in sleep; and when they have caught one, they tie it up over the fire, and as it shrivels in the heat the owner sickens. This is done, not out of any grudge towards the sufferer, but purely as a matter of business. The wizard does not care whose soul he has captured, and will readily restore it to its owner, if only he is paid for doing so. Some sorcerers keep regular asylums for strayed souls, and anybody who has lost or mislaid his own soul can always have another one from the asylum on payment of the usual fee. No blame whatever attaches to men who keep these private asylums or set traps for passing souls; it is their profession, and in the exercise of it they are actuated by no harsh or unkindly feelings. But there are also wretches who from pure spite or for the sake of lucre set and bait traps with the deliberate purpose of catching the soul of a particular man; and in the bottom of the pot, hidden by the bait, are knives and sharp hooks which tear and rend the poor soul, either killing it outright or mauling it so as to impair the health of its owner when it succeeds in escaping and returning to him. Miss Kingsley knew a Kruman who became very anxious about his soul, because for several nights he had smelt in his dreams the savoury smell of smoked crawfish seasoned with red pepper. Clearly some ill-wisher had set a trap baited with this dainty for his dream-soul, intending to do him grievous bodily, or rather spiritual, harm; and for the next few nights great pains were taken to keep his soul from straying abroad in his sleep. In the sweltering heat of the tropical night he lay sweating and snorting under a blanket, his nose and mouth tied up with a handkerchief to prevent the escape of his precious soul. In Hawaii there were sorcerers who caught souls of living people, shut them up in calabashes, and gave them to people to eat. By squeezing a captured soul in their hands they discovered the place where people had been secretly buried.

Nowhere perhaps is the art of abducting human souls more carefully cultivated or carried to higher perfection than in the Malay Peninsula. Here the methods by which the wizard works his will are various, and so too are his motives. Sometimes he desires to destroy an enemy, sometimes to win the love of a cold or bashful beauty. Thus, to take an instance of the latter sort of charm, the following are the directions given for securing the soul of one whom you wish to render distraught. When the moon, just risen, looks red above the eastern horizon, go out, and standing in the moonlight, with the big toe of your right foot on the big toe of your left, make a speaking-trumpet of your right hand and recite through it the following words:

'*OM. I loose my shaft, I loose it and the moon clouds over,*
 I loose it, and the sun is extinguished.
 I loose it, and the stars burn dim.
 But it is not the sun, moon, and stars that I shoot at,
 It is the stalk of the heart of that child of the congregation,
                So-and-so.

 Cluck! cluck! soul of So-and-so, come and walk with me,
 Come and sit with me,
 Come and sleep and share my pillow.
 Cluck! cluck! soul.'

Repeat this thrice and after every repetition blow through your hollow fist. Or you may catch the soul in your turban, thus. Go out on the night of the full moon and the two succeeding nights; sit down on an ant-hill facing the moon, burn incense, and recite the following incantation:

> '*I bring you a betel leaf to chew,*
> *Dab the lime on to it, Prince Ferocious,*
> *For Somebody, Prince Distraction's daughter, to chew.*
> *Somebody at sunrise be distraught for love of me,*
> *Somebody at sunset be distraught for love of me.*
> *As you remember your parents, remember me;*
> *As you remember your house and house-ladder, remember me;*
> *When thunder rumbles, remember me;*
> *When wind whistles, remember me;*
> *When the heavens rain, remember me;*
> *When the cocks crow, remember me;*
> *When the dial-bird tells its tales, remember me;*
> *When you look up at the sun, remember me;*
> *When you look up at the moon, remember me,*
> *For in that self-same moon I am there.*
> *Cluck! cluck! soul of Somebody come hither to me.*
> *I do not mean to let you have my soul,*
> *Let your soul come hither to mine.*'

Now wave the end of your turban towards the moon seven times each night. Go home and put it under your pillow, and if you want to wear it in the daytime, burn incense and say, 'It is not a turban that I carry in my girdle, but the soul of Somebody.'

The Indians of the Nass River, in British Columbia, are impressed with a belief that a physician may swallow his patient's soul by mistake. A doctor who is believed to have done so is made by the other members of the faculty to stand over the patient, while one of them thrusts his fingers down the doctor's throat, another kneads him in the stomach with his knuckles, and a third slaps him on the back. If the soul is not in him after all, and if the same process has been repeated upon all the medical men without success, it is concluded that the soul must be in the head-doctor's box. A party of doctors, therefore, waits upon him at his house and requests him to produce his box. When he has done so and arranged its contents on a new mat, they take the votary of Aesculapius and hold him up by the heels with his head in a hole in the floor. In this position they wash his head, and 'any water remaining from the ablution is taken and poured upon the sick man's head.' No doubt the lost soul is in the water.

§ 3. *The Soul as a Shadow and a Reflection.*—But the spiritual dangers I have enumerated are not the only ones which beset the savage. Often he regards his shadow or reflection as his soul, or at all events as a vital part of himself, and as such it is necessarily a source of danger to him. For if it is trampled upon, struck, or stabbed, he will feel the injury as if it were done to his person; and if it is detached from him entirely (as he believes that it may be) he will die. In the island of Wetar there are magicians who can make a man ill by stabbing his shadow with a pike or hacking it with a sword. After Sankara had destroyed the Buddhists in India, it is said that he journeyed to Nepaul, where he had some difference of opinion with the Grand Lama. To prove his supernatural powers, he soared into the air. But as he mounted up, the Grand Lama, perceiving his shadow swaying and wavering on the ground, struck his knife into it and down fell Sankara and broke his neck.

In the Banks Islands there are some stones of a remarkably long shape which go by the name of 'eating ghosts,' because certain powerful and dangerous ghosts are believed to lodge in them. If a man's shadow falls on one of these stones, the ghost will draw his soul out from him, so that he will die. Such stones, therefore, are set in a house to guard it; and a messenger sent to a house by the absent owner will call out the name of the sender, lest the watchful ghost in the stone should fancy that he came with evil intent and should do him a mischief. At a funeral in China, when the lid is about to be placed on the coffin, most of the bystanders, with the exception of the nearest kin, retire a few steps or even retreat to another room, for a person's health is believed to be endangered by allowing his shadow to be enclosed in a coffin. And when the coffin is about to be lowered into the grave most of the spectators recoil to a little distance lest their shadows should fall into the grave and harm should thus be done to their persons. The geomancer and his assistants stand on the side of the grave which is turned away from the sun; and the grave-diggers and coffin-bearers attach their shadows firmly to their persons by tying a strip of cloth tightly round their waists. Nor is it human beings alone who are thus liable to be injured by means of their shadows. Animals are to some extent in the same predicament. A small snail, which frequents the neighbourhood of the limestone hills in Perak, is believed to suck the blood of cattle through their shadows; hence the beasts grow lean and sometimes die from loss of blood. The ancients supposed that in Arabia, if a hyaena trod on a man's shadow, it deprived him of the power of speech and motion; and that if a dog, standing on a roof in the moonlight, cast a shadow on the ground and a hyaena trod on it, the dog would fall down as if dragged with a rope. Clearly in these cases the shadow, if not equivalent to the soul, is at least regarded as a living part of the man or the animal, so that injury done to the shadow is felt by the person or animal as if it were done to his body.

Conversely, if the shadow is a vital part of a man or an animal, it may under certain circumstances be as hazardous to be touched by it as it would be to come into contact with the person or animal. Hence the savage makes it a rule to shun the shadow of certain persons whom for various reasons he regards as sources of dangerous influence. Amongst the dangerous classes he commonly ranks mourners and women in general, but especially his mother-in-law. The Shuswap Indians think that the shadow of a mourner falling upon a person would make him sick. Amongst the Kurnai of Victoria novices at the initiation were cautioned not to let a woman's shadow fall across them, as this would make them thin, lazy, and stupid. An Australian native is said to have once nearly died of fright because the shadow of his mother-in-law fell on his legs as he lay asleep under a tree. The awe and dread with which the untutored savage contemplates his mother-in-law are amongst the most familiar facts of anthropology. In the Yuin tribes of New South Wales the rule which forbade a man to hold any communication with his wife's mother was very strict. He might not look at her or even in her direction. It was a ground of divorce if his shadow happened to fall on his mother-in-law: in that case he had to leave his wife, and she returned to her parents. In New Britain the native imagination fails to conceive the extent and nature of the calamities which would result from a man's accidentally speaking to his wife's mother; suicide of one or both would probably be the only course open to them. The most solemn form of oath a New Briton can take is, 'Sir, if I am not telling the truth, I hope I may shake hands with my mother-in-law.'

Where the shadow is regarded as so intimately bound up with the life of the man that its loss entails debility or death, it is natural to expect that its diminution should be regarded with solicitude and apprehension, as betokening a corresponding decrease in the vital energy of its owner. In Amboyna and Uliase, two islands near the equator, where necessarily there is little or no shadow cast at noon, the people make it a rule not to go out of the house at mid-day, because they fancy that by doing so a man may lose the shadow of his soul. The Mangaians tell of a mighty warrior, Tukaitawa, whose strength waxed and waned with the length of his shadow. In the morning, when his shadow fell longest, his strength was greatest; but as the shadow shortened towards noon his strength ebbed with it, till exactly at noon it reached its lowest point; then, as the shadow stretched out in the afternoon, his strength returned. A certain hero discovered the secret of Tukaitawa's strength and slew him at noon. The savage Besisis of the Malay Peninsula fear to bury their dead at noon, because they fancy that the shortness of their shadows at that hour would sympathetically shorten their own lives.

Nowhere, perhaps, does the equivalence of the shadow to the life or soul come out more clearly than in some customs practised to this day in South-eastern Europe. In modern Greece, when the foundation of a new building is being laid, it is the custom to kill a cock, a ram, or a lamb, and to let its blood flow on the foundation-stone, under which the animal is afterwards buried. The object of the sacrifice is to give strength and stability to the building. But sometimes, instead of killing an animal, the builder entices a man to the foundation-stone, secretly measures his body, or a part of it, or his shadow, and buries the measure under the foundation-stone; or he lays the foundation-stone upon the man's shadow. It is believed that the man will die within the year. The Roumanians of Transylvania think that he whose shadow is thus immured will die within forty days; so persons passing by a building which is in course of erection may hear a warning cry, 'Beware, lest they take thy shadow!' Not long ago there were still shadow-traders whose business it was to provide architects with the shadows necessary for securing their walls. In these cases the measure of the shadow is looked on as equivalent to the shadow itself, and to bury it is to bury the life or soul of the man, who, deprived of it, must die. Thus the custom is a substitute for the old practice of immuring a living person in the walls, or crushing him under the foundation-stone of a new building, in order to give strength and durability to the structure, or more definitely in order that the angry ghost may haunt the place and guard it against the intrusion of enemies.

As some peoples believe a man's soul to be in his shadow, so other (or the same) peoples believe it to be in his reflection in water or a mirror. Thus 'the Andamanese do not regard their shadows but their reflections (in any mirror) as their souls.' When the Motumotu of New Guinea first saw their likenesses in a looking-glass, they thought that their reflections were their souls. In New Caledonia the old men are of opinion that a person's reflection in water or a mirror is his soul; but the younger men, taught by the Catholic priests, maintain that it is a reflection and nothing more, just like the reflection of palm-trees in the water. The reflection-soul, being external to the man, is exposed to much the same dangers as the shadow-soul. The Zulus will not look into a dark pool because they think there is a beast in it which will take away their reflections, so that they die. The Basutos say that crocodiles have the power of thus killing a man by dragging his reflection under water. When one of them dies suddenly and from no apparent cause, his relatives will allege that a crocodile must have taken his shadow some time when he crossed a stream. In Saddle Island, Melanesia, there is a pool 'into which if any one looks he dies; the malignant spirit takes hold of his life by means of his reflection on the water.'

We can now understand why it was a maxim both in ancient India and ancient Greece not to look at one's reflection in water, and why the Greeks regarded it as an omen of death if a man dreamed of seeing himself so reflected. They feared that the water-spirits would drag the person's reflection or soul under water, leaving him soulless to perish. This was probably the origin of the classical story of the beautiful Narcissus, who languished and died through seeing his reflection in the water.

Further, we can now explain the widespread custom of covering up mirrors or turning them to the wall after a death has taken place in the house. It is feared that the soul, projected out of the person in the shape of his reflection in the mirror, may be carried off by the ghost of the departed, which is commonly supposed to linger about the house till the burial. The custom is thus exactly parallel to the Aru custom of not sleeping in a house after a death for fear that the soul, projected out of the body in a dream, may meet the ghost and be carried off by it. The reason why sick people should not see themselves in a mirror, and why the mirror in a sick-room is therefore covered up, is also plain; in time of sickness, when the soul might take flight so easily, it is particularly dangerous to project it out of the body by means of the reflection in a mirror. The rule is therefore precisely parallel to the rule observed by some peoples of not allowing sick people to sleep; for in sleep the soul is projected out of the body, and there is always a risk that it may not return.

As with shadows and reflections, so with portraits; they are often believed to contain the soul of the person portrayed. People who hold this belief are naturally loth to have their likenesses taken; for if the portrait is the soul, or at least a vital part of the person portrayed, whoever possesses the portrait will be able to exercise a fatal influence over the original of it. Thus the Esquimaux of Bering Strait believe that persons dealing in witchcraft have the power of stealing a person's shade, so that without it he will pine away and die. Once at a village on the lower Yukon River an explorer had set up his camera to get a picture of the people as they were moving about among their houses. While he was focussing the instrument, the headman of the village came up and insisted on peeping under the cloth. Being allowed to do so, he gazed intently for a minute at the moving figures on the ground glass, then suddenly withdrew his head and bawled at the top of his voice to the people, 'He has all of your shades in this box.' A panic ensued among the group, and in an instant they disappeared helter-skelter into their houses. The Tepehuanes of Mexico stood in mortal terror of the camera, and five days' persuasion was necessary to induce them to pose for it. When at last they consented, they looked like criminals about to be executed. They believed that by photographing people the artist could carry off their souls and devour them at his leisure moments. They said that, when the pictures reached his country, they would die or some other evil would befall them. When Dr. Catat and some companions were exploring the Bara country on the west coast of Madagascar, the people suddenly became hostile. The day before the travellers, not without difficulty, had photographed the royal family, and now found themselves accused of taking the souls of the natives for the purpose of selling them when they returned to France. Denial was vain; in compliance with the custom of the country they were obliged to catch the souls, which were then put into a basket and ordered by Dr. Catat to return to their respective owners.

Some villagers in Sikhim betrayed a lively horror and hid away whenever the lens of a camera, or 'the evil eye of the box' as they called it, was turned on them. They thought it took away their souls with their pictures, and so put it in the power of the owner of the pictures to cast spells on them, and they alleged that a photograph of the scenery blighted the landscape. Until the reign of the late King of Siam no Siamese coins were ever stamped with the image of the king, 'for at that time there was a strong prejudice against the making of portraits in any medium. Europeans who travel into the jungle have, even at the present time, only to point a camera at a crowd to procure its instant dispersion. When a copy of the face of a person is made and taken away from him, a portion of his life goes with the picture. Unless the sovereign had been blessed with the years of a Methuselah he could scarcely have permitted his life to be distributed in small pieces together with the coins of the realm.'

Beliefs of the same sort still linger in various parts of Europe. Not very many years ago some old women in the Greek island of Carpathus were very angry at having their likenesses drawn, thinking that in consequence they would pine and die. There are persons in the West of Scotland 'who refuse to have their likenesses taken lest it prove unlucky; and give as instances the cases of several of their friends who never had a day's health after being photographed.'

§ 1. *Taboos on Intercourse with Strangers.* — So much for the primitive conceptions of the soul and the dangers to which it is exposed. These conceptions are not limited to one people or country; with variations of detail they are found all over the world, and survive, as we have seen, in modern Europe. Beliefs so deep-seated and so widespread must necessarily have contributed to shape the mould in which the early kingship was cast. For if every person was at such pains to save his own soul from the perils which threatened it on so many sides, how much more carefully must *he* have been guarded upon whose life hung the welfare and even the existence of the whole people, and whom therefore it was the common interest of all to preserve? Therefore we should expect to find the king's life protected by a system of precautions or safeguards still more numerous and minute than those which in primitive society every man adopts for the safety of his own soul. Now in point of fact the life of the early kings is regulated, as we have seen and shall see more fully presently, by a very exact code of rules. May we not then conjecture that these rules are in fact the very safeguards which we should expect to find adopted for the protection of the king's life? An examination of the rules themselves confirms this conjecture. For from this it appears that some of the rules observed by the kings are identical with those observed by private persons out of regard for the safety of their souls; and even of those which seem peculiar to the king, many, if not all, are most readily explained on the hypothesis that they are nothing but safeguards or lifeguards of the king. I will now enumerate some of these royal rules or taboos, offering on each of them such comments and explanations as may serve to set the original intention of the rule in its proper light.

As the object of the royal taboos is to isolate the king from all sources of danger, their general effect is to compel him to live in a state of seclusion, more or less complete, according to the number and stringency of the rules he observes. Now of all sources of danger none are more dreaded by the savage than magic and witchcraft, and he suspects all strangers of practising these black arts. To guard against the baneful influence exerted voluntarily or involuntarily by strangers is therefore an elementary dictate of savage prudence. Hence before strangers are allowed to enter a district, or at least before they are permitted to mingle freely with the inhabitants, certain ceremonies are often performed by the natives of the country for the purpose of disarming the strangers of their magical powers, of counteracting the baneful influence which is believed to emanate from them, or of disinfecting, so to speak, the tainted atmosphere by which they are supposed to be surrounded. Thus, when the ambassadors sent by Justin II, Emperor of the East, to conclude a peace with the Turks had reached their destination, they were received by shamans, who subjected them to a ceremonial purification for the purpose of exorcising all harmful influence. Having deposited the goods brought by the ambassadors in an open place, these wizards carried burning branches of incense round them, while they rang a bell and beat on a tambourine, snorting and falling into a state of frenzy in their efforts to dispel the powers of evil. Afterwards they purified the ambassadors themselves by leading them through the flames. In the island of Nanumea (South Pacific) strangers from ships or from other islands were not allowed to communicate with the people until they all, or a few as representatives of the rest, had been taken to each of the four temples in the island, and prayers offered that the god would avert any disease or treachery which these strangers might have brought with them. Meat offerings were also laid upon the altars, accompanied by songs and dances in honour of the god. While these ceremonies were going on, all the people except the priests and their attendants kept out of sight. Amongst the Ot Danoms of Borneo it is the custom that strangers entering the territory should pay to the natives a certain sum, which is spent in the sacrifice of buffaloes or pigs to the spirits of the land and water, in order to reconcile them to the presence of the strangers, and to induce them not to withdraw their favour from the people of the country, but to bless the rice-harvest, and so forth. The men of a certain district in Borneo, fearing to look upon a European traveller lest he should make them ill, warned their wives and children not to go near him.

Those who could not restrain their curiosity killed fowls to appease the evil spirits and smeared themselves with the blood. 'More dreaded,' says a traveller in Central Borneo, 'than the evil spirits of the neighbourhood are the evil spirits from a distance which accompany travellers. When a company from the middle Mahakam river visited me among the Blu-u Kayans in the year 1897, no woman showed herself outside her house without a burning bundle of *plehiding* bark, the stinking smoke of which drives away evil spirits.'

When Crevaux was travelling in South America he entered a village of the Apalai Indians. A few moments after his arrival some of the Indians brought him a number of large black ants, of a species whose bite is painful, fastened on palm leaves. Then all the people of the village, without distinction of age or sex, presented themselves to him, and he had to sting them all with the ants on their faces, thighs, and other parts of their bodies. Sometimes, when he applied the ants too tenderly, they called out 'More! more!' and were not satisfied till their skin was thickly studded with tiny swellings like what might have been produced by whipping them with nettles. The object of this ceremony is made plain by the custom observed in Amboyna and Uliase of sprinkling sick people with pungent spices, such as ginger and cloves, chewed fine, in order by the prickling sensation to drive away the demon of disease which may be clinging to their persons. In Java a popular cure for gout or rheumatism is to rub Spanish pepper into the nails of the fingers and toes of the sufferer; the pungency of the pepper is supposed to be too much for the gout or rheumatism, who accordingly departs in haste. So on the Slave Coast the mother of a sick child sometimes believes that an evil spirit has taken possession of the child's body, and in order to drive him out she makes small cuts in the body of the little sufferer and inserts green peppers or spices in the wounds, believing that she will thereby hurt the evil spirit and force him to be gone. The poor child naturally screams with pain, but the mother hardens her heart in the belief that the demon is suffering equally.

It is probable that the same dread of strangers, rather than any desire to do them honour, is the motive of certain ceremonies which are sometimes observed at their reception, but of which the intention is not directly stated. In the Ongtong Java Islands, which are inhabited by Polynesians, the priests or sorcerers seem to wield great influence. Their main business is to summon or exorcise spirits for the purpose of averting or dispelling sickness, and of procuring favourable winds, a good catch of fish, and so on. When strangers land on the islands, they are first of all received by the sorcerers, sprinkled with water, anointed with oil, and girt with dried pandanus leaves. At the same time sand and water are freely thrown about in all directions, and the newcomer and his boat are wiped with green leaves. After this ceremony the strangers are introduced by the sorcerers to the chief. In Afghanistan and in some parts of Persia the traveller, before he enters a village, is frequently received with a sacrifice of animal life or food, or of fire and incense. The Afghan Boundary Mission, in passing by villages in Afghanistan, was often met with fire and incense. Sometimes a tray of lighted embers is thrown under the hoofs of the traveller's horse, with the words, 'You are welcome.' On entering a village in Central Africa Emin Pasha was received with the sacrifice of two goats; their blood was sprinkled on the path and the chief stepped over the blood to greet Emin. Sometimes the dread of strangers and their magic is too great to allow of their reception on any terms. Thus when Speke arrived at a certain village, the natives shut their doors against him, 'because they had never before seen a white man nor the tin boxes that the men were carrying: "Who knows," they said, "but that these very boxes are the plundering Watuta transformed and come to kill us? You cannot be admitted." No persuasion could avail with them, and the party had to proceed to the next village.'

The fear thus entertained of alien visitors is often mutual. Entering a strange land the savage feels that he is treading enchanted ground, and he takes steps to guard against the demons that haunt it and the magical arts of its inhabitants. Thus on going to a strange land the Maoris performed certain ceremonies to make it 'common,' lest it might have been previously 'sacred.' When Baron Miklucho-Maclay was approaching a village on the Maclay Coast of New Guinea, one of the natives who accompanied him broke a branch from a tree and going aside whispered to it for a while; then stepping up to each member of the party, one after another, he spat something upon his back and gave him some blows with the branch. Lastly, he went into the forest and buried the branch under withered leaves in the thickest part of the jungle. This ceremony was believed to protect the party against all treachery and danger in the village they were approaching. The idea probably was that the malignant influences were drawn off from the persons into the branch and buried with it in the depths of the forest. In Australia, when a strange tribe has been invited into a district and is approaching the encampment of the tribe which owns the land, 'the strangers carry lighted bark or burning sticks in their hands, for the purpose, they say, of clearing and purifying the air.' When the Toradjas are on a head-hunting expedition and have entered the enemy's country, they may not eat any fruits which the foe has planted nor any animal which he has reared until they have first committed an act of hostility, as by burning a house or killing a man. They think that if they broke this rule they would receive something of the soul or spiritual essence of the enemy into themselves, which would destroy the mystic virtue of their talismans.

Again, it is believed that a man who has been on a journey may have contracted some magic evil from the strangers with whom he has associated. Hence, on returning home, before he is re-admitted to the society of his tribe and friends, he has to undergo certain purificatory ceremonies. Thus the Bechuanas 'cleanse or purify themselves after journeys by shaving their heads, etc., lest they should have contracted from strangers some evil by witchcraft or sorcery.' In some parts of western Africa, when a man returns home after a long absence, before he is allowed to visit his wife, he must wash his person with a particular fluid, and receive from the sorcerer a certain mark on his forehead, in order to counteract any magic spell which a stranger woman may have cast on him in his absence, and which might be communicated through him to the women of his village. Two Hindoo ambassadors, who had been sent to England by a native prince and had returned to India, were considered to have so polluted themselves by contact with strangers that nothing but being born again could restore them to purity. 'For the purpose of regeneration it is directed to make an image of pure gold of the female power of nature, in the shape either of a woman or of a cow. In this statue the person to be regenerated is enclosed, and dragged through the usual channel. As a statue of pure gold and of proper dimensions would be too expensive, it is sufficient to make an image of the sacred *Yoni*, through which the person to be regenerated is to pass.' Such an image of pure gold was made at the prince's command, and his ambassadors were born again by being dragged through it.

When precautions like these are taken on behalf of the people in general against the malignant influence supposed to be exercised by strangers, it is no wonder that special measures are adopted to protect the king from the same insidious danger. In the middle ages the envoys who visited a Tartar Khan were obliged to pass between two fires before they were admitted to his presence, and the gifts they brought were also carried between the fires. The reason assigned for the custom was that the fire purged away any magic influence which the strangers might mean to exercise over the Khan. When subject chiefs came with their retinues to visit Kalamba (the most powerful chief of the Bashilange in the Congo Basin) for the first time or after being rebellious, they have to bathe, men and women together, in two brooks on two successive days, passing the nights under the open sky in the market-place. After the second bath they proceed, entirely naked, to the house of Kalamba, who makes a long white mark on the breast and forehead of each of them. Then they return to the market-place and dress, after which they undergo the pepper ordeal. Pepper is dropped into the eyes of each of them, and while this is being done the sufferer has to make a confession of all his sins, to answer all questions that may be put to him, and to take certain vows. This ends the ceremony, and the strangers are now free to take up their quarters in the town for as long as they choose to remain.

§ 2. *Taboos on Eating and Drinking*. — In the opinion of savages the acts of eating and drinking are attended with special danger; for at these times the soul may escape from the mouth, or be extracted by the magic arts of an enemy present. Among the Ewe-speaking peoples of the Slave Coast 'the common belief seems to be that the indwelling spirit leaves the body and returns to it through the mouth; hence, should it have gone out, it behoves a man to be careful about opening his mouth, lest a homeless spirit should take advantage of the opportunity and enter his body. This, it appears, is considered most likely to take place while the man is eating.' Precautions are therefore adopted to guard against these dangers. Thus of the Bataks it is said that 'since the soul can leave the body, they always take care to prevent their soul from straying on occasions when they have most need of it. But it is only possible to prevent the soul from straying when one is in the house. At feasts one may find the whole house shut up, in order that the soul may stay and enjoy the good things set before it.' The Zafimanelo in Madagascar lock their doors when they eat, and hardly any one ever sees them eating. The Warua will not allow any one to see them eating and drinking, being doubly particular that no person of the opposite sex shall see them doing so. 'I had to pay a man to let me see him drink; I could not make a man let a woman see him drink.' When offered a drink they often ask that a cloth may be held up to hide them whilst drinking.

If these are the ordinary precautions taken by common people, the precautions taken by kings are extraordinary. The king of Loango may not be seen eating or drinking by man or beast under pain of death. A favourite dog having broken into the room where the king was dining, the king ordered it to be killed on the spot. Once the king's own son, a boy of twelve years old, inadvertently saw the king drink. Immediately the king ordered him to be finely apparelled and feasted, after which he commanded him to be cut in quarters, and carried about the city with a proclamation that he had seen the king drink. 'When the king has a mind to drink, he has a cup of wine brought; he that brings it has a bell in his hand, and as soon as he has delivered the cup to the king, he turns his face from him and rings the bell, on which all present fall down with their faces to the ground, and continue so till the king has drunk. . . . His eating is much in the same style, for which he has a house on purpose, where his victuals are set upon a bensa or table: which he goes to, and shuts the door: when he has done, he knocks and comes out. So that none ever see the king eat or drink. For it is believed that if any one should, the king shall immediately die.' The remnants of his food are buried, doubtless to prevent them from falling into the hands of sorcerers, who by means of these fragments might cast a fatal spell over the monarch. The rules observed by the neighbouring king of Cacongo were similar; it was thought that the king would die if any of his subjects were to see him drink. It is a capital offence to see the king of Dahomey at his meals.

When he drinks in public, as he does on extraordinary occasions, he hides himself behind a curtain, or handkerchiefs are held up round his head, and all the people throw themselves with their faces to the earth. When the king of Bunyoro in Central Africa went to drink milk in the dairy, every man must leave the royal enclosure and all the women had to cover their heads till the king returned. No one might see him drink. One wife accompanied him to the dairy and handed him the milk-pot, but she turned away her face while he drained it.

§ 3. *Taboos on showing the Face.* — In some of the preceding cases the intention of eating and drinking in strict seclusion may perhaps be to hinder evil influences from entering the body rather than to prevent the escape of the soul. This certainly is the motive of some drinking customs observed by natives of the Congo region. Thus we are told of these people that 'there is hardly a native who would dare to swallow a liquid without first conjuring the spirits. One of them rings a bell all the time he is drinking; another crouches down and places his left hand on the earth; another veils his head; another puts a stalk of grass or a leaf in his hair, or marks his forehead with a line of clay. This fetish custom assumes very varied forms. To explain them, the black is satisfied to say that they are an energetic mode of conjuring spirits.' In this part of the world a chief will commonly ring a bell at each draught of beer which he swallows, and at the same moment a lad stationed in front of him brandishes a spear 'to keep at bay the spirits which might try to sneak into the old chief's body by the same road as the beer.' The same motive of warding off evil spirits probably explains the custom observed by some African sultans of veiling their faces. The Sultan of Darfur wraps up his face with a piece of white muslin, which goes round his head several times, covering his mouth and nose first, and then his forehead, so that only his eyes are visible. The same custom of veiling the face as a mark of sovereignty is said to be observed in other parts of Central Africa. The Sultan of Wadai always speaks from behind a curtain; no one sees his face except his intimates and a few favoured persons.

§ 4. *Taboos on quitting the House.* — By an extension of the like precaution kings are sometimes forbidden ever to leave their palaces; or, if they are allowed to do so, their subjects are forbidden to see them abroad. The fetish king of Benin, who was worshipped as a deity by his subjects, might not quit his palace. After his coronation the king of Loango is confined to his palace, which he may not leave. The king of Onitsha 'does not step out of his house into town unless a human sacrifice is made to propitiate the gods: on this account he never goes out beyond the precincts of his premises.' Indeed we are told that he may not quit his palace under pain of death or of giving up one or more slaves to be executed in his presence. As the wealth of the country is measured in slaves, the king takes good care not to infringe this law. Yet once a year at the Feast of Yams, the king is allowed, and even required by custom, to dance before his people outside the high mud wall of the palace. In dancing he carries a great weight, generally a sack of earth, on his back to prove that he is still able to support the burden and cares of state. Were he unable to discharge this duty, he would be immediately deposed and perhaps stoned. The kings of Ethiopia were worshipped as gods, but were mostly kept shut up in their palaces. On the mountainous coast of Pontus there dwelt in antiquity a rude and warlike people named the Mosyni or Mosynoeci, through whose rugged country the Ten Thousand marched on their famous retreat from Asia to Europe. These barbarians kept their king in close custody at the top of a high tower, from which after his election he was never more allowed to descend. Here he dispensed justice to his people; but if he offended them, they punished him by stopping his rations for a whole day, or even starving him to death. The kings of Sabaea or Sheba, the spice country of Arabia, were not allowed to go out of their palaces; if they did so, the mob stoned them to death. But at the top of the palace there was a window with a chain attached to it. If any man deemed he had suffered wrong, he pulled the chain, and the king perceived him and called him in and gave judgment.

§ 5. *Taboos on leaving Food over*. — Again, magic mischief may be wrought upon a man through the remains of the food he has partaken of, or the dishes out of which he has eaten. On the principles of sympathetic magic a real connexion continues to subsist between the food which a man has in his stomach and the refuse of it which he has left untouched, and hence by injuring the refuse you can simultaneously injure the eater. Among the

Narrinyeri of South Australia every adult is constantly on the look-out for bones of beasts, birds, or fish, of which the flesh has been eaten by somebody, in order to construct a deadly charm out of them. Every one is therefore careful to burn the bones of the animals which he has eaten, lest they should fall into the hands of a sorcerer. Too often, however, the sorcerer succeeds in getting hold of such a bone, and when he does so he believes that he hast he power of life and death over the man, woman, or child who ate the flesh of the animal. To put the charm in operation he makes a paste of red ochre and fish oil, inserts in it the eye of a cod and a small piece of the flesh of a corpse, and having rolled the compound into a ball sticks it on the top of the bone. After being left for some time in the bosom of a dead body, in order that it may derive a deadly potency by contact with corruption, the magical implement is set up in the ground near the fire, and as the ball melts, so the person against whom the charm is directed wastes with disease; if the ball is melted quite away, the victim will die. When the bewitched man learns of the spell that is being cast upon him, he endeavours to buy the bone from the sorcerer, and if he obtains it he breaks the charm by throwing the bone into a river or lake. In Tana, one of the New Hebrides, people bury or throw into the sea the leavings of their food, lest these should fall into the hands of the disease-makers. For if a disease-maker finds the remnants of a meal, say the skin of a banana, he picks it up and burns it slowly in the fire. As it burns, the person who ate the banana falls ill and sends to the disease-maker, offering him presents if he will stop burning the banana skin. In New Guinea the natives take the utmost care to destroy or conceal the husks and other remains of their food, lest these should be found by their enemies and used by them for the injury or destruction of the eaters. Hence they burn their leavings, throw them into the sea, or otherwise put them out of harm's way.

From a like fear, no doubt, of sorcery, no one may touch the food which the king of Loango leaves upon his plate; it is buried in a hole in the ground. And no one may drink out of the king's vessel. In antiquity the Romans used immediately to break the shells of eggs and of snails which they had eaten, in order to prevent enemies from making magic with them. The common practice, still observed among us, of breaking egg-shells after the eggs have been eaten may very well have originated in the same superstition.

The superstitious fear of the magic that may be wrought on a man through the leavings of his food has had the beneficial effect of inducing many savages to destroy refuse which, if left to rot, might through its corruption have proved a real, not a merely imaginary, source of disease and death. Nor is it only the sanitary condition of a tribe which has benefited by this superstition; curiously enough the same baseless dread, the same false notion of causation, has indirectly strengthened the moral bonds of hospitality, honour, and good faith among men who entertain it. For it is obvious that no one who intends to harm a man by working magic on the refuse of his food will himself partake of that food, because if he did so he would, on the principles of sympathetic magic, suffer equally with his enemy from any injury done to the refuse. This is the idea which in primitive society lends sanctity to the bond produced by eating together; by participation in the same food two men give, as it were, hostages for their good behaviour; each guarantees the other that he will devise no mischief against him, since, being physically united with him by the common food in their stomachs, any harm he might do to his fellow would recoil on his own head with precisely the same force with which it fell on the head of his victim. In strict logic, however, the sympathetic bond lasts only so long as the food is in the stomach of each of the parties. Hence the covenant formed by eating together is less solemn and durable than the covenant formed by transfusing the blood of the covenanting parties into each other's veins, for this transfusion seems to knit them together for life.

CHAPTER XX

TABOOED PERSONS

§ 1. *Chiefs and Kings tabooed.* — We have seen that the Mikado's food was cooked every day in new pots and served up in new dishes; both pots and dishes were of common clay, in order that they might be broken or laid aside after they had been once used. They were generally broken, for it was believed that if any one else ate his food out of these sacred dishes, his mouth and throat would become swollen and inflamed. The same ill effect was thought to be experienced by any one who should wear the Mikado's clothes without his leave; he would have swellings and pains all over his body. In Fiji there is a special name (*kana lama*) for the disease supposed to be caused by eating out of a chief's dishes or wearing his clothes. 'The throat and body swell, and the impious person dies. I had a fine mat given to me by a man who durst not use it because Thakombau's eldest son had sat upon it. There was always a family or clan of commoners who were exempt from this danger. I was talking about this once to Thakombau. "Oh yes," said he. "Here, So-and-so! come and scratch my back." The man scratched; he was one of those who could do it with impunity.' The name of the men thus highly privileged was *Na nduka ni*, or the dirt of the chief.

In the evil effects thus supposed to follow upon the use of the vessels or clothes of the Mikado and a Fijian chief we see that other side of the god-man's character to which attention has been already called. The divine person is a source of danger as well as of blessing; he must not only be guarded, he must also be guarded against. His sacred organism, so delicate that a touch may disorder it, is also, as it were, electrically charged with a powerful magical or spiritual force which may discharge itself with fatal effect on whatever comes in contact with it. Accordingly the isolation of the man-god is quite as necessary for the safety of others as for his own. His magical virtue is in the strictest sense of the word contagious: his divinity is a fire, which, under proper restraints, confers endless blessings, but, if rashly touched or allowed to break bounds, burns and destroys what it touches. Hence the disastrous effects supposed to attend a breach of taboo; the offender has thrust his hand into the divine fire, which shrivels up and consumes him on the spot.

The Nubas, for example, who inhabit the wooded and fertile range of Jebel Nuba in Eastern Africa, believe that they would die if they entered the house of their priestly king; however, they can evade the penalty of their intrusion by baring the left shoulder and getting the king to lay his hand on it. And were any man to sit on a stone which the king has consecrated to his own use, the transgressor would die within the year. The Cazembes of Angola regard their king as so holy that no one can touch him without being killed by the magical power which pervades his sacred person. But since contact with him is sometimes unavoidable, they have devised a means whereby the sinner can escape with his life. Kneeling down before the king he touches the back of the royal hand with the back of his own, then snaps his fingers; afterwards he lays the palm of his hand on the palm of the king's hand, then snaps his fingers again. This ceremony is repeated four or five times, and averts the imminent danger of death. In Tonga it was believed that if any one fed himself with his own hands after touching the sacred person of a superior chief or anything that belonged to him, he would swell up and die; the sanctity of the chief, like a virulent poison, infected the hands of his inferior, and, being communicated through them to the food, proved fatal to the eater. A commoner who had incurred this danger could disinfect himself by performing a certain ceremony, which consisted in touching the sole of a chief's foot with the palm and back of each of his hands, and afterwards rinsing his hands in water. If there was no water near, he rubbed his hands with the juicy stem of a plantain or banana. After that he was free to feed himself with his own hands without danger of being attacked by the malady which would otherwise follow from eating with tabooed or sanctified hands. But until the ceremony of expiation or disinfection had been performed, if he wished to eat, he had either to get some one to feed him, or else to go down on his knees and pick up the food from the ground with his mouth like a beast. He might not even use a toothpick himself, but might guide the hand of another person holding the toothpick. The Tongans were subject to induration of the liver and certain forms of scrofula, which they often attributed to a failure to perform the requisite expiation after having inadvertently touched a chief or his belongings. Hence they often went through the ceremony as a precaution, without knowing that they had done anything to call for it. The king of Tonga could not refuse to play his part in the rite by presenting his foot to such as desired to touch it, even when they applied to him at an inconvenient time. A fat unwieldy king, who perceived his subjects approaching with this intention, while he chanced to be taking his walks abroad, has been sometimes seen to waddle as fast as his legs could carry him out of their way, in order to escape the importunate and not wholly disinterested expression of their homage. If any one fancied he might have already unwittingly eaten with tabooed hands, he sat down before the chief, and, taking the chief's foot, pressed it against his own stomach, that the food in his belly might not injure him, and that he might not swell up and die. Since scrofula was regarded by the Tongans as a result of eating with tabooed hands, we may conjecture that persons who suffered from it among them often resorted to the touch or pressure of the king's foot as a cure for their malady. The analogy of the custom with the old English practice of bringing scrofulous patients to the king to be healed by his touch is sufficiently obvious, and suggests, as I have already pointed out elsewhere, that among our own remote ancestors scrofula may have obtained its name of the King's Evil from a belief, like that of the Tongans, that it was caused as well as cured by contact with the divine majesty of kings.

In New Zealand the dread of the sanctity of chiefs was at least as great as in Tonga. Their ghostly power, derived from an ancestral spirit, diffused itself by contagion over everything they touched, and could strike dead all who rashly or unwittingly meddled with it. For instance, it once happened that a New Zealand chief of high rank and great sanctity had left the remains of his dinner by the wayside. A slave, a stout, hungry fellow, coming up after the chief had gone, saw the unfinished dinner, and ate it up without asking questions. Hardly had he finished when he was informed by a horror-stricken spectator that the food of which he had eaten was the chief's. 'I knew the unfortunate delinquent well. He was remarkable for courage, and had signalised himself in the wars of the tribe,' but 'no sooner did he hear the fatal news than he was seized by the most extraordinary convulsions and cramp in the stomach, which never ceased till he died, about sundown the same day. He was a strong man, in the prime of life, and if any pakeha [European] freethinker should have said he was not killed by the *tapu* of the chief, which had been communicated to the food by contact, he would have been listened to with feelings of contempt for his ignorance and inability to understand plain and direct evidence.' This is not a solitary case. A Maori woman having eaten of some fruit, and being afterwards told that the fruit had been taken from a tabooed place, exclaimed that the spirit of the chief, whose sanctity had been thus profaned, would kill her. This was in the afternoon, and next day by twelve o'clock she was dead. A Maori chief's tinder-box was once the means of killing several persons; for, having been lost by him, and found by some men who used it to light their pipes, they died of fright on learning to whom it had belonged. So, too, the garments of a high New Zealand chief will kill any one else who wears them. A chief was observed by a missionary to throw down a precipice a blanket which he found too heavy to carry. Being asked by the missionary why he did not leave it on a tree for the use of a future traveller, the chief replied that 'it was the fear of its being taken by another which caused him to throw it where he did, for if it were worn, his tapu' (that is, his spiritual power communicated by contact to the blanket and through the blanket to the man) 'would kill the person.' For a similar reason a Maori chief would not blow a fire with his mouth; for his sacred breath would communicate its sanctity to the fire, which would pass it on to the pot on the fire, which would pass it on to the meat in the pot, which would pass it on to the man who ate the meat, which was in the pot, which stood on the fire, which was breathed on by the chief; so that the eater, infected by the chief's breath conveyed through these intermediaries, would surely die.

Thus in the Polynesian race, to which the Maoris belong, superstition erected round the persons of sacred chiefs a real, though at the same time purely imaginary barrier, to transgress which actually entailed the death of the transgressor whenever he became aware of what he had done. This fatal power of the imagination working through superstitious terrors is by no means confined to one race; it appears to be common among savages. For example, among the aborigines of Australia a native will die after the infliction of even the most superficial wound, if only he believes that the weapon which inflicted the wound had been sung over and thus endowed with magical virtue. He simply lies down, refuses food, and pines away. Similarly among some of the Indian tribes of Brazil, if the medicine-man predicted the death of any one who had offended him, 'the wretch took to his hammock instantly in such full expectation of dying, that he would neither eat nor drink, and the prediction was a sentence which faith effectually executed.'

§ 2. *Mourners tabooed.* — Thus regarding his sacred chiefs and kings as charged with a mysterious spiritual force which so to say explodes at contact, the savage naturally ranks them among the dangerous classes of society, and imposes upon them the same sort of restraints that he lays on manslayers, menstruous women, and other persons whom he looks upon with a certain fear and horror. For example, sacred kings and priests in Polynesia were not allowed to touch food with their hands, and had therefore to be fed by others; and as we have just seen, their vessels, garments, and other property might not be used by others on pain of disease and death. Now precisely the same observances are exacted by some savages from girls at their first menstruation, women after childbirth, homicides, mourners, and all persons who have come into contact with the dead. Thus, for example, to begin with the last class of persons, among the Maoris any one who had handled a corpse, helped to convey it to the grave, or touched a dead man's bones, was cut off from all intercourse and almost all communication with mankind. He could not enter any house, or come into contact with any person or thing, without utterly be-devilling them. He might not even touch food with his hands, which had become so frightfully tabooed or unclean as to be quite useless. Food would be set for him on the ground, and he would then sit or kneel down, and, with his hands carefully held behind his back, would gnaw at it as best he could. In some cases he would be fed by another person, who with outstretched arm contrived to do it without touching the tabooed man; but the feeder was himself subjected to many severe restrictions, little less onerous than those which were imposed upon the other. In almost every populous village there lived a degraded wretch, the lowest of the low, who earned a sorry pittance by thus waiting upon the defiled. Clad in rags, daubed from head to foot with red ochre and stinking shark oil, always solitary and silent, generally old, haggard, and wizened, often half crazed, he might be seen sitting motionless all day apart from the common path or thoroughfare of the village, gazing with lack-lustre eyes on the

busy doings in which he might never take a part. Twice a day a
dole of food would be thrown on the ground before him to munch
as well as he could without the use of his hands; and at night,
huddling his greasy tatters about him, he would crawl into some
miserable lair of leaves and refuse, where, dirty, cold, and hungry,
he passed, in broken ghost-haunted slumbers, a wretched night
as a prelude to another wretched day. Such was the only human
being deemed fit to associate at arm's length with one who had
paid the last offices of respect and friendship to the dead. And
when, the dismal term of his seclusion being over, the mourner
was about to mix with his fellows once more, all the dishes he had
used in his seclusion were diligently smashed, and all the garments
he had worn were carefully thrown away, lest they should spread
the contagion of his defilement among others, just as the vessels
and clothes of sacred kings and chiefs are destroyed or cast away
for a similar reason. So complete in these respects is the analogy
which the savage traces between the spiritual influences that
emanate from divinities and from the dead, between the odour
of sanctity and the stench of corruption.

The rule which forbids persons who have been in contact with
the dead to touch food with their hands would seem to have been
universal in Polynesia. Thus in Samoa 'those who attended the
deceased were most careful not to handle food, and for days were
fed by others as if they were helpless infants. Baldness and the
loss of teeth were supposed to be the punishment inflicted by the
household god if they violated the rule.' Again, in Tonga,
'no person can touch a dead chief without being taboo'd for ten
lunar months, except chiefs, who are only taboo'd for three, four,
or five months, according to the superiority of the dead chief;
except again it be the body of Tooitonga [the great divine chief],
and then even the greatest chief would be taboo'd ten months.
. . . During the time a man is taboo'd he must not feed himself
with his own hands, but must be fed by somebody else: he must
not even use a toothpick himself, but must guide another person's
hand holding the toothpick. If he is hungry and there is no one
to feed him, he must go down upon his hands and knees, and pick
up his victuals with his mouth: and if he infringes upon any of
these rules, it is firmly expected that he will swell up and die.'

Among the Shuswap of British Columbia widows and widowers

in mourning are secluded and forbidden to touch their own head
or body; the cups and cooking-vessels which they use may be used
by no one else. They must build a sweat-house beside a creek,
sweat there all night and bathe regularly, after which they must
rub their bodies with branches of spruce. The branches may not
be used more than once, and when they have served their purpose
they are stuck into the ground all round the hut. No hunter would
come near such mourners, for their presence is unlucky. If their
shadow were to fall on any one, he would be taken ill at once.
They employ thorn bushes for bed and pillow, in order to keep
away the ghost of the deceased; and thorn bushes are also laid
all around their beds. This last precaution shows clearly what the
spiritual danger is which leads to the exclusion of such persons
from ordinary society; it is simply a fear of the ghost who is
supposed to be hovering near them. In the Mekeo district of
British New Guinea a widower loses all his civil rights and
becomes a social outcast, an object of fear and horror, shunned
by all. He may not cultivate a garden, nor show himself in public,
nor traverse the village, nor walk on the roads and paths. Like
a wild beast he must skulk in the long grass and the bushes; and
if he sees or hears any one coming, especially a woman, he must
hide behind a tree or a thicket. If he wishes to fish or hunt, he
must do it alone and at night. If he would consult any one, even
the missionary, he does so by stealth and at night; he seems to
have lost his voice and speaks only in whispers. Were he to join
a party of fishers or hunters, his presence would bring misfortune
on them; the ghost of his dead wife would frighten away the fish
or the game. He goes about everywhere and at all times armed
with a tomahawk to defend himself, not only against wild boars
in the jungle, but against the dreaded spirit of his departed spouse,
who would do him an ill turn if she could; for all the souls of the
dead are malignant and their only delight is to harm the living.

§ 3. *Women tabooed at Menstruation and Childbirth.* — In
general, we may say that the prohibition to use the vessels,
garments, and so forth of certain persons, and the effects supposed
to follow an infraction of the rule, are exactly the same whether
the persons to whom the things belong are sacred or what we
might call unclean and polluted. As the garments which have
been touched by a sacred chief kill those who handle them, so do

the things which have been touched by a menstruous woman. An Australian black-fellow, who discovered that his wife had lain on his blanket at her menstrual period, killed her and died of terror himself within a fortnight. Hence Australian women at these times are forbidden under pain of death to touch anything that men use, or even to walk on a path that any man frequents. They are also secluded at childbirth, and all vessels used by them during their seclusion are burned. In Uganda the pots which a woman touches, while the impurity of childbirth or of menstruation is on her, should be destroyed; spears and shields defiled by her touch are not destroyed but only purified. 'Among all the Déné and most other American tribes, hardly any other being was the object of so much dread as a menstruating woman. As soon as signs of that condition made themselves apparent in a young girl she was carefully segregated from all but female company, and had to live by herself in a small hut away from the gaze of the villagers or of the male members of the roving band. While in that awful state, she had to abstain from touching anything belonging to man, or the spoils of any venison or other animal, lest she would thereby pollute the same, and condemn the hunters to failure, owing to the anger of the game thus slighted. Dried fish formed her diet, and cold water, absorbed through a drinking tube, was her only beverage. Moreover, as the very sight of her was dangerous to society, a special skin bonnet, with fringes falling over her face down to her breast, hid her from the public gaze, even some time after she had recovered her normal state.' Among the Bribri Indians of Costa Rica a menstruous woman is regarded as unclean. The only plates she may use for her food are banana leaves, which, when she has done with them, she throws away in some sequestered spot; for were a cow to find them and eat them, the animal would waste away and perish. And she drinks out of a special vessel for a like reason; because if any one drank out of the same cup after her, he would surely die.

Among many peoples similar restrictions are imposed on women in childbed and apparently for similar reasons; at such periods women are supposed to be in a dangerous condition which would infect any person or thing they might touch; hence they are put into quarantine until, with the recovery of their health and strength, the imaginary danger has passed away. Thus, in

Tahiti a woman after childbirth was secluded for a fortnight or three weeks in a temporary hut erected on sacred ground; during the time of her seclusion she was debarred from touching provisions, and had to be fed by another. Further, if any one else touched the child at this period, he was subjected to the same restrictions as the mother until the ceremony of her purification had been performed. Similarly in the island of Kadiak, off Alaska, a woman about to be delivered retires to a miserable low hovel built of reeds, where she must remain for twenty days after the birth of her child, whatever the season may be, and she is considered so unclean that no one will touch her, and food is reached to her on sticks. The Bribri Indians regard the pollution of childbed as much more dangerous even than that of menstruation. When a woman feels her time approaching, she informs her husband, who makes haste to build a hut for her in a lonely spot. There she must live alone, holding no converse with anybody save her mother or another woman. After her delivery the medicine-man purifies her by breathing on her and laying an animal, it matters not what, upon her. But even this ceremony only mitigates her uncleanness into a state considered to be equivalent to that of a menstruous woman; and for a full lunar month she must live apart from her housemates, observing the same rules with regard to eating and drinking as at her monthly periods. The case is still worse, the pollution is still more deadly, if she has had a miscarriage or has been delivered of a stillborn child. In that case she may not go near a living soul: the mere contact with things she has used is exceedingly dangerous: her food is handed to her at the end of a long stick. This lasts generally for three weeks, after which she may go home, subject only to the restrictions incident to an ordinary confinement.

Some Bantu tribes entertain even more exaggerated notions of the virulent infection spread by a woman who has had a miscarriage and has concealed it. An experienced observer of these people tells us that the blood of childbirth 'appears to the eyes of the South Africans to be tainted with a pollution still more dangerous than that of the menstrual fluid. The husband is excluded from the hut for eight days of the lying-in period, chiefly from fear that he might be contaminated by this secretion. He dare not take his child in his arms for the three first months after the birth. But the secretion of childbed is particularly terrible when it is the product of a miscarriage, especially *a concealed miscarriage*. In this case it is not merely the man who is threatened or killed, it is the whole country, it is the sky itself which suffers. By a curious association of ideas a physiological fact causes cosmic troubles!' As for the disastrous effect which a miscarriage may have on the whole country I will quote the words of a medicine-man and rain-maker of the Ba-Pedi tribe: 'When a woman has had a miscarriage, when she has allowed her blood to flow, and has hidden the child, it is enough to cause the burning winds to blow and to parch the country with heat. The rain no longer falls, for the country is no longer in order. When the rain approaches the place where the blood is, it will not dare to approach. It will fear and remain at a distance. That woman has committed a great fault. She has spoiled the country of the chief, for she has hidden blood which had not yet been well congealed to fashion a man. That blood is taboo. It should never drip on the road! The chief will assemble his men and say to them, "Are you in order in your villages?" Some one will answer, "Such and such a woman was pregnant and we have not yet seen the child which she has given birth to." Then they go and arrest the woman. They say to her, "Show us where you have hidden it." They go and dig at the spot, they sprinkle the hole with a decoction of two sorts of roots prepared in a special pot. They take a little of the earth of this grave, they throw it into the river, then they bring back water from the river and sprinkle it where she shed her blood. She herself must wash every day with the medicine. Then the country will be moistened again (by rain). Further, we (medicine-men) summon the women of the country; we tell them to prepare a ball of the earth which contains the blood. They bring it to us one morning. If we wish to prepare medicine with which to sprinkle the whole country, we crumble this earth to powder; at the end of five days we send little boys and little girls, girls that yet know nothing of women's affairs and have not yet had relations with men. We put the medicine in the horns of oxen, and these children go to all the fords, to all the entrances of the country. A little girl turns up the soil with her mattock, the others dip a branch in the horn and sprinkle the inside of the hole saying, "Rain! rain!" So we remove the misfortune which the women have brought on the roads; the rain will be able to come. The country is purified!'

§ 4. *Warriors tabooed.* — Once more, warriors are conceived by the savage to move, so to say, in an atmosphere of spiritual danger which constrains them to practise a variety of superstitious observances quite different in their nature from those rational precautions which, as a matter of course, they adopt against foes of flesh and blood. The general effect of these observances is to place the warrior, both before and after victory, in the same state of seclusion or spiritual quarantine in which, for his own safety, primitive man puts his human gods and other dangerous characters. Thus when the Maoris went out on the war-path they were sacred or taboo in the highest degree, and they and their friends at home had to observe strictly many curious customs over and above the numerous taboos of ordinary life. They became, in the irreverent language of Europeans who knew them in the old fighting days, 'tabooed an inch thick'; and as for the leader of the expedition, he was quite unapproachable. Similarly, when the Israelites marched forth to war they were bound by certain rules of ceremonial purity identical with rules observed by Maoris and Australian black-fellows on the war-path. The vessels they used were sacred, and they had to practise continence and a custom of personal cleanliness of which the original motive, if we may judge from the avowed motive of savages who conform to the same custom, was a fear lest the enemy should obtain the refuse of their persons, and thus be enabled to work their destruction by magic. Among some Indian tribes of North America a young warrior in his first campaign had to conform to certain customs, of which two were identical with the observances imposed by the same Indians on girls at their first menstruation: the vessels he ate and drank out of might be touched by no other person, and he was forbidden to scratch his head or any other part of his body with his fingers; if he could not help scratching himself, he had to do it with a stick. The latter rule, like the one which forbids a tabooed person to feed himself with his own fingers, seems to rest on the supposed sanctity or pollution, whichever we choose to call it, of the tabooed hands. Moreover, among these Indian tribes the men on the war-path had always to sleep at night with their faces turned towards their own country; however uneasy the

K

posture, they might not change it. They might not sit upon the bare ground, nor wet their feet, nor walk on a beaten path if they could help it; when they had no choice but to walk on a path, they sought to counteract the ill effect of doing so by doctoring their legs with certain medicines or charms which they carried with them for the purpose. No member of the party was permitted to step over the legs, hands, or body of any other member who chanced to be sitting or lying on the ground; and it was equally forbidden to step over his blanket, gun, tomahawk, or anything that belonged to him. If this rule was inadvertently broken, it became the duty of the member whose person or property had been stepped over to knock the other member down, and it was similarly the duty of that other to be knocked down peaceably and without resistance. The vessels out of which the warriors ate their food were commonly small bowls of wood or birch bark, with marks to distinguish the two sides; in marching from home the Indians invariably drank out of one side of the bowl, and in returning they drank out of the other. When on their way home they came within a day's march of the village, they hung up all their bowls on trees, or threw them away on the prairie, doubtless to prevent their sanctity or defilement from being communicated with disastrous effects to their friends, just as we have seen that the vessels and clothes of the sacred Mikado, of women at childbirth and menstruation, and of persons defiled by contact with the dead are destroyed or laid aside for a similar reason. The first four times that an Apache Indian goes out on the war-path, he is bound to refrain from scratching his head with his fingers and from letting water touch his lips. Hence he scratches his head with a stick, and drinks through a hollow reed or cane. Stick and reed are attached to the warrior's belt and to each other by a leathern thong. The rule not to scratch their heads with their fingers, but to use a stick for the purpose instead, was regularly observed by Ojebways on the war-path.

With regard to the Creek Indians and kindred tribes we are told they 'will not cohabit with women while they are out at war; they religiously abstain from every kind of intercourse even with their own wives, for the space of three days and nights before they go to war, and so after they return home, because they are to sanctify themselves.' Among the Ba-Pedi and Ba-Thonga tribes of South Africa not only have the warriors to abstain from women, but the people left behind in the villages are also bound to continence; they think that any incontinence on their part would cause thorns to grow on the ground traversed by the warriors, and that success would not attend the expedition.

Why exactly many savages have made it a rule to refrain from women in time of war, we cannot say for certain, but we may conjecture that their motive was a superstitious fear lest, on the principles of sympathetic magic, close contact with women should infect them with feminine weakness and cowardice. Similarly some savages imagine that contact with a woman in childbed enervates warriors and enfeebles their weapons. Indeed the Kayans of Central Borneo go so far as to hold that to touch a loom or women's clothes would so weaken a man that he would have no success in hunting, fishing, and war. Hence it is not merely sexual intercourse with women that the savage warrior sometimes shuns; he is careful to avoid the sex altogether. Thus among the hill tribes of Assam, not only are men forbidden to cohabit with their wives during or after a raid, but they may not eat food cooked by a woman; nay, they should not address a word even to their own wives. Once a woman, who unwittingly broke the rule by speaking to her husband while he was under the war taboo, sickened and died when she learned the awful crime she had committed.

§ 5. *Manslayers tabooed.* — If the reader still doubts whether the rules of conduct which we have just been considering are based on superstitious fears or dictated by a rational prudence, his doubts will probably be dissipated when he learns that rules of the same sort are often imposed even more stringently on warriors after the victory has been won and when all fear of the living corporeal foe is at an end. In such cases one motive for the inconvenient restrictions laid on the victors in their hour of triumph is probably a dread of the angry ghosts of the slain; and that the fear of the vengeful ghosts does influence the behaviour of the slayers is often expressly affirmed. The general effect of the taboos laid on sacred chiefs, mourners, women at childbirth, men on the war-path, and so on, is to seclude or isolate the tabooed persons from ordinary society, this effect being attained by a variety of rules, which oblige the men or women to live in

separate huts or in the open air, to shun the commerce of the
sexes, to avoid the use of vessels employed by others, and so
forth. Now the same effect is produced by similar means in the
case of victorious warriors, particularly such as have actually
shed the blood of their enemies. In the island of Timor, when a
warlike expedition has returned in triumph bringing the heads of
the vanquished foe, the leader of the expedition is forbidden by
religion and custom to return at once to his own house. A special
hut is prepared for him, in which he has to reside for two months,
undergoing bodily spiritual purification. During this time he may
not go to his wife nor feed himself; the food must be put into his
mouth by another person. That these observances are dictated
by fear of the ghosts of the slain seems certain; for from another
account of the ceremonies performed on the return of a successful
head-hunter in the same island we learn that sacrifices are offered
on this occasion to appease the soul of the man whose head has
been taken; the people think that some misfortune would befall
the victor were such offerings omitted. Moreover, a part of the
ceremony consists of a dance accompanied by a song, in which
the death of the slain man is lamented and his forgiveness is
entreated. 'Be not angry,' they say, 'because your head is here
with us; had we been less lucky, our heads might now have been
exposed in your village. We have offered the sacrifice to appease
you. Your spirit may now rest and leave us at peace. Why were
you our enemy? Would it not have been better that we should
remain friends? Then your blood would not have been spilt and
your head would not have been cut off.' The people of Paloo in
Central Celebes take the heads of their enemies in war and afterwards propitiate the souls of the slain in the temple.

Among the tribes at the mouth of the Wanigela River, in New
Guinea, 'a man who has taken life is considered to be impure
until he has undergone certain ceremonies: as soon as possible
after the deed he cleanses himself and his weapon. This satis-
factorily accomplished, he repairs to his village and seats himself
on the logs of sacrificial staging. No one approaches him or takes
any notice whatever of him. A house is prepared for him which
is put in charge of two or three small boys as servants. He may
eat only toasted bananas, and only the centre portion of them —
the ends being thrown away. On the third day of his seclusion a

small feast is prepared by his friends, who also fashion some new perineal bands for him. This is called *ivi poro*. The next day the man dons all his best ornaments and badges for taking life, and sallies forth fully armed and parades the village. The next day a hunt is organised, and a kangaroo selected from the game captured. It is cut open and the spleen and liver rubbed over the back of the man. He then walks solemnly down to the nearest water, and standing straddle-legs in it washes himself. All the young untried warriors swim between his legs. This is supposed to impart courage and strength to them. The following day, at early dawn, he dashes out of his house, fully armed, and calls aloud the name of his victim. Having satisfied himself that he has thoroughly scared the ghost of the dead man, he returns to his house. The beating of flooring-boards and the lighting of fires is also a certain method of scaring the ghost. A day later his purification is finished. He can then enter his wife's house.'

In Windessi, Dutch New Guinea, when a party of head-hunters has been successful, and they are nearing home, they announce their approach and success by blowing on triton shells. Their canoes are also decked with branches. The faces of the men who have taken a head are blackened with charcoal. If several have taken part in killing the same victim, his head is divided among them. They always time their arrival so as to reach home in the early morning. They come rowing to the village with a great noise, and the women stand ready to dance in the verandahs of the houses. The canoes row past the *room sram* or house where the young men live; and as they pass, the murderers throw as many pointed sticks or bamboos at the wall or the roof as there were enemies killed. The day is spent very quietly. Now and then they drum or blow on the conch; at other times they beat the walls of the houses with loud shouts to drive away the ghosts of the slain. So the Yabim of New Guinea believe that the spirit of a murdered man pursues his murderer and seeks to do him a mischief. Hence they drive away the spirit with shouts and the beating of drums. When the Fijians had buried a man alive, as they often did, they used at nightfall to make a great uproar by means of bamboos, trumpet-shells, and so forth, for the purpose of frightening away his ghost, lest he should attempt to return to his old home. And to render his house unattractive to him they dismantled it and clothed it with everything that to their ideas seemed most repulsive. On the evening of the day on which they had tortured a prisoner to death, the American Indians were wont to run through the village with hideous yells, beating with sticks on the furniture, the walls, and the roofs of the huts to prevent the angry ghost of their victim from settling there and taking vengeance for the torments that his body had endured at their hands. 'Once,' says a traveller, 'on approaching in the night a village of Ottawas, I found all the inhabitants in confusion: they were all busily engaged in raising noises of the loudest and most inharmonious kind. Upon inquiry, I found that a battle had been lately fought between the Ottawas and the Kickapoos, and that the object of all this noise was to prevent the ghosts of the departed combatants from entering the village.'

Among the Basutos 'ablution is specially performed on return from battle. It is absolutely necessary that the warriors should rid themselves, as soon as possible, of the blood they have shed, or the shades of their victims would pursue them incessantly, and disturb their slumbers. They go in a procession, and in full armour, to the nearest stream. At the moment they enter the water, a diviner, placed higher up, throws some purifying substances into the current. This is, however, not strictly necessary. The javelins and battle-axes also undergo the process of washing.' Among the Bageshu of East Africa a man who has killed another may not return to his own house on the same day, though he may enter the village and spend the night in a friend's house. He kills a sheep and smears his chest, his right arm, and his head with the contents of the animal's stomach. His children are brought to him and he smears them in like manner. Then he smears each side of the doorway with the tripe and entrails, and finally throws the rest of the stomach on the roof of his house. For a whole day he may not touch food with his hands, but picks it up with two sticks and conveys it to his mouth. His wife is not under any such restrictions. She may even go to mourn for the man whom her husband has killed, if she wishes to do so. Among the Angoni, to the north of the Zambesi, warriors who have slain foes on an expedition smear their bodies and faces with ashes, hang garments of their victims on their persons, and tie bark ropes round their necks, so that the ends hang down over their shoulders or breasts. This costume they wear for three days after their return, and rising at break of day they run through the village uttering frightful yells to drive away the ghosts of the slain, which, if they were not thus banished from the houses, might bring sickness and misfortune on the inmates.

In some of these accounts nothing is said of an enforced seclusion, at least after the ceremonial cleansing, but some South African tribes certainly require the slayer of a very gallant foe in war to keep apart from his wife and family for ten days after he has washed his body in running water. He also receives from the tribal doctor a medicine which he chews with his food. When a Nandi of East Africa has killed a member of another tribe, he paints one side of his body, spear, and sword red, and the other side white. For four days after the slaughter he is considered unclean and may not go home. He has to build a small shelter by a river and live there; he may not associate with his wife or sweetheart, and he may eat nothing but porridge, beef, and goat's flesh. At the end of the fourth day he must purify himself by taking a strong purge made from the bark of the *segetet* tree and by drinking goat's milk mixed with blood. Among the Bantu tribes of Kavirondo, when a man has killed an enemy in warfare he shaves his head on his return home, and his friends rub a medicine, which generally consists of goat's dung, over his body to prevent the spirit of the slain man from troubling him. Exactly the same custom is practised for the same reason by the Wageia of East Africa. With the Ja-Luo of Kavirondo the custom is somewhat different. Three days after his return from the fight the warrior shaves his head. But before he may enter his village he has to hang a live fowl, head uppermost, round his neck; then the bird is decapitated and its head left hanging round his neck. Soon after his return a feast is made for the slain man, in order that his ghost may not haunt his slayer. In the Pelew Islands, when the men return from a warlike expedition in which they have taken a life, the young warriors who have been out fighting for the first time, and all who handled the slain, are shut up in the large council-house and become tabooed. They may not quit the edifice, nor bathe, nor touch a woman, nor eat fish; their food is limited to coco-nuts and syrup. They rub themselves with charmed leaves and chew charmed betel. After three days they go together to bathe as near as possible to the spot where the man was killed.

Among the Natchez Indians of North America young braves who had taken their first scalps were obliged to observe certain rules of abstinence for six months. They might not sleep with their wives nor eat flesh; their only food was fish and hasty-pudding. If they broke these rules, they believed that the soul of the man they had killed would work their death by magic, that they would gain no more successes over the enemy, and that the least wound inflicted on them would prove mortal. When a Choctaw had killed an enemy and taken his scalp, he went into mourning for a month, during which he might not comb his hair, and if his head itched he might not scratch it except with a little stick which he wore fastened to his wrist for the purpose. This ceremonial mourning for the enemies they had slain was not uncommon among the North American Indians.

Thus we see that warriors who have taken the life of a foe in battle are temporarily cut off from free intercourse with their fellows, and especially with their wives, and must undergo certain rites of purification before they are readmitted to society. Now if the purpose of their seclusion and of the expiatory rites which they have to perform is, as we have been led to believe, no other than to shake off, frighten, or appease the angry spirit of the slain man, we may safely conjecture that the similar purification of homicides and murderers, who have imbrued their hands in the blood of a fellow-tribesman, had at first the same significance, and that the idea of a moral or spiritual regeneration symbolised by the washing, the fasting, and so on, was merely a later interpretation put upon the old custom by men who had out-grown the primitive modes of thought in which the custom originated. The conjecture will be confirmed if we can show that savages have actually imposed certain restrictions on the murderer of a fellow-tribesman from a definite fear that he is haunted by the ghost of his victim. This we can do with regard to the Omahas of North America. Among these Indians the kinsmen of a murdered man had the right to put the murderer to death, but sometimes they waived their right in consideration of presents which they consented to accept. When the life of the murderer was spared, he had to observe certain stringent rules for a period which varied from two to four years. He must walk barefoot, and he might eat no warm food, nor raise his voice, nor look around. He was compelled to pull his robe about him and to have it tied at the neck even in hot weather; he might not let it hang loose or fly open. He might not move his hands about, but had to keep them close to his body. He might not comb his hair, and it might not be blown about by the wind. When the tribe went out hunting, he was obliged to pitch his tent about a quarter of a mile from the rest of the people 'lest the ghost of his victim should raise a high wind, which might cause damage.' Only one of his kindred was allowed to remain with him at his tent. No one wished to eat with him, for they said, 'If we eat with him whom Wakanda hates, Wakanda will hate us.' Sometimes he wandered at night crying and lamenting his offence. At the end of his long isolation the kinsmen of the murdered man heard his crying and said, 'It is enough. Begone, and walk among the crowd. Put on moccasins and wear a good robe.' Here the reason alleged for keeping the murderer at a considerable distance from the hunters gives the clue to all the other restrictions laid on him: he was haunted and therefore dangerous. The ancient Greeks believed that the soul of a man who had just been killed was wroth with his slayer and troubled him; wherefore it was needful even for the involuntary homicide to depart from his country for a year until the anger of the dead man had cooled down; nor might the slayer return until sacrifice had been offered and ceremonies of purification performed. If his victim chanced to be a foreigner, the homicide had to shun the native country of the dead man as well as his own. The legend of the matricide Orestes, how he roamed from place to place pursued by the Furies of his murdered mother, and none would sit at meat with him, or take him in, till he had been purified, reflects faithfully the real Greek dread of such as were still haunted by an angry ghost.

§ 6. *Hunters and Fishers tabooed.* — In savage society the hunter and the fisherman have often to observe rules of abstinence and to submit to ceremonies of purification of the same sort as those which are obligatory on the warrior and the manslayer; and though we cannot in all cases perceive the exact purpose which these rules and ceremonies are supposed to serve, we may with some probability assume that, just as the dread of the spirits of his enemies is the main motive for the seclusion and purification of the warrior who hopes to take or has already taken their lives, so the huntsman or fisherman who complies with similar customs is principally actuated by a fear of the spirits of the beasts, birds, or fish which he has killed or intends to kill. For the savage commonly conceives animals to be endowed with souls and intelligences like his own, and hence he naturally treats them with similar respect. Just as he attempts to appease the ghosts of the men he has slain, so he essays to propitiate the spirits of the animals he has killed. These ceremonies of propitiation will be described later on in this work; here we have to deal, first, with the taboos observed by the hunter and the fisherman before or during the hunting and fishing seasons, and, second, with the ceremonies of purification which have to be practised by these men on returning with their booty from a successful chase.

While the savage respects, more or less, the souls of all animals, he treats with particular deference the spirits of such as are either especially useful to him or formidable on account of their size, strength, or ferocity. Accordingly the hunting and killing of these valuable or dangerous beasts are subject to more elaborate rules and ceremonies than the slaughter of comparatively useless and insignificant creatures. Thus the Indians of Nootka Sound prepared themselves for catching whales by observing a fast for a week, during which they ate very little, bathed in the water several times a day, sang, and rubbed their bodies, limbs, and faces with shells and bushes till they looked as if they had been severely torn with briars. They were likewise required to abstain from any commerce with their women for the like period, this last condition being considered indispensable to their success. A chief who failed to catch a whale has been known to attribute his failure to a breach of chastity on the part of his men. It should be remarked that the conduct thus prescribed as a preparation for whaling is precisely that which in the same tribe of Indians was required of men about to go on the war-path. Rules of the same sort are, or were formerly, observed by Malagasy whalers. For eight days before they went to sea the crew of a whaler used to fast, abstaining from women and liquor, and confessing their most secret faults to each other; and if any man was found to have sinned deeply, he was forbidden to share in the expedition. In the island of Mabuiag continence was imposed on the people both before they went to hunt the dugong and while the turtles were pairing. The turtle-season lasts during parts of October and November; and if at that time unmarried persons had sexual intercourse with each other, it was believed that when the canoe approached the floating turtle, the male would separate from the female and both would dive down in different directions. So at Mowat in New Guinea men have no relation with women when the turtle are coupling, though there is considerable laxity of morals at other times. In the island of Uap, one of the Caroline group, every fisherman plying his craft lies under a most strict taboo during the whole of the fishing season, which lasts for six or eight weeks. Whenever he is on shore he must spend all his time in the men's clubhouse, and under no pretext whatever may he visit his own house or so much as look upon the faces of his wife and womenkind. Were he but to steal a glance at them, they think that flying fish must inevitably bore out his eyes at night. If his wife, mother, or daughter brings any gift for him or wishes to talk with him, she must stand down towards the shore with her back turned to the men's clubhouse. Then the fisherman may go out and speak to her, or with his back turned to her he may receive what she has brought him; after which he must return at once to his rigorous confinement. Indeed the fishermen may not even join in dance and song with the other men of the clubhouse in the evening; they must keep to themselves and be silent. In Mirzapur, when the seed of the silkworm is brought into the house, the Kol or Bhuiyar puts it in a place which has been carefully plastered with holy cow-dung to bring good luck. From that time the owner must be careful to avoid ceremonial impurity. He must give up cohabitation with his wife; he may not sleep on a bed, nor shave himself, nor cut his nails, nor anoint himself with oil, nor eat food cooked with butter, nor tell lies, nor do anything else that he deems wrong. He vows to Singarmati Devi that, if the worms are duly born, he will make her an offering. When the cocoons open and the worms appear, he assembles the women of the house and they sing the same song as at the birth of a baby, and red lead is smeared on the parting of the hair of all the married women of the neighbourhood. When the worms pair, rejoicings are made as at a marriage. Thus the silkworms are treated as far as possible like human beings. Hence the custom which prohibits the commerce of the sexes while the worms are hatching may be only an extension, by analogy, of the rule which is observed by many races, that the husband may not cohabit with his wife during pregnancy and lactation.

In the island of Nias the hunters sometimes dig pits, cover them lightly over with twigs, grass, and leaves, and then drive the game into them. While they are engaged in digging the pits, they have to observe a number of taboos. They may not spit, or the game would turn back in disgust from the pits. They may not laugh, or the sides of the pit would fall in. They may eat no salt, prepare no fodder for swine, and in the pit they may not scratch themselves, for if they did, the earth would be loosened and would collapse. And the night after digging the pit they may have no intercourse with a woman, or all their labour would be in vain.

This practice of observing strict chastity as a condition of success in hunting and fishing is very common among rude races; and the instances of it which have been cited render it probable that the rule is always based on a superstition rather than on a consideration of the temporary weakness which a breach of the custom may entail on the hunter or fisherman. In general it appears to be supposed that the evil effect of incontinence is not so much that it weakens him, as that, for some reason or other, it offends the animals, who in consequence will not suffer themselves to be caught. A Carrier Indian of British Columbia, used to separate from his wife for a full month before he set traps for bears, and during this time he might not drink from the same vessel as his wife, but had to use a special cup made of birch bark. The neglect of these precautions would cause the game to escape after it had been snared. But when he was about to snare martens, the period of continence was cut down to ten days.

An examination of all the many cases in which the savage bridles his passions and remains chaste from motives of superstition, would be instructive, but I cannot attempt it now.

I will only add a few miscellaneous examples of the custom before passing to the ceremonies of purification which are observed by the hunter and fisherman after the chase and the fishing are over. The workers in the salt-pans near Siphoum, in Laos, must abstain from all sexual relations at the place where they are at work; and they may not cover their heads nor shelter themselves under an umbrella from the burning rays of the sun. Among the Kachins of Burma, the ferment used in making beer is prepared by two women, chosen by lot, who during the three days that the process lasts may eat nothing acid and may have no conjugal relations with their husbands; otherwise it is supposed that the beer would be sour. Among the Masai honey-wine is brewed by a man and a woman who live in a hut set apart for them till the wine is ready for drinking. But they are strictly forbidden to have sexual intercourse with each other during this time; it is deemed essential that they should be chaste for two days before they begin to brew and for the whole of the six days that the brewing lasts. The Masai believe that were the couple to commit a breach of chastity, not only would the wine be undrinkable but the bees which made the honey would fly away. Similarly they require that a man who is making poison should sleep alone and observe other taboos which render him almost an outcast. The Wandorobbo, a tribe of the same region as the Masai, believe that the mere presence of a woman in the neighbourhood of a man who is brewing poison would deprive the poison of its venom, and that the same thing would happen if the wife of the poison-maker were to commit adultery while her husband was brewing the poison. In this last case it is obvious that a rationalistic explanation of the taboo is impossible. How could the loss of virtue in the poison be a physical consequence of the loss of virtue in the poison-maker's wife? Clearly the effect which the wife's adultery is supposed to have on the poison is a case of sympathetic magic; her misconduct sympathetically affects her husband at his work at a distance. We may, accordingly, infer with some confidence that the rule of continence imposed on the poison-maker himself is also a simple case of sympathetic magic, and not, as a civilised reader might be disposed to conjecture, a wise precaution designed to prevent him from accidentally poisoning his wife.

Among the Ba-Pedi and Ba-thonga tribes of South Africa, when the site of a new village has been chosen and the houses are building, all the married people are forbidden to have conjugal relations with each other. If it were discovered that any couple had broken this rule, the work of building would immediately be stopped, and another site chosen for the village. For they think that a breach of chastity would spoil the village which was growing up, that the chief would grow lean and perhaps die, and that the guilty woman would never bear another child. Among the Chams of Cochin-China, when a dam is made or repaired on a river for the sake of irrigation, the chief who offers the traditional sacrifices and implores the protection of the deities on the work, has to stay all the time in a wretched hovel of straw, taking no part in the labour, and observing the strictest continence; for the people believe that a breach of his chastity would entail a breach of the dam. Here, it is plain, there can be no idea of maintaining the mere bodily vigour of the chief for the accomplishment of a task in which he does not even bear a hand.

If the taboos or abstinences observed by hunters and fishermen before and during the chase are dictated, as we have seen reason to believe, by superstitious motives, and chiefly by a dread of offending or frightening the spirits of the creatures whom it is proposed to kill, we may expect that the restraints imposed after the slaughter has been perpetrated will be at least as stringent, the slayer and his friends having now the added fear of the angry ghosts of his victims before their eyes. Whereas on the hypothesis that the abstinences in question, including those from food, drink, and sleep, are merely salutary precautions for maintaining the men in health and strength to do their work, it is obvious that the observance of these abstinences or taboos after the work is done, that is, when the game is killed and the fish caught, must be wholly superfluous, absurd, and inexplicable. But as I shall now show, these taboos often continue to be enforced or even increased in stringency after the death of the animals, in other words, after the hunter or fisher has accomplished his object by making his bag or landing his fish. The rationalistic theory of them therefore breaks down entirely; the hypothesis of super-stition is clearly the only one open to us.

Among the Inuit or Esquimaux of Bering Strait 'the dead bodies of various animals must be treated very carefully by the hunter who obtains them, so that their shades may not be offended and bring bad luck or even death upon him or his people.' Hence the Unalit hunter who has had a hand in the killing of a white whale, or even has helped to take one from the net, is not allowed to do any work for the next four days, that being the time during which the shade or ghost of the whale is supposed to stay with its body. At the same time no one in the village may use any sharp or pointed instrument for fear of wounding the whale's shade, which is believed to be hovering invisible in the neighbourhood; and no loud noise may be made lest it should frighten or offend the ghost. Whoever cuts a whale's body with an iron axe will die. Indeed the use of all iron instruments is forbidden in the village during these four days.

These same Esquimaux celebrate a great annual festival in December, when the bladders of all the seals, whales, walrus, and white bears that have been killed in the year are taken into the assembly-house of the village. They remain there for several days, and so long as they do so the hunters avoid all intercourse with women, saying that if they failed in that respect the shades of the dead animals would be offended. Similarly among the Aleuts of Alaska the hunter who had struck a whale with a charmed spear would not throw again, but returned at once to his home and separated himself from his people in a hut specially constructed for the purpose, where he stayed for three days without food or drink and without touching or looking upon a woman. During this time of seclusion he snorted occasionally in imitation of the wounded and dying whale, in order to prevent the whale which he had struck from leaving the coast. On the fourth day he emerged from his seclusion and bathed in the sea, shrieking in a hoarse voice and beating the water with his hands. Then, taking with him a companion, he repaired to that part of the shore where he expected to find the whale stranded. If the beast was dead, he at once cut out the place where the death-wound had been inflicted. If the whale was not dead, he again returned to his home and continued washing himself until the whale died. Here the hunter's imitation of the wounded whale is probably intended by means of homoeopathic magic to make the beast die in earnest. Once more the soul of the grim polar bear is offended if the taboos which concern him are not observed. His soul tarries for three days near the spot where it left his body, and during these days the Esquimaux are particularly careful to conform rigidly to the laws of taboo, because they believe that punishment overtakes the transgressor who sins against the soul of a bear far more speedily than him who sins against the souls of the sea-beasts.

When the Kayans have shot one of the dreaded Bornean panthers, they are very anxious about the safety of their souls, for they think that the soul of a panther is almost more powerful than their own. Hence they step eight times over the carcase of the dead beast reciting the spell, 'Panther, thy soul under my soul.' On returning home they smear themselves, their dogs, and their weapons with the blood of fowls in order to calm their souls and hinder them from fleeing away; for, being themselves fond of the flesh of fowls, they ascribe the same taste to their souls. For eight days afterwards they must bathe by day and by night before going out again to the chase. Among the Hottentots, when a man has killed a lion, leopard, elephant or rhinoceros, he is esteemed a great hero, but has to remain at home quite idle for three days, during which his wife may not come near him; she is also enjoined to restrict herself to a poor diet and to eat no more than is barely necessary to keep her in health. Similarly the Lapps deem it the height of glory to kill a bear, which they consider the king of beasts. Nevertheless, all the men who take part in the slaughter are regarded as unclean, and must live by themselves for three days in a hut or tent made specially for them, where they cut up and cook the bear's carcase. The reindeer which brought in the carcase on a sledge must not be driven by a woman for a whole year; indeed, according to one account, it may not be used by anybody for that period. Before the men go into the tent where they are to be secluded, they strip themselves of the garments they had worn in killing the bear, and their wives spit the red juice of alder bark in their faces. They enter the tent not by the ordinary door but by an opening at the back. When the bear's flesh has been cooked, a portion of it is sent by the hands of two men to the women, who may not approach the men's tent while the cooking is going on.

The men who convey the flesh to the women pretend to be strangers bringing presents from a foreign land; the women keep up the pretence and promise to tie red threads round the legs of the strangers. The bear's flesh may not be passed in to the women through the door of their tent, but must be thrust in at a special opening made by lifting up the hem of the tent-cover. When the three days' seclusion is over and the men are at liberty to return to their wives, they run, one after the other, round the fire, holding the chain by which pots are suspended over it. This is regarded as a form of purification; they may now leave the tent by the ordinary door and rejoin the women. But the leader of the party must still abstain from cohabitation with his wife for two days more.

Again, the Caffres are said to dread greatly the boa-constrictor or an enormous serpent resembling it; 'and being influenced by certain superstitious notions they even fear to kill it. The man who happened to put it to death, whether in self-defence or otherwise, was formerly required to lie in a running stream of water during the day for several weeks together; and no beast whatever was allowed to be slaughtered at the hamlet to which he belonged, until this duty had been fully performed. The body of the snake was then taken and carefully buried in a trench, dug close to the cattle-fold, where its remains, like those of a chief, were henceforward kept perfectly undisturbed. The period of penance, as in the case of mourning for the dead, is now happily reduced to a few days.' In Madras it is considered a great sin to kill a cobra. When this has happened, the people generally burn the body of the serpent, just as they burn the bodies of human beings. The murderer deems himself polluted for three days. On the second day milk is poured on the remains of the cobra. On the third day the guilty wretch is free from pollution.

In these last cases the animal whose slaughter has to be atoned for is sacred, that is, it is one whose life is commonly spared from motives of superstition. Yet the treatment of the sacrilegious slayer seems to resemble so closely the treatment of hunters and fishermen who have killed animals for food in the ordinary course of business, that the ideas on which both sets of customs are based may be assumed to be substantially the same. Those ideas, if I am right, are the respect which the savage feels for the souls of beasts, especially valuable or formidable beasts, and the dread which he entertains of their vengeful ghosts. Some confirmation of this view may be drawn from the ceremonies observed by fishermen of Annam when the carcase of a whale is washed ashore. These fisherfolk, we are told, worship the whale on account of the benefits they derive from it. There is hardly a village on the sea-shore which has not its small pagoda, containing the bones, more or less authentic, of a whale. When a dead whale is washed ashore, the people accord it a solemn burial. The man who first caught sight of it acts as chief mourner, performing the rites which as chief mourner and heir he would perform for a human kinsman. He puts on all the garb of woe, the straw hat, the white robe with long sleeves turned inside out, and the other paraphernalia of full mourning. As next of kin to the deceased he presides over the funeral rites. Perfumes are burned, sticks of incense kindled, leaves of gold and silver scattered, crackers let off. When the flesh has been cut off and the oil extracted, the remains of the carcase are buried in the sand. Afterwards a shed is set up and offerings are made in it. Usually some time after the burial the spirit of the dead whale takes possession of some person in the village and declares by his mouth whether he is a male or female.

CHAPTER XXI

TABOOED THINGS

§ 1. *The Meaning of Taboo.* — Thus in primitive society the rules of ceremonial purity observed by divine kings, chiefs, and priests agree in many respects with the rules observed by homicides, mourners, women in childbed, girls at puberty, hunters and fishermen, and so on. To us these various classes of persons appear to differ totally in character and condition; some of them we should call holy, others we might pronounce unclean and polluted. But the savage makes no such moral distinction between them; the conceptions of holiness and pollution are not yet differentiated in his mind. To him the common feature of all these persons is that they are dangerous and in danger, and the danger in which they stand and to which they expose others is what we should call spiritual or ghostly, and therefore imaginary. The danger, however, is not less real because it is imaginary; imagination acts upon a man as really as does gravitation, and may kill him as certainly as a dose of prussic acid. To seclude these persons from the rest of the world so that the dreaded spiritual danger shall neither reach them nor spread from them, is the object of the taboos which they have to observe. These taboos act, so to say, as electrical insulators to preserve the spiritual force with which these persons are charged from suffering or inflicting harm by contact with the outer world.

To the illustrations of these general principles which have been already given I shall now add some more, drawing my examples, first, from the class of tabooed things, and, second, from the class of tabooed words; for in the opinion of the savage both things and words may, like persons, be charged or electrified, either temporarily or permanently, with the mysterious virtue of taboo, and may therefore require to be banished for a longer or shorter time from the familiar usage of common life. And the examples will be chosen with special reference to those sacred chiefs, kings and priests, who, more than anybody else, live fenced about by taboo as by a wall. Tabooed things will be illustrated in the present chapter, and tabooed words in the next.

§ 2. *Iron Tabooed.* — In the first place we may observe that the awful sanctity of kings naturally leads to a prohibition to touch their sacred persons. Thus it was unlawful to lay hands on the person of a Spartan king: no one might touch the body of the king or queen of Tahiti: it is forbidden to touch the person of the king of Siam under pain of death; and no one may touch the king of Cambodia, for any purpose whatever, without his express command. In July 1874 the king was thrown from his carriage and lay insensible on the ground, but not one of his suite dared to touch him; a European coming to the spot carried the injured monarch to his palace. Formerly no one might touch the king of Corea; and if he deigned to touch a subject, the spot touched became sacred, and the person thus honoured had to wear a visible mark (generally a cord of red silk) for the rest of his life. Above all, no iron might touch the king's body. In 1800 King Tieng-tsong-tai-oang died of a tumour in the back, no one dreaming of employing the lancet, which would probably have saved his life. It is said that one king suffered terribly from an abscess in the lip, till his physician called in a jester, whose pranks made the king laugh heartily, and so the abscess burst. Roman and Sabine priests might not be shaved with iron but only with bronze razors or shears; and whenever an iron graving-tool was brought into the sacred grove of the Arval Brothers at Rome for the purpose of cutting an inscription in stone, an expiatory sacrifice of a lamb and a pig must be offered, which was repeated when the graving-tool was removed from the grove. As a general rule iron might not be brought into Greek sanctuaries. In Crete sacrifices were offered to Menedemus without the use of iron, because the legend ran that Menedemus had been killed by an iron weapon in the Trojan war. The Archon of Plataea might not touch iron; but once a year, at the annual commemoration of the men who fell at the battle of Plataea, he was allowed to carry a sword wherewith to sacrifice a bull. To this day a Hottentot priest never uses an iron knife, but always a sharp splint of quartz, in sacrificing an animal or circumcising a lad. Among the Ovambo of South-west Africa custom requires that lads should be circumcised with a sharp flint; if none is to hand, the operation may be performed with iron, but the iron must afterwards be buried. Amongst the Moquis of Arizona stone knives, hatchets, and so on have passed out of common use, but are retained in religious ceremonies. After the Pawnees had ceased to use stone arrow-heads for ordinary purposes, they still employed them to slay the sacrifices, whether human captives or buffalo and deer. Amongst the Jews no iron tool was used in building the Temple at Jerusalem or in making an altar. The old wooden bridge (*Pons Sublicius*) at Rome, which was considered sacred, was made and had to be kept in repair without the use of iron or bronze. It was expressly provided by law that the temple of Jupiter Liber at Furfo might be repaired with iron tools. The council chamber at Cyzicus was constructed of wood without any iron nails, the beams being so arranged that they could be taken out and replaced.

This superstitious objection to iron perhaps dates from that early time in the history of society when iron was still a novelty, and as such was viewed by many with suspicion and dislike. For everything new is apt to excite the awe and dread of the savage. 'It is a curious superstition,' says a pioneer in Borneo, 'this of the Dusuns, to attribute anything — whether good or bad, lucky or unlucky — that happens to them to something novel which has arrived in their country. For instance, my living in Kindram has caused the intensely hot weather we have experienced of late.' The unusually heavy rains which happened to follow the English survey of the Nicobar Islands in the winter of 1886–1887 were imputed by the alarmed natives to the wrath of the spirits at the theodolites, dumpy-levellers, and other strange instruments which had been set up in so many of their favourite haunts; and some of them proposed to soothe the anger of the spirits by sacrificing a pig. In the seventeenth century a succession of bad seasons excited a revolt among the Esthonian peasantry, who traced the origin of the evil to a water-mill, which put a stream to some inconvenience by checking its flow. The first introduction of iron ploughshares into Poland having been followed by a succession of bad harvests, the farmers attributed the badness of the crops to the iron ploughshares, and discarded them for the old wooden ones. To this day the primitive Baduwis of Java, who live chiefly by husbandry, will use no iron tools in tilling their fields.

The general dislike of innovation, which always makes itself strongly felt in the sphere of religion, is sufficient by itself to account for the superstitious aversion to iron entertained by kings and priests and attributed by them to the gods; possibly this aversion may have been intensified in places by some such accidental cause as the series of bad seasons which cast discredit on iron ploughshares in Poland. But the disfavour in which iron is held by the gods and their ministers has another side. Their antipathy to the metal furnishes men with a weapon which may be turned against the spirits when occasion serves. As their dislike of iron is supposed to be so great that they will not approach persons and things protected by the obnoxious metal, iron may obviously be employed as a charm for banning ghosts and other dangerous spirits. And often it is so used. Thus in the Highlands of Scotland the great safeguard against the elfin race is iron, or, better yet, steel. The metal in any form, whether as a sword, a knife, a gun-barrel, or what not, is all-powerful for this purpose. Whenever you enter a fairy dwelling you should always remember to stick a piece of steel, such as a knife, a needle, or a fish-hook, in the door; for then the elves will not be able to shut the door till you come out again. So too when you have shot a deer and are bringing it home at night, be sure to thrust a knife into the carcase, for that keeps the fairies from laying their weight on it. A knife or a nail in your pocket is quite enough to prevent the fairies from lifting you up at night. Nails in the front of a bed ward off elves from women 'in the straw' and from their babes; but to make quite sure it is better to put the smoothing-iron under the bed, and the reaping-hook in the window. If a bull has fallen over a rock and been killed, a nail stuck into it will preserve the flesh from the fairies. Music discoursed on a Jew's harp keeps the elfin women away from the hunter, because the tongue of the instrument is of steel. In Morocco iron is considered a great protection against demons; hence it is usual to place a knife or dagger under a sick man's pillow. The Singhalese believe that they are constantly surrounded by evil spirits, who lie in wait to do them harm. A peasant would not dare to carry good food, such as cakes or roast meat, from one place to another without putting an iron nail on it to prevent a demon from taking possession of the viands and so making the eater ill. No sick person, whether man or woman, would venture out of the house without a bunch of keys or a knife in his hand, for without such a talisman he would fear that some devil might take advantage of his weak state to slip into his body. And if a man has a large sore on his body he tries to keep a morsel of iron on it as a protection against demons. On the Slave Coast when a mother sees her child gradually wasting away, she concludes that a demon has entered into the child, and takes her measures accordingly. To lure the demon out of the body of her offspring, she offers a sacrifice of food; and while the devil is bolting it, she attaches iron rings and small bells to her child's ankles and hangs iron chains round his neck. The jingling of the iron and the tinkling of the bells are supposed to prevent the demon, when he has concluded his repast, from entering again into the body of the little sufferer. Hence many children may be seen in this part of Africa weighed down with iron ornaments.

§ 3. *Sharp Weapons tabooed.* — There is a priestly king to the north of Zengwih in Burma, revered by the Sotih as the highest spiritual and temporal authority, into whose house no weapon or cutting instrument may be brought. This rule may perhaps be explained by a custom observed by various peoples after a death; they refrain from the use of sharp instruments so long as the ghost of the deceased is supposed to be near, lest they should wound it. Thus among the Esquimaux of Bering Strait 'during the day on which a person dies in the village no one is permitted to work, and the relatives must perform no labour during the three following days. It is especially forbidden during this period to cut with any edged instrument, such as a knife or an axe; and the use of pointed instruments, like needles or bodkins, is also forbidden. This is said to be done to avoid cutting or injuring the shade, which may be present at any time during this period, and, if accidentally injured by any of these things, it would become very angry and bring sickness or death to the people. The relatives must also be very careful at this time not to make any loud or harsh noises that may startle or anger the shade.' We have seen that in like manner after killing a white whale these Esquimaux abstain from the use of cutting or pointed instruments for four days, lest they should unwittingly cut or stab the whale's ghost. The same taboo is sometimes observed by them when there is a sick person in the village, probably from a fear of injuring his shade which may be hovering outside of his body. After a death the Roumanians of Transylvania are careful not to leave a knife lying with the sharp edge uppermost so long as the corpse remains in the house, 'or else the soul will be forced to ride on the blade.' For seven days after a death, the corpse being still in the house, the Chinese abstain from the use of knives and needles, and even of chopsticks, eating their food with their fingers. On the third, sixth, ninth, and fortieth days after the funeral the old Prussians and Lithuanians used to prepare a meal, to which, standing at the door, they invited the soul of the deceased. At these meals they sat silent round the table and used no knives, and the women who served up the food were also without knives. If any morsels fell from the table they were left lying there for the lonely souls that had no living relations or friends to feed them. When the meal was over the priest took a broom and swept the souls out of the house, saying, 'Dear souls, ye have eaten and drunk. Go forth, go forth.' We can now understand why no cutting instrument may be taken into the house of the Burmese pontiff. Like so many priestly kings, he is probably regarded as divine, and it is therefore right that his sacred spirit should not be exposed to the risk of being cut or wounded whenever it quits his body to hover invisible in the air or to fly on some distant mission.

§ 4. *Blood tabooed.* — We have seen that the Flamen Dialis was forbidden to touch or even name raw flesh. At certain times a Brahman teacher is enjoined not to look on raw flesh, blood, or persons whose hands have been cut off. In Uganda the father of twins is in a state of taboo for some time after the birth; among other rules he is forbidden to kill anything or to see blood. In the Pelew Islands when a raid has been made on a village and a head carried off, the relations of the slain man are tabooed and have to submit to certain observances in order to escape the wrath of his ghost. They are shut up in the house, touch no raw flesh, and chew betel over which an incantation has been uttered by the exorcist. After this the ghost of the slaughtered man goes away to the enemy's country in pursuit of his murderer. The taboo is probably based on the common belief that the soul or spirit of the animal is in the blood. As tabooed persons are believed to be in a perilous state — for example, the relations of the slain man are liable to attacks of his indignant ghost — it is especially necessary to isolate them from contact with spirits; hence the prohibition to touch raw meat. But as usual the taboo is only the special enforcement of a general precept; in other words, its observance is particularly enjoined in circumstances which seem urgently to call for its application, but apart from such circumstances the prohibition is also observed, though less strictly, as a common rule of life. Thus some of the Esthonians will not taste blood because they believe that it contains the animal's soul, which would enter the body of the person who tasted the blood. Some Indian tribes of North America, 'through a strong principle of religion, abstain in the strictest manner from eating the blood of any animal, as it contains the life and spirit of the beast.' Jewish hunters poured out the blood of the game they had killed and covered it up with dust. They would not taste the blood, believing that the soul or life of the animal was in the blood, or actually was the blood.

It is a common rule that royal blood may not be shed upon

the ground. Hence when a king or one of his family is to be put to death a mode of execution is devised by which the royal blood shall not be spilt upon the earth. About the year 1688 the generalissimo of the army rebelled against the king of Siam and put him to death 'after the manner of royal criminals, or as princes of the blood are treated when convicted of capital crimes, which is by putting them into a large iron caldron, and pounding them to pieces with wooden pestles, because none of their royal blood must be spilt on the ground, it being, by their religion, thought great impiety to contaminate the divine blood by mixing it with earth.' When Kublai Khan defeated and took his uncle Nayan, who had rebelled against him, he caused Nayan to be put to death by being wrapt in a carpet and tossed to and fro till he died, 'because he would not have the blood of his Line Imperial spilt upon the ground or exposed in the eye of Heaven and before the Sun.' 'Friar Ricold mentions the Tartar maxim: "One Khan will put another to death to get possession of the throne, but he takes great care that the blood be not spilt. For they say that it is highly improper that the blood of the Great Khan should be spilt upon the ground; so they cause the victim to be smothered somehow or other." The like feeling prevails at the court of Burma, where a peculiar mode of execution without bloodshed is reserved for princes of the blood.'

The reluctance to spill royal blood seems to be only a particular case of a general unwillingness to shed blood or at least to allow it to fall on the ground. Marco Polo tells us that in his day persons caught in the streets of Cambaluc (Peking) at unseasonable hours were arrested, and if found guilty of a misdemeanour were beaten with a stick. 'Under this punishment people sometimes die, but they adopt it in order to eschew bloodshed, for their *Bacsis* say that it is an evil thing to shed man's blood.' In West Sussex people believe that the ground on which human blood has been shed is accursed and will remain barren for ever. Among some primitive peoples, when the blood of a tribesman has to be spilt it is not suffered to fall upon the ground, but is received upon the bodies of his fellow-tribesmen. Thus in some Australian tribes boys who are being circumcised are laid on a platform, formed by the living bodies of the tribesmen; and when a boy's tooth is knocked out as an initiatory ceremony, he is seated on the shoulders of a man, on whose breast the blood flows and may not be wiped away. 'Also the Gauls used to drink their enemies' blood and paint themselves therewith. So also they write that the old Irish were wont; and so have I seen some of the Irish do, but not their enemies' but friends' blood, as, namely, at the execution of a notable traitor at Limerick, called Murrogh O'Brien, I saw an old woman, which was his foster-mother, take up his head whilst he was quartered and suck up all the blood that ran thereout, saying that the earth was not worthy to drink it, and therewith also steeped her face and breast and tore her hair, crying out and shrieking most terribly.' Among the Latuka of Central Africa the earth on which a drop of blood has fallen at child-birth is carefully scraped up with an iron shovel, put into a pot along with the water used in washing the mother, and buried tolerably deep outside the house on the left-hand side. In West Africa, if a drop of your blood has fallen on the ground, you must carefully cover it up, rub and stamp it into the soil; if it has fallen on the side of a canoe or a tree, the place is cut out and the chip destroyed. One motive of these African customs may be a wish to prevent the blood from falling into the hands of magicians, who might make an evil use of it. That is admittedly the reason why people in West Africa stamp out any blood of theirs which has dropped on the ground or cut out any wood that has been soaked with it. From a like dread of sorcery natives of New Guinea are careful to burn any sticks, leaves, or rags which are stained with their blood; and if the blood has dripped on the ground they turn up the soil and if possible light a fire on the spot. The same fear explains the curious duties discharged by a class of men called *ramanga* or 'blue blood' among the Betsileo of Madagascar. It is their business to eat all the nail-parings and to lick up all the spilt blood of the nobles. When the nobles pare their nails, the parings are collected to the last scrap and swallowed by these *ramanga*. If the parings are too large, they are minced small and so gulped down. Again, should a nobleman wound himself, say in cutting his nails or treading on something, the *ramanga* lick up the blood as fast as possible. Nobles of high rank hardly go anywhere without these humble attendants; but if it should happen that there are none of them present, the cut nails and the spilt blood are carefully collected to be afterwards swallowed by the *ramanga*. There is scarcely a nobleman of any pretensions who does not strictly observe this custom, the intention of which probably is to prevent these parts of his person from falling into the hands of sorcerers, who on the principles of contagious magic could work him harm thereby.

The general explanation of the reluctance to shed blood on the ground is probably to be found in the belief that the soul is in the blood, and that therefore any ground on which it may fall necessarily becomes taboo or sacred. In New Zealand anything upon which even a drop of a high chief's blood chances to fall becomes taboo or sacred to him. For instance, a party of natives having come to visit a chief in a fine new canoe, the chief got into it, but in doing so a splinter entered his foot, and the blood trickled on the canoe, which at once became sacred to him. The owner jumped out, dragged the canoe ashore opposite the chief's house, and left it there. Again, a chief in entering a missionary's house knocked his head against a beam, and the blood flowed. The natives said that in former times the house would have belonged to the chief. As usually happens with taboos of universal application, the prohibition to spill the blood of a tribesman on the ground applies with peculiar stringency to chiefs and kings, and is observed in their case long after it has ceased to be observed in the case of others.

§ 5. *The Head tabooed.* — Many peoples regard the head as peculiarly sacred; the special sanctity attributed to it is sometimes explained by a belief that it contains a spirit which is very sensitive to injury or disrespect. Thus the Yorubas hold that every man has three spiritual inmates, of whom the first, called Olori, dwells in the head and is the man's protector, guardian, and guide. Offerings are made to this spirit, chiefly of fowls, and some of the blood mixed with palm-oil is rubbed on the forehead. The Karens suppose that a being called the *tso* resides in the upper part of the head, and while it retains its seat no harm can befall the person from the efforts of the seven *Kelahs*, or personified passions. 'But if the *tso* becomes heedless or weak certain evil to the person is the result. Hence the head is carefully attended to, and all possible pains are taken to provide such dress and attire as will be pleasing to the *tso*.' The Siamese think that

a spirit called *khuan* or *kwun* dwells in the human head, of which
it is the guardian spirit. The spirit must be carefully protected
from injury of every kind; hence the act of shaving or cutting
the hair is accompanied with many ceremonies. The *kwun* is
very sensitive on points of honour, and would feel mortally
insulted if the head in which he resides were touched by the
hand of a stranger. The Cambodians esteem it a grave offence
to touch a man's head; some of them will not enter a place where
anything whatever is suspended over their heads; and the meanest
Cambodian would never consent to live under an inhabited room.
Hence the houses are built of one story only; and even the
Government respects the prejudice by never placing a prisoner in
the stocks under the floor of a house, though the houses are raised
high above the ground. The same superstition exists amongst the
Malays; for an early traveller reports that in Java people 'wear
nothing on their heads, and say that nothing must be on their
heads . . . and if any person were to put his hand upon their
head they would kill him; and they do not build houses with
storeys, in order that they may not walk over each other's heads.'

The same superstition as to the head is found in full force
throughout Polynesia. Thus of Gattanewa, a Marquesan chief,
it is said that 'to touch the top of his head, or anything which
had been on his head, was sacrilege. To pass over his head was
an indignity never to be forgotten. The son of a Marquesan
high priest has been seen to roll on the ground in an agony of
rage and despair, begging for death, because some one had
desecrated his head and deprived him of his divinity by sprinkling
a few drops of water on his hair. But it was not the Marquesan
chiefs only whose heads were sacred. The head of every Marquesan
was taboo, and might neither be touched nor stepped over by
another; even a father might not step over the head of his sleeping
child; women were forbidden to carry or touch anything that
had been in contact with, or had merely hung over, the head of
their husband or father. No one was allowed to be over the head
of the king of Tonga. In Tahiti any one who stood over the
king or queen, or passed his hand over their heads, might be put
to death. Until certain rites were performed over it, a Tahitian
infant was especially taboo; whatever touched the child's
head, while it was in this state, became sacred and was deposited

in a consecrated place railed in for the purpose at the child's house. If a branch of a tree touched the child's head, the tree was cut down; and if in its fall it injured another tree so as to penetrate the bark, that tree also was cut down as unclean and unfit for use. After the rites were performed these special taboos ceased; but the head of a Tahitian was always sacred, he never carried anything on it, and to touch it was an offence. So sacred was the head of a Maori chief that 'if he only touched it with his fingers, he was obliged immediately to apply them to his nose, and snuff up the sanctity which they had acquired by the touch, and thus restore it to the part from whence it was taken.' On account of the sacredness of his head a Maori chief 'could not blow the fire with his mouth, for the breath being sacred, communicated his sanctity to it, and a brand might be taken by a slave, or a man of another tribe, or the fire might be used for other purposes, such as cooking, and so cause his death.'

§ 6. *Hair tabooed.* — When the head was considered so sacred that it might not even be touched without grave offence, it is obvious that the cutting of the hair must have been a delicate and difficult operation. The difficulties and dangers which, on the primitive view, beset the operation are of two kinds. There is first the danger of disturbing the spirit of the head, which may be injured in the process and may revenge itself upon the person who molests him. Secondly, there is the difficulty of disposing of the shorn locks. For the savage believes that the sympathetic connexion which exists between himself and every part of his body continues to exist even after the physical connexion has been broken, and that therefore he will suffer from any harm that may befall the severed parts of his body, such as the clippings of his hair or the parings of his nails. Accordingly he takes care that these severed portions of himself shall not be left in places where they might either be exposed to accidental injury or fall into the hands of malicious persons who might work magic on them to his detriment or death. Such dangers are common to all, but sacred persons have more to fear from them than ordinary people, so the precautions taken by them are proportionately stringent. The simplest way of evading the peril is not to cut the hair at all; and this is the expedient adopted where the risk is thought to be more than usually great. The Frankish kings were never allowed to crop their hair; from their childhood upwards they had to keep it unshorn. To poll the long locks that floated on their shoulders would have been to renounce their right to the throne. When the wicked brothers Clotaire and Childebert coveted the kingdom of their dead brother Clodomir, they inveigled into their power their little nephews, the two sons of Clodomir; and having done so, they sent a messenger bearing scissors and a naked sword to the children's grandmother, Queen Clotilde, at Paris. The envoy showed the scissors and the sword to Clotilde, and bade her choose whether the children should be shorn and live or remain unshorn and die. The proud queen replied that if her grandchildren were not to come to the throne she would rather see them dead than shorn. And murdered they were by their ruthless uncle Clotaire with his own hand. The king of Ponape, one of the Caroline Islands, must wear his hair long, and so must his grandees. Among the Hos, a negro tribe of West Africa, 'there are priests on whose head no razor may come during the whole of their lives. The god who dwells in the man forbids the cutting of his hair on pain of death. If the hair is at last too long, the owner must pray to his god to allow him at least to clip the tips of it. The hair is in fact conceived as the seat and lodging-place of his god, so that were it shorn the god would lose his abode in the priest.' The members of a Masai clan, who are believed to possess the art of making rain, may not pluck out their beards, because the loss of their beards would, it is supposed, entail the loss of their rain-making powers. The head chief and the sorcerers of the Masai observe the same rule for a like reason: they think that were they to pull out their beards, their super-natural gifts would desert them.

Again, men who have taken a vow of vengeance sometimes keep their hair unshorn till they have fufilled their vow. Thus of the Marquesans we are told that 'occasionally they have their head entirely shaved, except one lock on the crown, which is worn loose or put up in a knot. But the latter mode of wearing the hair is only adopted by them when they have a solemn vow, as to revenge the death of some near relation, etc. In such case the lock is never cut off until they have fulfilled their promise.' A similar custom was sometimes observed by the ancient Germans; among the Chatti the young warriors never clipped

their hair or their beard till they had slain an enemy. Among
the Toradjas, when a child's hair is cut to rid it of vermin, some
locks are allowed to remain on the crown of the head as a refuge
for one of the child's souls. Otherwise the soul would have no
place in which to settle, and the child would sicken. The Karo-
Bataks are much afraid of frightening away the soul of a child;
hence when they cut its hair, they always leave a patch unshorn,
to which the soul can retreat before the shears. Usually this lock
remains unshorn all through life, or at least up to manhood.

§ 7. *Ceremonies at Hair-cutting.* — But when it becomes
necessary to crop the hair, measures are taken to lessen the
dangers which are supposed to attend the operation. The chief
of Namosi in Fiji always ate a man by way of precaution when
he had had his hair cut. 'There was a certain clan that had to
provide the victim, and they used to sit in solemn council among
themselves to choose him. It was a sacrificial feast to avert evil
from the chief.' Amongst the Maoris many spells were uttered
at hair-cutting; one, for example, was spoken to consecrate the
obsidian knife with which the hair was cut; another was pronounced to avert the thunder and lightning which hair-cutting was
believed to cause. 'He who had had his hair cut is in immediate
charge of the Atua (spirit); he is removed from the contact and
society of his family and his tribe; he dare not touch his food
himself; it is put into his mouth by another person; nor can he
for some days resume his accustomed occupations or associate
with his fellow-men.' The person who cuts the hair is also
tabooed; his hands having been in contact with a sacred head, he
may not touch food with them or engage in any other employment;
he is fed by another person with food cooked over a sacred fire.
He cannot be released from the taboo before the following day,
when he rubs his hands with potato or fern root which has been
cooked on a sacred fire; and this food having been taken to the
head of the family in the female line and eaten by her, his hands
are freed from the taboo. In some parts of New Zealand the most
sacred day of the year was that appointed for hair-cutting; the
people assembled in large numbers on that day from all the
neighbourhood.

§ 8. *Disposal of Cut Hair and Nails.* — But even when the hair
and nails have been safely cut, there remains the difficulty of

disposing of them, for their owner believes himself liable to suffer from any harm that may befall them. The notion that a man may be bewitched by means of the clippings of his hair, the parings of his nails, or any other severed portion of his person is almost world-wide and attested by evidence too ample, too familiar, and too tedious in its uniformity to be here analysed at length. The general idea on which the superstition rests is that of the sympathetic connexion supposed to persist between a person and everything that has once been part of his body or in any way closely related to him. A very few examples must suffice. They belong to that branch of sympathetic magic which may be called contagious. Dread of sorcery, we are told, formed one of the most salient characteristics of the Marquesan islanders in the old days. The sorcerer took some of the hair, spittle, or other bodily refuse of the man he wished to injure, wrapped it up in a leaf, and placed the packet in a bag woven of threads or fibres, which were knotted in an intricate way. The whole was then buried with certain rites, and thereupon the victim wasted away of a languishing sickness which lasted twenty days. His life, however, might be saved by discovering and digging up the buried hair, spittle, or what not; for as soon as this was done the power of the charm ceased. A Maori sorcerer intent on bewitching somebody sought to get a tress of his victim's hair, the parings of his nails, some of his spittle, or a shred of his garment. Having obtained the object, whatever it was, he chanted certain spells and curses over it in a falsetto voice and buried it in the ground. As the thing decayed, the person to whom it had belonged was supposed to waste away. When an Australian blackfellow wishes to get rid of his wife, he cuts off a lock of her hair in her sleep, ties it to his spear-thrower, and goes with it to a neighbouring tribe, where he gives it to a friend. His friend sticks the spear-thrower up every night before the camp fire, and when it falls down it is a sign that the wife is dead. The way in which the charm operates was explained to Dr. Howitt by a Wirajuri man. 'You see,' he said, 'when a blackfellow doctor gets hold of something belonging to a man and roasts it with things, and sings over it, the fire catches hold of the smell of the man, and that settles the poor fellow.'

The Huzuls of the Carpathians imagine that if mice get a person's shorn hair and make a nest of it, the person will suffer from headache or even become idiotic. Similarly in Germany it is a common notion that if birds find a person's cut hair, and build their nests with it, the person will suffer from headache; sometimes it is thought that he will have an eruption on the head. The same superstition prevails, or used to prevail, in West Sussex.

Again it is thought that cut or combed-out hair may disturb the weather by producing rain and hail, thunder and lightning. We have seen that in New Zealand a spell was uttered at hair-cutting to avert thunder and lightning. In the Tyrol, witches are supposed to use cut or combed-out hair to make hailstones or thunderstorms with. Thlinkeet Indians have been known to attribute stormy weather to the rash act of a girl who had combed her hair outside of the house. The Romans seem to have held similar views, for it was a maxim with them that no one on shipboard should cut his hair or nails except in a storm, that is, when the mischief was already done. In the Highlands of Scotland it is said that no sister should comb her hair at night if she have a brother at sea. In West Africa, when the Mani of Chitombe or Jumba died, the people used to run in crowds to the corpse and tear out his hair, teeth, and nails, which they kept as a rain-charm, believing that otherwise no rain would fall. The Makoko of the Anzikos begged the missionaries to give him half their beards as a rain-charm.

If cut hair and nails remain in sympathetic connexion with the person from whose body they have been severed, it is clear that they can be used as hostages for his good behaviour by any one who may chance to possess them; for on the principles of contagious magic he has only to injure the hair or nails in order to hurt simultaneously their original owner. Hence when the Nandi have taken a prisoner they shave his head and keep the shorn hair as a surety that he will not attempt to escape; but when the captive is ransomed, they return his shorn hair with him to his own people.

To preserve the cut hair and nails from injury and from the dangerous uses to which they may be put by sorcerers, it is necessary to deposit them in some safe place. The shorn locks of a Maori chief were gathered with much care and placed in an adjoining cemetery. The Tahitians buried the cuttings of their hair at the temples. In the streets of Soku a modern traveller

L

observed cairns of large stones piled against walls with tufts of human hair inserted in the crevices. On asking the meaning of this, he was told that when any native of the place polled his hair he carefully gathered up the clippings and deposited them in one of these cairns, all of which were sacred to the fetish and therefore inviolable. These cairns of sacred stones, he further learned, were simply a precaution against witchcraft, for if a man were not thus careful in disposing of his hair, some of it might fall into the hands of his enemies, who would, by means of it, be able to cast spells over him and so compass his destruction. When the top-knot of a Siamese child has been cut with great ceremony, the short hairs are put into a little vessel made of plantain leaves and set adrift on the nearest river or canal. As they float away, all that was wrong or harmful in the child's disposition is believed to depart with them. The long hairs are kept till the child makes a pilgrimage to the holy Footprint of Buddha on the sacred hill at Prabat. They are then presented to the priests, who are supposed to make them into brushes with which they sweep the Footprint; but in fact so much hair is thus offered every year that the priests cannot use it all, so they quietly burn the superfluity as soon as the pilgrims' backs are turned. The cut hair and nails of the Flamen Dialis were buried under a lucky tree. The shorn tresses of the Vestal Virgins were hung on an ancient lotus-tree.

Often the clipped hair and nails are stowed away in any secret place, not necessarily in a temple or cemetery or at a tree, as in the cases already mentioned. Thus in Swabia you are recommended to deposit your clipped hair in some spot where neither sun nor moon can shine on it, for example in the earth or under a stone. In Danzig it is buried in a bag under the threshold. In Ugi, one of the Solomon Islands, men bury their hair lest it should fall into the hands of an enemy, who would make magic with it and so bring sickness or calamity on them. The same fear seems to be general in Melanesia, and has led to a regular practice of hiding cut hair and nails. The same practice prevails among many tribes of South Africa, from a fear lest wizards should get hold of the severed particles and work evil with them. The Caffres carry still further this dread of allowing any portion of themselves to fall into the hands of an enemy; for not only do they bury their cut hair and nails in a secret spot, but when one of them cleans the head of another he preserves the vermin which he catches, 'carefully delivering them to the person to whom they originally appertained, supposing, according to their theory, that as they derived their support from the blood of the man from whom they were taken, should they be killed by another, the blood of his neighbour would be in his possession, thus placing in his hands the power of some super-human influence.'

Sometimes the severed hair and nails are preserved, not to prevent them from falling into the hands of a magician, but that the owner may have them at the resurrection of the body, to which some races look forward. Thus the Incas of Peru 'took extreme care to preserve the nail-parings and the hairs that were shorn off or torn out with a comb; placing them in holes or niches in the walls; and if they fell out, any other Indian that saw them picked them up and put them in their places again. I very often asked different Indians, at various times, why they did this, in order to see what they would say, and they all replied in the same words saying, "Know that all persons who are born must return to life" (they have no word to express resuscitation), "and the souls must rise out of their tombs with all that belonged to their bodies. We, therefore, in order that we may not have to search for our hair and nails at a time when there will be much hurry and confusion, place them in one place, that they may be brought together more conveniently, and, whenever it is possible, we are also careful to spit in one place." ' Similarly the Turks never throw away the parings of their nails, but carefully stow them in cracks of the walls or of the boards, in the belief that they will be needed at the resurrection. The Armenians do not throw away their cut hair and nails and extracted teeth, but hide them in places that are esteemed holy, such as a crack in the church wall, a pillar of the house, or a hollow tree. They think that all these severed portions of themselves will be wanted at the resurrection, and that he who has not stowed them away in a safe place will have to hunt about for them on the great day. In the village of Drumconrath in Ireland there used to be some old women who, having ascertained from Scripture that the hairs of their heads were all numbered by the Almighty, expected to have to account for them at the day of judgment. In order to be able to do so they stuffed the severed hair away in the thatch of their cottages.

Some people burn their loose hair to save it from falling into the hands of sorcerers. This is done by the Patagonians and some of the Victorian tribes. In the Upper Vosges they say that you should never leave the clippings of your hair and nails lying about, but burn them to hinder the sorcerers from using them against you. For the same reason Italian women either burn their loose hairs or throw them into a place where no one is likely to look for them. The almost universal dread of witchcraft induces the West African negroes, the Makololo of South Africa, and the Tahitians to burn or bury their shorn hair. In the Tyrol many people burn their hair lest the witches should use it to raise thunderstorms; others burn or bury it to prevent the birds from lining their nests with it, which would cause the heads from which the hair came to ache.

This destruction of the hair and nails plainly involves an inconsistency of thought. The object of the destruction is avowedly to prevent these severed portions of the body from being used by sorcerers. But the possibility of their being so used depends upon the supposed sympathetic connexion between them and the man from whom they were severed. And if this sympathetic connexion still exists, clearly these severed portions cannot be destroyed without injury to the man.

§ 9. *Spittle tabooed.* — The same fear of witchcraft which has led so many people to hide or destroy their loose hair and nails has induced other or the same people to treat their spittle in a like fashion. For on the principles of sympathetic magic the spittle is part of the man, and whatever is done to it will have a corresponding effect on him. A Chilote Indian, who has gathered up the spittle of an enemy, will put it in a potato, and hang the potato in the smoke, uttering certain spells as he does so in the belief that his foe will waste away as the potato dries in the smoke. Or he will put the spittle in a frog and throw the animal into an inaccessible, unnavigable river, which will make the victim quake and shake with ague. The natives of Urewera, a district of New Zealand, enjoyed a high reputation for their skill in magic. It was said that they made use of people's spittle to bewitch them. Hence visitors were careful to conceal their spittle, lest they should furnish these wizards with a handle for working them harm. Similarly among some tribes of South Africa no man will spit when an enemy is near, lest his foe should find the spittle and give it to a wizard, who would then mix it with magical ingredients so as to injure the person from whom it fell. Even in a man's own house his saliva is carefully swept away and obliterated for a similar reason.

If common folk are thus cautious, it is natural that kings and chiefs should be doubly so. In the Sandwich Islands chiefs were attended by a confidential servant bearing a portable spittoon, and the deposit was carefully buried every morning to put it out of the reach of sorcerers. On the Slave Coast, for the same reason, whenever a king or chief expectorates, the saliva is scrupulously gathered up and hidden or buried. The same precautions are taken for the same reason with the spittle of the chief of Tabali in Southern Nigeria.

The magical use to which spittle may be put marks it out, like blood or nail-parings, as a suitable material basis for a covenant, since by exchanging their saliva the covenanting parties give each other a guarantee of good faith. If either of them afterwards forswears himself, the other can punish his perfidy by a magical treatment of the perjurer's spittle which he has in his custody. Thus when the Wajagga of East Africa desire to make a covenant, the two parties will sometimes sit down with a bowl of milk or beer between them, and after uttering an incantation over the beverage they each take a mouthful of the milk or beer and spit it into the other's mouth. In urgent cases, when there is no time to spend on ceremony, the two will simply spit into each other's mouth, which seals the covenant just as well.

§ 10. *Foods tabooed.* — As might have been expected, the superstitions of the savage cluster thick about the subject of food; and he abstains from eating many animals and plants, wholesome enough in themselves, which for one reason or another he fancies would prove dangerous or fatal to the eater. Examples of such abstinence are too familiar and far too numerous to quote. But if the ordinary man is thus deterred by superstitious fear from partaking of various foods, the restraints of this kind which are laid upon sacred or tabooed persons, such as kings and priests, are still more numerous and stringent. We have already seen that the Flamen Dialis was forbidden to eat or even name several plants and animals, and that the flesh diet of Egyptian kings was restricted to veal and goose. In antiquity many priests and many kings of barbarous peoples abstained wholly from a flesh diet. The *Gangas* or fetish priests of the Loango Coast are forbidden to eat or even see a variety of animals and fish, in consequence of which their flesh diet is extremely limited; often they live only on herbs and roots, though they may drink fresh blood. The heir to the throne of Loango is forbidden from infancy to eat pork; from early childhood he is interdicted the use of the *cola* fruit in company; at puberty he is taught by a priest not to partake of fowls except such as he has himself killed and cooked; and so the number of taboos goes on increasing with his years. In Fernando Po the king after installation is forbidden to eat *cocco* (*arum acaule*), deer, and porcupine, which are the ordinary foods of the people. The head chief of the Masai may eat nothing but milk, honey, and the roasted livers of goats; for if he partook of any other food he would lose his power of soothsaying and of compounding charms.

§ 11. *Knots and Rings tabooed*. — We have seen that among the many taboos which the Flamen Dialis at Rome had to observe, there was one that forbade him to have a knot on any part of his garments, and another that obliged him to wear no ring unless it were broken. In like manner Moslem pilgrims to Mecca are in a state of sanctity or taboo and may wear on their persons neither knots nor rings. These rules are probably of kindred significance, and may conveniently be considered together. To begin with knots, many people in different parts of the world entertain a strong objection to having any knot about their person at certain critical seasons, particularly childbirth, marriage, and death. Thus among the Saxons of Transylvania, when a woman is in travail all knots on her garments are untied, because it is believed that this will facilitate her delivery, and with the same intention all the locks in the house, whether on doors or boxes, are unlocked. The Lapps think that a lying-in woman should have no knot on her garments, because a knot would have the effect of making the delivery difficult and painful. In the East Indies this super-stition is extended to the whole time of pregnancy; the people believe that if a pregnant woman were to tie knots, or braid, or make anything fast, the child would thereby be constricted or the woman would herself be 'tied up' when her time came. Nay, some of them enforce the observance of the rule on the father as well as the mother of the unborn child. Among the Sea Dyaks neither of the parents may bind up anything with string or make anything fast during the wife's pregnancy. In the Toumbuluh tribe of North Celebes a ceremony is performed in the fourth or fifth month of a woman's pregnancy, and after it her husband is forbidden, among many other things, to tie any fast knots and to sit with his legs crossed over each other.

In all these cases the idea seems to be that the tying of a knot would, as they say in the East Indies, 'tie up' the woman, in other words, impede and perhaps prevent her delivery, or delay her convalescence after the birth. On the principles of homoeopathic or imitative magic the physical obstacle or impediment of a knot on a cord would create a corresponding obstacle or impediment in the body of the woman. That this is really the explanation of the rule appears from a custom observed by the Hos of West Africa at a difficult birth. When a woman is in hard labour and cannot bring forth, they call in a magician to her aid. He looks at her and says, 'The child is bound in the womb, that is why she cannot be delivered.' On the entreaties of her female relations he then promises to loose the bond so that she may bring forth. For that purpose he orders them to fetch a tough creeper from the forest, and with it he binds the hands and feet of the sufferer on her back. Then he takes a knife and calls out the woman's name, and when she answers he cuts through the creeper with a knife, saying, 'I cut through today thy bonds and thy child's bonds.' After that he chops up the creeper small, puts the bits in a vessel of water, and bathes the woman with the water. Here the cutting of the creeper with which the woman's hands and feet are bound is a simple piece of homoeopathic or imitative magic: by releasing her limbs from their bonds the magician imagines that he simultaneously releases the child in her womb from the trammels which impede its birth. The same train of thought underlies a practice observed by some peoples of opening all locks, doors, and so on, while a birth is taking place in the house. We have seen that at such a time the Germans of Transylvania open all the locks, and the same thing is done also in Voigtland and Mecklenburg. In north-western Argyllshire superstitious people used to open every lock in the house at childbirth. In the island of Salsette near Bombay, when a woman is in hard labour, all locks or doors or drawers are opened with a key to facilitate her delivery. Among the Mandelings of Sumatra the lids of all chests, boxes, pans, and so forth are opened; and if this does not produce the desired effect, the anxious husband has to strike the projecting ends of some of the house-beams in order to loosen them; for they think that 'everything must be open and loose to facilitate the delivery.' In Chittagong, when a woman cannot bring her child to the birth, the midwife gives orders to throw all doors and windows wide open, to uncork all bottles, to remove the bungs from all casks, to unloose the cows in the stall, the horses in the stable, the watch-dog in his kennel, to set free sheep, fowls, ducks, and so forth. This universal liberty accorded to the animals and even to inanimate things is, according to the people, an infallible means of ensuring the woman's delivery and allowing the babe to be born. In the island of Saghalien, when a woman is in labour, her husband undoes everything that can be undone. He loosens the plaits of his hair and the laces of his shoes. Then he unties whatever is tied in the house or its vicinity. In the courtyard he takes the axe out of the log in which it is stuck; he unfastens the boat, if it is moored to a tree, he withdraws the cartridges from his gun, and the arrows from his crossbow.

Again, we have seen that a Toumbuluh man abstains not only from tying knots, but also from sitting with crossed legs during his wife's pregnancy. The train of thought is the same in both cases. Whether you cross threads in tying a knot, or only cross your legs in sitting at your ease, you are equally, on the principles of homoeopathic magic, crossing or thwarting the free course of things, and your action cannot but check and impede whatever may be going forward in your neighbourhood. Of this important truth the Romans were fully aware. To sit beside a pregnant woman or a patient under medical treatment with clasped hands, says the grave Pliny, is to cast a malignant spell over the person, and it is worse still if you nurse your leg or legs with your clasped hands, or lay one leg over the other. Such postures were regarded by the old Romans as a let and hindrance to business of every sort, and at a council of war or a meeting of magistrates, at prayers and sacrifices, no man was suffered to cross his legs or clasp his hands. The stock instance of the dreadful consequences that might flow from doing one or the other was that of Alcmena, who travailed with Hercules for seven days and seven nights, because the goddess Lucina sat in front of the house with clasped hands and crossed legs, and the child could not be born until the goddess had been beguiled into changing her attitude. It is a Bulgarian superstition that if a pregnant woman is in the habit of sitting with crossed legs, she will suffer much in childbed. In some parts of Bavaria, when conversation comes to a standstill and silence ensues, they say, 'Surely somebody has crossed his legs.'

The magical effect of knots in trammelling and obstructing human activity was believed to be manifested at marriage not less than at birth. During the Middle Ages, and down to the eighteenth century, it seems to have been commonly held in Europe that the consummation of marriage could be prevented by any one who, while the wedding ceremony was taking place, either locked a lock or tied a knot in a cord, and then threw the lock or the cord away. The lock or the knotted cord had to be flung into water; and until it had been found and unlocked, or untied, no real union of the married pair was possible. Hence it was a grave offence, not only to cast such a spell, but also to steal or make away with the material instrument of it, whether lock or knitted cord. In the year 1718 the parliament of Bordeaux sentenced some one to be burned alive for having spread desolation through a whole family by means of knotted cords; and in 1705 two persons were condemned to death in Scotland for stealing certain charmed knots which a woman had made, in order thereby to mar the wedded happiness of Spalding of Ashintilly. The belief in the efficacy of these charms appears to have lingered in the Highlands of Perthshire down to the end of the eighteenth century, for at that time it was still customary in the beautiful parish of Logierait, between the river Tummel and the river Tay, to unloose carefully every knot in the clothes of the bride and bridegroom before the celebration of the marriage ceremony. We meet with the same superstition and the same custom at the present day in Syria. The persons who help a Syrian bridegroom to don his wedding garments take care that no knot is tied on them and no button buttoned, for they believe that a button buttoned or a knot tied would put it within the power of his enemies to deprive him of

his nuptial rights by magical means. The fear of such charms is
diffused all over North Africa at the present day. To render a
bridegroom impotent the enchanter has only to tie a knot in a
handkerchief which he had previously placed quietly on some
part of the bridegroom's body when he was mounted on horseback ready to fetch his bride: so long as the knot in the
handkerchief remains tied, so long will the bridegroom remain
powerless to consummate the marriage.

The maleficent power of knots may also be manifested in the
infliction of sickness, disease, and all kinds of misfortune. Thus
among the Hos of West Africa a sorcerer will sometimes curse his
enemy and tie a knot in a stalk of grass, saying, 'I have tied up
So-and-so in this knot. May all evil light upon him! When he
goes into the field, may a snake bite him! When he goes to the
chase, may a ravening beast attack him! And when he steps into a
river, may the water sweep him away! When it rains, may the
lightning strike him! May evil nights be his!' It is believed that
in the knot the sorcerer has bound up the life of his enemy. In the
Koran there is an allusion to the mischief of 'those who puff into
the knots,' and an Arab commentator on the passage explains
that the words refer to women who practise magic by tying knots
in cords, and then blowing and spitting upon them. He goes on to
relate how, once upon a time, a wicked Jew bewitched the prophet
Mohammed himself by tying nine knots on a string, which he then
hid in a well. So the prophet fell ill, and nobody knows what
might have happened if the archangel Gabriel had not opportunely revealed to the holy man the place where the knotted cord
was concealed. The trusty Ali soon fetched the baleful thing from
the well; and the prophet recited over it certain charms, which
were specially revealed to him for the purpose. At every verse of
the charms a knot untied itself, and the prophet experienced a
certain relief.

If knots are supposed to kill, they are also supposed to cure.
This follows from the belief that to undo the knots which are
causing sickness will bring the sufferer relief. But apart from this
negative virtue of maleficent knots, there are certain beneficent
knots to which a positive power of healing is ascribed. Pliny tells
us that some folk cured diseases of the groin by taking a thread
from a web, tying seven or nine knots on it, and then fastening

it to the patient's groin; but to make the cure effectual it was necessary to name some widow as each knot was tied. O'Donovan describes a remedy for fever employed among the Turcomans. The enchanter takes some camel hair and spins it into a stout thread, droning a spell the while. Next he ties seven knots on the thread, blowing on each knot before he pulls it tight. This knotted thread is then worn as a bracelet on his wrist by the patient. Every day one of the knots is untied and blown upon, and when the seventh knot is undone the whole thread is rolled up into a ball and thrown into a river, bearing away (as they imagine) the fever with it.

Again knots may be used by an enchantress to win a lover and attach him firmly to herself. Thus the love-sick maid in Virgil seeks to draw Daphnis to her from the city by spells and by tying three knots on each of three strings of different colours. So an Arab maiden, who had lost her heart to a certain man, tried to gain his love and bind him to herself by tying knots in his whip; but her jealous rival undid the knots. On the same principle magic knots may be employed to stop a runaway. In Swazieland you may often see grass tied in knots at the side of the footpaths. Every one of these knots tells of a domestic tragedy. A wife has run away from her husband, and he and his friends have gone in pursuit, binding up the paths, as they call it, in this fashion to prevent the fugitive from doubling back over them. A net, from its affluence of knots, has always been considered in Russia very efficacious against sorcerers; hence in some places, when a bride is being dressed in her wedding attire, a fishing-net is flung over her to keep her out of harm's way. For a similar purpose the bridegroom and his companions are often girt with pieces of net, or at least with tight-drawn girdles, for before a wizard can begin to injure them he must undo all the knots in the net, or take off the girdles. But often a Russian amulet is merely a knotted thread. A skein of red wool wound about the arms and legs is thought to ward off agues and fevers; and nine skeins, fastened round a child's neck, are deemed a preservative against scarlatina. In the Tver Government a bag of a special kind is tied to the neck of the cow which walks before the rest of a herd, in order to keep off wolves; its force binds the maw of the ravening beast. On the same principle, a padlock is carried thrice round a herd of horses before they go afield in the spring, and the bearer locks and un-locks it as he goes, saying, 'I lock from my herd the mouths of the grey wolves with this steel lock.'

Knots and locks may serve to avert not only wizards and wolves but death itself. When they brought a woman to the stake at St. Andrews in 1572 to burn her alive for a witch, they found on her a white cloth like a collar, with strings and many knots on the strings. They took it from her, sorely against her will, for she seemed to think that she could not die in the fire, if only the cloth with the knotted strings was on her. When it was taken away, she said, 'Now I have no hope of myself.' In many parts of England it is thought that a person cannot die so long as any locks are locked or bolts shot in the house. It is therefore a very common practice to undo all locks and bolts when the sufferer is plainly near his end, in order that his agony may not be unduly prolonged. For example, in the year 1863, at Taunton, a child lay sick of scarlatina and death seemed inevitable. 'A jury of matrons was, as it were, empanelled, and to prevent the child "dying hard" all the doors in the house, all the drawers, all the boxes, all the cup-boards were thrown wide open, the keys taken out, and the body of the child placed under a beam, whereby a sure, certain, and easy passage into eternity could be secured.' Strange to say, the child declined to avail itself of the facilities for dying so obligingly placed at its disposal by the sagacity and experience of the British matrons of Taunton; it preferred to live rather than give up the ghost just then.

The rule which prescribes that at certain magical and religious ceremonies the hair should hang loose and the feet should be bare is probably based on the same fear of trammelling and impeding the action in hand, whatever it may be, by the presence of any knot or constriction, whether on the head or on the feet of the performer. A similar power to bind and hamper spiritual as well as bodily activities is ascribed by some people to rings. Thus in the island of Carpathus people never button the clothes they put upon a dead body and they are careful to remove all rings from it; 'for the spirit, they say, can even be detained in the little finger, and cannot rest.' Here it is plain that even if the soul is not definitely supposed to issue at death from the finger-tips, yet the ring is conceived to exercise a certain constrictive influence which detains and imprisons the immortal spirit in spite of its efforts to escape from the tabernacle of clay; in short the ring, like the knot, acts as a spiritual fetter. This may have been the reason of an ancient Greek maxim, attributed to Pythagoras, which forbade people to wear rings. Nobody might enter the ancient Arcadian sanctuary of the Mistress at Lycosura with a ring on his or her finger. Persons who consulted the oracle of Faunus had to be chaste, to eat no flesh, and to wear no rings.

On the other hand, the same constriction which hinders the egress of the soul may prevent the entrance of evil spirits; hence we find rings used as amulets against demons, witches, and ghosts. In the Tyrol it is said that a woman in childbed should never take off her wedding-ring, or spirits and witches will have power over her. Among the Lapps, the person who is about to place a corpse in the coffin receives from the husband, wife, or children of the deceased a brass ring, which he must wear fastened to his right arm until the corpse is safely deposited in the grave. The ring is believed to serve the person as an amulet against any harm which the ghost might do to him. How far the custom of wearing finger-rings may have been influenced by, or even have sprung from, a belief in their efficacy as amulets to keep the soul in the body, or demons out of it, is a question which seems worth considering. Here we are only concerned with the belief in so far as it seems to throw light on the rule that the Flamen Dialis might not wear a ring unless it were broken. Taken in conjunction with the rule which forbade him to have a knot on his garments, it points to a fear that the powerful spirit embodied in him might be trammelled and hampered in its goings-out and comings-in by such corporeal and spiritual fetters as rings and knots.

CHAPTER XXII

TABOOED WORDS

§ 1. *Personal Names tabooed.* — Unable to discriminate clearly between words and things, the savage commonly fancies that the link between a name and the person or thing denominated by it is not a mere arbitrary and ideal association, but a real and substantial bond which unites the two in such a way that magic may be wrought on a man just as easily through his name as through his hair, his nails, or any other material part of his person. In fact, primitive man regards his name as a vital portion of himself and takes care of it accordingly. Thus, for example, the North American Indian 'regards his name, not as a mere label, but as a distinct part of his personality, just as much as are his eyes or his teeth, and believes that injury will result as surely from the malicious handling of his name as from a wound inflicted on any part of his physical organism. This belief was found among the various tribes from the Atlantic to the Pacific, and has occasioned a number of curious regulations in regard to the concealment and change of names.' Some Esquimaux take new names when they are old, hoping thereby to get a new lease of life. The Tolampoos of Celebes believe that if you write a man's name down you can carry off his soul along with it. Many savages at the present day regard their names as vital parts of themselves, and therefore take great pains to conceal their real names, lest these should give to evil-disposed persons a handle by which to injure their owners.

Thus, to begin with the savages who rank at the bottom of the social scale, we are told that the secrecy with which among the Australian aborigines personal names are often kept from general knowledge 'arises in great measure from the belief that an enemy, who knows your name, has in it something which he can use magically to your detriment.' 'An Australian black,' says another writer, 'is always very unwilling to tell his real name, and there is no doubt that this reluctance is due to the fear that through his name he may be injured by sorcerers.' Amongst the tribes of Central Australia every man, woman, and child has, besides a personal name which is in common use, a secret or sacred name which is bestowed by the older men upon him or her soon after birth, and which is known to none but the fully initiated members of the group. This secret name is never mentioned except upon the most solemn occasions; to utter it in the hearing of women or of men of another group would be a most serious breach of tribal custom, as serious as the most flagrant case of sacrilege among ourselves. When mentioned at all, the name is spoken only in a whisper, and not until the most elaborate precautions have been taken that it shall be heard by no one but members of the group. 'The native thinks that a stranger knowing his secret name would have special power to work him ill by means of magic.'

The same fear seems to have led to a custom of the same sort amongst the ancient Egyptians, whose comparatively high civilisation was strangely dashed and chequered with relics of the lowest savagery. Every Egyptian received two names, which were known respectively as the true name and the good name, or the great name and the little name; and while the good or little name was made public, the true or great name appears to have been carefully concealed. A Brahman child receives two names, one for common use, the other a secret name which none but his father and mother should know. The latter is only used at ceremonies such as marriage. The custom is intended to protect the person against magic, since a charm only becomes effectual in combination with the real name. Similarly, the natives of Nias believe that harm may be done to a person by the demons who hear his name pronounced. Hence the names of infants, who are especially exposed to the assaults of evil spirits, are never spoken; and often in haunted spots, such as the gloomy depths of the forest, the banks of a river, or beside a bubbling spring, men will abstain from calling each other by their names for a like reason.

The Indians of Chiloe keep their names secret and do not like to have them uttered aloud; for they say that there are fairies or imps on the mainland or neighbouring islands who, if they knew folk's names, would do them an injury: but so long as they do not know the names, these mischievous sprites are powerless. The Araucanians will hardly ever tell a stranger their names because they fear that he would thereby acquire some supernatural power over themselves. Asked his name by a stranger, who is ignorant of their superstitions, an Araucanian will answer, 'I have none.' When an Ojebway is asked his name, he will look at some bystander and ask him to answer. 'This reluctance arises from an impression they receive when young, that if they repeat their own names it will prevent their growth, and they will be small in stature. On account of this unwillingness to tell their names, many strangers have fancied that they either have no names or have forgotten them.'

In this last case no scruple seems to be felt about communicating a man's name to strangers, and no ill effects appear to be dreaded as a consequence of divulging it; harm is only done when a name is spoken by its owner. Why is this? and why in particular should a man be thought to stunt his growth by uttering his own name? We may conjecture that to savages who act and think thus a person's name only seems to be a part of himself when it is uttered with his own breath; uttered by the breath of others it has no vital connexion with him, and no harm can come to him through it. Whereas, so these primitive philosophers may have argued, when a man lets his own name pass his lips, he is parting with a living piece of himself, and if he persists in so reckless a course he must certainly end by dissipating his energy and shattering his constitution. Many a broken-down debauchee, many a feeble frame wasted with disease, may have been pointed out by these simple moralists to their awe-struck disciples as a fearful example of the fate that must sooner or later overtake the profligate who indulges immoderately in the seductive habit of mentioning his own name.

However we may explain it, the fact is certain that many a savage evinces the strongest reluctance to pronounce his own name, while at the same time he makes no objection at all to other people pronouncing it, and will even invite them to do so for him in order to satisfy the curiosity of an inquisitive stranger. Thus in some parts of Madagascar it is taboo for a person to tell his own name, but a slave or attendant will answer for him. The same curious inconsistency, as it may seem to us, is recorded of some tribes of American Indians. Thus we are told that 'the name of an American Indian is a sacred thing, not to be divulged by the owner himself without due consideration. One may ask a warrior of any tribe to give his name, and the question will be met with either a point-blank refusal or the more diplomatic evasion that he cannot understand what is wanted of him. The moment a friend approaches, the warrior first interrogated will whisper what is wanted, and the friend can tell the name, receiving a reciprocation of the courtesy from the other.' This general statement applies, for example, to the Indian tribes of British Columbia, as to whom it is said that 'one of their strangest prejudices, which appears to pervade all tribes alike, is a dislike to telling their names—thus you never get a man's right name from himself; but they will tell each other's names without hesitation.' In the whole of the East Indian Archipelago the etiquette is the same. As a general rule no one will utter his own name. To enquire, 'What is your name?' is a very indelicate question in native society. When in the course of administrative or judicial business a native is asked his name, instead of replying he will look at his comrade to indicate that he is to answer for him, or he will say straight out, 'Ask him.' The superstition is current all over the East Indies without exception, and it is found also among the Motu and Motumotu tribes, the Papuans of Finsch Haven in North New Guinea, the Nufoors of Dutch New Guinea, and the Melanesians of the Bismarck Archipelago. Among many tribes of South Africa men and women never mention their names if they can get any one else to do it for them, but they do not absolutely refuse when it cannot be avoided.

Sometimes the embargo laid on personal names is not permanent; it is conditional on circumstances, and when these change it ceases to operate. Thus when the Nandi men are away on a foray, nobody at home may pronounce the names of the absent warriors; they must be referred to as birds. Should a child so far forget itself as to mention one of the distant ones by name, the mother would rebuke it, saying, 'Don't talk of the birds who are in the heavens.' Among the Bangala of the Upper Congo, while a man is fishing and when he returns with his catch, his proper name is in abeyance and nobody may mention it. Whatever the fisherman's real name may be, he is called *mwele* without distinction. The reason is that the river is full of spirits, who, if they heard the fisherman's real name, might so work against him that he would catch little or nothing. Even when he has caught his fish and landed them, the buyer must still not address him by his proper name, but must only call him *mwele*; for even then, if the spirits were to hear his proper name, they would either bear it in mind and serve him out another day, or they might so mar the fish he had caught that he would get very little for them. Hence the fisherman can extract heavy damages from anybody who mentions his name, or can compel the thoughtless speaker to relieve him of the fish at a good price so as to restore his luck. When the Sulka of New Britain are near the territory of their enemies the Gaktei, they take care not to mention them by their proper name, believing that were they to do so, their foes would attack and slay them. Hence in these circumstances they speak of the Gaktei as *o lapsiek*, that is, 'the rotten tree-trunks,' and they imagine that by calling them that they make the limbs of their dreaded enemies ponderous and clumsy like logs. This example illustrates the extremely materialistic view which these savages take of the nature of words; they suppose that the mere utterance of an expression signifying clumsiness will homoeopathically affect with clumsiness the limbs of their distant foemen. Another illustration of this curious misconception is furnished by a Caffre superstition that the character of a young thief can be reformed by shouting his name over a boiling kettle of medicated water, then clapping a lid on the kettle and leaving the name to steep in the water for several days. It is not in the least necessary that the thief should be aware of the use that is being made of his name behind his back; the moral reformation will be effected without his knowledge.

When it is deemed necessary that a man's real name should be kept secret, it is often customary, as we have seen, to call him by a surname or nickname. As distinguished from the real or primary names, these secondary names are apparently held to be no part of the man himself, so that they may be freely used and divulged to everybody without endangering his safety thereby. Sometimes in order to avoid the use of his own name a man will be called after his child. Thus we are informed that 'the Gippsland blacks objected strongly to let any one outside the tribe know their names, lest their enemies, learning them, should make them vehicles of incantation, and so charm their lives away. As children were not thought to have enemies, they used to speak of a man as "the father, uncle, or cousin of So-and-so," naming the child; but on all occasions abstained from mentioning the name of a grown-up person.' The Alfoors of Poso in Celebes will not pronounce their own names. Among them, accordingly, if you wish to ascertain a person's name, you ought not to ask the man himself, but should enquire of others. But if this is impossible, for example, when there is no one else near, you should ask him his child's name, and then address him as the 'Father of So-and-so.' Nay, these Alfoors are shy of uttering the names even of children; so when a boy or girl has a nephew or niece, he or she is addressed as 'Uncle of So-and-so,' or 'Aunt of So-and-so.' In pure Malay society, we are told, a man is never asked his name, and the custom of naming parents after their children is adopted only as a means of avoiding the use of the parents' own names. The writer who makes this statement adds in confirmation of it that childless persons are named after their younger brothers. Among the land Dyaks children as they grow up are called, according to their sex, the father or mother of a child of their father's or mother's younger brother or sister, that is, they are called the father or mother of what we should call their first cousin. The Caffres used to think it discourteous to call a bride by her own name, so they would call her 'the Mother of So-and-so,' even when she was only betrothed, far less a wife and a mother. Among the Kukis and Zemis or Kacha Nagas of Assam parents drop their names after the birth of a child and are named Father and Mother of So-and-so. Childless couples go by the name of 'the childless father,' 'the childless mother,' 'the father of no child,' 'the mother of no child.' The widespread custom of naming a father after his child has sometimes been supposed to spring from a desire on the father's part to assert his paternity, apparently as a means of obtaining those rights over his children which had previously, under a system of mother-kin, been possessed by the mother. But this explanation does not account for the parallel custom of naming the mother after her child, which seems commonly to coexist with the practice of naming the father after the child. Still less, if possible, does it apply to the customs of calling childless couples the father and mother of children which do not exist, of naming people after their younger brothers, and of designating children as the uncles and aunts of So-and-so, or as the fathers and mothers of their first cousins. But all these practices are explained in a simple and natural way if we suppose that they originate in a reluctance to utter the real names of persons addressed or directly referred to. That reluctance is probably based partly on a fear of attracting the notice of evil spirits, partly on a dread of revealing the name to sorcerers, who would thereby obtain a handle for injuring the owner of the name.

§ 2. *Names of Relations tabooed.* — It might naturally be expected that the reserve so commonly maintained with regard to personal names would be dropped or at least relaxed among relations and friends. But the reverse of this is often the case. It is precisely the persons most intimately connected by blood and especially by marriage to whom the rule applies with the greatest stringency. Such people are often forbidden, not only to pronounce each other's names, but even to utter ordinary words which resemble or have a single syllable in common with these names. The persons who are thus mutually debarred from mentioning each other's names are especially husbands and wives, a man and his wife's parents, and a woman and her husband's father. For example, among the Caffres a woman may not publicly pronounce the birth-name of her husband or of any of his brothers, nor may she use the interdicted word in its ordinary sense. If her husband, for instance, be called u-Mpaka, from *impaka*, a small feline animal, she must speak of that beast by some other name. Further, a Caffre wife is forbidden to pronounce even mentally the names of her father-in-law and of all her husband's male relations in the ascending line; and whenever the emphatic syllable of any of their names occurs in another word, she must avoid it by substituting either an entirely new word, or, at least, another syllable in its place. Hence this custom has given rise to an almost distinct language among the women, which the Caffres call 'women's speech.' The interpretation of this 'women's speech' is naturally very difficult, 'for no definite rules can be given for the formation of these substituted words, nor is it possible to form a dictionary of them, their number being so great — since there may be many women, even in the same tribe, who would be no more at liberty to use the substitutes employed by some others, than they are to use the original words themselves.' A Caffre man, on his side, may not mention the name of his mother-in-law, nor may she pronounce his; but he is free to utter words in which the emphatic syllable of her name occurs. A Kirghiz woman dares not pronounce the names of the older relations of her husband, nor even use words which resemble them in sound. For example, if one of these relations is called Shepherd, she may not speak of sheep, but must call them 'the bleating ones'; if his name is Lamb, she must refer to lambs as 'the young bleating ones.' In Southern India wives believe that to tell their husband's name or to pronounce it even in a dream would bring him to an untimely end. Among the Sea Dyaks a man may not pronounce the name of his father-in-law or mother-in-law without incurring the wrath of the spirits. And since he reckons as his father-in-law and mother-in-law not only the father and mother of his own wife, but also the fathers and mothers of his brothers' wives and sisters' husbands, and likewise the fathers and mothers of all his cousins, the number of tabooed names may be very considerable and the opportunities of error correspondingly numerous. To make confusion worse confounded, the names of persons are often the names of common things, such as moon, bridge, barley, cobra, leopard; so that when any of a man's many fathers-in-law and mothers-in-law are called by such names, these common words may not pass his lips. Among the Alfoors of Minahassa, in Celebes, the custom is carried still further so as to forbid the use even of words which merely resemble the personal names in sound. It is especially the name of a father-in-law which is thus laid under an interdict. If he, for example, is called Kalala, his son-in-law may not speak of a horse by its common name *kawalo*; he must call it a 'riding-beast' (*sasakajan*). So among the Alfoors of the island of Buru it is taboo to mention the names of parents and parents-in-law, or even to speak of common objects by words which resemble these names in sound. Thus, if your mother-in-law is called Dalu, which means 'betel,' you may not ask for betel by its ordinary name, you must ask for 'red mouth'; if you want betel-leaf, you may not say betel-leaf (*dalu 'mun*), you must say *karon fenna*. In the same island it is also taboo to mention the name of an elder brother in his presence. Transgressions of these rules are punished with fines. In Sunda it is thought that a particular crop would be spoilt if a man were to mention the names of his father and mother.

Among the Nufoors of Dutch New Guinea persons who are related to each other by marriage are forbidden to mention each other's names. Among the connexions whose names are thus tabooed are wife, mother-in-law, father-in-law, your wife's uncles and aunts and also her grand-uncles and grand-aunts, and the whole of your wife's or your husband's family in the same generation as yourself, except that men may mention the names of their brothers-in-law, though women may not. The taboo comes into operation as soon as the betrothal has taken place and before the marriage has been celebrated. Families thus connected by the betrothal of two of their members are not only forbidden to pronounce each other's names; they may not even look at each other, and the rule gives rise to the most comical scenes when they happen to meet unexpectedly. And not merely the names themselves, but any words that sound like them are scrupulously avoided and other words used in their place. If it should chance that a person has inadvertently uttered a forbidden name, he must at once throw himself on the floor and say, 'I have mentioned a wrong name. I throw it through the chinks of the floor in order that I may eat well.'

In the western islands of Torres Straits a man never mentioned the personal names of his father-in-law, mother-in-law, brother-in-law, and sister-in-law; and a woman was subject to the same restrictions. A brother-in-law might be spoken of as the husband or brother of some one whose name it was lawful to mention; and similarly a sister-in-law might be called the wife of So-and-so. If a man by chance used the personal name of his brother-in-law, he was ashamed and hung his head. His shame was only relieved when he made a present as compensation to the man whose name he had taken in vain. The same compensation was made to a sister-in-law, a father-in-law, and a mother-in-law for the accidental mention of their names. Among the natives who inhabit the coast of the Gazelle Peninsula in New Britain to mention the name of a brother-in-law is the grossest possible affront you can offer to him; it is a crime punishable with death. In the Banks' Islands, Melanesia, the taboos laid on the names of persons connected by marriage are very strict. A man will not mention the name of his father-in-law, much less the name of his mother-in-law, nor may he name his wife's brother; but he may name his wife's sister — she is nothing to him. A woman may not name her father-in-law, nor on any account her son-in-law. Two people whose children have intermarried are also debarred from mentioning each other's names. And not only are all these persons forbidden to utter each other's names; they may not even pronounce ordinary words which chance to be either identical with the names or to have any syllables in common with them. Thus we hear of a native of these islands who might not use the common words for 'pig' and 'to die', because these words occurred in the polysyllabic name of his son-in-law; and we are told of another unfortunate who might not pronounce the everyday words for 'hand' and 'hot' on account of his wife's brother's name, and who was even debarred from mentioning the number 'one,' because the word for 'one' formed part of the name of his wife's cousin.

The reluctance to mention the names or even syllables of the names of persons connected with the speaker by marriage can hardly be separated from the reluctance evinced by so many people to utter their own names or the names of the dead or of chiefs and kings; and if the reticence as to these latter names springs mainly from superstition, we may infer that the reticence as to the former has no better foundation. That the savage's unwillingness to mention his own name is based, at least in part, on a superstitious fear of the ill use that might be made of it by his foes, whether human or spiritual, has already been shown. It remains to examine the similar usage in regard to the names of the dead and of royal personages.

§ 3. *Names of the Dead tabooed.* — The custom of abstaining from all mention of the names of the dead was observed in antiquity by the Albanians of the Caucasus, and at the present day it is in full force among many savage tribes. Thus we are told that one of the customs most rigidly observed and enforced amongst the Australian aborigines is never to mention the name of a deceased person, whether male or female; to name aloud one who has departed this life would be a gross violation of their most sacred prejudices, and they carefully abstain from it. The chief motive for this abstinence appears to be a fear of evoking the ghost, although the natural unwillingness to revive past sorrows undoubtedly operates also to draw the veil of oblivion over the names of the dead. Once Mr. Oldfield so terrified a native by shouting out the name of a deceased person, that the man fairly took to his heels and did not venture to show himself again for several days. At their next meeting he bitterly reproached the rash white man for his indiscretion: 'nor could I,' adds Mr. Oldfield, 'induce him by any means to utter the awful sound of a dead man's name, for by so doing he would have placed himself in the power of the malign spirits.' Among the aborigines of Victoria the dead were very rarely spoken of, and then never by their names; they were referred to in a subdued voice as 'the lost one' or 'the poor fellow that is no more.' To speak of them by name would, it was supposed, excite the malignity of Couit-gil, the spirit of the departed, which hovers on earth for a time before it departs for ever towards the setting sun. Of the tribes on the Lower Murray River we are told that when a person dies 'they carefully avoid mentioning his name; but if compelled to do so, they pronounce it in a very low whisper, so faint that they imagine the spirit cannot hear their voice.' Among the tribes of Central Australia no one may utter the name of the deceased during the period of mourning, unless it is absolutely necessary to do so, and then it is only done in a whisper for fear of disturbing and annoying the man's spirit which is walking about in ghostly form. If the ghost hears his name mentioned he concludes that his kinsfolk are not mourning for him properly; if their grief were genuine they could not bear to bandy his name about. Touched to the quick by their hard-hearted indifference, the indignant ghost will come and trouble them in dreams.

The same reluctance to utter the names of the dead appears to prevail among all the Indian tribes of America from Hudson's Bay Territory to Patagonia. Among the Goajiros of Colombia to mention the dead before his kinsmen is a dreadful offence, which is often punished by death; for if it happen on the *rancho* of the deceased, in presence of his nephew or uncle, they will assuredly kill the offender on the spot if they can. But if he escapes, the penalty resolves itself into a heavy fine, usually of two or more oxen.

A similar reluctance to mention the names of the dead is reported of peoples so widely separated from each other as the Samoyeds of Siberia and the Todas of Southern India; the Mongols of Tartary and the Tuaregs of the Sahara; the Ainos of Japan and the Akamba and Nandi of Eastern Africa; the Tinguianes of the Philippines and the inhabitants of the Nicobar Islands, of Borneo, of Madagascar, and of Tasmania. In all cases, even where it is not expressly stated, the fundamental reason for this avoidance is probably the fear of the ghost. That this is the real motive with the Tuaregs we are positively informed. They dread the return of the dead man's spirit, and do all they can to avoid it by shifting their camp after a death, ceasing for ever to pronounce the name of the departed, and eschewing everything that might be regarded as an evocation or recall of his soul. Hence they do not, like the Arabs, designate individuals by adding to their personal names the names of their fathers; they never speak of So-and-so, son of So-and-so; they give to every man a name which will live and die with him. So among some of the Victorian tribes in Australia personal names were rarely perpetuated, because the natives believed that any one who adopted the name of a deceased person would not live long; probably his ghostly namesake was supposed to come and fetch him away to the spirit-land.

The same fear of the ghost, which moves people to suppress his old name, naturally leads all persons who bear a similar name to exchange it for another, lest its utterance should attract the attention of the ghost, who cannot reasonably be expected to discriminate between all the different applications of the same name. Thus we are told that in the Adelaide and Encounter Bay tribes of South Australia the repugnance to mentioning the names of those who have died lately is carried so far, that persons who bear the same name as the deceased abandon it, and either adopt temporary names or are known by any others that happen to belong to them. A similar custom prevails among some of the Queensland tribes; but the prohibition to use the names of the dead is not permanent, though it may last for many years. In some Australian tribes the change of name thus brought about is permanent; the old name is laid aside for ever, and the man is known by his new name for the rest of his life, or at least until he is obliged to change it again for a like reason. Among the North American Indians all persons, whether men or women, who bore the name of one who had just died were obliged to abandon it and to adopt other names, which was formally done at the first ceremony of mourning for the dead. In some tribes to the east of the Rocky Mountains this change of name lasted only during the season of mourning, but in other tribes on the Pacific Coast of North America it seems to have been permanent.

Sometimes by an extension of the same reasoning all the near relations of the deceased change their names, whatever they may happen to be, doubtless from a fear that the sound of the familiar names might lure back the vagrant spirit to its old home. Thus in some Victorian tribes the ordinary names of all the next of kin were disused during the period of mourning, and certain general terms, prescribed by custom, were substituted for them. To call a mourner by his own name was considered an insult to the departed, and often led to fighting and bloodshed. Among Indian tribes of North-western America near relations of the deceased often change their names 'under an impression that spirits will be attracted back to earth if they hear familiar names often repeated.' Among the Kiowa Indians the name of the dead is never spoken in the presence of the relatives, and on the death of any member of a family all the others take new names. This custom was noted by Raleigh's colonists on Roanoke Island more than three centuries ago. Among the Lengua Indians not only is a dead man's name never mentioned, but all the survivors change their names also. They say that Death has been among them and has carried off a list of the living, and that he will soon come back for more victims; hence in order to defeat his fell purpose they change their names, believing that on his return Death, though he has got them all on his list, will not be able to identify them under their new names, and will depart to pursue the search elsewhere. Nicobarese mourners take new names in order to escape the unwelcome attentions of the ghost; and for the same purpose they disguise themselves by shaving their heads so that the ghost is unable to recognise them.

Further, when the name of the deceased happens to be that of some common object, such as an animal, or plant, or fire, or water, it is sometimes considered necessary to drop that word in ordinary speech and replace it by another. A custom of this sort, it is plain, may easily be a potent agent of change in language; for where it prevails to any considerable extent many words must constantly become obsolete and new ones spring up. And this tendency has been remarked by observers who have recorded the custom in Australia, America, and elsewhere. For example, with regard to the Australian aborigines it has been noted that 'the dialects change with almost every tribe. Some tribes name their children after natural objects; and when the person so named dies, the word is never again mentioned; another word has therefore to be invented for the object after which the child is called.' The writer gives as an instance the case of a man whose name Karla signified 'fire'; when Karla died, a new word for fire had to be introduced. 'Hence,' adds the writer, 'the language is always changing.' Again, in the Encounter Bay tribe of South Australia, if a man of the name of Ngnke, which means 'water,' were to die, the whole tribe would be obliged to use some other word to express water for a considerable time after his decease. The writer who records this custom surmises that it may explain the presence of a number of synonyms in the language of the tribe. This conjecture is confirmed by what we know of some Victorian tribes whose speech comprised a regular set of synonyms to be used instead of the common terms by all members of a tribe in times of mourning. For instance, if a man called Waa ('crow') departed this life, during the period of mourning for him nobody might call a crow a *waa*; everybody had to speak of the bird as a *narrapart*. When a person who rejoiced in the title of Ringtail Opossum (*weearn*) had gone the way of all flesh, his sorrowing relations and the tribe at large were bound for a time to refer to ringtail opossums by the more sonorous name of *manuungkuurt*. If the community were plunged in grief for the loss of a respected female who bore the honourable name of Turkey Bustard, the proper name for turkey bustards, which was *barrim barrim*, went out, and *tillit tilliitsh* came in. And so *mutatis mutandis* with the names of Black Cockatoo, Grey Duck, Gigantic Crane, Kangaroo, Eagle, Dingo, and the rest.

A similar custom used to be constantly transforming the language of the Abipones of Paraguay, amongst whom, however, a word once abolished seems never to have been revived. New words, says the missionary Dobrizhoffer, sprang up every year like mushrooms in a night, because all words that resembled the names of the dead were abolished by proclamation and others coined in their place. The mint of words was in the hands of the old women of the tribe, and whatever term they stamped with their approval and put into circulation was immediately accepted without a murmur by high and low alike, and spread like wildfire through every camp and settlement of the tribe. You would be astonished, says the same missionary, to see how meekly the whole nation acquiesces in the decision of a withered old hag, and how completely the old familiar words fall instantly out of use and are never repeated either through force of habit or forgetfulness. In the seven years that Dobrizhoffer spent among these Indians the native word for jaguar was changed thrice, and the words for crocodile, thorn, and the slaughter of cattle underwent similar though less varied vicissitudes. As a result of this habit, the vocabularies of the missionaries teemed with erasures, old words having constantly to be struck out as obsolete and new ones inserted in their place. In many tribes of British New Guinea the names of persons are also the names of common things. The people believe that if the name of a deceased person is pronounced, his spirit will return, and as they have no wish to see it back among them the mention of his name is tabooed and a new word is created to take its place, whenever the name happens to be a common term of the language. Consequently many words are permanently lost or revived with modified or new meanings. In the Nicobar Islands a similar practice has similarly affected the speech of the natives. 'A most singular custom,' says Mr. de Roepstorff, 'prevails among them which one would suppose must most effectually hinder the "making of history," or, at any rate, the transmission of historical narrative. By a strict rule, which has all the sanction of Nicobar superstition, no man's name may be mentioned after his death! To such a length is this carried that when, as very frequently happens, the man rejoiced in the name of "Fowl," "Hat," "Fire," "Road," etc., in its Nicobarese equivalent, the use of these words is carefully eschewed for the future, not only as being the personal designation of the deceased, but even as the names of the common things they represent; the words die out of the language, and either new vocables are coined to express the thing intended, or a substitute for the disused word is found in other Nicobarese dialects or in some foreign tongue. This extraordinary custom not only adds an element of instability to the language, but destroys the continuity of political life, and renders the record of past events precarious and vague, if not impossible.'

That a superstition which suppresses the names of the dead must cut at the very root of historical tradition has been remarked by other workers in this field. 'The Klamath people,' observes Mr. A. S. Gatschet, 'possess no historic traditions going further back in time than a century, for the simple reason that there was a strict law prohibiting the mention of the person or acts of a

deceased individual by *using his name*. This law was [...]
observed among the Californians no less than among the
Oregonians, and on its transgression the death penalty could be
inflicted. This is certainly enough to suppress all historical knowledge within a people. How can history be written without names?'

In many tribes, however, the power of this superstition to blot
out the memory of the past is to some extent weakened and
impaired by a natural tendency of the human mind. Time, which
wears out the deepest impressions, inevitably dulls, if it does not
wholly efface, the print left on the savage mind by the mystery
and horror of death. Sooner or later, as the memory of his loved
ones fades away, he becomes more willing to speak of them, and
thus their rude names may sometimes be rescued by the philosophic enquirer before they have vanished, like autumn leaves or
winter snows, into the vast undistinguished limbo of the past.
In some of the Victorian tribes the prohibition to mention the
names of the dead remained in force only during the period of
mourning; in the Port Lincoln tribe of South Australia it lasted
many years. Among the Chinook Indians of North America
'custom forbids the mention of a dead man's name, at least till
many years have elapsed after the bereavement.' Among the
Puyallup Indians the observance of the taboo is relaxed after
several years, when the mourners have forgotten their grief; and
if the deceased was a famous warrior, one of his descendants, for
instance a great-grandson, may be named after him. In this tribe
the taboo is not much observed at any time except by the relations
of the dead. Similarly the Jesuit missionary Lafitau tells us that
the name of the departed and similar names of the survivors were,
so to say, buried with the corpse until, the poignancy of their
grief being abated, it pleased the relations to 'lift up the tree and
raise the dead.' By raising the dead they meant bestowing the
name of the departed upon some one else, who thus became to all
intents and purposes a reincarnation of the deceased, since on
the principles of savage philosophy the name is a vital part, if
not the soul, of the man.

Among the Lapps, when a woman was with child and near the
time of her delivery, a deceased ancestor or relation used to appear
to her in a dream, and inform her what dead person was to be
born again in her infant, and whose name the child was therefore

If the woman had no such dream, it fell to the father or the relatives to determine the name by divination or by consulting a wizard. Among the Khonds a birth is celebrated on the seventh day after the event by a feast given to the priest and to the whole village. To determine the child's name the priest drops grains of rice into a cup of water, naming with each grain a deceased ancestor. From the movements of the seed in the water, and from observations made on the person of the infant, he pronounces which of his progenitors has reappeared in him, and the child generally, at least among the northern tribes, receives the name of that ancestor. Among the Yorubas, soon after a child has been born, a priest of Ifa, the god of divination, appears on the scene to ascertain what ancestral soul has been reborn in the infant. As soon as this has been decided, the parents are told that the child must conform in all respects to the manner of life of the ancestor who now animates him or her, and if, as often happens, they profess ignorance, the priest supplies the necessary information. The child usually receives the name of the ancestor who has been born again in him.

§ 4. *Names of Kings and other Sacred Persons tabooed.* — When we see that in primitive society the names of mere commoners, whether alive or dead, are matters of such anxious care, we need not be surprised that great precautions should be taken to guard from harm the names of sacred kings and priests. Thus the name of the king of Dahomey is always kept secret, lest the knowledge of it should enable some evil-minded person to do him a mischief. The appellations by which the different kings of Dahomey have been known to Europeans are not their true names, but mere titles, or what the natives call 'strong names.' The natives seem to think that no harm comes of such titles being known, since they are not, like the birth-names, vitally connected with their owners. In the Galla kingdom of Ghera the birth-name of the sovereign may not be pronounced by a subject under pain of death, and common words which resemble it in sound are changed for others. Among the Bahima of Central Africa, when the king dies, his name is abolished from the language, and if his name was that of an animal, a new appellation must be found for the creature at once. For example, the king is often called a lion; hence at the death of a king named Lion a new name for lions in general has to be coined. In Siam it used to be difficult to ascertain the king's real name, since it was carefully kept secret from fear of sorcery; any one who mentioned it was clapped into gaol. The king might only be referred to under certain high-sounding titles, such as 'the august,' 'the perfect,' 'the supreme,' 'the great emperor,' ' descendant of the angels,' and so on. In Burma it was accounted an impiety of the deepest dye to mention the name of the reigning sovereign; Burmese subjects, even when they were far from their country, could not be prevailed upon to do so; after his accession to the throne the king was known by his royal titles only.

Among the Zulus no man will mention the name of the chief of his tribe or the names of the progenitors of the chief, so far as he can remember them; nor will he utter common words which coincide with or merely resemble in sound tabooed names. In the tribe of the Dwandwes there was a chief called Langa, which means the sun; hence the name of the sun was changed from *langa* to *gala*, and so remains to this day, though Langa died more than a hundred years ago. Again, in the Xnumayo tribe the word meaning 'to herd cattle' was changed from *alusa* or *ayusa* to *kagesa*, because u-Mayusi was the name of the chief. Besides these taboos, which were observed by each tribe separately, all the Zulu tribes united in tabooing the name of the king who reigned over the whole nation. Hence, for example, when Panda was king of Zululand, the word for 'a root of a tree,' which is *impando*, was changed to *nxabo*. Again, the word for 'lies' or 'slander' was altered from *amacebo* to *amakwata*, because *amacebo* contains a syllable of the name of the famous King Cetchwayo. These substitutions are not, however, carried so far by the men as by the women, who omit every sound even remotely resembling one that occurs in a tabooed name. At the king's kraal, indeed, it is sometimes difficult to understand the speech of the royal wives, as they treat in this fashion the names not only of the king and his forefathers, but even of his and their brothers back for generations. When to these tribal and national taboos we add those family taboos on the names of connexions by marriage which have been already described, we can easily understand how it comes about that in Zululand every tribe has words peculiar to itself, and that the women have a considerable

vocabulary of their own. Members, too, of one family may be
debarred from using words employed by those of another. The
women of one kraal, for instance, may call a hyaena by its
ordinary name; those of the next may use the common substitute;
while in a third the substitute may also be unlawful and another
term may have to be invented to supply its place. Hence the
Zulu language at the present day almost presents the appearance
of being a double one; indeed, for multitudes of things it
possesses three or four synonyms, which through the blending of
tribes are known all over Zululand.

In Madagascar a similar custom everywhere prevails and has
resulted, as among the Zulus, in producing certain dialectic
differences in the speech of the various tribes. There are no
family names in Madagascar, and almost every personal name is
drawn from the language of daily life and signifies some common
object or action or quality, such as a bird, a beast, a tree, a plant,
a colour, and so on. Now, whenever one of these common words
forms the name or part of the name of the chief of the tribe, it
becomes sacred and may no longer be used in its ordinary
signification as the name of a tree, an insect, or what not. Hence
a new name for the object must be invented to replace the one
which has been discarded. It is easy to conceive what confusion
and uncertainty may thus be introduced into a language when it
is spoken by many little local tribes each ruled by a petty chief
with his own sacred name. Yet there are tribes and people who
submit to this tyranny of words as their fathers did before them
from time immemorial. The inconvenient results of the custom
are especially marked on the western coast of the island, where, on
account of the large number of independent chieftains, the names
of things, places, and rivers have suffered so many changes that
confusion often arises, for when once common words have been
banned by the chiefs the natives will not acknowledge to have
ever known them in their old sense.

But it is not merely the names of living kings and chiefs which
are tabooed in Madagascar; the names of dead sovereigns are
equally under a ban, at least in some parts of the island. Thus
among the Sakalavas, when a king has died, the nobles and people
meet in council round the dead body and solemnly choose a new
name by which the deceased monarch shall be henceforth known.

After the new name has been adopted, the old name by which the king was known during his life becomes sacred and may not be pronounced under pain of death. Further, words in the common language which bear any resemblance to the forbidden name also become sacred and have to be replaced by others. Persons who uttered these forbidden words were looked on not only as grossly rude, but even as felons; they had committed a capital crime. However, these changes of vocabulary are confined to the district over which the deceased king reigned; in the neighbouring districts the old words continue to be employed in the old sense.

The sanctity attributed to the persons of chiefs in Polynesia naturally extended also to their names, which on the primitive view are hardly separable from the personality of their owners. Hence in Polynesia we find the same systematic prohibition to utter the names of chiefs or of common words resembling them which we have already met with in Zululand and Madagascar. Thus in New Zealand the name of a chief is held so sacred that, when it happens to be a common word, it may not be used in the language, and another has to be found to replace it. For example, a chief to the southward of East Cape bore the name of Maripi, which signified a knife, hence a new word (*nekra*) for knife was introduced, and the old one became obsolete. Elsewhere the word for water (*wai*) had to be changed, because it chanced to be the name of the chief, and would have been desecrated by being applied to the vulgar fluid as well as to his sacred person. This taboo naturally produced a plentiful crop of synonyms in the Maori language, and travellers newly arrived in the country were sometimes puzzled at finding the same things called by quite different names in neighbouring tribes. When a king comes to the throne in Tahiti, any words in the language that resemble his name in sound must be changed for others. In former times, if any man were so rash as to disregard this custom and to use the forbidden words, not only he but all his relations were immediately put to death. But the changes thus introduced were only temporary; on the death of the king the new words fell into disuse, and the original ones were revived.

In ancient Greece the names of the priests and other high officials who had to do with the performance of the Eleusinian mysteries might not be uttered in their lifetime. To pronounce them was a legal offence. The pedant in Lucian tells how he fell in with these august personages haling along to the police court a ribald fellow who had dared to name them, though well he knew that ever since their consecration it was unlawful to do so, because they had become anonymous, having lost their old names and acquired new and sacred titles. From two inscriptions found at Eleusis it appears that the names of the priests were committed to the depths of the sea; probably they were engraved on tablets of bronze or lead, which were then thrown into deep water in the Gulf of Salamis. The intention doubtless was to keep the names a profound secret; and how could that be done more surely than by sinking them in the sea? what human vision could spy them glimmering far down in the dim depths of the green water? A clearer illustration of the confusion between the incorporeal and the corporeal, between the name and its material embodiment, could hardly be found than in this practice of civilised Greece.

§ 5. *Names of Gods tabooed.* — Primitive man creates his gods in his own image. Xenophanes remarked long ago that the complexion of negro gods was black and their noses flat; that Thracian gods were ruddy and blue-eyed; and that if horses, oxen, and lions only believed in gods and had hands wherewith to portray them, they would doubtless fashion their deities in the form of horses, and oxen, and lions. Hence just as the furtive savage conceals his real name because he fears that sorcerers might make an evil use of it, so he fancies that his gods must likewise keep their true names secret, lest other gods or even men should learn the mystic sounds and thus be able to conjure with them. Nowhere was this crude conception of the secrecy and magical virtue of the divine name more firmly held or more fully developed than in ancient Egypt, where the superstitions of a dateless past were embalmed in the hearts of the people hardly less effectually than the bodies of cats and crocodiles and the rest of the divine menagerie in their rock-cut tombs. The conception is well illustrated by a story which tells how the subtle Isis wormed his secret name from Ra, the great Egyptian god of the sun. Isis, so runs the tale, was a woman mighty in words, and she was weary of the world of men, and yearned after the world of the gods. And she meditated in her heart, saying, 'Cannot I by virtue of the great name of Ra make myself a goddess and reign like him in heaven and earth?' For Ra had many names, but the great name which gave him all power over gods and men was known to none but himself. Now the god was by this time grown old; he slobbered at the mouth and his spittle fell upon the ground. So Isis gathered up the spittle and the earth with it, and kneaded thereof a serpent and laid it in the path where the great god passed every day to his double kingdom after his heart's desire. And when he came forth according to his wont, attended by all his company of gods, the sacred serpent stung him, and the god opened his mouth and cried, and his cry went up to heaven. And the company of gods cried, 'What aileth thee? and the gods shouted, 'Lo and behold!' But he could not answer; his jaws rattled, his limbs shook, the poison ran through his flesh as the Nile floweth over the land. When the great god had stilled his heart, he cried to his followers, 'Come to me, O my children, offspring of my body. I am a prince, the son of a prince, the divine seed of a god. My father devised my name; my father and my mother gave me my name, and it remained hidden in my body since my birth, that no magician might have magic power over me. I went out to behold that which I have made, I walked in the two lands which I have created, and lo! something stung me. What it was, I know not. Was it fire? was it water? My heart is on fire, my flesh trembleth, all my limbs do quake. Bring me the children of the gods with healing words and understanding lips, whose power reacheth to heaven.' Then came to him the children of the gods, and they were very sorrowful. And Isis came with her craft, whose mouth is full of the breath of life, whose spells chase pain away, whose word maketh the dead to live. She said, 'What is it, divine Father? what is it?' The holy god opened his mouth, he spake and said, 'I went upon my way, I walked after my heart's desire in the two regions which I have made to behold that which I have created, and lo! a serpent that I saw not stung me. Is it fire? is it water? I am colder than water, I am hotter than fire, all my limbs sweat, I tremble, mine eye is not steadfast, I behold not the sky, the moisture bedeweth my face as in summer-time.' Then spake Isis, 'Tell me thy name, divine Father, for the man shall live who is called by his name.' Then answered Ra, 'I created the heavens and the earth, I ordered the mountains, I made the great and wide sea, I stretched out the two horizons like a curtain. I am he who openeth his eyes and it is light, and who shutteth them and it is dark. At his command the Nile riseth, but the gods know not his name. I am Khepera in the morning, I am Ra at noon, I am Tum at eve.' But the poison was not taken away from him; it pierced deeper, and the great god could no longer walk. Then said Isis to him, 'That was not thy name that thou spakest unto me. Oh tell me, that the poison may depart; for he shall live whose name is named.' Now the poison burned like fire, it was hotter than the flame of fire. The god said, 'I consent that Isis shall search into me, and that my name shall pass from my breast into hers.' Then the god hid himself from the gods, and his place in the ship of eternity was empty. Thus was the name of the great god taken from him, and Isis, the witch, spake, 'Flow away poison, depart from Ra. It is I, even I, who overcome the poison and cast it to the earth; for the name of the great god hath been taken away from him. Let Ra live and let the poison die.' Thus spake great Isis, the queen of the gods, she who knows Ra and his true name.

From this story it appears that the real name of the god, with which his power was inextricably bound up, was supposed to be lodged, in an almost physical sense, somewhere in his breast, from which Isis extracted it by a sort of surgical operation and transferred with all its supernatural powers to herself. In Egypt attempts like that of Isis to appropriate the power of a high god by possessing herself of his name were not mere legends of the mythical beings of a remote past; every Egyptian magician aspired to wield like powers by similar means. For it was believed that he who possessed the true name possessed the very being of god or man, and could force even a deity to obey him as a slave obeys his master. Thus the art of the magician consisted in obtaining from the gods a revelation of their sacred names, and he left no stone unturned to accomplish his end. When once a god in a moment of weakness or forgetfulness had imparted to the wizard the wondrous lore, the deity had no choice but to submit humbly to the man or pay the penalty of his contumacy.

The belief in the magic virtue of divine names was shared by the Romans. When they sat down before a city, the priests addressed the guardian deity of the place in a set form of prayer or incantation, inviting him to abandon the beleaguered city and come over to the Romans, who would treat him as well as or better than he had ever been treated in his old home. Hence the name of the guardian deity of Rome was kept a profound secret, lest the enemies of the republic might lure him away, even as the Romans themselves had induced many gods to desert, like rats, the falling fortunes of cities that had sheltered them in happier days. Nay, the real name, not merely of its guardian deity, but of the city itself, was wrapt in mystery and might never be uttered, not even in the sacred rites. A certain Valerius Soranus, who dared to divulge the priceless secret, was put to death or came to a bad end. In like manner, it seems, the ancient Assyrians were forbidden to mention the mystic names of their cities; and down to modern times the Cheremiss of the Caucasus keep the names of their communal villages secret from motives of superstition.

If the reader has had the patience to follow this examination of the superstitions attaching to personal names, he will probably agree that the mystery in which the names of royal personages are so often shrouded is no isolated phenomenon, no arbitrary expression of courtly servility and adulation, but merely the particular application of a general law of primitive thought, which includes within its scope common folk and gods as well as kings and priests.

CHAPTER XXIII

OUR DEBT TO THE SAVAGE

IT would be easy to extend the list of royal and priestly taboos, but the instances collected in the preceding pages may suffice as specimens. To conclude this part of our subject it only remains to state summarily the general conclusions to which our enquiries have thus far conducted us. We have seen that in savage or barbarous society there are often found men to whom the superstition of their fellows ascribes a controlling influence over the general course of nature. Such men are accordingly adored and

treated as gods. Whether these human divinities also hold
temporal sway over the lives and fortunes of their adorers, or
whether their functions are purely spiritual and supernatural, in
other words, whether they are kings as well as gods or only the
latter, is a distinction which hardly concerns us here. Their
supposed divinity is the essential fact with which we have to deal.
In virtue of it they are a pledge and guarantee to their worshippers
of the continuance and orderly succession of those physical
phenomena upon which mankind depends for subsistence.
Naturally, therefore, the life and health of such a god-man are
matters of anxious concern to the people whose welfare and even
existence are bound up with his; naturally he is constrained by
them to conform to such rules as the wit of early man has devised
for averting the ills to which flesh is heir, including the last ill,
death. These rules, as an examination of them has shown, are
nothing but the maxims with which, on the primitive view, every
man of common prudence must comply if he would live long in
the land. But while in the case of ordinary men the observance
of the rules is left to the choice of the individual, in the case of
the god-man it is enforced under penalty of dismissal from his
high station, or even of death. For his worshippers have far too
great a stake in his life to allow him to play fast and loose with
it. Therefore all the quaint superstitions, the old-world maxims,
the venerable saws which the ingenuity of savage philosophers
elaborated long ago, and which old women at chimney corners
still impart as treasures of great price to their descendants
gathered round the cottage fire on winter evenings — all these
antique fancies clustered, all these cobwebs of the brain were
spun about the path of the old king, the human god, who,
immeshed in them like a fly in the toils of a spider, could hardly
stir a limb for the threads of custom, 'light as air but strong as
links of iron,' that crossing and recrossing each other in an endless maze bound him fast within a network of observances from
which death or deposition alone could release him.

Thus to students of the past the life of the old kings and priests
teems with instruction. In it was summed up all that passed for
wisdom when the world was young. It was the perfect pattern
after which every man strove to shape his life; a faultless model
constructed with rigorous accuracy upon the lines laid down by

a barbarous philosophy. Crude and false as that philosophy may seem to us, it would be unjust to deny it the merit of logical consistency. Starting from a conception of the vital principle as a tiny being or soul existing in, but distinct and separable from, the living being, it deduces for the practical guidance of life a system of rules which in general hangs well together and forms a fairly complete and harmonious whole. The flaw — and it is a fatal one — of the system lies not in its reasoning, but in its premises; in its conception of the nature of life, not in any irrelevancy of the conclusions which it draws from that conception. But to stigmatise these premises as ridiculous because we can easily detect their falseness, would be ungrateful as well as unphilosophical. We stand upon the foundation reared by the generations that have gone before, and we can but dimly realise the painful and prolonged efforts which it has cost humanity to struggle up to the point, no very exalted one after all, which we have reached. Our gratitude is due to the nameless and forgotten toilers, whose patient thought and active exertions have largely made us what we are. The amount of new knowledge which one age, certainly which one man, can add to the common store is small, and it argues stupidity or dishonesty, besides ingratitude, to ignore the heap while vaunting the few grains which it may have been our privilege to add to it. There is indeed little danger at present of undervaluing the contributions which modern times and even classical antiquity have made to the general advancement of our race. But when we pass these limits, the case is different. Contempt and ridicule or abhorrence and denunciation are too often the only recognition vouchsafed to the savage and his ways. Yet of the benefactors whom we are bound thankfully to commemorate, many, perhaps most, were savages. For when all is said and done our resemblances to the savage are still far more numerous than our differences from him; and what we have in common with him, and deliberately retain as true and useful, we owe to our savage forefathers who slowly acquired by experience and transmitted to us by inheritance those seemingly fundamental ideas which we are apt to regard as original and intuitive. We are like heirs to a fortune which has been handed down for so many ages that the memory of those who built it up is lost, and its possessors for the time being regard it as having been an original and unalterable possession of their race since the beginning of the world. But reflection and enquiry should satisfy us that to our predecessors we are indebted for much of what we thought most our own, and that their errors were not wilful extravagances or the ravings of insanity, but simply hypotheses, justifiable as such at the time when they were propounded, but which a fuller experience has proved to be inadequate. It is only by the successive testing of hypotheses and rejection of the false that truth is at last elicited. After all, what we call truth is only the hypothesis which is found to work best. Therefore in reviewing the opinions and practices of ruder ages and races we shall do well to look with leniency upon their errors as inevitable slips made in the search for truth, and to give them the benefit of that indulgence which we ourselves may one day stand in need of: *cum excusatione itaque veteres audiendi sunt.*

CHAPTER XXIV

THE KILLING OF THE DIVINE KING

§ 1. *The Mortality of the Gods.* — Man has created gods in his own likeness and being himself mortal he has naturally supposed his creatures to be in the same sad predicament. Thus the Greenlanders believed that a wind could kill their most powerful god, and that he would certainly die if he touched a dog. When they heard of the Christian God, they kept asking if he never died, and being informed that he did not, they were much surprised, and said that he must be a very great god indeed. In answer to the enquiries of Colonel Dodge, a North American Indian stated that the world was made by the Great Spirit. Being asked which Great Spirit he meant, the good one or the bad one, 'Oh, neither of *them*,' replied he, 'the Great Spirit that made the world is dead long ago. He could not possibly have lived as long as this.' A tribe in the Philippine Islands told the Spanish conquerors that the grave of the Creator was upon the top of Mount Cabunian. Heitsi-eibib, a god or divine hero of the Hottentots, died several times and came to life again. His graves are generally to be met with in narrow defiles between mountains. When the Hottentots pass one of them, they throw a stone on it for good luck, sometimes muttering 'Give us plenty of cattle.' The grave of Zeus, the great god of Greece, was shown to visitors in Crete as late as about the beginning of our era. The body of Dionysus was buried at Delphi beside the golden statue of Apollo, and his tomb bore the inscription, 'Here lies Dionysus dead, the son of Semele.' According to one account, Apollo himself was buried at Delphi; for Pythagoras is said to have carved an inscription on his tomb, setting forth how the god had been killed by the python and buried under the tripod.

The great gods of Egypt themselves were not exempt from the common lot. They too grew old and died. But when at a later time the discovery of the art of embalming gave a new lease of life to the souls of the dead by preserving their bodies for an indefinite time from corruption, the deities were permitted to share the benefit of an invention which held out to gods as well as to men a reasonable hope of immortality. Every province then had the tomb and mummy of its dead god. The mummy of Osiris was to be seen at Mendes; Thinis boasted of the mummy of Anhouri; and Heliopolis rejoiced in the possession of that of Toumou. The high gods of Babylon also, though they appeared to their worshippers only in dreams and visions, were conceived to be human in their bodily shape, human in their passions, and human in their fate; for like men they were born into the world, and like men they loved and fought and died.

§ 2. *Kings killed when their Strength fails.* — If the high gods, who dwell remote from the fret and fever of this earthly life, are yet believed to die at last, it is not to be expected that a god who lodges in a frail tabernacle of flesh should escape the same fate, though we hear of African kings who have imagined themselves immortal by virtue of their sorceries. Now primitive peoples, as we have seen, sometimes believe that their safety and even that of the world is bound up with the life of one of these god-men or human incarnations of the divinity. Naturally, therefore, they take the utmost care of his life, out of a regard for their own. But no amount of care and precaution will prevent the man-god from growing old and feeble and at last dying. His worshippers have to lay their account with this sad necessity and to meet it as best they can. The danger is a formidable one; for if the course of nature is dependent on the man-god's life, what catastrophes may not be expected from the gradual enfeeblement of his powers and their final extinction in death? There is only one way of averting these dangers. The man-god must be killed as soon as he shows symptoms that his powers are beginning to fail, and his soul must be transferred to a vigorous successor before it has been seriously impaired by the threatened decay. The advantages of thus putting the man-god to death instead of allowing him to die of old age and disease are, to the savage, obvious enough. For if the man-god dies what we call a natural death, it means, according to the savage, that his soul has either voluntarily departed from his body and refuses to return, or more commonly that it has been extracted, or at least detained in its wanderings, by a demon or sorcerer. In any of these cases the soul of the man-god is lost to his worshippers, and with it their prosperity is gone and their very existence endangered. Even if they could arrange to catch the soul of the dying god as it left his lips or his nostrils and so transfer it to a successor, this would not effect their purpose; for, dying of disease, his soul would necessarily leave his body in the last stage of weakness and exhaustion, and so enfeebled it would continue to drag out a languid, inert existence in any body to which it might be transferred. Whereas by slaying him his worshippers could, in the first place, make sure of catching his soul as it escaped and transferring it to a suitable successor; and, in the second place, by putting him to death before his natural force was abated, they would secure that the world should not fall into decay with the decay of the man-god. Every purpose, therefore, was answered, and all dangers averted by thus killing the man-god and transferring his soul, while yet at its prime, to a vigorous successor.

The mystic kings of Fire and Water in Cambodia are not allowed to die a natural death. Hence when one of them is seriously ill and the elders think that he cannot recover, they stab him to death. The people of Congo believed, as we have seen, that if their pontiff the Chitomé were to die a natural death, the world would perish, and the earth, which he alone sustained by his power and merit, would immediately be annihilated. Accordingly when he fell ill and seemed likely to die, the man who was destined to be his successor entered the pontiff's house with a rope or a club and strangled or clubbed him to death. The Ethiopian kings of Meroe were worshipped as gods; but whenever the priests chose, they sent a messenger to the king, ordering him to die, and alleging an oracle of the gods as their authority for the command. This command the kings always obeyed down to the reign of Ergamenes, a contemporary of Ptolemy II., King of Egypt. Having received a Greek education which emancipated him from the superstitions of his countrymen, Ergamenes ventured to disregard the command of the priests, and, entering the Golden Temple with a body of soldiers, put the priests to the sword.

Customs of the same sort appear to have prevailed in this part of Africa down to modern times. In some tribes of Fazoql the king had to administer justice daily under a certain tree. If from sickness or any other cause he was unable to discharge this duty for three whole days, he was hanged on the tree in a noose, which contained two razors so arranged that when the noose was drawn tight by the weight of the king's body they cut his throat.

A custom of putting their divine kings to death at the first symptoms of infirmity or old age prevailed until lately, if indeed it is even now extinct and not merely dormant, among the Shilluk of the White Nile, and in recent years it has been carefully investigated by Dr. C. G. Seligman. The reverence which the Shilluk pay to their king appears to arise chiefly from the conviction that he is a reincarnation of the spirit of Nyakang, the semi-divine hero who founded the dynasty and settled the tribe in their present territory. It is a fundamental article of the Shilluk creed that the spirit of the divine or semi-divine Nyakang is incarnate in the reigning king, who is accordingly himself invested to some extent with the character of a divinity. But while the Shilluk hold their kings in high, indeed religious reverence and take every precaution against their accidental death, nevertheless they cherish 'the conviction that the king must not be allowed to become ill or senile, lest with his diminishing vigour the cattle should sicken and fail to bear their increase, the crops should rot in the fields, and man, stricken with disease, should die in ever-increasing numbers.' To prevent these calamities it used to be the regular custom with the Shilluk to put the king to death whenever he showed signs of ill-health or failing strength. One of the fatal symptoms of decay was taken to be an incapacity to satisfy the sexual passions of his wives, of whom he has very many, distributed in a large number of houses at Fashoda. When this ominous weakness manifested itself, the wives reported it to the chiefs, who are popularly said to have intimated to the king his doom by spreading a white cloth over his face and knees as he lay slumbering in the heat of the sultry afternoon. Execution soon followed the sentence of death. A hut was specially built for the occasion: the king was led into it and lay down with his head resting on the lap of a nubile virgin: the door of the hut was then walled up; and the couple were left without food, water, or fire to die of hunger and suffocation. This was the old custom, but it was abolished some five generations ago on account of the excessive sufferings of one of the kings who perished in this way. It is said that the chiefs announce his fate to the king, and that afterwards he is strangled in a hut which has been specially built for the occasion.

From Dr. Seligman's enquiries it appears that not only was the Shilluk king liable to be killed with due ceremony at the first symptoms of incipient decay, but even while he was yet in the prime of health and strength he might be attacked at any time by a rival and have to defend his crown in a combat to the death. According to the common Shilluk tradition any son of a king had the right thus to fight the king in possession and, if he succeeded in killing him, to reign in his stead. As every king had a large harem and many sons, the number of possible candidates for the throne at any time may well have been not inconsiderable, and the reigning monarch must have carried his life in his hand. But the attack on him could only take place with any prospect of success at night; for during the day the king surrounded himself with his friends and bodyguards, and an aspirant to the throne could hardly hope to cut his way through them and strike home. It was otherwise at night. For then the guards were dismissed and the king was alone in his enclosure with his favourite wives, and there was no man near to defend him except a few herdsmen, whose huts stood a little way off. The hours of darkness were therefore the season of peril for the king. It is said that he used to pass them in constant watchfulness, prowling round his huts fully armed, peering into the blackest shadows, or himself standing silent and alert, like a sentinel on duty, in some dark corner. When at last his rival appeared, the fight would take place in grim silence, broken only by the clash of spears and shields, for it was a point of honour with the king not to call the herdsmen to his assistance.

Like Nyakang himself, their founder, each of the Shilluk kings after death is worshipped at a shrine, which is erected over his grave, and the grave of a king is always in the village where he was born. The tomb-shrine of a king resembles the shrine of Nyakang, consisting of a few huts enclosed by a fence; one of the huts is built over the king's grave, the others are occupied by the guardians of the shrine. Indeed the shrines of Nyakang and the shrines of the kings are scarcely to be distinguished from each other, and the religious rituals observed at all of them are identical in form and vary only in matters of detail, the variations being due apparently to the far greater sanctity attributed to the shrines of Nyakang. The grave-shrines of the kings are tended by certain old men or women, who correspond to the guardians of the shrines of Nyakang. They are usually widows or old men-servants of the deceased king, and when they die they are succeeded in their office by their descendants. Moreover, cattle are dedicated to the grave-shrines of the kings and sacrifices are offered at them just as at the shrines of Nyakang.

In general the principal element in the religion of the Shilluk would seem to be the worship which they pay to their sacred or divine kings, whether dead or alive. These are believed to be animated by a single divine spirit, which has been transmitted from the semi-mythical, but probably in substance historical, founder of the dynasty through all his successors to the present day. Hence, regarding their kings as incarnate divinities on whom the welfare of men, of cattle, and of the corn implicitly depends, the Shilluk naturally pay them the greatest respect and take every care of them; and however strange it may seem to us, their custom of putting the divine king to death as soon as he shows signs of ill-health or failing strength springs directly from their profound veneration for him and from their anxiety to preserve him, or rather the divine spirit by which he is animated, in the most perfect state of efficiency: nay, we may go further and say that their practice of regicide is the best proof they can give of the high regard in which they hold their kings. For they believe, as we have seen, that the king's life or spirit is so sympathetically bound up with the prosperity of the whole country, that if he fell ill or grew senile the cattle would sicken and cease to multiply, the crops would rot in the fields, and men would perish of widespread disease. Hence, in their opinion, the only way of averting these calamities is to put the king to death while he is still hale and hearty, in order that the divine spirit which he has inherited from his predecessors may be transmitted in turn by him to his successor while it is still in full vigour and has not yet been impaired by the weakness of disease and old age. In this connexion the particular symptom which is commonly said to seal the king's death-warrant is highly significant; when he can no longer satisfy the passions of his numerous wives, in other words, when he has ceased, whether partially or wholly, to be able to reproduce his kind, it is time for him to die and to make room for a more vigorous successor. Taken along with the other reasons which are alleged for putting the king to death, this one suggests that the fertility of men, of cattle, and of the crops is believed to depend sympathetically on the generative power of the king, so that the complete failure of that power in him would involve a corresponding failure in men, animals, and plants, and would thereby entail at no distant date the entire extinction of all life, whether human, animal, or vegetable. No wonder, that with such a danger before their eyes the Shilluk should be most careful not to let the king die what we should call a natural death of sickness or old age. It is characteristic of their attitude towards the death of the kings that they refrain from speaking of it as death: they do not say that a king has died but simply that he has 'gone away' like his divine ancestors Nyakang and Dag, the two first kings of the dynasty, both of whom are reported not to have died but to have disappeared. The similar legends of the mysterious disappearance of early kings in other lands, for example at Rome and in Uganda, may well point to a similar custom of putting them to death for the purpose of preserving their life.

On the whole the theory and practice of the divine kings of the Shilluk correspond very nearly to the theory and practice of the priests of Nemi, the Kings of the Wood, if my view of the latter is correct. In both we see a series of divine kings on whose life the fertility of men, of cattle, and of vegetation is believed to depend, and who are put to death, whether in single combat or otherwise, in order that their divine spirit may be transmitted to their successors in full vigour, uncontaminated by the weakness and decay of sickness or old age, because any such degeneration on the part of the king would, in the opinion of his worshippers, entail a corresponding degeneration on mankind, on cattle, and on the crops. Some points in this explanation of the custom of putting divine kings to death, particularly the method of transmitting their divine souls to their successors, will be dealt with more fully in the sequel. Meantime we pass to other examples of the general practice.

The Dinka are a congeries of independent tribes in the valley of the White Nile. They are essentially a pastoral people, passionately devoted to the care of their numerous herds of oxen, though they also keep sheep and goats, and the women cultivate small quantities of millet and sesame. For their crops and above all for their pastures they depend on the regularity of the rains: in seasons of prolonged drought they are said to be reduced to great extremities. Hence the rain-maker is a very important personage among them to this day; indeed the men in authority whom travellers dub chiefs or sheikhs are in fact the actual or potential rain-makers of the tribe or community. Each of them is believed to be animated by the spirit of a great rain-maker, which has come down to him through a succession of rain-makers; and in virtue of this inspiration a successful rain-maker enjoys very great power and is consulted on all important matters. Yet in spite, or rather in virtue, of the high honour in which he is held, no Dinka rain-maker is allowed to die a natural death of sickness or old age; for the Dinka believe that if such an untoward event were to happen, the tribe would suffer from disease and famine, and the herds would not yield their increase. So when a rain-maker feels that he is growing old and infirm, he tells his children that he wishes to die. Among the Agar Dinka a large grave is dug and the rain-maker lies down in it, surrounded by his friends and relatives. From time to time he speaks to the people, recalling the past history of the tribe, reminding them how he has ruled and advised them, and instructing them how they are to act in the future. Then, when he has concluded his admonition, he bids them cover him up. So the earth is thrown down on him as he lies in the grave, and he soon dies of suffocation. Such, with minor variations, appears to be the regular end of the honourable career of a rain-maker in all the Dinka tribes. The Khor-Adar Dinka told Dr. Seligman that when they have dug the grave for their rain-maker they strangle him in his house. The father and paternal uncle of one of Dr. Seligman's informants had both been rain-makers and both had been killed in the most regular and orthodox fashion. Even if a rain-maker is quite young he will be put to death should he seem likely to perish of disease. Further, every precaution is taken to prevent a rain-maker from dying an accidental death, for such an end, though not nearly so serious a matter as death from illness or old age, would be sure to entail sickness on the tribe. As soon as a rain-maker is killed, his valuable spirit is supposed to pass to a suitable successor, whether a son or other near blood relation.

In the Central African kingdom of Bunyoro down to recent years custom required that as soon as the king fell seriously ill or began to break up from age, he should die by his own hand; for, according to an old prophecy, the throne would pass away from the dynasty if ever the king were to die a natural death. He killed himself by draining a poisoned cup. If he faltered or were too ill to ask for the cup, it was his wife's duty to administer the poison. When the king of Kibanga, on the Upper Congo, seems near his end, the sorcerers put a rope round his neck, which they draw gradually tighter till he dies. If the king of Gingiro happens to be wounded in war, he is put to death by his comrades, or, if they fail to kill him, by his kinsfolk, however hard he may beg for mercy. They say they do it that he may not die by the hands of his enemies. The Jukos are a heathen tribe of the Benue river, a great tributary of the Niger. In their country 'the town of Gatri is ruled by a king who is elected by the big men of the town as follows. When in the opinion of the big men the king has reigned long enough, they give out that "the king is sick" — a formula understood by all to mean that they are going to kill him, though the intention is never put more plainly. They then decide who is to be the next king. How long he is to reign is settled by the influential men at a meeting; the question is put and answered by each man throwing on the ground a little piece of stick for each year he thinks the new king should rule. The king is then told, and a great feast prepared, at which the king gets drunk on guinea-corn beer. After that he is speared, and the man who was chosen becomes king. Thus each Juko king knows that he cannot have very many more years to live, and that he is certain of his predecessor's fate. This, however, does not seem to frighten candidates. The same custom of king-killing is said to prevail at Quonde and Wukari as well as at Gatri.' In the three Hausa kingdoms of Gobir, Katsina, and Daura, in Northern Nigeria, as soon as a king showed signs of failing health or growing infirmity, an official who bore the title of Killer of the Elephant appeared and throttled him.

The Matiamvo is a great king or emperor in the interior of Angola. One of the inferior kings of the country, by name Challa, gave to a Portuguese expedition the following account of the manner in which the Matiamvo comes by his end. 'It has been customary,' he said, 'for our Matiamvos to die either in war or by a violent death, and the present Matiamvo must meet this last fate, as, in consequence of his great exactions, he has lived long enough. When we come to this understanding, and decide that he should be killed, we invite him to make war with our enemies, on which occasion we all accompany him and his family to the war, when we lose some of our people. If he escapes unhurt, we return to the war again and fight for three or four days. We then suddenly abandon him and his family to their fate, leaving him in the enemy's hands. Seeing himself thus deserted, he causes his throne to be erected, and, sitting down, calls his family around him. He then orders his mother to approach; she kneels at his feet; he first cuts off her head, then decapitates his sons in succession, next his wives and relatives, and, last of all, his most beloved wife, called Anacullo. This slaughter being accomplished, the Matiamvo, dressed in all his pomp, awaits his own death, which immediately follows, by an officer sent by the powerful neighbouring chiefs, Caniquinha and Canica. This officer first cuts off his legs and arms at the joints, and lastly he cuts off his head; after which the head of the officer is struck off. All the potentates retire from the encampment, in order not to witness his death. It is my duty to remain and witness his death, and to mark the place where the head and arms have been deposited by the two great chiefs, the enemies of the Matiamvo. They also take possession of all the property belonging to the deceased monarch and his family, which they convey to their own residence. I then provide for the funeral of the mutilated remains of the late Matiamvo, after which I retire to his capital and proclaim the new government. I then return to where the head, legs, and arms have been deposited, and, for forty slaves, I ransom them, together with the merchandise and other property belonging to the deceased, which I give up to the new Matiamvo, who has been proclaimed. This is what has happened to many Matiamvos, and what must happen to the present one.'

It appears to have been a Zulu custom to put the king to death as soon as he began to have wrinkles or grey hairs. At least this seems implied in the following passage written by one who resided for some time at the court of the notorious Zulu tyrant Chaka, in the early part of the nineteenth century: 'The extraordinary violence of the king's rage with me was mainly occasioned by that absurd nostrum, the hair oil, with the notion of which Mr. Farewell had impressed him as being a specific for removing all indications of age. From the first moment of his having heard that such a preparation was attainable, he evinced a solicitude to procure it, and on every occasion never forgot to remind us of his anxiety respecting it; more especially on our departure on the mission his injunctions were particularly directed to this object. It will be seen that it is one of the barbarous customs of the Zoolas in their choice or election of their kings that he must neither have wrinkles nor grey hairs, as they are both distinguishing marks of disqualification for becoming a monarch of a warlike people. It is also equally indispensable that their king should never exhibit those proofs of having become unfit and incompetent to reign; it is therefore important that they should conceal these indications so long as they possibly can. Chaka had become greatly apprehensive of the approach of grey hairs; which would at once be the signal for him to prepare to make his exit from this sublunary world, it being always followed by the death of the monarch.' The writer to whom we are indebted for this instructive anecdote of the hair oil omits to specify the mode in which a grey-haired and wrinkled Zulu chief used 'to make his exit from this sublunary world'; but on analogy we may conjecture that he was killed.

The custom of putting kings to death as soon as they suffered from any personal defect prevailed two centuries ago in the Caffre kingdom of Sofala. We have seen that these kings of Sofala were regarded as gods by their people, being entreated to give rain or sunshine, according as each might be wanted. Nevertheless a slight bodily blemish, such as the loss of a tooth, was considered a sufficient cause for putting one of these god-men to death, as we learn from the following passage of an old Portuguese historian: 'It was formerly the custom of the kings of this land to commit suicide by taking poison when any disaster or natural physical defect fell upon them, such as impotence, infectious disease, the loss of their front teeth, by which they were disfigured, or any other deformity or affliction. To put an end to such defects they killed themselves, saying that the king should be free from any blemish, and if not, it was better for his honour that he should die and seek another life where he would be made whole, for there everything was perfect. But the Quiteve (king) who reigned when I was in those parts would not imitate his predecessors in this, being discreet and dreaded as he was; for having lost a front tooth he caused it to be proclaimed throughout the kingdom that all should be aware that he had lost a tooth and should recognise him when they saw him without it, and if his predecessors killed themselves for such things they were very foolish, and he would not do so; on the contrary, he would be very sorry when the time came for him to die a natural death, for his life was very necessary to preserve his kingdom and defend it from his enemies; and he recommended his successors to follow his example.'

The king of Sofala who dared to survive the loss of his front tooth was thus a bold reformer like Ergamenes, king of Ethiopia. We may conjecture that the ground for putting the Ethiopian kings to death was, as in the case of the Zulu and Sofala kings, the appearance on their person of any bodily defect or sign of decay; and that the oracle which the priests alleged as the authority for the royal execution was to the effect that great calamities would result from the reign of a king who had any blemish on his body; just as an oracle warned Sparta against a 'lame reign,' that is, the reign of a lame king. It is some confirmation of this conjecture that the kings of Ethiopia were chosen for their size, strength, and beauty long before the custom of killing them was abolished. To this day the Sultan of Wadai must have no obvious bodily defect, and the king of Angoy cannot be crowned if he has a single blemish, such as a broken or a filed tooth or the scar of an old wound. According to the Book of Acaill and many other authorities no king who was afflicted with a personal blemish might reign over Ireland at Tara. Hence, when the great King Cormac Mac Art lost one eye by an accident, he at once abdicated.

Many days' journey to the north-east of Abomey, the old capital of Dahomey, lies the kingdom of Eyeo. 'The Eyeos are governed by a king, no less absolute than the king of Dahomey, yet subject to a regulation of state, at once humiliating and extraordinary. When the people have conceived an opinion of his ill-government, which is sometimes insidiously infused into them by the artifice of his discontented ministers, they send a deputation to him with a present of parrots' eggs, as a mark of its authenticity, to represent to him that the burden of government must have so far fatigued him that they consider it full time for him to repose from his cares and indulge himself with a little sleep. He thanks his subjects for their attention to his ease, retires to his own apartment as if to sleep, and there gives directions to his women to strangle him. This is immediately executed, and his son quietly ascends the throne upon the usual terms of holding the reins of government no longer than whilst he merits the approbation of the people.' About the year 1774, a king of Eyeo, whom his ministers attempted to remove in the customary manner, positively refused to accept the proffered parrots' eggs at their hands, telling them that he had no mind to take a nap, but on the contrary was resolved to watch for the benefit of his subjects. The ministers, surprised and indignant at his recalcitrancy, raised a rebellion, but were defeated with great slaughter, and thus by his spirited conduct the king freed himself from the tyranny of his councillors and established a new precedent for the guidance of his successors. However, the old custom seems to have revived and persisted until late in the nineteenth century, for a Catholic missionary, writing in 1884, speaks of the practice as if it were still in vogue. Another missionary, writing in 1881, thus describes the usage of the Egbas and the Yorubas of West Africa: 'Among the customs of the country one of the most curious is unquestionably that of judging and punishing the king. Should he have earned the hatred of his people by exceeding his rights, one of his councillors, on whom the heavy duty is laid, requires of the prince that he shall "go to sleep," which means simply "take poison and die." If his courage fails him at the supreme moment, a friend renders him this last service, and quietly, without betraying the secret, they prepare the people for the news of the king's death. In Yoruba the thing is managed a little differently. When a son is born to the king of Oyo, they make a model of the infant's right foot in clay and keep it in the house of the elders (*ogboni*). If the king fails to observe the customs of the country, a messenger, without speaking a word, shows him his child's foot. The king knows what that means. He takes poison and goes to sleep.' The old Prussians acknowledged as their supreme lord a ruler who governed them in the name of the gods, and was known as 'God's Mouth.' When he felt himself weak and ill, if he wished to leave a good name behind him, he had a great heap made of thorn-bushes and straw, on which he mounted and delivered a long sermon to the people, exhorting them to serve the gods and promising to go to the gods and speak for the people. Then he took some of the perpetual fire which burned in front of the holy oak-tree, and lighting the pile with it burned himself to death.

§ 3. *Kings killed at the End of a Fixed Term.* — In the cases hitherto described, the divine king or priest is suffered by his people to retain office until some outward defect, some visible symptom of failing health or advancing age, warns them that he is no longer equal to the discharge of his divine duties; but not until such symptoms have made their appearance is he put to death. Some peoples, however, appear to have thought it unsafe to wait for even the slightest symptom of decay and have preferred to kill the king while he was still in the full vigour of life. Accordingly, they have fixed a term beyond which he might not reign, and at the close of which he must die, the term fixed upon being short enough to exclude the probability of his degenerating physically in the interval. In some parts of Southern India the period fixed was twelve years. Thus, according to an old traveller, in the province of Quilacare, 'there is a Gentile house of prayer, in which there is an idol which they hold in great account, and every twelve years they celebrate a great feast to it, whither all the Gentiles go as to a jubilee. This temple possesses many lands and much revenue: it is a very great affair. This province has a king over it, who has not more than twelve years to reign from jubilee to jubilee. His manner of living is in this wise, that is to say: when the twelve years are completed, on the day of this feast there assemble together innumerable people, and much money is spent in giving food to Bramans. The king has a wooden scaffolding made, spread over with silken hangings: and on that day he goes to bathe at a tank with great ceremonies and sound of music, after that he comes to the idol and prays to it, and mounts on to the scaffolding, and there before all the people he takes some very sharp knives, and begins to cut off his nose, and then his ears, and his lips, and all his members, and as much flesh off himself as he can; and he throws it away very hurriedly until so much of his blood is spilled that he begins to faint, and then he cuts his throat himself. And he performs this sacrifice to the idol, and whoever desires to reign other twelve years and undertake this martyrdom for love of the idol, has to be present looking on at this: and from that place they raise him up as king.'

The king of Calicut, on the Malabar coast, bears the title of Samorin or Samory. He 'pretends to be of a higher rank than the Brahmans, and to be inferior only to the invisible gods; a pretention that was acknowledged by his subjects, but which is held as absurd and abominable by the Brahmans, by whom he is only treated as a Sudra.' Formerly the Samorin had to cut his throat in public at the end of a twelve years' reign. But towards the end of the seventeenth century the rule had been modified as follows: 'Many strange customs were observed in this country in former times, and some very odd ones are still continued. It was an ancient custom for the Samorin to reign but twelve years, and no longer. If he died before his term was expired, it saved him a troublesome ceremony of cutting his own throat, on a publick scaffold erected for the purpose. He first made a feast for all his nobility and gentry, who are very numerous. After the feast he saluted his guests, and went on the scaffold, and very decently cut his own throat in the view of the assembly, and his body was, a little while after, burned with great pomp and ceremony, and the grandees elected a new Samorin. Whether that custom was a religious or a civil ceremony, I know not, but it is now laid aside. And a new custom is followed by the modern Samorins, that jubilee is proclaimed throughout his dominions, at the end of twelve years, and a tent is pitched for him in a spacious plain, and a great feast is celebrated for ten or twelve days, with mirth and jollity, guns firing night and day, so at the end of the feast any four of the guests that have a mind to gain a crown by a desperate action, in fighting their way through 30 or 40,000 of his guards, and kill the Samorin in his tent, he that kills him succeeds him in his empire. In anno 1695, one of those jubilees happened, and the tent pitched near Pennany, a seaport of his, about fifteen leagues to the southward of Calicut. There were but three men that would venture on that desperate action, who fell in, with sword and target, among the guard, and, after they had killed and wounded many, were themselves killed. One of the desperadoes had a nephew of fifteen or sixteen years of age, that kept close by his uncle in the attack on the guards, and, when he saw him fall, the youth got through the guards into the tent, and made a stroke at his Majesty's head, and had certainly despatched him if a large brass lamp which was burning over his head had not marred the blow; but, before he could make another, he was killed by the guards; and, I believe, the same Samorin reigns yet. I chanced to come that time along the coast and heard the guns for two or three days and nights successively.'

The English traveller, whose account I have quoted, did not himself witness the festival he describes, though he heard the sound of the firing in the distance. Fortunately, exact records of these festivals and of the number of men who perished at them have been preserved in the archives of the royal family at Calicut. In the latter part of the nineteenth century they were examined by Mr. W. Logan, with the personal assistance of the reigning king, and from his work it is possible to gain an accurate conception both of the tragedy and of the scene where it was periodically enacted down to 1743, when the ceremony took place for the last time.

The festival at which the king of Calicut staked his crown and his life on the issue of battle was known as the 'Great Sacrifice.' It fell every twelfth year, when the planet Jupiter was in retrograde motion in the sign of the Crab, and it lasted twenty-eight days, culminating at the time of the eighth lunar asterism in the month of Makaram. As the date of the festival was determined by the position of Jupiter in the sky, and the interval between two festivals was twelve years, which is roughly Jupiter's period of revolution round the sun, we may conjecture that the splendid planet was supposed to be in a special sense the king's star and to rule his destiny, the period of its revolution in heaven corresponding to the period of his reign on earth. However that may be, the ceremony was observed with great pomp at the Tirunavayi temple, on the north bank of the Ponnani River. The spot is close to the present railway line. As the train rushes by, you can just catch a glimpse of the temple, almost hidden behind a clump of trees on the river bank. From the western gateway of the temple a perfectly straight road, hardly raised above the level of the surrounding rice-fields and shaded by a fine avenue, runs for half a mile to a high ridge with a precipitous bank, on which the outlines of three or four terraces can still be traced. On the topmost of these terraces the king took his stand on the eventful day. The view which it commands is a fine one. Across the flat expanse of the rice-fields, with the broad placid river winding through them, the eye ranges eastward to high tablelands, their lower slopes embowered in woods, while afar off looms the great chain of the western Ghauts, and in the furthest distance the Neilgherries or Blue Mountains, hardly distinguishable from the azure of the sky above.

But it was not to the distant prospect that the king's eyes naturally turned at this crisis of his fate. His attention was arrested by a spectacle nearer at hand. For all the plain below was alive with troops, their banners waving gaily in the sun, the white tents of their many camps standing sharply out against the green and gold of the rice-fields. Forty thousand fighting men or more were gathered there to defend the king. But if the plain swarmed with soldiers, the road that cuts across it from the temple to the king's stand was clear of them. Not a soul was stirring on it. Each side of the way was barred by palisades, and from the palisades on either hand a long hedge of spears, held by strong arms, projected into the empty road, their blades meeting in the middle and forming a glittering arch of steel. All was now ready. The king waved his sword. At the same moment a great chain of massy gold, enriched with bosses, was placed on an elephant at his side. That was the signal. On the instant a stir might be seen half a mile away at the gate of the temple. A group of swordsmen, decked with flowers and smeared with ashes, has stepped out from the crowd. They have just partaken of their last meal on earth, and they now receive the last blessings and farewells of their friends. A moment more and they are coming down the lane of spears, hewing and stabbing right and left at the spearmen, winding and turning and writhing among the blades as if they had no bones in their bodies. It is all in vain. One after the other they fall, some nearer the king, some farther off, content to die, not for the shadow of a crown, but for the mere sake of approving their dauntless valour and swordsmanship to the world. On the last days of the festival the same magnificent display of gallantry, the same useless sacrifice of life was repeated again and again. Yet perhaps no sacrifice is wholly useless which proves that there are men who prefer honour to life.

'It is a singular custom in Bengal,' says an old native historian of India, 'that there is little of hereditary descent in succession to the sovereignty. . . . Whoever kills the king, and succeeds in placing himself on that throne, is immediately acknowledged as king; all the *amirs*, *wazirs*, soldiers, and peasants instantly obey and submit to him, and consider him as being as much their sovereign as they did their former prince, and obey his orders implicitly. The people of Bengal say, "We are faithful to the throne; whoever fills the throne we are obedient and true to it." ' A custom of the same sort formerly prevailed in the little kingdom of Passier, on the northern coast of Sumatra. The old Portuguese historian De Barros, who informs us of it, remarks with surprise that no wise man would wish to be king of Passier, since the monarch was not allowed by his subjects to live long. From time to time a sort of fury seized the people, and they marched through the streets of the city chanting with loud voices the fatal words, 'The king must die!' When the king heard that song of death he knew that his hour had come. The man who struck the fatal blow was of the royal lineage, and as soon as he had done the deed of blood and seated himself on the throne he was regarded as the legitimate king, provided that he contrived to maintain his seat peaceably for a single day. This, however, the regicide did not always succeed in doing. When Fernão Peres d'Andrade, on a voyage to China, put in at Passier for a cargo of spices, two kings were massacred, and that in the most peaceable and orderly manner, without the smallest sign of tumult or sedition in the city, where everything went on in its usual course, as if the murder or execution of a king were a matter of everyday occurrence. Indeed, on one occasion three kings were raised to the dangerous elevation and followed each other on the dusty road of death in a single day. The people defended the custom, which they esteemed very laudable and even of divine institution, by saying that God would never allow so high and mighty a being as a king, who reigned as his vicegerent on earth, to perish by violence unless for his sins he thoroughly deserved it. Far away from the tropical island of Sumatra a rule of the same sort appears to have obtained among the old Slavs. When the captives Gunn and Jarmerik contrived to slay the king and queen of the Slavs and made their escape, they were pursued by the barbarians, who shouted after them that if they would only come back they would reign instead of the murdered monarch, since by a public statute of the ancients the succession to the throne fell to the king's assassin. But the flying regicides turned a deaf ear to promises which they regarded as mere baits to lure them back to destruction; they continued their flight, and the shouts and clamour of the barbarians gradually died away in the distance.

When kings were bound to suffer death, whether at their own hands or at the hands of others, on the expiration of a fixed term of years, it was natural that they should seek to delegate the painful duty, along with some of the privileges of sovereignty, to a substitute who should suffer vicariously in their stead. This expedient appears to have been resorted to by some of the princes of Malabar. Thus we are informed by a native authority on that country that 'in some places all powers both executive and judicial were delegated for a fixed period to natives by the sovereign. This institution was styled *Thalavettiparothiam* or authority obtained by decapitation. . . . It was an office tenable for five years during which its bearer was invested with supreme despotic powers within his jurisdiction. On the expiry of the five years the man's head was cut off and thrown up in the air amongst a large concourse of villagers, each of whom vied with the other in trying to catch it in its course down. He who succeeded was nominated to the post for the next five years.'

When once kings, who had hitherto been bound to die a violent death at the end of a term of years, conceived the happy thought of dying by deputy in the persons of others, they would very naturally put it in practice; and accordingly we need not wonder at finding so popular an expedient, or traces of it, in many lands. Scandinavian traditions contain some hints that of old the Swedish kings reigned only for periods of nine years, after which they were put to death or had to find a substitute to die in their stead. Thus Aun or On, king of Sweden, is said to have sacrificed to Odin for length of days and to have been answered by the god that he should live so long as he sacrificed one of his sons every ninth year. He sacrificed nine of them in this manner, and would have sacrificed the tenth and last, but the Swedes would not allow him. So he died and was buried in a mound at Upsala. Another indication of a similar tenure of the crown occurs in a curious legend of the deposition and banishment of Odin. Offended at his misdeeds, the other gods outlawed and exiled him, but set up in his place a substitute, Oller by name, a cunning wizard, to whom they accorded the symbols both of royalty and of godhead. The deputy bore the name of Odin, and reigned for nearly ten years, when he was driven from the throne, while the real Odin came to his own again. His discomfited rival retired to Sweden and was afterwards slain in an attempt to repair his shattered fortunes. As gods are often merely men who loom large through the mists of tradition, we may conjecture that this Norse legend preserves a confused reminiscence of ancient Swedish kings who reigned for nine or ten years together, then abdicated, delegating to others the privilege of dying for their country. The great festival which was held at Upsala every nine years may have been the occasion on which the king or his deputy was put to death. We know that human sacrifices formed part of the rites.

There are some grounds for believing that the reign of many ancient Greek kings was limited to eight years, or at least that at the end of every period of eight years a new consecration, a fresh outpouring of the divine grace, was regarded as necessary in order to enable them to discharge their civil and religious duties. Thus it was a rule of the Spartan constitution that every eighth year

the ephors should choose a clear and moonless night and sitting
down observe the sky in silence. If during their vigil they saw a
meteor or shooting star, they inferred that the king had sinned
against the deity, and they suspended him from his functions until
the Delphic or Olympic oracle should reinstate him in them.
This custom, which has all the air of great antiquity, was not
suffered to remain a dead letter even in the last period of the
Spartan monarchy; for in the third century before our era a
king, who had rendered himself obnoxious to the reforming party,
was actually deposed on various trumped-up charges, among
which the allegation that the ominous sign had been seen in the
sky took a prominent place.

   If the tenure of the regal office was formerly limited among
the Spartans to eight years, we may naturally ask, why was that
precise period selected as the measure of a king's reign? The
reason is probably to be found in those astronomical considerations which determined the early Greek calendar. The difficulty
of reconciling lunar with solar time is one of the standing puzzles
which has taxed the ingenuity of men who are emerging from
barbarism. Now an octennial cycle is the shortest period at the
end of which sun and moon really mark time together after
overlapping, so to say, throughout the whole of the interval.
Thus, for example, it is only once in every eight years that the
full moon coincides with the longest or shortest day; and as this
coincidence can be observed with the aid of a simple dial, the
observation is naturally one of the first to furnish a base for a
calendar which shall bring lunar and solar times into tolerable,
though not exact, harmony. But in early days the proper adjustment of the calendar is a matter of religious concern, since on
it depends a knowledge of the right seasons for propitiating the
deities whose favour is indispensable to the welfare of the
community. No wonder, therefore, that the king, as the chief
priest of the state, or as himself a god, should be liable to
deposition or death at the end of an astronomical period. When
the great luminaries had run their course on high, and were about
to renew the heavenly race, it might well be thought that the king
should renew his divine energies, or prove them unabated, under
pain of making room for a more vigorous successor. In Southern
India, as we have seen, the king's reign and life terminated with

the revolution of the planet Jupiter round the sun. In Greece, on the other hand, the king's fate seems to have hung in the balance at the end of every eight years, ready to fly up and kick the beam as soon as the opposite scale was loaded with a falling star.

Whatever its origin may have been, the cycle of eight years appears to have coincided with the normal length of the king's reign in other parts of Greece besides Sparta. Thus Minos, king of Cnossus in Crete, whose great palace has been unearthed in recent years, is said to have held office for periods of eight years together. At the end of each period he retired for a season to the oracular cave on Mount Ida, and there communed with his divine father Zeus, giving him an account of his kingship in the years that were past, and receiving from him instructions for his guidance in those which were to come. The tradition plainly implies that at the end of every eight years the king's sacred powers needed to be renewed by intercourse with the godhead, and that without such a renewal he would have forfeited his right to the throne.

Without being unduly rash we may surmise that the tribute of seven youths and seven maidens whom the Athenians were bound to send to Minos every eight years had some connexion with the renewal of the king's power for another octennial cycle. Traditions varied as to the fate which awaited the lads and damsels on their arrival in Crete; but the common view appears to have been that they were shut up in the labyrinth, there to be devoured by the Minotaur, or at least to be imprisoned for life. Perhaps they were sacrificed by being roasted alive in a bronze image of a bull, or of a bull-headed man, in order to renew the strength of the king and of the sun, whom he personated. This at all events is suggested by the legend of Talos, a bronze man who clutched people to his breast and leaped with them into the fire, so that they were roasted alive. He is said to have been given by Zeus to Europa, or by Hephaestus to Minos, to guard the island of Crete, which he patrolled thrice daily. According to one account he was a bull, according to another he was the sun. Probably he was identical with the Minotaur, and stripped of his mythical features was nothing but a bronze image of the sun represented as a man with a bull's head. In order to renew the solar fires, human victims may have been sacrificed to the idol by being roasted in its hollow body or placed on its sloping hands and allowed to roll into a pit of fire. It was in the latter fashion that the Carthaginians sacrificed their offspring to Moloch. The children were laid on the hands of a calf-headed image of bronze, from which they slid into a fiery oven, while the people danced to the music of flutes and timbrels to drown the shrieks of the burning victims. The resemblance which the Cretan traditions bear to the Carthaginian practice suggests that the worship associated with the names of Minos and the Minotaur may have been powerfully influenced by that of a Semitic Baal. In the tradition of Phalaris, tyrant of Agrigentum, and his brazen bull we may have an echo of similar rites in Sicily, where the Carthaginian power struck deep roots.

In the province of Lagos the Ijebu tribe of the Yoruba race is divided into two branches, which are known respectively as the Ijebu Ode and the Ijebu Remon. The Ode branch of the tribe is ruled by a chief who bears the title of Awujale and is surrounded by a great deal of mystery. Down to recent times his face might not be seen even by his own subjects, and if circumstances obliged him to communicate with them he did so through a screen which hid him from view. The other or Remon branch of the Ijebu tribe is governed by a chief, who ranks below the Awujale. Mr. John Parkinson was informed that in former times this subordinate chief used to be killed with ceremony after a rule of three years. As the country is now under British protection the custom of putting the chief to death at the end of a three years' reign has long been abolished, and Mr. Parkinson was unable to ascertain any particulars on the subject.

At Babylon, within historical times, the tenure of the kingly office was in practice lifelong, yet in theory it would seem to have been merely annual. For every year at the festival of Zagmuk the king had to renew his power by seizing the hands of the image of Marduk in his great temple of Esagil at Babylon. Even when Babylon passed under the power of Assyria, the monarchs of that country were expected to legalise their claim to the throne every year by coming to Babylon and performing the ancient ceremony at the New Year festival, and some of them found the obligation so burdensome that rather than discharge it they renounced the title of king altogether and contented themselves with the humbler one of Governor. Further, it would appear that in remote times, though not within the historical period, the kings of Babylon or their barbarous predecessors forfeited not merely their crown but their life at the end of a year's tenure of office. At least this is the conclusion to which the following evidence seems to point. According to the historian Berosus, who as a Babylonian priest spoke with ample knowledge, there was annually celebrated in Babylon a festival called the Sacaea. It began on the sixteenth day of the month Lous, and lasted for five days, during which masters and servants changed places, the servants giving orders and the masters obeying them. A prisoner condemned to death was dressed in the king's robes, seated on the king's throne, allowed to issue whatever commands he pleased, to eat, drink, and enjoy himself, and to lie with the king's concubines. But at the end of the five days he was stripped of his royal robes, scourged, and hanged or impaled. During his brief term of office he bore the title of Zoganes. This custom might perhaps have been explained as merely a grim jest perpetrated in a season of jollity at the expense of an unhappy criminal. But one circumstance — the leave given to the mock king to enjoy the king's concubines — is decisive against this interpretation. Considering the jealous seclusion of an oriental despot's harem we may be quite certain that permission to invade it would never have been granted by the despot, least of all to a condemned criminal, except for the very gravest cause. This cause could hardly be other than that the condemned man was about to die in the king's stead, and that to make the substitution perfect it was necessary he should enjoy the full rights of royalty during his brief reign. There is nothing surprising in this substitution. The rule that the king must be put to death either on the appearance of any symptom of bodily decay or at the end of a fixed period is certainly one which, sooner or later, the kings would seek to abolish or modify. We have seen that in Ethiopia, Sofala, and Eyeo the rule was boldly set aside by enlightened monarchs; and that in Calicut the old custom of killing the king at the end of twelve years was changed into a permission granted to any one at the end of the twelve years' period to attack the king, and, in the event of killing him, to reign in his stead; though, as the king took care at these times to be surrounded by his guards, the permission was little more than a form. Another way of modifying the stern old rule is seen in the Babylonian custom just described. When the time drew near for the king to be put to death (in Babylon this appears to have been at the end of a single year's reign) he abdicated for a few days, during which a temporary king reigned and suffered in his stead. At first the temporary king may have been an innocent person, possibly a member of the king's own family; but with the growth of civilisation the sacrifice of an innocent person would be revolting to the public sentiment, and accordingly a condemned criminal would be invested with the brief and fatal sovereignty. In the sequel we shall find other examples of a dying criminal representing a dying god. For we must not forget that, as the case of the Shilluk kings clearly shows, the king is slain in his character of a god or a demigod, his death and resurrection, as the only means of perpetuating the divine life unimpaired, being deemed necessary for the salvation of his people and the world.

A vestige of a practice of putting the king to death at the end of a year's reign appears to have survived in the festival called Macahity, which used to be celebrated in Hawaii during the last month of the year. About a hundred years ago a Russian voyager described the custom as follows: 'The taboo Macahity is not unlike to our festival of Christmas. It continues a whole month, during which the people amuse themselves with dances, plays, and sham-fights of every kind. The king must open this festival wherever he is. On this occasion his majesty dresses himself in his richest cloak and helmet, and is paddled in a canoe along the shore, followed sometimes by many of his subjects. He embarks early, and must finish his excursion at sunrise. The strongest and most expert of the warriors is chosen to receive him on his landing. The warrior watches the canoe along the beach; and as soon as the king lands, and has thrown off his cloak, he darts his spear at him, from a distance of about thirty paces, and the king must either catch the spear in his hand, or suffer from it: there is no jesting in the business. Having caught it, he carries it under his arm, with the sharp end downwards, into the temple or *heavoo*. On his entrance, the assembled multitude begin their sham-fights, and immediately the air is obscured by clouds of spears, made for the occasion with blunted ends. Hamamea [the king] has been frequently advised to abolish this ridiculous ceremony, in which he risks his life every year; but to no effect. His answer always is, that he is as able to catch a spear as any one on the island is to throw it at him. During the Macahity, all punishments are remitted throughout the country; and no person can leave the place in which he commences these holidays, let the affair be ever so important.'

That a king should regularly have been put to death at the close of a year's reign will hardly appear improbable when we learn that to this day there is still a kingdom in which the reign and the life of the sovereign are limited to a single day. In Ngoio, a province of the ancient kingdom of Congo, the rule obtains that the chief who assumes the cap of sovereignty is always killed on the night after his coronation. The right of succession lies with the chief of the Musurongo; but we need not wonder that he does not exercise it, and that the throne stands vacant. 'No one likes to lose his life for a few hours' glory on the Ngoio throne.'

CHAPTER XXV

TEMPORARY KINGS

IN some places the modified form of the old custom of regicide which appears to have prevailed at Babylon has been further softened down. The king still abdicates annually for a short time and his place is filled by a more or less nominal sovereign; but at the close of his short reign the latter is no longer killed, though sometimes a mock execution still survives as a memorial of the time when he was actually put to death. To take examples. In the month of Méac (February) the king of Cambodia annually abdicated for three days. During this time he performed no act of authority, he did not touch the seals, he did not even receive the revenues which fell due. In his stead there reigned a temporary king called Sdach Méac, that is, King February. The office of temporary king was hereditary in a family distantly connected with the royal house, the sons succeeding the fathers and the

N

younger brothers the elder brothers just as in the succession to the real sovereignty. On a favourable day fixed by the astrologers the temporary king was conducted by the mandarins in triumphal procession. He rode one of the royal elephants, seated in the royal palanquin, and escorted by soldiers who, dressed in appropriate costumes, represented the neighbouring peoples of Siam, Annam, Laos, and so on. In place of the golden crown he wore a peaked white cap, and his regalia, instead of being of gold encrusted with diamonds, were of rough wood. After paying homage to the real king, from whom he received the sovereignty for three days, together with all the revenues accruing during that time (though this last custom has been omitted for some time), he moved in procession round the palace and through the streets of the capital. On the third day, after the usual procession, the temporary king gave orders that the elephants should trample under foot the 'mountain of rice,' which was a scaffold of bamboo surrounded by sheaves of rice. The people gathered up the rice, each man taking home a little with him to secure a good harvest. Some of it was also taken to the king, who had it cooked and presented to the monks.

In Siam on the sixth day of the moon in the sixth month (the end of April) a temporary king is appointed, who for three days enjoys the royal prerogatives, the real king remaining shut up in his palace. The temporary king sends his numerous satellites in all directions to seize and confiscate whatever they can find in the bazaar and open shops; even the ships and junks which arrive in harbour during the three days are forfeited to him and must be redeemed. He goes to a field in the middle of the city, whither they bring a gilded plough drawn by gaily-decked oxen. After the plough has been anointed and the oxen rubbed with incense, the mock king traces nine furrows with the plough, followed by aged dames of the palace scattering the first seed of the season. As soon as the nine furrows are drawn, the crowd of spectators rushes in and scrambles for the seed which has just been sown, believing that, mixed with the seed-rice, it will ensure a plentiful crop. Then the oxen are unyoked, and rice, maize, sesame, sago, bananas, sugar-cane, melons, and so on, are set before them; whatever they eat first will, it is thought, be dear in the year following, though some people interpret the omen in the opposite sense. During this time the temporary king stands leaning against a tree with his right foot resting on his left knee. From standing thus on one foot he is popularly known as King Hop; but his official title is Phaya Phollathep, 'Lord of the Heavenly Hosts.' He is a sort of Minister of Agriculture: all disputes about fields, rice, and so forth, are referred to him. There is moreover another ceremony in which he personates the king. It takes place in the second month (which falls in the cold season) and lasts three days. He is conducted in procession to an open space opposite the Temple of the Brahmans, where there are a number of poles dressed like May-poles, upon which the Brahmans swing. All the while that they swing and dance, the Lord of the Heavenly Hosts has to stand on one foot upon a seat which is made of bricks plastered over, covered with a white cloth, and hung with tapestry. He is supported by a wooden frame with a gilt canopy, and two Brahmans stand one on each side of him. The dancing Brahmans carry buffalo horns with which they draw water from a large copper cauldron and sprinkle it on the spectators; this is supposed to bring good luck, causing the people to dwell in peace and quiet, health and prosperity. The time during which the Lord of the Heavenly Hosts has to stand on one foot is about three hours. This is thought 'to prove the dispositions of the Devattas and spirits.' If he lets his foot down 'he is liable to forfeit his property and have his family enslaved by the king; as it is believed to be a bad omen, portending destruction to the state, and instability to the throne. But if he stand firm he is believed to have gained a victory over evil spirits, and he has moreover the privilege, ostensibly at least, of seizing any ship which may enter the harbour during these three days, and taking its contents, and also of entering any open shop in the town and carrying away what he chooses.'

Such were the duties and privileges of the Siamese King Hop down to about the middle of the nineteenth century or later. Under the reign of the late enlightened monarch this quaint personage was to some extent both shorn of the glories and relieved of the burden of his office. He still watches, as of old, the Brahmans rushing through the air in a swing suspended between two tall masts, each some ninety feet high; but he is allowed to sit instead of stand, and, although public opinion still expects him to keep his right foot on his left knee during the whole of the ceremony, he would incur no legal penalty were he, to the great chagrin of the people, to put his weary foot to the ground. Other signs, too, tell of the invasion of the East by the ideas and civilisation of the West. The thoroughfares that lead to the scene of the performance are blocked with carriages: lamp-posts and telegraph posts, to which eager spectators cling like monkeys, rise above the dense crowd; and, while a tatterdemalion band of the old style, in gaudy garb of vermilion and yellow, bangs and tootles away on drums and trumpets of an antique pattern, the procession of bare-footed soldiers in brilliant uniforms steps briskly along to the lively strains of a modern military band playing 'Marching through Georgia.'

On the first day of the sixth month, which was regarded as the beginning of the year, the king and people of Samarcand used to put on new clothes and cut their hair and beards. Then they repaired to a forest near the capital where they shot arrows on horseback for seven days. On the last day the target was a gold coin, and he who hit it had the right to be king for one day. In Upper Egypt on the first day of the solar year by Coptic reckoning, that is, on the tenth of September, when the Nile has generally reached its highest point, the regular government is suspended for three days and every town chooses its own ruler. This temporary lord wears a sort of tall fool's cap and a long flaxen beard, and is enveloped in a strange mantle. With a wand of office in his hand and attended by men disguised as scribes, executioners, and so forth, he proceeds to the Governor's house. The latter allows himself to be deposed; and the mock king, mounting the throne, holds a tribunal, to the decisions of which even the governor and his officials must bow. After three days the mock king is condemned to death; the envelope or shell in which he was encased is committed to the flames, and from its ashes the Fellah creeps forth. The custom perhaps points to an old practice of burning a real king in grim earnest. In Uganda the brothers of the king used to be burned, because it was not lawful to shed the royal blood.

The Mohammedan students of Fez, in Morocco, are allowed to appoint a sultan of their own, who reigns for a few weeks, and is known as *Sultan t-tulba,* 'the Sultan of the Scribes.' This brief authority is put up for auction and knocked down to the highest bidder. It brings some substantial privileges with it, for the holder is freed from taxes thenceforward, and he has the right of asking a favour from the real sultan. That favour is seldom refused; it usually consists in the release of a prisoner. Moreover, the agents of the student-sultan levy fines on the shopkeepers and householders, against whom they trump up various humorous charges. The temporary sultan is surrounded with the pomp of a real court, and parades the streets in state with music and shouting, while a royal umbrella is held over his head. With the so-called fines and free-will offerings, to which the real sultan adds a liberal supply of provisions, the students have enough to furnish forth a magnificent banquet; and altogether they enjoy themselves thoroughly, indulging in all kinds of games and amusements. For the first seven days the mock sultan remains in the college; then he goes about a mile out of the town and encamps on the bank of the river, attended by the students and not a few of the citizens. On the seventh day of his stay outside the town he is visited by the real sultan, who grants him his request and gives him seven more days to reign, so that the reign of 'the Sultan of the Scribes' nominally lasts three weeks. But when six days of the last week have passed the mock sultan runs back to the town by night. This temporary sultanship always falls in spring, about the beginning of April. Its origin is said to have been as follows. When Mulai Rasheed II was fighting for the throne in 1664 or 1665, a certain Jew usurped the royal authority at Taza. But the rebellion was soon suppressed through the loyalty and devotion of the students. To effect their purpose they resorted to an ingenious stratagem. Forty of them caused themselves to be packed in chests which were sent as a present to the usurper. In the dead of night, while the unsuspecting Jew was slumbering peacefully among the packing-cases, the lids were stealthily raised, the brave forty crept forth, slew the usurper, and took possession of the city in the name of the real sultan, who, to mark his gratitude for the help thus rendered him in time of need, conferred on the students the right of annually appointing a sultan of their own. The narrative has all the air of a fiction devised to explain an old custom, of which the real meaning and origin had been forgotten.

A custom of annually appointing a mock king for a single day was observed at Lostwithiel in Cornwall down to the sixteenth century. On 'little Easter Sunday,' the freeholders of the town and manor assembled together, either in person or by their deputies, and one among them, as it fell to his lot by turn, gaily attired and gallantly mounted, with a crown on his head, a sceptre in his hand, and a sword borne before him, rode through the principal street to the church, dutifully attended by all the rest on horseback. The clergyman in his best robes received him at the churchyard stile and conducted him to hear divine service. On leaving the church he repaired, with the same pomp, to a house provided for his reception. Here a feast awaited him and his suite, and being set at the head of the table he was served on bended knees, with all the rites due to the estate of a prince. The ceremony ended with the dinner, and every man returned home.

Sometimes the temporary king occupies the throne, not annually, but once for all at the beginning of each reign. Thus in the kingdom of Jambi in Sumatra it is the custom that at the beginning of a new reign a man of the people should occupy the throne and exercise the royal prerogatives for a single day. The origin of the custom is explained by a tradition that there were once five royal brothers, the four elder of whom all declined the throne on the ground of various bodily defects, leaving it to their youngest brother. But the eldest occupied the throne for one day, and reserved for his descendants a similar privilege at the beginning of every reign. Thus the office of temporary king is hereditary in a family akin to the royal house. In Bilaspur it seems to be the custom, after the death of a Rajah, for a Brahman to eat rice out of the dead Rajah's hand, and then to occupy the throne for a year. At the end of the year the Brahman receives presents and is dismissed from the territory, being forbidden apparently to return. 'The idea seems to be that the spirit of the Rájá enters into the Bráhman who eats the *khír* (rice and milk) out of his hand when he is dead, as the Brahman is apparently carefully watched during the whole year, and not allowed to go away.' The same or a similar custom is believed to obtain among the hill states about Kangra. The custom of banishing the Brahman who represents the king may be a substitute for putting him to death. At the installation of a prince of Carinthia a peasant, in whose family the office was hereditary, ascended a marble stone which stood surrounded by meadows in a spacious valley; on his right stood a black mother-cow, on his left a lean ugly mare. A rustic crowd gathered about him. Then the future prince, dressed as a peasant and carrying a shepherd's staff, drew near, attended by courtiers and magistrates. On perceiving him the peasant called out, 'Who is this whom I see coming so proudly along?' The people answered, 'The prince of the land.' The peasant was then prevailed on to surrender the marble seat to the prince on condition of receiving sixty pence, the cow and mare, and exemption from taxes. But before yielding his place he gave the prince a light blow on the cheek.

Some points about these temporary kings deserve to be specially noticed before we pass to the next branch of the evidence. In the first place, the Cambodian and Siamese examples show clearly that it is especially the divine or magical functions of the king which are transferred to his temporary substitute. This appears from the belief that by keeping up his foot the temporary king of Siam gained a victory over the evil spirits, whereas by letting it down he imperilled the existence of the state. Again, the Cambodian ceremony of trampling down the 'mountain of rice,' and the Siamese ceremony of opening the ploughing and sowing, are charms to produce a plentiful harvest, as appears from the belief that those who carry home some of the trampled rice, or of the seed sown, will thereby secure a good crop. Moreover, when the Siamese representative of the king is guiding the plough, the people watch him anxiously, not to see whether he drives a straight furrow, but to mark the exact point on his leg to which the skirt of his silken robe reaches; for on that is supposed to hang the state of the weather and the crops during the ensuing season. If the Lord of the Heavenly Hosts hitches up his garment above his knee, the weather will be wet and heavy rains will spoil the harvest. If he lets it trail to his ankle, a drought will be the consequence. But fine weather and heavy crops will follow if the hem of his robe hangs exactly half-way down the calf of his leg. So closely is the course of nature, and with it the weal or woe of the people, dependent on the minutest act or gesture of the king's representative. But the task of making the crops grow, thus deputed to the temporary kings, is one of the magical functions regularly supposed to be discharged by kings in primitive society. The rule that the mock king must stand on one foot upon a raised seat in the rice-field was perhaps originally meant as a charm to make the crop grow high; at least this was the object of a similar ceremony observed by the old Prussians. The tallest girl, standing on one foot upon a seat, with her lap full of cakes, a cup of brandy in her right hand and a piece of elm-bark or linden-bark in her left, prayed to the god Waizganthos that the flax might grow as high as she was standing. Then, after draining the cup, she had it refilled, and poured the brandy on the ground as an offering to Waizganthos, and threw down the cakes for his attendant sprites. If she remained steady on one foot throughout the ceremony, it was an omen that the flax crop would be good; but if she let her foot down, it was feared that the crop might fail. The same significance perhaps attaches to the swinging of the Brahmans, which the Lord of the Heavenly Hosts had formerly to witness standing on one foot. On the principles of homoeopathic or imitative magic it might be thought that the higher the priests swing the higher will grow the rice. For the ceremony is described as a harvest festival, and swinging is practised by the Letts of Russia with the avowed intention of influencing the growth of the crops. In the spring and early summer, between Easter and St. John's Day (the summer solstice), every Lettish peasant is said to devote his leisure hours to swinging diligently; for the higher he rises in the air the higher will his flax grow that season.

In the foregoing cases the temporary king is appointed annually in accordance with a regular custom. But in other cases the appointment is made only to meet a special emergency, such as to relieve the real king from some actual or threatened evil by diverting it to a substitute, who takes his place on the throne for a short time. The history of Persia furnishes instances of such occasional substitutes for the Shah. Thus Shah Abbas the Great, being warned by his astrologers in the year 1591 that a serious danger impended over him, attempted to avert the omen by abdicating the throne and appointing a certain unbeliever named Yusoofee, probably a Christian, to reign in his stead. The substitute was accordingly crowned, and for three days, if we may trust the Persian historians, he enjoyed not only the name and the state but the power of the king. At the end of his brief reign he was put to death; the decree of the stars was fulfilled by this sacrifice; and Abbas, who re-ascended his throne in a most propitious hour, was promised by his astrologers a long and glorious reign.

CHAPTER XXVI

SACRIFICE OF THE KING'S SON

A POINT to notice about the temporary kings described in the foregoing chapter is that in two places (Cambodia and Jambi) they come of a stock which is believed to be akin to the royal family. If the view here taken of the origin of these temporary kingships is correct, we can easily understand why the king's substitute should sometimes be of the same race as the king. When the king first succeeded in getting the life of another accepted as a sacrifice instead of his own, he would have to show that the death of that other would serve the purpose quite as well as his own would have done. Now it was as a god or demigod that the king had to die; therefore the substitute who died for him had to be invested, at least for the occasion, with the divine attributes of the king. This, as we have just seen, was certainly the case with the temporary kings of Siam and Cambodia; they were invested with the supernatural functions, which in an earlier stage of society were the special attributes of the king. But no one could so well represent the king in his divine character as his son, who might be supposed to share the divine afflatus of his father. No one, therefore, could so appropriately die for the king and, through him, for the whole people, as the king's son.

We have seen that according to tradition, Aun or On, King of Sweden, sacrificed nine of his sons to Odin at Upsala in order that his own life might be spared. After he had sacrificed his second son he received from the god an answer that he should live so long as he gave him one of his sons every ninth year. When he had sacrificed his seventh son, he still lived, but was so feeble that he could not walk but had to be carried in a chair. Then he offered up his eighth son, and lived nine years more, lying in his bed. After that he sacrificed his ninth son, and lived another nine years, but so that he drank out of a horn like a weaned child. He now wished to sacrifice his only remaining son to Odin, but the Swedes would not allow him. So he died and was buried in a mound at Upsala.

In ancient Greece there seems to have been at least one kingly house of great antiquity of which the eldest sons were always liable to be sacrificed in room of their royal sires. When Xerxes was marching through Thessaly at the head of his mighty host to attack the Spartans at Thermopylae, he came to the town of Alus. Here he was shown the sanctuary of Laphystian Zeus, about which his guides told him a strange tale. It ran somewhat as follows. Once upon a time the king of the country, by name Athamas, married a wife Nephele, and had by her a son called Phrixus and a daughter named Helle. Afterwards he took to himself a second wife called Ino, by whom he had two sons, Learchus and Melicertes. But his second wife was jealous of her step-children, Phrixus and Helle, and plotted their death. She went about very cunningly to compass her bad end. First of all she persuaded the women of the country to roast the seed corn secretly before it was committed to the ground. So next year no crops came up and the people died of famine. Then the king sent messengers to the oracle at Delphi to enquire the cause of the dearth. But the wicked stepmother bribed the messenger to give out as the answer of the god that the dearth would never cease till the children of Athamas by his first wife had been sacrificed to Zeus. When Athamas heard that, he sent for the children, who were with the sheep. But a ram with a fleece of gold opened his lips, and speaking with the voice of a man warned the children of their danger. So they mounted the ram and fled with him over land and sea. As they flew over the sea, the girl slipped from the animal's back, and falling into water was drowned. But her brother Phrixus was brought safe to the land of Colchis, where reigned a child of the Sun. Phrixus married the king's daughter, and she bore him a son Cytisorus. And there he sacrificed the ram with the golden fleece to Zeus the God of Flight; but some will have it that he sacrificed the animal to Laphystian Zeus. The golden fleece itself he gave to his wife's father, who nailed it to an oak tree, guarded by a sleepless dragon in a sacred grove of Ares. Meanwhile at home an oracle had commanded that King Athamas himself should be sacrificed as an expiatory offering for the whole country. So the people decked him with garlands like a victim and led him to the altar, where they were just about to sacrifice him when he was rescued either by his grandson Cytisorus, who arrived in the nick of time from Colchis, or by Hercules, who brought tidings that the king's son Phrixus was yet alive. Thus Athamas was saved, but afterwards he went mad, and mistaking his son Learchus for a wild beast shot him dead. Next he attempted the life of his remaining son Melicertes, but the child was rescued by his mother Ino, who ran and threw herself and him from a high rock into the sea. Mother and son were changed into marine divinities, and the son received special homage in the isle of Tenedos, where babes were sacrificed to him. Thus bereft of wife and children the unhappy Athamas quitted his country, and on enquiring of the oracle where he should dwell was told to take up his abode wherever he should be entertained by wild beasts. He fell in with a pack of wolves devouring sheep, and when they saw him they fled and left him the bleeding remnants of their prey. In this way the oracle was fulfilled. But because King Athamas had not been sacrificed as a sin-offering for the whole country, it was divinely decreed that the eldest male scion of his family in each generation should be sacrificed without fail, if ever he set foot in the town-hall, where the offerings were made to Laphystian Zeus by one of the house of Athamas. Many of the family, Xerxes was informed, had fled to foreign lands to escape this doom; but some of them had returned long afterwards, and being caught by the sentinels in the act of entering the town-hall were wreathed as victims, led forth in procession, and sacrificed. These instances appear to have been notorious, if not frequent; for the writer of a dialogue attributed to Plato, after speaking of the immolation of human victims by the Carthaginians, adds that such practices were not unknown among the Greeks, and he refers with horror to the sacrifices offered on Mount Lycaeus and by the descendants of Athamas.

The suspicion that this barbarous custom by no means fell into disuse even in later days is strengthened by a case of human sacrifice which occurred in Plutarch's time at Orchomenus, a very ancient city of Boeotia, distant only a few miles across the plain from the historian's birthplace. Here dwelt a family of which the men went by the name of Psoloeis or 'Sooty,' and the women by the name of Oleae or 'Destructive.' Every year at the festival of the Agrionia the priest of Dionysus pursued these women with a drawn sword, and if he overtook one of them he had the right to slay her. In Plutarch's lifetime the right was actually exercised by a priest Zoilus. The family thus liable to furnish at least one human victim every year was of royal descent, for they traced their lineage to Minyas, the famous old king of Orchomenus, the monarch of fabulous wealth, whose stately treasury, as it is called, still stands in ruins at the point where the long rocky hill of Orchomenus melts into the vast level expanse of the Copaic plain. Tradition ran that the king's three daughters long despised the other women of the country for yielding to the Bacchic frenzy, and sat at home in the king's house scornfully plying the distaff and the loom, while the rest, wreathed with flowers, their dishevelled locks streaming to the wind, roamed in ecstasy the barren mountains that rise above Orchomenus, making the solitude of the hills to echo to the wild music of cymbals and tambourines. But in time the divine fury infected even the royal damsels in their quiet chamber; they were seized with a fierce longing to partake of human flesh, and cast lots among themselves which should give up her child to furnish a cannibal feast. The lot fell on Leucippe, and she surrendered her son Hippasus, who was torn limb from limb by the three. From these misguided women sprang the Oleae and the Psoloeis, of whom the men were said to be so called because they wore sad-coloured raiment in token of their mourning and grief.

Now this practice of taking human victims from a family of royal descent at Orchomenus is all the more significant because Athamas himself is said to have reigned in the land of Orchomenus even before the time of Minyas, and because over against the city there rises Mount Laphystius, on which, as at Alus in Thessaly, there was a sanctuary of Laphystian Zeus, where, according to tradition, Athamas purposed to sacrifice his two children Phrixus and Helle. On the whole, comparing the traditions about Athamas with the custom that obtained with regard to his descendants in historical times, we may fairly infer that in Thessaly and probably in Boeotia there reigned of old a dynasty of which the kings were liable to be sacrificed for the good of the country to the god called Laphystian Zeus, but that they contrived to shift the fatal responsibility to their offspring, of whom the eldest son was regularly destined to the altar. As time went on, the cruel custom was so far mitigated that a ram was accepted as a vicarious sacrifice in room of the royal victim, provided always that the prince abstained from setting foot in the town-hall where the sacrifices were offered to Laphystian Zeus by one of his kinsmen. But if he were rash enough to enter the place of doom, to thrust himself wilfully, as it were, on the notice of the god who had good-naturedly winked at the substitution of a ram, the ancient obligation which had been suffered to lie in abeyance recovered all its force, and there was no help for it but he must die. The tradition which associated the sacrifice of the king or his children with a great dearth points clearly to the belief, so common among primitive folk, that the king is responsible for the weather and the crops, and that he may justly pay with his life for the inclemency of the one or the failure of the other. Athamas and his line, in short, appear to have united divine or magical with royal functions; and this view is strongly supported by the claims to divinity which Salmoneus, the brother of Athamas, is said to have set up. We have seen that this presumptuous mortal professed to be no other than Zeus himself, and to wield the thunder and lightning, of which he made a trumpery imitation by the help of tinkling kettles and blazing torches. If we may judge from analogy, his mock thunder and lightning were no mere scenic exhibition designed to deceive and impress the beholders; they were enchantments practised by the royal magician for the purpose of bringing about the celestial phenomena which they feebly mimicked.

Among the Semites of Western Asia the king, in a time of national danger, sometimes gave his own son to die as a sacrifice for the people. Thus Philo of Byblus, in his work on the Jews, says: 'It was an ancient custom in a crisis of great danger that the ruler of a city or nation should give his beloved son to die for the whole people, as a ransom offered to the avenging demons; and the children thus offered were slain with mystic rites. So Cronus, whom the Phoenicians call Israel, being king of the land and having an only-begotten son called Jeoud (for in the Phoenician tongue Jeoud signifies "only-begotten"), dressed him in royal robes and sacrificed him upon an altar in a time of war, when the country was in great danger from the enemy.' When the king of Moab was besieged by the Israelites and hard beset, he took his eldest son, who would have reigned in his stead, and offered him for a burnt offering on the wall.

CHAPTER XXVII

SUCCESSION TO THE SOUL

To the view that in early times, and among barbarous races, kings have frequently been put to death at the end of a short reign, it may be objected that such a custom would tend to the extinction of the royal family. The objection may be met by observing, first, that the kingship is often not confined to one family, but may be shared in turn by several; second, that the office is frequently not hereditary, but is open to men of any family, even to foreigners, who may fulfil the requisite conditions, such as marrying a princess or vanquishing the king in battle; and, third, that even if the custom did tend to the extinction of a dynasty, that is not a consideration which would prevent its observance among people less provident of the future and less heedful of human life than ourselves. Many races, like many individuals, have indulged in practices which must in the end destroy them. The Polynesians seem regularly to have killed two-thirds of their children. In some parts of East Africa the proportion of infants massacred at birth is said to be the same. Only children born in certain presentations are allowed to live. The Jagas, a conquering tribe in Angola, are reported to have put to death all their children, without exception, in order that the women might not be cumbered with babies on the march. They recruited their numbers by adopting boys and girls of thirteen or fourteen years of age, whose parents they had killed and eaten. Among the Mbaya Indians of South America the women used to murder all their children except the last, or the one they believed to be the last. If one of them had another child afterwards, she killed it. We need not wonder that this practice entirely destroyed a branch of the Mbaya nation, who had been for many years the most formidable enemies of the Spaniards. Among the Lengua Indians of the Gran Chaco, the missionaries discovered what they describe as 'a carefully planned system of racial suicide, by the practice of infanticide by abortion, and other methods.' Nor is infanticide the only mode in which a savage tribe commits suicide. A lavish use of the poison ordeal may be equally effective. Some time ago a small tribe named Uwet came down from the hill country, and settled on the left branch of the Calabar river in West Africa. When the missionaries first visited the place, they found the population considerable, distributed into three villages. Since then the constant use of the poison ordeal has almost extinguished the tribe. On one occasion the whole population took poison to prove their innocence. About half perished on the spot, and the remnant, we are told, still continuing their superstitious practice, must soon become extinct. With such examples before us we need not hesitate to believe that many tribes have felt no scruple or delicacy in observing a custom which tends to wipe out a single family. To attribute such scruples to them is to commit the common, the perpetually repeated mistake of judging the savage by the standard of European civilisation. If any of my readers set out with the notion that all races of men think and act much in the same way as educated Englishmen, the evidence of superstitious belief and custom collected in this work should suffice to disabuse him of so erroneous a prepossession.

The explanation here given of the custom of killing divine persons assumes, or at least is readily combined with, the idea that the soul of the slain divinity is transmitted to his successor. Of this transmission I have no direct proof except in the case of the Shilluk, among whom the practice of killing the divine king prevails in a typical form, and with whom it is a fundamental article of faith that the soul of the divine founder of the dynasty is immanent in every one of his slain successors. But if this is the only actual example of such a belief which I can adduce, analogy seems to render it probable that a similar succession to the soul of the slain god has been supposed to take place in other instances, though direct evidence of it is wanting. For it has been already shown that the soul of the incarnate deity is often supposed to transmigrate at death into another incarnation; and if this takes place when the death is a natural one, there seems no reason why it should not take place when the death has been brought about by violence. Certainly the idea that the soul of a dying person may be transmitted to his successor is perfectly familiar to primitive peoples. In Nias the eldest son usually succeeds his father in the chieftainship. But if from any bodily or mental defect the eldest son is disqualified for ruling, the father determines in his lifetime which of his sons shall succeed him. In order, however, to establish his right of succession, it is necessary that the son upon whom his father's choice falls shall catch in his mouth or in a bag the last breath, and with it the soul, of the dying chief. For whoever catches his last breath is chief equally with the appointed successor. Hence the other brothers, and sometimes also strangers, crowd round the dying man to catch his soul as it passes. The houses in Nias are raised above the ground on posts, and it has happened that when the dying man lay with his face on the floor, one of the candidates has bored a hole in the floor and sucked in the chief's last breath through a bamboo tube. When the chief has no son, his soul is caught in a bag, which is fastened to an image made to represent the deceased; the soul is then believed to pass into the image.

Sometimes it would appear that the spiritual link between a king and the souls of his predecessors is formed by the possession of some part of their persons. In Southern Celebes the regalia often consist of corporeal portions of deceased rajahs, which are treasured as sacred relics and confer the right to the throne. Similarly among the Sakalavas of Southern Madagascar a vertebra of the neck, a nail, and a lock of hair of a deceased king are placed in a crocodile's tooth and carefully kept along with the similar relics of his predecessors in a house set apart for the purpose. The possession of these relics constitutes the right to the throne. A legitimate heir who should be deprived of them would lose all his authority over the people, and on the contrary a usurper who should make himself master of the relics would be acknowledged king without dispute. When the Alake or king of Abeokuta in West Africa dies, the principal men decapitate his body, and placing the head in a large earthen vessel deliver it to the new sovereign; it becomes his fetish, and he is bound to pay it honours. Sometimes, in order apparently that the new sovereign may inherit more surely the magical and other virtues of the royal line, he is required to eat a piece of his dead predecessor. Thus at Abeokuta not only was the head of the late king presented to his successor, but the tongue was cut out and given him to eat. Hence, when the natives wish to signify that the sovereign reigns, they say, 'He has eaten the king.' A custom of the same sort is still practised at Ibadan, a large town in the interior of Lagos, West Africa. When the king dies his head is cut off and sent to his nominal suzerain, the Alafin of Oyo, the paramount king of Yoruba land; but his heart is eaten by his successor. This ceremony was performed not very many years ago at the accession of a new king of Ibadan.

Taking the whole of the preceding evidence into account, we may fairly suppose that when the divine king or priest is put to death his spirit is believed to pass into his successor. In point of fact, among the Shilluk of the White Nile, who regularly kill their divine kings, every king on his accession has to perform a ceremony which appears designed to convey to him the same sacred and worshipful spirit which animated all his predecessors, one after the other, on the throne.

CHAPTER XXVIII

THE KILLING OF THE TREE-SPIRIT

§ 1. *The Whitsuntide Mummers.* — It remains to ask what light the custom of killing the divine king or priest sheds upon the special subject of our enquiry. In an earlier part of this work we saw reason to suppose that the King of the Wood at Nemi was regarded as an incarnation of a tree-spirit or of the spirit of vegetation, and that as such he would be endowed, in the belief of his worshippers, with a magical power of making the trees to bear fruit, the crops to grow, and so on. His life must therefore have been held very precious by his worshippers, and was probably hedged in by a system of elaborate precautions or taboos like those by which, in so many places, the life of the man-god has been guarded against the malignant influence of demons and sorcerers. But we have seen that the very value attached to the life of the man-god necessitates his violent death as the only means of preserving it from the inevitable decay of age. The same reasoning would apply to the King of the Wood; he, too, had to be killed in order that the divine spirit, incarnate in him, might be transferred in its integrity to his successor. The rule that he held office till a stronger should slay him might be supposed to secure both the preservation of his divine life in full vigour and its transference to a suitable successor as soon as that vigour began to be impaired. For so long as he could maintain his position by the strong hand, it might be inferred that his natural force was not abated; whereas his defeat and death at the hands of another proved that his strength was beginning to fail and that it was time his divine life should be lodged in a less dilapidated tabernacle. This explanation of the rule that the King of the Wood had to be slain by his successor at least renders that rule perfectly intelligible. It is strongly supported by the theory and practice of the Shilluk, who put their divine king to death at the first signs of failing health, lest his decrepitude should entail a corresponding failure of vital energy on the corn, the cattle, and men. Moreover, it is countenanced by the analogy of the Chitomé, upon whose life the existence of the world was supposed to hang, and who was therefore slain by his successor as soon as he showed signs of breaking up. Again, the terms on which in later times the King of Calicut held office are identical with those attached to the office of King of the Wood, except that whereas the former might be assailed by a candidate at any time, the King of Calicut might only be attacked once every twelve years. But as the leave granted to the King of Calicut to reign so long as he could defend himself against all comers was a mitigation of the old rule which set a fixed term to his life, so we may conjecture that the similar permission granted to the King of the Wood was a mitigation of an older custom of putting him to death at the end of a definite period. In both cases the new rule gave to the god-man at least a chance for his life, which under the old rule was denied him; and people probably reconciled themselves to the change by reflecting that so long as the god-man could maintain himself by the sword against all assaults, there was no reason to apprehend that the fatal decay had set in.

The conjecture that the King of the Wood was formerly put to death at the expiry of a fixed term, without being allowed a chance for his life, will be confirmed if evidence can be adduced of a custom of periodically killing his counterparts, the human representatives of the tree-spirit, in Northern Europe. Now in point of fact such a custom has left unmistakable traces of itself in the rural festivals of the peasantry. To take examples.

At Niederpöring, in Lower Bavaria, the Whitsuntide representative of the tree-spirit — the *Pfingstl* as he was called — was clad from top to toe in leaves and flowers. On his head he wore a high pointed cap, the ends of which rested on his shoulders, only two holes being left in it for his eyes. The cap was covered with water-flowers and surmounted with a nosegay of peonies. The sleeves of his coat were also made of water-plants, and the rest of his body was enveloped in alder and hazel leaves. On each side of him marched a boy holding up one of the *Pfingstl's* arms. These two boys carried drawn swords, and so did most of the others who formed the procession. They stopped at every house where they hoped to receive a present; and the people, in hiding, soused the leaf-clad boy with water. All rejoiced when he was well drenched. Finally he waded into the brook up to his middle; whereupon one of the boys, standing on the bridge, pretended to cut off his head. At Wurmlingen, in Swabia, a score of young fellows dress themselves on Whit-Monday in white shirts and white trousers, with red scarves round their waists and swords hanging from the scarves. They ride on horseback into the wood, led by two trumpeters blowing their trumpets. In the wood they cut down leafy oak branches, in which they envelop from head to foot him who was the last of their number to ride out of the village. His legs, however, are encased separately, so that he may be able to mount his horse again. Further, they give him a long artificial neck, with an artificial head and a false face on the top of it. Then a May-tree is cut, generally an aspen or beech about ten feet high; and being decked with coloured handkerchiefs and ribbons it is entrusted to a special 'May-bearer.' The cavalcade then returns with music and song to the village. Amongst the personages who figure in the procession are a Moorish king with a sooty face and a crown on his head, a Dr. Iron-Beard, a corporal, and an executioner. They halt on the village green, and each of the characters makes a speech in rhyme. The executioner announces that the leaf-clad man has been condemned to death, and cuts off his false head. Then the riders race to the May-tree, which has been set up a little way off. The first man who succeeds in wrenching it from the ground as he gallops past keeps it with all its decorations. The ceremony is observed every second or third year.

In Saxony and Thüringen there is a Whitsuntide ceremony called 'chasing the Wild Man out of the bush,' or 'fetching the Wild Man out of the wood.' A young fellow is enveloped in leaves or moss and called the Wild Man. He hides in the wood and the other lads of the village go out to seek him. They find him, lead him captive out of the wood, and fire at him with blank muskets. He falls like dead to the ground, but a lad dressed as a doctor bleeds him, and he comes to life again. At this they rejoice, and, binding him fast on a waggon, take him to the village, where they tell all the people how they have caught the Wild Man. At every house they receive a gift. In the Erzgebirge the following custom was annually observed at Shrovetide about the beginning of the seventeenth century. Two men disguised as Wild Men, the one in brushwood and moss, the other in straw, were led about the streets, and at last taken to the market-place, where they were chased up and down, shot and stabbed. Before falling they reeled about with strange gestures and spirted blood on the people from bladders which they carried. When they were down, the huntsmen placed them on boards and carried them to the ale-house, the miners marching beside them and winding blasts on their mining tools as if they had taken a noble head of game. A very similar Shrovetide custom is still observed near Schluckenau in Bohemia. A man dressed up as a Wild Man is chased through several streets till he comes to a narrow lane across which a cord is stretched. He stumbles over the cord and, falling to the ground, is overtaken and caught by his pursuers. The executioner runs up and stabs with his sword a bladder filled with blood which the Wild Man wears round his body; so the Wild Man dies, while a stream of blood reddens the ground. Next day a straw-man, made up to look like the Wild Man, is placed on a litter, and, accompanied by a great crowd, is taken to a pool into which it is thrown by the executioner. The ceremony is called 'burying the Carnival.'

In Semic (Bohemia) the custom of beheading the King is observed on Whit-Monday. A troop of young people disguise themselves; each is girt with a girdle of bark and carries a wooden sword and a trumpet of willow-bark. The King wears a robe of tree-bark adorned with flowers, on his head is a crown of bark decked with flowers and branches, his feet are wound about with ferns, a mask hides his face, and for a sceptre he has a hawthorn switch in his hand. A lad leads him through the village by a rope fastened to his foot, while the rest dance about, blow their trumpets, and whistle. In every farmhouse the King is chased round the room, and one of the troop, amid much noise and outcry, strikes with his sword a blow on the King's robe of bark till it rings again. Then a gratuity is demanded. The ceremony of decapitation, which is here somewhat slurred over, is carried out with a greater semblance of reality in other parts of Bohemia. Thus in some villages of the Königgrätz district on Whit-Monday the girls assemble under one lime-tree and the young men under another, all dressed in their best and tricked out with ribbons. The young men twine a garland for the Queen, and the girls another for the King. When they have chosen the King and Queen they all go in procession two and two, to the ale-house, from the balcony of which the crier proclaims the names of the King and Queen. Both are then invested with the insignia of their office and are crowned with the garlands, while the music plays up. Then some one gets on a bench and accuses the King of various offences, such as ill-treating the cattle. The King appeals to witnesses and a trial ensues, at the close of which the judge, who carries a white wand as his badge of office, pronounces a verdict of 'Guilty' or 'Not guilty.' If the verdict is 'Guilty,' the judge breaks his wand, the King kneels on a white cloth, all heads are bared, and a soldier sets three or four hats, one above the other, on his Majesty's head. The judge then pronounces the word 'Guilty' thrice in a loud voice, and orders the crier to behead the King. The crier obeys by striking off the King's hats with his wooden sword.

But perhaps, for our purpose, the most instructive of these

mimic executions is the following Bohemian one. In some places of the Pilsen district (Bohemia) on Whit-Monday the King is dressed in bark, ornamented with flowers and ribbons; he wears a crown of gilt paper and rides a horse, which is also decked with flowers. Attended by a judge, an executioner, and other characters, and followed by a train of soldiers, all mounted, he rides to the village square, where a hut or arbour of green boughs has been erected under the May-trees, which are firs, freshly cut, peeled to the top, and dressed with flowers and ribbons. After the dames and maidens of the village have been criticised and a frog beheaded, the cavalcade rides to a place previously determined upon, in a straight, broad street. Here they draw up in two lines and the King takes to flight. He is given a short start and rides off at full speed, pursued by the whole troop. If they fail to catch him he remains King for another year, and his companions must pay his score at the ale-house in the evening. But if they overtake and catch him he is scourged with hazel rods or beaten with the wooden swords and compelled to dismount. Then the executioner asks, 'Shall I behead this King?' The answer is given, 'Behead him'; the executioner brandishes his axe, and with the words 'One, two, three, let the King headless be!' he strikes off the King's crown. Amid the loud cries of the bystanders the King sinks to the ground; then he is laid on a bier and carried to the nearest farmhouse.

In most of the personages who are thus slain in mimicry it is impossible not to recognise representatives of the tree-spirit or spirit of vegetation, as he is supposed to manifest himself in spring. The bark, leaves, and flowers in which the actors are dressed, and the season of the year at which they appear, show that they belong to the same class as the Grass King, King of the May, Jack-in-the-Green, and other representatives of the vernal spirit of vegetation which we examined in an earlier part of this work. As if to remove any possible doubt on this head, we find that in two cases these slain men are brought into direct connexion with May-trees, which are the impersonal, as the May King, Grass King, and so forth, are the personal representatives of the tree-spirit. The drenching of the *Pfingstl* with water and his wading up to the middle into the brook are, therefore, no doubt rain-charms like those which have been already described.

But if these personages represent, as they certainly do, the spirit of vegetation in spring, the question arises, Why kill them? What is the object of slaying the spirit of vegetation at any time and above all in spring, when his services are most wanted? The only probable answer to this question seems to be given in the explanation already proposed of the custom of killing the divine king or priest. The divine life, incarnate in a material and mortal body, is liable to be tainted and corrupted by the weakness of the frail medium in which it is for a time enshrined; and if it is to be saved from the increasing enfeeblement which it must necessarily share with its human incarnation as he advances in years, it must be detached from him before, or at least as soon as, he exhibits signs of decay, in order to be transferred to a vigorous successor. This is done by killing the old representative of the god and conveying the divine spirit from him to a new incarnation. The killing of the god, that is, of his human incarnation, is therefore merely a necessary step to his revival or resurrection in a better form. Far from being an extinction of the divine spirit, it is only the beginning of a purer and stronger manifestation of it. If this explanation holds good of the custom of killing divine kings and priests in general, it is still more obviously applicable to the custom of annually killing the representative of the tree-spirit or spirit of vegetation in spring. For the decay of plant life in winter is readily interpreted by primitive man as an enfeeblement of the spirit of vegetation: the spirit has, he thinks, grown old and weak and must therefore be renovated by being slain and brought to life in a younger and fresher form. Thus the killing of the representative of the tree-spirit in spring is regarded as a means to promote and quicken the growth of vegetation. For the killing of the tree-spirit is associated always (we must suppose) implicitly, and sometimes explicitly also, with a revival or resurrection of him in a more youthful and vigorous form. So in the Saxon and Thüringen custom, after the Wild Man has been shot he is brought to life again by a doctor; and in the Wurmlingen ceremony there figures a Dr. Iron-Beard, who probably once played a similar part; certainly in another spring ceremony, which will be described presently, Dr. Iron-Beard pretends to restore a dead man to life. But of this revival or resurrection of the god we shall have more to say anon.

The points of similarity between these North European personages and the subject of our enquiry — the King of the Wood or priest of Nemi — are sufficiently striking. In these northern maskers we see kings, whose dress of bark and leaves along with the hut of green boughs and the fir-trees, under which they hold their court, proclaim them unmistakably as, like their Italian counterpart, Kings of the Wood. Like him they die a violent death, but like him they may escape from it for a time by their bodily strength and agility; for in several of these northern customs the flight and pursuit of the king is a prominent part of the ceremony, and in one case at least if the king can outrun his pursuers he retains his life and his office for another year. In this last case the king in fact holds office on condition of running for his life once a year, just as the King of Calicut in later times held office on condition of defending his life against all comers once every twelve years, and just as the priest of Nemi held office on condition of defending himself against any assault at any time. In every one of these instances the life of the god-man is prolonged on condition of his showing, in a severe physical contest of fight or flight, that his bodily strength is not decayed, and that, therefore, the violent death, which sooner or later is inevitable, may for the present be postponed. With regard to flight it is noticeable that flight figured conspicuously both in the legend and in the practice of the King of the Wood. He had to be a runaway slave in memory of the flight of Orestes, the traditional founder of the worship; hence the Kings of the Wood are described by an ancient writer as 'both strong of hand and fleet of foot.' Perhaps if we knew the ritual of the Arician grove fully we might find that the king was allowed a chance for his life by flight, like his Bohemian brother. I have already conjectured that the annual flight of the priestly king of Rome (*regifugium*) was at first a flight of the same kind; in other words, that he was originally one of those divine kings who are either put to death after a fixed period or allowed to prove by the strong hand or the fleet foot that their divinity is vigorous and unimpaired. One more point of resemblance may be noted between the Italian King of the Wood and his northern counterparts. In Saxony and Thüringen the representative of the tree-spirit, after being killed, is brought to life again by a doctor. This is exactly what legend affirmed to have happened to the first

King of the Wood at Nemi, Hippolytus or Virbius, who after he had been killed by his horses was restored to life by the physician Aesculapius. Such a legend tallies well with the theory that the slaying of the King of the Wood was only a step to his revival or resurrection in his successor.

§ 2. *Burying the Carnival.* — Thus far I have offered an explanation of the rule which required that the priest of Nemi should be slain by his successor. The explanation claims to be no more than probable; our scanty knowledge of the custom and of its history forbids it to be more. But its probability will be augmented in proportion to the extent to which the motives and modes of thought which it assumes can be proved to have operated in primitive society. Hitherto the god with whose death and resurrection we have been chiefly concerned has been the tree-god. But if I can show that the custom of killing the god and the belief in his resurrection originated, or at least existed, in the hunting and pastoral stage of society, when the slain god was an animal, and that it survived into the agricultural stage, when the slain god was the corn or a human being representing the corn, the probability of my explanation will have been considerably increased. This I shall attempt to do in the sequel, and in the course of the discussion I hope to clear up some obscurities which still remain, and to answer some objections which may have suggested themselves to the reader.

We start from the point at which we left off — the spring customs of European peasantry. Besides the ceremonies already described there are two kindred sets of observances in which the simulated death of a divine or supernatural being is a conspicuous feature. In one of them the being whose death is dramatically represented is a personification of the Carnival; in the other it is Death himself. The former ceremony falls naturally at the end of the Carnival, either on the last day of that merry season, namely Shrove Tuesday, or on the first day of Lent, namely Ash Wednesday. The date of the other ceremony — the Carrying or Driving out of Death, as it is commonly called — is not so uniformly fixed. Generally it is the fourth Sunday in Lent, which hence goes by the name of Dead Sunday; but in some places the celebration falls a week earlier, in others, as among the Czechs of Bohemia, a week later, while in certain German villages of

Moravia it is held on the first Sunday after Easter. Perhaps, as has been suggested, the date may originally have been variable, depending on the appearance of the first swallow or some other herald of the spring. Some writers regard the ceremony as Slavonic in its origin. Grimm thought it was a festival of the New Year with the old Slavs, who began their year in March. We shall first take examples of the mimic death of the Carnival, which always falls before the other in the calendar.

At Frosinone, in Latium, about half-way between Rome and Naples, the dull monotony of life in a provincial Italian town is agreeably broken on the last day of the Carnival by the ancient festival known as the *Radica*. About four o'clock in the afternoon the town band, playing lively tunes and followed by a great crowd, proceeds to the Piazza del Plebiscito, where is the Sub-Prefecture as well as the rest of the Government buildings. Here, in the middle of the square, the eyes of the expectant multitude are greeted by the sight of an immense car decked with many-coloured festoons and drawn by four horses. Mounted on the car is a huge chair, on which sits enthroned the majestic figure of the Carnival, a man of stucco about nine feet high with a rubicund and smiling countenance. Enormous boots, a tin helmet like those which grace the heads of officers of the Italian marine, and a coat of many colours embellished with strange devices, adorn the outward man of this stately personage. His left hand rests on the arm of the chair, while with his right he gracefully salutes the crowd, being moved to this act of civility by a string which is pulled by a man who modestly shrinks from publicity under the mercy-seat. And now the crowd, surging excitedly round the car, gives vent to its feelings in wild cries of joy, gentle and simple being mixed up together and all dancing furiously the *Saltarello*. A special feature of the festival is that every one must carry in his hand what is called a *radica* ('root'), by which is meant a huge leaf of the aloe or rather the agave. Any one who ventured into the crowd without such a leaf would be unceremoniously hustled out of it, unless indeed he bore as a substitute a large cabbage at the end of a long stick or a bunch of grass curiously plaited. When the multitude, after a short turn, has escorted the slow-moving car to the gate of the Sub-Prefecture, they halt, and the car, jostling over the uneven ground, rumbles into the courtyard. A hush now falls on the crowd, their subdued voices sounding, according to the description of one who has heard them, like the murmur of a troubled sea. All eyes are turned anxiously to the door from which the Sub-Prefect himself and the other representatives of the majesty of the law are expected to issue and pay their homage to the hero of the hour. A few moments of suspense and then a storm of cheers and hand-clapping salutes the appearance of the dignitaries, as they file out and, descending the staircase, take their place in the procession. The hymn of the Carnival is now thundered out, after which, amid a deafening roar, aloe leaves and cabbages are whirled aloft and descend impartially on the heads of the just and the unjust, who lend fresh zest to the proceedings by engaging in a free fight. When these preliminaries have been concluded to the satisfaction of all concerned, the procession gets under way. The rear is brought up by a cart laden with barrels of wine and policemen, the latter engaged in the congenial task of serving out wine to all who ask for it, while a most internecine struggle, accompanied by a copious discharge of yells, blows, and blasphemy, goes on among the surging crowd at the cart's tail in their anxiety not to miss the glorious opportunity of intoxicating themselves at the public expense. Finally, after the procession has paraded the principal streets in this majestic manner, the effigy of Carnival is taken to the middle of a public square, stripped of his finery, laid on a pile of wood, and burnt amid the cries of the multitude, who thundering out once more the song of the Carnival fling their so-called 'roots' on the pyre and give themselves up without restraint to the pleasures of the dance.

In the Abruzzi a pasteboard figure of the Carnival is carried by four grave-diggers with pipes in their mouths and bottles of wine slung at their shoulder-belts. In front walks the wife of the Carnival dressed in mourning and dissolved in tears. From time to time the company halts, and while the wife addresses the sympathising public, the grave-diggers refresh the inner man with a pull at the bottle. In the open square the mimic corpse is laid on a pyre, and to the roll of drums, the shrill screams of the women, and the gruffer cries of the men a light is set to it. While the figure burns, chestnuts are thrown about among the crowd. Sometimes the Carnival is represented by a straw-man at the top of a pole which is borne through the town by a troop of mummers in the course of the afternoon. When evening comes on, four of the mummers hold out a quilt or sheet by the corners, and the figure of the Carnival is made to tumble into it. The procession is then resumed, the performers weeping crocodile tears and emphasising the poignancy of their grief by the help of saucepans and dinner bells. Sometimes, again, in the Abruzzi the dead Carnival is personified by a living man who lies in a coffin, attended by another who acts the priest and dispenses holy water in great profusion from a bathing tub.

At Lerida, in Catalonia, the funeral of the Carnival was witnessed by an English traveller in 1877. On the last Sunday of the Carnival, a grand procession of infantry, cavalry, and maskers of many sorts, some on horseback and some in carriages, escorted the grand car of His Grace Pau Pi, as the effigy was called, in triumph through the principal streets. For three days the revelry ran high, and then at midnight on the last day of the Carnival the same procession again wound through the streets, but under a different aspect and for a different end. The triumphal car was exchanged for a hearse, in which reposed the effigy of his dead Grace: a troop of maskers, who in the first procession had played the part of Students of Folly with many a merry quip and jest, now, robed as priests and bishops, paced slowly along holding aloft huge lighted tapers and singing a dirge. All the mummers wore crape, and all the horsemen carried blazing flambeaux. Down the high street, between the lofty, many-storeyed and balconied houses, where every window, every balcony, every housetop was crammed with a dense mass of spectators, all dressed and masked in fantastic gorgeousness, the procession took its melancholy way. Over the scene flashed and played the shifting cross-lights and shadows from the moving torches: red and blue Bengal lights flared up and died out again; and above the trampling of the horses and the measured tread of the marching multitude rose the voices of the priests chanting the requiem, while the military bands struck in with the solemn roll of the muffled drums. On reaching the principal square the procession halted, a burlesque funeral oration was pronounced over the defunct Pau Pi, and the lights were extinguished. Immediately the devil and his angels darted from the crowd, seized the body and fled away with it, hotly pursued by the whole multitude, yelling, screaming, and cheering. Naturally the fiends were overtaken and dispersed; and the sham corpse, rescued from their clutches, was laid in a grave that had been made ready for its reception. Thus the Carnival of 1877 at Lerida died and was buried.

A ceremony of the same sort is observed in Provence on Ash Wednesday. An effigy called Caramantran, whimsically attired, is drawn in a chariot or borne on a litter, accompanied by the populace in grotesque costumes, who carry gourds full of wine and drain them with all the marks, real or affected, of intoxication. At the head of the procession are some men disguised as judges and barristers, and a tall gaunt personage who masquerades as Lent; behind them follow young people mounted on miserable hacks and attired as mourners who pretend to bewail the fate that is in store for Caramantran. In the principal square the procession halts, the tribunal is constituted, and Caramantran placed at the bar. After a formal trial he is sentenced to death amid the groans of the mob: the barrister who defended him embraces his client for the last time: the officers of justice do their duty: the condemned is set with his back to a wall and hurried into eternity under a shower of stones. The sea or a river receives his mangled remains. Throughout nearly the whole of the Ardennes it was and still is customary on Ash Wednesday to burn an effigy which is supposed to represent the Carnival, while appropriate verses are sung round about the blazing figure. Very often an attempt is made to fashion the effigy in the likeness of the husband who is reputed to be least faithful to his wife of any in the village. As might perhaps have been anticipated, the distinction of being selected for portraiture under these painful circumstances has a slight tendency to breed domestic jars, especially when the portrait is burnt in front of the house of the gay deceiver whom it represents, while a powerful chorus of caterwauls, groans, and other melodious sounds bears public testimony to the opinion which his friends and neighbours entertain of his private virtues. In some villages of the Ardennes a young man of flesh and blood, dressed up in hay and straw, used to act the part of Shrove Tuesday (*Mardi Gras*), as the personification of the Carnival is often called in France after the last day of the period which he personates. He was brought before a mock tribunal, and being condemned to death was placed with his back to a wall, like a soldier at a military execution, and fired at with blank cartridges. At Vrigne-aux-Bois one of these harmless buffoons, named Thierry, was accidentally killed by a wad that had been left in a musket of the firing-party. When poor Shrove Tuesday dropped under the fire, the applause was loud and long, he did it so naturally; but when he did not get up again, they ran to him and found him a corpse. Since then there have been no more of these mock executions in the Ardennes.

In Normandy on the evening of Ash Wednesday it used to be the custom to hold a celebration called the Burial of Shrove Tuesday. A squalid effigy scantily clothed in rags, a battered old hat crushed down on his dirty face, his great round paunch stuffed with straw, represented the disreputable old rake who, after a long course of dissipation, was now about to suffer for his sins. Hoisted on the shoulders of a sturdy fellow, who pretended to stagger under the burden, this popular personification of the Carnival promenaded the streets for the last time in a manner the reverse of triumphal. Preceded by a drummer and accompanied by a jeering rabble, among whom the urchins and all the tag-rag and bobtail of the town mustered in great force, the figure was carried about by the flickering light of torches to the discordant din of shovels and tongs, pots and pans, horns and kettles, mingled with hootings, groans, and hisses. From time to time the procession halted, and a champion of morality accused the broken-down old sinner of all the excesses he had committed and for which he was now about to be burned alive. The culprit, having nothing to urge in his own defence, was thrown on a heap of straw, a torch was put to it, and a great blaze shot up, to the delight of the children who frisked round it screaming out some old popular verses about the death of the Carnival. Sometimes the effigy was rolled down the slope of a hill before being burnt. At Saint-Lô the ragged effigy of Shrove Tuesday was followed by his widow, a big burly lout dressed as a woman with a crape veil, who emitted sounds of lamentation and woe in a stentorian voice. After being carried about the streets on a litter attended by a crowd of maskers, the figure was thrown into the River Vire. The final scene has been graphically described by Madame Octave Feuillet as she witnessed it in her childhood some sixty years ago. 'My parents invited friends to see, from the top of the tower of Jeanne Couillard, the funeral procession passing. It was there that, quaffing lemonade — the only refreshment allowed because of the fast — we witnessed at nightfall a spectacle of which I shall always preserve a lively recollection. At our feet flowed the Vire under its old stone bridge. On the middle of the bridge lay the figure of Shrove Tuesday on a litter of leaves, surrounded by scores of maskers dancing, singing, and carrying torches. Some of them in their motley costumes ran along the parapet like fiends. The rest, worn out with their revels, sat on the posts and dozed. Soon the dancing stopped, and some of the troop, seizing a torch, set fire to the effigy, after which they flung it into the river with redoubled shouts and clamour. The man of straw, soaked with resin, floated away burning down the stream of the Vire, lighting up with its funeral fires the woods on the bank and the battlements of the old castle in which Louis XI and Francis I had slept. When the last glimmer of the blazing phantom had vanished, like a falling star, at the end of the valley, every one withdrew, crowd and maskers alike, and we quitted the ramparts with our guests.'

In the neighbourhood of Tübingen on Shrove Tuesday a straw-man, called the Shrovetide Bear, is made up; he is dressed in a pair of old trousers, and a fresh black-pudding or two squirts filled with blood are inserted in his neck. After a formal condemnation he is beheaded, laid in a coffin, and on Ash Wednesday is buried in the churchyard. This is called 'Burying the Carnival.' Amongst some of the Saxons of Transylvania the Carnival is hanged. Thus at Braller on Ash Wednesday or Shrove Tuesday two white and two chestnut horses draw a sledge on which is placed a straw-man swathed in a white cloth; beside him is a cart-wheel which is kept turning round. Two lads disguised as old men follow the sledge lamenting. The rest of the village lads, mounted on horseback and decked with ribbons, accompany the procession, which is headed by two girls crowned with evergreen and drawn in a waggon or sledge. A trial is held under a tree, at which lads disguised as soldiers pronounce sentence of death. The two old men try to rescue the straw-man and to fly with him, but to no purpose; he is caught by the two girls and handed over to the executioner, who hangs him on a tree. In vain the old men try to climb up the tree and take him down; they always tumble down, and at last in despair they throw themselves on the ground and weep and howl for the hanged man. An official then makes a speech in which he declares that the Carnival was condemned to death because he had done them harm, by wearing out their shoes and making them tired and sleepy. At the 'Burial of Carnival' in Lechrain, a man dressed as a woman in black clothes is carried on a litter or bier by four men; he is lamented over by men disguised as women in black clothes, then thrown down before the village dung-heap, drenched with water, buried in the dung-heap, and covered with straw. On the evening of Shrove Tuesday the Esthonians make a straw figure called *metsik* or 'wood-spirit'; one year it is dressed with a man's coat and hat, next year with a hood and a petticoat. This figure is stuck on a long pole, carried across the boundary of the village with loud cries of joy, and fastened to the top of a tree in the wood. The ceremony is believed to be a protection against all kinds of misfortune.

Sometimes at these Shrovetide or Lenten ceremonies the resurrection of the pretended dead person is enacted. Thus, in some parts of Swabia on Shrove Tuesday Dr. Iron-Beard professes to bleed a sick man, who thereupon falls as dead to the ground; but the doctor at last restores him to life by blowing air into him through a tube. In the Harz Mountains, when Carnival is over, a man is laid on a baking-trough and carried with dirges to a grave; but in the grave a glass of brandy is buried instead of the man. A speech is delivered and then the people return to the village-green or meeting-place, where they smoke the long clay pipes which are distributed at funerals. On the morning of Shrove Tuesday in the following year the brandy is dug up and the festival begins by every one tasting the spirit which, as the phrase goes, has come to life again.

§ 3. *Carrying out Death.* — The ceremony of 'Carrying out Death' presents much the same features as 'Burying the Carnival'; except that the carrying out of Death is generally followed by a ceremony, or at least accompanied by a profession, of bringing in Summer, Spring, or Life. Thus in Middle Franken, a province of Bavaria, on the fourth Sunday in Lent, the village urchins used to make a straw effigy of Death, which they carried about with burlesque pomp through the streets, and afterwards burned with loud cries beyond the bounds. The Frankish custom is thus described by a writer of the sixteenth century: 'At Mid-Lent, the season when the church bids us rejoice, the young people of my native country make a straw image of Death, and fastening it to a pole carry it with shouts to the neighbouring villages. By some they are kindly received, and after being refreshed with milk, peas, and dried pears, the usual food of that season, are sent home again. Others, however, treat them with anything but hospitality; for, looking on them as harbingers of misfortune, to wit of death, they drive them from their boundaries with weapons and insults.' In the villages near Erlangen, when the fourth Sunday in Lent came round, the peasant girls used to dress themselves in all their finery with flowers in their hair. Thus attired they repaired to the neighbouring town, carrying puppets which were adorned with leaves and covered with white cloths. These they took from house to house in pairs, stopping at every door where they expected to receive something, and singing a few lines in which they announced that it was Mid-Lent and that they were about to throw Death into the water. When they had collected some trifling gratuities they went to the River Regnitz and flung the puppets representing Death into the stream. This was done to ensure a fruitful and prosperous year; further, it was considered a safeguard against pestilence and sudden death. At Nuremberg girls of seven to eighteen years of age go through the streets bearing a little open coffin, in which is a doll hidden under a shroud. Others carry a beech branch, with an apple fastened to it for a head, in an open box. They sing, 'We carry Death into the water, it is well,' or 'We carry Death into the water, carry him in and out again.' In some parts of Bavaria down to 1780 it was believed that a fatal epidemic would ensue if the custom of 'Carrying out Death' were not observed.

In some villages of Thüringen, on the fourth Sunday of Lent, the children used to carry a puppet of birchen twigs through the village, and then threw it into a pool, while they sang, 'We carry the old Death out behind the herdsman's old house; we have got Summer, and Kroden's (?) power is destroyed.' At Debschwitz or Dobschwitz, near Gera, the ceremony of 'Driving out Death' is or was annually observed on the first of March. The young people make up a figure of straw or the like materials, dress it in old clothes, which they have begged from houses in the village, and

o

carry it out and throw it into the river. On returning to the village they break the good news to the people, and receive eggs and other victuals as a reward. The ceremony is or was supposed to purify the village and to protect the inhabitants from sickness and plague. In other villages of Thüringen, in which the population was originally Slavonic, the carrying out of the puppet is accompanied with the singing of a song, which begins, 'Now we carry Death out of the village and Spring into the village.' At the end of the seventeenth and beginning of the eighteenth century the custom was observed in Thüringen as follows. The boys and girls made an effigy of straw or the like materials, but the shape of the figure varied from year to year. In one year it would represent an old man, in the next an old woman, in the third a young man, and in the fourth a maiden, and the dress of the figure varied with the character it personated. There used to be a sharp contest as to where the effigy was to be made, for the people thought that the house from which it was carried forth would not be visited with death that year. Having been made, the puppet was fastened to a pole and carried by a girl if it represented an old man, but by a boy if it represented an old woman. Thus it was borne in procession, the young people holding sticks in their hands and singing that they were driving out Death. When they came to water they threw the effigy into it and ran hastily back, fearing that it might jump on their shoulders and wring their necks. They also took care not to touch it, lest it should dry them up. On their return they beat the cattle with the sticks, believing that this would make the animals fat or fruitful. Afterwards they visited the house or houses from which they had carried the image of Death, where they received a dole of half-boiled peas. The custom of 'Carrying out Death' was practised also in Saxony. At Leipsic the bastards and public women used to make a straw effigy of Death every year at Mid-Lent. This they carried through all the streets with songs and showed it to the young married women. Finally they threw it into the River Parthe. By this ceremony they professed to make the young wives fruitful, to purify the city, and to protect the inhabitants for that year from plague and other epidemics.

Ceremonies of the same sort are observed at Mid-Lent in Silesia. Thus in many places the grown girls with the help of the young men dress up a straw figure with women's clothes and carry it out of the village towards the setting sun. At the boundary they strip it of its clothes, tear it in pieces, and scatter the fragments about the fields. This is called 'Burying Death.' As they carry the image out, they sing that they are about to bury Death under an oak, that he may depart from the people. Sometimes the song runs that they are bearing Death over hill and dale to return no more. In the Polish neighbourhood of Gross-Strehlitz the puppet is called Goik. It is carried on horseback and thrown into the nearest water. The people think that the ceremony protects them from sickness of every sort in the coming year. In the districts of Wohlau and Guhrau the image of Death used to be thrown over the boundary of the next village. But as the neighbours feared to receive the ill-omened figure, they were on the look-out to repel it, and hard knocks were often exchanged between the two parties. In some Polish parts of Upper Silesia the effigy, representing an old woman, goes by the name of Marzana, the goddess of death. It is made in the house where the last death occurred, and is carried on a pole to the boundary of the village, where it is thrown into a pond or burnt. At Polkwitz the custom of 'Carrying out Death' fell into abeyance; but an outbreak of fatal sickness which followed the intermission of the ceremony induced the people to resume it.

In Bohemia the children go out with a straw-man, representing Death, to the end of the village, where they burn it, singing —

'*Now carry we Death out of the village,*   *Welcome, dear Summer,*
The new Summer into the village,   *Green little corn.*'

At Tabor in Bohemia the figure of Death is carried out of the town and flung from a high rock into the water, while they sing —

'*Death swims on the water,*   *And do thou, O holy Marketa,*
Summer will soon be here,   *Give us a good year*
We carried Death away for you,   *For wheat and for rye.*'
We brought the Summer.

In other parts of Bohemia they carry Death to the end of the village, singing —

> '*We carry Death out of the village,*
> *And the New Year into the village.*
> *Dear Spring, we bid you welcome,*
> *Green grass, we bid you welcome.*'

Behind the village they erect a pyre, on which they burn the straw figure, reviling and scoffing at it the while. Then they return, singing —

> '*We have carried away Death,*
> *And brought Life back.*
> *He has taken up his quarters in the village,*
> *Therefore sing joyous songs.*'

In some German villages of Moravia, as in Jassnitz and Seitendorf, the young folk assemble on the third Sunday in Lent and fashion a straw-man, who is generally adorned with a fur cap and a pair of old leathern hose, if such are to be had. The effigy is then hoisted on a pole and carried by the lads and lasses out into the open fields. On the way they sing a song, in which it is said that they are carrying Death away and bringing dear Summer into the house, and with Summer the May and the flowers. On reaching an appointed place they dance in a circle round the effigy with loud shouts and screams, then suddenly rush at it and tear it to pieces with their hands. Lastly, the pieces are thrown together in a heap, the pole is broken, and fire is set to the whole. While it burns the troop dances merrily round it, rejoicing at the victory won by Spring; and when the fire has nearly died out they go to the householders to beg for a present of eggs wherewith to hold a feast, taking care to give as a reason for the request that they have carried Death out and away.

The preceding evidence shows that the effigy of Death is often regarded with fear and treated with marks of hatred and abhorrence. Thus the anxiety of the villagers to transfer the figure from their own to their neighbours' land, and the reluctance of the latter to receive the ominous guest, are proof enough of the dread which it inspires. Further, in Lusatia and Silesia the puppet is sometimes made to look in at the window of a house, and it is believed that some one in the house will die within the year unless his life is redeemed by the payment of money. Again, after throwing the effigy away, the bearers sometimes run home lest

Death should follow them, and if one of them falls in running, it is believed that he will die within the year. At Chrudim, in Bohemia, the figure of Death is made out of a cross, with a head and mask stuck at the top, and a shirt stretched out on it. On the fifth Sunday in Lent the boys take this effigy to the nearest brook or pool, and standing in a line throw it into the water. Then they all plunge in after it; but as soon as it is caught no one more may enter the water. The boy who did not enter the water or entered it last will die within the year, and he is obliged to carry the Death back to the village. The effigy is then burned. On the other hand, it is believed that no one will die within the year in the house out of which the figure of Death has been carried; and the village out of which Death has been driven is sometimes supposed to be protected against sickness and plague. In some villages of Austrian Silesia on the Saturday before Dead Sunday an effigy is made of old clothes, hay, and straw, for the purpose of driving Death out of the village. On Sunday the people, armed with sticks and straps, assemble before the house where the figure is lodged. Four lads then draw the effigy by cords through the village amid exultant shouts, while all the others beat it with their sticks and straps. On reaching a field which belongs to a neighbouring village they lay down the figure, cudgel it soundly, and scatter the fragments over the field. The people believe that the village from which Death has been thus carried out will be safe from any infectious disease for the whole year.

§ 4. *Bringing in Summer.* — In the preceding ceremonies the return of Spring, Summer, or Life, as a sequel to the expulsion of Death, is only implied or at most announced. In the following ceremonies it is plainly enacted. Thus in some parts of Bohemia the effigy of Death is drowned by being thrown into the water at sunset; then the girls go out into the wood and cut down a young tree with a green crown, hang a doll dressed as a woman on it, deck the whole with green, red, and white ribbons, and march in procession with their *Lito* (Summer) into the village, collecting gifts and singing —

> ' *Death swims in the water,*
> *Spring comes to visit us,*
> *With eggs that are red,*
> *With yellow pancakes.*

> *We carried Death out of the village,*
> *We are carrying Summer into the village.'*

In many Silesian villages the figure of Death, after being treated with respect, is stript of its clothes and flung with curses into the water, or torn to pieces in a field. Then the young folk repair to a wood, cut down a small fir-tree, peel the trunk, and deck it with festoons of evergreens, paper roses, painted egg-shells, motley bits of cloth, and so forth. The tree thus adorned is called Summer or May. Boys carry it from house to house singing appropriate songs and begging for presents. Among their songs is the following:

> *' We have carried Death out,*
> *We are bringing the dear Summer back,*
> *The Summer and the May,*
> *And all the flowers gay.'*

Sometimes they also bring back from the wood a prettily adorned figure, which goes by the name of Summer, May, or the Bride; in the Polish districts it is called Dziewanna, the goddess of spring.

At Eisenach on the fourth Sunday in Lent young people used to fasten a straw-man, representing Death, to a wheel, which they trundled to the top of a hill. Then setting fire to the figure they allowed it and the wheel to roll down the slope. Next they cut a tall fir-tree, tricked it out with ribbons, and set it up in the plain. The men then climbed the tree to fetch down the ribbons. In Upper Lusatia the figure of Death, made of straw and rags, is dressed in a veil furnished by the last bride and a shirt provided by the house in which the last death took place. Thus arrayed the figure is stuck on the end of a long pole and carried at full speed by the tallest and strongest girl, while the rest pelt the effigy with sticks and stones. Whoever hits it will be sure to live through the year. In this way Death is carried out of the village and thrown into the water or over the boundary of the next village. On their way home each one breaks a green branch and carries it gaily with him till he reaches the village, when he throws it away. Sometimes the young people of the next village, upon whose land the figure has been thrown, run after them and hurl it back, not wishing to have Death among them. Hence the two parties occasionally come to blows.

In these cases Death is represented by the puppet which is thrown away, Summer or Life by the branches or trees which are brought back. But sometimes a new potency of life seems to be attributed to the image of Death itself, and by a kind of resurrection it becomes the instrument of the general revival. Thus in some parts of Lusatia women alone are concerned in carrying out Death, and suffer no male to meddle with it. Attired in mourning, which they wear the whole day, they make a puppet of straw, clothe it in a white shirt, and give it a broom in one hand and a scythe in the other. Singing songs and pursued by urchins throwing stones, they carry the puppet to the village boundary, where they tear it in pieces. Then they cut down a fine tree, hang the shirt on it, and carry it home singing. On the Feast of Ascension the Saxons of Braller, a village of Transylvania, not far from Hermannstadt, observe the ceremony of 'Carrying out Death' in the following manner. After morning service all the school-girls repair to the house of one of their number, and there dress up the Death. This is done by tying a threshed-out sheaf of corn into a rough semblance of a head and body, while the arms are simulated by a broomstick thrust through it horizontally. The figure is dressed in the holiday attire of a young peasant woman, with a red hood, silver brooches, and a profusion of ribbons at the arms and breast. The girls bustle at their work, for soon the bells will be ringing to vespers, and the Death must be ready in time to be placed at the open window, that all the people may see it on their way to church. When vespers are over, the longed-for moment has come for the first procession with the Death to begin; it is a privilege that belongs to the school-girls alone. Two of the older girls seize the figure by the arms and walk in front: all the rest follow two and two. Boys may take no part in the procession, but they troop after it gazing with open-mouthed admiration at the 'beautiful Death.' So the procession goes through all the streets of the village, the girls singing the old hymn that begins —

> *'Gott mein Vater, deine Liebe*
> *Reicht so weit der Himmel ist,'*

to a tune that differs from the ordinary one. When the procession has wound its way through every street, the girls go to another house, and having shut the door against the eager prying crowd of boys who follow at their heels, they strip the Death and pass the naked truss of straw out of the window to the boys, who pounce on it, run out of the village with it without singing, and fling the dilapidated effigy into the neighbouring brook. This done, the second scene of the little drama begins. While the boys were carrying away the Death out of the village, the girls remained in the house, and one of them is now dressed in all the finery which had been worn by the effigy. Thus arrayed she is led in procession through all the streets to the singing of the same hymn as before. When the procession is over they all betake themselves to the house of the girl who played the leading part. Here a feast awaits them from which also the boys are excluded. It is a popular belief that the children may safely begin to eat gooseberries and other fruit after the day on which Death has thus been carried out; for Death, which up to that time lurked especially in gooseberries, is now destroyed. Further, they may now bathe with impunity out of doors. Very similar is the ceremony which, down to recent years, was observed in some of the German villages of Moravia. Boys and girls met on the afternoon of the first Sunday after Easter, and together fashioned a puppet of straw to represent Death. Decked with bright-coloured ribbons and cloths, and fastened to the top of a long pole, the effigy was then borne with singing and clamour to the nearest height, where it was stript of its gay attire and thrown or rolled down the slope. One of the girls was next dressed in the gauds taken from the effigy of Death, and with her at its head the procession moved back to the village. In some villages the practice is to bury the effigy in the place that has the most evil reputation of all the country-side: others throw it into running water.

In the Lusatian ceremony described above, the tree which is brought home after the destruction of the figure of Death is plainly equivalent to the trees or branches which, in the preceding customs, were brought back as representatives of Summer or Life, after Death had been thrown away or destroyed. But the transference of the shirt worn by the effigy of Death to the tree clearly indicates that the tree is a kind of revivification, in a new form, of the destroyed effigy. This comes out also in the Transylvanian and Moravian customs: the dressing of a girl in the clothes worn by the Death, and the leading her about the village to the same song which had been sung when the Death was being carried about, show that she is intended to be a kind of resuscitation of the being whose effigy has just been destroyed. These examples therefore suggest that the Death whose demolition is represented in these ceremonies cannot be regarded as the purely destructive agent which we understand by Death. If the tree which is brought back as an embodiment of the reviving vegetation of spring is clothed in the shirt worn by the Death which has just been destroyed, the object certainly cannot be to check and counteract the revival of vegetation : it can only be to foster and promote it. Therefore the being which has just been destroyed — the so-called Death — must be supposed to be endowed with a vivifying and quickening influence, which it can communicate to the vegetable and even the animal world. This ascription of a life-giving virtue to the figure of Death is put beyond a doubt by the custom, observed in some places, of taking pieces of the straw effigy of Death and placing them in the fields to make the crops grow, or in the manger to make the cattle thrive. Thus in Spachendorf, a village of Austrian Silesia, the figure of Death, made of straw, brushwood, and rags, is carried with wild songs to an open place outside the village and there burned, and while it is burning a general struggle takes place for the pieces, which are pulled out of the flames with bare hands. Each one who secures a fragment of the effigy ties it to a branch of the largest tree in his garden, or buries it in his field, in the belief that this causes the crops to grow better. In the Troppau district of Austrian Silesia the straw figure which the boys make on the fourth Sunday in Lent is dressed by the girls in woman's clothes and hung with ribbons, necklace, and garlands. Attached to a long pole it is carried out of the village, followed by a troop of young people of both sexes, who alternately frolic, lament, and sing songs. Arrived at its destination — a field outside the village — the figure is stripped of its clothes and ornaments ; then the crowd rushes at it and tears it to bits, scuffling for the fragments. Every one tries to get a wisp of the straw of which the effigy was made, because such a wisp, placed in the manger, is believed to make the cattle thrive. Or the straw is put in the hens' nest, it being supposed that this prevents the hens from carrying away their eggs, and makes them brood much better. The same attribution of a fertilising power to the figure of Death appears in the belief that if the bearers of the figure, after throwing it away, beat cattle with their sticks, this will render the beasts fat or prolific. Perhaps the sticks had been previously used to beat the Death, and so had acquired the fertilising power ascribed to the effigy. We have seen, too, that at Leipsic a straw effigy of Death was shown to young wives to make them fruitful.

It seems hardly possible to separate from the May-trees the trees or branches which are brought into the village after the destruction of the Death. The bearers who bring them in profess to be bringing in the Summer, therefore the trees obviously represent the Summer; indeed in Silesia they are commonly called the Summer or the May, and the doll which is sometimes attached to the Summer-tree is a duplicate representative of the Summer, just as the May is sometimes represented at the same time by a May-tree and a May Lady. Further, the Summer-trees are adorned like May-trees with ribbons and so on; like May-trees, when large, they are planted in the ground and climbed up; and like May-trees, when small, they are carried from door to door by boys or girls singing songs and collecting money. And as if to demonstrate the identity of the two sets of customs the bearers of the Summer-tree sometimes announce that they are bringing in the Summer and the May. The customs, therefore, of bringing in the May and bringing in the Summer are essentially the same; and the Summer-tree is merely another form of the May-tree, the only distinction (besides that of name) being in the time at which they are respectively brought in; for while the May-tree is usually fetched in on the first of May or at Whitsuntide, the Summer-tree is fetched in on the fourth Sunday in Lent. Therefore, if the May-tree is an embodiment of the tree-spirit or spirit of vegetation, the Summer-tree must likewise be an embodiment of the tree-spirit or spirit of vegetation. But we have seen that the Summer-tree is in some cases a revivification of the effigy of Death. It follows, therefore, that in these cases the effigy called Death must be an embodiment of the tree-spirit or spirit of vegetation. This inference is confirmed, first, by the vivifying and fertilising influence which the fragments of the effigy of Death are believed to exercise both on vegetable and on animal life; for this influence, as we saw in an earlier part of this work, is supposed to be a special attribute of the tree-spirit. It is confirmed, secondly, by observing that the effigy of Death is sometimes decked with leaves or made of twigs, branches, hemp, or a threshed-out sheaf of corn; and that sometimes it is hung on a little tree and so carried about by girls collecting money, just as is done with the May-tree and the May Lady, and with the Summer-tree and the doll attached to it. In short, we are driven to regard the expulsion of Death and the bringing in of Summer as, in some cases at least, merely another form of that death and revival of the spirit of vegetation in spring which we saw enacted in the killing and resurrection of the Wild Man. The burial and resurrection of the Carnival is probably another way of expressing the same idea. The interment of the representative of the Carnival under a dung-heap is natural, if he is supposed to possess a quickening and fertilising influence like that ascribed to the effigy of Death. The Esthonians, indeed, who carry the straw figure out of the village in the usual way on Shrove Tuesday, do not call it the Carnival, but the Wood-spirit (*Metsik*), and they clearly indicate the identity of the effigy with the wood-spirit by fixing it to the top of a tree in the wood, where it remains for a year, and is besought almost daily with prayers and offerings to protect the herds; for like a true wood-spirit the *Metsik* is a patron of cattle. Sometimes the *Metsik* is made of sheaves of corn.

Thus we may fairly conjecture that the names Carnival, Death, and Summer are comparatively late and inadequate expressions for the beings personified or embodied in the customs with which we have been dealing. The very abstractness of the names bespeaks a modern origin; for the personification of times and seasons like the Carnival and Summer, or of an abstract notion like death, is not primitive. But the ceremonies themselves bear the stamp of a dateless antiquity; therefore we can hardly help supposing that in their origin the ideas which they embodied were of a more simple and concrete order. The notion of a tree, perhaps of a particular kind of tree (for some savages have no word for tree in general), or even of an individual tree, is sufficiently concrete to supply a basis from which by a gradual process of generalisation the wider idea of a spirit of vegetation might be reached. But this general idea of vegetation would readily be confounded with the season in which it manifests itself; hence the substitution of Spring, Summer, or May for the tree-spirit or spirit of vegetation would be easy and natural. Again, the concrete notion of the dying tree or dying vegetation would by a similar process of generalisation glide into a notion of death in general; so that the practice of carrying out the dying or dead vegetation in spring, as a preliminary to its revival, would in time widen out into an attempt to banish Death in general from the village or district. The view that in these spring ceremonies Death meant originally the dying or dead vegetation of winter has the high support of W. Mannhardt; and he confirms it by the analogy of the name Death as applied to the spirit of the ripe corn. Commonly the spirit of the ripe corn is conceived, not as dead, but as old, and hence it goes by the name of the Old Man or the Old Woman. But in some places the last sheaf cut at harvest, which is generally believed to be the seat of the corn spirit, is called 'the Dead One': children are warned against entering the corn-fields because Death sits in the corn; and, in a game played by Saxon children in Transylvania at the maize harvest, Death is represented by a child completely covered with maize leaves.

§ 5. *Battle of Summer and Winter.* — Sometimes in the popular customs of the peasantry the contrast between the dormant powers of vegetation in winter and their awakening vitality in spring takes the form of a dramatic contest between actors who play the parts respectively of Winter and Summer. Thus in the towns of Sweden on May Day two troops of young men on horseback used to meet as if for mortal combat. One of them was led by a representative of Winter clad in furs, who threw snowballs and ice in order to prolong the cold weather. The other troop was commanded by a representative of Summer covered with fresh leaves and flowers. In the sham fight which followed the party of Summer came off victorious, and the ceremony ended with a feast. Again, in the region of the middle Rhine, a representative of Summer clad in ivy combats a representative of Winter clad in straw or moss and finally gains a victory over him. The vanquished foe is thrown to the ground and stripped of his casing of straw, which is torn to pieces and scattered about, while the youthful comrades of the two champions sing a song to commemorate the defeat of Winter by Summer. Afterwards they carry about a summer garland or branch and collect gifts of eggs and bacon from house to house. Sometimes the champion who acts the part of Summer is dressed in leaves and flowers and wears a chaplet of flowers on his head. In the Palatinate this mimic conflict takes place on the fourth Sunday in Lent. All over Bavaria the same drama used to be acted on the same day, and it was still kept up in some places down to the middle of the nineteenth century or later. While Summer appeared clad all in green, decked with fluttering ribbons, and carrying a branch in blossom or a little tree hung with apples and pears, Winter was muffled up in a cap and mantle of fur and bore in his hand a snow-shovel or a flail. Accompanied by their respective retinues dressed in corresponding attire, they went through all the streets of the village, halting before the houses and singing staves of old songs, for which they received presents of bread, eggs, and fruit. Finally, after a short struggle, Winter was beaten by Summer and ducked in the village well or driven out of the village with shouts and laughter into the forest.

At Goepfritz in Lower Austria, two men personating Summer and Winter used to go from house to house on Shrove Tuesday, and were everywhere welcomed by the children with great delight. The representative of Summer was clad in white and bore a sickle; his comrade, who played the part of Winter, had a fur cap on his head, his arms and legs were swathed in straw, and he carried a flail. In every house they sang verses alternately. At Drömling in Brunswick, down to the present time, the contest between Summer and Winter is acted every year at Whitsuntide by a troop of boys and a troop of girls. The boys rush singing, shouting, and ringing bells from house to house to drive Winter away; after them come the girls singing softly and led by a May Bride, all in bright dresses and decked with flowers and garlands to represent the genial advent of spring. Formerly the part of Winter was played by a straw-man which the boys carried with them; now it is acted by a real man in disguise.

Among the central Esquimaux of North America the contest between representatives of summer and winter, which in Europe has long degenerated into a mere dramatic performance, is still kept up as a magical ceremony of which the avowed intention is to influence the weather. In autumn, when storms announce the approach of the dismal Arctic winter, the Esquimaux divide themselves into two parties called respectively the ptarmigans and the ducks, the ptarmigans comprising all persons born in winter, and the ducks all persons born in summer. A long rope of seal-skin is then stretched out, and each party laying hold of one end of it seeks by tugging with might and main to drag the other party over to its side. If the ptarmigans get the worst of it, then summer has won the game and fine weather may be expected to prevail through the winter.

§ 6. *Death and Resurrection of Kostrubonko.* — In Russia funeral ceremonies like those of 'Burying the Carnival' and 'Carrying out Death' are celebrated under the names, not of Death or the Carnival, but of certain mythic figures, Kostrubonko, Kostroma, Kupalo, Lada, and Yarilo. These Russian ceremonies are observed both in spring and at midsummer. Thus 'in Little Russia it used to be the custom at Eastertide to celebrate the funeral of a being called Kostrubonko, the deity of the spring. A circle was formed of singers who moved slowly around a girl who lay on the ground as if dead, and as they went they sang:

> " *Dead, dead is our Kostrubonko!*
> *Dead, dead is our dear one!*"

until the girl suddenly sprang up, on which the chorus joyfully exclaimed:

> "*Come to life, come to life has our Kostrubonko!*
> *Come to life, come to life has our dear one!*"'

On the Eve of St. John (Midsummer Eve) a figure of Kupalo is made of straw and 'is dressed in woman's clothes, with a necklace and a floral crown. Then a tree is felled, and, after being decked with ribbons, is set up on some chosen spot. Near this tree, to which they give the name of Marena [Winter or Death], the straw figure is placed, together with a table, on which stand spirits and viands. Afterwards a bonfire is lit, and the young men and maidens jump over it in couples, carrying the figure with them. On the next day they strip the tree and the figure of their ornaments, and throw them both into a stream.' On St. Peter's Day, the twenty-ninth of June, or on the following Sunday, 'the Funeral of Kostroma' or of Lada or of Yarilo is celebrated in

Russia. In the Governments of Penza and Simbirsk the funeral used to be represented as follows. A bonfire was kindled on the twenty-eighth of June, and on the next day the maidens chose one of their number to play the part of Kostroma. Her companions saluted her with deep obeisances, placed her on a board, and carried her to the bank of a stream. There they bathed her in the water, while the oldest girl made a basket of lime-tree bark and beat it like a drum. Then they returned to the village and ended the day with processions, games, and dances. In the Murom district Kostroma was represented by a straw figure dressed in woman's clothes and flowers. This was laid in a trough and carried with songs to the bank of a lake or river. Here the crowd divided into two sides, of which the one attacked and the other defended the figure. At last the assailants gained the day, stripped the figure of its dress and ornaments, tore it in pieces, trod the straw of which it was made under foot, and flung it into the stream; while the defenders of the figure hid their faces in their hands and pretended to bewail the death of Kostroma. In the district of Kostroma the burial of Yarilo was celebrated on the twenty-ninth or thirtieth of June. The people chose an old man and gave him a small coffin containing a Priapus-like figure representing Yarilo. This he carried out of the town, followed by women chanting dirges and expressing by their gestures grief and despair. In the open fields a grave was dug, and into it the figure was lowered amid weeping and wailing, after which games and dances were begun, 'calling to mind the funeral games celebrated in old times by the pagan Slavonians.' In Little Russia the figure of Yarilo was laid in a coffin and carried through the streets after sunset surrounded by drunken women, who kept repeating mournfully, 'He is dead! he is dead!' The men lifted and shook the figure as if they were trying to recall the dead man to life. Then they said to the women, 'Women, weep not. I know what is sweeter than honey.' But the women continued to lament and chant, as they do at funerals. 'Of what was he guilty? He was so good. He will arise no more. O how shall we part from thee? What is life without thee? Arise, if only for a brief hour. But he rises not, he rises not.' At last the Yarilo was buried in a grave.

§ 7. *Death and Revival of Vegetation.* — These Russian customs are plainly of the same nature as those which in Austria and

Germany are known as 'Carrying out Death.' Therefore if the interpretation here adopted of the latter is right, the Russian Kostrubonko, Yarilo, and the rest must also have been originally embodiments of the spirit of vegetation, and their death must have been regarded as a necessary preliminary to their revival. The revival as a sequel to the death is enacted in the first of the ceremonies described, the death and resurrection of Kostrubonko. The reason why in some of these Russian ceremonies the death of the spirit of vegetation is celebrated at midsummer may be that the decline of summer is dated from Midsummer Day, after which the days begin to shorten, and the sun sets out on his downward journey:

> *'To the darksome hollows*
> *Where the frosts of winter lie.'*

Such a turning-point of the year, when vegetation might be thought to share the incipient though still almost imperceptible decay of summer, might very well be chosen by primitive man as a fit moment for resorting to those magic rites by which he hopes to stay the decline, or at least to ensure the revival, of plant life.

But while the death of vegetation appears to have been represented in all, and its revival in some, of these spring and midsummer ceremonies, there are features in some of them which can hardly be explained on this hypothesis alone. The solemn funeral, the lamentations, and the mourning attire, which often characterise these rites, are indeed appropriate at the death of the beneficent spirit of vegetation. But what shall we say of the glee with which the effigy is often carried out, of the sticks and stones with which it is assailed, and the taunts and curses which are hurled at it? What shall we say of the dread of the effigy evinced by the haste with which the bearers scamper home as soon as they have thrown it away, and by the belief that some one must soon die in any house into which it has looked? This dread might perhaps be explained by a belief that there is a certain infectiousness in the dead spirit of vegetation which renders its approach dangerous. But this explanation, besides being rather strained, does not cover the rejoicings which often attend the carrying out of Death. We must therefore recognise two distinct and seemingly opposite features in these ceremonies: on the one hand, sorrow for the death, and affection and respect for the dead; on the other hand, fear and hatred of the dead, and rejoicings at his death. How the former of these features is to be explained I have attempted to show: how the latter came to be so closely associated with the former is a question which I shall try to answer in the sequel.

§ 8. *Analogous Rites in India.* — In the Kanagra district of India there is a custom observed by young girls in spring which closely resembles some of the European spring ceremonies just described. It is called the *Ralî Ka melâ*, or fair of Ralî, the *Ralî* being a small painted earthen image of Siva or Pârvatî. The custom is in vogue all over the Kanagra district, and its celebration, which is entirely confined to young girls, lasts through most of Chet (March-April) up to the Sankrânt of Baisâkh (April). On a morning in March all the young girls of the village take small baskets of *dûb* grass and flowers to an appointed place, where they throw them in a heap. Round this heap they stand in a circle and sing. This goes on every day for ten days, till the heap of grass and flowers has reached a fair height. Then they cut in the jungle two branches, each with three prongs at one end, and place them, prongs downwards, over the heap of flowers, so as to make two tripods or pyramids. On the single uppermost points of these branches they get an image-maker to construct two clay images, one to represent Siva, and the other Pârvatî. The girls then divide themselves into two parties, one for Siva and one for Pârvatî, and marry the images in the usual way, leaving out no part of the ceremony. After the marriage they have a feast, the cost of which is defrayed by contributions solicited from their parents. Then at the next Sankrânt (Baisâkh) they all go together to the river-side, throw the images into a deep pool, and weep over the place, as though they were performing funeral obsequies. The boys of the neighbourhood often tease them by diving after the images, bringing them up, and waving them about while the girls are crying over them. The object of the fair is said to be to secure a good husband.

That in this Indian ceremony the deities Siva and Pârvatî are conceived as spirits of vegetation seems to be proved by the placing of their images on branches over a heap of grass and flowers. Here, as often in European folk-custom, the divinities of vegetation are represented in duplicate, by plants and by puppets.

The marriage of these Indian deities in spring corresponds to the European ceremonies in which the marriage of the vernal spirits of vegetation is represented by the King and Queen of May, the May Bride, Bridegroom of the May, and so forth. The throwing of the images into the water, and the mourning for them, are the equivalents of the European customs of throwing the dead spirit of vegetation under the name of Death, Yarilo, Kostroma, and the rest, into the water and lamenting over it. Again, in India, as often in Europe, the rite is performed exclusively by females. The notion that the ceremony helps to procure husbands for the girls can be explained by the quickening and fertilising influence which the spirit of vegetation is believed to exert upon the life of man as well as of plants.

§ 9. *The Magic Spring.* — The general explanation which we have been led to adopt of these and many similar ceremonies is that they are, or were in their origin, magical rites intended to ensure the revival of nature in spring. The means by which they were supposed to effect this end were imitation and sympathy. Led astray by his ignorance of the true causes of things, primitive man believed that in order to produce the great phenomena of nature on which his life depended he had only to imitate them, and that immediately by a secret sympathy or mystic influence the little drama which he acted in forest glade or mountain dell, on desert plain or wind-swept shore, would be taken up and repeated by mightier actors on a vaster stage. He fancied that by masquerading in leaves and flowers he helped the bare earth to clothe herself with verdure, and that by playing the death and burial of winter he drove that gloomy season away, and made smooth the path for the footsteps of returning spring. If we find it hard to throw ourselves even in fancy into a mental condition in which such things seem possible, we can more easily picture to ourselves the anxiety which the savage, when he first began to lift his thoughts above the satisfaction of his merely animal wants, and to meditate on the causes of things, may have felt as to the continued operation of what we now call the laws of nature. To us, familiar as we are with the conception of the uniformity and regularity with which the great cosmic phenomena succeed each other, there seems little ground for apprehension that the causes which produce these effects will cease to operate, at least within the near future. But this confidence in the stability of nature is bred only by the experience which comes of wide observation and long tradition; and the savage, with his narrow sphere of observation and his short-lived tradition, lacks the very elements of that experience which alone could set his mind at rest in face of the ever-changing and often menacing aspects of nature. No wonder, therefore, that he is thrown into a panic by an eclipse, and thinks that the sun or the moon would surely perish, if he did not raise a clamour and shoot his puny shafts into the air to defend the luminaries from the monster who threatens to devour them. No wonder he is terrified when in the darkness of night a streak of sky is suddenly illumined by the flash of a meteor, or the whole expanse of the celestial arch glows with the fitful light of the Northern Streamers. Even phenomena which recur at fixed and uniform intervals may be viewed by him with apprehension, before he has come to recognise the orderliness of their recurrence. The speed or slowness of his recognition of such periodic or cyclic changes in nature will depend largely on the length of the particular cycle. The cycle, for example, of day and night is everywhere, except in the polar regions, so short and hence so frequent that men probably soon ceased to discompose themselves seriously as to the chance of its failing to recur, though the ancient Egyptians, as we have seen, daily wrought enchantments to bring back to the east in the morning the fiery orb which had sunk at evening in the crimson west. But it was far otherwise with the annual cycle of the seasons. To any man a year is a considerable period, seeing that the number of our years is but few at the best. To the primitive savage, with his short memory and imperfect means of marking the flight of time, a year may well have been so long that he failed to recognise it as a cycle at all, and watched the changing aspects of earth and heaven with a perpetual wonder, alternately delighted and alarmed, elated and cast down, according as the vicissitudes of light and heat, of plant and animal life, ministered to his comfort or threatened his existence. In autumn when the withered leaves were whirled about the forest by the nipping blast, and he looked up at the bare boughs, could he feel sure that they would ever be green again? As day by day the sun sank lower and lower in the sky, could he be certain that the luminary would ever retrace his heavenly road? Even the waning moon, whose pale sickle rose thinner and thinner every night over the rim of the eastern horizon, may have excited in his mind a fear lest, when it had wholly vanished, there should be moons no more.

These and a thousand such misgivings may have thronged the fancy and troubled the peace of the man who first began to reflect on the mysteries of the world he lived in, and to take thought for a more distant future than the morrow. It was natural, therefore, that with such thoughts and fears he should have done all that in him lay to bring back the faded blossom to the bough, to swing the low sun of winter up to his old place in the summer sky, and to restore its orbed fullness to the silver lamp of the waning moon. We may smile at his vain endeavours if we please, but it was only by making a long series of experiments, of which some were almost inevitably doomed to failure, that man learned from experience the futility of some of his attempted methods and the fruitfulness of others. After all, magical ceremonies are nothing but experiments which have failed and which continue to be repeated merely because, for reasons which have already been indicated, the operator is unaware of their failure. With the advance of knowledge these ceremonies either cease to be performed altogether or are kept up from force of habit long after the intention with which they were instituted has been forgotten. Thus fallen from their high estate, no longer regarded as solemn rites on the punctual performance of which the welfare and even the life of the community depend, they sink gradually to the level of simple pageants, mummeries, and pastimes, till in the final stage of degeneration they are wholly abandoned by older people, and, from having once been the most serious occupation of the sage, become at last the idle sport of children. It is in this final stage of decay that most of the old magical rites of our European forefathers linger on at the present day, and even from this their last retreat they are fast being swept away by the rising tide of those multitudinous forces, moral, intellectual, and social, which are bearing mankind onward to a new and unknown goal. We may feel some natural regret at the disappearance of quaint customs and picturesque ceremonies, which have preserved to an age often deemed dull and prosaic something of the flavour and freshness of the olden time, some breath of the springtime of the world; yet our regret will be lessened when we remember that these pretty pageants, these now innocent diversions, had their origin in ignorance and superstition; that if they are a record of human endeavour, they are also a monument of fruitless ingenuity, of wasted labour, and of blighted hopes; and that for all their gay trappings — their flowers, their ribbons, and their music — they partake far more of tragedy than of farce.

The interpretation which, following in the footsteps of W. Mannhardt, I have attempted to give of these ceremonies has been not a little confirmed by the discovery, made since this book was first written, that the natives of Central Australia regularly practise magical ceremonies for the purpose of awakening the dormant energies of nature at the approach of what may be called the Australian spring. Nowhere apparently are the alternations of the seasons more sudden and the contrasts between them more striking than in the deserts of Central Australia, where at the end of a long period of drought the sandy and stony wilderness, over which the silence and desolation of death appear to brood, is suddenly, after a few days of torrential rain, transformed into a landscape smiling with verdure and peopled with teeming multitudes of insects and lizards, of frogs and birds. The marvellous change which passes over the face of nature at such times has been compared even by European observers to the effect of magic; no wonder, then, that the savage should regard it as such in very deed. Now it is just when there is promise of the approach of a good season that the natives of Central Australia are wont especially to perform those magical ceremonies of which the avowed intention is to multiply the plants and animals they use as food. These ceremonies, therefore, present a close analogy to the spring customs of our European peasantry not only in the time of their celebration, but also in their aim; for we can hardly doubt that in instituting rites designed to assist the revival of plant life in spring our primitive forefathers were moved, not by any sentimental wish to smell at early violets, or pluck the rathe primrose, or watch yellow daffodils dancing in the breeze, but by the very practical consideration, certainly not formulated in abstract terms, that the life of man is inextricably bound up with that of plants, and that if they were to perish he could not survive. And as the faith of the Australian savage in the efficacy of his magic rites is confirmed by observing that their performance is invariably followed, sooner or later, by that increase of vegetable and animal life which it is their object to produce, so, we may suppose, it was with European savages in the olden time. The sight of the fresh green in brake and thicket, of vernal flowers blowing on mossy banks, of swallows arriving from the south, and of the sun mounting daily higher in the sky, would be welcomed by them as so many visible signs that their enchantments were indeed taking effect, and would inspire them with a cheerful confidence that all was well with a world which they could thus mould to suit their wishes. Only in autumn days, as summer slowly faded, would their confidence again be dashed by doubts and misgivings at symptoms of decay, which told how vain were all their efforts to stave off for ever the approach of winter and of death.

CHAPTER XXIX

THE MYTH OF ADONIS

THE spectacle of the great changes which annually pass over the face of the earth has powerfully impressed the minds of men in all ages, and stirred them to meditate on the causes of transformations so vast and wonderful. Their curiosity has not been purely disinterested; for even the savage cannot fail to perceive how intimately his own life is bound up with the life of nature, and how the same processes which freeze the stream and strip the earth of vegetation menace him with extinction. At a certain stage of development men seem to have imagined that the means of averting the threatened calamity were in their own hands, and that they could hasten or retard the flight of the seasons by magic art. Accordingly they performed ceremonies and recited spells to make the rain to fall, the sun to shine, animals to multiply, and the fruits of the earth to grow. In course of time the slow advance of knowledge, which has dispelled so many cherished illusions, convinced at least the more thoughtful portion of mankind that the alternations of summer and winter, of spring and autumn, were not merely the result of their own magical rites, but that some deeper cause, some mightier power, was at work behind the shifting scenes of nature. They now pictured to themselves the growth and decay of vegetation, the birth and death of living creatures, as effects of the waxing or waning strength of divine beings, of gods and goddesses, who were born and died, who married and begot children, on the pattern of human life.

Thus the old magical theory of the seasons was displaced, or rather supplemented, by a religious theory. For although men now attributed the annual cycle of change primarily to corresponding changes in their deities, they still thought that by performing certain magical rites they could aid the god, who was the principle of life, in his struggle with the opposing principle of death. They imagined that they could recruit his failing energies and even raise him from the dead. The ceremonies which they observed for this purpose were in substance a dramatic representation of the natural processes which they wished to facilitate; for it is a familiar tenet of magic that you can produce any desired effect by merely imitating it. And as they now explained the fluctuations of growth and decay, of reproduction and dissolution, by the marriage, the death, and the rebirth or revival of the gods, their religious or rather magical dramas turned in great measure on these themes. They set forth the fruitful union of the powers of fertility, the sad death of one at least of the divine partners, and his joyful resurrection. Thus a religious theory was blended with a magical practice. The combination is familiar in history. Indeed, few religions have ever succeeded in wholly extricating themselves from the old trammels of magic. The inconsistency of acting on two opposite principles, however it may vex the soul of the philosopher, rarely troubles the common man; indeed he is seldom even aware of it. His affair is to act, not to analyse the motives of his action. If mankind had always been logical and wise, history would not be a long chronicle of folly and crime.

Of the changes which the seasons bring with them, the most striking within the temperate zone are those which affect vegetation. The influence of the seasons on animals, though great, is not nearly so manifest. Hence it is natural that in the magical dramas designed to dispel winter and bring back spring the emphasis should be laid on vegetation, and that trees and plants should figure in them more prominently than beasts and birds. Yet the two sides of life, the vegetable and the animal, were not dissociated in the minds of those who observed the ceremonies. Indeed they commonly believed that the tie between the animal and the vegetable world was even closer than it really is; hence they often combined the dramatic representation of reviving plants with a real or a dramatic union of the sexes for the purpose of furthering at the same time and by the same act the multiplication of fruits, of animals, and of men. To them the principle of life and fertility, whether animal or vegetable, was one and indivisible. To live and to cause to live, to eat food and to beget children, these were the primary wants of men in the past, and they will be the primary wants of men in the future so long as the world lasts. Other things may be added to enrich and beautify human life, but unless these wants are first satisfied, humanity itself must cease to exist. These two things, therefore, food and children, were what men chiefly sought to procure by the performance of magical rites for the regulation of the seasons.

Nowhere, apparently, have these rites been more widely and solemnly celebrated than in the lands which border the eastern Mediterranean. Under the names of Osiris, Tammuz, Adonis, and Attis, the peoples of Egypt and Western Asia represented the yearly decay and revival of life, especially of vegetable life, which they personified as a god who annually died and rose again from the dead. In name and detail the rites varied from place to place: in substance they were the same. The supposed death and resurrection of this oriental deity, a god of many names but of essentially one nature, is now to be examined. We begin with Tammuz or Adonis.

The worship of Adonis was practised by the Semitic peoples of Babylonia and Syria, and the Greeks borrowed it from them as early as the seventh century before Christ. The true name of the deity was Tammuz: the appellation of Adonis is merely the Semitic *Adon*, 'lord,' a title of honour by which his worshippers addressed him. But the Greeks through a misunderstanding converted the title of honour into a proper name. In the religious literature of Babylonia Tammuz appears as the youthful spouse or lover of Ishtar, the great mother goddess, the embodiment of the reproductive energies of nature. The references to their connexion with each other in myth and ritual are both fragmentary and obscure, but we gather from them that every year Tammuz was believed to die, passing away from the cheerful earth to the gloomy subterranean world, and that every year his divine mistress journeyed in quest of him 'to the land from which there is no returning, to the house of darkness, where dust lies on door and bolt.' During her absence the passion of love ceased to operate: men and beasts alike forgot to reproduce their kinds: all life was threatened with extinction. So intimately bound up with the goddess were the sexual functions of the whole animal kingdom that without her presence they could not be discharged. A messenger of the great god Ea was accordingly despatched to rescue the goddess on whom so much depended. The stern queen of the infernal regions, Allatu or Eresh-Kigal by name, reluctantly allowed Ishtar to be sprinkled with the Water of Life and to depart, in company probably with her lover Tammuz, that the two might return together to the upper world, and that with their return all nature might revive.

Laments for the departed Tammuz are contained in several Babylonian hymns, which liken him to plants that quickly fade. He is

'*A tamarisk that in the garden has drunk no water,*
  Whose crown in the field has brought forth no blossom.
A willow that rejoiced not by the watercourse,
A willow whose roots were torn up.
A herb that in the garden had drunk no water.'

His death appears to have been annually mourned, to the shrill music of flutes, by men and women about midsummer in the month named after him, the month of Tammuz. The dirges were seemingly chanted over an effigy of the dead god, which was washed with pure water, anointed with oil, and clad in a red robe, while the fumes of incense rose into the air, as if to stir his dormant senses by their pungent fragrance and wake him from the sleep of death. In one of these dirges, inscribed *Lament of the Flutes for Tammuz*, we seem still to hear the voices of the singers chanting the sad refrain and to catch, like far-away music, the wailing notes of the flutes:

'*At his vanishing away she lifts up a lament,*
  "*Oh my child!*" *at his vanishing away she lifts up a lament;*

"My Damu!" at his vanishing away she lifts up a lament.
  "My enchanter and priest!" at his vanishing away she lifts up a
    lament,
At the shining cedar, rooted in a spacious place,
  In Eanna, above and below, she lifts up a lament.
Like the lament that a house lifts up for its master, lifts she up a
  lament,
  Like the lament that a city lifts up for its lord, lifts she up a lament.
Her lament is the lament for a herb that grows not in the bed,
  Her lament is the lament for the corn that grows not in the ear.
Her chamber is a possession that brings not forth a possession,
  A weary woman, a weary child, forspent.
Her lament is for a great river, where no willows grow,
  Her lament is for a field, where corn and herbs grow not.
Her lament is for a pool, where fishes grow not.
  Her lament is for a thicket of reeds, where no reeds grow.
Her lament is for woods, where tamarisks grow not.
  Her lament is for a wilderness where no cypresses (?) grow.
Her lament is for the depth of a garden of trees, where honey and
  wine grow not.
  Her lament is for meadows, where no plants grow.
Her lament is for a palace, where length of life grows not.'

The tragical story and the melancholy rites of Adonis are better known to us from the descriptions of Greek writers than from the fragments of Babylonian literature or the brief reference of the prophet Ezekiel, who saw the women of Jerusalem weeping for Tammuz at the north gate of the temple. Mirrored in the glass of Greek mythology, the oriental deity appears as a comely youth beloved by Aphrodite. In his infancy the goddess hid him in a chest, which she gave in charge to Persephone, queen of the nether world. But when Persephone opened the chest and beheld the beauty of the babe, she refused to give him back to Aphrodite, though the goddess of love went down herself to hell to ransom her dear one from the power of the grave. The dispute between the two goddesses of love and death was settled by Zeus, who decreed that Adonis should abide with Persephone in the under world for one part of the year, and with Aphrodite in the upper world for another part. At last the fair youth was killed in hunting by a wild boar, or by the jealous Ares, who turned himself into the likeness of a boar in order to compass the death of his rival.

Bitterly did Aphrodite lament her loved and lost Adonis. In this form of the myth, the contest between Aphrodite and Persephone for the possession of Adonis clearly reflects the struggle between Ishtar and Allatu in the land of the dead, while the decision of Zeus that Adonis is to spend one part of the year under ground and another part above ground is merely a Greek version of the annual disappearance and reappearance of Tammuz.

CHAPTER XXX

ADONIS IN SYRIA

THE myth of Adonis was localised and his rites celebrated with much solemnity at two places in Western Asia. One of these was Byblus on the coast of Syria, the other was Paphos in Cyprus. Both were great seats of the worship of Aphrodite, or rather of her Semitic counterpart, Astarte; and of both, if we accept the legends, Cinyras, the father of Adonis, was king. Of the two cities Byblus was the more ancient; indeed it is claimed to be the oldest city in Phoenicia, and to have been founded in the early ages of the world by the great god El, whom Greeks and Romans identified with Cronus and Saturn respectively. However that may have been, in historical times it ranked as a holy place, the religious capital of the country, the Mecca or Jerusalem of the Phoenicians. The city stood on a height beside the sea, and contained a great sanctuary of Astarte, where in the midst of a spacious open court, surrounded by cloisters and approached from below by staircases, rose a tall cone or obelisk, the holy image of the goddess. In this sanctuary the rites of Adonis were celebrated. Indeed the whole city was sacred to him, and the River Nahr Ibrahim, which falls into the sea a little to the south of Byblus, bore in antiquity the name of Adonis. This was the kingdom of Cinyras. From the earliest to the latest times the city appears to have been ruled by kings, assisted perhaps by a senate or council of elders.

The last king of Byblus bore the ancient name of Cinyras, and was beheaded by Pompey the Great for his tyrannous excesses. His legendary namesake Cinyras is said to have founded a sanctuary of Aphrodite, that is, of Astarte, at a place on Mount Lebanon, distant a day's journey from the capital. The spot was probably Aphaca, at the source of the River Adonis, half-way between Byblus and Baalbec; for at Aphaca there was a famous grove and sanctuary of Astarte which Constantine destroyed on account of the flagitious character of the worship. The site of the temple has been discovered by modern travellers near the miserable village which still bears the name of Afka at the head of the wild, romantic, wooded gorge of the Adonis. The hamlet stands among groves of noble walnut-trees on the brink of the lyn. A little way off the river rushes from a cavern at the foot of a mighty amphitheatre of towering cliffs to plunge in a series of cascades into the awful depths of the glen. The deeper it descends, the ranker and denser grows the vegetation, which, sprouting from the crannies and fissures of the rocks, spreads a green veil over the roaring or murmuring stream in the tremendous chasm below. There is something delicious, almost intoxicating, in the freshness of these tumbling waters, in the sweetness and purity of the mountain air, in the vivid green of the vegetation. The temple, of which some massive hewn blocks and a fine column of Syenite granite still mark the site, occupied a terrace facing the source of the river and commanding a magnificent prospect. Across the foam and the roar of the waterfalls you look up to the cavern and away to the top of the sublime precipices above. So lofty is the cliff that the goats which creep along its ledges to browse on the bushes appear like ants to the spectator hundreds of feet below. Seaward the view is especially impressive when the sun floods the profound gorge with golden light, revealing all the fantastic buttresses and rounded towers of its mountain rampart, and falling softly on the varied green of the woods which clothe its depths. It was here that, according to the legend, Adonis met Aphrodite for the first or the last time, and here his mangled body was buried. A fairer scene could hardly be imagined for a story of tragic love and death. Yet, sequestered as the valley is and must always have been, it is not wholly deserted. A convent or a village may be observed here and there standing out against the sky on the top of some beetling crag, or clinging to the face of a nearly perpendicular cliff high above the foam and the din of the river; and at evening the lights that twinkle through the gloom betray the presence of human habitations on slopes which might seem inaccessible to man. In antiquity the whole of the lovely vale appears to have been dedicated to Adonis, and to this day it is haunted by his memory; for the heights which shut it in are crested at various points by ruined monuments of his worship, some of them overhanging the dreadful abysses, down which it turns the head dizzy to look and see the eagles wheeling about their nests far below. One such monument exists at Ghineh. The face of a great rock, above a roughly hewn recess, is here carved with figures of Adonis and Aphrodite. He is portrayed with spear in rest, awaiting the attack of a boar, while she is seated in an attitude of sorrow. Her grief-stricken figure may well be the mourning Aphrodite of the Lebanon described by Macrobius, and the recess in the rock is perhaps her lover's tomb. Every year, in the belief of his worshippers, Adonis was wounded to death on the mountains, and every year the face of nature itself was dyed with his sacred blood. So year by year the Syrian damsels lamented his untimely fate, while the red anemone, his flower, bloomed among the cedars of Lebanon, and the river ran red to the sea, fringing the winding shores of the blue Mediterranean, whenever the wind set inshore, with a sinuous band of crimson.

CHAPTER XXXI

ADONIS IN CYPRUS

THE island of Cyprus lies but one day's sail from the coast of Syria. Indeed, on fine summer evenings its mountains may be descried looming low and dark against the red fires of sunset. With its rich mines of copper and its forests of firs and stately cedars, the island naturally attracted a commercial and maritime people like the Phoenicians; while the abundance of its corn, its wine, and its oil must have rendered it in their eyes a Land of Promise by comparison with the niggardly nature of their own rugged coast, hemmed in between the mountains and the sea. Accordingly they settled in Cyprus at a very early date and remained there long after the Greeks had also established themselves on its shores; for we know from inscriptions and coins that Phoenician kings reigned at Citium, the Chittim of the Hebrews, down to the time of Alexander the Great. Naturally the Semitic colonists brought their gods with them from the mother-land. They worshipped Baal of the Lebanon, who may well have been Adonis, and at Amathus on the south coast they instituted the rites of Adonis and Aphrodite, or rather Astarte. Here, as at Byblus, these rites resembled the Egyptian worship of Osiris so closely that some people even identified the Adonis of Amathus with Osiris.

But the great seat of the worship of Aphrodite and Adonis in Cyprus was Paphos on the south-western side of the island. Among the petty kingdoms into which Cyprus was divided from the earliest times until the end of the fourth century before our era Paphos must have ranked with the best. It is a land of hills and billowy ridges, diversified by fields and vineyards and inter-sected by rivers, which in the course of ages have carved for themselves beds of such tremendous depth that travelling in the interior is difficult and tedious. The lofty range of Mount Olympus (the modern Troodos), capped with snow the greater part of the year, screens Paphos from the northerly and easterly winds and cuts it off from the rest of the island. On the slopes of the range the last pine-woods of Cyprus linger, sheltering here and there monasteries in scenery not unworthy of the Apennines. The old city of Paphos occupied the summit of a hill about a mile from the sea; the newer city sprang up at the harbour some ten miles off. The sanctuary of Aphrodite at Old Paphos (the modern Kuklia) was one of the most celebrated shrines in the ancient world. According to Herodotus, it was founded by Phoenician colonists from Ascalon; but it is possible that a native goddess of fertility was worshipped on the spot before the arrival of the Phoenicians, and that the newcomers identified her with their own Baalath or Astarte, whom she may have closely resembled. If two deities were thus fused in one, we may suppose that they were both varieties of that great goddess of motherhood and fertility whose worship appears to have been spread all over Western Asia from a very early time. The supposition is confirmed as well by the archaic shape of her image as by the licentious character of her rites; for both that shape and those rites were

shared by her with other Asiatic deities. Her image was simply
a white cone or pyramid. In like manner, a cone was the emblem
of Astarte at Byblus, of the native goddess whom the Greeks
called Artemis at Perga in Pamphylia, and of the sun-god
Heliogabalus at Emesa in Syria. Conical stones, which apparently
served as idols, have also been found at Golgi in Cyprus, and in
the Phoenician temples of Malta; and cones of sandstone came
to light at the shrine of the 'Mistress of Torquoise' among the
barren hills and frowning precipices of Sinai.

In Cyprus it appears that before marriage all women were
formerly obliged by custom to prostitute themselves to strangers
at the sanctuary of the goddess, whether she went by the name of
Aphrodite, Astarte, or what not. Similar customs prevailed in
many parts of Western Asia. Whatever its motive, the practice
was clearly regarded, not as an orgy of lust, but as a solemn
religious duty performed in the service of that great Mother
Goddess of Western Asia whose name varied, while her type
remained constant, from place to place. Thus at Babylon every
woman, whether rich or poor, had once in her life to submit to
the embraces of a stranger at the temple of Mylitta, that is, of
Ishtar or Astarte, and to dedicate to the goddess the wages earned
by this sanctified harlotry. The sacred precinct was crowded
with women waiting to observe the custom. Some of them had to
wait there for years. At Heliopolis or Baalbec in Syria, famous
for the imposing grandeur of its ruined temples, the custom of
the country required that every maiden should prostitute herself
to a stranger at the temple of Astarte, and matrons as well as
maids testified their devotion to the goddess in the same manner.
The emperor Constantine abolished the custom, destroyed the
temple, and built a church in its stead. In Phoenician temples
women prostituted themselves for hire in the service of religion,
believing that by this conduct they propitiated the goddess and
won her favour. 'It was a law of the Amorites, that she who was
about to marry should sit in fornication seven days by the gate.'
At Byblus the people shaved their heads in the annual mourning
for Adonis. Women who refused to sacrifice their hair had to
give themselves up to strangers on a certain day of the festival,
and the money which they thus earned was devoted to the goddess.
A Greek inscription found at Tralles in Lydia proves that the

practice of religious prostitution survived in that country as late as the second century of our era. It records of a certain woman, Aurelia Aemilia by name, not only that she herself served the god in the capacity of a harlot at his express command, but that her mother and other female ancestors had done the same before her; and the publicity of the record, engraved on a marble column which supported a votive offering, shows that no stain attached to such a life and such a parentage. In Armenia the noblest families dedicated their daughters to the service of the goddess Anaitis in her temple at Acilisena, where the damsels acted as prostitutes for a long time before they were given in marriage. Nobody scrupled to take one of these girls to wife when her period of service was over. Again, the goddess Ma was served by a multitude of sacred harlots at Comana in Pontus, and crowds of men and women flocked to her sanctuary from the neighbouring cities and country to attend the biennial festivals or to pay their vows to the goddess.

If we survey the whole of the evidence on this subject, some of which has still to be laid before the reader, we may conclude that a great Mother Goddess, the personification of all the reproductive energies of nature, was worshipped under different names but with a substantial similarity of myth and ritual by many peoples of Western Asia; that associated with her was a lover, or rather series of lovers, divine yet mortal, with whom she mated year by year, their commerce being deemed essential to the propagation of animals and plants, each in their several kind; and further, that the fabulous union of the divine pair was simulated and, as it were, multiplied on earth by the real, though temporary, union of the human sexes at the sanctuary of the goddess for the sake of thereby ensuring the fruitfulness of the ground and the increase of man and beast.

At Paphos the custom of religious prostitution is said to have been instituted by King Cinyras, and to have been practised by his daughters, the sisters of Adonis, who, having incurred the wrath of Aphrodite, mated with strangers and ended their days in Egypt. In this form of the tradition the wrath of Aphrodite is probably a feature added by a later authority, who could only regard conduct which shocked his own moral sense as a punishment inflicted by the goddess instead of as a sacrifice regularly enjoined by her on all her devotees. At all events the story indicates that the princesses of Paphos had to conform to the custom as well as women of humble birth.

Among the stories which were told of Cinyras, the ancestor of the priestly kings of Paphos and the father of Adonis, there are some that deserve our attention. In the first place, he is said to have begotten his son Adonis in incestuous intercourse with his daughter Myrrha at a festival of the corn-goddess, at which women robed in white were wont to offer corn-wreaths as first-fruits of the harvest and to observe strict chastity for nine days. Similar cases of incest with a daughter are reported of many ancient kings. It seems unlikely that such reports are without foundation, and perhaps equally improbable that they refer to mere fortuitous outbursts of unnatural lust. We may suspect that they are based on a practice actually observed for a definite reason in certain special circumstances. Now in countries where the royal blood was traced through women only, and where consequently the king held office merely in virtue of his marriage with an hereditary princess, who was the real sovereign, it appears to have often happened that a prince married his own sister, the princess royal, in order to obtain with her hand the crown which otherwise would have gone to another man, perhaps to a stranger. May not the same rule of descent have furnished a motive for incest with a daughter? For it seems a natural corollary from such a rule that the king was bound to vacate the throne on the death of his wife, the queen, since he occupied it only by virtue of his marriage with her. When the marriage terminated, his right to the throne terminated with it and passed at once to his daughter's husband. Hence if the king desired to reign after his wife's death, the only way in which he could legitimately continue to do so was by marrying his daughter, and thus prolonging through her the title which had formerly been his through her mother.

Cinyras is said to have been famed for his exquisite beauty and to have been wooed by Aphrodite herself. Thus it would appear, as scholars have already observed, that Cinyras was in a sense a duplicate of his handsome son Adonis, to whom the inflammable goddess also lost her heart. Further, these stories of the love of Aphrodite for two members of the royal house of Paphos can

P

hardly be dissociated from the corresponding legend told of Pygmalion, a Phoenician king of Cyprus, who is said to have fallen in love with an image of Aphrodite and taken it to his bed. When we consider that Pygmalion was the father-in-law of Cinyras, that the son of Cinyras was Adonis, and that all three, in successive generations, are said to have been concerned in a love-intrigue with Aphrodite, we can hardly help concluding that the early Phoenician kings of Paphos, or their sons, regularly claimed to be not merely the priests of the goddess but also her lovers, in other words, that in their official capacity they personated Adonis. At all events Adonis is said to have reigned in Cyprus, and it appears to be certain that the title of Adonis was regularly borne by the sons of all the Phoenician kings of the island. It is true that the title strictly signified no more than 'lord'; yet the legends which connect these Cyprian princes with the goddess of love make it probable that they claimed the divine nature as well as the human dignity of Adonis. The story of Pygmalion points to a ceremony of a sacred marriage in which the king wedded the image of Aphrodite, or rather of Astarte. If that was so, the tale was in a sense true, not of a single man only, but of a whole series of men, and it would be all the more likely to be told of Pygmalion, if that was a common name of Semitic kings in general, and of Cyprian kings in particular. Pygmalion, at all events, is known as the name of the famous king of Tyre from whom his sister Dido fled; and a king of Citium and Idalium in Cyprus, who reigned in the time of Alexander the Great, was also called Pygmalion, or rather Pumiyathon, the Phoenician name which the Greeks corrupted into Pygmalion. Further, it deserves to be noted that the names Pygmalion and Astarte occur together in a Punic inscription on a gold medallion which was found in a grave at Carthage; the characters of the inscription are of the earliest type. As the custom of religious prostitution at Paphos is said to have been founded by King Cinyras and observed by his daughters, we may surmise that the kings of Paphos played the part of the divine bridegroom in a less innocent rite than the form of marriage with a statue; in fact, that at certain festivals each of them had to mate with one or more of the sacred harlots of the temple, who played Astarte to his Adonis. If that was so, there is more truth than has commonly been supposed in the reproach cast by the Christian fathers that the Aphrodite worshipped by Cinyras was a common whore. The fruit of their union would rank as sons and daughters of the deity, and would in time become the parents of gods and goddesses, like their fathers and mothers before them. In this manner Paphos, and perhaps all sanctuaries of the great Asiatic goddess where sacred prostitution was practised, might be well stocked with human deities, the offspring of the divine king by his wives, concubines, and temple harlots. Any one of these might probably succeed his father on the throne or be sacrificed in his stead whenever stress of war or other grave junctures called, as they sometimes did, for the death of a royal victim. Such a tax, levied occasionally on the king's numerous progeny for the good of the country, would neither extinguish the divine stock nor break the father's heart, who divided his paternal affection among so many. At all events, if, as there seems reason to believe, Semitic kings were often regarded at the same time as hereditary deities, it is easy to understand the frequency of Semitic personal names which imply that the bearers of them were the sons or daughters, the brothers or sisters, the fathers or mothers of a god, and we need not resort to the shifts employed by some scholars to evade the plain sense of the words. This interpretation is confirmed by a parallel Egyptian usage; for in Egypt, where the kings were worshipped as divine, the queen was called 'the wife of the god' or 'the mother of the god,' and the title 'father of the god' was borne not only by the king's real father but also by his father-in-law. Similarly, perhaps, among the Semites any man who sent his daughter to swell the royal harem may have been allowed to call himself 'the father of the god.'

If we may judge by his name, the Semitic king who bore the name of Cinyras was, like King David, a harper; for the name of Cinyras is clearly connected with the Greek *cinyra*, 'a lyre,' which in its turn comes from the Semitic *kinnor*, 'a lyre,' the very word applied to the instrument on which David played before Saul. We shall probably not err in assuming that at Paphos as at Jerusalem the music of the lyre or harp was not a mere pastime designed to while away an idle hour, but formed part of the service of religion, the moving influence of its melodies being perhaps set down, like the effect of wine, to the direct inspiration of a deity. Certainly at Jerusalem the regular clergy of the temple prophesied to the music of harps, of psalteries, and of cymbals; and it appears that the irregular clergy also, as we may call the prophets, depended on some such stimulus for inducing the ecstatic state which they took for immediate converse with the divinity. Thus we read of a band of prophets coming down from a high place with a psaltery, a timbrel, a pipe, and a harp before them, and prophesying as they went. Again, when the united forces of Judah and Ephraim were traversing the wilderness of Moab in pursuit of the enemy, they could find no water for three days, and were like to die of thirst, they and the beasts of burden. In this emergency the prophet Elisha, who was with the army, called for a minstrel and bade him play. Under the influence of the music he ordered the soldiers to dig trenches in the sandy bed of the waterless waddy through which lay the line of march. They did so, and next morning the trenches were full of the water that had drained down into them underground from the desolate, forbidding mountains on either hand. The prophet's success in striking water in the wilderness resembles the reported success of modern dowsers, though his mode of procedure was different. Incidentally he rendered another service to his countrymen. For the skulking Moabites from their lairs among the rocks saw the red sun of the desert reflected in the water, and taking it for the blood, or perhaps rather for an omen of the blood, of their enemies, they plucked up heart to attack the camp and were defeated with great slaughter.

Again, just as the cloud of melancholy which from time to time darkened the moody mind of Saul was viewed as an evil spirit from the Lord vexing him, so on the other hand the solemn strains of the harp, which soothed and composed his troubled thoughts, may well have seemed to the hag-ridden king the very voice of God or of his good angel whispering peace. Even in our own day a great religious writer, himself deeply sensitive to the witchery of music, has said that musical notes, with all their power to fire the blood and melt the heart, cannot be mere empty sounds and nothing more; no, they have escaped from some higher sphere, they are outpourings of eternal harmony, the voice of angels, the Magnificat of saints. It is thus that the rude imaginings of primitive man are transfigured and his feeble lispings echoed with a rolling reverberation in the musical prose of Newman. Indeed the influence of music on the development of religion is a subject which would repay a sympathetic study. For we cannot doubt that this, the most intimate and affecting of all the arts, has done much to create as well as to express the religious emotions, thus modifying more or less deeply the fabric of belief to which at first sight it seems only to minister. The musician has done his part as well as the prophet and the thinker in the making of religion. Every faith has its appropriate music, and the difference between the creeds might almost be expressed in musical notation. The interval, for example, which divides the wild revels of Cybele from the stately ritual of the Catholic Church is measured by the gulf which severs the dissonant clash of cymbals and tambourines from the grave harmonies of Palestrina and Handel. A different spirit breathes in the difference of the music.

CHAPTER XXXII

THE RITUAL OF ADONIS

AT the festivals of Adonis, which were held in Western Asia and in Greek lands, the death of the god was annually mourned, with a bitter wailing, chiefly by women; images of him, dressed to resemble corpses, were carried out as to burial and then thrown into the sea or into springs; and in some places his revival was celebrated on the following day. But at different places the ceremonies varied somewhat in the manner and apparently also in the season of their celebration. At Alexandria images of Aphrodite and Adonis were displayed on two couches; beside them were set ripe fruits of all kinds, cakes, plants growing in flower-pots, and green bowers twined with anise. The marriage of the lovers was celebrated one day, and on the morrow women attired as mourners, with streaming hair and bared breasts, bore the image of the dead Adonis to the sea-shore and committed it to the waves. Yet they sorrowed not without hope, for they sang that the lost one would come back again. The date at which this Alexandrian ceremony was observed is not expressly stated; but from the mention of the ripe fruits it has been inferred that it took place in late summer. In the great Phoenician sanctuary of Astarte at Byblus the death of Adonis was annually mourned, to the shrill wailing notes of the flute, with weeping, lamentation, and beating of the breast; but next day he was believed to come to life again and ascend up to heaven in the presence of his worshippers. The disconsolate believers, left behind on earth, shaved their heads as the Egyptians did on the death of the divine bull Apis; women who could not bring themselves to sacrifice their beautiful tresses had to give themselves up to strangers on a certain day of the festival, and to dedicate to Astarte the wages of their shame.

This Phoenician festival appears to have been a vernal one, for its date was determined by the discolouration of the River Adonis, and this has been observed by modern travellers to occur in spring. At that season the red earth washed down from the mountains by the rain tinges the water of the river, and even the sea, for a great way with a blood-red hue, and the crimson stain was believed to be the blood of Adonis, annually wounded to death by the boar on Mount Lebanon. Again, the scarlet anemone is said to have sprung from the blood of Adonis, or to have been stained by it; and as the anemone blooms in Syria about Easter, this may be thought to show that the festival of Adonis, or at least one of his festivals, was held in spring. The name of the flower is probably derived from Naaman ('darling'), which seems to have been an epithet of Adonis. The Arabs still call the anemone 'wounds of the Naaman.' The red rose also was said to owe its hue to the same sad occasion; for Aphrodite, hastening to her wounded lover, trod on a bush of white roses; the cruel thorns tore her tender flesh, and her sacred blood dyed the white roses for ever red. It would be idle, perhaps, to lay much weight on evidence drawn from the calendar of flowers, and in particular to press an argument so fragile as the bloom of the rose. Yet so far as it counts at all, the tale which links the damask rose with the death of Adonis points to a summer rather than to a spring celebration of his passion. In Attica, certainly, the festival fell at the height of summer. For the fleet which Athens fitted out against Syracuse, and by the destruction of which her power was permanently crippled, sailed at midsummer, and by an ominous coincidence the sombre rites of Adonis were being celebrated at the very time. As the troops marched down to the harbour to embark, the streets through which they passed were lined with coffins and corpse-like effigies, and the air was rent with the noise of women wailing for the dead Adonis. The circumstances cast a gloom over the sailing of the most splendid armament that Athens ever sent to sea. Many ages afterwards, when the Emperor Julian made his first entry into Antioch, he found in like manner the gay, the luxurious capital of the East plunged in mimic grief for the annual death of Adonis; and if he had any presentiment of coming evil, the voices of lamentation which struck upon his ear must have seemed to sound his knell.

The resemblance of these ceremonies to the Indian and European ceremonies which I have described elsewhere is obvious. In particular, apart from the somewhat doubtful date of its celebration, the Alexandrian ceremony is almost identical with the Indian. In both of them the marriage of two divine beings, whose affinity with vegetation seems indicated by the fresh plants with which they are surrounded, is celebrated in effigy, and the effigies are afterwards mourned over and thrown into the water. From the similarity of these customs to each other and to the spring and midsummer customs of modern Europe we should naturally expect that they all admit of a common explanation. Hence, if the explanation which I have adopted of the latter is correct, the ceremony of the death and resurrection of Adonis must also have been a dramatic representation of the decay and revival of plant life. The inference thus based on the resemblance of the customs is confirmed by the following features in the legend and ritual of Adonis. His affinity with vegetation comes out at once in the common story of his birth. He was said to have been born from a myrrh-tree, the bark of which bursting, after a ten months' gestation, allowed the lovely infant to come forth. According to some, a boar rent the bark with his tusk and so opened a passage for the babe. A faint rationalistic colour was given to the legend by saying that his mother was a woman named Myrrh, who had been turned into a myrrh-tree soon after she had conceived the child. The use of myrrh as incense at the festival of Adonis may have given rise to the fable. We have seen that incense was burnt at the corresponding Babylonian rites, just as it was burnt by the idolatrous Hebrews in honour of the Queen of Heaven, who was no other than Astarte. Again, the story that Adonis spent half, or according to others a third, of the year in the lower world and the rest of it in the upper world, is explained most simply and naturally by supposing that he represented vegetation, especially the corn, which lies buried in the earth half the year and reappears above the ground the other half. Certainly of the annual phenomena of nature there is none which suggests so obviously the idea of death and resurrection as the disappearance and reappearance of vegetation in autumn and spring. Adonis has been taken for the sun; but there is nothing in the sun's annual course within the temperate and tropical zones to suggest that he is dead for half or a third of the year and alive for the other half or two-thirds. He might, indeed, be conceived as weakened in winter, but dead he could not be thought to be; his daily reappearance contradicts the supposition. Within the Arctic Circle, where the sun annually disappears for a continuous period which varies from twenty-four hours to six months according to the latitude, his yearly death and resurrection would certainly be an obvious idea; but no one except the unfortunate astronomer Bailly has maintained that the Adonis worship came from the Arctic regions. On the other hand, the annual death and revival of vegetation is a conception which readily presents itself to men in every stage of savagery and civilisation; and the vastness of the scale on which this ever-recurring decay and regeneration takes place, together with man's intimate dependence on it for subsistence, combine to render it the most impressive annual occurrence in nature, at least within the temperate zones. It is no wonder that a phenomenon so important, so striking, and so universal should, by suggesting similar ideas, have given rise to similar rites in many lands. We may, therefore, accept as probable an explanation of the Adonis worship which accords so well with the facts of nature and with the analogy of similar rites in other lands. Moreover, the explanation is countenanced by a considerable body of opinion amongst the ancients themselves, who again and again interpreted the dying and reviving god as the reaped and sprouting grain.

The character of Tammuz or Adonis as a corn-spirit comes out plainly in an account of his festival given by an Arabic writer of the tenth century. In describing the rites and sacrifices observed at the different seasons of the year by the heathen Syrians of Harran, he says: 'Tammuz (July). In the middle of this month is the festival of el-Bûgât, that is, of the weeping women, and this is the Tâ-uz festival, which is celebrated in honour of the god Tâ-uz. The women bewail him, because his lord slew him so cruelly, ground his bones in a mill, and then scattered them to the wind. The women (during this festival) eat nothing which has been ground in a mill, but limit their diet to steeped wheat, sweet vetches, dates, raisins, and the like.' Tâ-uz, who is no other than Tammuz, is here like Burns's John Barleycorn:

> '*They wasted o'er a scorching flame*
> *The marrow of his bones;*
> *But a miller us'd him worst of all,*
> *For he crush'd him between two stones.*'

This concentration, so to say, of the nature of Adonis upon the cereal crops is characteristic of the stage of culture reached by his worshippers in historical times. They had left the nomadic life of the wandering hunter and herdsman far behind them; for ages they had been settled on the land, and had depended for their subsistence mainly on the products of tillage. The berries and roots of the wilderness, the grass of the pastures, which had been matters of vital importance to their ruder forefathers, were now of little moment to them: more and more their thoughts and energies were engrossed by the staple of their life, the corn; more and more accordingly the propitiation of the deities of fertility in general and of the corn-spirit in particular tended to become the central feature of their religion. The aim they set before themselves in celebrating the rites was thoroughly practical. It was no vague poetical sentiment which prompted them to hail with joy the rebirth of vegetation and to mourn its decline. Hunger, felt or feared, was the mainspring of the worship of Adonis.

It has been suggested by Father Lagrange that the mourning for Adonis was essentially a harvest rite designed to propitiate the corn-god, who was then either perishing under the sickles of the reapers or being trodden to death under the hoofs of the oxen on the threshing-floor. While the men slew him, the women wept crocodile tears at home to appease his natural indignation by a show of grief for his death. The theory fits in well with the dates of the festivals, which fell in spring or summer; for spring and summer, not autumn, are the seasons of the barley and wheat harvests in the lands which worshipped Adonis. Further, the hypothesis is confirmed by the practice of the Egyptian reapers, who lamented, calling upon Isis, when they cut the first corn; and it is recommended by the analogous customs of many hunting tribes, who testify great respect for the animals which they kill and eat.

Thus interpreted the death of Adonis is not the natural decay of vegetation in general under the summer heat or the winter cold; it is the violent destruction of the corn by man, who cuts it down on the field, stamps it to pieces on the threshing-floor, and grinds it to powder in the mill. That this was indeed the principal aspect in which Adonis presented himself in later times to the agricultural peoples of the Levant, may be admitted; but whether from the beginning he had been the corn and nothing but the corn, may be doubted. At an earlier period he may have been to the herdsman, above all, the tender herbage which sprouts after rain, offering rich pasture to the lean and hungry cattle. Earlier still he may have embodied the spirit of the nuts and berries which the autumn woods yield to the savage hunter and his squaw. And just as the husbandman must propitiate the spirit of the corn which he consumes, so the herdsman must appease the spirit of the grass and leaves which his cattle munch, and the hunter must soothe the spirit of the roots which he digs, and of the fruits which he gathers from the bough. In all cases the propitiation of the injured and angry sprite would naturally comprise elaborate excuses and apologies, accompanied by loud lamentations at his decease whenever, through some deplorable accident or necessity, he happened to be murdered as well as robbed. Only we must bear in mind that the savage hunter and herdsman of those early days had probably not yet attained to the abstract idea of vegetation in general; and that accordingly, so far as Adonis existed for them at all, he must have been the *Adon* or lord of each individual tree and plant rather than a personification of vegetable life as a whole. Thus there would be as many Adonises as there were trees and shrubs, and each of them might expect to receive satisfaction for any damage done to his person or property. And year by year, when the trees were deciduous, every Adonis would seem to bleed to death with the red leaves of autumn and to come to life again with the fresh green of spring.

There is some reason to think that in early times Adonis was sometimes personated by a living man who died a violent death in the character of the god. Further, there is evidence which goes to show that among the agricultural peoples of the Eastern Mediterranean, the corn-spirit, by whatever name he was known, was often represented, year by year, by human victims slain on the harvest-field. If that was so, it seems likely that the propitiation of the corn-spirit would tend to fuse to some extent with the worship of the dead. For the spirits of these victims might be thought to return to life in the ears which they had fattened with their blood, and to die a second death at the reaping of the corn. Now the ghosts of those who have perished by violence are surly and apt to wreak their vengeance on their slayers whenever an opportunity offers. Hence the attempt to appease the souls of the slaughtered victims would naturally blend, at least in the popular conception. with the attempt to pacify the slain corn-spirit. And as the dead came back in the sprouting corn, so they might be thought to return in the spring flowers, waked from their long sleep by the soft vernal airs. They had been laid to their rest under the sod. What more natural than to imagine that the violets and the hyacinths, the roses and the anemones, sprang from their dust, were empurpled or incarnadined by their blood, and contained some portion of their spirit?

> '*I sometimes think that never blows so red*
> *The Rose as where some buried Caesar bled;*
> *That every Hyacinth the Garden wears*
> *Dropt in her Lap from some once lovely Head.*

> '*And this reviving Herb whose tender Green*
> *Fledges the River-Lip on which we lean—*
> *Ah, lean upon it lightly, for who knows*
> *From what once lovely Lip it springs unseen?*'

In the summer after the battle of Landen, the most sanguinary battle of the seventeenth century in Europe, the earth, saturated with the blood of twenty thousand slain, broke forth into millions of poppies, and the traveller who passed that vast sheet of scarlet might well fancy that the earth had indeed given up her dead. At Athens a great Commemoration of the Dead fell in spring about the middle of March, when the early flowers are in bloom. Then the dead were believed to rise from their graves and go about the streets, vainly endeavouring to enter the temples and dwellings, which were barred against these perturbed spirits with ropes, buckthorn, and pitch. The name of the festival, according to the most obvious and natural interpretation, means the Festival of Flowers, and the title would fit well with the substance of the ceremonies if at that season the poor ghosts were indeed thought to creep from the narrow house with the opening flowers. There may therefore be a measure of truth in the theory of Renan, who saw in the Adonis worship a dreamy voluptuous cult of death, conceived not as the King of Terrors, but as an insidious enchanter who lures his victims to himself and lulls them into an eternal sleep. The infinite charm of nature in the Lebanon, he thought, lends itself to religious emotions of this sensuous, visionary sort, hovering vaguely between pain and pleasure, between slumber and tears. It would doubtless be a mistake to attribute to Syrian peasants the worship of a conception so purely abstract as that of death in general. Yet it may be true that in their simple minds the thought of the reviving spirit of vegetation was blent with the very concrete notion of the ghosts of the dead, who come to life again in spring days with the early flowers, with the tender green of the corn and the many-tinted blossoms of the trees. Thus their views of the death and resurrection of nature would be coloured by their views of the death and resurrection of man, by their personal sorrows and hopes and fears. In like manner we cannot doubt that Renan's theory of Adonis was itself deeply tinged by passionate memories, memories of the slumber akin to death which sealed his own eyes on the slopes of the Lebanon, memories of the sister who sleeps in the land of Adonis never again to wake with the anemones and the roses.

CHAPTER XXXIII

THE GARDENS OF ADONIS

PERHAPS the best proof that Adonis was a deity of vegetation and especially of the corn, is furnished by the gardens of Adonis, as they were called. These were baskets or pots filled with earth, in which wheat, barley, lettuces, fennel, and various kinds of flowers were sown and tended for eight days, chiefly or exclusively by women. Fostered by the sun's heat, the plants shot up rapidly, but having no root they withered as rapidly away, and at the end of the eight days were carried out with the images of the dead Adonis, and flung with them into the sea or into springs.

These gardens of Adonis are most naturally interpreted as representatives of Adonis or manifestations of his power; they represented him, true to his original nature, in vegetable form, while the images of him, with which they were carried out and cast into the water, portrayed him in his later human shape. All these Adonis ceremonies, if I am right, were originally intended as charms to promote the growth or revival of vegetation; and the principle by which they were supposed to produce this effect was homoeopathic or imitative magic. For ignorant people suppose that by mimicking the effect which they desire to produce they actually help to produce it; thus by sprinkling water they make rain, by lighting a fire they make sunshine, and so on. Similarly, by mimicking the growth of crops they hope to ensure a good harvest. The rapid growth of the wheat and barley in the gardens of Adonis was intended to make the corn shoot up; and the throwing of the gardens and of the images into the water was a charm to secure a due supply of fertilising rain. The same, I take it, was the object of throwing the effigies of Death and the Carnival into water in the corresponding ceremonies of modern Europe. Certainly the custom of drenching with water a leaf-clad person, who undoubtedly personifies vegetation, is still resorted to in Europe for the express purpose of producing rain. Similarly the custom of throwing water on the last corn cut at harvest, or on the person who brings it home (a custom observed in Germany and France, and till lately in England and Scotland), is in some places practised with the avowed intent to procure rain for the next year's crops. Thus in Wallachia and amongst the Roumanians in Transylvania, when a girl is bringing home a crown made of the last ears of corn cut at harvest, all who meet her hasten to throw water on her, and two farm-servants are placed at the door for the purpose; for they believe that if this were not done, the crops next year would perish from drought. At the spring ploughing in Prussia, when the ploughmen and sowers returned in the evening from their work in the fields, the farmer's wife and the servants used to splash water over them. The ploughmen and sowers retorted by seizing every one, throwing them into the pond, and ducking them under the water. The farmer's wife might claim exemption on payment of a forfeit, but every one else had to be ducked. By observing this custom they hoped to ensure a due supply of rain for the seed.

The opinion that the gardens of Adonis are essentially charms to promote the growth of vegetation, especially of the crops, and that they belong to the same class of customs as those spring and midsummer folk-customs of modern Europe which I have described elsewhere, does not rest for its evidence merely on the intrinsic probability of the case. Fortunately we are able to show that gardens of Adonis (if we may use the expression in a general sense) are still planted, first, by a primitive race at their sowing season, and, second, by European peasants at midsummer. Amongst the Oraons and Mundas of Bengal, when the time comes for planting out the rice which has been grown in seed-beds, a party of young people of both sexes go to the forest and cut a young Karma-tree, or the branch of one. Bearing it in triumph they return dancing, singing, and beating drums, and plant it in the middle of the village dancing-ground. A sacrifice is offered to the tree; and next morning the youth of both sexes, linked arm-in-arm, dance in a great circle round the Karma-tree, which is decked with strips of coloured cloth and sham bracelets and necklets of plaited straw. As a preparation for the festival, the daughters of the head-man of the village cultivate blades of barley in a peculiar way. The seed is sown in moist, sandy soil, mixed with turmeric, and the blades sprout and unfold of a pale-yellow or primrose colour. On the day of the festival the girls take up these blades and carry them in baskets to the dancing ground, where, prostrating themselves reverentially, they place some of the plants before the Karma-tree. Finally, the Karma-tree is taken away and thrown into a stream or tank. The meaning of planting these barley blades and then presenting them to the Karma-tree is hardly open to question. Trees are supposed to exercise a quickening influence upon the growth of crops, and amongst the very people in question — the Mundas or Mundaris — 'the grove deities are held responsible for the crops.' Therefore, when at the season for planting out the rice the Mundas bring in a tree and treat it with so much respect, their object can only be to foster thereby the growth of the rice which is about to be planted out; and the custom of causing barley blades to sprout rapidly and then presenting them to the tree must be intended to subserve the same purpose, perhaps by reminding the tree-spirit of his duty towards the crops, and stimulating his activity by this visible example of rapid vegetable growth. The throwing of the Karma-tree into the water is to be interpreted as a rain-charm. Whether the barley blades are also thrown into the water is not said; but if my interpretation of the custom is right, probably they are so. A distinction between this Bengal custom and the Greek rites of Adonis is that in the former the tree-spirit appears in his original form as a tree; whereas in the Adonis worship he appears in human form, represented as a dead man, though his vegetable nature is indicated by the gardens of Adonis, which are, so to say, a secondary manifestation of his original power as a tree-spirit.

Gardens of Adonis are cultivated also by the Hindoos, with the intention apparently of ensuring the fertility both of the earth and of mankind. Thus at Oodeypoor in Rajputana a festival is held in honour of Gouri, or Isani, the goddess of abundance. The rites begin when the sun enters the sign of the Ram, the opening of the Hindoo year. An image of the goddess Gouri is made of earth, and a smaller one of her husband Iswara, and the two are placed together. A small trench is next dug, barley is sown in it, and the ground watered and heated artificially till the grain sprouts, when the women dance round it hand in hand, invoking the blessing of Gouri on their husbands. After that the young corn is taken up and distributed by the women to the men, who wear it in their turbans. In these rites the distribution of the barley shoots to the men, and the invocation of a blessing on their husbands by the wives, point clearly to the desire of offspring as one motive for observing the custom. The same motive probably explains the use of gardens of Adonis at the marriage of Brahmans in the Madras Presidency. Seeds of five or nine sorts are mixed and sown in earthen pots, which are made specially for the purpose and are filled with earth. Bride and bridegroom water the seeds both morning and evening for four days; and on the fifth day the seedlings are thrown, like the real gardens of Adonis, into a tank or river.

In Sardinia the gardens of Adonis are still planted in connexion with the great Midsummer festival which bears the name of St. John. At the end of March or on the first of April a young man of the village presents himself to a girl, and asks her to be his *comare* (gossip or sweetheart), offering to be her *compare*. The invitation is considered as an honour by the girl's family, and is gladly accepted. At the end of May the girl makes a pot of the bark of the cork-tree, fills it with earth, and sows a handful of wheat and barley in it. The pot being placed in the sun and often watered, the corn sprouts rapidly and has a good head by Midsummer Eve (St. John's Eve, the twenty-third of June). The pot is then called *Erme* or *Nenneri*. On St. John's Day the young man and the girl, dressed in their best, accompanied by a long retinue and preceded by children gambolling and frolicking, move in procession to a church outside the village. Here they break the pot by throwing it against the door of the church. Then they sit down in a ring on the grass and eat eggs and herbs to the music of flutes. Wine is mixed in a cup and passed round, each one drinking as it passes. Then they join hands and sing 'Sweethearts of St. John' (*Compare e comare di San Giovanni*) over and over again, the flutes playing the while. When they tire of singing they stand up and dance gaily in a ring till evening. This is the general Sardinian custom. As practised at Ozieri it has some special features. In May the pots are made of cork-bark and planted with corn, as already described. Then on the Eve of St. John the window-sills are draped with rich cloths, on which the pots are placed, adorned with crimson and blue silk and ribbons of various colours. On each of the pots they used formerly to place a statuette or cloth doll dressed as a woman, or a Priapus-like figure made of paste; but this custom, rigorously forbidden by the Church, has fallen into disuse. The village swains go about in a troop to look at the pots and their decorations and to wait for the girls, who assemble on the public square to celebrate the festival. Here a great bonfire is kindled, round which they dance and make merry. Those who wish to be 'Sweethearts of St. John' act as follows. The young man stands on one side of the bonfire and the girl on the other, and they, in a manner, join hands by each grasping one end of a long stick, which they pass three times backwards and forwards across the fire, thus thrusting their hands thrice rapidly into the flames. This seals their relationship to each other. Dancing and music go on till late at night. The correspondence of these Sardinian pots of grain to the gardens of Adonis seems complete, and the images formerly placed in them answer to the images of Adonis which accompanied his gardens.

Customs of the same sort are observed at the same season in Sicily. Pairs of boys and girls become gossips of St. John on St. John's Day by drawing each a hair from his or her head and performing various ceremonies over them. Thus they tie the hairs together and throw them up in the air, or exchange them over a potsherd, which they afterwards break in two, preserving each a fragment with pious care. The tie formed in the latter way is supposed to last for life. In some parts of Sicily the gossips of St. John present each other with plates of sprouting corn, lentils, and canary seed, which have been planted forty days before the festival. The one who receives the plate pulls a stalk of the young plants, binds it with a ribbon, and preserves it among his or her greatest treasures, restoring the platter to the giver. At Catania the gossips exchange pots of basil and great cucumbers; the girls tend the basil, and the thicker it grows the more it is prized.

In these midsummer customs of Sardinia and Sicily it is possible that, as Mr. R. Wünsch supposes, St. John has replaced Adonis. We have seen that the rites of Tammuz or Adonis were commonly celebrated about midsummer; according to Jerome, their date was June.

In Sicily gardens of Adonis are still sown in spring as well as in summer, from which we may perhaps infer that Sicily as well as

Syria celebrated of old a vernal festival of the dead and risen god. At the approach of Easter, Sicilian women sow wheat, lentils, and canary-seed in plates, which they keep in the dark and water every two days. The plants soon shoot up; the stalks are tied together with red ribbons, and the plates containing them are placed on the sepulchres which, with the effigies of the dead Christ, are made up in Catholic and Greek churches on Good Friday, just as the gardens of Adonis were placed on the grave of the dead Adonis. The practice is not confined to Sicily, for it is observed also at Cosenza in Calabria, and perhaps in other places. The whole custom — sepulchres as well as plates of sprouting grain — may be nothing but a continuation, under a different name, of the worship of Adonis.

Nor are these Sicilian and Calabrian customs the only Easter ceremonies which resemble the rites of Adonis. 'During the whole of Good Friday a waxen effigy of the dead Christ is exposed to view in the middle of the Greek churches and is covered with fervent kisses by the thronging crowd, while the whole church rings with melancholy, monotonous dirges. Late in the evening, when it has grown quite dark, this waxen image is carried by the priests into the street on a bier adorned with lemons, roses, jessamine, and other flowers, and there begins a grand procession of the multitude, who move in serried ranks, with slow and solemn step, through the whole town. Every man carries his taper and breaks out into doleful lamentation. At all the houses which the procession passes there are seated women with censers to fumigate the marching host. Thus the community solemnly buries its Christ as if he had just died. At last the waxen image is again deposited in the church, and the same lugubrious chants echo anew. These lamentations, accompanied by a strict fast, continue till midnight on Saturday. As the clock strikes twelve, the bishop appears and announces the glad tidings that "Christ is risen," to which the crowd replies, "He is risen indeed," and at once the whole city bursts into an uproar of joy, which finds vent in shrieks and shouts, in the endless discharge of carronades and muskets, and the explosion of fire-works of every sort. In the very same hour people plunge from the extremity of the fast into the enjoyment of the Easter lamb and neat wine.'

In like manner the Catholic Church has been accustomed to

bring before its followers in a visible form the death and resurrection of the Redeemer. Such sacred dramas are well fitted to impress the lively imagination and to stir the warm feelings of a susceptible southern race, to whom the pomp and pageantry of Catholicism are more congenial than to the colder temperament of the Teutonic peoples.

When we reflect how often the Church has skilfully contrived to plant the seeds of the new faith on the old stock of paganism, we may surmise that the Easter celebration of the dead and risen Christ was grafted upon a similar celebration of the dead and risen Adonis, which, as we have seen reason to believe, was celebrated in Syria at the same season. The type, created by Greek artists, of the sorrowful goddess with her dying lover in her arms, resembles and may have been the model of the *Pietà* of Christian art, the Virgin with the dead body of her divine Son in her lap, of which the most celebrated example is the one by Michael Angelo in St. Peter's. That noble group, in which the living sorrow of the mother contrasts so wonderfully with the languor of death in the son, is one of the finest compositions in marble. Ancient Greek art has bequeathed to us few works so beautiful, and none so pathetic.

In this connexion a well-known statement of Jerome may not be without significance. He tells us that Bethlehem, the traditionary birthplace of the Lord, was shaded by a grove of that still older Syrian Lord, Adonis, and that where the infant Jesus had wept, the lover of Venus was bewailed. Though he does not expressly say so, Jerome seems to have thought that the grove of Adonis had been planted by the heathen after the birth of Christ for the purpose of defiling the sacred spot. In this he may have been mistaken. If Adonis was indeed, as I have argued, the spirit of the corn, a more suitable name for his dwelling-place could hardly be found than Bethlehem, 'the House of Bread,' and he may well have been worshipped there at his House of Bread long ages before the birth of Him who said, 'I am the bread of life.' Even on the hypothesis that Adonis followed rather than preceded Christ at Bethlehem, the choice of his sad figure to divert the allegiance of Christians from their Lord cannot but strike us as eminently appropriate when we remember the similarity of the rites which commemorated the death and resurrection of the two.

One of the earliest seats of the worship of the new god was Antioch, and at Antioch, as we have seen, the death of the old god was annually celebrated with great solemnity. A circumstance which attended the entrance of Julian into the city at the time of the Adonis festival may perhaps throw some light on the date of its celebration. When the emperor drew near to the city he was received with public prayers as if he had been a god, and he marvelled at the voices of a great multitude who cried that the Star of Salvation had dawned upon them in the East. This may doubtless have been no more than a fulsome compliment paid by an obsequious Oriental crowd to the Roman emperor. But it is also possible that the rising of a bright star regularly gave the signal for the festival, and that as chance would have it the star emerged above the rim of the eastern horizon at the very moment of the emperor's approach. The coincidence, if it happened, could hardly fail to strike the imagination of a superstitious and excited multitude, who might thereupon hail the great man as the deity whose coming was announced by the sign in the heavens. Or the emperor may have mistaken for a greeting to himself the shouts which were addressed to the star. Now Astarte, the divine mistress of Adonis, was identified with the planet Venus, and her changes from a morning to an evening star were carefully noted by the Babylonian astronomers, who drew omens from her alternate appearance and disappearance. Hence we may conjecture that the festival of Adonis was regularly timed to coincide with the appearance of Venus as the Morning or Evening Star. But the star which the people of Antioch saluted at the festival was seen in the East; therefore, if it was indeed Venus, it can only have been the Morning Star. At Aphaca in Syria, where there was a famous temple of Astarte, the signal for the celebration of the rites was apparently given by the flashing of a meteor, which on a certain day fell like a star from the top of Mount Lebanon into the river Adonis. The meteor was thought to be Astarte herself, and its flight through the air might naturally be interpreted as the descent of the amorous goddess to the arms of her lover. At Antioch and elsewhere the appearance of the Morning Star on the day of the festival may in like manner have been hailed as the coming of the goddess of love to wake her dead leman from his earthy bed. If that were so, we may surmise that it was the Morning Star which guided the wise men of the East to Bethlehem, the hallowed spot which heard, in the language of Jerome, the weeping of the infant Christ and the lament for Adonis.

CHAPTER XXXIV

THE MYTH AND RITUAL OF ATTIS

ANOTHER of those gods whose supposed death and resurrection struck such deep roots into the faith and ritual of Western Asia is Attis. He was to Phrygia what Adonis was to Syria. Like Adonis, he appears to have been a god of vegetation, and his death and resurrection were annually mourned and rejoiced over at a festival in spring. The legends and rites of the two gods were so much alike that the ancients themselves sometimes identified them. Attis was said to have been a fair young shepherd or herdsman beloved by Cybele, the Mother of the Gods, a great Asiatic goddess of fertility, who had her chief home in Phrygia. Some held that Attis was her son. His birth, like that of many other heroes, is said to have been miraculous. His mother, Nana, was a virgin, who conceived by putting a ripe almond or a pomegranate in her bosom. Indeed in the Phrygian cosmogony an almond figured as the father of all things, perhaps because its delicate lilac blossom is one of the first heralds of spring, appearing on the bare boughs before the leaves have opened. Such tales of virgin mothers are relics of an age of childish ignorance when men had not yet recognized the intercourse of the sexes as the true cause of offspring. Two different accounts of the death of Attis were current. According to the one he was killed by a boar, like Adonis. According to the other he unmanned himself under a pine-tree, and bled to death on the spot. The latter is said to have been the local story told by the people of Pessinus, a great seat of the worship of Cybele, and the whole legend of which the story forms a part is stamped with a character of rudeness and savagery that speaks strongly for its antiquity. Both tales might claim the support of custom, or rather both were probably invented to explain certain customs observed by the worshippers. The story of the self-mutilation of Attis is clearly an attempt to account for the self-mutilation of his priests, who regularly castrated themselves on entering the service of the goddess. The story of his death by the boar may have been told to explain why his worshippers, especially the people of Pessinus, abstained from eating swine. In like manner the worshippers of Adonis abstained from pork, because a boar had killed their god. After his death Attis is said to have been changed into a pine-tree.

The worship of the Phrygian Mother of the Gods was adopted by the Romans in 204 B.C. towards the close of their long struggle with Hannibal. For their drooping spirits had been opportunely cheered by a prophecy, alleged to be drawn from that convenient farrago of nonsense, the Sibylline Books, that the foreign invader would be driven from Italy if the great Oriental goddess were brought to Rome. Accordingly ambassadors were despatched to her sacred city Pessinus in Phrygia. The small black stone which embodied the mighty divinity was entrusted to them and conveyed to Rome, where it was received with great respect and installed in the temple of Victory on the Palatine Hill. It was the middle of April when the goddess arrived, and she went to work at once. For the harvest that year was such as had not been seen for many a long day, and in the very next year Hannibal and his veterans embarked for Africa. As he looked his last on the coast of Italy, fading behind him in the distance, he could not foresee that Europe, which had repelled the arms, would yet yield to the gods, of the Orient. The vanguard of the conquerors had already encamped in the heart of Italy before the rearguard of the beaten army fell sullenly back from its shores.

We may conjecture, though we are not told, that the Mother of the Gods brought with her the worship of her youthful lover or son to her new home in the West. Certainly the Romans were familiar with the Galli, the emasculated priests of Attis, before the close of the Republic. These unsexed beings, in their Oriental costume, with little images suspended on their breasts, appear to have been a familiar sight in the streets of Rome, which they traversed in procession, carrying the image of the goddess and chanting their hymns to the music of cymbals and tambourines, flutes and horns, while the people, impressed by the fantastic show and moved by the wild strains, flung alms to them in abundance, and buried the image and its bearers under showers of roses. A further step was taken by the Emperor Claudius when he incorporated the Phrygian worship of the sacred tree, and with it probably the orgiastic rites of Attis, in the established religion of Rome. The great spring festival of Cybele and Attis is best known to us in the form in which it was celebrated at Rome; but as we are informed that the Roman ceremonies were also Phrygian, we may assume that they differed hardly, if at all, from their Asiatic original. The order of the festival seems to have been as follows.

On the twenty-second day of March, a pine-tree was cut in the woods and brought into the sanctuary of Cybele, where it was treated as a great divinity. The duty of carrying the sacred tree was entrusted to a guild of Tree-bearers. The trunk was swathed like a corpse with woollen bands and decked with wreaths of violets, for violets were said to have sprung from the blood of Attis, as roses and anemones from the blood of Adonis; and the effigy of a young man, doubtless Attis himself, was tied to the middle of the stem. On the second day of the festival, the twenty-third of March, the chief ceremony seems to have been a blowing of trumpets. The third day, the twenty-fourth of March, was known as the Day of Blood: the Archigallus or high-priest drew blood from his arms and presented it as an offering. Nor was he alone in making this bloody sacrifice. Stirred by the wild barbaric music of clashing cymbals, rumbling drums, droning horns, and screaming flutes, the inferior clergy whirled about in the dance with waggling heads and streaming hair, until, rapt into a frenzy of excitement and insensible to pain, they gashed their bodies with potsherds or slashed them with knives in order to bespatter the altar and the sacred tree with their flowing blood. The ghastly rite probably formed part of the mourning for Attis and may have been intended to strengthen him for the resurrection. The Australian aborigines cut themselves in like manner over the graves of their friends for the purpose, perhaps, of enabling them to be born again. Further, we may conjecture, though we are not expressly told, that it was on the same Day of Blood and for the same purpose that the novices sacrificed their virility. Wrought up to the highest pitch of religious excitement they dashed the severed portions of themselves against the image of the cruel goddess.

These broken instruments of fertility were afterwards reverently wrapt up and buried in the earth or in subterranean chambers sacred to Cybele, where, like the offering of blood, they may have been deemed instrumental in recalling Attis to life and hastening the general resurrection of nature, which was then bursting into leaf and blossom in the vernal sunshine. Some confirmation of this conjecture is furnished by the savage story that the mother of Attis conceived by putting in her bosom a pomegranate sprung from the severed genitals of a man-monster named Agdestis, a sort of double of Attis.

If there is any truth in this conjectural explanation of the custom, we can readily understand why other Asiatic goddesses of fertility were served in like manner by eunuch priests. These feminine deities required to receive from their male ministers, who personated the divine lovers, the means of discharging their beneficent functions: they had themselves to be impregnated by the life-giving energy before they could transmit it to the world. Goddesses thus ministered to by eunuch priests were the great Artemis of Ephesus and the great Syrian Astarte of Hierapolis, whose sanctuary, frequented by swarms of pilgrims and enriched by the offerings of Assyria and Babylonia, of Arabia and Phoenicia, was perhaps in the days of its glory the most popular in the East. Now the unsexed priests of this Syrian goddess resembled those of Cybele so closely that some people took them to be the same. And the mode in which they dedicated themselves to the religious life was similar. The greatest festival of the year at Hierapolis fell at the beginning of spring, when multitudes thronged to the sanctuary from Syria and the regions round about. While the flutes played, the drums beat, and the eunuch priests slashed themselves with knives, the religious excitement gradually spread like a wave among the crowd of onlookers, and many a one did that which he little thought to do when he came as a holiday spectator to the festival. For man after man, his veins throbbing with the music, his eyes fascinated by the sight of the streaming blood, flung his garments from him, leaped forth with a shout, and seizing one of the swords which stood ready for the purpose, castrated himself on the spot. Then he ran through the city, holding the bloody pieces in his hand, till he threw them into one of the houses which he passed in his mad career. The household thus honoured had to furnish him with a suit of female attire and female ornaments, which he wore for the rest of his life. When the tumult of emotion had subsided, and the man had come to himself again, the irrevocable sacrifice must often have been followed by passionate sorrow and lifelong regret. This revulsion of natural human feeling after the frenzies of a fanatical religion is powerfully depicted by Catullus in a celebrated poem.

The parallel of these Syrian devotees confirms the view that in the similar worship of Cybele the sacrifice of virility took place on the Day of Blood at the vernal rites of the goddess, when the violets, supposed to spring from the red drops of her wounded lover, were in bloom among the pines. Indeed the story that Attis unmanned himself under a pine-tree was clearly devised to explain why his priests did the same beside the sacred violet-wreathed tree at his festival. At all events, we can hardly doubt that the Day of Blood witnessed the mourning for Attis over an effigy of him which was afterwards buried. The image thus laid in the sepulchre was probably the same which had hung upon the tree. Throughout the period of mourning the worshippers fasted from bread, nominally because Cybele had done so in her grief for the death of Attis, but really perhaps for the same reason which induced the women of Harran to abstain from eating anything ground in a mill while they wept for Tammuz. To partake of bread or flour at such a season might have been deemed a wanton profanation of the bruised and broken body of the god. Or the fast may possibly have been a preparation for a sacramental meal.

But when night had fallen, the sorrow of the worshippers was turned to joy. For suddenly a light shone in the darkness: the tomb was opened: the god had risen from the dead; and as the priest touched the lips of the weeping mourners with balm, he softly whispered in their ears the glad tidings of salvation. The resurrection of the god was hailed by his disciples as a promise that they too would issue triumphant from the corruption of the grave. On the morrow, the twenty-fifth day of March, which was reckoned the vernal equinox, the divine resurrection was celebrated with a wild outburst of glee. At Rome, and probably elsewhere, the celebration took the form of a carnival. It was the Festival of Joy (*Hilaria*). A universal licence prevailed. Every man might say and do what he pleased. People went about the streets in disguise. No dignity was too high or too sacred for the humblest citizen to assume with impunity. In the reign of Commodus a band of conspirators thought to take advantage of the masquerade by dressing in the uniform of the Imperial Guard, and so, mingling with the crowd of merrymakers, to get within stabbing distance of the emperor. But the plot miscarried. Even the stern Alexander Severus used to relax so far on the joyous day as to admit a pheasant to his frugal board. The next day, the twenty-sixth of March, was given to repose, which must have been much needed after the varied excitements and fatigues of the preceding days. Finally, the Roman festival closed on the twenty-seventh of March with a procession to the brook Almo. The silver image of the goddess, with its face of jagged black stone, sat in a waggon drawn by oxen. Preceded by the nobles walking barefoot, it moved slowly, to the loud music of pipes and tambourines, out by the Porta Capena, and so down to the banks of the Almo, which flows into the Tiber just below the walls of Rome. There the high-priest, robed in purple, washed the waggon, the image, and the other sacred objects in the water of the stream. On returning from their bath, the wain and the oxen were strewn with fresh spring flowers. All was mirth and gaiety. No one thought of the blood that had flowed so lately. Even the eunuch priests forgot their wounds.

Such, then, appears to have been the annual solemnisation of the death and resurrection of Attis in spring. But besides these public rites, his worship is known to have comprised certain secret or mystic ceremonies, which probably aimed at bringing the worshipper, and especially the novice, into closer communication with his god. Our information as to the nature of these mysteries and the date of their celebration is unfortunately very scanty, but they seem to have included a sacramental meal and a baptism of blood. In the sacrament the novice became a partaker of the mysteries by eating out of a drum and drinking out of a cymbal, two instruments of music which figured prominently in the thrilling orchestra of Attis. The fast which accompanied the mourning for the dead god may perhaps have been designed to prepare the body of the communicant for the reception of the blessed sacrament by purging it of all that could defile by contact the sacred elements. In the baptism the devotee, crowned with gold and wreathed with fillets, descended into a pit, the mouth of which was covered with a wooden grating. A bull, adorned with garlands of flowers, its forehead glittering with gold leaf, was then driven on to the grating and there stabbed to death with a consecrated spear. Its hot reeking blood poured in torrents through the apertures, and was received with devout eagerness by the worshipper on every part of his person and garments, till he emerged from the pit, drenched, dripping, and scarlet from head to foot, to receive the homage, nay the adoration, of his fellows as one who had been born again to eternal life and had washed away his sins in the blood of the bull. For some time afterwards the fiction of a new birth was kept up by dieting him on milk like a new-born babe. The regeneration of the worshipper took place at the same time as the regeneration of his god, namely at the vernal equinox. At Rome the new birth and the remission of sins by the shedding of the bull's blood appear to have been carried out above all at the sanctuary of the Phrygian goddess on the Vatican Hill, at or near the spot where the great basilica of St. Peter's now stands; for many inscriptions relating to the rites were found when the church was being enlarged in 1608 or 1609. From the Vatican as a centre this barbarous system of superstition seems to have spread to other parts of the Roman empire. Inscriptions found in Gaul and Germany prove that provincial sanctuaries modelled their ritual on that of the Vatican. From the same source we learn that the testicles as well as the blood of the bull played an important part in the ceremonies. Probably they were regarded as a powerful charm to promote fertility and hasten the new birth.

CHAPTER XXXV

ATTIS AS A GOD OF VEGETATION

THE original character of Attis as a tree-spirit is brought out plainly by the part which the pine-tree plays in his legend, his ritual, and his monuments. The story that he was a human being transformed into a pine-tree is only one of those transparent attempts at rationalising old beliefs which meet us so frequently in mythology. The bringing in of the pine-tree from the woods, decked with violets and woollen bands, is like bringing in the May-tree or Summer-tree in modern folk-custom; and the effigy which was attached to the pine-tree was only a duplicate representative of the tree-spirit Attis. After being fastened to the tree, the effigy was kept for a year and then burned. The same thing appears to have been sometimes done with the Maypole; and in like manner the effigy of the corn-spirit, made at harvest, is often preserved till it is replaced by a new effigy at next year's harvest. The original intention of such customs was no doubt to maintain the spirit of vegetation in life throughout the year. Why the Phrygians should have worshipped the pine above other trees we can only guess. Perhaps the sight of its changeless, though sombre, green cresting the ridges of the high hills above the fading splendour of the autumn woods in the valleys may have seemed to their eyes to mark it out as the seat of a diviner life, of something exempt from the sad vicissitudes of the seasons, constant and eternal as the sky which stooped to meet it. For the same reason, perhaps, ivy was sacred to Attis; at all events, we read that his eunuch priests were tattooed with a pattern of ivy leaves. Another reason for the sanctity of the pine may have been its usefulness. The cones of the stone-pine contain edible nut-like seeds, which have been used as food since antiquity, and are still eaten, for example, by the poorer classes in Rome. Moreover, a wine was brewed from these seeds, and this may partly account for the orgiastic nature of the rites of Cybele, which the ancients compared to those of Dionysus. Further, pine-cones were regarded as symbols or rather instruments of fertility. Hence at the festival of the Thesmophoria they were thrown, along with pigs and other agents or emblems of fecundity, into the sacred vaults of Demeter for the purpose of quickening the ground and the wombs of women.

Like tree-spirits in general, Attis was apparently thought to wield power over the fruits of the earth or even to be identical with the corn. One of his epithets was 'very fruitful': he was addressed as the 'reaped green (or yellow) ear of corn'; and the story of his sufferings, death, and resurrection was interpreted as the ripe grain wounded by the reaper, buried in the granary, and coming to life again when it is sown in the ground. A statue of him in the Lateran Museum at Rome clearly indicates his relation to the fruits of the earth, and particularly to the corn; for it represents him with a bunch of ears of corn and fruit in his hand, and a wreath of pine-cones, pomegranates, and other fruits on his head, while from the top of his Phrygian cap ears of corn are sprouting. On a stone urn, which contained the ashes of an Archigallus or high-priest of Attis, the same idea is expressed in a slightly different way. The top of the urn is adorned with ears of corn carved in relief, and it is surmounted by the figure of a cock, whose tail consists of ears of corn. Cybele in like manner was conceived as a goddess of fertility who could make or mar the fruits of the earth; for the people of Augustodunum (Autun) in Gaul used to cart her image about in a waggon for the good of the fields and vineyards, while they danced and sang before it, and we have seen that in Italy an unusually fine harvest was attributed to the recent arrival of the Great Mother. The bathing of the image of the goddess in a river may well have been a rain-charm to ensure an abundant supply of moisture for the crops.

CHAPTER XXXVI

HUMAN REPRESENTATIVES OF ATTIS

FROM inscriptions it appears that both at Pessinus and Rome the high-priest of Cybele regularly bore the name of Attis. It is therefore a reasonable conjecture that he played the part of his namesake, the legendary Attis, at the annual festival. We have seen that on the Day of Blood he drew blood from his arms, and this may have been an imitation of the self-inflicted death of Attis under the pine-tree. It is not inconsistent with this supposition that Attis was also represented at these ceremonies by an effigy; for instances can be shown in which the divine being is first represented by a living person and afterwards by an effigy, which is then burned or otherwise destroyed. Perhaps we may go a step farther and conjecture that this mimic killing of the priest, accompanied by a real effusion of his blood, was in Phrygia, as it has been elsewhere, a substitute for a human sacrifice which in earlier times was actually offered.

A reminiscence of the manner in which these old representatives of the deity were put to death is perhaps preserved in the famous story of Marsyas. He was said to be a Phrygian satyr of Silenus, according to others a shepherd or herdsman, who played sweetly on the flute. A friend of Cybele, he roamed the country with the disconsolate goddess to soothe her grief for the death of Attis. The composition of the Mother's Air, a tune played on the flute in honour of the Great Mother Goddess, was attributed to him by the people of Celaenae in Phrygia. Vain of his skill, he challenged Apollo to a musical contest, he to play on the flute and Apollo on the lyre. Being vanquished, Marsyas was tied up to a pine-tree and flayed or cut limb from limb either by the victorious Apollo or by a Scythian slave. His skin was shown at Celaenae in historical times. It hung at the foot of the citadel in a cave from which the river Marsyas rushed with an impetuous and noisy tide to join the Maeander. So the Adonis bursts full-born from the precipices of the Lebanon; so the blue river of Ibreez leaps in a crystal jet from the red rocks of the Taurus; so the stream, which now rumbles deep underground, used to gleam for a moment on its passage from darkness to darkness in the dim light of the Corycian cave. In all these copious fountains, with their glad promise of fertility and life, men of old saw the hand of God and worshipped him beside the rushing river with the music of its tumbling waters in their ears. At Celaenae, if we can trust tradition, the piper Marsyas, hanging in his cave, had a soul for harmony even in death; for it is said that at the sound of his native Phrygian melodies the skin of the dead satyr used to thrill, but that if the musician struck up an air in praise of Apollo it remained deaf and motionless.

In this Phrygian satyr, shepherd, or herdsman who enjoyed the friendship of Cybele, practised the music so characteristic of her rites, and died a violent death on her sacred tree, the pine, may we not detect a close resemblance to Attis, the favourite shepherd or herdsman of the goddess, who is himself described as a piper, is said to have perished under a pine-tree, and was annually represented by an effigy hung, like Marsyas, upon a pine? We may conjecture that in old days the priest who bore the name and played the part of Attis at the spring festival of Cybele was regularly hanged or otherwise slain upon the sacred tree, and that this barbarous custom was afterwards mitigated into the form in which it is known to us in later times, when the priest merely drew blood from his body under the tree and attached an effigy instead of himself to its trunk. In the holy grove at Upsala men and animals were sacrificed by being hanged upon the sacred trees. The human victims dedicated to Odin were regularly put to death by hanging or by a combination of hanging and stabbing, the man being strung up to a tree or a gallows and then wounded with a spear. Hence Odin was called the Lord of the Gallows or the God of the Hanged, and he is represented sitting under a gallows tree. Indeed he is said to have been sacrificed to himself in the ordinary way, as we learn from the weird verses of the *Havamal*, in which the god describes how he acquired his divine power by learning the magic runes:

> '*I know that I hung on the windy tree*
> *For nine whole nights,*
> *Wounded with the spear, dedicated to Odin,*
> *Myself to myself.*'

The Bagobos of Mindanao, one of the Philippine Islands, used annually to sacrifice human victims for the good of the crops in a similar way. Early in December, when the constellation Orion appeared at seven o'clock in the evening, the people knew that the time had come to clear their fields for sowing and to sacrifice a slave. The sacrifice was presented to certain powerful spirits as payment for the good year which the people had enjoyed, and to ensure the favour of the spirits for the coming season. The victim was led to a great tree in the forest; there he was tied with his back to the tree and his arms stretched high above his head, in the attitude in which ancient artists portrayed Marsyas hanging on the fatal tree. While he thus hung by the arms, he was slain by a spear thrust through his body at the level of the armpits. Afterwards the body was cut clean through the middle at the waist, and the upper part was apparently allowed to dangle for a little from the tree, while the under part wallowed in blood on the ground. The two portions were finally cast into a shallow trench beside the tree. Before this was done, anybody who wished might cut off a piece of flesh or a lock of hair from the corpse and carry it to the grave of some relation whose body was being consumed by a ghoul. Attracted by the fresh corpse, the ghoul would leave the mouldering old body in peace. These sacrifices have been offered by men now living.

In Greece the great goddess Artemis herself appears to have been annually hanged in effigy in her sacred grove of Condylea among the Arcadian hills, and there accordingly she went by the name of the Hanged One. Indeed a trace of a similar rite may perhaps be detected even at Ephesus, the most famous of her sanctuaries, in the legend of a woman who hanged herself and was thereupon dressed by the compassionate goddess in her own divine garb and called by the name of Hecate. Similarly, at Melite in Phthia, a story was told of a girl named Aspalis who hanged herself, but who appears to have been merely a form of Artemis. For after her death her body could not be found, but an image of her was discovered standing beside the image of Artemis, and the people bestowed on it the title of Hecaerge or Far-shooter, one of the regular epithets of the goddess. Every year the virgins sacrificed a young goat to the image by hanging it, because Aspalis was said to have hanged herself. The sacrifice may have been a substitute for hanging an image or a human representative of Artemis. Again, in Rhodes the fair Helen was worshipped under the title of Helen of the Tree, because the queen of the island had caused her handmaids, disguised as Furies, to string her up to a bough. That the Asiatic Greeks sacrificed animals in this fashion is proved by coins of Ilium, which represent an ox or cow hanging on a tree and stabbed with a knife by a man, who sits among the branches or on the animal's back. At Hierapolis also the victims were hung on trees before they were burnt. With these Greek and Scandinavian parallels before us we can hardly dismiss as wholly improbable the conjecture that in Phrygia a man-god may have hung year by year on the sacred but fatal tree.

CHAPTER XXXVII

ORIENTAL RELIGIONS IN THE WEST

THE worship of the Great Mother of the Gods and her lover or son was very popular under the Roman Empire. Inscriptions prove that the two received divine honours, separately or conjointly, not only in Italy, and especially at Rome, but also in the provinces, particularly in Africa, Spain, Portugal, France, Germany and Bulgaria. Their worship survived the establishment of Christianity by Constantine; for Symmachus records the recurrence of the festival of the Great Mother, and in the days of Augustine her effeminate priests still paraded the streets and squares of Carthage with whitened faces, scented hair, and mincing gait, while, like the mendicant friars of the Middle Ages, they begged alms from the passers-by. In Greece, on the other hand, the bloody orgies of the Asiatic goddess and her consort appear to have found little favour. The barbarous and cruel character of the worship, with its frantic excesses, was doubtless repugnant to the good taste and humanity of the Greeks, who seem to have preferred the kindred but gentler rites of Adonis. Yet the same features which shocked and repelled the Greeks may have positively attracted the less refined Romans and barbarians of the West. The ecstatic frenzies, which were mistaken for divine inspiration, the mangling of the body, the theory of a new birth and the remission of sins through the shedding of blood, have all their origin in savagery, and they naturally appealed to peoples in whom the savage instincts were still strong. Their true character was indeed often disguised under a decent veil of allegorical or philosophical interpretation, which probably sufficed to impose upon the rapt and enthusiastic worshippers, reconciling even the more cultivated of them to things which otherwise must have filled them with horror and disgust.

The religion of the Great Mother, with its curious blending of crude savagery with spiritual aspirations, was only one of a multitude of similar Oriental faiths which in the later days of paganism spread over the Roman Empire, and by saturating the

European peoples with alien ideals of life gradually undermined the whole fabric of ancient civilisation. Greek and Roman society was built on the conception of the subordination of the individual to the community, of the citizen to the state; it set the safety of the commonwealth, as the supreme aim of conduct, above the safety of the individual whether in this world or in a world to come. Trained from infancy in this unselfish ideal, the citizens devoted their lives to the public service and were ready to lay them down for the common good; or if they shrank from the supreme sacrifice, it never occurred to them that they acted otherwise than basely in preferring their personal existence to the interests of their country. All this was changed by the spread of Oriental religions which inculcated the communion of the soul with God and its eternal salvation as the only objects worth living for, objects in comparison with which the prosperity and even the existence of the state sank into insignificance. The inevitable result of this selfish and immoral doctrine was to withdraw the devotee more and more from the public service, to concentrate his thoughts on his own spiritual emotions, and to breed in him a contempt for the present life which he regarded merely as a probation for a better and an eternal. The saint and the recluse, disdainful of earth and rapt in ecstatic contemplation of heaven, became in popular opinion the highest ideal of humanity, displacing the old ideal of the patriot and hero who, forgetful of self, lives and is ready to die for the good of his country. The earthly city seemed poor and contemptible to men whose eyes beheld the City of God coming in the clouds of heaven. Thus the centre of gravity, so to say, was shifted from the present to a future life, and however much the other world may have gained, there can be little doubt that this one lost heavily by the change. A general disintegration of the body politic set in. The ties of the state and the family were loosened; the structure of society tended to resolve itself into its individual elements and thereby to relapse into barbarism; for civilisation is only possible through the active co-operation of the citizens and their willingness to subordinate their private interests to the common good. Men refused to defend their country and even to continue their kind. In their anxiety to save their own souls and the souls of others, they were content to leave the material world, which they identified with the principle of evil, to perish around them. This obsession lasted for a thousand years. The revival of Roman law, of the Aristotelian philosophy, of ancient art and literature at the close of the Middle Ages, marked the return of Europe to native ideals of life and conduct, to saner, manlier views of the world. The long halt in the march of civilisation was over. The tide of Oriental invasion had turned at last. It is ebbing still.

Among the gods of eastern origin who in the decline of the ancient world competed against each other for the allegiance of the West was the old Persian deity Mithra. The immense popularity of his worship is attested by the monuments illustrative of it which have been found scattered in profusion all over the Roman Empire. In respect both of doctrines and of rites the cult of Mithra appears to have presented many points of resemblance not only to the religion of the Mother of the Gods but also to Christianity. The similarity struck the Christian doctors themselves and was explained by them as a work of the devil, who sought to seduce the souls of men from the true faith by a false and insidious imitation of it. So to the Spanish conquerors of Mexico and Peru many of the native heathen rites appeared to be diabolical counterfeits of the Christian sacraments. With more probability the modern student of comparative religion traces such resemblances to the similar and independent workings of the mind of man in his sincere, if crude, attempts to fathom the secret of the universe, and to adjust his little life to its awful mysteries. However that may be, there can be no doubt that the Mithraic religion proved a formidable rival to Christianity, combining as it did a solemn ritual with aspirations after moral purity and a hope of immortality. Indeed the issue of the conflict between the two faiths appears for a time to have hung in the balance. An instructive relic of the long struggle is preserved in our festival of Christmas, which the Church seems to have borrowed directly from its heathen rival. In the Julian calendar the twenty-fifth of December was reckoned the winter solstice, and it was regarded as the Nativity of the Sun, because the day begins to lengthen and the power of the sun to increase from that turning-point of the year. The ritual of the nativity, as it appears to have been celebrated in Syria and Egypt, was remarkable. The celebrants retired into certain inner shrines, from which at midnight they issued with a loud cry, 'The Virgin has brought forth! The light is waxing!' The Egyptians even represented the new-born sun by the image of an infant which on his birthday, the winter solstice, they brought forth and exhibited to his worshippers. No doubt the Virgin who thus conceived and bore a son on the twenty-fifth of December was the great Oriental goddess whom the Semites called the Heavenly Virgin or simply the Heavenly Goddess; in Semitic lands she was a form of Astarte. Now Mithra was regularly identified by his worshippers with the Sun, the Unconquered Sun, as they called him; hence his nativity also fell on the twenty-fifth of December. The Gospels say nothing as to the day of Christ's birth, and accordingly the early Church did not celebrate it. In time, however, the Christians of Egypt came to regard the sixth of January as the date of the Nativity, and the custom of commemorating the birth of the Saviour on that day gradually spread until by the fourth century it was universally established in the East. But at the end of the third or the beginning of the fourth century the Western Church, which had never recognised the sixth of January as the day of the Nativity, adopted the twenty-fifth of December as the true date, and in time its decision was accepted also by the Eastern Church. At Antioch the change was not introduced till about the year 375 A.D.

What considerations led the ecclesiastical authorities to institute the festival of Christmas? The motives for the innovation are stated with great frankness by a Syrian writer, himself a Christian. 'The reason,' he tells us, 'why the fathers transferred the celebration of the sixth of January to the twenty-fifth of December was this. It was a custom of the heathen to celebrate on the same twenty-fifth of December the birthday of the Sun, at which they kindled lights in token of festivity. In these solemnities and festivities the Christians also took part. Accordingly when the doctors of the Church perceived that the Christians had a leaning to this festival, they took counsel and resolved that the true Nativity should be solemnised on that day and the festival of the Epiphany on the sixth of January, Accordingly, along with this custom, the practice has prevailed of kindling fires till the sixth.' The heathen origin of Christmas is plainly hinted at, if not tacitly admitted, by Augustine when he exhorts his Christian brethren not to celebrate that solemn day like the heathen on account of the sun, but on account of him who made the sun. In like manner Leo the Great rebuked the pestilent belief that Christmas was solemnised because of the birth of the new sun, as it was called, and not because of the nativity of Christ.

Thus it appears that the Christian Church chose to celebrate the birthday of its Founder on the twenty-fifth of December in order to transfer the devotion of the heathen from the Sun to him who was called the Sun of Righteousness. If that was so, there can be no intrinsic improbability in the conjecture that motives of the same sort may have led the ecclesiastical authorities to assimilate the Easter festival of the death and resurrection of their Lord to the festival of the death and resurrection of another Asiatic god which fell at the same season. Now the Easter rites still observed in Greece, Sicily, and southern Italy bear in some respects a striking resemblance to the rites of Adonis, and I have suggested that the Church may have consciously adapted the new festival to its heathen predecessor for the sake of winning souls to Christ. But this adaptation probably took place in the Greek-speaking rather than in the Latin-speaking parts of the ancient world; for the worship of Adonis, while it flourished among the Greeks, appears to have made little impression on Rome and the West. Certainly it never formed part of the official Roman religion. The place which it might have taken in the affections of the vulgar was already occupied by the similar but more barbarous worship of Attis and the Great Mother. Now the death and resurrection of Attis were officially celebrated at Rome on the twenty-fourth and twenty-fifth of March, the latter being regarded as the spring equinox, and therefore as the most appropriate day for the revival of a god of vegetation who had been dead or sleeping throughout the winter. But according to an ancient and widespread tradition Christ suffered on the twenty-fifth of March, and accordingly some Christians regularly celebrated the Crucifixion on that day without any regard to the state of the moon. This custom was certainly observed in Phrygia, Cappadocia, and Gaul, and there seem to be grounds for thinking that at one time it was followed also in Rome. Thus the tradition which placed the death of Christ on the twenty-fifth of March was ancient and deeply rooted. It is all the more remarkable because astronomical considerations prove that it can have had no historical foundation. The inference appears to be inevitable that the passion of Christ must have been arbitrarily referred to that date in order to harmonise with an older festival of the spring equinox. This is the view of the learned ecclesiastical historian Mgr. Duchesne, who points out that the death of the Saviour was thus made to fall upon the very day on which, according to a widespread belief, the world had been created. But the resurrection of Attis, who combined in himself the characters of the divine Father and the divine Son, was officially celebrated at Rome on the same day. When we remember that the festival of St. George in April has replaced the ancient pagan festival of the Parilia; that the festival of St. John the Baptist in June has succeeded to a heathen Midsummer festival of water; that the festival of the Assumption of the Virgin in August has ousted the festival of Diana; that the feast of All Souls in November is a continuation of an old heathen feast of the dead; and that the Nativity of Christ himself was assigned to the winter solstice in December because that day was deemed the Nativity of the Sun; we can hardly be thought rash or unreasonable in conjecturing that the other cardinal festival of the Christian church — the solemnisation of Easter — may have been in like manner, and from like motives of edification, adapted to a similar celebration of the Phrygian god Attis at the vernal equinox.

At least it is a remarkable coincidence, if it is nothing more, that the Christian and the heathen festivals of the divine death and resurrection should have been solemnised at the same season and in the same places. For the places which celebrated the death of Christ at the spring equinox were Phrygia, Gaul, and apparently Rome, that is, the very regions in which the worship of Attis either originated or struck deepest root. It is difficult to regard the coincidence as purely accidental. If the vernal equinox, the season at which in the temperate regions the whole face of nature testifies to a fresh outburst of vital energy, has been viewed from of old as the time when the world was annually created afresh in the resurrection of a god, nothing could be more natural than to place the resurrection of the new deity at the same cardinal point of the year. Only it is to be observed that if the death of Christ was dated on the twenty-fifth of March, his resurrection, according to Christian tradition, must have happened on the twenty-seventh of March, which is just two days later than the vernal equinox of the Julian calendar and the resurrection of Attis. A similar displacement of two days in the adjustment of Christian to heathen celebrations occurs in the festivals of St. George and the Assumption of the Virgin. However, another Christian tradition, followed by Lactantius and perhaps by the practice of the Church in Gaul, placed the death of Christ on the twenty-third and his resurrection on the twenty-fifth of March. If that was so, his resurrection coincided exactly with the resurrection of Attis.

In point of fact it appears from the testimony of an anonymous Christian, who wrote in the fourth century of our era, that Christians and pagans alike were struck by the remarkable coincidence between the death and resurrection of their respective deities, and that the coincidence formed a theme of bitter controversy between the adherents of the rival religions, the pagans contending that the resurrection of Christ was a spurious imitation of the resurrection of Attis, and the Christians asserting with equal warmth that the resurrection of Attis was a diabolical counterfeit of the resurrection of Christ. In these unseemly bickerings the heathen took what to a superficial observer might seem strong ground by arguing that their god was the older and therefore presumably the original, not the counterfeit, since as a general rule an original is older than its copy. This feeble argument the Christians easily rebutted. They admitted, indeed, that in point of time Christ was the junior deity, but they triumphantly demonstrated his real seniority by falling back on the subtlety of Satan, who on so important an occasion had surpassed himself by inverting the usual order of nature.

Taken altogether, the coincidences of the Christian with the heathen festivals are too close and too numerous to be accidental. They mark the compromise which the Church in the hour of its triumph was compelled to make with its vanquished yet still dangerous rivals. The inflexible Protestantism of the primitive missionaries, with their fiery denunciations of heathendom, had been exchanged for the supple policy, the easy tolerance, the comprehensive charity of shrewd ecclesiastics, who clearly perceived that if Christianity was to conquer the world it could do so only by relaxing the too rigid principles of its Founder, by widening a little the narrow gate which leads to salvation. In this respect an instructive parallel might be drawn between the history of Christianity and the history of Buddhism. Both systems were in their origin essentially ethical reforms born of the generous ardour, the lofty aspirations, the tender compassion of their noble Founders, two of those beautiful spirits who appear at rare intervals on earth like beings come from a better world to support and guide our weak and erring nature. Both preached moral virtue as the means of accomplishing what they regarded as the supreme object of life, the eternal salvation of the individual soul, though by a curious antithesis the one sought that salvation in a blissful eternity, the other in a final release from suffering, in annihilation. But the austere ideals of sanctity which they inculcated were too deeply opposed not only to the frailties but to the natural instincts of humanity ever to be carried out in practice by more than a small number of disciples, who consistently renounced the ties of the family and the state in order to work out their own salvation in the still seclusion of the cloister. If such faiths were to be nominally accepted by whole nations or even by the world, it was essential that they should first be modified or transformed so as to accord in some measure with the prejudices, the passions, the superstitions of the vulgar. This process of accommodation was carried out in after ages by followers who, made of less ethereal stuff than their masters, were for that reason the better fitted to mediate between them and the common herd. Thus as time went on, the two religions, in exact proportion to their growing popularity, absorbed more and more of those baser elements which they had been instituted for the very purpose of suppressing. Such spiritual decadences are inevitable. The world cannot live at the level of its great men. Yet it would be unfair to the generality of our kind to ascribe wholly to their intellectual and moral weakness the gradual divergence of Buddhism and Christianity from their primitive patterns. For it should never be forgotten that by their glorification of poverty and celibacy both these religions struck straight at the root not merely of civil society but of human existence. The blow was parried by the wisdom or the folly of the vast majority of mankind, who refused to purchase a chance of saving their souls with the certainty of extinguishing the species.

CHAPTER XXXVIII

THE MYTH OF OSIRIS

IN ancient Egypt the god whose death and resurrection were annually celebrated with alternate sorrow and joy was Osiris, the most popular of all Egyptian deities; and there are good grounds for classing him in one of his aspects with Adonis and Attis as a personification of the great yearly vicissitudes of nature, especially of the corn. But the immense vogue which he enjoyed for many ages induced his devoted worshippers to heap upon him the attributes and powers of many other gods; so that it is not always easy to strip him, so to say, of his borrowed plumes and to restore them to their proper owners.

The story of Osiris is told in a connected form only by Plutarch, whose narrative has been confirmed and to some extent amplified in modern times by the evidence of the monuments.

Osiris was the offspring of an intrigue between the earth-god Seb (Keb or Geb, as the name is sometimes transliterated) and the sky-goddess Nut. The Greeks identified his parents with their own deities Cronus and Rhea. When the sun-god Ra perceived that his wife Nut had been unfaithful to him, he declared with a curse that she should be delivered of the child in no month and no year. But the goddess had another lover, the god Thoth or Hermes, as the Greeks called him, and he playing at draughts with the moon won from her a seventy-second part of every day, and having compounded five whole days out of these parts he added them to the Egyptian year of three hundred and sixty days. This was the mythical origin of the five supplementary days which the Egyptians annually inserted at the end of every year in order to establish a harmony between lunar and solar time. On these five days, regarded as outside the year of twelve months, the curse of the sun-god did not rest, and accordingly Osiris was born on the first of them. At his nativity a voice rang out proclaiming that the Lord of All had come into the world. Some say that a certain Pamyles heard a voice from the temple at Thebes bidding him announce with a shout that a great king, the beneficent Osiris, was born. But Osiris was not the only child of his mother. On the second of the supplementary days she gave birth to the elder Horus, on the third to the god Set, whom the Greeks called Typhon, on the fourth to the goddess Isis, and on the fifth to the goddess Nephthys. Afterwards Set married his sister Nephthys, and Osiris married his sister Isis.

Reigning as a king on earth, Osiris reclaimed the Egyptians from savagery, gave them laws, and taught them to worship the gods. Before his time the Egyptians had been cannibals. But Isis, the sister and wife of Osiris, discovered wheat and barley growing wild, and Osiris introduced the cultivation of these grains amongst his people, who forthwith abandoned cannibalism and took kindly to a corn diet. Moreover, Osiris is said to have been the first to gather fruit from trees, to train the vine to poles, and to tread the grapes. Eager to communicate these beneficent discoveries to all mankind, he committed the whole government of Egypt to his wife Isis, and travelled over the world, diffusing the blessings of civilisation and agriculture wherever he went. In countries where a harsh climate or niggardly soil forbade the cultivation of the vine, he taught the inhabitants to console themselves for the want of wine by brewing beer from barley. Loaded with the wealth that had been showered upon him by grateful nations, he returned to Egypt, and on account of the benefits he had conferred on mankind he was unanimously hailed and worshipped as a deity. But his brother Set (whom the Greeks called Typhon) with seventy-two others plotted against him. Having taken the measure of his good brother's body by stealth, the bad brother Typhon fashioned and highly decorated a coffer of the same size, and once when they were all drinking and making merry he brought in the coffer and jestingly promised to give it to the one whom it should fit exactly. Well, they all tried one after the other, but it fitted none of them. Last of all Osiris stepped into it and lay down. On that the conspirators ran and slammed the lid down on him, nailed it fast, soldered it with molten lead, and flung the coffer into the Nile. This happened on the seventeenth day of the month Athyr, when the sun is in the sign of the Scorpion, and in the eight-and-twentieth year of the reign or the life of Osiris. When Isis heard of it she sheared off a lock of her hair, put on mourning attire, and wandered disconsolately up and down, seeking the body.

By the advice of the god of wisdom she took refuge in the papyrus swamps of the Delta. Seven scorpions accompanied her in her flight. One evening when she was weary she came to the house of a woman, who, alarmed at the sight of the scorpions, shut the door in her face. Then one of the scorpions crept under the door and stung the child of the woman that he died. But when Isis heard the mother's lamentation, her heart was touched, and she laid her hands on the child and uttered her powerful spells; so the poison was driven out of the child and he lived. Afterwards Isis herself gave birth to a son in the swamps. She had conceived him while she fluttered in the form of a hawk over the corpse of her dead husband. The infant was the younger Horus, who in his youth bore the name of Harpocrates, that is, the child Horus. Him Buto, the goddess of the north, hid from the wrath of his wicked uncle Set. Yet she could not guard him from all mishap; for one day when Isis came to her little son's hiding-place she found him stretched lifeless and rigid on the ground: a scorpion had stung him. Then Isis prayed to the sun-god Ra for help. The god hearkened to her and staid his bark in the sky, and sent down Thoth to teach her the spell by which she might restore her son to life. She uttered the words of power, and straightway the poison flowed from the body of Horus, air passed into him, and he lived. Then Thoth ascended up into the sky and took his place once more in the bark of the sun, and the bright pomp passed onward jubilant.

Meantime the coffer containing the body of Osiris had floated down the river and away out to sea, till at last it drifted ashore at Byblus, on the coast of Syria. Here a fine *erica*-tree shot up suddenly and enclosed the chest in its trunk. The king of the country, admiring the growth of the tree, had it cut down and made into a pillar of his house; but he did not know that the coffer with the dead Osiris was in it. Word of this came to Isis and she journeyed to Byblus, and sat down by the well, in humble guise, her face wet with tears. To none would she speak till the king's handmaidens came, and them she greeted kindly, and braided their hair, and breathed on them from her own divine body a wondrous perfume. But when the queen beheld the braids of her handmaidens' hair and smelt the sweet smell that emanated from them, she sent for the stranger woman and took her into her house and made her the nurse of her child. But Isis gave the babe her finger instead of her breast to suck, and at night she began to burn all that was mortal of him away, while she herself in the likeness of a swallow fluttered round the pillar that contained her dead brother, twittering mournfully. But the queen spied what she was doing and shrieked out when she saw her child in flames, and thereby she hindered him from becoming immortal. Then the goddess revealed herself and begged for the pillar of the roof, and they gave it her, and she cut the coffer out of it, and fell upon it and embraced it and lamented so loud that the younger of the king's children died of fright on the spot. But the trunk of the tree she wrapped in fine linen, and poured ointment on it, and gave it to the king and queen, and the wood stands in a temple of Isis and is worshipped by the people of Byblus to this day. And Isis put the coffer in a boat and took the eldest of the king's children with her and sailed away. As soon as they were alone, she opened the chest, and laying her face on the face of her brother she kissed him and wept. But the child came behind her softly and saw what she was about, and she turned and looked at him in anger, and the child could not bear her look and died; but some say that it was not so, but that he fell into the sea and was drowned. It is he whom the Egyptians sing of at their banquets under the name of Maneros.

But Isis put the coffer by and went to see her son Horus at the city of Buto, and Typhon found the coffer as he was hunting a boar one night by the light of a full moon. And he knew the body, and rent it into fourteen pieces, and scattered them abroad. But Isis sailed up and down the marshes in a shallop made of papyrus, looking for the pieces; and that is why when people sail in shallops made of papyrus, the crocodiles do not hurt them, for they fear or respect the goddess. And that is the reason, too, why there are many graves of Osiris in Egypt, for she buried each limb as she found it. But others will have it that she buried an image of him in every city, pretending it was his body, in order that Osiris might be worshipped in many places, and that if Typhon searched for the real grave he might not be able to find it. However, the genital member of Osiris had been eaten by the fishes, so Isis made an image of it instead, and the image is used by the Egyptians at their festivals to this day. 'Isis,' writes the historian Diodorus Siculus, 'recovered all the parts of the body except the genitals; and because she wished that her husband's grave should be unknown and honoured by all who dwell in the land of Egypt, she resorted to the following device. She moulded human images out of wax and spices, corresponding to the stature of Osiris, round each one of the parts of his body. Then she called in the priests according to their families and took an oath of them all that they would reveal to no man the trust she was about to repose in them. So to each of them privately she said that to them alone she entrusted the burial of the body, and reminding them of the benefits they had received she exhorted them to bury the body in their own land to honour Osiris as a God. She also besought them to dedicate one of the animals of their country, whichever they chose, and to honour it in life as they had formerly honoured Osiris, and when it died to grant it obsequies like his. And because she would encourage the priests in their own interest to bestow the aforesaid honours, she gave them a third part of the land to be used by them in the service and worship of the gods. Accordingly it is said that the priests, mindful of the benefits of Osiris, desirous of gratifying the queen, and moved by the prospect of gain, carried out all the injunctions of Isis. Wherefore to this day each of the priests imagines that Osiris is buried in his country, and they honour the beasts that were consecrated in the beginning, and when the animals die the priests renew at their burial the mourning for Osiris. But the sacred bulls, the one called Apis and the other Mnevis, were dedicated to Osiris, and it was ordained that they should be worshipped as gods in common by all the Egyptians, since these animals above all others had helped the discoverers of corn in sowing the seed and procuring the universal benefits of agriculture.'

Such is the myth or legend of Osiris, as told by Greek writers and eked out by more or less fragmentary notices or allusions in native Egyptian literature. A long inscription in the temple at Denderah has preserved a list of the god's graves, and other texts mention the parts of his body which were treasured as holy relics in each of the sanctuaries. Thus his heart was at Athribis, his backbone at Busiris, his neck at Letopolis, and his head at

Memphis. As often happens in such cases, some of his divine limbs were miraculously multiplied. His head, for example, was at Abydos as well as at Memphis, and his legs, which were remarkably numerous, would have sufficed for several ordinary mortals. In this respect, however, Osiris was nothing to St. Denys, of whom no less than seven heads, all equally genuine, are extant.

According to native Egyptian accounts, which supplement that of Plutarch, when Isis had found the corpse of her husband Osiris, she and her sister Nephthys sat down beside it and uttered a lament which in after ages became the type of all Egyptian lamentations for the dead. 'Come to thy house', they wailed, 'Come to thy house. O god On! come to thy house, thou who hast no foes. O fair youth, come to thy house, that thou mayest see me. I am thy sister, whom thou lovest; thou shalt not part from me. O fair boy, come to thy house. . . . I see thee not, yet doth my heart yearn after thee and mine eyes desire thee. Come to her who loves thee, who loves thee, Unnefer, thou blessed one! Come to thy sister, come to thy wife, to thy wife, thou whose heart stands still. Come to thy housewife. I am thy sister by the same mother, thou shalt not be far from me. Gods and men have turned their faces towards thee and weep for thee together. . . . I call after thee and weep, so that my cry is heard to heaven, but thou hearest not my voice; yet am I thy sister, whom thou didst love on earth; thou didst love none but me, my brother! my brother!' This lament for the fair youth cut off in his prime reminds us of the laments for Adonis. The title of Unnefer or 'the Good Being' bestowed on him marks the beneficence which tradition universally ascribed to Osiris; it was at once his commonest title and one of his names as king.

The lamentations of the two sad sisters were not in vain. In pity for her sorrow the sun-god Ra sent down from heaven the jackal-headed god Anubis, who, with the aid of Isis and Nephthys, of Thoth and Horus, pieced together the broken body of the murdered god, swathed it in linen bandages, and observed all the other rites which the Egyptians were wont to perform over the bodies of the departed. Then Isis fanned the cold clay with her wings: Osiris revived, and thenceforth reigned as king over the dead in the other world. There he bore the titles of Lord of the Underworld, Lord of Eternity, Ruler of the Dead. There, too, in the great Hall of the Two Truths, assisted by forty-two assessors, one from each of the principal districts of Egypt, he presided as judge at the trial of the souls of the departed, who made their solemn confession before him, and, their heart having been weighed in the balance of justice, received the reward of virtue in a life eternal or the appropriate punishment of their sins.

In the resurrection of Osiris the Egyptians saw the pledge of a life everlasting for themselves beyond the grave. They believed that every man would live eternally in the other world if only his surviving friends did for his body what the gods had done for the body of Osiris. Hence the ceremonies observed by the Egyptians over the human dead were an exact copy of those which Anubis, Horus, and the rest had performed over the dead god. 'At every burial there was enacted a representation of the divine mystery which had been performed of old over Osiris, when his son, his sisters, his friends were gathered round his mangled remains and succeeded by their spells and manipulations in converting his broken body into the first mummy, which they afterwards reanimated and furnished with the means of entering on a new individual life beyond the grave. The mummy of the deceased was Osiris; the professional female mourners were his two sisters Isis and Nephthys; Anubis, Horus, all the gods of the Osirian legend gathered about the corpse.' In this way every dead Egyptian was identified with Osiris and bore his name. From the Middle Kingdom onwards it was the regular practice to address the deceased as 'Osiris So-and-So,' as if he were the god himself, and to add the standing epithet 'true of speech,' because true speech was characteristic of Osiris. The thousands of inscribed and pictured tombs that have been opened in the valley of the Nile prove that the mystery of the resurrection was performed for the benefit of every dead Egyptian; as Osiris died and rose again from the dead, so all men hoped to arise like him from death to life eternal.

Thus according to what seems to have been the general native tradition Osiris was a good and beloved king of Egypt, who suffered a violent death but rose from the dead and was henceforth worshipped as a deity. In harmony with this tradition he was regularly represented by sculptors and painters in human and regal form as a dead king, swathed in the wrappings of a mummy, but wearing on his head a kingly crown and grasping in one of his hands, which were left free from the bandages, a kingly sceptre. Two cities above all others were associated with his myth or memory. One of them was Busiris in Lower Egypt, which claimed to possess his backbone; the other was Abydos in Upper Egypt, which gloried in the possession of his head. Encircled by the nimbus of the dead yet living god, Abydos, originally an obscure place, became from the end of the Old Kingdom the holiest spot in Egypt; his tomb there would seem to have been to the Egyptians what the Church of the Holy Sepulchre at Jerusalem is to Christians. It was the wish of every pious man that his dead body should rest in hallowed earth near the grave of the glorified Osiris. Few indeed were rich enough to enjoy this inestimable privilege; for, apart from the cost of a tomb in the sacred city, the mere transport of mummies from great distances was both difficult and expensive. Yet so eager were many to absorb in death the blessed influence which radiated from the holy sepulchre that they caused their surviving friends to convey their mortal remains to Abydos, there to tarry for a short time, and then to be brought back by river and interred in the tombs which had been made ready for them in their native land. Others had cenotaphs built or memorial tablets erected for themselves near the tomb of their dead and risen Lord, that they might share with him the bliss of a joyful resurrection.

PRINTED BY PURNELL AND SONS, LTD.
PAULTON (SOMERSET) AND LONDON